THEOLOGICAL DICTIONARY

OF THE

OLD TESTAMENT

EDITED BY

G. JOHANNES BOTTERWECK

AND

HELMER RINGGREN

Translator

JOHN T. WILLIS

Abilene Christian College

Volume II

גָּלָה ־ בדל

bdl – gālāh

Revised Edition

WILLIAM B. EERDMANS PUBLISHING COMPANY

GRAND RAPIDS, MICHIGAN

THEOLOGICAL DICTIONARY OF THE OLD TESTAMENT

COPYRIGHT © 1975 BY WILLIAM B. EERDMANS PUBLISHING CO.

Revised edition 1977
Translated from
THEOLOGISCHES WÖRTERBUCH ZUM ALTEN TESTAMENT
Lieferungen 5-9
Published 1972, 1973 by
VERLAG W. KOHLHAMMER GMBH STUTTGART, W. GERMANY

Library of Congress Cataloging in Publication Data

Botterweck, G   Johannes.
    Theological dictionary of the Old Testament.

    Includes bibliographical references.
    Translation of Theologisches Wörterbuch zum
Alten Testament.
        1. Bible.   O. T.—Dictionaries—Hebrew.
    2. Hebrew language—Dictionaries—English.
    I. Ringgren, Helmer, 1917–   joint author.
    II. Title.

BS440.B5713   221.3   73-76170
ISBN 0–8028–2338-6 (set)

Printed in the United States of America

NOTE TO THE REVISED ENGLISH EDITION

The present edition incorporates a number of corrections and revisions suggested by the original contributors, by reviewers, by Geoffrey W. Bromiley, and by David Green, to each of whom the publishers wish to express sincere gratitude.

CONTRIBUTORS

Ch. Barth, Mainz
B. Beck, Bonn
Jan Bergman, Linköping
Karl-Heinz Bernhardt, Berlin
G. Johannes Botterweck, Bonn (Editor)
N. P. Bratsiotis, Agia-Paraskevi-Attikis, Greece
Ronald E. Clements, Cambridge, England
W. Dommershausen, Trier
H. Eising, Münster
H.-J. Fabry, Bonn
David N. Freedman, Ann Arbor
H. F. Fuhs, Cologne
J. Gamberoni, Paderborn
M. Görg, Bochum
H. Haag, Tübingen
Vinzenz Hamp, Munich
R. Hentschke, Berlin
Harry A. Hoffner, Chicago
Alfred Jepsen, Greifswald
Diether Kellermann, Tübingen
H. Kosmala, Cheltenham, England
J. Lundbom, Berkeley
J. C. de Moor, Kampen
R. Mosis, Freiburg
M. J. Mulder, Amsterdam
Magnus Ottosson, Uppsala
Benedikt Otzen, Aarhus, Denmark
Horst Dietrich Preuss, Göttingen
Helmer Ringgren, Uppsala (Editor)
Josef Scharbert, Munich
O. Schilling (†), Bochum
K.-D. Schunk, Rostock
J. Schüpphaus, Bonn
Horst Seebass, Münster
M. Tsevat, Cincinnati
Siegfried Wagner, Leipzig
Gerhard Wallis, Halle
M. Weinfeld, Jerusalem
Hans-Jürgen Zobel, Halle

CONTENTS

Contents

ABBREVIATIONS

AANLR	*Atti dell'Accademia Nazionale dei Lincei, Rendiconti*
AASOR	*Annual of the American Schools of Oriental Research*
AB	*The Anchor Bible*
ABAW	*Abhandlungen der Akademie der Wissenschaften*, Berlin
ABL	R. F. Harper, *Assyrian and Babylonian Letters*, 1-14, Chicago, 1892-1914
ABR	*Australian Biblical Review*, Melbourne
ABRT	J. Craig, *Assyrian and Babylonian Religious Texts*, Leipzig, 1895-97
abs.	absolute
acc.	accusative
AcOr	*Acta Orientalia*
act.	active
adj.	adjective
adv.	adverb
ÄF	*Ägyptologische Forschungen*, Glückstadt
AfK	*Archiv für Kulturgeschichte*
AFNW	*Arbeitsgemeinschaft für Forschung des Landes Nordrhein-Westfalen*
AfO	*Archiv für Orientforschung*
ÄgAbh	*Ägyptologische Abhandlungen*
AH	*Analecta Hymnica*, ed. G. Dreves and C. Blume, Leipzig, 1886-1922
AHAW	*Abhandlungen der Heidelberger Akademie der Wissenschaften*
AHDO	*Archives d'Histoire du Droit Oriental*
AHw	W. von Soden, *Akkadisches Handwörterbuch*
AION	*Annali dell'Istituto Universitario Orientale di Napoli*
AJA	*American Journal of Archaeology*
AJSL	*The American Journal of Semitic Languages and Literatures*
Akk.	Akkadian
AKM	*Abhandlungen zur Kunde des Morgenlandes* (Leipzig), Wiesbaden
AN	J. J. Stamm, *Die akkadische Namengebung. MVÄG*, 44 (1939)
AnAcScFen	*Annales Academiae Scientiarum Fennicae*
AnAeg	*Analecta Aegyptiaca*
AnBibl	*Analecta Biblica*, Rome
AncIsr	R. de Vaux, *Ancient Israel: Its Life and Institutions*, trans. 1961
ANEP	*The Ancient Near East in Pictures*, ed. J. B. Pritchard, Princeton, 1954, [2]1969
ANET	*Ancient Near Eastern Texts Relating to the Old Testament*, ed. J. B. Pritchard, [2]1955, [3]1969
AnOr	*Analecta Orientalia*
AnSt	*Anatolian Studies*, London
ANVAO	*Avhandlinger utgitt av det Norske Videnskaps-Akademi i Oslo*
AO	*Der Alte Orient*, Leipzig
AOAT	*Alter Orient und Altes Testament*, Neukirchen-Vluyn
AOB	*Altorientalische Bilder zum Alten Testament*, ed. H. Gressmann, [2]1927
AOT	*Altorientalische Texte zum Alten Testament*, ed. H. Gressmann, [2]1926
AP	A. E. Cowley, *Aramaic Papyri of the Fifth Century B.C.*, Oxford, 1923
APAW	*Abhandlungen der Preussische Akademie der Wissenschaften*, Berlin
APNM	H. B. Huffmon, *Amorite Personal Names in the Mari Texts*, Baltimore, 1965
Arab.	Arabic
Aram.	Aramaic
ArbT	*Arbeiten zur Theologie*, Stuttgart
ARM	*Archives Royales de Mari*, Paris
ArOr	*Archiv Orientální*, Prague
ARW	*Archiv für Religionswissenschaft*, Leipzig, Berlin
ASAW	*Abhandlungen der Sächsischen Akademie der Wissenschaften in Leipzig*
ASKT	P. Haupt, *Akkadische und Sumerische Keilschrifttexte*, Leipzig, 1882
Assyr.	Assyrian
ASTI	*Annual of the Swedish Theological Institute in Jerusalem*, Leiden
AT	Alte Testament

ATA	*Alttestamentliche Abhandlungen*, Münster
ATD	*Das Alte Testament Deutsch*
AThANT	*Abhandlungen zur Theologie des Alten und Neuen Testaments*, Zurich
ATR	*Anglican Theological Review*, Evanston
Aug	*Augustinianum*
AuS	G. Dalman, *Arbeit und Sitte in Palästina*, 1928-1942
BA	*The Biblical Archaeologist*, New Haven
Bab.	Babylonian
BAfO	*Beihefte zur Archiv für Orientforschung*
BAH	*Bibliothèque Archéologique et Historique*, Paris
BASOR	*Bulletin of the American Schools of Oriental Research*
BAss	*Beiträge zu Assyriologie*
BBB	*Bonner Biblische Beiträge*
BDB	Brown-Driver-Briggs, *A Hebrew and English Lexicon of the Old Testament*
BE	Babylonian Expedition of the University of Pennsylvania, Philadelphia
BeO	*Bibbia e Oriente*
BethM	*Beth Mikra*
BETL	*Bibliotheca Ephemeridum Theologicarum Lovaniensium*
BFChTh	*Beiträge zur Förderung Christlicher Theologie*, Gütersloh
BHHW	*Biblisch-Historisches Handwörterbuch*, ed. L. Rost and B. Reicke, 1962ff.
BHK	*Biblia Hebraica*, ed. R. Kittel
BHS	*Biblia Hebraica Stuttgartensia*, ed. K. Elliger and W. Rudolph, 1968ff.
BHTh	*Beiträge zur Historischen Theologie*, Tübingen
Bibl	*Biblica*, Rome
BiblRes	*Biblical Research*
BietOr	*Biblica et Orientalia*
BiLe	*Bibel und Leben*
BiLi	*Bibel und Liturgie*
BIN	*Babylonian Inscriptions in the Collection of James B. Nies*, New Haven
BiOr	*Bibliotheca Orientalis*, Leiden
BJRL	*Bulletin of the John Rylands Library*, Manchester
BK	*Biblischer Kommentar zum Alten Testament*, ed. M. Noth and H. W. Wolff
BL	*Bibel-Lexikon*, ed. H. Haag
BLA	H. Bauer-P. Leander, *Grammatik des Biblisch-Aramäischen*, 1927
Blachère-Chouémi	R. Blachère-M. Chouémi-C. Denizeau, *Dictionnaire Arabe-Français-Anglais*
BLe	H. Bauer-P. Leander, *Historische Grammatik der hebräischen Sprache*, 1922
BMAP	E. G. Kraeling, *The Brooklyn Museum Aramaic Papyri*, 1953
BMB	*Bulletin du Musée de Beyrouth*
Bo	Unpublished Boğazköy tablets (with catalog number)
BoSt	*Boghazköi Studien*
BOT	*De Boeken van het Oude Testament*, ed. Grossow, van der Ploeg, *et al.*
BRL	K. Galling, *Biblisches Reallexikon*, 1937
BS	*Bibliotheca Sacra*, Dallas
BSAW	*Berichte über die Verhandlungen der Sächsischen Akademie der Wissenschaften zu Leipzig*
BSGW	*Berichte der Sächsischen Gesellschaft der Wissenschaften*
BSt	*Biblische Studien*, Neukirchen
BT	*The Bible Translator*, London
BThH	*Biblisch-Theologisches Handwörterbuch zur Lutherbibel und zu neueren Übersetzungen*, ed. E. Osterloh and H. Engeland
BuA	B. Meissner, *Babylonien und Assyrien*, I 1920, II 1925
BuK	*Bibel und Kirche*
BVC	*Bible et Vie Chrétienne*
BWA(N)T	*Beiträge zur Wissenschaft vom Alten (und Neuen) Testament*, Stuttgart
BWL	W. G. Lambert, *Babylonian Wisdom Literature*, Oxford, 1960

BZ	*Biblische Zeitschrift*, Paderborn
BZAW	*Beihefte zur Zeitschrift für die Alttestamentliche Wissenschaft*, Berlin
BZfr	*Biblische Zeitfragen*
BZTS	*Bonner Zeitschrift für Theologie und Seelsorge*
CAD	*The Assyrian Dictionary of the Oriental Institute of the University of Chicago*, 1956ff.
CahRB	*Cahiers de la Revue Biblique*
CahTD	*Cahiers du Groupe F. Thureau-Dangin*, I, Paris, 1960
CANES	*Corpus of Ancient Near Eastern Seals in North American Collections*, I, Washington, 1948
CAT	*Commentaire de l'Ancien Testament*
CBQ	*Catholic Biblical Quarterly*
CBSC	*The Cambridge Bible for Schools and Colleges*
CChr	*Corpus Christianorum*, Turnhout
CD A, B	Damascus Document, Manuscript A, B
CH	Codex Hammurabi
ChrÉg	*Chronique d'Égypte*
CIH	*Corpus Inscriptionum Himjariticarum* (=*CIS*, IV)
CIS	*Corpus Inscriptionum Semiticarum*, 1881ff.
CML	G. R. Driver, *Canaanite Myths and Legends*, Edinburgh, 1956
CollBG	*Collationes Brugenses et Gandavenses*, Gent
comm.	commentary
ComViat	*Communio Viatorum*, Prague
conj.	conjecture
const.	construct
ContiRossini	K. Conti Rossini, *Chrestomathia Arabica meridionalis epigraphica*, 1931
Copt.	Coptic
COT	*Commentaar op het Oude Testament*, ed. G. C. Aalders, Kampen
CRAI	*Comptes-rendus de l'Académie des Inscriptions et Belles-Lettres*, Paris
CRRA	*Compte Rendu de . . . Recontre Assyriologique Internationale*
CT	Cuneiform Texts from Babylonian Tablets, etc. in the British Museum, London, 1896ff.
CT	*The Egyptian Coffin Texts*, ed. A. de Buck and A. H. Gardiner, 1935ff.
CTA	A. Herdner, *Corpus des Tablettes en Cunéiformes Alphabétiques Découvertes à Ras Shamra-Ugarit* I/II, Paris, 1963
CTM	*Concordia Theological Monthly*, St. Louis
CultBibl	*Cultura Bíblica*, Segovia
CW	*Die Christliche Welt*
DACL	F. Cabrol-H. Leclercq, *Dictionnaire d'Archéologie Chrétienne et Liturgie*, Paris, 1907ff.
DB	*Dictionnaire de la Bible*
DBS	*Dictionnaire de la Bible, Supplément*, ed. L. Pirot, A. Robert, H. Cazelles, and A. Feuillet, 1928ff.
DISO	Ch. F. Jean-J. Hoftijzer, *Dictionnaire des Inscriptions Sémitiques de l'Ouest*, Leiden, 1965
diss.	dissertation
DissAbs	*Dissertation Abstracts*
DJD	*Discoveries in the Judaean Desert*, 1955ff.
DLZ	*Deutsche Literaturzeitung*
DN	name of a deity
DTT	*Dansk Teologisk Tidsskrift*, Copenhagen
EA	Tell el-Amarna Tablets
EB	*Die Heilige Schrift in deutscher Übersetzung. Echter-Bibel*, Würzburg
EGA	R. M. Boehmer, *Die Entwicklung der Glyptik während der Akkad-Zeit*, Berlin, 1965
Egyp.	Egyptian

Einl.	Einleitung
EJ	*Encyclopaedia Judaica*
EKL	*Evangelisches Kirchenlexikon,* Göttingen, I 1956, II 1958
EMiqr	*Entsiqlopēdiā Miqrā'it–Encyclopaedia Biblica,* Jerusalem
EnEl	Enuma Elish
Eng.	English
ErfThSt	*Erfurter Theologische Studien*
ErJb	*Eranos-Jahrbuch*
EstBíb	*Estudios Bíblicos,* Madrid
EstEcl	*Estudios Eclesiásticos*
Ethiop.	Ethiopic
ETL	*Ephemerides Theologicae Lovanienses*
EvQ	*The Evangelical Quarterly*
EvTh	*Evangelische Theologie,* Munich
ExpT	*The Expository Times,* London
FreibThSt	*Freiburger Theologische Studien*
FRLANT	*Forschungen zur Religion und Literatur des Alten und Neuen Testaments,* Göttingen
FzB	*Forschung zur Bibel*
gen.	genitive
GesB	W. Gesenius-F. Buhl, *Hebräisches und aramäisches Handwörterbuch,* [17]1921
GF	A. Alt, *The God of the Fathers,* trans. in *Essays on Old Testament History and Religion* (1966), 1-77
GGA	*Göttingische Gelehrte Anzeigen*
GHK	*Hand-Kommentar zum Alten Testament,* ed. W. Nowack, Göttingen
Gilg	Gilgamesh Epic
GK	W. Gesenius-E. Kautzsch, *Hebräische Grammatik,* [28]1909 (=Kautzsch-Cowley, *Gesenius' Hebrew Grammar,* [2]1910)
Gk.	Greek
Gl	Inscriptions in the E. Glaser collection (Old South Arabic)
GLECS	*Comptes Rendus du Groupe Linguistique d'Études Chamito-Sémitiques,* Paris
Greg	*Gregorianum*
GSAT	*Gesammelte Studien zum Alten Testament*
HAT	*Handbuch zum Alten Testament,* ed. O. Eissfeldt, 1st series
Ḫatt.	Ḫattic
HAW	*Handbuch der Altertumswissenschaft,* ed. W. Otto, Munich, 1929ff.
Heb.	Hebrew
Hitt.	Hittite
HNT	*Handbuch zum Neuen Testament,* ed. G. Bornkamm
HO	*Handbuch der Orientalistik,* ed. B. Spuler, Leiden, 1952ff.
HSAT	*Die Heilige Schrift des Alten Testaments,* ed. E. Kautsch-A. Bertholet, [4]1922/23
HThR	*Harvard Theological Review*
HUCA	*Hebrew Union College Annual,* Cincinnati
IB	*The Interpreter's Bible,* ed. G. A. Buttrick, 1951-57
ICC	*The International Critical Commentary*
IDB	*The Interpreter's Dictionary of the Bible,* ed. G. A. Buttrick, I-IV, 1962
IEJ	*Israel Exploration Journal,* Jerusalem
ILC	J. Pedersen, *Israel. Its Life and Culture,* 1926, [3]1953, 4 vols. in 2
impf.	imperfect
impv.	imperative
In	*Interpretation*
inf.	infinitive
in loc.	on this passage
Introd.	Introduction (to)
IPN	M. Noth, *Die israelitischen Personennamen. BWANT,* 3/10, 1928

IrishThQ	*Irish Theological Quarterly*, Maynooth
JA	*Journal Asiatique*, Paris
Ja	Enumeration according to A. Jamme (Old South Arabic)
JAOS	*Journal of the American Oriental Society*
JBL	*Journal of Biblical Literature*
JBR	*Journal of Bible and Religion*, Boston
JCS	*Journal of Cuneiform Studies*, New Haven
JEA	*Journal of Egyptian Archaeology*, London
JEOL	*Jaarbericht... Ex Oriente Lux*, Leiden
JES	*Journal of Ecumenical Studies*
JJS	*Journal of Jewish Studies*, London
JNES	*Journal of Near Eastern Studies*, Chicago
JNWSL	*Journal of Northwest Semitic Languages*
JoPh	*The Journal of Philology*
JPOS	*Journal of the Palestine Oriental Society*, Jerusalem
JQR	*Jewish Quarterly Review*
JR	*Journal of Religion*, Chicago
JRAS	*Journal of the Royal Asiatic Society of Great Britain and Ireland*, London
JRH	*Journal of Religion and Health*
JSOR	*Journal of the Society of Oriental Research*, Toronto
JSS	*Journal of Semitic Studies*, Manchester
JThC	*Journal for Theology and the Church*
JTS	*Journal of Theological Studies*, Oxford
Jud	*Judaica*
K	Tablets in the Kouyunjik collection of the British Museum
KAI	H. Donner-W. Röllig, *Kanaanäische und aramäische Inschriften*, I ²1966, II ²1968, III ²1969
KAR	E. Ebeling, *Keilinschriften aus Assur religiösen Inhalts*, 1915-19
KAT	*Kommentar zum Alten Testament*, ed. E. Sellin, continued by J. Herrmann
KAV	O. Schroeder, *Keilinschriften aus Assur verschiedenen Inhalts*
KB	*Keilinschriftliche Bibliothek*, ed. E. Schrader
KBL	L. Koehler-W. Baumgartner, *Hebräisches und aramäisches Lexikon zum Alten Testament*, ²1958, ³1967ff.
KBo	*Keilschrifttexte aus Boghazköy*
KHC	*Kurzer Handcommentar zum Alten Testament*, ed. K. Marti
KlSchr	*Kleine Schriften* (A. Alt, 1953-59; O. Eissfeldt, 1962ff.)
KUB	*Keilschrifturkunden aus Boghazköi*
KuD	*Kerygma und Dogma*, Göttingen
Lane	E. W. Lane, *An Arabic-English Lexicon*, London, 1863-1893
Lat.	Latin
LD	*Lectio Divina*
Leslau, *Contributions*	W. Leslau, *Ethiopic and South Arabic Contributions to the Hebrew Lexicon* (1958)
Levy, *WTM*	J. Levy, *Wörterbuch über die Talmudim und Midraschim*, ²1924=1963
LexSyr	C. Brockelmann, *Lexicon Syriacum*, ²1968
LidzEph	M. Lidzbarski, *Ephemeris für semitische Epigraphik*, 1900-1915
LidzNE	M. Lidzbarski, *Handbuch der nordsemitischen Epigraphik*, 1898
lit.	literally
LRSt	*Leipziger Rechtswissenschaftliche Studien*
LSS	*Leipziger Semitischen Studien*
LThK	*Lexikon für Theologie und Kirche*, 1930-38, ²1957ff.
LUÅ	*Lunds Universitets Årsskrift*
LXX	Septuagint
MAOG	*Mitteilungen der Altorientalischen Gesellschaft*, Leipzig
MBPAR	*Münchener Beiträge zur Papyrusforschung und Antiken Rechtsgeschichte*
MDAI	*Mitteilungen des Deutschen Archäologischen Instituts in Kairo*, Wiesbaden

MdD	E. S. Drower-R. Macuch, *Mandaic Dictionary*, Oxford, 1963
MDOG	*Mitteilungen der Deutschen Orient-Gesellschaft*, Berlin
MeyerK	*Kritisch-exegetischer Kommentar über das Neue Testament*, initiated by H. A. W. Meyer, Göttingen
MIFAO	*Mémoires publiés par les membres de l'Institut Français d'Archéologie Orientale au Caire*, Cairo
MIO	*Mitteilungen des Instituts für Orientforschung*, Berlin
MKAW	*Mededelingen der Kon. Nederlandse Akademie van Wetenschappen*, Amsterdam
MKPAW	*Monatsberichte der Königlich-Preussischen Akademie der Wissenschaften*, Berlin
MPG	*Patrologia Graeca*, ed. J. P. Migne, Paris
MPL	*Patrologia Latina*, ed. J. P. Migne, Paris
ms.	manuscript
MT	Massoretic Text
MThS	*Münchener Theologische Studien*
MThZ	*Münchener Theologische Zeitschrift*
Mus	*Le Muséon, Revue d'Études Orientales*
MUSJ	*Mélanges de l'Université St. Joseph*, Beirut
MVÄG	*Mitteilungen der Vorderasiatisch-Ägyptischen Gesellschaft* (Berlin), Leipzig
n.d.	no date
NedGTT	*Nederduitse Gereformeerde Teologiese Tydskrif*
NedThT	*Nederlands Theologisch Tijdschrift*, Wageningen
NKZ	*Neue Kirchliche Zeitschrift*, Erlangen, Leipzig
n.n.	no name
NovT	*Novum Testamentum*, Leiden
NRTh	*Nouvelle Revue Théologique*, Paris
NSI	G. A. Cooke, *A Text-Book of North-Semitic Inscriptions*, Oxford, 1903
NTS	*New Testament Studies*, Cambridge
NTT	*Norsk Teologisk Tidsskrift*, Oslo
obj.	object
OECT	*Oxford Editions of Cuneiform Texts*, London, 1923ff.
OIP	*Oriental Institute Publications*, Chicago, 1924ff.
OLP	*Orientalia Lovaniensia Periodica*
OLZ	*Orientalistische Literaturzeitung* (Leipzig), Berlin
Or	*Orientalia. Commentarii periodici Pontificii Instituti Biblici*, Rome
OrAnt	*Oriens Antiquus*
OrNeer	*Orientalia Neerlandica*, Leiden
OTL	*The Old Testament Library*
OTS	*Oudtestamentische Studiën*, Leiden
OuTWP	*De Ou Testamentiese Werkgemeenskap in Suid-Afrika*, Pretoria
PAAJR	*Proceedings of the American Academy for Jewish Research*
par.	parallel/and parallel passages
pass.	passive
PBS	*Publications of the Babylonian Section of the University Museum*, Philadelphia
PEQ	*Palestine Exploration Quarterly*, London
perf.	perfect
Phoen.	Phoenician
PJ	*Palästinajahrbuch*, Berlin
PN	name of a person
PN	H. Ranke, *Die ägyptischen Personennamen*, 1935-1952
PNU	F. Gröndahl, *Personennamen der Texte aus Ugarit*, Rome, 1967
prep.	preposition
PRU	*Le Palais Royal d'Ugarit*, ed. Cl. Schaeffer, Paris
PSBA	*Proceedings of the Society of Biblical Archaeology*, Bloomsbury (London)

ptcp.   participle
Pun.   Punic
PV   *Parole di Vita*
PW   A. Pauly-G. Wissowa, *Real-Encyclopädie der classischen Altertums-
               wissenschaft,* 1894ff.
Pyr.   Pyramid Texts, ed. K. Sethe
QuaestDisp   *Quaestiones Disputatae,* ed. K. Rahner and H. Schlier, 1959ff.
R   H. C. Rawlinson, *The Cuneiform Inscriptions of Western Asia,* London, 1861-
               1909
RA   *Revue d'Assyriologie et d'Archéologie Orientale,* Paris
RAC   *Reallexikon für Antike und Christentum,* ed. Th. Klauser, 1941ff.
RÄR   H. Bonnet, *Reallexikon der ägyptischen Religionsgeschichte*
RB   *Revue Biblique,* Paris
RdM   *Die Religionen der Menschheit,* ed. C. M. Schröder
RE   *Real-Enzyklopädie für protestantische Theologie und Kirche,* ³1896-1913
RÉg   *Revue d'Égyptologie*
repr.   reprint, reprinted
RES   *Revue des Études Sémitiques,* Paris
RES (with
   number)   *Répertoire d'Épigraphie Sémitique*
RevQ   *Revue de Qumrân,* Paris
RevRéf   *La Revue Réformee*
RGG   *Die Religion in Geschichte und Gegenwart,* ³1957-1965
RHA   *Revue Hittite et Asianique,* Paris
RHJE   *Revue de l'Histoire Juive en Égypte*
RHPR   *Revue d'Histoire et de Philosophie Religieuses,* Strasbourg, Paris
RHR   *Revue de l'Histoire des Religions,* Paris
RivBibl   *Rivista Biblica,* Rome
RLA   *Reallexikon der Assyriologie,* ed. G. Ebeling and B. Meissner, Berlin, I 1932,
               II 1938, III 1, 2 1957/59
RLR   *Revue de Linguistique Romane*
RLV   *Reallexikon der Vorgeschichte,* ed. Max Ebert, Berlin, 1924-1932
RoB   *Religion och Bibel. Nathan Söderblom-Sällskapets Årsbok*
RS   Ras Shamra
RScR   *Revue des Sciences Religieuses*
RSO   *Rivista degli Studi Orientali,* Rome
RSPT   *Revue des Sciences Philosophiques et Théologiques,* Paris
RT   *Recueil de Travaux relatifs à la philologie et à l'archéologie égyptiennes et
               assyriennes*
RTP   *Revue de Théologie et de Philosophie,* Lausanne
Ry   Enumeration in G. Ryckmans, *Inscriptions sudarabes* I-XVII;
               Le Muséon, 40-72
SAHG   A. Falkenstein-W. von Soden, *Sumerische und akkadische Hymnen und Gebete*
SAK   *Die sumerischen und akkadischen Königsinschriften,* ed. F. Thureau-Dangin
               (=*VAB,* I)
SAT   *Die Schriften des Alten Testaments in Auswahl,* trans. and ed. H. Gunkel, *et al.,*
               Göttingen
SAW   *Sitzungsberichte der Österreichischen Akademie der Wissenschaften in Wien*
SBAW   *Sitzungsberichte der Bayerischen Akademie der Wissenschaften,* Munich
SBM   *Stuttgarter Biblische Monographien*
SBS   *Stuttgarter Bibel-Studien*
SBT   *Studies in Biblical Theology*
SchThU   *Schweizerische Theologische Umschau,* Bern
ScrHier   *Scripta Hierosolymitana. Publications of the Hebrew University,* Jerusalem
SDAW   *Sitzungsberichte der Deutschen Akademie der Wissenschaften zu Berlin*
SEÅ   *Svensk Exegetisk Årsbok,* Lund

Sem	*Semitica*
Seux	J. M. Seux, *Epithètes Royales Akkadiennes et Sumériennes,* Paris, 1968
SG	F. Delitzsch, *Sumerische Grammatik*
SgV	*Sammlung gemeinverständlicher Vorträge und Schriften aus dem Gebiet der Theologie und Religionsgeschichte,* Tübingen
SJT	*Scottish Journal of Theology,* Edinburgh
SL	A. Deimel, *Šumerisches Lexikon,* Rome, 1925-1937
SMSR	*Studi e Materiali di Storia delle Religioni* (Rome), Bologna
SNumen	*Supplements to Numen*
SNVAO	*Skrifter utgitt av Det Norske Videnskaps-Akademi i Oslo*
Soq.	Soqoṭri
SPAW	*Sitzungsberichte der Preussischen Akademie der Wissenschaften zu Berlin*
SSAW	*Sitzungsberichte der Sächsischen Akademie der Wissenschaften zu Leipzig*
SSN	*Studia Semitica Neerlandica*
StANT	*Studien zum Alten und Neuen Testament,* Munich
St.-B.	H. L. Strack-P. Billerbeck, *Kommentar zum Neuen Testament aus Talmud und Midrasch,* 1923-1961
StOr	*Studia Orientalia,* Helsinki
StSem	*Studi Semitici*
StTh	*Studia Theologica,* Lund, Aarhus
StudGen	*Studium Generale,* Heidelberg
subj.	subject
subst.	substantive
suf.	suffix
Sum.	Sumerian
SVT	*Supplements to Vetus Testamentum,* Leiden
Synt	C. Brockelmann, *Hebräische Syntax*
Syr.	Syriac
Syr	*Syria. Revue d'Art Oriental et d'Archéologie,* Paris
TAik	*Teologinen Aikakauskirja*
TCL	*Textes Cunéiformes du Musée du Louvre*
TDNT	*Theological Dictionary of the New Testament,* ed. G. Kittel and G. Friedrich, trans. G. Bromiley
TDOT	*Theological Dictionary of the Old Testament*
TGUOS	*Transactions of the Glasgow University Oriental Society*
Th.	Theologie
Theol.	Theology (of)
THAT	*Theologisches Handwörterbuch zum Alten Testament,* ed. E. Jenni and C. Westermann, Munich, 1971
ThB	*Theologische Bücherei*
Theol.Diss.	*Theologische Dissertationen,* Basel
ThLZ	*Theologische Literaturzeitung,* Leipzig, Berlin
ThR	*Theologische Rundschau,* Tübingen
ThSt	*Theologische Studien,* Zurich
ThStKr	*Theologische Studien und Kritiken,* Berlin
ThViat	*Theologia Viatorum*
ThZ	*Theologische Zeitschrift,* Basel
Tigr.	Tigrīnya (Tigriña)
trans.	translated
TrThSt	*Trierer Theologische Studien*
TrThZ	*Trierer Theologische Zeitschrift*
TS	*Theological Studies*
TüThQ	*Theologische Quartalschrift,* Tübingen, Stuttgart
TynB	*Tyndale Bulletin*
UET	*Ur Excavations. Texts,* London, 1928ff.
UF	*Ugarit-Forschungen*

Ugar.	Ugaritic
Urk.	*Urkunden des ägyptischen Altertums,* ed. G. Steindorff
UT	C. H. Gordon, *Ugaritic Textbook,* Rome, 1965
UUÅ	*Uppsala Universitets Årsskrift*
VAB	*Vorderasiatische Bibliothek*
VAS	*Vorderasiatische Schriftdenkmäler der königlichen Museen zu Berlin*
VD	*Verbum Domini,* Rome
VG	C. Brockelmann, *Grundriss der vergleichenden Grammatik der semitischen Sprachen,* 1908-1913
VT	*Vetus Testamentum,* Leiden
Vulg.	Vulgate
WbÄS	A. Erman-H. Grapow, *Wörterbuch der ägyptischen Sprache,* I-V
WbMyth	*Wörterbuch der Mythologie,* ed. H. W. Haussig
Whitaker	R. E. Whitaker, *A Concordance of the Ugaritic Literature,* 1972
WMANT	*Wissenschaftliche Monographien zum Alten und Neuen Testament,* Neukirchen
WO	*Die Welt des Orients,* Göttingen
WTM	J. Levy, *Wörterbuch über die Talmudim und Midraschim,* ²1924 = 1963
WUS	J. Aistleitner, *Wörterbuch der ugaritischen Sprache,* ³1967
WZ	*Wissenschaftliche Zeitschrift*
WZKM	*Wiener Zeitschrift für die Kunde des Morgenlandes*
ZA	*Zeitschrift für Assyriologie* (Leipzig), Berlin
ZÄS	*Zeitschrift für Ägyptische Sprache und Altertumskunde* (Leipzig), Berlin
ZAW	*Zeitschrift für die Alttestamentliche Wissenschaft* (Giessen), Berlin
ZDMG	*Zeitschrift der Deutschen Morgenländischen Gesellschaft* (Leipzig), Wiesbaden
ZDPV	*Zeitschrift des Deutschen Palästina-Vereins* (Leipzig, Stuttgart), Wiesbaden
ZE	*Zeitschrift für Ethnologie*
ZEE	*Zeitschrift für Evangelische Ethik,* Gütersloh
ZMR	*Zeitschrift für Missionskünde und Religionswissenschaft,* Berlin
ZNW	*Zeitschrift für die Neutestamentliche Wissenschaft* (Giessen), Berlin
ZRGG	*Zeitschrift für Religions- und Geistesgeschichte,* Cologne
ZS	*Zeitschrift für Semitistik und verwandte Gebiete,* Leipzig
ZST	*Zeitschrift für die Systematische Theologie* (Gütersloh), Berlin
ZThK	*Zeitschrift für Theologie und Kirche,* Tübingen
ZZ	*Die Zeichen der Zeit*
→	indicates cross-reference within this *Dictionary*

TRANSLITERATION OF HEBREW

CONSONANTS

Hebrew Consonant	Technical Usage	Nontechnical Usage
א	ʾ	ʾ
ב	b	b
ב	bh	bh
ג	g	g
ג	gh	gh
ד	d	d
ד	dh	dh
ה	h	h
ו	v, w	v
ז	z	z
ח	ch, ḥ	ch
ט	ṭ	t
י	y	y
כ	k	k
כ	kh	kh
ל	l	l
מ	m	m
נ	n	n
ס	s	s
ע	ʿ	ʿ
פ	p	p
פ	ph	ph
צ	ts, ṣ	ts
ק	q	q
ר	r	r
שׂ	ś	s
שׁ	sh, š	sh
ת	t	t
ת	th	th

VOWELS

Hebrew Vowel	Technical Usage	Nontechnical Usage
─	a	a
─	a	a
─	ā	a
─	e	e
─	e	e
─	ey	ey
─	ē	e
─	ê	e
─	e	e
─	i	i
─	î	i
─	o	o
─	o	o
─	ō	o
─	ô	o
─	u	u
─	û	u
─	ai	ai
─	āv	av
─	āi	ai
ה	h	h

בָּדַל bdl

Contents: I. Etymology, Occurrences. II. With a Modified Sacral Meaning. III. In the Priestly Account of Creation. IV. Setting Apart of the Priesthood. V. Separation Between Clean and Unclean. VI. Election and Apostasy. VII. In the Qumran Literature.

I. Etymology, Occurrences. Apparently the root *bdl* occurs only in Northwest and Southwest Semitic. There seems to be a connection between Ugar. *bdlm*, "merchant,"[1] and stem II, "to change, exchange," of the Arab. verb *badala*, "to replace."[2] It is more difficult to see a connection between Heb. *bdl*, "to separate (oneself), to make a distinction," and the same root in Arabic. Instead one might be tempted to revive some connection between Heb. *bdl* and the Arab. verb *batala*, "to separate" (cf. Heb. *bethulah*), as was done in the earlier lexicons. However, *bdl* may be related to *badala*.[3] This word seems to have come into Hebrew at a rather late period; it must be assumed that it was used especially in priestly circles, and that a special, almost technical meaning was attached to it. The verb appears 10 times in the niphal (almost exclusively in the Chronicler's History) and 31 times in the hiphil (most frequently in the Priestly legal literature).

II. With a Modified Sacral Meaning. The verb *bdl* is used predominantly in the Priestly literature and usually refers to sacral matters. If a writer wishes to describe a separation in a purely secular context, he usually uses the synonym *paradh*.[4] Passages that deal with the separation of warriors for or from battle are no exception (1 Ch. 12:9 [Eng. v. 8]; 2 Ch. 25:10). Even in these late texts there is a reminiscence of the idea that mustering for battle was a sacral act.[5]

bdl must be understood in a similar way in the Deuteronomic regulations concerning the setting apart of the cities of refuge (Dt. 4:41; 19:2,7). Although Deuteronomy strips this institution of its sacral character, the choice of words

---

bdl. J. Begrich, "Die priesterliche Tora," *Werden und Wesen des AT. BZAW,* 66 (1936), 63-88; S. R. Driver, "On Some Alleged Linguistic Affinities of the Elohist," *JoPh,* 11 (1882), 201-236; K. Elliger, *HAT,* 4 (1966), 277; H. Odeberg, *Trito-Isaiah* (Uppsala, 1931), 40f.; Pedersen, *ILC,* III-IV, 264-295; W. H. Schmidt, *Die Schöpfungsgeschichte der Priesterschrift. WMANT,* 17 (1964, ²1967).

[1] Gordon, *UT,* No. 448.
[2] See *KBL*³ and Eissfeldt, *JSS,* 5 (1960), 35f.
[3] *BDB, KBL*³.
[4] Driver, 219f.
[5] Von Rad, *Der Heilige Krieg* (⁴1965), 79-81.

would suggest that it originated in a religious context.[6] Finally the verb *bdl* occurs a couple of times in the Priestly sacrificial regulations with the simple meaning "to divide asunder" (Lev. 1:17; 5:8).

III. In the Priestly Account of Creation. *bdl* is used in a typical way in the Priestly account of creation (Gen. 1:4,6,7,14,18): the individual phases in creation are depicted as a separation of the different elements from one another: light from darkness, water from the firmament, day from night, etc. The author uses the word *bdl* in order to emphasize a major idea in the Priestly account of creation, viz., that the creator-God is a God of order rather than a mythological procreator.[7]

IV. Setting Apart of the Priesthood. The Priestly preference for the word *bdl* stands out clearly in postexilic texts which deal with the relationship of the priesthood to the rest of the people. Frequently these texts affirm that Yahweh (or Moses) has set apart the priesthood from the people (Nu. 8:14; 16:9; Dt. 10:8).[8] In other passages also the setting apart of individual priests is emphasized by the use of the verb *bdl* (Nu. 16:21; 1 Ch. 23:13; Ezr. 8:24; cf. 1 Ch. 25:1; Ezr. 10:16). *bdl* is used in a similar way in the realm of sacral law, although it is characterized by negative overtones here: whoever transgresses the law is separated from the community (Dt. 29:20[21]; Ezr. 10:8; → חרם *cherem*).

V. Separation Between Clean and Unclean. The important concept of clean and unclean is already apparent in these last-mentioned passages. The distinction between clean and unclean (and between sacred and profane, → קדשׁ *qādhash*), which was certainly observed from ancient times, is emphasized more and more in the postexilic period; the primary task of the priest is to distinguish between sacred and profane, between unclean and clean (Ezk. 22:26; cf. 44:23; Lev. 10:10; 11:47; cf. 20:25).[9] Special furnishings of the temple which serve to separate the holy from the common (the veil: Ex. 26:33; the wall of the temple: Ezk. 42:20) belong to the same category.

This emphasis on the distinction between clean and unclean in the postexilic period leads to the use of cleanness and holiness to express the nature of Israel in contrast to other nations (Ex. 19:6).[10] Thus *bdl* is used several times to denote Israel's separation from the heathen. In Ezr. 6:21, those who have returned from exile are characterized as people who have separated themselves from the pollutions of the peoples (Neh. 9:2; 10:29[28]). In a more concrete sense, *bdl* appears in connection with the separation of the Jews from their heathen wives (Ezr. 9:1; 10:11) and the expulsion of those of foreign descent (Neh. 13:3; cf. Isa. 56:3).[11]

---

[6] Cf. Greenberg, *JBL,* 78 (1959), 125-132.
[7] Schmidt, 99-103, 167-69.
[8] On the problems in Dt. 10:8, see von Rad, *ATD,* VIII, 57.
[9] Begrich, 66.
[10] Pedersen, 272ff.
[11] See also Odeberg, 40-42.

VI. Election and Apostasy. In a usage that follows the same train of thought but bears greater theological weight, *bdl* is used to express the idea of election (1 K. 8:53; Lev. 20:24,26). [12] In direct antithesis to this expression (probably formulated in Deuteronomistic circles), Isa. 59:2 says: "your iniquities have made a separation (*hayu mabhdilim*) between you and your God." This statement is made in answer to the question of whether Yahweh's arm is too short, in other words, whether Yahweh is able to fulfil the promise he made at the time he chose his people. And the answer seeks to make clear that Israel itself has, as it were, annulled this choice. In reality, the only time *bdl* is used in the figurative sense in the OT is in this passage.

VII. In the Qumran Literature. In the Qumran texts, the Priestly use of *bdl* is dominant. *bdl* occurs 24 times in the Damascus Document and the Manual of Discipline alone. It is found in the same contexts as it is in the OT: (1) separation between clean and unclean; (2) separation of the community from "the others"; and (3) expulsion of whoever transgresses the law from the community. [13]

Otzen

---

[12] See Vriezen, *Die Erwählung Israels* (Zürich, 1953), 37.
[13] Kuhn, *Konkordanz zu den Qumrántexten* (1960), 28.

בהל bhl; בֶּהָלָה behālāh

Contents: I. Etymology, Occurrences. II. "To Hasten." III. 1. "To Be Terrified" in General Usage; 2. "Terror" of the Numinous; 3. "Terror" of Death; 4. "Terror" of Yahweh.

I. Etymology, Occurrences. The root *bhl* has two meanings in both Hebrew and Aramaic: "to hasten" and "to be terrified." There have been numerous attempts to determine its original meaning by relating *bhl* to various Arabic roots, but they are dubious. [1] Palache thinks that possibly the original meaning was "to move suddenly and excitedly." [2] However, the view of Blau, who prefers

---

bhl. J. Becker, *Gottesfurcht im AT* (Rome, 1965); J. Blau, "Etymologische Untersuchungen auf Grund des palästinischen Arabisch," *VT,* 5 (1955), 337-344; A. Guillaume, *Prophecy and Divination* (London, 1938), 274; J. Hempel, *Gott und Mensch im AT. BWANT,* 3/2 (²1936), 3-27; B. Jordahn, "Schrecken, schrecklich," *BThH* (1954), 510-13; S. Plath, *Furcht Gottes* (1963); L. Wächter, *Der Tod im AT* (1967), 10-56; M. Wagner, *Die lexikalischen und grammatikalischen Aramaismen im alttestamentlichen Hebräisch. BZAW,* 96 (1966), 33.

[1] Blau, 339; Guillaume, 274.
[2] Palache, *Semantic Notes on the Hebrew Lexicon* (Leiden, 1959), 12f.

to assume that Heb. *bhl* is cognate with Arab. *bahara,* stem VII "to be breath-less," and to find here the common origin of both meanings,[3] is more acceptable. In Hebrew the meaning "to hasten" clearly came to be attached to the root *bhl* at a late period under Aramaic influence.[4] The verb *bhl* occurs 24 times in the niphal, 10 times in the piel, twice in the pual, and 3 times in the hiphil. We may add to this the corresponding Biblical Aram. verb *behal,* which appears 7 times in the pael, 3 times in the hithpeel, and once in the hithpaal. Finally, a noun *behalah* occurs 4 times in OT Hebrew.

II. "To Hasten." There are certain difficulties connected with delimiting the two meanings of the root *bhl* already mentioned: "be terrified" (or "terrify") and "hasten." The meaning "hasten" is confined primarily to late texts (Prov., Est., and Ch.). The use of *bhl* in this sense is typical in the Wisdom Literature, especially in passages that warn against rash actions (Eccl. 5:1 [Eng. v. 2]; 7:9 [both in the piel]; Prov. 28:22 [niphal]; 20:21 [pual], where it is necessary to emend the text with *BHK*). In the other passages where *bhl* means "to hasten," it simply refers to people who are brought in or carried away in haste (2 Ch. 26:20; Est. 6:14 [both hiphil]; 2 Ch. 35:21; Est. 2:9 [both piel]; Est. 8:14); cf. the substantival infinitive in Biblical Aram. *hithbehalah,* "haste" (Dnl. 2:25; 3:24; 6:20[19]) and the Biblical Aram. noun *behilu* (Ezr. 4:23). In this connection, Eccl. 8:3 is dubious: usually *'al tibbahel* is rendered "do not act rashly."[5] How-ever, Wildeboer[6] is possibly correct in translating "do not tremble."[7]

III. 1. *"To Be Terrified" in General Usage.* As has already been mentioned, however, the predominant meaning of the verb *bhl* is "be terrified" (in the hiphil and Biblical Aramaic hithpaal; "terrify" in the piel, hiphil, and Biblical Aramaic pael). The noun *behalah* also belongs to this semantic field. Often this terror is connected with the unexpected or is brought about by an event that breaks into human reality in a threatening manner.[8] It is seldom used to denote a person's fear of someone else (Gen. 45:3); more often it describes fear in battle (niphal: Jgs. 20:41; 2 S. 4:1; piel: 2 Ch. 32:18; Dnl. 11:44; and Ezr. 4:4).

2. *"Terror" of the Numinous.* But more frequently the root *bhl* denotes the terror that comes upon a man who knows he is confronted by the numinous. 1 S. 28:21 is typical: Saul is terrified by the supernatural appearance of Samuel. In the Biblical Aramaic of the book of Daniel, *bhl* repeatedly denotes man's reaction to strange visions (Dnl. 4:2,16[5,19]; 5:6,9,10; 7:15,28 [mostly pael]; cf. 1QGenAp 2:3). When the plaintiff of Ps. 6:3f.(2f.) says that his bones and

---

3 Blau, 339.

4 Wagner, 33.

5 On the problem of the beginning of this expression, see the comms., and H. L. Gins-berg, *PAAJR,* 21 (1952), 52.

6 Wildeboer, *KHC,* 17 (1898), 150.

7 See below.

8 Cf. Jordahn, 511.

his soul are terrified (RSV "troubled"), this is certainly connected with the idea that his enemies are demonic *poʿale ʾaven,* "workers of iniquity, evildoers," who have brought his sickness upon him. [9] If the explanation of Eccl. 8:3 mentioned above is correct, this verse warns against terrified withdrawal because of a divine oath.

3. *"Terror" of Death.* Faced with sudden, unexpected, and premature death, the Israelite felt that he was in the presence of a sinister power. The noun *behalah* denotes simply the terror associated or even identical with sudden death (Lev. 26:16; Ps. 78:33; Jer. 15:8; Isa. 65:23; cf. the synonyms *ballahah, baʿath,* and → אימה *ʾemāh,* which also denote [the terror of] death in Job 18:14; Ps. 18:5 [4]; Job 15:24; Dt. 32:25; Ps. 55:5[4]; 88:16[15]). [10]

4. *"Terror" of Yahweh.* This fear of death lies behind the terror man has of Yahweh. The verb *bhl* is used to describe man's terror of Yahweh in approximately 20 passages. It is used in certain psalms of the man whom God has forsaken (Ps. 30:8 [7]; 90:7; 104:29). But it is more characteristic of the book of Job, where it refers to the man who knows that he has been delivered into the hands of an arbitrary God (Job 4:5; 21:6; 23:15f.). This word is found most frequently, however, in contexts that speak of Yahweh punishing man. It is used to denote the punishment of individuals (Ps. 6:11[10]; Job 22:10) or of Israel (Jer. 15:8; Ezk. 7:27) only in a few passages. It applies to the divine punishment of Israel's enemies much more often. It is no accident that *bhl* is often used in connection with descriptions of the day of Yahweh: the sudden, unexpected, and ominous evoke sudden terror (Ps. 48:6[5]; 83:16,18[15,17]; 2:5; Ex. 15:15; Isa. 13:8; 21:3; Zeph. 1:18; Jer. 51:32; Ezk. 26:18). Several of these passages use the anxiety and trembling connected with birth to emphasize the physical effects of terror.

Otzen

---

[9] Cf. Mowinckel, *Psalmenstudien,* I (Oslo, 1921), 10f.
[10] Cf. also Pedersen, *ILC,* III-IV, 477ff., and Wächter, 10ff.

בְּהֵמָה behēmāh;   בְּהֵמוֹת behēmôth

Contents: I. 1. Etymology; 2. Occurrences; 3. Stereotyped Phrases; 4. LXX. II. Attempts at Classification: 1. In J; 2. In P; 3. Beasts of Burden or Riding Animals; 4. Dangerous Wild Animals. III. God, Man, and Animal: 1. Cultic Regulations; 2. Family and Tribal Relationship; 3. Connection with Creation and Fate; 4. Distinction Between 'adham and behemah. IV. behēmôth: 1. Definition; 2. The Existence of Hippopotami in Palestine, Syria, and Egypt; 3. The Egyptian Hippopotamus Cult; 4. Behemoth in Job 40:15ff.

I. 1. *Etymology.* The etymology of *behemah*, "beast, cattle, domestic animal, game," is uncertain: Ugar. *ʔbn yḫlq bhmt, UT* 19, 450a, "our enemy will destroy the cattle";[1] Arab. *bahīmat*, "animal," pl. "large cattle," *bah(a)m*, "lamb, sheep";[2] Aram. *bhm(y)th;*[3] Middle Heb. "domestic animal," *bhm*, "drover";

---

behēmāh. F. S. Bodenheimer, *The Animals of Palestine* (Jerusalem, 1935); Dalman, *AuS,* VI (1939), 171, and often (Index, 380); J. Hempel, "Gott, Mensch und Tier im AT," *ZST,* 9 (1932), 211-249=*Apoxysmata. BZAW,* 81 (1961), 198-229; M.-L. Henry, *Das Tier im religiösen Bewusstsein des alttestamentlichen Menschen. SgV,* 220/221 (1958); W. Kornfeld, "Reine und unreine Tiere im AT," *Kairos,* 7 (1965), 134-147; W. Krebs, "Zur kultischen Kohabitation mit Tieren im Alten Orient," *Forschungen und Fortschritte,* 37 (1963), 19-21; W. Pangritz, *Das Tier in der Bibel* (Munich-Basel, 1963); additional literature is given under → אֲרִי *'arî.*
On IV: H. Altenmüller, *Jagd im Alten Ägypten* (1967); H. Bonnet, *RÄR,* 528-530; B. Brentjes, "Gelegentlich gehaltene Wildtiere des Alten Orients," *WZ* Halle-Wittenberg (1962), 703-732; S. T. Byington, "Hebrew Marginalia," *JBL,* 64 (1945), 345ff.; G. R. Driver, "Leviathan and Behemoth," *VT,* 1 (1951), 314; *idem,* "Mythical Monsters in the OT," *Proceedings of the Twenty-second Congress of Orientalists,* II (1957), 113-15; *idem,* "Mythical Monsters in the OT," *Studi Orientalistici in onore di Giorgio Levi Della Vida,* I (Rome, 1956), 234-249; J. Feliks, *The Animal World of the Bible* (Tel Aviv, 1962), 95; G. Fohrer, *KAT,* XVI (1963), 551ff.; H. Gunkel, *Schöpfung und Chaos in Urzeit und Endzeit* (1895, ²1921), 61ff.; J. Guttmann, "Leviathan, Behemoth and Ziz: Jewish Messianic Symbols in Art," *HUCA,* 39 (1968), 219-230; G. Haas, "On the Occurrence of Hippopotamus in the Iron Age of the Coastal Area of Israel (Tell Qasīleh)," *BASOR,* 132 (1953), 30-34; G. Hölscher, *HAT,* 17 (²1952), 94ff.; P. Humbert, "Le modernisme de Job," *SVT,* 3 (1955), 150-161, esp. 152; O. Kaiser, *Die mythische Bedeutung des Meeres in Ägypten, Ugarit und Israel. BZAW,* 78 (1959, ²1962), 149ff.; H. Kees, "Zu den Krokodil- und Nilpferdkulten im Nordwestdelta Ägyptens," *Studi in memoria di I. Rosellini,* II (Pisa, 1955), 142-152 + Tables XIV, XV; *idem,* "Der Krokodilgott des 6. oberägyptischen Gaues" (*SBO* III), *AnBibl,* 12 (Rome, 1959), 161-64; J. Lewy, "Influences ḥurrites sur Israel," *RES* (1938), 48-75, esp. 65-67; A. Ohler, *Mythologische Elemente im AT* (1969), 101ff.; E. Ruprecht, "Das Nilpferd im Hiobbuch. Beobachtungen zu der sogenannten zweiten Gottesrede," *VT,* 21 (1971), 209-231; T. Säve-Söderbergh, *An Egyptian Representation of Hippopotamus Hunting as a Religious Motiv. Horae Soederblomianae,* 3 (Uppsala, 1953); A. Schultens, *Commentarius in Librum Jobi* (Halae Magdeburgicae, 1773), 919-929.

[1] Virolleaud.
[2] Blachère-Chouémi; on Ethiopic, cf. Leslau, *Contributions,* 12.
[3] *DISO,* 32.

Mandean *b'hym'*, "ass." [4] To derive *behemah* from *bhm*, "dumb, mute" (cf. Arab. *'abham*, "dumb, mute"), is hardly justified. It is more likely that Albright is correct [5] in deriving it from Ugar. *bmt*, "back," Akk. *bāmtu*, "half," "half of a slope," "middle part of the back," [6] Heb. *bmh*, "back," "high place," "burial-place or cult place" (cf. *bhn*, "thumb"? "toe"). [7]

2. *Occurrences*. *behemah* occurs in the OT 188 times, or not counting three conjectural passages (Isa. 30:6; Joel 1:18; Job 12:7) 185 times, distributed as follows:

Gen. 20 times; Ex. 18 times; Lev. 31 times; Nu. 15 times; Dt. 18 times; Josh. 4 times; Jgs. and 1 S. once each; 1 and 2 K. 4 times; Isa. 5 times; Jer. 18 times; Ezk. 12 times; Joel, Jonah, and Zec. 3 times each; Job 3 times; Prov. twice; Eccl. 4 times; Ezr. twice; Neh. 5 times; and 2 Ch. once. *behemah* is used as a subject 10 times and as an object 37 times.

3. *Stereotyped Phrases*. Among the stereotyped phrases using *behemah*, such as expressions in the construct state and adverbial expressions, we find the following: (a) *behemath ha'arets*, "the beasts of the earth," or *behemah 'asher 'al ha'arets*, "the beasts that are on the earth," Lev. 11:2; Dt. 28:26; Isa. 18:6; Jer. 7:33; 15:3; 16:4; 19:7; 34:20; Job 35:11; (b) *behemath hassadheh*, "the beasts of the field," etc., Ex. 9:19 (twice); 1 S. 17:44; Joel 1:20; 2:22; Ps. 8:8 (Eng. v. 7); (c) *bahamoth ya'ar*, which is equivalent to *chayetho ya'ar*, "the beasts of the forest," Mic. 5:7(8); (d) the formula *'adham-behemah*, "man-beast," or *me'adham (ve)'adh behemah*, "from man (even) to beast," is used as a comprehensive statement 20 times in Exodus and Numbers, 24 times in the Prophets, and 3 times in the Psalms. [8]

4. *LXX*. The LXX translates *behemah* mostly by *ktĕnos*, "animal," *tetrápous*, "four-footed animal," and *thēríon*, "beast."

II. Attempts at Classification.

1. *In J*. In Gen. 2:19, the Yahwist mentions only two classes of animals, viz., *chayyath hassadheh*, "beast of the field," and *'oph hashshamayim*, "bird of the air (lit. heaven)"; but in 2:20 the first man designates three classes, viz., *behemah*, "cattle," *'oph hashshamayim*, "birds of the air," and *chayyath hassadheh*, "beast of the field." Although we cannot be sure whether *chayyath*

---

[4] *MdD*, 46a.

[5] Albright, *SVT*, 4 (1957), 256f.

[6] *AHw*, 101b.

[7] Cf. *BLe*, § 600j.

[8] On the curse formula *lema'akhal le'oph ulebhehemath ha'arets*, "food for birds and for the beasts of the earth," etc., and on the combinations *chayyah, behemah, remes*, "living creatures, beasts, creeping things," or *deghath hayyam, 'oph shamayim, behemah (chayyah, remes)*, "fish of the sea, birds of the heavens, beasts (living creatures, creeping things)," see below.

hassadheh in vv. 19 and 20 refers to the same class of animals, it is obvious that the order of these classes is different in the two verses. According to 2:5, for lack of rain and cultivation the field (open country, *sadheh;* 2:4b, *'erets,* "earth") produced neither wild plants (*siach*) nor useful or cultivated plants (*'esebh*). Thus in 2:19, *chayyath hassadheh* still denotes land animals in general, while in the three classes of 2:20, a distinction is made between *behemah,* "domestic animals," and *chayyath hassadheh,* "wild animals."

The Yahwist does not mention fish or aquatic animals. "The region in which he lives is composed of land in which plants sprung up after a rain, beasts of the field, birds, husbandman and his wife." [9]

J does not yet know or use *remes,* "creeping things." The occurrences of this word in 1:24-26; 7:14; 8:17,19 are from P; and 6:7a; 7:8,23a are probably redactional additions in the style of P. [10]

The narrative of the creation of animals on the earth (which, however, says nothing about God breathing into their nostrils the breath of life) and of the giving of their names in Gen. 2:18-20 shows a high estimation of animals as possible companions of man. But it defines their inability to fill this role by describing how man autonomously gave names to all the animals in harmony with their nature and function, and realizing finally that for man there was found no "helper of his kind (RSV, fit for him)", *'ezer keneghdo* (cf. v. 18), and thus clearly throws into bold relief the "sovereignty of human nature." [11]

The undifferentiated terminology of *chayyath hassadheh,* "beast of the field," in 2:19 also appears in Gen. 3:1,14: the serpent was more subtle *mikkol chayyath hassadheh,* "than any beast of the field"; but it belongs to the "beasts of the field" which God had created, i.e., to the land animals. According to 3:14, the serpent is reproved by the *'arur*-formula, the curse formula: it is "banished from the fellowship of the animal world," [12] excommunicated from among the *behemah,* "cattle," and *chayyath hassadheh,* "beasts of the field," which agrees with the differentiation in 2:20: it is cursed and banned from the community of domesticated and wild land animals. [13] Then in the flood narrative the Yahwist distinguishes between clean and unclean *behemah,* "animals," and *'oph,* "birds" (7:2; 8:20; → טהר *tāhēr*).

2. *In P.* The Priestly narrative of creation divides animals into different classes according to the day on which each is created: water and air animals on the fifth day (Gen. 1:20-23), and land animals on the sixth day (vv. 24f.). Here the real principle of classification is an animal's natural habitat and movement: water–air (heaven)–earth. In the account of the creation of land animals, what God says (1:24) differs from what he does (v. 25) in the order and precise wording (v. 24: comprehensive category *nephesh chayyah,* "living creatures";

---

[9] H. Gunkel, *Genesis* (³1910=⁷1966), 29.

[10] Procksch, Gunkel, etc.

[11] A. Dillmann; cf. Westermann, *BK,* I, 309-312.

[12] O. Procksch, *KAT,* I, 34.

[13] Cf. W. Schottroff, *WMANT,* 30 (1969), 142-47; and also Westermann, *BK,* I, 349ff.

main types, *behemah*, "cattle," *remes*, "creeping things," *chayetho 'erets*, "beasts of the earth"; v. 25 lacks a comprehensive category, and has the main types *chayyath ha'arets*, "beasts of the earth," *behemah*, and *kol remes ha'adhamah*, "everything that creeps upon the ground").

These variations may be explained in different ways: either there was no stereotyped systematized order for classifying animals, or the account of what God did differed from the account of what God said for stylistic reasons, e.g., the writer made the third member in v. 24, *chayetho 'erets*, the first member in v. 25, and then mentioned *behemah* before *kol remes ha'adhamah*, to produce a crescendo effect. *behemah* here seems to mean four-footed domestic animals, large and small livestock, while *chayyath ha'arets* probably denotes wild animals; by way of contrast, in 2:19(J) *chayyath hassadheh* means land animals.

There is also a classification according to natural habitat, water–air–land, in God's transfer of dominion from himself to man in Gen. 1:26: *deghath hayyam*, "the fish of the sea," *'oph hashshamayim*, "the birds of the air," *kol ([chayyath] ha'arets) behemah*, "all ([the beasts] of the earth) the cattle," *kol haremes haromes 'al ha'arets*, "every creeping thing that creeps upon the earth."

This tripartite classification of land animals corresponds to what we find in Gen. 1:24f., but the order is different. The only similarity is that *behemah* is mentioned first in both vv. 24 and 26. According to the word of blessing in v. 28b, man's dominion extends over fish, birds, and "every living thing that moves upon the earth." This last group could be divided into the subspecies *chayyath ha'arets*, "beasts of the earth," and *haromes 'al ha'arets*, "that which creeps upon the earth."

The reference to food (grass and plants) for the animals in 1:30 explicitly names *chayyath ha'arets, kol 'oph hashshamayim*, "every bird of the air," *romes 'al ha'arets*, "that which creeps on the earth," and *chayyah 'asher bo nephesh*, "that which has the breath of life," which probably are to be identified with the three classes of v. 24. It is impossible to say why *behemah* is omitted here.

No constant classification of animals can be detected in the Priestly account of the flood: 6:20; 8:17; otherwise 7:14,21; 8:1; 9:10; cf. also the addition in 6:7a.

The cultic legal regulations in Leviticus are repeatedly concerned with classifying the *behemah*. According to Lev. 1:2, the offering for the burnt-offering must be taken from domestic animals, *behemah*, from the cattle, → בקר *bāqār*, and from the small livestock (sheep, goats), *tso'n*. Here the redactor has systematically classified *behemah* as the main type, and *baqar* and *tso'n* as the subspecies. [14] In the regulations concerning touching an unclean thing in connection with the sin-offering in Lev. 5:2f., we find the classifications *chayyah*, "beast," *behemah*, "cattle," and *sherets*, "swarming things." According to Lev. 7:21, a person who has become unclean by touching an unclean thing (man, beast, small animal [*sherets*, MT has *sheqets*, "abomination"]) is forbidden to eat the sacrifice of the peace-offering.

In the laws concerning cleanness, the cultic classification of clean and un-

---

[14] Elliger: Po[1].

clean, or of what can be eaten and what cannot, is also based on the broad classification of living creatures on the basis of their natural habitat.

Thus Lev. 11:2b-23 (cf. Dt. 14:3-21) distinguishes between land animals, *kol behemah 'asher 'al ha'arets,* "all the beasts that are on the earth," 11:2b-8 (par. Dt. 14:4-8), marine animals, 11:9-12 (par. Dt. 14:9f.), and flying creatures, 11:13-23 (par. Dt. 14:11-20). Lev. 11:2 subsumes these three groups under the general classification *chayyah,* "living things," but Dt. 14:3 forbids the eating of any abominable thing (abomination), → תועבה *tô'ēbhāh.* [15] The lists of forbidden *behemah* in Leviticus and Deuteronomy correspond, except that Lev. 11:4-8 and Dt. 14:6-8 reverse the hare and the rock-badger. However, Lev. 11:3 states only two criteria for *behemah* that can be eaten (those that part the hoof and are cloven-footed, and those that chew the cud), while Dt. 14:4f. gives a detailed list of animals that part the hoof and are cloven-footed, and that chew the cud (ox, sheep, young goat, hart ['*ayyal*], gazelle [*tsebhi*], roebuck [*yachmur*], wild goat ['*aqqo*], bison [antelope, *dishon*], wild sheep [*te'o*], and mountain-goat [type of gazelle, *zemer*]). On uncleanness incurred by touching the carcass of *behemah* that do not part the hoof, are not cloven-footed, and do not chew the cud, cf. Lev. 11:24,39. In the subscript of the main redaction in 11:46f., we find a different classification: beasts, birds, creatures that move through the waters, and creatures that swarm (*shoretseth*) upon the earth. Perhaps the marine animals stand in the third position here (instead of in the second, as in 11:9-12) because of the length of the expression used to describe them. [16] The admonition in Lev. 20:25 for a person to make a distinction between clean and unclean *behemah* and '*oph,* "birds," and not to make himself abominable, may be an addition based on Lev. 11. [17] It is not clear why marine animals are not mentioned in this passage.

3. *Beasts of Burden or Riding Animals. behemah* is used in referring to a single riding animal in Neh. 2:12,14: Nehemiah rides on a *behemah* in order to inspect the city walls during the night. The *behemah* here could have been a horse or a mule. [18]

In Isa. 46:1 *chayyah* and *behemah* (RSV "beasts and cattle") occur as pack-animals or beasts of burden for the idols of Bel and Nebo which are pulled along, and which "bow down" and "stoop." [19] In Isa. 30:6 (the text of which is uncertain), the *bahamoth* of the Negeb could mean the asses and camels which carry riches and treasures on their backs or humps.

According to Hab. 2:17, the violence done to Lebanon and the destruction of the beasts of burden (*shodh behemoth*) will revert back to the heathen emperor responsible for this. The reference here is to the plundering of Lebanon and the ruthless exploitation of beasts of burden and draught-animals in the removal of timber from Lebanon.

---

[15] Cf. Elliger, *HAT,* 4 (1966), 143, 241; P. Humbert, *ZAW,* 72 (1960), 217-237.
[16] Thus Elliger, 148.
[17] Elliger: Ph³.
[18] Cf. W. Rudolph, *HAT,* 20 (1949), *in loc.*
[19] On the text, cf. C. F. Whitley, *VT,* 11 (1961), 459.

4. *Dangerous Wild Animals. behemah* is used in connection with "serpent" to denote a wild and dangerous animal. Yahweh announces to those who are "no people" (*lo' 'am,* Babylonians or Philistines?) that he will send "the teeth of beasts against them, with venom of crawling things of the dust" (Dt. 32:24). With this one should compare the *chayyath hassadheh,* "beasts of the field," in Lev. 26:22, which shall rob disobedient people of their children, destroy their cattle, and even decimate the adults. A curse formula *lema'akhal 'oph hash-shamayim ulebhehemath ha'arets,* "may he (they) be food for the birds of the air and for the beasts of the earth," or something similar, is used to announce that Israel will be oppressed by her enemies and suffer a humiliating death when her dead bodies shall become food for the birds of the air and for the beasts of the earth, and no one will frighten them away (Dt. 28:26). Jer. 7:33 and 19:7 threaten a similar fate on those who offer human sacrifices at the places of sacrifice in Topheth. According to 15:3 and 16:4, those who have not been buried and those whose corpses have been desecrated by wild beasts will increase even more: "the sword to slay, the dogs to tear, and the birds of the air and the beasts of the earth to devour and destroy." Jer. 34:20 threatens those who violate the covenant in similar terms. According to Isa. 18:6, the Assyrians will be left to "the birds of prey of the mountains" (*'et harim*) during the summer, and to the beasts of the earth during the winter. Here the predatory character of the beasts is made clear by *'et harim* (cf. also Goliath's scoffing at David in 1 S. 17:44).

III. God, Man, and Animal. The relationship between God, man, and animal is described in the OT under different rubrics.

1. *Cultic Regulations.* a. Acting shamefully with an animal in the form of sexual intercourse (*shokhebh 'im behemah,* "lying with a beast") is in the Book of the Covenant a crime punishable by death (Ex. 22:18[19]), and in the Shechemite Dodecalog a crime punishable by a curse (Dt. 27:21). The Holiness Code expands this regulation and demands that the beast (*behemah*) be killed (*haragh,* Lev. 20:15). The same punishment applies to a woman's incest with an animal (*qarabh 'el kol behemah leribh'ah,* "[if a woman] approaches any beast and lies with it," 20:16). The codicil in Lev. 18:23 makes no reference to a penalty of death for a man, woman, or beast involved in this crime, but merely labels this act a "defilement" (*tame'*) or a perversion (*tebhel*).

W. Krebs thinks that the prohibition against acting shamefully with an animal or against committing incest with an animal, using the word *behemah,* originally could have been directed against a cohabitation of women and animals practiced in the ancient Near East and Egypt by certain animal and fertility cults.

Apparently the killing of the beast in Lev. 20:15 assumes that the community shares in the guilt for the crime, and therefore it must punish the offenders. [20] The difference in terminology here should be noted: a guilty man or woman is

---

[20] Cf. Elliger, 276.

to be "put to death" (*moth yumath*), whereas a *behemah* is to be "killed" (*haragh*).

Henry [21] calls attention to Aliyan Baal's love for a young cow in Ugaritic mythology. [22]

Because of his virility, the ram (he-goat) of Mendes was called "procreator in Anep, impregnator in the province of Mendes." [23] According to Cosmas women stripped themselves before him, and according to Pindar and Herodas they had sexual intercourse with him. The father of Ramses II and III was said to be the god Ptah, in the form of the ram of Mendes, who cohabited with their mother. [24]

In Hittite law, a man who cohabited with a cow (Table II, § 73), sheep (§ 74), swine, or dog (§ 85) was to be punished; a man who cohabited with a horse or a mule was not punished, but lost his civil rights (§ 86).

b. The law against hybridization in Lev. 19:19, according to which a cow (*behemah*) was not allowed to copulate with a breed of cattle different from its own (or a field was not to be sown with two different kinds of seed, or a person was not to wear a garment made of two different kinds of cloth), is based on very ancient cultic concepts. According to Elliger, these three regulations were inserted in the redaction of Ph². [25] Dt. 22:9-11 refers to other kinds of hybridization, and seems to represent a later reinterpretation. These various kinds of hybridization could point back to different spheres of activity and areas of worship of various deities originally.

c. According to the interpretation in the addition in Dt. 4:16-18, the law against making images in Yahwism forbids the manufacture of any likeness of men, beasts, and heavenly bodies. In addition to the beasts of the earth, 4:17f. also mentions birds, creeping things, and fish.

Ezekiel sees depicted on the walls in the outer court various kinds of *sheqets*, "loathsome things" (or *shiqqutsim*, "detested things"), which are further interpreted as *remes ubhehemah*, "creeping things and beasts" (Ezk. 8:7-12). It is impossible to determine the cultic significance of these symbols. Gaster thinks they had something to do with the celebration of the mysteries. [26] Albright believes they are part of a syncretistic cult like the Osiris cult. [27] Zimmerli begins by pointing out that *sheqets*, "loathsome," and *tame'*, "unclean," are synonymous, and concludes that these symbols are connected with the worship of various creatures that were not supposed to be eaten. [28]

---

[21] Henry, 28.
[22] *CTA*, 5 [I* AB], V, 18ff.
[23] Brugsch, *Thes.*, 626.
[24] The evidence is given in *RÄR*, 868f. ("Widder" ["ram"]).
[25] Elliger, *HAT*, 4, 255.
[26] T. H. Gaster, *JBL*, 60 (1941), 289-310.
[27] W. F. Albright, *Archaeology and the Religion of Israel* (⁴1956), 166f.
[28] W. Zimmerli, *BK*, XIII/1, 217.

d. Israel's belief in the reality of creation led to the idea that the firstborn of man and beast were to be given to God (→ בכור *bᵉkhôr;* cf. Ex. 13:2,12,15; Nu. 3:13[45]; 8:17; 18:15). The Levites play a special role as substitutes for the firstborn in this system. It should be mentioned that according to Lev. 27:9f. an animal (*behemah*) that has been promised as a sacrifice may not be exchanged, since it is "holy," for an animal that has been promised and exchanged defiles the sanctuary. The priest establishes the monetary value of an unclean animal that cannot be sacrificed to be paid into the temple treasury (27:11). The codicil in Lev. 27:26f. on the redemptive value of animals that are dedicated to the Lord decrees that the firstborn of the *behemah* cannot be dedicated to Yahweh, since it (whether ox, *shor,* or small animal, *seh*) belongs to Yahweh; unclean animals can be redeemed. The so-called devoted thing (man, *'adham;* beast, *behemah;* and inherited field, *sedheh 'achuzzatho*) cannot be redeemed or sold (27:28).

2. *Family and Tribal Relationship.* There is an intimate family and tribal relationship between man and animal.

a. The intimate relationship and association of animals with the family is expressed in the Sabbath commandment in Ex. 20:10, where *behemah* is placed after "maidservant" and before "sojourner." Dt. 5:14 contains a detailed list, viz., *shor,* "ox," *chamor,* "ass," and *kol behemah,* "any cattle." In Lev. 25:2-7 also, cattle are mentioned along with male slaves, female slaves, hired servants (*sakhir*), and sojourners as those who are to enjoy that which grows wild in the Sabbatical Year. Even wild beasts (*chayyah bᵉ'artsekha,* "the beasts in your land," vv. 6f.) who are not considered part of the family and who are not employed in its service are not excluded from enjoying this yield.

Gen. 47:17f. states that during the famine all the money and animals of the Egyptians became Pharaoh's possession. For a year, Joseph gave the Egyptians food in exchange for flocks, herds, asses (v. 17), and herds of cattle (v. 18).

b. According to Ex. 22:9(10), a person must give security and, if necessary, restitution for an animal that his neighbor has entrusted to him if it dies or is hurt or is driven away. This verse specifically mentions "an ass or an ox or small livestock, or any beast." Here *kol behemah* could be understood as a collective term for large livestock (ox or ass as work animals) and small.

The *jus talionis* (law of retribution) for killing and for inflicting bodily injury (cf. Ex. 21:23-25; Dt. 19:21) is interpreted differently in Lev. 24:18,21, where *nephesh tachath naphesh,* "life for life," refers to *behemah,* but then a clear distinction is made between *nephesh 'adham,* "a man's life (lit. soul)," and *nephesh behemah:* when one kills a beast, he must make it good (*shillem,* piel), but when one kills a man he must be "put to death" (*moth yumath*).

c. In other passages also animals always appear in close connection with the family, the tribe, and the army. According to Gen. 34:23, Hamor and Shechem hope by submitting to circumcision to share in the property of the great family of Jacob, i.e., in their cattle, property, and beasts. Esau took to Seir his wives, sons, daughters, and all the members of his household, his cattle, all his beasts, and all his property which he had acquired (Gen. 36:6). In Josh. 21:2, the Levites also have pasture lands for their cattle (*behemah*); Nu. 35:3 says they have pasture lands for their cattle, livestock (*rekhush*), and all their beasts (*kol chayyah*). In Nu. 32:26, little ones, wives, flocks, and cattle remain behind, while the men go to battle in the land across the Jordan.

Cattle are thus also part of the spoil (Nu. 31:9; an addition), which is divided (31:26,47). *behemah* are specified as part of the spoil (*shalal*) and the devoted thing in Dt. 2:35; 3:7; 20:14; cf. 13:16(15). According to Jgs. 20:48, the ban in its more rigorous form meant the destruction of men and beasts, while in its more liberal form the people were allowed to take cattle and other spoils as booty (Josh. 8:2,27; 11:14). Neh. 9:37 says that God set the Persians over Israel, and they had power over their bodies and over their cattle at their pleasure, so that the Israelites are in great distress because of high taxes and military service.

d. The description of Hezekiah's wealth in 2 Ch. 32:28f. mentions stalls for all kinds of cattle (*behemah*), and also rich possessions of herds of *tso'n ubhaqar*, "sheep and cattle." According to Ezr. 1:4,6, gifts for the temple (and for those who returned home willingly) included not only silver, gold, and other costly wares, but also beasts.

e. According to 2 K. 3:17, *miqneh* and *behemah* followed the Israelite army in the campaign against Mesha of Moab. *miqneh* and *behemah* are interpreted as livestock and beasts of burden respectively. But the meanings of these two words are not so clear, because mules and asses (and camels) could be included in the "herds" as well as *tso'n*, "sheep," and *baqar*, "cattle."

3. *Connection with Creation and Fate.* The connection of men and beasts with creation and fate in prosperity and calamity is expressed in phrases like *'adham ubhehemah*, "man and beast," or *me'adham ve'adh behemah*, "from man to beast."

a. These expressions are used in the accounts of the plagues in Egypt to convey the idea of the completeness of the affliction (Ex. 8:13,14b[17,18b]; 9:9,10,19,22,25). Ex. 11:5; 12:12,29; Ps. 135:8 speak of the death of man and beast on the passover night. Neither man nor beast will remain alive if they touch the mountain of God (Ex. 19:13). (Cf. Nu. 31:26,47 on the distribution of the spoil.) According to Zeph. 1:3, man and beast, birds and fish will be swept away (*'aseph*) by divine judgment. In connection with *hikhrith*, "cut off," *hishchith*, "destroy," *hishbith*, "cut off," etc., the complete desolation of land and habitation to waste (*shammah, shemamah, chorbah*) is characterized as an act of divine anger or judgment (Jer. 7:20; 9:9[10]; 12:4; 21:6; 27:5; 36:29; 50:3; 51:62). According to Jer. 21:6, Yahweh will smite the inhabitants of Jerusalem, both man and beast, with a great pestilence that they may die.

Ezk. 14:13,17,19 give examples of sanctions of divine punishment against a sinful land: through famine (v. 13), sword (v. 17), and pestilence (v. 19) Yahweh will cut off from it (*hikhratti mimmennah*) man and beast. In an addition (14:21), [29] this principle of sanction is applied to Jerusalem. The formula of the *kareth* = punishment (cutting off) of man and beast is expanded to include Edom in 25:13, and is illustrated by *unethattiha chorbah*, "and I will make it desolate." The second oracle of doom against Egypt in 29:8,9a announces that Yahweh will bring a sword, the destruction of man and beast, a desolation, and a wasting upon the land. 29:9b-12 expands this sanction further (in statements parallel to those describing the fate of Israel and Jerusalem): neither man nor beast shall pass through it, it shall be uninhabited forty years, and the Egyptians will be scattered among the nations. According to Ezk. 32:13, Yahweh will destroy (by the sword of the Babylonian king) all the beasts of Pharaoh, so that the Nile will no longer be troubled by the foot of man or the hoofs of beasts.

Because the building of the temple has been neglected, Yahweh will bring a drought upon men and cattle, according to Hag. 1:11 (cf. also Zec. 8:10). And according to Zec. 14:15, a plague will fall on horses, mules, camels, asses, and whatever beasts may be in the enemy camp, because of a divine dread (12:4). Joel describes in detail how the beasts groan, the herds of cattle are perplexed, and the flocks of small livestock are dismayed because of a drought and a locust plague (Joel 1:18). The wild beasts, *bahamoth hassadheh*, cry to God (1:20). According to Jonah 3:7 the king's proclamation to fast applies to man and beast, herd and flock (*tso'n*); man and beast (as part of the household) must wear sackcloth (3:8).

b. The salvation oracles in Jeremiah announce that Judah and Jerusalem, which had become a desolation without man and beast, will again be inhabited, and will receive wealth and peace (Jer. 32:43; 33:10,12). Yahweh will again make the house of Israel fruitful (*vezara'ti*) with the seed of man and the seed of beast (31:27). Ezk. 36:11 also announces that man and beast will be multiplied for the time of salvation. A type of blessing formula (cf. Gen. 1:22,28; Lev. 26:9) was added to this in a later expansion (v. 10). Zec. 2:8(4) also contains the promise of blessing upon the multitude of men and cattle. According to the salvation oracle in Joel 2:21-24, the beasts need fear no longer, "for the pastures of the wilderness are green" (2:22).

In the formula of blessing in Dt. 28:3-6, "the fruit of your body, the fruit of your ground, the fruit of your beasts," as well as "the increase of your cattle (*'alaphekha*) and the young of your flock (*tso'n*)," are mentioned as objects of blessing (v. 4). This should be compared with 28:11 in the series of verbal blessings in 28:7-12a. Plöger thinks "the fruit of your beasts . . ." was added by the Deuteronomistic redactor. [30] Dt. 30:9 speaks of prospering abundantly in the fruit of the body, of the cattle, and of the ground. According to 7:14 there will be no barrenness, not even among the cattle. And 28:51 says the enemies sent by Yahweh will eat the fruit of Israel and will leave nothing, until they have caused Israel to perish.

---

[29] Cf. van den Born, Fohrer, and Zimmerli *in loc.*
[30] J. Plöger, *BBB,* 26 (1967), 141ff., 145ff.

c. Cattle enjoy special divine care: God causes grass to grow in the field for cattle (Dt. 11:15). "He gives to the beasts their food, and to the young ravens which cry" (Ps. 147:9; cf. 104:27f.; 145:15f.). The prosperity of the land with good harvests, herds of cattle, and increased numbers of people is a blessing from God (Ps. 107:38).

In the order of creation, God has placed sheep (*tso'nah*), oxen ('*alaphim*), the beasts of the field, birds, and fish under man's dominion (Ps. 8:8f.[7f.]). The beast of the forest (*chayetho ya'ar*) and the cattle (*behemoth*) on a thousand hills belong to God (Ps. 50:10); therefore, he does not want the flesh of bulls and the blood of goats, but a sacrifice of thanksgiving (v. 14). Heaven and earth, wild beasts (*chayyah*) and tame (*behemah*), birds and reptiles are to praise God (Ps. 148:10).

According to Sir. 7:22 man is to care personally for his cattle. Prov. 27:23 charges man to give attention to his flocks and herds; 12:10 says a righteous man has regard for "the life (lit. soul) of his beast" (*nephesh behemto*), but the mercy of the wicked is cruel. Hab. 2:17 refers to the mistreatment of beasts, which probably means the inconsiderate exploitation of beasts of burden (*behemah*) in the transportation of timber by the heathen world power.

4. *Distinction Between 'adham and behemah.* a. The distinction between man and beast is already evident in the story of man's naming of the animals, and in that among the animals "there was not found a helper fit for" man (Gen. 2:18-20). Similarly, the *jus talionis* (law of retribution) states that the punishment for killing a man shall be death, but the punishment for killing a beast will be restitution (Lev. 24:18-21).

b. Ps. 49:13,21 (12,20) reflects an assumed disparaging distinction between man and beast by describing a beast as a "dumb animal": man in his pomp is "like an ox without understanding" (read *kabbaqar lo' yabhin*), and like a cow that "is dumb" or that "is destroyed" (*damah* II or III). When "his heart is embittered" and "his kidneys are pricked," i.e., when he is consumed with brooding and despair, the godly man is "foolish" (→ בער *ba'ar*) and "without understanding" (*lo' 'edha'*), like a beast before God (Ps. 73:22; cf. also 94:8). In Job 18:3, Bildad protests against Job's reproach of his friends' lack of understanding (17:4) by asking: "Why are we counted as cattle (*kabbehemah*)? Why are we stupid[31] in your sight?" Man should not protest with a loud wailing; instead, he must be conscious that he is unique, and that God "has taught him before the beasts (or, more than the beasts) of the earth" and "has made him wise before (more than?) the birds of the air" (Job 35:11). Yet beasts and fish can teach man about the Creator and Lord of every living thing (Job 12:7f.).

c. On the other hand, Eccl. 3:18 states that God has made man and beast equal in death, without giving man any advantage over the beasts (3:19). This gives rise to the sarcastic question in 3:21: "Who knows whether 'the spirit of

---

[31] F. Stier: niphal of *tmm*.

man' (*ruach bene ha'adham*) goes upward, and 'the spirit of the beast' (*ruach habbehemah*) goes down to the earth?" Indeed, it is precisely in the mutuality of the common death of man and beast that the nothingness of man is made clear, and that man's hope of compensation and justice is disappointed [32] (see also Sir. 40:11).

IV. beḥemôth.

1. *Definition.* Ever since Bochart, [33] *behemoth* has been translated "hippopotamus," and has been derived from Egyp. *pʒ-iḥ-mw,* [34] even though only the individual elements of this composite word can be identified in Egyptian. The pl. *behemoth* is usually explained as a *pl. extensivus* (pl. of extension). [35] According to Gunkel, "there is no reason to regard this word as non-Semitic." [36] The plural form, above all, would seem to indicate that a particularly large animal (a giant beast or monster) was intended. And then, perhaps because of popular etymological reminiscences of the "water ox" or the "river ox," the meaning "hippopotamus" (*Hippopotamus amphibius*) has been maintained. [37]

On the basis of textual emendations, G. R. Driver has advanced the thesis that in Job 40:15 the supplementary gloss *'asher 'asithi* (*'immakh*), "which I made (as I made you)," is a corruption of *'mśk* from *'msh,* "crocodile," and that the *rēshîth beḥēmôth,* "chief of beasts," is the crocodile. [38] In another work, he clarifies his point more fully by translating Job 40:15: "Behold now: the crocodile, chief of beasts; he eats grass like cattle." [39] Schultens inclines to the view that the *behemoth* is the elephant, [40] and suggests other deviating interpretations.

2. *The Existence of Hippopotami in Palestine, Syria, and Egypt.* Recent discoveries provide information concerning the existence of hippopotami in Palestine. According to Haas, bones and teeth of hippopotami have been found at Tel Aviv (Tell Qasîleh) dating from the twelfth to the fourth centuries B.C., and at Ugarit dating from the fourteenth to the thirteenth centuries B.C. Under the Greek temple at Tell Sūkās, archeologists have found bones of hippopotami near figurines of an ass and of a cow in Early Bronze Age and Early Iron Age strata, which "prove that hippopotami actually lived in Syria at least in the third century B.C." [41]

---

[32] Cf. Hertzberg, *KAT,* XVII/4, 110f.

[33] S. Bochart, *Hierozoicon sive de animalibus sacrae scripturae* (London, 1663), II lib. V, cap. XV.

[34] So recently Hölscher, *HAT,* 17, 95f.; Fohrer, *KAT,* XVI, 522.

[35] *GK,* § 124b.

[36] Gunkel, *Schöpfung und Chaos,* 64.

[37] Contra A. Lewy, 65-67, who wants to derive *behemoth* from Hurrian.

[38] G. R. Driver, *VT,* 1, 314, and *Twenty-second Congress of Orientalists,* II, 113-15.

[39] G. R. Driver, *Studi Orientalistici,* 234ff.; cf. also G. Richter, *Textstudien zum Buche Hiob. BWANT,* 3/7 (1927), 86f.

[40] Cf. on this E. Stauffer, *ThLZ,* 76 (1951), 667-674 on 1QpHab 3:9f.

[41] *AfO,* 21 (1966), 195.

It is often assumed that isolated hippopotami wandered "along the coast to the Philistine plain, or followed Pharaoh Necho's canal to the Gulf of Suez and followed the coast to Ezion-geber, and then followed the valley to the Dead Sea," but "in either case it could have got into the swamp of the upper Jordan and lived in lonely comfort till it died of old age." [42]

The Egyptian hippopotamus is found today, but only south of Dongola between the second and third cataracts of the Nile; however, evidence from Egyptian texts and representations [43] indicates that it must have lived in Lower Egypt also.

3. *The Egyptian Hippopotamus Cult.* The symbol of the royal hunter as a "harpooner" (*mśnw*) of the hippopotamus is attested as early as Den (earlier read Udimu) (First Dynasty) in numerous representations: the king in enormous stature, surrounded by several assistants, is standing up in a papyrus boat and is thrusting his spear into the mouth of the hippopotamus, which is wide open, gasping for air. Texts and illustrations also reveal the existence of a "festival of the white female hippopotamus" (*ḥb ḥḏ.t*) (originally from Lower Egypt). E.g., an inscription on the Horus temple of Edfu tells of a battle between the gods Horus and Seth: Horus pursues Seth, who has taken the form of a red hippopotamus, and conquers him by thrusting a harpoon through his nose. (However, according to Kees, [44] in the original festival act the conquered hippopotamus was not a Sethic [male] animal, but a white female hippopotamus.) In the Ptolemaic period, the harpooning of Seth (in the form of a hippopotamus), the opponent of Horus, is represented by ten harpoons on the walls of the temple of Edfu. In the ritual of the victory celebration on the twenty-first of Mechir, the dismemberment of a placenta in the form of a hippopotamus is depicted as the defeat of Seth. In the different portrayals of the harpooning of Seth (in the form of a hippopotamus), a hunting trophy (e.g., a carved thigh) is brought to a well-known Osiris cult place and then venerated as an Osiris relic.

In the harpooning of the evil, male hippopotamus there was seen a victory of the king or the god "over all evil powers before the enthronement of the king." But the festival of the white, female hippopotamus is a "celebration in honour of the wild beast that has become a good and benign goddess." [45] The contrasting structures of the more agrarian Lower Egypt and nomadic Upper Egypt have left their impression on these two motifs; they have great religious significance, "because they are intimately linked with the rites guaranteeing the maintenance of the Egyptian cosmos." [46]

4. *Behemoth in Job 40:15ff.* The only passage in the OT where *behemoth* has the meaning "giant beast," "sea monster," or "hippopotamus" is Job 40:15ff.

---

[42] Byington, 346.
[43] Cf. Säve-Söderbergh and Kees.
[44] Kees, 144.
[45] Säve-Söderbergh, 55f.
[46] *Ibid.,* 56.

The extent of the pericope beginning with 40:15 is variously understood. [47] Three units can be delineated on the basis of style and content: 40:15-24; 40:25–41:3(4) (Eng. 41:1-11[12]); and 41:4(5)-26 (Eng. vv. 12[13]-34).

Whereas Job 40:15-24 gives a relatively realistic description of a sea monster in the form of a hippopotamus, the Leviathan pericopes in 40:25ff. (41:1ff.) and 41:4ff. (12ff.) are different in style and content. In 41:4ff. (12ff.), Leviathan takes on legendary and mythical features of an invincible fire-breathing crocodile-dragon. Ruprecht thinks that 40:15-31(40:15–41:7) is a homogeneous pericope, and that 41:1-3(9-11) is the conclusion of the second part of God's speech in 40:2–41:3(40:2–41:11). Thus, for him *livyathan,* "Leviathan," must be "an additional name for this monster (*behemoth*), this hippopotamus, and not the name of another animal, perhaps the crocodile," [48] "although one cannot exclude the possibility that 40:25ff.[41:1ff.] has reference to the crocodile." [49]

The pericope concerning the giant beast or sea monster in the form of a hippopotamus reaches its peak in the question: "Who is it (read *mi hu'*) that can take him in his eyes (or [?] by his eyeteeth [*beshinav*]), [50] or that can pierce his nose with a harpoon?" (Job 40:24). How can man comprehend God's world order or exalt himself against God when he is not even able to subdue a hippopotamus? This theme pervades the entire description in 40:15-23: in spite of the plural intensification, this monster *behemoth* eats grass like an ox; it has power and strength in its loins and in the muscles of its belly; its bones are like "tubes of bronze" and "bars of iron" (vv. 15b-20). It lies under lotus (?) and poplar, in the concealment of reed and marsh, and is not frightened if the river becomes turbulent (vv. 21-23). Vv. 19f., the text of which is uncertain, emphasize the peculiar position of the *behemoth* as the beginning or firstborn (*re'shith*) of the work of creation. In a temporal *re'shith, behemoth* could be one of the great sea monsters of Gen. 1:21. [51] Job 41:25(33) says there is none like Leviathan upon earth.

Irrespective of 40:19f. and the somewhat hyperbolic description of *behemoth* in 40:15-24, conclusive arguments cannot be given to support the view that *behemoth* is a zoological designation for the hippopotamus or to deny the mythical interpretation of *behemoth* in the sense of → ים *yām,* "sea," → לויתן *livyāthān,* "Leviathan," → תנין *tannîn,* "serpent, sea monster," etc. Therefore, Ruprecht's threefold explanation of the term *behemoth* (a real, naturalistic beast, a mythical enemy of the creator-god, and mythico-historical great powers) survives the test of scrutiny. We must assume that the poet of Job 40:15 knew the Egyptian hippopotamus cults and assimilated Egyptian terminology in his presentation. [52]

---

[47] Cf. the comms., and also Westermann, *BHTh,* 23 (1956), 93-96, and Ruprecht, 209-231.

[48] Ruprecht, 220.

[49] *Ibid.,* 221.

[50] G. H. B. Wright, E. Ruprecht.

[51] Cf. P. Humbert, "Trois notes sur Genèse I," *Festschrift S. Mowinckel* (Oslo, 1955), 85-96.

[52] Humbert, *SVT,* 3, 152; Fohrer, *in loc.;* Ruprecht; etc.

In the Apocalyptic Literature, *behemoth* appears along with Leviathan as a mythical beast of the End Time. According to 1 En. 60:7-9, Leviathan lives in the abyss of the sea above the fountains of water, while Behemoth receives a desolate wilderness, Dendain (cf. also 4 Esd. 6:49-52 and the Apocalypse of Bar. 29:4). [53]

Botterweck

_____

[53] On the Jewish tradition, in addition to F. Weber, *Jüdische Theologie* (1897), 202, 402, cf. esp. Guttmann.

_____

בּוֹא *bô';* אָתָה *'āthāh*

Contents: I. Range of Meaning. II. 1. The Coming (qal) of Man to God, to the Priest, and to the Man of God; 2. The Bringing (hiphil) of Man to God, to the Priest, and to the Man of God. III. *bo'* (qal and hiphil) in the Wisdom Literature, and in Blessings and Curses. IV. Coming (qal) and Bringing (hiphil) into the Land. V. *bo'* As "fulfilling." VI. 1. *bo'* in Laments; 2. *bo'* in Prayers. VII. *bo'* (hiphil) As a Term for God's Guidance in History. VIII. 1. The Coming Judgment; 2. The Fulfilled Judgment. IX. 1. The Coming and Fulfilled Salvation; 2. The Coming Bringer of Salvation. X. Yahweh As the Coming One.

I. Range of Meaning. Occurring 2532 times (1969 times in the qal, 539 times in the hiphil, and 24 times in the hophal), *bo'* is one of the most frequently used verbs in the OT, [1] and is at the head of verbs expressing motion. The majority of examples belong to the secular sphere (approximately 1630 times in the qal, 330 times in the hiphil, and 7 times in the hophal). The variety of meanings conveyed by *bo'* is demonstrated already in that the LXX had to use over 150 different words and phrases to translate it. [2]

'athah, which properly is to be included in a study of *bo',* appears 19 times in the qal and twice in the hiphil; 7 of its occurrences in the qal are relevant in theological considerations. Since *'athah* is also found in Ugaritic, it should no

_____

bo'. E. Jenni, "'Kommen' im theologischen Sprachgebrauch des AT," *Wort-Gebot-Glaube. W. Eichrodt zum 80. Geburtstag. AThANT,* 59 (1970), 251-261; J. Jeremias, *Theophanie. Die Geschichte einer alttestamentlichen Gattung. WMANT,* 10 (1965); S. Mowinckel, *He That Cometh* (Oxford, ²1959); G. Pidoux, *Le Dieu qui vient* (Neuchâtel/Paris, 1947); J. G. Plöger, *Literarkritische, formgeschichtliche und stilkritische Untersuchungen zum Deuteronomium. BBB,* 26 (1967); F. Schnutenhaus, "Das Kommen und Erscheinen Gottes im AT," *ZAW,* 76 (1964), 1-21.

On the general idea: W. H. Schmidt, *Alttestamentlicher Glaube und seine Umwelt* (1968), 38ff., 148ff.

On *'āthāh* (*'ᵃthā'*), cf. *TDNT,* IV, 467ff. (Kuhn); and M. Wagner, *Die lexikalischen und grammatikalischen Aramaismen im alttestamentlichen Hebräisch. BZAW,* 96 (1966), No. 31.

[1] Jenni, 252, "Allerweltswort."

[2] On some of these, see *TDNT,* II, 667, 927; V, 861f., 864; and W. Mundle, *Theol. Begriffslexikon zum NT,* II/1 (1969), 803-808.

longer be regarded as an Aramaic loanword. At Qumran *'athah* has not been found thus far, but *bo'* appears many times, where, in addition to its ordinary usages, it refers mostly to entering into or bringing into the group, the coming judgment and salvation (1QS 11:13!), the coming bringer of salvation, or going into battle (1QM).

In the OT *bo'* manifests a widely diversified range of meaning (cf. Ugar. *b'*) within the expressions for a movement directed toward a certain goal in space and time: "to go into" (frequently in contrast to → יצא *yātsā'*, "to go out," or → שׁוּב *shûbh*, "to return"), Gen. 7:1,13; 24:31; 1 K. 3:7; 2 Ch. 23:7; etc., which is the most frequent meaning; "to come" (toward or to), Gen. 14:5; 1 S. 13:8; also in Lachish, *KAI,* 193.11, 20; "to come into," Gen. 19:3; Jgs. 19:22f.; also "... to a place," 2 K. 24:10; "to arrive at, come to, attain to," Jgs. 16:2; 2 S. 23:19; etc.; "to add to, come up to," Ex. 22:14 (Eng. v. 15); 1 S. 17:12; "to go into," Jgs. 6:19; "to go through" (the sea or fire), Ex. 14:16,22,28, etc.; "to get into something" (e.g., bloodguilt), 1 S. 25:26,33; "to attain to," 2 S. 23:23; 1 Ch. 11:21; "to come into contact with, come near," Lev. 21:11; Nu. 6:6; "to break in," Ps. 79:1; "to come before someone," Isa. 1:23; "to draw near, march out" (militarily), Josh. 14:11; etc.; "to come back, return, come home," 2 S. 19:31(30); Ezk. 36:8; "to come to," Jer. 2:31. The meaning of *bo'* is also expanded and used figuratively: "to come upon someone," Dt. 30:1; Jer. 12:12; etc.; "to come to, belong to," Nu. 32:19; "to come (have a chance) to speak," Prov. 18:17; "to go to one's fathers" = "to be buried," only in Gen. 15:15 (but cf. 1 K. 13:22; Isa. 57:2)[3]; "to come into one's days" = "to become old" (frequently with → זקן *zāqēn),* Gen. 18:11; 24:1(J); in Dt. also; "to go down (= to return) (of the sun),"[4] Gen. 15:17; Ex. 17:12; Jer. 15:9; Eccl. 1:5; also 1QM 18:5; but in general the combination of *bo'* and *yatsa'* can also denote man's conduct: Josh. 14:11; 1 K. 3:7; etc.[5] *bo'* is also used of having sexual relations with a woman, Gen. 6:4; 16:2,4; Dt. 22:13; Cant. 5:1; etc.; but not in P; Josh. 23:12 as apostasy from Yahweh; with a harlot: Jgs. 16:1; Ezk. 23:44.

bo' is also used as a kind of auxiliary verb in combination with a second verb, and in this case expresses intention ("I come and get" = "I will get"; "I will come and judge" = "I will come in order to judge," etc.), 1 K. 13:25; 2 K. 18:32; Isa. 36:17; Ps. 102:14(13); etc.

'athah (qal) basically has the same shades of meaning as *bo'*: "to come, come back, come upon someone, go, go with." The range of meaning of *bo'* can be well illustrated by Dnl. 11:6-45 (cf. 8:6,17), where the verb appears with a frequency typical of the historical reflections in Daniel and where almost a word-play is carried on with *bo'* (come near, come up, come in, arrive, bring, come to an end). In theological contexts,[6] *bo'* (qal) is used especially in the sense of "come, go in, come in, and fulfil."

---

[3] On the customary terminology, cf. → אב *'ābh,* III.3.a.

[4] → אור *'ôr,* II.1.c; cf. E. Kutsch, *ZAW,* 83 (1971), 18.

[5] On the legal use of *bo'* in Ex. 21:3, see S. M. Paul, *Studies in the Book of the Covenant. SVT,* 18 (Leiden, 1970), 47f.

[6] See II-X below.

In the hiphil, *bo'* usually means "to bring" (also, into judgment, Eccl. 11:9), "to cause to come," "to bring in," "to bring something upon (*'al*) someone," "to bring (the army) home," "to bring one home as a wife," Dt. 21:12; Jgs. 12:9; frequently it means "to offer" or "to bring up" in connection with sacrifices or gifts (before someone: *'al*); it also means "to make the sun go down," Am. 8:9; "to get, to receive."

According to the MT, *'athah* is found in the hiphil in Isa. 21:14 and Jer. 12:9. However, both texts are uncertain; but cf. Job 37:22 (read the hiphil) and Ps. 68:32(31).

The hophal of *bo'* functions as the passive of the hiphil: "to be brought," "to lead to." [7]

II. 1. *The Coming (qal) of Man to God, to the Priest, and to the Man of God.* The use of *bo'* in the theologically filled or theologically related sphere should be understood in the broadest sense possible, not merely, e.g., of the coming of God to man. [8] *bo'* is also used quite often of man's coming to God. This coming is made concrete as a coming to the sanctuary, or to the priest or man of God (prophet).

That *bo'* was a commonly used verb for the coming of man to the sanctuary (cf. 1 K. 1:28,32 for the use of *bo'* in connection with an audience before a king), and for his entering into its sacral sphere and the community gathered there, [9] is proved by the abundance of occurrences (in the perf., impf., impv., and ptcp.) and is emphasized by the assimilation of this verb in the cult polemic. The cult polemic also contains the word → יצא *yātsā'*, "to go out," which is the antithesis of *bo'* (Ex. 28:35; Lev. 16:17; 2 K. 11:9; Ezk. 46:2,8-10). A person comes to the temple of Yahweh and enters into it to worship, but especially to sacrifice. He comes to pray to Yahweh, for he hears the prayers of all flesh that come to him (Ps. 65:3[2]; no textual emendation is necessary here). There are examples of this use of *bo'* in Dt. 29:6(7); 31:11; 2 S. 7:18; 1 K. 14:28 and par.; Isa. 30:29; Jer. 7:10 (cf. *habba'im*, "those who enter these gates," which occurs frequently in Jer.: 7:2; 17:20; 22:2; etc.; cf. Gen. 23:10,18[P]); 22:4; Ezk. 46:9. Characteristically, it frequently has this sense in the Psalms: 5:8(7); 40:8(7); 42:3 (2); 66:13; 71:16; etc.; perhaps it also has this meaning in Ps. 73:17; [10] 1 Ch. 16:29; 2 Ch. 29:17; 23:6: only the priests are allowed to enter because they are holy; 30:4f.,8 (the celebration of the Passover in Jerusalem); Ezr. 2:68. Lam. 1:4 speaks of people coming to a festival on Zion. Jeremiah is debarred from

---

[7] On the qal of *bo'* with the meaning "bring," see M. Dahood, *Psalms*, I, 262; II, 110; III, 61f., 323. For some examples from the extensive material from the ancient Near East on the coming of the deity, see Jeremias, 73ff., and also A. Ohler, *Mythologische Elemente im AT* (1969), 13ff., 146ff., etc. However, the actual understanding of the cult, the festivals, the divine images, etc., should be investigated more closely on this point. Some examples also appear in *RLA, s.v.* "Gott." For Egypt, examples may be found in E. Hornung, *Der Eine und die Vielen* (1971).

[8] So Jenni.

[9] Kraus, *BK*, XV, 319.

[10] On 22:32(30) see *ibid., in loc.*

coming to the house of the Lord (36:5; cf. 2 Ch. 7:2). For a specified period of time a woman who had given birth to a child was not allowed to enter the sanctuary (Lev. 12:4). The distribution of these occurrences outside the Psalter (the concluding phrase in Hos. 9:4 is a gloss) makes it clear that this use of *bo'* originated, for the most part, in the Deuteronomic-Deuteronomistic and post-Deuteronomistic period, which is also confirmed by the use of *bo'* in the Deuteronomistic redaction of the book of Jeremiah (cf. Dt. 12:5,26).

Certain conditions seem to have been connected with the "entering" into the sanctuary (cf. the examples in the Psalms). The → צדקה *ts^edhāqāh*, "righteousness," of the potential cultic participants was ascertained (cf. also Isa. 26:2; then Ps. 5:8[7]; 118:19f.; as well as Pss. 15 and 24). An oath of purification in the temple is mentioned (even if only on a special occasion) in Solomon's litany as a self-imprecation (→ אלה *'ālāh*) before the altar of burnt-offering (1 K. 8:31 [Deuteronomistic]; cf. 2 Ch. 6:22). Before the temple was built, people came, e.g., to the Mount of Olives, where it was customary to worship *'elohim*, "God" (2 S. 15:32). Thus *bo'* was used in a cultic sense even in an earlier period, which is emphasized by *KAI*, 27.5f. and *DISO*, 32. Those who entered *beshem yhvh*, "in the name of Yahweh" (Ps. 118:26; those also who had returned from battle? 1 S. 17:45), [11] were blessed. Late prophetic oracles promise that those who were lost in the land of Assyria and those who were driven out to the land of Egypt will come and worship Yahweh on the holy mountain at Jerusalem (Isa. 27:13; 35:10; 51:11; also the hymnic v. 9 of the later Ps. 86). Even (*gam*) foreigners come to the house of Yahweh to pray (1 K. 8:41 [Deuteronomistic]; 2 Ch. 6:32) (in this connection the distance, 1 K. 8:42, should be noted), and then Yahweh is inclined to hear them. Those of the heathen who survive (Zec. 14:16) will also come there, and all flesh will come to worship (Isa. 66:23; cf. 65:3).

But no eunuch shall enter into the cultic community (Dt. 23:2[1]; cf. 23:2-9 [1-8]). The role the adoption of this exclusion played particularly in late prophetic eschatology is clear from Isa. 52:1; 56:1; Ezk. 44:9; also Neh. 13:1 and (with a different orientation) Lam. 1:10.

The idea that *bo'* is a commonly used technical term of the cultic language is illustrated further by its use in describing one's "coming" to heathen cult places or foreign gods (Hos. 9:10; 2 K. 10:21; 2 Ch. 23:17). People "come" to the → במה *bāmāh*, "high place" (Ezk. 20:29), the temple of Dagon (1 S. 5:5), and the house of *ba'al berith* (or El-berith) (Jgs. 9:46). When Moab comes to his sanctuary, he will not prevail, because Yahweh threatens judgment (Isa. 16:12). Thus, the "coming" to the deity (cf. Isa. 1:12; → פנים *pānîm*, "face"; → ראה *rā'āh*, "to see") originally would have had reference to people "coming" to his presence in the cult image, an understanding that is impossible for Israel (Dt. 12:5,26; etc.).

bo' also appears as a cult term in the prophetic polemic against the cult. Frequently the prophetic polemic appears in the form of a perverted cultic decree (Isa. 1:12; Hos. 4:15; Am. 4:4; 5:5; cf. Hos. 9:4,10), and elsewhere also it is characterized by cult terminology (→ דרש *dārash*, "to seek"; *chayah, chayyim,*

---

11 See further H. A. Brongers, *ZAW*, 77 (1965), 2-4.

"to live, life"; *chaphets,* "to delight in"; *chashabh,* "to think, consider"; *ratsah, ratson,* "to accept, acceptance").

Priestly texts mention the coming of Moses, Aaron, or the priest to the → אֹהֶל מוֹעֵד *ʾōhel môʿēdh,* "tent of meeting," [12] or to its door, and thus their coming before Yahweh (Lev. 15:14; cf. 16:23; Nu. 4:5). Specific regulations are given to the priests when they come into the tent of meeting (Ex. 28:29f.,35,43; 29:30; 30:20; 40:32; Lev. 10:9; 16:2f.,17,23). [13]

According to the ancient text, Ex. 34:34f., Moses put on a mask (*masveh*) after he had gone in unto Yahweh (cf. Nu. 7:89); according to Ex. 33:9 (cf. v. 8 in vv. 7-11) the cloud (→ עָנָן *ʿānān*) descended when Moses went in (the situation is different in Ex. 40:35[P]). [14] It should not be surprising if we also find in the book of Ezekiel specific statements concerning the coming of the → נָשִׂיא *nāśîʾ,* "prince," and of the people, as well as of the priest, to Yahweh in his new temple (Ezk. 42:14; 44:17,21,27; 46:8-10).

The pertinent expressions in Dt. 17:9 (to the Levitical priests) and Lev. 13:16; 14:35; 15:14; Dt. 26:3, show that people go to the priest of Yahweh when they come to the sanctuary. Conversely, the priest "comes" to give his judgment concerning the leprosy (→ נֶגַע *neghaʿ*) of a house (Lev. 14:44). Further, the OT contains detailed statements as to where priests (particularly the high priest) or Nazirites are not allowed to come (=draw near, come in contact with), e.g., especially not close to a dead body (Lev. 21:11; Nu. 6:6; Ezk. 44:25).

Finally, people come to the man of God (→ אִישׁ *ʾîsh*), the prophet, e.g., to Ahijah of Shiloh (1 K. 14:3,5), Elisha (2 K. 4:42), and Ezekiel (Ezk. 14:4,7; 20:1,3). Their purpose is to inquire of Yahweh (Ezk. 14:7), who answers (Ezk. 14:4) or gives information (1 K. 14) through the prophet. However, if anyone does this while worshipping foreign gods (Ezk. 14:3; → גִּלּוּלִים *gillûlîm*), Yahweh will answer with judgment.

In his wish for Ruth, Boaz describes the result of her emigration (*baʾth*) to Israel, i.e., to the realm of Yahweh's protection, in cultic terminology (*tachath kephanav,* "under his wings," Ruth 2:12). [15]

In the earlier period, one "came" to Yahweh by joining his army. Those who did not do so were reproved (Jgs. 5:23). Some texts speak of *boʾ babberith,* "entering into the *berith*" (Jer. 34:10; 2 Ch. 15:12; cf. Neh. 10:30[29] with → אָלָה *ʾālāh,* "curse," and → שְׁבוּעָה *shebhûʿāh,* "oath"). Man's coming to God is made concrete here as entering into the *berith,* which should be translated "enter into a commitment" in these passages (cf. → עָמַד *ʿāmādh,* "stand," in 2 K. 23:3, and → עָבַר *ʿābhar,* "enter," in Dt. 29:11[12]; the hiphil is used differently in 1 S. 20:8 in describing the *berith* between David and Jonathan; on this subject cf. also 1QS 2:12,18; 5:8; CD A 2:2; etc.). It is difficult to determine

---

[12] *TDOT,* I, 123-130.

[13] On the *boʾ,* "coming," of the priest as a technical term, see B. Jacob, *ZAW,* 18 (1898), 290.

[14] On the use of *boʾ,* "go in," and *yatsaʾ,* "go out," in Ex. 33:7-11 and elsewhere, cf. Plöger, 174-184.

[15] On this figure, cf. Rudolph, *KAT,* XVII/1, 49.

whether *boʾ* here was originally connected with the rite described in Gen. 15:7 (Jer. 34:18!). This derivation no longer has any relevance in the texts mentioned here.

2. *The Bringing (hiphil) of Man to God, to the Priest, and to the Man of God.* The hiphil of *boʾ* also occurs frequently as a fixed term in cult terminology, and is used to denote the bringing of sacrifices, firstfruits, etc., by men in general, and the bringing of sacrifices by priests (it is hardly necessary to cite examples; already in J, Gen. 4:3f.; then naturally esp. in P; but also in Dt.; 2 K. 12:5[4]; Isa. 66:20; Jer. 17:26; etc.; Mal. 1:13; cf. the bringing of taxes, 2 Ch. 24:6,9; cf. 31:10). Several times the hiphil of *boʾ* is used to describe the bringing of materials to the priests for sacrifice (Lev. 2:2; 5:12; etc.), the bringing of tithes (Dt. 12:6; Mal. 3:10; etc.), of the bringing of gifts to be used in building the → אהל מועד *ʾōhel môʿēdh*, "tent of meeting" (Ex. 35:21ff.; 36:3; cf. 2 Ch. 24:14). On the Sabbath one must not bring anything into Jerusalem (Neh. 13:15ff.; cf. Jer. 17:27; CD B 11:6ff.). The ark was brought to Jerusalem and later brought into the temple (1 K. 8:6; 1 Ch. 13:5,12; 16:1; etc.; also cf. on all these points the appropriate phrases using *boʾ* in the hophal: Lev. 6:23[30]; 10:18; 16:27 [→ דם *dām*, "blood," → כפר *kāphar*, "to make atonement"]; 2 K. 12:17[16]). Lepers are to be brought to the priest (Lev. 13:2,9; 14:2), and unclean vessels are to be put (brought) into water (11:32). Money must be brought to the house of God, and there it may be used, e.g., to defray expenses for repairing the temple under Jehoash (2 K. 12:5,10,14[4,9,13]; 2 Ch. 34:9,14).

The hiphil also appears in cult polemical texts (Am. 4:4; Isa. 1:13; 43:23). One is not to bring any graven image into his house (Dt. 7:26), nor is he to bring the hire of a harlot (*ʾethnan*, a word used in OT polemical contexts only from Hosea on) into the house of God (Dt. 23:19[18]), although of course he is to bring the needy into his house (Isa. 58:7). And when the worshipper in a psalm asks Yahweh to send out his light and truth in order that they might bring the worshipper to Yahweh's holy mountain and to his dwelling (Ps. 43:3, hiphil), the cultic use of *boʾ* in this passage makes one think of its use to denote guidance.[16]

The (singular) statement of Yahweh to his people in Ex. 19:4, *vaʾabhiʾ ʾethekhem ʾelai*, "and I brought you to myself," is later, but is also fixed by cult terminology.[17] After all that has been said, it must be concluded that this statement not only refers to a bringing to the "mountain" (v. 3), but also reflects cultic events, an element missing in Dt. 32:11.

III. boʾ (qal and hiphil) in the Wisdom Literature, and in Blessings and Curses. The Wisdom Literature is characterized by a concept of order.[18] It

---

[16] See below, VII.

[17] On this passage, see now L. Perlitt, *Bundestheologie im AT. WMANT,* 36 (1969), 18, 167-181; A. Deissler, "Das Priestertum im AT," *Der priesterliche Dienst,* I (1970), 9-80, esp. pp. 67-72 with literature.

[18] See H. D. Preuss, *EvTh,* 30 (1970), 393-417; G. von Rad, *Wisdom in Israel* (trans. 1972), 74ff.

attempts to understand the world as order and gives guidance for life, i.e., for its realization, in this order. The connection between conduct and reward in particular is fundamental to this order,[19] and *bo'* (in the perf., impf. and ptcp. of the qal and of the hiphil) is often used to establish this connection: "When pride comes, then comes disgrace," Prov. 11:2; cf. from the earlier Wisdom Literature Prov. 10:24; 11:27; 18:3,6; 24:25,34 (cf. 6:11); 26:2 (an undeserved curse does not alight or come to pass). In these passages, *bo'* can often be translated "fulfil." However, the subject matter indicates that it would be more correct to translate it "come of necessity," "come necessarily," "encompass," etc., because *bo'* conveys the idea of entering into and moving within that realm of activity which affects destiny.[20]

From the later Wisdom Literature, Prov. 3:25; 6:11,15 should be mentioned. That *bo'* was an important technical term for this concept is further indicated by its occurrence in the Wisdom Psalms (Ps. 37:15; 49:20[19]; cf. 35:8; 109:17; also Job 2:11; 4:5, *bo' 'al*, "come upon"; 29:13; Sir. 3:11). The author of Ecclesiastes also takes up this theme, but he places it in the midst of his critical reflections on Wisdom (2:16; 5:14f.[15f.]; 11:8).

This wisdom concept also plays a role in the idea of the "coming" of calamity or of mercy upon someone (Ps. 119:77 without *'al*, "upon"; cf. Gen. 42:21; Jer. 2:3; Dnl. 9:13; Job 42:11; Jgs. 9:23f.).[21] Jgs. 9:23f. affirms that violence (→ חמס *chāmās*) and blood (→ דם *dām*) of the slain overtakes the slayer, or rather, clings to him.[22] Israel saw no conflict between the concept of deed and consequence and belief in a providential guidance of Yahweh.

Yahweh also stands behind the strength of a blessing or the power of a curse even when this is not expressly stated (cf. Dt. 28:2; etc.). Thus, here also it is appropriate to mention the effects of the blessing (→ ברכה *berākhāh*) and the curse (→ אלה *'ālāh;* → ארר *'ārar;* → קללה *qelālāh;* cf. Dt. 28:2,15 with *bo'* ["shall come upon you"] as thematic introductions of old passages, 28:3-6,16-19; see also 28:45; 30:1). 28:2a and 15b have a parallelistic structure and are part of the original introductions, and v. 45 is not a later addition. In contrast to the earlier and original independent passages, the introductory formulas are Deuteronomic. They connect blessing and curse with the covenant, a connection that had not been made previously. Dt. 29:1-20(2-21) (and 21-27[22-28]) refers back to 28:15. These sections are Deuteronomistic and intend to represent the fulfilment of the curse as already having taken place (cf. vv. 19 and 26 [20 and 27]; cf. further 30:7 from another stratum).[23] It is worthy of note that Deuteronomy does not speak of the blessing (the relation of 30:1-10 is disputed). Dt. 30:1 uses "blessing and curse" to indicate the sum total of Yahweh's deeds (cf. "all these things" in v. 1a; Josh. 8:34: words of blessing and curse in the law; Dt. 30:19f.: life and

---

[19] For the literature, see *EvTh,* 30 (1970), 398.

[20] K. Koch, *ZThK,* 52 (1955), 1-42; G. von Rad, *OT Theol,* I (trans. 1962), 296ff.

[21] On this subject, cf. K. Koch, *VT,* 12 (1962), 397.

[22] Koch, *ZThK,* 52, 23; on p. 24 he deals with Gen. 30:33 and with the problem of translating *thabho'* in that passage; on *bo' 'al,* "come upon," see further Josh. 23:15; Isa. 47:9; Am. 4:2.

[23] Cf. L. Perlitt, *Bundestheologie,* 23-30.

death). Ps. 3:9(8) and 109:17 should also be mentioned in this connection as contrasts.

The "coming" of the blessing and especially of the curse represents one way in which the Deuteronomic and Deuteronomistic historians endeavored to interpret history. Lev. 26, e.g., does not know this use of bo'. Thus Wisdom Literature and OT blessings and curses have several things in common. They are both connected with the concept of order and with the condition of salvation assumed by it or disrupted and then restored by it. Also at one time an original magical idea of the "coming" of a positive or negative consequence stood behind both of them. In Israel, this idea was given new meaning because of its relationship to Yahweh without completely destroying its uniqueness. [24] This can be supported e.g., by the reference to the effects of the curse water in Nu. 5:22 (with bo').

The hiphil of bo' is also used in this connection: Jacob does not want to bring a curse upon himself (Gen. 27:12, E); on the blessing, cf. 1 S. 25:27. Yahweh brought upon the land all the curses that "are written in this book" because his people served other gods (Dt. 29:26[27]). Yahweh brought upon the fathers "all the words of this covenant" (Jer. 11:8; on the understanding of the covenant, cf. the Deuteronomistic history!). On the other hand, Jeremiah prays that Yahweh might bring the day of calamity upon those who persecute him (Jer. 17:18; cf. 18:22). One person brings sin upon another (Gen. 20:9; Ex. 32:21). The concluding statement in Ecclesiastes (which was added for theological reasons) emphasizes that Yahweh will bring every deed into judgment (12:14; cf. 11:9).

IV. Coming (qal) and Bringing (hiphil) into the Land. The theological evaluation of the land (→ ארץ 'erets) is very important in the theology of Deuteronomy and the Deuteronomistic history. The Deuteronomist has created numerous formulas in order to affirm the uniqueness and dignity of the land (→ נחלה nachⁱlāh, "possession, inheritance"; → נתן nāthan, "to give"; → עבר 'ābhar, "to pass over, pass through"), [25] and has put them in the mouth of Yahweh or, more accurately, of Moses. In keeping with the perspective of the speaker's line of argumentation, the book of Deuteronomy, it is true, usually speaks of the gift of the land as being in the future, but it also apostrophizes it as a past event or as present. Israel came, comes, or especially will come into the land in order to possess (→ ירש yārash) it. In this way Yahweh fulfils the oath (→ שבע shābhaʿ) which he swore to the fathers. [26]

Deuteronomy and the literature influenced by it use the qal perfect, imperfect, infinitive, and participle of the verb bo' to emphasize that there are no natural or substantial original connections between Israel and its land. On the contrary, there was a time when Israel was not yet in the land. This is clear from statements in the OT to the effect that first of all the people "came" into the land, and received it as a gracious gift of Yahweh who "brought" Israel therein. Thus, Yahweh's historical guidance of Israel into the land he had promised and

---

[24] Cf. J. Hempel, *BZAW,* 81 (1961), 31ff.

[25] See Driver, *Deuteronomy, ICC,* LXXVIII-LXXXIV.

[26] → אב *'ābh* III.3.c; → אדמה *'ⁱdhāmāh* III.3.a.

sworn to give them is expressed by *boʼ* in the qal and the hiphil.[27] Under Yah-weh's guidance, Moses brought Israel up to the land and Joshua brought them into the land. The book of Deuteronomy in particular emphasizes that this is a saving gift of Yahweh. Therefore, the land with its gifts is a historical gift of Yahweh into which Israel was led and which was given to them. Thus, here also the line of argumentation in Deuteronomy is similar to that in Hosea.

In Deuteronomy, references to Israel's coming into the land (usually stated as being in the future because of the fiction that Moses is the speaker) are often completed by the statement, "to take possession of it" (→ ירשׁ *yārash*), Dt. 7:1; 9:5; 11:10,29; 12:29; 23:21(20); then also 28:21,63; 30:16 (*boʼ* always as a qal ptcp.; on *yarash,* "to possess," cf. also Am. 2:10, Deuteronomistic); also Dt. 1:8 (impv.); 11:8 (perf.); 17:14 (impf.; cf. also CD A 8:14). Here *boʼ* appears in what are generally considered to be Deuteronomic pareneses (8:1; cf. 4:1,5, Deuteronomistic; further in 26:1 with *ki,* "when"; 27:3 with *ʼasher,* "when"; in texts independent of Deuteronomy, Lev. 14:34; Nu. 15:2 not using *yarash,* "to possess," but *nathan,* "to give"; Lev. 19:23 using only *thabhoʼu* with *ki,* "when"), but it also occurs in concrete references (Dt. 23:21[20]). Israel is not (from its beginning or by nature) a people of the land into which they come; therefore, they are not to act like the peoples of the land (12:9; 18:9; but cf. 31:16 as a continuing divine oracle). The passages in Dt. 28ff. use *boʼ* in the expansions of the old curse oracles[28] in 28:16-18, and as a threat in 28:21,63 and 30:16, in order to articulate the severity of a calamity or a loss: Yahweh will take back this gift of salvation which is so important to the Deuteronomist and his hearers. In any case, Israel came into the land only because of Yahweh's faithfulness, and not because of the righteousness of the people (9:1,5). If 6:18 makes this coming dependent on obedience, still the book of Deuteronomy demands that this obedience always be renewed (cf. the Deuteronomistic history in Josh. 1:11; 18:3; similarly Jgs. 18:9) "in this realm of promises fulfilled."[29]

boʼ is given a more specific hostile connotation in Deuteronomy by its con-nection with *yarash,* "to possess" (cf. Dt. 1:8), while its less frequent connections with *nathan,* "to give," or with the oath to the fathers (the latter appears only in 6:18f.; 8:1; 11:9 [but this verse contrasts rather strongly with 11:8]; 26:3; 6:23; hiphil inf. with the oath to the fathers),[30] indicate a "more peaceful" con-cept. The expression "until you came to this place" emphasizes the idea that it was Yahweh who caused his people to come and who brought his people into the land. This phrase points to Yahweh's guidance reflected in this activity (1:31; 9:7; 11:5: always used in the pl. address), which is the important thing to the Deuteronomist. Ex. 16:35 should also be mentioned here. It contains two parallel statements about Israel eating the manna in the wilderness. One says that they ate it until they came to the habitable land, and the other that they ate it until they came to the border of Canaan. Although this verse would seem to belong

---

[27] See VII below.
[28] See III above.
[29] W. Zimmerli, *Man and His Hope in the OT* (trans. 1971), 72.
[30] Cf. the reflections of N. Lohfink, *Das Hauptgebot. AnBibl,* 20 (1963), 82.

to the early part of the period of the wilderness wanderings, it describes the forty years of wandering as already having taken place. The passage is significant for the present discussion because the two sources lying behind it (P and J) use *'adh bo'am* in the same way as the above-mentioned passages in Deuteronomy. Consequently, it is likely that J also already knew *bo'* in the sense of "coming into the (promised) land," although he did not use it as a key word in this group of motifs (as Dt. does).

The coming into the land is already connected with the obedience that would be necessary in the future (from the perspective assumed in Dt.), or with the punishment of the loss of the land in case of disobedience, in Dt. 27:3; 28:21,63 (cf. 6:1; 8:1). This emphasis, then, is especially typical of Deuteronomistic thought (4:1,5 and 30:16; 31:20f. in the Deuteronomistic framework of the Song of Moses): Yahweh warns Israel against apostasy because he knows the thoughts of the people before he gives them the land (31:21). To be sure, Israel is to "come" into the land, but is not to be mixed with the peoples living in it (Josh. 23:7, Deuteronomistic).

Stereotyped expressions of the Deuteronomist can also be recognized elsewhere in texts that have been influenced by Deuteronomic or Deuteronomistic thought: Ex. 12:25; Lev. 23:10; 25:2; Jer. 32:23. Ezr. 9:11 and Neh. 9:15,23f. have also been influenced by Deuteronomic thought.

Naturally, the "coming" into the promised land, the "bringing" into the wilderness, etc., are mentioned frequently in the murmuring stories (→ לוּן *lûn,* "to lodge"), because these accounts are also concerned with Israel coming into the land or with Yahweh bringing them into the land. The people ask Moses and Aaron why they had brought the → קָהָל *qāhāl,* "assembly," of Yahweh or "us" into this evil place (Nu. 20:4, P; on v. 5, cf. Ex. 17:3 and the hiphil in Nu. 14:3 and 20:4; Dathan and Abiram against Moses according to Nu. 16:14, J). Aaron (Nu. 20:24: addition to P; cf. v. 26) and Moses (Dt. 4:21, Deuteronomistic) shall not enter into the land (Nu. 20:12, P). Because of the murmuring of the people in connection with the sending of the spies, only Caleb will come into the land (Nu. 14:30: addition to P; cf. also 32:9 as a late note; but see Nu. 14:24[J] with the emphasis on that which follows "my servant Caleb," and Nu. 13:27,30; also 14:8[P]), or Yahweh will bring into the land only the children of the generation that murmured (Nu. 14:31[P]). Moses implores Yahweh not to carry out his punishment on the murmuring people lest foreigners say that he is not able (!) to bring Israel into the land (thus Nu. 14:16 in a speech of Moses [a Deuteronomic addition to J?] and Dt. 9:28). Ezk. 20:15 (using the hiphil of *bo'* and significantly reinterpreting Yahweh's oath) and Ps. 95:11 (qal) refer to the murmuring tradition.

Frequently in the murmuring stories also *bo'* stands in antithesis to *yatsa',* "to go out." [31]

The idea of the coming (*bo',* qal) of the people into the land is based on the

---

[31] Cf. some examples of this in G. W. Coats, *Rebellion in the Wilderness* (Nashville/New York, 1968), 29f., 89f.

concept that Yahweh has brought (*bo'*, hiphil) them into the land (cf. Dt. 8:7-10 with its elaborate description of the gift). Thus, this combination of "coming" and "bringing" appears in Ex. 6:8(P); Dt. 7:1; 11:29; Jer. 2:7; 23:23 with Deuteronomistic terminology; and also in Nu. 15:18 with Deuteronomistic terminology, where the *'ani mebhi'*, "I bring," even refers to Moses. [32] It is Yahweh who brings the people into the land, according to Dt. 6:10f.; 11:29; 7:1; 8:7; 9:4,28; 30:5. The pre-Deuteronomic manner of stating this idea occurs in Nu. 32:17, and is fundamentally different from the Deuteronomic.

It is because of the influence of Deuteronomic and Deuteronomistic thought, then, that several passages refer to the idea that Yahweh brought (hiphil; cf. also → יצא *yātsā'*, "to go out"; → עבר *'ābhar,* "to pass over"; → עלה *'ālāh,* "to go up") his people into the land: Ex. 23:20, with Deuteronomistic terminology (except for "angel of Yahweh"); 13:5,11; 15:17, with clear Deuteronomistic influence; Dt. 1:20; 4:1, with characteristic connection with the concept of obedience; Ezk. 20:28, with reference to Yahweh's oath (to the fathers?); Ps. 78:54, presenting the gift of the land as an affirmation of divine guidance (cf. Ezk. 20:10). At the same time, Lev. 18:3 and 20:22, which contain the phrase *'ani mebhi'*, "I am bringing," with Yahweh as the speaker, are among the few passages using this participial expression in connection with a positive emphasis. [33] When Joshua receives the promise that he will bring the people into the land (cf. Nu. 27:17 [P]), [34] as Yahweh had sworn (Dt. 31:23), he also receives the promise that Yahweh will be with him (→ את *'ēth,* and cf. on this emphasis Dt. 31:6f.).

Accordingly, *bo'* in the sense of "come into" (qal) and "bring into" (hiphil) the land is a motif word or a key word of salvation history (cf. by way of analogy Jonah 1:3,8; also 3:4) in texts influenced by Deuteronomic (Dt. 26:3!) and Deuteronomistic (1:8!) thought. Dt. 12:9 shows that for the Deuteronomist the coming into the land was not the conclusion of Israel's way with Yahweh.

bo' appears in an analogous context in the exilic prophets (Ezk.!) when they promise or discuss the possibility of the return to the land of Israel. Also the question as to whether the people should go (*bo'*) to Egypt or not, which is discussed in detail in Jer. 42f. and which is important to Jeremiah, is due in part to the high regard for the land given by Yahweh, and not merely to the problem of the recognition of Nebuchadnezzar as Yahweh's instrument of punishment (Jer. 25:9; 27:6; → עבר *'ābhar,* "to pass over").

Wijngaards presents a completely different view of the Deuteronomic and Deuteronomistic theology of the land [35] (frequently appealing to *bo'* in the qal and hiphil). The title of his book (*The Dramatization of Salvific History in the Deuteronomic Schools*) and concluding section ("The Cultic Occupation of the Land") indicate the kind of interpretation he advocates, an interpretation that could not be followed here.

---

[32] On this text as a late passage, see Noth, *ATD, in loc.*

[33] Cf. VIII below.

[34] Cf. Plöger, 178f.

[35] J. N. M. Wijngaards, *The Dramatization of Salvific History in the Deuteronomic Schools. OTS,* 16 (Leiden, 1969), 68-105.

V. bo' As "Fulfilling." By "bringing" his people into the land as he had promised and sworn, Yahweh fulfils his oath and his promise. To be sure, the use of *bo'* in the sense of "fulfil" does not appear in Deuteronomy, which otherwise is characterized by a stereotyped use of *bo'*, [36] but it occurs not infrequently in other passages, especially in the Deuteronomistic history and later.

In Josh. 21:45 the Deuteronomist states that "all came to pass" (*hakkol ba'*) and nothing of the good word of Yahweh which he had spoken to the house of Israel had failed (→ נפל *nāphal*). V. 43 shows that the fulfilled word is the promise of the land, the oath to the fathers (thus Deuteronomic and Deuteronomistic), [37] which a comparison with Josh. 1 (Deuteronomistic) also confirms. It declares the history of divine guidance. Josh. 23:14f. begins the same way, but its significance is in asserting that now also Yahweh will "bring upon you" every evil word until he has destroyed his people from off the good land he gave them. The possession of the land depends on Israel's obedience (thus the concept is esp. Deuteronomic and Deuteronomistic).

Additional examples also show the interest of the Deuteronomic and Deuteronomistic theology in the "fulfilment" of that which Yahweh had said, be it good or bad. Everything the man of God says surely comes true (1 S. 9:6, *bo' yabho'*). If a prophet announces Yahweh's word, this will be demonstrated by its fulfilment (Dt. 18:22). But the OT also knows that predictions of false prophets can come true (Dt. 13:3[2]), so that further investigation is necessary (v. 3c [2c]) to identify a false prophet. But the means of identification mentioned here ("if he says, 'Let us go after other gods'") is not very helpful, because a "false" prophet hardly would have called on Israelite people to follow other gods. [38] Within the Deuteronomistic history, Jgs. 13:12,17; 1 S. 2:34; 10:7 (with *bo'*) also speak of the fulfilment of things or signs (→ אות *'ôth*) which had been predicted; on the sign in 1 S. 10:7f. and its fulfilment, cf. Ex. 4:8f. and Jgs. 6:17-21 (here without *bo'*, however), and also 1 S. 9:6. Also, according to Jer. 28:9, one can recognize the true prophet by the fulfilment (*bebho'*) of his word of salvation (!). On the other hand, the people mock when there is no fulfilment of a threat (17:15). In Hab. 2:3, Habakkuk receives Yahweh's assurance that his vision (→ חזון *chāzôn*) will yet certainly (*bo' yabho'*, "it will surely come"; cf. 1 S. 9:6) be fulfilled. Because Ezekiel's hearers do not believe his word (Ezk. 33:30-33), Yahweh also has to assure him that it will certainly be fulfilled and then ("when this comes") they will know that a prophet has been in their midst (v. 33; cf. also 24:14,24; 30:9; 39:8; in 24:14 *ba'ah* is probably an addition; [39] 33:30-33 is almost dominated by a wordplay on *bo'*). The exilic text, Isa. 13:22, is also related to these texts. The same is true of 42:9, where Deutero-Isaiah has Yahweh say that that which Yahweh had announced earlier came to pass, and consequently one could and should rely on the new things that he now declares.

---

[36] See IV below.
[37] Cf. under IV, and → אדמה *'adhāmāh* III.3.a.
[38] On this problem, cf. E. Osswald, *Falsche Prophetie im AT* (1962), 23-26, with literature.
[39] W. Zimmerli, *BK*, XIII, 558f.

In its review of Israel's history, three times Ps. 105 refers to something Yahweh had spoken that had been fulfilled (vv. 31,34), even when it consisted only in predictions of the man Joseph (v. 19). [40]

This survey shows that Israel gave great consideration to the question of the fulfilment of the words of Yahweh, in particular from the period of (Deuteronomy and) the Deuteronomistic history on, and that the problem was especially intensified by the exile (cf. Ezk. and Deutero-Isaiah). Job 6:8, where Job desires the fulfilment (bo') of his request, does not convey the same idea under consideration here.

The hiphil of bo' is also used to express the fulfilment of that which has been threatened or promised (Josh. 23:15, Deuteronomistic; 2 K. 19:25; Isa. 31:2; 46:11; 48:15; Jer. 25:13; 40:3; Ezk. 38:17; also CD A 7:10, but otherwise in 1QS 1:7: to fulfil precepts). [41] Fulfilment of something that has been said earlier is also a sign, indeed, it is a part of divine guidance. [42] Yahweh fulfils a prayer (Ps. 105:40) and brings to pass something that someone has asked him (1 Ch. 4:10). He brings upon Abraham that which he had promised him (so J in a monolog of Yahweh, which is characteristic of his style: Gen. 18:19).

VI. 1. bo' in Laments. A few texts use bo' (qal) in a lament or prayer to Yahweh. In laments, worshippers bring before Yahweh various distresses which have come (always perf.), to move him to intervene. In a popular lament, the people spread out before him the calamities that have come upon them in spite of their having not forgotten him (Ps. 44:18[17]). In a funeral dirge (cf. Am. 5:2), Jeremiah laments: "Death has entered our palaces," and Yahweh has done it (Jer. 9:20f.[21f.]); or Yahweh himself (or Jeremiah?) laments over his devastated land: destroyers have come (12:12; cf. 8:7). Jerusalem had to watch while the nations came and invaded her sanctuary (Lam. 1:10: bo' occurs twice here in a "tragic wordplay"; [43] cf. 2:7), and she laments: "our end had come" (Lam. 4:18; cf. Am. 8:2; Ezk. 7:2,6). Daniel recognizes (Dnl. 9:13) that the calamity has come, as it is written in the law of Moses (cf. Ezr. 9:13; Neh. 9:28,33; Jer. 12:1; Lam. 1:18: consequently the prayer or repentance in Dnl. 9 is clearly dependent on the Deuteronomistic literature). The outcry (→ צְעָקָה tseʿāqāh) over the sins of Sodom has come before Yahweh, and he will go down to see whether the people of Sodom have done according to this outcry (Gen. 18:21[J]). And in particular the lament of the children of Israel has come before Yahweh, as he himself affirms in a direct address, and he intervenes (Ex. 3:9[E]; v. 7 uses → שָׁמַע shāmaʿ, "to hear"; cf. 1 S. 9:16). In view of this, an individual can also bring his own special lament before Yahweh in the hope that he will intervene to save (Ps. 102:14[13]: "Thou wilt arise and have pity on Zion; it is the time to favor her" ["the appointed time has come"–an addition?]). A worshipper also asks Yahweh not to enter into judgment with his servant (Ps. 143:2; [44] cf. Job 9:32).

---

[40] On bo' here in the sense of "bring," see Dahood, Psalms, III, 61f.
[41] See even more precise information under VII below.
[42] See VII below.
[43] Rudolph, KAT, XVII, 1-3, 213.
[44] On the qal in this passage, cf. Dahood, Psalms, III, 323.

2. *bo' in Prayers.* Since Yahweh answers prayers, all flesh comes to him, i.e., to Zion, to the sanctuary (Ps. 65:2f.[1f.]; there is no justification for emending the text here to the hiphil); [45] each brings his own sin to God. The concept of the coming of all peoples to Zion (cf. Isa. 2:3f. and par.; 24:15; 60:1ff.; Ps. 22:28ff. [27ff.]) also appears hymnically in the lament as a motif of answering prayer (Ps. 86:9). Prayers and laments can come before Yahweh from the sanctuary (Ps. 18:7[6]; 79:11; 88:3[2]; 102:2[1]; 119:170; also Jonah 2:8[7]), and the worshipper says: "Let thy mercy come to me (*yebho'uni*), that I may live" (Ps. 119:77; cf. v. 41); or he prays that all the evil of his enemies may come before Yahweh (Lam. 1:22). Even before making his petitions, the worshipper in Ps. 40:8(7) says in gratitude: "Lo, I have come; in the book it is written of me what is to be done" [46] (cf. Jer. 3:22, *'athanu,* "we come," to be understood cultically? cf. Hos. 6:1, an expression meaning conversion, but in antithesis to Jer. 2:31); see also the postexilic text, Jer. 50:5: the return of Israel and Judah to Yahweh and to his everlasting covenant in view of the destruction of Babylon. [47]

The hiphil of *bo'* also occurs in these same senses. "Hear, O Yahweh, the voice of Judah, and bring him in to his people" (Dt. 33:7). [48] One may also compare the prayer that Yahweh may bring the day of recompense (Lam. 1:21).

VII. bo' (hiphil) As a Term for God's Guidance in History. Several times already [49] we have had occasion to call attention to the use of the hiphil of *bo'* in theologically significant statements. But here again we must mention that it is not uncommon for the OT writers to use the idea of Yahweh "bringing" or "causing to come" in order to express their faith in Yahweh's dominion over history. Yahweh fulfils that which he has threatened, he brings to pass what he has promised, he causes that for which a person prays to take place (Gen. 18:19 [J]; Josh. 23:15 [Deuteronomistic]; 2 K. 19:25; Isa. 31:2; 48:15; Jer. 25:13; 40:3; Ezk. 38:17; Ps. 105:40; 1 Ch. 4:10). In this way Yahweh shapes time as a time curve, as a course directed toward a goal; he guides it toward its goal and demonstrates that he is its lord, because he shapes history over the span of threat or promise to fulfilment.

For judicious historical and theological reasons these assertions increase in Deuteronomistic texts (Josh. 23:15; 24:7; 1 K. 9:9; 2 K. 19:25; cf. 2 Ch. 7:22), in texts in Jeremiah influenced by Deuteronomistic thought (Jer. 15:8; 23:8; 25:13; 32:42; 44:2; 49:8), and in Ezekiel (Ezk. 14:22; 20:10; 38:16; 39:2), all texts having to do generally with the occurrence of punishment that had been threatened, which is a subject of contemplation in the exile. In contrast, a major emphasis in Deutero-Isaiah [50] is that now Yahweh also brings to reality the salva-

---

[45] Cf. *ibid.,* II, 110.

[46] So Kraus, *BK,* XV, *in loc.*

[47] On Ps. 69:28(27), see under VIII below.

[48] See H.-J. Zobel, *Stammesspruch und Geschichte. BZAW,* 95 (1965), 77f., who points out on p. 29 that *'am* and *bo'* are also to be found in Gen. 49:10; see also under IX below.

[49] See under II-VI above, and also under VIII-IX below.

[50] Cf. A. Zillessen, *ZAW,* 26 (1906), 256.

tion he had promised, raising up Cyrus as his instrument of salvation (Isa. 43:5f.; 46:11; 48:15; 49:22). The quotations, imitations, and new interpretations of this concept in Trito-Isaiah should be noted in comparison (Isa. 56:7; 60:9; 66:20; also 58:7; 60:17). Other texts that use the hiphil of *bo'* to articulate a belief in divine guidance and in an explanation of history are Dt. 26:9 (!); 29:26(27); 2 S. 7:18; 17:14 (!); cf. 1 Ch. 17:16; Isa. 37:26; Ps. 66:11; 78:71; Neh. 1:9; 13:18; 2 Ch. 33:11; Dnl. 9:12,14 (cf. Neh. 1:9); see also Dt. 33:7; Ps. 43:3.

A completely different use of the hiphil of *bo'* appears in a group of texts in Ezekiel (Ezk. 8:3,7,14,16; 11:1,24; 43:5; with a suffix in 40:17,28,32,35,48; 41:1; 42:1; 44:4; 46:19). Here several times Yahweh or his hand (40:1,4, hophal; cf. 37:1; → יד *yādh*) or even the "man" (*ha'ish*) brings Ezekiel to different places, and also leads him (cf. also → לקח *lāqach*, "to take," and → נשא *nāśā'*, "to lift up"). Early in the book (Ezk. 3), this means "mysteriously the inside of a normal self-motivation of the prophet seen from the outside," [51] but then it comes to be used with intensification and in chapters 8, 11 and 40ff. is represented as more than a real journey–it is a "vision." The extent to which this is a stylistic device cannot be discussed here.

VIII. 1. *The Coming Judgment.* Of course, ultimately it is always Yahweh who comes anew to his people in an approaching judgment or salvation as the one who acts. Nevertheless, in the following sections a distinction is made between passages that speak (!) of judgment which is coming or has been brought (VIII), passages that speak of salvation which is coming or has been brought (IX) (for the sake of better clarification), and passages that speak of the coming of Yahweh himself (X) (because of the unique importance of the texts with which we must deal here). In dealing with the coming of Yahweh, it is necessary also to differentiate between goal, purpose, and point of departure on the one hand, and to determine the manner of his coming on the other.

In the OT it is predominantly the prophets who were active in the period between 750 and 587 B.C. (cf. already Elisha, 2 K. 8:1) that announce the approaching judgment of Yahweh as an event of destruction in the world. In making such announcements, not infrequently they use the verb *bo'* (and not *'athah*), and usually in the form of the so-called *perfect propheticum* (prophetic perfect). [52] Announcements of judgment appear both as words of Yahweh (messenger oracle) and as words of the prophet, in which *bo'*, of course, usually occurs in the announcements of judgment, and only rarely in the reasons given for it.

"The end (→ קץ *qēts*) has come (*ba'*) upon my people Israel" (Am. 8:2). With this message, Amos states quite harshly and blatantly that which he himself in other places transforms into what may at least possibly be an admonition (5:4-6, 14f.; etc.), and which other prophets after him proclaim less radically (but cf. Ezk. 7:2,6; in v. 6, this expression is repeated chiastically). *bo'* appears in the

---

[51] Zimmerli, *BK*, XIII, 206.

[52] See Brockelmann, *Synt.*, 40f.; F. Rundgren, *Das hebräische Verbum* (Stockholm, 1961), 90.

announcement of judgment on the house of Eli in 1 S. 2:31, and in Isaiah's announcement of judgment on Hezekiah in 2 K. 20:17 (cf. Isa. 39:6). The expression *yamim ba'im* is found already in the book of Amos (→ יום *yôm,* "day"), [53] viz., in Am. 4:2 in the announcement of judgment upon (*'al*) the women of Samaria, and in 8:11 (but with a disruption in the context; from Amos?) in connection with a general announcement of judgment. [54]

Hos. 9:7 states that the days of recompense (→ פקד *pāqadh*) would come, and thus attempts to fix these "days" concretely (which is typical for the OT understanding of time) and especially to fill them with content. Amos uses *bo'* only in direct words of Yahweh. Hosea uses it in a prophetic oracle and in the quotation of a "song of repentance" by the people which supposes that Yahweh will "come" as the rain (Hos. 6:3; but cf. 10:12). According to Micah, the plague of Yahweh comes upon Judah (Mic. 1:9), the day of visitation which the "watchmen" of Judah have seen (7:4?). [55] Before salvation can come, the daughter of Zion must come to Babylon (4:10); but this will be only a temporary exile (4:9f.; hardly from Micah; for a different view cf. Jer. 4:31; 10:17). According to Isaiah, Yahweh comes in a judgment assembly in order to judge (different from Deutero-Isaiah) the elders of his people (Isa. 3:14; cf. Job 22:4). Isaiah proclaims his "Woe!" to those who (as Isa. quotes them) do not believe that the judgment which had been announced will come to pass (*qarabh,* "draw near," *bo'*), and scoff at it (5:19; cf. 14:31). According to 19:1, [56] Yahweh comes to judge Egypt, and according to 30:27, the name (→ שם *shēm;* so here only; an addition?) of Yahweh comes from afar to judge Assyria. According to Isa. 7:17, Isaiah tells Ahaz that Yahweh will bring (*bo',* hiphil) days ("by the king of Assyria," probably a gloss) such as have not come (*bo',* qal) since the division of the kingdom. This verse is an announcement of judgment. According to 2 K. 19:28 (Isa. 37:29), Isaiah announces that Yahweh will turn Assyria back on the way by which she came by putting a ring in her nose. As is often the case in announcements of judgment against foreign nations, this announcement of judgment against Assyria means also salvation for Israel. [57]

Also, from the time of Zephaniah on, the day of Yahweh (→ יום *yôm*) and thus the day of Yahweh's fierce anger (Zeph. 2:2) is spoken of in connection with *bo'*. [58] According to Zephaniah, one should still seek Yahweh to the best of his ability, because it may be possible (cf. Am. 5:15) for him to be delivered in this way (Zeph. 2:3). Jeremiah makes this day of Yahweh concrete as a day of calamity upon (usually with *'al*) Egypt (46:21). Ezekiel proclaims that the day of distress is near (Ezk. 7:7,10), that the day draws near (7:12), that the day of punishment has come upon the prince in Israel (21:30[25]), and that the "day" of the Ammonites has come (21:34[29]). According to Malachi, the day

53 *TDNT,* II, 947.

54 On *yamim ba'im* in announcements of salvation, see under IX below.

55 But cf. Robinson, *HAT,* 14 (³1964), 148f.

56 See under X below.

57 See IX below.

58 On the "coming of the day" with the meaning "to die," see L. Černý, *The Day of Yahweh and some relevant problems* (Prague, 1948), 23; Pidoux, 14.

that comes will be judgment upon the ungodly, but salvation for those who fear
the name of Yahweh (3:19[4:1]), and Elijah will be sent to turn the hearts
(thoughts) of the people (3:24[4:6]). The day of Yahweh comes as a destruction
from → שַׁדַּי shaddai, "the Almighty" (Joel 1:15; Isa. 13:6, transferred to Babylon,
not from Isaiah; cf. perhaps also Am. 5:9), and before his coming the sun
and the moon are darkened (Joel 4:15[3:15]). The nations are to depart and
come and gather for judgment (Joel 4:11[3:11]). → עלה 'ālāh, "go up," bo',
"come," and → קבץ qābhats, "gather," here belong to the group of words having
to do with "summons to battle," or more precisely with "advancing" [59] (bo' also
has this sense in Jer. 49:14; 50:26; Isa. 13:2; Joel 4:11,13[3:11,13]). [60] This day
of Yahweh is coming and is near (Joel 2:1). According to later texts, it comes as
judgment upon Babylon (Isa 13:9), as the day of Babylon's visitation (Jer. 50:27,
31); for the end of Babylon has come (Jer. 51:13). The destroyer has come upon
Babylon, his "harvest" will soon come (Jer. 51:33). The changing concrete contents and relationship of the Day of Yahweh in the prophets from Am. 5:18f.
on indicate the historical development of the announcements of judgment in the
prophets. [61]

In the book of Jeremiah, the expression yamim ba'im, "the days are coming,"
in the announcements of judgment upon Israel appears only in speeches of
Yahweh, and there it occurs rather frequently (Jer. 7:32; cf. 19:6; 48:12, against
Moab; 51:52, concerning the images of Babylon; cf. 51:47; here always with
lakhen, "therefore"; without lakhen against Israel, 9:24[25]; against Ammon,
49:2 [many scholars delete lakhen here and in 48:12]). Jeremiah calls attention
to the early period of Israel's history as a warning to his audience that evil will
come (tabho') upon those who are unfaithful now (Jer. 2:3). The people deny
that this warning against them is correct (5:12), especially since the false prophets
support them in this view (Jer. 23:17; cf. Mic. 3:11). But shepherds will come
against God's people from the north and will pasture, each in his place (Jer. 6:3);
a people is coming from the north (6:22; cf. 13:20; 50:41; → צפון tsāphôn).
The destruction is coming, regardless of whether Jehoiakim was willing to accept
Jeremiah's message of judgment that Nebuchadnezzar was coming (25:8-11)
(36:29; cf. the people's attitude in 21:13). At all events, the Chaldeans will come
to Jerusalem (32:29; cf. 21:13), and this is quite certain (36:29).

Of course, later oracles concerning foreign nations speak of the coming judgment: destroyers will come against Babylon from Yahweh (Jer. 51:48,53,56),
the "butcher" will certainly come from the north against Egypt (46:20,22). The
day of destruction is coming upon the Philistines (47:4). Destroyers will come
upon Ammon (49:9) and Moab (48:8). Mourning will come upon Gaza (47:5).
A report (cf. Dnl. 11:44) will come against Babylon as an announcement of Yah-

---

[59] See R. Bach, Die Aufforderung zur Flucht und zum Kampf im alttestamentlichen
Prophetenspruch. WMANT, 9 (1962), 63.

[60] On these texts and their forms, cf. Bach, 51-91.

[61] On this see K.-D. Schunck, VT, 14 (1964), 319-330; H. D. Preuss, Jahweglaube und
Zukunftserwartung. BWANT, 5/7 (1968), 170-79 with literature; on p. 176 he also deals with
the phrase yamim ba'im, "the days are coming"; on the combination of the day of Yahweh
and bo', see Zimmerli, BK, XIII, 167f.

weh's judgment upon Babylon, which will bring about the deliverance of the exiles (Jer. 51:46).

Just as Ezekiel speaks until 587 B.C. of the coming end (Ezk. 7:2,5,6,10; cf. Gen. 6:13[P] as an oracle of Yahweh at the beginning of the flood), in which Yahweh will show himself to be Yahweh, so the prophet also knows that anguish will come from it (7:25). Robbers shall come and profane Yahweh's sanctuary (7:22). Because of the message of judgment that will come and will be fulfilled (*ba'ah* occurs twice here), Ezekiel must sigh (21:12[7]). By shedding blood, Jerusalem has brought near her time ("days and years") which is coming (22:3f.). Oholibah's former paramours will now come against her with hostility and warfare (23:24). It is clear that *bo'* was selected here as a contrast to its meaning *coire cum femina*, "have sexual relations with a woman." The judged Israel will bear witness of Yahweh in the lands into which they come, as they tell of the punishment that has come upon them because of their sins (12:16). To be sure, those of Israel who have rebelled against Yahweh will be delivered from the exile, but they will not return to the land of Israel (20:38; cf. also v. 35: the use of *bo'* in the hiphil here actually reminds one of the divine guidance into the land!). [62] This will happen also to the false prophets (13:9). Among the late oracles concerning foreign nations in Ezekiel, there is an oracle of judgment announcing that the sword will "come" upon Egypt (30:4; cf. the assurance in v. 9).

Deutero-Isaiah uses *bo'* almost exclusively in announcements of salvation. [63] Correspondingly, however, he announces that a calamity will come upon Babylon (47:11), which its sorcerers, who otherwise always explain whence and why something happens (? v. 13 at the end), cannot prevent. All they can do is stand forth (v. 13)–in spite of this, the calamity will come irresistibly and suddenly (*bha'; thabho'*). Through Malachi (3:1), Yahweh announces the coming of the angel of the covenant (has the text here been disturbed?) for the judgment of purification.

God also ordained that Ahaziah would go to Joram for Ahaziah's destruction (2 Ch. 22:7), whereas the wrath of Yahweh did not come upon Hezekiah (32:26) because he humbled himself.

In a lament, one psalmist prays that the ungodly might not receive the salvation (*tsedhaqah*, "righteousness," RSV "acquittal") of Yahweh (Ps. 69:28[27]: *'al yabho'u be*).

2. *The Fulfilled Judgment.* Frequently the threats of coming judgment also use the hiphil of *bo'*. This brings out even more clearly that it is Yahweh who causes the judgment to come or who brings the judgment (cf. the use of the pass. for God as the subj. in the NT and in Dnl.; cf. already Jer. 27:22; Ezk. 30:11; etc.).

Usually it is Yahweh himself who declares that he will cause calamity to come (impf. or perf.) as judgment upon an individual, his people or its leaders, or

---

[62] See under V above.
[63] See under IX below.

upon a foreign nation (Ex. 11:1[J]; 1 K. 21:29; Isa. 66:4; Jer. 11:23; 23:12; 48:44; 49:32,36f.; Ezk. 5:17; 7:24; 11:8; 14:17; cf. 33:2). Yahweh will bring Nebuchadnezzar (Jer. 25:9), he will bring the lovers of Oholibah together against her (Ezk. 23:22; cf. also Jer. 20:5; Ezk. 31:9), he will bring the prince of Israel to Babylon (Ezk. 12:13; cf. 17:20), he will bring his people into the wilderness of the peoples and will enter into judgment with them there (Ezk. 20:35,37; cf. also Lev. 26:25,36,41), he will cause a third of his people as a refined remnant to go through the fire once again (Zec. 13:9).

All this becomes particularly clear in the announcement *hineni mebhi'*, "behold, I am bringing," as a divine statement from the mouth of Yahweh himself, which occasionally is strengthened even more by the divine I (*'ani* or *'anokhi*). This phrase appears 29 times in the OT (with *hineni*), usually in announcements of the negative type (it occurs only 4 times in announcements of salvation); [64] and its distribution through the OT indicates that it is found most often in Jeremiah, Ezekiel, and the Deuteronomistic literature (Gen. 6:17[P]; Ex. 10:4 [J]; 1 K. 14:10; 21:21; 2 K. 21:12; 22:16,20; Jer. 4:6; 5:15; 6:19; 11:11; 19:3, 15; 35:17; 39:16; 42:17; 45:5; 49:5; 51:64; Ezk. 6:3; 26:7; 28:7; 29:8; 2 Ch. 34:24,28). [65]

IX. 1. *The Coming and Fulfilled Salvation.* In promises of the salvation which is coming or which will be brought, [66] *bo'* (used later in the perf., impf., and ptcp. in this sense) does not appear before Amos, [67] and after Amos it is also missing in Hosea. In promises of salvation, in Amos we encounter *bo'* only in the expression *yamim ba'im,* "the days are coming," in the disputed verse, 9:13. [68] *yamim ba'im* stands at the beginning of a promise of salvation frequently in the book of Jeremiah (16:14 and 23:7 with *lakhen* [these two texts are hardly from Jer.]; without *lakhen,* 23:5; 30:3; 31:27,31,38[31:27,38 are hardly from Jer.; 33:14 is also secondary]). Isa. 14:2 (a part of the exilic introduction to 14:5ff. in 14:1-2,3-4a) promises that the peoples will bring Israel back to its place (hiphil).

In the book of Micah, 4:8 (here *bo'* and *'athah* stand in parallelism; this is a late text) promises the return of the former dominion, the kingdom of the daughter of Zion. 7:11f. (the genuineness of which is disputed) promises that the day will come when the walls will be built.

In Isa. 1–39, *bo'* occurs in promises of salvation only in late, non-Isaianic texts: 35:10 (cf. 51:11) and 35:4. [69] In 27:6 a promise of salvation is introduced by an isolated *habba'im,* while 27:13 promises that those who were lost in the land of Assyria and those who were driven out of the land of Egypt will come to worship Yahweh on his holy mountain at Jerusalem. In 37:34f., Yahweh prom-

---

[64] See VII and IX.

[65] See K. Koch, *Growth of the Biblical Tradition* (trans. 1969), 213f.

[66] See also II and VII above.

[67] On Gen. 49:10, see 2 below.

[68] See U. Kellermann, *EvTh,* 29 (1969), 169-183; and H. W. Wolff, *BK,* XIV/2, *in loc.;* but see also I. Willi-Plein, *Vorformen der Schriftexegese innerhalb des AT. BZAW,* 123 (1971), 57.

[69] See under X below.

ises Hezekiah through Isaiah that the king of Assyria will return (*yashubh*) on the way that he came (*ba'*), and will not come (*lo' yabho'*) "into this city."

In Zephaniah, *bo'* appears in promises of salvation only once in the hiphil (3:20): Yahweh promises his people, "at that time I will bring you home, and gather you together" (hardly from Zeph.). In the book of Jeremiah, Hananiah promises [70] that Yahweh will bring those who had gone to Babylon back to Zion (28:4), and Jeremiah promises that the diaspora will come to Zion (31:12). Yahweh will console those who come weeping (with tears of joy?) (31:9; [71] cf. 50:4). Since Yahweh wants to bring (hiphil) the faithless to Zion, they should return (3:14: an admonition motivated by a promise). Out of only four passages that use *hineni mebhi'*, "behold, I am bringing," as an introduction to a promise of salvation in an oracle of Yahweh using the direct address, two are found in Jeremiah (the other two are in Ezk. 37:5: gift of the spirit; and Zec. 3:8: "my servant the Branch"). In Jer. 31:8 (cf. also v. 9), Yahweh promises to bring Israel from the north country. In 32:42, in his answer to Jeremiah's prayer, he promises that he will bring the good which he had promised upon the people just as he had brought the evil upon them (cf. Josh. 23:15, Deuteronomistic). A (secondary) historical survey says that aliens will come upon the sanctuary of the house of Yahweh (Jer. 51:51; in the context of a promise of salvation). The promise in Jer. 16:19-21 that the nations will come to Yahweh when they recognize the mendacity of their self-made gods, presupposes Deutero-Isaiah and does not originate from Jeremiah.

bo' appears frequently in Ezekiel's promises of salvation (just as it does in his threats of judgment). 11:16 contains a promise to those who have come into various countries (cf. 36:20f. as a negative background for vv. 22ff.; and 20:42, hiphil, with the affirmation that Judah will know that Yahweh is the Lord). These who were scattered shall come back into the land (so the addition, 11:18), and shall remove from it all their abominations and idols. Also, according to many interpreters, the word of judgment against the prince in Israel in 21:32(27) ends with a promise ("until he who has → מִשְׁפָּט *mishpāt*, 'justice,' comes"?). [72] After the man who had escaped from Jerusalem comes to Ezekiel to tell him that the city has fallen (Ezk. 33:21f.; cf. 24:25f.), Ezekiel's preaching changes completely to the promise of coming salvation. Yahweh will gather his flock and bring it into its land (34:13, hiphil; cf. 36:24; 37:21), and his people will soon come home (*labho'*, 36:8). A spirit (→ רוּחַ *rûach*) will cause the people who think they are dead (37:11) to live, and by the word of Ezekiel (! cf. Isa. 40:6,8; 55:8-11) it will come from the four winds (Ezk. 37:9f.; cf. 2:2; 3:24). Even though God will go up against the land of Israel and come or be brought to Jerusalem (38:11,13,18; 39:2, hiphil; cf. Joel 4:11a[3:11a], qal), [73] Yahweh

---

[70] On *yamim ba'im* in Jeremiah, see above.

[71] So Rudolph, *HAT, in loc.*

[72] Cf. below on Gen. 49:10; on the traditio-historical interpretation of Ezk. 21:32(27), see U. Kellermann, *Messias und Gesetz. BSt,* 61 (1971), 32f.

[73] On *bo'* in Ezk. 38f., see H.-M. Lutz, *Jahwe, Jerusalem und die Völker. WMANT,* 27 (1968), 115; and on the verb *bo'*, H. Fredriksson, *Jahwe als Krieger* (Lund, 1945), 9, 11, 23-25, 29, 36, 44, 85.

will show his holiness and magnificence and will make himself known before the nations (Ezk. 38:23). Ezekiel sees the *kebhodh yhvh,* "glory of Yahweh" (→ כבוד *kābhôdh*), coming into the new temple (43:4; cf. 10:18f. by way of contrast) there to remain, so that later also this gate will remain shut because he has entered it (44:2; cf. Zec. 2:14[10]!), and he sees that the wonderful river going out of the temple brings life wherever it goes (47:9, where *bo'* appears several times).

In order to understand the similarities and differences between Ezekiel and Deutero Isaiah, a comparison with Isa. 40:10 is appropriate: according to Deutero-Isaiah, Yahweh himself is the one coming. That which Deutero-Isaiah has to say about the *kabhodh,* "glory," of Yahweh is found in Isa. 40:5 (*nighlah,* "shall be revealed"). Since Yahweh himself will come with might (Isa. 40:10), [74] in the opinion of Deutero-Isaiah the final salvation to Israel in the exile will take place when the people are delivered from Babylon. Yahweh has raised up Cyrus as the instrument of eschatological salvation (Isa. 45:1), and he has come (41:25, *'athah*). Thus the ransomed of Yahweh also will return and come to Zion with singing (51:11; cf. 35:10 and Ps. 126:6, *bo' yabho'*). Moreover, her children will be brought up on the arms of the peoples (Isa. 49:22, hiphil; cf. 60:4 as a reapplication), for Yahweh will say to the north and to the south: "Bring my sons from afar" (43:6, hiphil; cf. also v. 5). Besides, Yahweh's divine nature is demonstrated in particular by his having brought about what he had promised, [75] that which he had said (42:9), even suddenly (48:3). Thus, in the court scenes between Yahweh and the foreign nations or their gods, the foreign nations are invited to come and declare the things to come (*habba'oth,* 41:22; in 41:23 and 44:7 [*ha*]*'othiyyoth* [the article occurs only in 41:23]; the text of 45:11 should be emended to *ha'othi*). Also, 41:5 uses *'athah* when speaking of "coming" to these legal proceedings, while 45:20 and 50:2 use *bo'* (cf. also → נגש *nāghash,* "to draw near," and → קבץ *qābhats,* "to assemble"; cf. also Isa. 3:14).

After a dispute with the people who think the time to rebuild the temple has not yet come (Hag. 1:2), Haggai not only admonishes them (1:4ff.), but also calls to their attention the promise of the salvation that was breaking in upon them at that time (2:5-10,15-19), in order to inspire them to take courage. Consequently, when Zerubbabel, Joshua, and the remnant of the people actually "come" and resume the work on the temple (1:14), Haggai attributes this to the working of the divine spirit. The wretched condition of the new temple will be remedied by the treasures of all nations, whose coming to the temple is promised by Haggai (2:7).

Here, as in Ezra (Ezr. 3:8; 8:35), those who had "come" from the Babylonian captivity play a peculiar role.

For Zechariah also, the fulfilment of the promise that men shall come from afar to build the temple of Yahweh will be evidence of his credibility (Zec. 6:15; cf. 8:22). The promise that Yahweh will bring his people home (8:8, hiphil; cf. also 10:10) obviously could be repeated again and again. The coming day for

---

[74] See also under X below.
[75] See under IV above.

(*le*) Yahweh will be the time when all the spoil that had been taken from Jerusalem will be divided in the midst of the city (14:1). [76]

The situation that necessitated such promises (cf. Isa. 59:9ff. and v. 14 with *bo'*) is also reflected in texts in Trito-Isaiah which (as in Deutero-Isaiah earlier) frequently are put in the form of an answer to a complaint. "Salvation comes" (Isa. 62:11; cf. 56:1). Through his intervention, Yahweh will turn the negative situation into salvation: "my year of retaliation has come." As a contrast to the judgment that fell upon Edom, salvation will break forth upon Israel (63:4 cj.; cf. Jer. 51:46). Yahweh even promises that he himself will come (Isa. 59:20; 66:18) in order to redeem and to gather all nations and tongues. [77] Since Yahweh will bring the foreigners who have been converted to him to his holy mountain (Isa. 56:7, hiphil) and will make them joyful in his house of prayer, the promise to Jerusalem can also sound similar ("your light comes," 60:1; cf. vv. 4-6, which speak of different groups of people coming to Zion; further 49:18 and 60:9-11, as well as 66:20, hiphil). Indeed, in the coming situation of salvation, Yahweh will bring to Zion gold instead of bronze, silver instead of iron, etc. (60:17, hiphil). According to Mal. 3:23f. (4:5f.) (secondary), Yahweh will send Elijah, who will convert the people before the great and terrible day of Yahweh comes (Mal. 3:19-21[4:1-3]). [78]

The eschatologizing addition to Ps. 22 (vv. 28-32[27-31]) [79] speaks of the eschatological deliverance of Israel: afterward men shall come and proclaim Yahweh's → צדקה *ts⁼dhāqāh*, "righteousness, deliverance," to the coming generation (vv. 31f.[30f.]).

Finally, Dnl. 9:24 asserts that after 70 weeks (of years) Yahweh will bring everlasting salvation (hiphil).

2. *The Coming Bringer of Salvation.* Gen. 49:10 ('*adh ki yabho' shiloh*) and Zec. 9:9 (*hinneh malkekh yabho' lakh;* cf. 2:14[10]; also 3:8, hiphil) belong to a peculiar line of tradition, viz., texts that promise the coming of a bringer of salvation. Ezk. 21:32(27) and especially Dnl. 7:13 (*kebhar 'enash 'atheh havah*) should also be reckoned among them.

Gen. 49:10 is part of the blessing of Judah (49:8-12), which was handed down by the Yahwist (cf. the similar text in Nu. 24:15-19) and is not unimportant for his theology. [80] The text-critical matters in this passage are quite complicated, and we cannot be sure whether '*adh* is to be interpreted as "his throne," because the meaning of the alleged Ugaritic equivalent '*d* is disputed, [81] and this translation presents new problems. Therefore, it seems preferable to attempt an interpretation of this verse that is based on the present Hebrew text and requires the

---

[76] On Zec. 2:14(10) and 14:5, see X below.

[77] On this see H.-P. Müller, *BZAW,* 109 (1969), 220f.

[78] On Mal. 3:1-2, see X below.

[79] See J. Becker, *Israel deutet seine Psalmen* (1966), 49f.

[80] See Mowinckel, 13; Preuss, *Jahweglaube . . . ,* 133-35 with literature; M. Rehm, *Der königliche Messias* (1968), 19-23 with literature.

[81] For a different interpretation, see L. Sabottka, *Bibl,* 51 (1970), 225-29.

fewest possible hypotheses. The symbol of leadership and authority, and thus the authority itself, shall not depart from Judah "until *yabho' shiloh.*" Above all, the connection of this phrase with *'adh ki* can indeed lead one to suppose "that only the previously mentioned Judah can be the subject of the sentence." [82] But *shiloh* could be the subject only if it could be understood in some way other than as a place name, which is very doubtful. Thus, the only conclusion that can be drawn is that it refers to the place Shiloh. V. 10 is not (like v. 8) to be characterized as an oracle of blessing, but rather as an oracle of salvation or a promise. Shiloh cannot be destroyed yet and (or!) must still have great importance (in spite of destruction) while Judah has a ruling position, which will increase in strength but will not attain its ultimate goal. [83] A look at the theology of J, which in other passages also reveals an emphatic positive attitude toward the Davidic-Solomonic empire and especially toward David, suggests that Gen. 49:10 contains a theological interpretation of a situation from the time of David which can be connected with some historical event. It may be a later attempt to give a theological interpretation of an act of David or an act David was expected to perform, i.e., a *vaticinium ex eventu,* a traditional ancient oracle which was taken over by J, and may come from the time after David had already been crowned king in Hebron but was still ruling over Judah only (2 S. 2:4). The author of this oracle expected that ultimately David would extend his rule (v. 10d!) over the other tribes also, by "coming" to (entering into?) Shiloh, a town that did not belong to Judah, but is mentioned here as representative of the northern tribes because it was an important sanctuary of those tribes. Moreover, this verse may reflect the desire to restore to Shiloh its old position of honor. [84] Consequently, Gen. 49:10 is one of the texts of the OT (cf. the oracles in Nu. 24) that exhibit a positive attitude toward the rule of David and wish to see it expanded. Authors of ancient texts tried to glorify David in oracles that they placed at an earlier period, and thus these texts stand at the beginning of the development of texts having a "messianic" tint. The *bo'* in v. 10 represents a step toward a later messianic understanding of this section. As a result of the "coming" of this ruler, a condition of complete salvation was expected. In harmony with this, the present oracle (cf. v. 11) connects other royal ideological, messianic texts with its own contemporary messianism.

Ezk. 21:32b(27b) (cf. also 23:24b) has assimilated Gen. 49:10 into later interpretation. To be sure, whether this verse represents a positive promise [85] or its reversal to a "message of complete calamity" [86] is controversial.

In Zec. 9:9f. (cf. 2:14[10]; 3:8, hiphil; and Zeph. 3:14-17), this promise is given to the daughter of Zion (as a cult community?) in the form of a message proclaimed by a herald: *hinneh malkekh yabho' lakh,* "Lo, your king comes to

---

[82] Zobel, *BZAW,* 95, 13.

[83] J. Lindblom, *SVT,* 1 (1953), 83, with arguments for this interpretation of *'adh ki;* the coming will be fulfilment, it will be climax: Eissfeldt, *SVT,* 4 (1957), 141.

[84] G. von Rad, *OT Theol,* II (trans. 1965), 13.

[85] W. L. Moran, *Bibl,* 39 (1958), 405-425.

[86] Zimmerli, *BK,* XIII, 496.

you." Within the history of the tradition of "messianic prophecies," Zec. 9:9f. is clearly a late text. It is possible that it belongs to the period of the campaigns of Alexander the Great; if so, it is thought to be the antithesis to 9:1-8: the real bringer of salvation comes in humility and lowliness (v. 9), not as a warlike world conqueror; and the object of his work is the end of weapons and wars (v. 10; cf. Isa. 2:4). Thus, Jerusalem certainly will not be subjected to a new foreign power, but this city of Jerusalem is promised especially to the coming king alone (as a correction of and in opposition to 2:14[10]?). This king, then, will not create peace among the nations by conquests (but cf. 9:1-8,11-17 as the frame-work). The relationship of this passage to Gen. 49:10 is clear not only from the common use of *bo'*, but also from the similar figures of peace. Zec. 9:9f. reminds us of other texts from the series of so-called "messianic prophecies" (Isa. 9:4[5]; 11:10; Mic. 5:3[4]). But what is critical is the reapplication of earlier concepts in Zec. 9:9f.: this king is in need of help himself, and receives his law from God. He is poor (→ עני *'ānî*), and thus also needy, with respect to God. He comes in on an ass, which, in this context at least, is an attempt to emphasize once again his lowliness. Through him Yahweh (v. 10; the change of person merely falsifies) creates the peace of eschatological salvation, which, here at least, takes place in a genuinely peaceful way. Gen. 49:11 produces an aftereffect. Weapons will be eliminated, and the eschatological king of salvation in Zec. 9:9f. also has the prophetic office of proclaiming (v. 10). The "messianic" concept in the OT has also undergone a history, in the process of which it has experienced extensive reinterpretation.

According to Dnl. 7:13, the son of man "comes" only after (!) the enemy powers are defeated and God passes judgment. [87] Thus, here *'athah* has nothing to do with coming to a legal proceeding (like *bo'* in Isa. 3:14 and in Deutero-Isaiah). [88] Dnl. 7:9-14 sketches a judgment scene. Vv. 9f. and 13f. (the latter being the culminating point of the chapter) are in rhythmic prose. The judgment will come first on the fourth beast. The end begins with his destruction. After the fourth beast, the other beasts will be judged; in fact, they succumb together with him. It is not until this point that one "like a son of man" (→ בן־אדם *ben 'ādhām*) "comes" with the clouds of heaven. Against the four beasts, which come from below and out of the sea and thus are characterized as powers hostile to God, and as corporate personalities represent the kingdoms and powers personified by them, one similar to a man now arises and comes from heaven. Therefore, he also probably should be interpreted as a corporate personality, i.e., as the people of God who will now inherit the coming kingdom of God. Thus, "one man from heaven" is the personified antithesis to the kingdoms of the world and represents the coming kingdom of God of the new world. It is impossible (at least thus far) and ultimately even unnecessary to get behind this concept in Dnl. 7 from a religio-historical point of view, especially since the eschatologiza-tion of the prototype of this figure which is to be disclosed or postulated reveals a peculiarity characteristic of the Yahweh faith. However, Dnl. 7:13 is not based

[87] W. H. Schmidt, *KuD,* 15 (1969), 33.
[88] Contra the reflections of Jenni, 259, n. 42.

on the expectation of a Davidic messiah. There is no mention of an eschatological bringer of salvation anywhere else in the book of Daniel. [89]

Therefore, *bo'* and *'athah* are used in Zec. 9:9 and Dnl. 7:13 of the eschatological coming of the eschatological mediator of salvation, and of the corporate personality symbolizing the kingdom of God, respectively. Gen. 49:10 and other texts of a "messianic" type prepare the way for this use of these words.

X. Yahweh As the Coming One. The ark (→ ארון *'arôn*) of Yahweh comes into the Israelite camp (1 S. 4:6; 2 S. 6:17, hiphil), where it is greeted with → תרועה *terû'āh*, "shouting." When the Philistines hear about this, they say that *'elohim*, "god" (*'elohehem*, "their god"?) has come into the camp (1 S. 4:7). This understanding of the ark is not restricted to the Philistine way of thinking (cf. Nu. 10:35f.); it probably presupposes a connection between Yahweh and the ark. Thus, the appearance of the ark has severe consequences for Dagon: when the ark appears, Yahweh himself "comes." [90]

According to old texts, Yahweh comes to a man in a dream (Gen. 20:3[E]; 31:24[E]; perhaps also 1 S. 3:10 and Nu. 22:9,20[E]; cf. v. 8[J]; on this subject, cf. → חלם *chālam*). Yahweh comes through his messenger (→ מלאך *mal'ākh*, Josh. 5:14; Jgs. 6:11; 13:6-10; 13:3 [which, however, uses *vayyera'*, "and... appeared," instead of *bo'*]), and this is interpreted as an (originally pre-Israelite?) cult etiology. It is described as an unusual event, and Yahweh's coming has a "more or less positive" effect. [91] The messenger is closely connected with Yahweh and yet is contrasted with him to a certain extent. The belief that when a man of God, a prophet, or an angel (less perhaps a priest, Lev. 13:33-53) comes to a man, in essence God himself comes with his message, is further reflected when the direct identification of God and his messenger is specifically emphasized or even implied (Nu. 22:38; 1 S. 2:27; 13:11; 16:2; 2 S. 24:13,18; 1 K. 13:1; 17:18 [this verse contains the typical Deuteronomistic interpretation]; then also 2 K. 9:11; 20:14 and par.; 23:17f.; Jer. 40:6; 2 Ch. 12:5; 16:7; 25:7; and on down to Dnl. 9:23; 10:12-14,20; on 10:20, cf. also 1 S. 17:45). The early type of Yahweh's coming in his messenger is taken up again in the late text, Mal. 3:1f. [92] Here, Yahweh's coming is never something harmless.

Nor is Yahweh's coming something that is obvious, as the old text from the law concerning the altar in the Book of the Covenant, Ex. 20:24b, shows: "in every (cult?) place (→ מקום *māqôm;* this word is to be so translated here in spite of the article) where I cause my name to be remembered (→ זכר *zākhar*), I will come (*'abho'*) to you and bless you." In the blessing of the priest, Yahweh promises to come to the one who is blessed, promising his presence in the priestly blessing. Thus, these verses too have been characterized as a divine oracle. Conrad considers them to be a priestly redaction, and is inclined to attribute v. 24b to the same redaction. [93]

---

[89] See further H. D. Preuss, *Texte aus dem Danielbuch. Calwer Predigthilfen,* VI (1971).
[90] See H. D. Preuss, *Verspottung fremder Religionen im AT. BWANT,* 5/12 (1971), 74-80.
[91] Jenni, 254.
[92] See below.
[93] D. Conrad, *Studien zum Altargesetz* (diss., Marburg, 1968), 11f., 20.

Was a specific "coming" of Yahweh fundamental to the history of Israel with her God? It is natural, first of all, to think of Yahweh's appearance at Sinai. But in the biblical accounts of this event, *bo'* in the sense of the coming of God occurs only in explanatory framework passages (Ex. 19:9; 20:20). → ירד *yāradh,* "to go down," is used frequently to describe Yahweh's appearance at Sinai. In Ex. 19:9 *ba'* is a participle in an oracle of Yahweh, and in 20:20 *ba' ha'elohim* occurs in an oracle of Moses to the people. 19:9 looks forward and emphasizes the position of Moses; 20:20 looks back and gives an explanation, while the description of the theophany itself in 19:16-25 does not use *bo'*. 20:20 draws parenetic conclusions from that which was experienced (19:16,19[E]), while this encounter with God is extrapolated to the corresponding fear of God, which recalls the use of Elohistic elements.[94] The view that 19:9 is from J[95] is unlikely, as linguistic usage indicates. J here uses *yaradh,* "to go down," but nowhere else speaks of the "coming" of Yahweh or of an angel (messenger). Generally speaking, *bo'* and *yaradh* are not found together with Yahweh as the common subject, while e.g., *yatsa',* "to go out," and *yaradh* do occur in this way (cf. the different subjects of *bo'* and *yaradh* in Ex. 33:9, but the repetition of *yaradh* in Jgs. 5:13).

With regard to the Sinai tradition, two observations need to be made here. On the one hand, the old texts in the Sinai pericope by no means (or only very sparingly and later) interpret the appearance of God as a "coming" of Yahweh (God), but they speak more of a coming down (*yaradh,* e.g., Ex. 19:18; 34:5[J]). Thus, the mountain is the object on which Yahweh "comes." On the other hand, later texts speak of Yahweh's coming from (!) Sinai, or of a cultic or historical coming of Yahweh.[96] Perhaps this terminology reflects the original belief that Yahweh was localized on Sinai (or better, on the mountain of God) (Ex. 19:17 [E]!; cf. Jgs. 5:5; Ps. 68:9[8]), upon which he "descended," but did not "dwell," and whence he came to Palestine, but in a later period it was no longer assumed that he was connected with Sinai exclusively. Westermann uses the term "epiphany" here: Yahweh comes to help his people.[97] The later disinclination to use *yaradh* in the descriptions of theophanies[98] could also be explained in this way. Generally speaking, therefore, one should be cautious about accepting the view that the "coming" of God is a fundamental element in the Sinai tradition:[99] *bo'* and *yaradh* are not identical.[100]

The following basic[101] texts, all of which are hymnic and enriched by char-

---

[94] Cf. H. W. Wolff, *EvTh,* 29 (1969), 59-72.

[95] Chr. Barth, *EvTh,* 29 (1969), 529f.; cf. Beer, *HAT:* J[2].

[96] See below.

[97] C. Westermann, *Praise of God in the Psalms* (trans. 1965), 92; cf. also Schnutenhaus, 21.

[98] Jeremias, 106.

[99] G. von Rad, *Problem of the Hexateuch* (trans. 1966), 13ff.; also Jeremias, 154, who argues that there was a first "coming" of Yahweh from Sinai; and with both, Perlitt, *Bundestheologie,* 234.

[100] Contra Jeremias, 154f.

[101] So Jenni, 256.

acteristic explanatory material, speak of a "coming" of Yahweh from Sinai (!):
Dt. 33:2 (are bo' and 'athah used in parallelism here?[102] cf. Zec. 14:5); Ps. 68:18b
(17b; read ba' missinai, "[Yahweh] came from Sinai"; cf. 68:8f.[7f.]; also 68:32
[31]); [103] and Hab. 3:3; but also Isa. 63:1. [104]

The hymn in Dt. 33:2-5,26-29 extols the one (perhaps ever new!) coming of
Yahweh to help his people accomplish a variety of goals, but especially to give
them victory over their enemies (vv. 26f.,29). bo' is used with several other
verbs (→ זרח zārach, "to rise, dawn"; yāpha', hiphil, "to shine forth"; nāghāh,
"to shine"; also qum, "to rise," and ra'ah, niphal, "to appear"), and they help
clarify the meaning of bo' just as connections of places to each other help in
locating each place. Thus, in Dt. 33:2-5,26-29, bo' in the qal is used in almost
the same way that it is frequently used in the hiphil, viz., to express divine
guidance. [105] As in Jgs. 5:4f. (which uses yatsa', "to go out," however; cf. Isa.
42:13 and → צעד tsā'adh), Yahweh "comes" from Sinai to help his people in
battle (cf. Amun in the Kadesh Poem). [106] However, in contrast to Dt. 33:2,
Jgs. 5:4f. clearly refers to Yahweh coming only one time to help in a single
concrete battle, and also there are no other elements of a theophany in Dt.
33:2. [107] Teman in Hab. 3:3 points in a similar geographic direction. [108] This
passage celebrates the coming of Yahweh to give Israel victory over her enemies,
and the praise of Yahweh who came to fight for his people has made its way
into the cult lyric poetry here. [109] In spite of the disconnected context, [110] Ps.
68:18b(17b) reveals that and how the original idea of Yahweh coming to help
his people in battle was expanded (cf. Mal. 3:1) and made to refer to Yahweh
coming into his sanctuary in a cultic sense. [111]

A precise statement as to the place whence Yahweh comes is missing in Isa.
30:27, which says that Yahweh (only the shem, "name," seems to be secondary
here; should we read sham, "there"?) comes "from far" to judge Assyria and
to make Israel rejoice. It is missing also in Mic. 1:3 (a judgment against Israel;
but again, bo' does not occur in this passage, but yaradh, "to go down," and
yatsa', "to go out"). Thus, the prophetic threats of judgment in Amos (Am. 1:2
is to be understood differently) and Hosea do not speak of the coming of Yahweh, but they probably do in Isaiah and Micah. Further, in Isa. 30:27 and Mic.
1:3 (1:3-5a,6 is the context), the element of Yahweh's coming to fight is still
present, and the passage in Micah even refers to the effects of his coming on
nature.

---

102 But see KBL³ s.v. 'athah, and Jeremias, 63f., n. 5.
103 On the hiphil of 'athah, see KBL³ s.v.
104 On the phenomena accompanying Yahweh's coming, see Jeremias, passim; on fire,
see also TDNT, VI, 934ff.
105 See VII above.
106 A. Erman, Literature of the Ancient Egyptians (trans. 1927), 264.
107 Jeremias, 158f.
108 Ibid., 8.
109 On this process, see ibid., 118ff.; and Jenni, 256.
110 Jenni, 256, n. 25.
111 Cf. Jeremias, 160f.

Subsequently, then, several prophetic texts threaten that Yahweh will come to judge his enemies without reflecting on the place from which he will come. At the same time, the phenomena accompanying his coming are often similar to those found in the earlier descriptions of theophany. Yahweh comes to judge Egypt (Isa. 19:1) and to destroy her idols (→ אֱלִיל *'elil*), and he rises on a cloud. Yahweh will come against Jerusalem and will enter into it, even though the people in Jerusalem assume that no one can do this (Jer. 21:13; cf. 49:4). Thus, he will not "come" to Jerusalem "cultically" as he was usually thought to come; he will not come for his healing presence. He comes to judge the nations (Jer. 25:31, hardly from Jeremiah; but in v. 30 he comes to judge Israel!); he comes with (like?) fire, storm, and sword (Isa. 66:15f.; cf. 59:19); he comes to judge "from Edom" (Isa. 63:1; cf. 35:4). [112] Yahweh comes to judge the evildoers in Israel (Isa. 59:19f.). According to the prophetic oracle in Zec. 14:5, on the day of Yahweh (v. 1), "Yahweh my God" himself will come down *(yatsa'*, lit. "come out"; cf. Jgs. 5:4f.; Ezk. 43:1-5, "from the east"?) from heaven (?) to the Mount of Olives, and from there will come *(bo')* (he and all the "holy ones" with him) to fight and to judge the nations, and thus to save the people of God. The purpose of his coming is to dwell in Jerusalem (cf. Zec. 2:14[10]). Not only do Zec. 14:3 and 5 use different words for Yahweh's "coming," but they also have different content and purposes: the conquest of the nations is "preliminary to the final entrance of Yahweh into the city," when he will destroy the cult places of the idols (v. 5a). Mal. 3:1f. also threatens that Yahweh (or the angel of the covenant; this is probably an addition in v. 1c) will come to his temple with fire to judge his people. Isa. 59:19f.; 66:15f.; Mal. 3:1f., and to some extent Zec. 14:5 announce that Yahweh will come to judge evildoers in postexilic Israel. Thus, attempts were made to keep alive and to renew again and again hope in the final return of Yahweh to Zion, for which Israel yearned ever since the exile (cf. Ezk. 43:1ff.; Isa. 40:3-5).

This is emphasized by the exilic and postexilic promises that Yahweh will come to save his people. In Isa. 40:10, the joyous cry of the messenger of victory promises (cf. 62:11): Yahweh will come "with might" fighting to save his people, he will rule and bring his spoil home (vv. 9-11). Thus, this coming clearly is no longer merely a single historical event (cf. Ezk. 43:1ff.), but Deutero-Isaiah (like Ezk. 40ff.; also Hag. and Zec.) is living in a situation of realized eschatology (cf. Isa. 40:5) concerning the *kebhodh yhvh*, "glory of Yahweh" [113] (see also Isa. 52:10 and Zec. 9:9f.). Yahweh's word of promise to the daughter of Zion in Zec. 2:14(10): "for lo, I come (ptcp.) and I will dwell in the midst of you" (cf. Ezk. 43:7-9; Zec. 8:3; also 14:4f.), [114] also shows that in the late exilic and early postexilic period a belief in realized eschatology had arisen, which was convinced of the final eschatological Now, and thought that the new "coming"

---

[112] On this text, however, see *ibid.*, 125, n. 1.

[113] On the concepts of theophany in Deutero-Isaiah, see L. Köhler, *BZAW*, 37 (1923), 124-27; cf. also Westermann, *ATD*, XIX, 39, on the relationship of Isa. 40:9-11 to the "eschatological psalm of praise" in Deutero-Isaiah.

[114] Cf. also the evaluation by W. Zimmerli, *VT*, 18 (1968), 229-255.

of Yahweh would remain a final Now. In Zec. 2:14(10) *bo'* does not signify a "theophany," but is more an introductory auxiliary verb; [115] furthermore, the context (vv. 12-16[8-12]?) does not indicate a cultic setting, but a military situation. [116] Isa. 60:1 contains another word of salvation to the postexilic community of Zion: "your light (→ אור *'ôr*) has come, and the *kebhodh yhvh*, 'glory of Yahweh,' has arisen upon you" (cf. Isa. 40:10; 62:11). The coming of salvation is the coming of Yahweh, as he himself also promises that he will come for historical salvation (66:18, an appropriate revision of 66:15).

A few (!) texts, which "hardly made an impact in the history of OT theology," [117] have in mind a cultic event when they speak of the "coming" of Yahweh. However, the contexts in which they appear support the hypothesis that there was hardly a ritualistic, dramatic presentation of the theophany (by light, smoke cloud, or noise?) in the Israelite cult. Instead, one has to think of a "theophany" as a word event. [118]

The only text using *bo'* (vv. 7 and 9) that might cause one to think of a cultic entrance of Yahweh (in connection with the entrance of the ark?) [119] as the *melekh hakkabhodh*, "King of glory," is Ps. 24. However, the entire scene raises doubts as to whether that which is described in Ps. 24 reflects a regular and oft-repeated continuous rite.

Ps. 50:3, "our God comes, he does not keep silence," is interesting. This psalm is an admonition to God's people, and the purpose of Yahweh's coming is to judge. According to v. 2, Yahweh will come from Zion, and thus his coming is to be understood cultically. The theophany is actualized as a word event (vv. 1 and 7ff.). Here the coming of Yahweh is described in connection with the shining forth of brightness (→ כבוד *kābhôdh*) (cf. Dt. 33:2 without *kabhodh*, however; but also Ezk. 1:4ff.; 43:1ff.), but brightness and theophany appear in connection with one another for the first time in later texts; thus a preexilic dating of Ps. 50 encounters considerable difficulties. [120]

Frequently scholars cite Ps. 96:13 (cf. 1 Ch. 16:33) and 98:9 (both with *bo'*) as examples of a cult-dramatic realized theophany, but this is incorrect. Instead, these two texts state that Yahweh is coming to judge, which is similar to the description of his coming in Deutero-Isaiah. [121] There are other indications too that Pss. 96 and 98 presuppose Deutero-Isaiah. [122] As an eschatological hymn, Ps. 96 also contains the proclamation of Yahweh as the eschatological judge of the world, and has at most (like Ps. 98:9) "reminiscences of a description of a

---

[115] Jenni, 257, n. 33.

[116] On the relationship of Zec. 2:14(10) to 9:9f., cf. the reflections of M. Saebø, *Sacharja 9-14. WMANT,* 34 (1969), 184 and 315.

[117] Jenni, 253.

[118] Cf. H.-J. Kraus, *Worship in Israel* (trans. 1966), 229f.; *idem, BK,* XV, LXVIf., 144f.; also Schnutenhaus, 18.

[119] See Kraus, *BK,* XV, *in loc.*

[120] Cf. Jeremias, 63f., with additional literature.

[121] See IX above.

[122] Cf. Kraus, *BK,* XV, *in loc.* Dahood, *Psalms,* II, 357; Preuss, *Verspottung...,* 248f. on Ps. 96.

theophany." [123] "In the context (of 96:13), *bo'* is to be understood not cultically, but eschatologically." [124] The purpose of his coming is to assume dominion of the world, not to be present in the cult. Therefore it can be asked again whether *bo'* may not function here simply as an auxiliary verb. [125]

None of the descriptions of theophany in the OT describes Yahweh himself, but rather the results of his coming. Also, Yahweh's coming is never an end in itself, but he "comes" to do something. Here also, he makes himself known by his works. Accordingly, he comes, e.g., primarily not in his sanctuary or in the assembly of the heavenly council (as is often attested of the gods of Israel's neighbors), but "in the sphere of Israel's affliction." [126]

Ancient texts reveal that and how Yahweh's coming to fight (each time new and in a specific situation) was believed and experienced, and later how his coming to judge and to save was threatened, promised, experienced, and praised. Thus, in the OT God's "coming" does not always mean the same thing, and it never means something that can be brought about by man or that is at man's disposal. Israel expects the final coming of Yahweh who had come and is coming. A study of the use of *bo'* discloses only a part of the whole OT concept of Yahweh's coming (cf. further → יצא *yātsā'*, "to go out"; → ירד *yāradh,* "to go down"; etc.). Consequently, one should not speak too comprehensively of the "coming" of Yahweh when the OT chooses a variety of words to describe it.

In Dt. 32:17 the Song of Moses accuses Israel of having sacrificed to new gods (cf. already the reference to "new" gods in Jgs. 5:8) which they had never known and which had "come in" (*ba'u*) of late, gods their fathers had never worshipped. God's people are forbidden to go to these gods, and they are not to be brought into Israel. As "new" (→ חדש *chādhāsh*) gods, they had no history with Israel. Precisely here lay Yahweh's distinctiveness.

Preuss

בוז *bûz* → בזה *bāzāh*
בור *bôr* → באר *be'ēr*

---

[123] Jeremias, 112, n. 3; cf. Jenni, 258.
[124] Kraus, *BK,* XV, 668; cf. p. 679 on Ps. 98:9.
[125] Cf. Jenni, 258.
[126] Schnutenhaus, 17.

בּוֹשׁ *bôsh;* בּוּשָׁה *búshāh;*
בּשֶׁת *bōsheth;* מְבוּשִׁים *mᵉbhúshîm*

Contents: I. 1. Forms and Derivatives; 2. Ugaritic and Akkadian Parallels. II. Words with Similar Meaning, Original Meaning. III. *bosh* in the Prophetic Literature and in the Psalms: 1. Hosea; 2. Isaiah, Micah; 3. Jeremiah; 4. Zephaniah, Joel; 5. Deutero-Isaiah; 6. Psalms. IV. The Hiphil Forms.

I. 1. *Forms and Derivatives. bosh* is a primitive Semitic root with two radicals and a medial long vowel,[1] and occurs in the qal, hiphil (2 forms), and hithpolel. From it derive the nouns *bushah,* "shame" (4 times),[2] *bosheth,* "shame" (in my opinion, not the feeling of shame),[3] and *mebhushim,* "the pudenda of a male" (once; the derivation of *boshnah* in Hos. 10:6 cannot be determined absolutely). It is likely that a *bosh* II is to be distinguished from this *bosh;* cf. especially the polel forms in Ex. 32:1; Jgs. 5:28, and perhaps also the qal form in Ezr. 8:22.[4]

2. *Ugaritic and Akkadian Parallels.* From the other Semitic languages, the most interesting data for an analysis of OT words built from the root *bosh* are to be found in Akkadian. To be sure, this root is certainly exemplified in Ugaritic by the noun *btt,* "shame,"[5] but its use here does not allow a distinct definition of its meaning. At the same time, scholars are still debating the derivation of the verbal forms *bt* (impv.)[6] and *ybt*[7]; with Gray,[8] it seems to me that their relationship to *bosh* I is unlikely. It should be mentioned that in Middle Hebrew the meaning has shifted more to the subjective idea, to the feeling[9] (in Middle Hebrew the qal, piel, hithpael, and nithpael forms occur, but not the hiphil; *bosheth* retains the nuance "modesty," but it also denotes the reimbursement for a dishonor inflicted on someone). This word seems also to have become more closely connected with sexual shame in Middle Hebrew.[10]

In Akk. *bâšum* has the derivatives *bāštum, buštum, bayyišu,* and *ayyabāš* ("I will not be put to shame"). While the two latter derivatives are not very important to the present discussion, one can hardly ignore the use of the verb forms and

---

[1] Cf. von Soden, *AHw* on *bâšum.*

[2] *BLe,* § 452u: an abstract form of *bosh,* as *tubh* is an abstract form of *tobh,* according to the pattern of qutl abstracts.

[3] Thus *KBL³,* see below; *BLe,* § 452u: a qutl abstract.

[4] On this see *KBL³,* 112f.

[5] *CTA,* 4 [II AB], 51; III, 19, 21.

[6] *CTA,* 2 [III AB], IV, 28f.

[7] *CTA,* 2, IV, 31.

[8] J. Gray, *Legacy of Canaan. SVT,* 5 (²1965), 26.

[9] Cf. in particular J. Levy, *WTM, s.v. bwš.*

[10] Cf. perhaps Levy, *WTM,* 14, 157d, *mqwm bšth* of the modesty of the woman; *Kidd.* 81b, "she is ashamed to stand before him naked."

the first two derivatives. Von Soden observes that the meaning of the verb is seldom "to be ashamed" (late Bab.)[11]–this meaning is not mentioned in *CAD* (*ba'āšum,* II). But in general in the G-stem *bâšu* means "to come to shame" and in the D-stem "to put to shame." There does not seem to be a specific reference to sexual shame; rather, as in Hebrew, Akkadian texts speak of becoming exposed, e.g., by a creditor or in the gate.[12] But from the earliest to the latest stages of the language we encounter prayers in the style, "Let me/us not be put to shame," as well as in proper names.[13] The following proper names may serve as examples: (Old Bab.) *dSin-a-ia-ba-aš,* "O Sin, let me not be put to shame"; *A-ia-ba-aš-ì-lí,* "Let me not be put to shame, O my God," or the shortened form *A-a-ba-aš;* as feminine names, e.g. (Middle Bab.), *fAt-kal-ši-ul-a-ba-aš,* "I trusted in her and was not put to shame"; from Neo-Bab.: *La-ba-ši-i-li,* "Let me not be put to shame, O my God," and very beautifully *Nabû-alsi-ul-a-ba-aš,* "I appealed to Nabu and was not put to shame."[14] In the D-stem it is sufficient to mention the consequences of *bâšu* as examples: "otherwise we shall send an order (lit. tablet) of the prince and the *rābiṣu*-official, and we shall put you to shame (*nu-ba-aš-ka*) in the *kâru,* and you will no longer be our colleague."[15] Very meaningful also is the statement, "I (Ishtar) have given you encouragement, I will not let you come to shame."[16]

Apparently the noun *buštum,* corresponding to Heb. *bosheth,* has a very similar meaning.[17] It probably means "shame, dishonor," and in the negative (*lā buštum*) is a technical term for impudence, shamelessness. Here we may mention the following as examples: "... who covers the dishonor of the land" (*bu-ul-tim ša ma-ta-ti*);[18] "the king has given you an order, but you do not want to give (me the house) ... so you will have to give him (the house) [*a-n*]*a bu-uš-ti-ka,* to your dishonor."[19]

On the other hand, the meaning of *bāštum* is not found in Hebrew. It is that which is injured in the *bosh,* that which is protected when one is not put to shame, thus vitality[20] or fulness of life. *CAD* suggests "dignity,"[21] i.e., presumably that one can move about with uplifted head and be in full possession of the personality. Under certain circumstances this abundance of life can be summed up in sexual potency, e.g., "my dignity (*ba-aš-ti*) has been taken away, my virility has been jeopardized";[22] cf. quite simply *ṣubāt bal-ti,* "cloth of

---

11 Von Soden, *AHw,* 112.

12 *CAD,* II, 5f.

13 *CAD,* II, 5f.; *AHw,* 112; of course, the Old Akk. *E-ni-ba-aš* along with *E-ni/na-ba-ša-at* is uncertain, thus von Soden.

14 *CAD,* II, 6.

15 *TCL,* 19, 1:33 in connection with *CAD,* II, 6.

16 IV R, 61, Neo-Assyr. oracle for Esarhaddon, *CAD,* II, 6.

17 The meaning "dignity" assumed in *CAD,* II, 352, does not occur in von Soden, *AHw,* 143.

18 *AHw,* 143.

19 *CAD,* II, 352, with the correction of von Soden, 143.

20 *AHw.*

21 *CAD,* II, 142ff.

22 *CAD,* II, 142, following Lambert, *BWL,* 32:47, Ludlul I.

modesty." [23] But in general it means something like (Old Assyr.): "may they be satisfied by your (the deity's) abundance of life." Indeed *bāštum* is personified as a protective angel (?) [24] or a "protective spirit," [25] and thus appears in proper names, e.g., *A-bi-ba-áš-ti*, "my father is my *bāštum*"; as a feminine name, *ᶠA-lí-ba-aš-ti*, "Where is my *bāštum*?" or in Old Akk., *Era-ba-aš-ti*, "Era is my *bāštum*."

II. Words with Similar Meaning, Original Meaning. It is worthy of note that the root *bwš* and its derivatives play practically no role at all before the great literary prophets of the 8th century B.C. To be sure, we encounter the expression *'adh bosh*, "till shame" = "excessive," [26] in this period (Jgs. 3:25; 2 K. 2:17; 8:11); but it is indifferent and contributes nothing to the understanding of the word. Also this root appears (apart from the Psalms) in 1 S. 20:30 (*bosheth*); 2 S. 19:6 (Eng. v. 5) (*hobhish*); and perhaps Dt. 25:11 (*mebhushim*, pudenda of a male); but these few exceptions can only strengthen the overall impression, not diminish it. It is strengthened even more when we examine the parallel root → חפר *chāphēr*, "to be ashamed," which (apart from the Psalms) generally speaking does not occur before the literary prophets. Perhaps the situation is somewhat different with → נכלם *nikhlam*, "to be humiliated," which is used in parallelism with *bosh* quite frequently. Among the words or expressions having a meaning similar to *bosh* are *chathath*, "to be dismayed," *pachadh*, "to dread," *sugh 'achor*, "to turn away from," *chavar*, "to grow pale" (once), *nadhammah*, "to be silenced" (once), but also *shadhadh* in the pual, "to be devastated" (Jer. 9:18 [19]), *'abhadh*, "to perish" (Ps. 83:18[17]), and *kalah*, "to be destroyed" (Ps. 71:13). However, in reality only *chapher* and especially *nikhlam* appear in parallelism with *bosh* frequently. *nikhlam* occurs fairly often (7 times) in earlier passages; but this root, like *chēreph* (→ חרף *chāraph*), has a more active ring than *bosh*, and so means something like "to be dishonored, be put to shame." [27] By way of contrast, *bosh* expresses the idea that someone, a person, a city, a people, a professional organization, or the like, underwent an experience in which his (or its) former respected position and importance were overthrown. Someone risked something to a power, whether it be to another person, a country, or a god, and thus undertook a daring venture. Now he receives the consequences of that venture so that he must suffer the opposite of what he sought, viz., dishonor, and be put to shame, not because of some subjective act but because of something that was inherent in the risk he took. In short, *bosh* always has a passive connotation even in its causative forms; a person endures it. It is also worthy of note that this root is in no way oriented to sexual shame–Gen. 2:25 (hithpael) seems to mean, "they (the man and his wife) were not found in a state of shame as far as their nakedness was concerned." *bosh* denotes the human shame described above, an unsuccessful plan by one whose life is to plan, the breakdown of

---

[23] *AHw*, 112, contra *CAD*, II, 142.
[24] *AHw*.
[25] *CAD*.
[26] *KBL²*, 112.
[27] Cf. *KBL¹*.

an "ecstatic existence." And it looks almost as if this dimension of being human was discovered on the broader plain, i.e., outside the language of the Psalms, for the first time in the period of the great prophets. Of course, this observation is made with great reservations, because generally speaking the root *bosh* (as well as its derivatives) is seldom found outside the Psalms and Jeremiah. It is missing entirely in Amos, Nahum, Habakkuk, Malachi, Daniel, the Pentateuch, and the Deuteronomistic history. But it is noteworthy that the great prophets used this root in speaking of the catastrophe of their people before God, and that they broached this dimension at a crucial moment in the history of their people.

The basic characteristic of *bosh* appears already in 2 S. 19:6(5): when David was so deeply grieved over the death of Absalom that he had nothing to say to his victorious troops, not only was he treating them unjustly, but even worse he was ridiculing his troops and friends, for they had aligned themselves with a king who was legally inferior and deposed, and had been faithful to him in opposition to the man that the people had proclaimed king. Consequently, when David kept on grieving over Absalom's death, he left his troops in the lurch and made their fidelity absurd. Thus *bosh* means to be disgraced for something that has been undertaken. The same meaning also follows very clearly from 1 S. 20:30. When Jonathan took sides with David against Saul, Saul reviled him saying, "You son of a perverse rebellious woman, do I not know that you have chosen the son of Jesse to your own shame, and to the shame of your mother's nakedness? For as long as the son of Jesse lives upon the earth, neither you nor your kingdom shall be established." In my opinion the wording of the MT gives an excellent sense. Saul reproves his son not only because he "chose" David's interests above those of his father, thus committing a grave injustice against the reigning king (and especially against his own mother), but also because by turning away from the king Jonathan ran the risk that David would become king instead of him and that he would take over Jonathan's mother as his wife with the royal harem. Thus according to Saul's words the worst thing about Jonathan's action was not the injustice he had done the king, but that he had not thought things through carefully and thus had made a fool of himself. In short, the highly esteemed son of the king had acted shamefully, as when experienced caravans rely on unreliable watercourses and perish in the wilderness (Job 6:20).

III. bosh in the Prophetic Literature and in the Psalms.

1. *Hosea.* Clearly some of the great prophets retained the element of shame in describing the conduct of the states of Israel and Judah at the time of their catastrophe. While *bosh* and its derivatives are absent in Amos, they do appear in Hosea, Isaiah, and Micah. To be sure, we must read a form of *yabhesh,* "to be dry," in Hos. 13:15, and the context in 4:19 is so corrupt that one can do no more than hazard a guess as to the original text. But 10:6 says clearly, "Israel shall be put to shame because of his plan"; i.e., by worshipping the calf of Beth-aven, uttering mere words, swearing oaths, and making covenants, not only is the state acting unjustly before God, but also it is disgracing itself by its injustice

because the plans of this tiny state are trivialities to Assyria. What is meant is that in deference to their own intentions they lose Yahweh and thus are even more foolish. 9:10 has a similar meaning of *bosh:* Israel's coming to Baal-peor was not only an injustice to God, but also foolish. The prophet makes it clear that the people had not relied on that which was reliable and thus literally had consecrated themselves to shame.

2. *Isaiah, Micah.* That which Hosea merely suggests Isaiah declares fully in his oracle on Egypt in Isa. 30:1-5. Judah plans to make a league with Egypt, "but they do not ask of my mouth!" Thus they add sin to sin (v. 1b). But it is disgraceful for Judah to make a league with a nation which cannot help, but only desires to save its own skin. Instead of relying on Yahweh as a refuge and seeking shelter in his shadow (psalmic language, v. 2), the people commit the sin of choosing Pharaoh as a refuge and shadow, and reap nothing but shame (v. 3). Similarly, 20:5 says: "Then they (i.e., the Judeans) shall be dismayed and confounded because of Ethiopia their hope and of Egypt their boast." When Ashdod attempted to rebel against Assyria in 713 B.C., Judah also took the risk of turning against the greatly superior Assyrian empire, and this risk seemed to be a certainty by reliance on the power of Egypt. But the prophet declares that this risk will not be rewarded; everyone will come to shame because Egypt will not give sufficient help. 1:29 is not entirely clear because it has been handed down only in a fragment: "for 'you' shall be ashamed of the trees in which you delighted; and you shall be put to shame for the gardens which you have chosen." It still seems most likely that this passage has reference to holy trees and gardens. [28] Thus in her pride Judah adopted heathen practices in her cultic activities to embellish her existence, and in this way acted foolishly, pulling the foundation out from under her own feet. She acted contrary to the will of God and thus lost the power that alone was able to guarantee well-being.

bosh is not used in Micah with reference to the people. While it is impossible to draw any absolute conclusions from Mic. 1:11, 3:5-8 states that the prophets in whose mouths Yahweh has not put his word will be disgraced in their prophesying, inasmuch as they will not receive the word of Yahweh any more and the day will become night for them.

3. *Jeremiah.* Jeremiah continues the tradition of his predecessors, but differs from them in that he sees his personal existence completely intertwined with the catastrophe of his people and thus quite directly enters into the popular lament. The excellent oracle in Jer. 2:26ff. probably comes from the period before Josiah's reform: the house of Israel will be carried away like a thief who is caught in the act of stealing, for they say to a tree, "My father!" and to a stone, "My mother!" But in their distress they will be left alone with these symbols, and will have to endure the dishonor that Yahweh will not help them and they can do nothing.

In Jer. 2:36f. it says that Israel will be put to shame by Egypt just as they

---

[28] With Wildberger, *BK,* contra Fohrer, *Das Buch Jesaja, in loc.*

were put to shame by Assyria. The meaning of these verses seems to be: as Yahweh had not allowed the schemes of "Israel" against Assyria to succeed because she had rejected his protection, so now he will not help Israel against Egypt because she completely rejects his protection. The point is that a small state foolishly turns against a great power and thus will learn its lesson very quickly. It is remarkable that the prophet could speak to a foreign nation in a similar way (48:11-13). At the end of this quite original oracle, it says: "Then Moab shall be ashamed of Chemosh, as the house of Israel was ashamed of Bethel, their confidence." Now whether this wording is authentic or not (perhaps its poetic form can be restored following the LXX: *ubhosh mo'abh mikkemosh kebhosh beth yisra'el mibbeth 'el mibhtecham 'elav mibhtachim,* "then Moab shall be ashamed of Chemosh as the house of Israel was ashamed of Bethel on which they trusted securely"), in the context the meaning can only be this: as the sanctuary at Bethel [29] only fed the national self-confidence of Israel instead of speaking Yahweh's truth to Israel, so Chemosh only fed the national self-confidence of Moab and prevented the people from hearing the truth they needed. The lament of the people cited in the prophetic oracle in 3:24,25 points in the same direction: "But from our youth the shameful thing has devoured all for which our fathers labored, their flocks and their herds, their sons and their daughters. Let us lie down in our shame...." The view that *bosheth* here is used as a substitute for *ba'al,* "Baal," as it is in the gloss in 11:13, is attractive, but to me it does not really seem to be necessary. The poet says: the terrible loss the state of Israel suffered in its downfall did not in the final analysis exhibit the heroism of a nation fighting for its independence, but the distressing shame of a people that had forgotten its God and had fought with all its energies for nothing. Finally the oracle in 7:17-20 (v. 18aβ,γ, is a gloss) belongs here. Because Jerusalem and Judah secretly baked cakes for the queen of heaven even though Yahweh had made it known that he was going to destroy Judah, ultimately it was not Yahweh but they themselves who brought the terrible wrath upon them. Thus, after the catastrophe they will have to endure complete wrath, in which they will suffer similar things, and so the whole nation will be put to shame.

Jer. 9:18(19); 12:13; 14:4; 15:9; 31:19 (and 17:13, which is not authentic) move entirely in the sphere of popular laments. While 9:18(19); 31:19 (and 17:13) simply contain quotations, in the liturgy in 14:1–15:3 the prophet states that the farmers are ashamed and cover their heads (14:4) since they have nothing to offer because of the general drought, when they could have gained respect with a good harvest. 12:13 looks like a prophetic affirmation of guilt after a lament: the people reaped thorns instead of wheat, they tired themselves out for nothing, and they would be ashamed of their harvests–because of Yahweh's anger. In all these cases the shame is that the nation that lived in Yahweh's shadow was expected to be attractive, but was unattractive. This is also the background of the statements that appear in Jeremiah's own laments (17:18 and 20:11). In 17:18 we read: "Let those be put to shame who persecute me, but

---

[29] See Rudolph, *HAT, in loc.,* opposing the interpretation of Bethel as a god.

let me not be put to shame; let them be dismayed, but let me not be dismayed."
Jeremiah felt compelled to speak Yahweh's word concerning the catastrophe of
Judah and Jerusalem and because of this he was attacked personally. But since
he felt compelled to speak Yahweh's word, the only word that was really depend-
able, he was sure that Yahweh would protect him personally. It troubled him
immensely that this protection did not come (see esp. 15:15ff.), and this convinced him more than anything else of the immovability of Yahweh's will to bring
calamity. So also here, his request that his persecutors be put to shame is a prayer
that the word of Yahweh to the people would be manifested unambiguously *as*
the word of Yahweh. Shame is what was to be expected and demanded for his
persecutors, but it does not come; the word is merely spoken. Similarly, in 20:11
the prophet states that which he had expected, and then in 20:14ff. follows his
self-imprecation.

We must still examine the later interpretation of the book of Jeremiah.[30] In
Jer. 48:39 we read: "How Moab has turned away her neck on account of shame!"
(In my opinion this does not mean to show the back in a disgraceful manner, but
means not to show the face on account of shame;[31] cf. 2:26.) This shame is made
manifest by comparing Moab now with her former esteemed position. Nothing
more than this can be said because the text has not been handed down entirely
satisfactorily. 49:23 probably has something to do with political leagues made
between nations: "Hamath and Arpad were put to shame for they heard evil
tidings...: Damascus was asleep, she turned to flee...." This passage assumes a
situation in which either Damascus had gained control over Hamath and Arpad,
or these two cities considered Damascus to be their bulwark against an invading
enemy. Shame came upon Hamath and Arpad because the joyful city (v. 25)
gave up so quickly. Of course, the shame of Babylon will be even worse (according to 50:12), because formerly she had been the first of the nations, but she
will become the scum of the nations, dry and deserted; cf. also 51:47. 51:51 is
a popular lament.

4. *Zephaniah, Joel.* The work of Zephaniah also falls in the time of Jeremiah.
boshtam in 3:19 is probably a textual corruption, and the text of 3:5bβ is very
uncertain (see the LXX). However, it is very likely that the prophecy of the
future in 3:11 is genuine; it says: "On that day you (fem.) shall not be put to
shame because of the deeds by which you have rebelled against me; for then
I will remove from your midst your proudly exultant ones...." 2 K. 19:26=
Isa. 37:27 probably also comes from the same time, because the satire of the
daughter of Zion over the almost omnipotent Assyria in 2 K. 19:20b-28 seems to
presuppose the downfall of the Assyrian power *ca.* 630 B.C. and to fit better in
the time of Josiah than in the exilic-postexilic period.[32] This verse still reflects
the situation that existed before the fall of Assyria when the inhabitants of the
fortified cities were ashamed of their pitiable power (according to the will of

---

[30] On 6:15 and 8:12, see under IV, hiphil 2.
[31] Contra Rudolph, *HAT, in loc.*
[32] In particular contra Eissfeldt, *The OT* (trans. 1965), 425.

Yahweh), i.e., a genuine great power makes it clear with one blow that all small powers that boast against him are insignificant.

If scholars who date the prophet Joel in the last century before the fall of Jerusalem [33] are correct, then we must include Joel 2:26f.; 1:10f.,17 in the discussion at this point. Since these verses come from the realm of popular repentance, and on the one hand cannot be restricted to a specific date and on the other hand show affinities with Jer. 14:1–15:3, they may be mentioned here in any case. Now while 2:27 (2:26 text!) contains a familiar Psalm motif and can best be understood in connection with the language of the Psalms, 1:10f.,17 use *bosh* in a way that is quite original. [34] In my opinion, they use *bosh* to denote that which has brought shame, e.g., 1:10 says: "The fields are laid waste, the ground mourns; because the grain is destroyed, the wine brings shame, the oil is miserable." At first glance, the context seems to suggest that the meaning "to be spoiled, corrupted," lies behind the concept in *hobhish* here; [35] but in my opinion the idea is different. The wine in which one rejoices, which refreshes the heart, is put in the corner like disgraceful wine. The oil that is yet to be pressed out of withered fruit is dried up and in this sense is miserable, shameful (1:11). V. 12 means the same thing: the royal vine yields shame, one can no longer recognize that it is a royal plant. 1:17 seems to be most difficult: "The storehouses are desolate; the granaries are ruined, because the grain is shameful." I.e., it is not worth it to lay claim to the storage rooms for grain, because the grain is shamefully bad and must be destroyed quickly in order to keep from causing any further shame.

5. *Deutero-Isaiah.* The five passages in Ezekiel that use *bosh* (once *bushah*) are not very productive, and if the unauthentic passages in Deutero-Isaiah that use *bosh* and its derivatives (Isa. 42:17; 44:9,11; 45:16f.) are separated from the authentic (41:11; 49:23; 50:7; 54:4), there remains no unusually lofty use of this root in this prophet either. This is indeed very remarkable! 49:23 would seem to be classic for the preaching of Deutero-Isaiah as a whole–indeed, it was a unique expectation for his people who (as it seems) had ceased to exist as a people. How could one believe that the relatives of the people would actually be brought to Zion from all the ends of the earth and be cared for by kings? The prophet answers the question of the people as to why they had been put to shame while emphasizing the lack of faith inherent in such a question: the devastated people will not merely experience a *restitutio* (restoration) in Palestine–this would be too little. In addition, Yahweh will be worshiped on Zion as the God of the whole world. The risk of faith does not lead to shame, but to universalism. 54:4 follows a similar line of thought: Zion will not be put to shame–on the contrary! She will no longer remember the earlier shame of her youth and widowhood, because the husband of the daughter of Zion is the lord of the whole earth, i.e., because Yahweh did not spare his people the truth and

---

[33] Cf. most recently W. Rudolph, *HAT,* against the post-Nehemian dating of H. W. Wolff, *BK,* which is supported with detailed arguments.

[34] See also under IV below, hiphil 2.

[35] *KBL*³.

thus their destruction, he proved himself to be the only true God, who has no respect of persons. The destruction, which was connected with shame, is not shame in its outcome, but proof of the uniqueness of Yahweh. 41:11f. probably means that Yahweh applies his standards to Babylon just as he does to Israel. For when the city that claimed to have world dominion and world religion was angry with the people of Judah and brought a sacral lawsuit against them to prove that their God was no God, they demonstrated their complete ignorance of the Lord of the world who had made his people witnesses of his world dominion. Thus in their hubris they were destined to be put to shame.

However, while Israel and Zion had been smitten with calamity because they deserved it and as a result had become witnesses of their God, Isa. 50:4-9 speaks of one who was smitten with calamity and did not deserve it, but who could still say: "The Lord God helps me, ... therefore I have set my face like a flint, and I know that I shall not be put to shame." The speaker seems to have been subjected to public shame for the sake of Yahweh, and yet he knows that he will not be put to shame. He does not bring a complaint against Yahweh, he does not beg, he is not bitter, and he does not draw back. Moths may eat up others like an old garment, but no one will be able to declare him guilty: does this mean that the poem, 50:4-9, understands and describes the action of Yahweh as untrustworthy in the eyes of the world and of Israel and therefore true?

The passages in Isa. 42:17; 44:9,11, which state that those who make idols will be put to shame, are rather simple. 45:16f. seem to be a later interpretation of vv. 14f.

6. *Psalms.* In the Psalms, *bosh* is used in four different ways: (1) once in a lament in Ps. 44:16(15): shame has covered my face; (2) twice in affirmations of trust in Ps. 22:6(5) and 44:8(7) (hiphil 1); [36] (3) 13 times in petitions of a lament (e.g., "let me not ..."; twice in the hiphil) or as a supplement to and motivation for a petition (e.g., "may those who hope in thee not ..."); and (4) 16 times as a wish concerning the enemies of the worshipper; it is used in praise in Ps. 71:24 as a wish that had been fulfilled. (In my opinion, Ps. 14:6; 53:6[5] are not applicable, because these verses so far lack a generally accepted emendation.) In view of the very old Akkadian parallels the petition in the lament, which actually is an appropriate conclusion to the whole, is of particular interest.

If we suppose that an urgent petition not to be put to shame has a particular place in polytheism when the worshipper turns to one particular deity (and not to any other), then another interpretation seems to be more correct: with his petition the worshipper steps out of his community, which considers itself to be normal, and takes a risk in making a petition to a particular God. In a petition made before a king, the most important thing is that the loyalty of the (perhaps insignificant) petitioner might not be subjected to shame, but might meet with the king's approval and thus cause him to hear the petitioner's case. Likewise, in a prayer the most important thing is that God, who is infinitely

---

[36] See under IV.

superior to the king, might not expose the loyalty of one petitioning him to ridicule. Thus when a worshipper comes to Yahweh with the petition: "in thee I trust, let me not be put to shame" (25:2; cf. 22:6[5]; 25:20; 31:2[1]), the emphasis is on the worshipper's conviction that he will be established in his relationship to God by Yahweh himself. This relationship to God is always the important thing in the petition, and if it is not established his soul is humiliated even unto Sheol. It is the importance of this relationship to God that makes one's desire that his enemy be put to shame intelligible. Such a desire, then, is motivated not primarily by revenge, but by the fact that the falsehood with which the worshipper's enemies deal with him, and thus negatively the truth of God, shall be manifest in his enemies. For when they deny the worshipper's relationship to God, they actually judge this relationship falsely. The idea that they are able to regard life as death and death as life is intolerable and requires a clarification of reality, for it is dangerous for the community as a whole when "life" and "death" can be confused in such a way. Therefore, it is possible to think of the extent of the shame to be revealed to the enemies in quite different ways. The worshipper in Ps. 86 can say (v. 17): "Show me a sign of thy favor, that those who hate me may see and be put to shame." Ps. 31:18(17) reads quite differently: "Let me not be put to shame, O Lord, ... let the wicked be put to shame, let them go dumbfounded to Sheol." In any case, it seems to me that the interpretation that the worshipper here is demanding revenge is wrong. What he is requesting is a clear revelation of his God. For as long as God's truth is not indifferent, one must desire that falsehood be recognized as falsehood.

Among the examples in the Psalter, Ps. 119:80 is unique: "May my heart be blameless in thy statutes, that I may not be put to shame." Apparently, "being put to shame" is spiritualized here in the sense that if one is not complete in the commandments, he will be put to shame in all of them.

IV. The Hiphil Forms. We must still discuss some passages in which the hiphil forms of *bosh* occur. While the verbal forms of the regular hiphil form (hiphil 1) *hebhish* yield the expected causative meaning "to be put to shame" (Ps. 44:8[7]; 119:31,116; the text of 14:6; 53:6[5] is corrupt), apparently the participle has taken on a different meaning. Generally speaking, it seems to mean the worker of shame without designating (like the verbal forms) the nature of the shame that is caused. It almost loses its aspect of action and becomes a judgment on one's character. It denotes a type of person who may be contrasted with a *maskil,* "prudent (wise) person" (Prov. 10:5; 17:2; 14:35, according to the emended text), or with a good (prudent, *chayil*) wife (Prov. 12:4). Is the participle a word like "pest?"

On the other hand, the hiphil of *bosh* (hiphil 2) tainted by the hiphil of *yabhesh,* "to make dry, wither," seems to modify the qal in that the actor does not simply fall into shame passively, but brings it on himself and thus earns shame. [37] Thus a mother who plays the harlot brings shame on herself (Hos. 2:7[5]), and so does a thief who gets caught in the act of stealing (Jer. 2:26), and

---

[37] B. Duhm on Isa. 30:5; otherwise *KBL*[2], conjec.

Israel who says to a tree, "You are my father...!" This modification is also quite clear in Jer. 6:15 and 8:12 (cf. 8:9): the priests, wise men, and prophets, who should know the truth, bring shame upon themselves because they are not ashamed of their own false ideas and words. While Jer. 10:14 = 51:17; 46:24; 48:1 do not clearly convey this distinctive meaning, 50:2 seems to contain this same picture when it says that Bel the god of Babylon has been put to shame, and Marduk has been dismayed. Evidently the author means that the boasting of Babylon has brought shame upon them. The passages in Joel 1:10-12,17 in particular are to be explained in this way. [38] The meaning "to fail," which has been suggested for *bosh* in these passages, [39] indeed conveys the sense, but the original meaning remains clear: the wine flows weakly and is diluted, thus it is a shame. The vine, usually a royal plant, presents a picture of misery and is a disgrace to its owner. The usual joy of harvest, which is an institution in itself (cf. the "Christmas spirit"), has given way to despair because of shame, i.e., if the harvest festival were carried out in the normal way it would be too disgraceful for those participating in it to tolerate. And the grain is of such poor quality (1:17) that the people do not bring it into the storehouses, and so they are ruined. Thus these passages seem to form the transition to the only passage in which the hiphil 2 form of *bosh* replaces the normal form, viz., 2 S. 19:6(5). But the nuance in that verse seems to be that by lamenting over Absalom David not only brings shame on his soldiers and friends, but by his inconsistent behavior suffers shame and brings it on his servants, just as wine, grain, and oil suffered shame and thus ruined the usual festival joy.

Seebass

---

[38] See above under c.
[39] See *KBL²*.

בָּזָה *bāzāh;* בּוּז *bûz;* בּוּזָה *bûzāh*

Contents: I. Original Meaning: 1. Etymology; 2. Occurrences; 3. Forms. II. Man as Subject: 1. Social Aspect; 2. Sacral Legal Relationship; 3. Historico-Theological Function. III. Man as Object: 1. Disapproval As Contempt; 2. Despising Outsiders; 3. Contempt and Salvation.

I. Original Meaning.

1. *Etymology.* The root *bzh* (*bzy*) corresponds to the Old Bab. *buzzu'u(m)*, *buzzûm*, "to treat wickedly, unrighteously." [1] According to *CAD*, [2] the Old

---

bāzāh. G. Bertram, "μυκτηρίζω, ἐκμυκτηρίζω," *TDNT*, IV, 796-99; V. de Leeuw, *De Ebed Jahweh-Profetieën* (1956); J. L. Palache, *Semantic Notes on the Hebrew Lexicon* (1959); H. D. Preuss, *Verspottung fremder Religionen im AT. BWANT*, 5/12 (1971).

[1] *AHw*, I, 145b.
[2] *CAD*, II, 185a.

Babylonian form means more specifically "to press a person for money or services" without "illegal implications," while the Old Assyr. *bazā'u* means "to make (undue?) demands." [3] Irrespective of whether such a distinction is justified, it seems clear that this root means something more than a mental intention. The Arab. *bazā*, "to subjugate," also refers to an external activity. In the Syr. and Mandean *bs'* and Middle Heb. *bzh,* the meaning seems to have been weakened semantically to the specific aspect of a contemptuous attitude, but even these words imply an external activity in addition to the intention. The idea that Heb. *bazah* comes from **basā* (= Syr. *bᵉsā*) can hardly be defended. [4] Also the view that the root *bazaz,* which is related to *bazah,* was "originally identical with *bus,* 'trample,'" [5] simply cannot be accepted. The Egyptian language knows a verb *bwy* with the meaning "abhor," which "apparently was replaced at an early period by *bwt.*" [6] It also has *bw.t,* which means "abominable," "repulsive," and *bw.ty* in the New Kingdom, which means "abhorred." [7] Of course, there is no proof that these words have any semantic relationship to West Semitic languages: not only is the vocalization of the Egyptian words questionable, but also the feminine ending of the Egyptian does not correspond to the second strong consonant of our root. And yet, one cannot exclude the possibility that a short onomatopoetic word imitating the sound of loathing or of one disapproving conduct may be the common term lying behind these roots in the two languages.

2. *Occurrences.* According to Palache, *buz* is the later form which occurs only "in later books" with the exception of Gen. 38:23 and 2 K. 19:21, while the "older books" allegedly have *bazah.* [8] However, the spectrum of base-forms shows that *bazah* is also sufficiently represented in the later literature. Including the conjectures in Prov. 15:20; 27:7; and Ezk. 36:4f., the root *buz* appears 29 times, while the root *bazah* is found 43 times. Conjectures based on a different orientation have been suggested for Sir. 3:13,16. [9]

3. *Forms.* When they function as verbs, the roots *bazah* and *buz* belong to the linguistic phenomena in which "weak forms with the same meaning are built according to different classes from the same two strong consonants without any indication that either of the two forms is secondary." [10] In the original root, *bazah* is usually construed with the accusative and occurs only twice with *le* (2 S. 6:16; 1 Ch. 15:29), while *buz* ordinarily appears with *le* and is construed only three times with the accusative (Prov. 1:7; 23:22; 27:7). In addition to the passive participle of the original root, *bazuy, bazah* has the niphal ptcp. *nibhzeh.* The causative form of *bazah* in Est. 1:17 and the construction of *bazah* with *'al*

---

[3] *CAD,* II, 184b.
[4] Contra Brockelmann, *VG,* I, 153.
[5] Palache, 14.
[6] *WbÄS,* I, 453.
[7] *WbÄS,* I, 454.
[8] Palache, 14.
[9] *KBL³.*
[10] G. Bergsträsser, *Hebräische Grammatik,* II/2 (1929), 170.

in Neh. 2:19 are both late. The noun *bizzayon,* "contempt," in Est. 1:18 is derived from *bazah.* The nouns *buz,* "contempt," which occurs rather frequently, and *buzah,* "contempt," which appears only once (Neh. 3:36 [Eng. 4:4]), are from *buz.* Also *bozeh* in Prov. 15:20 should be emended to a substantive from *buz.* [11]

II. Man As Subject.

1. *Social Aspect.* In the book of Proverbs the social aspect of *buz* seems to be quite clear. He who is unwise shows disdain for his neighbor (Prov. 11:12), the fool despises his mother (15:20; 23:22), wisdom and instruction (1:7), and prudence of understanding (23:9). But he who shows disdain for his neighbor commits sin (14:21); the eye that looks on an aged mother with contempt falls victim to the birds of prey (30:17); he who refuses a word of admonition goes astray (13:13). People do not despise the hungry thief (6:30). *buz* is the same as a symptom of a destroyed social order: "he who is sated loathes honey" (27:7). The following words are used to express ideas antithetical to *buz: charesh,* "to be silent" (11:12); → ירא *yārē',* "to respect" (13:13); → חנן *chānan,* "to be kind" (14:21); → שׂמח *śāmēach,* "to be glad" (15:20); and → שׁמע *shāma',* "to hear" (23:22). In keeping with the relationship between the deed and the condition in the root *bazah,* here there is a necessary connection between the action that the community despises and its punishment as a recompense.

2. *Sacral Legal Relationship.* Every offense against the will of Yahweh implies a *bazah,* "contempt, despising," of Yahweh. David's adultery with Bathsheba is the result of despising the "word of Yahweh" (2 S. 12:9), and therefore God himself (v. 10). He who deliberately acts in opposition to the community founded by Yahweh despises the "word of Yahweh" and falls into the *kareth*-punishment (the punishment of being "utterly cut off," Nu. 15:31). He who despises Yahweh is devious in his ways (Prov. 14:2), is lightly esteemed (1 S. 2:30), and will die (Prov. 19:16). The words used to convey ideas antithetical to *bazah* here are → כבד *kābhēdh* in the piel, "to honor" (1 S. 2:30); → ירא *yārē',* "to fear" (Prov. 14:2); and → שׁמר *shāmar,* "to keep" (Prov. 19:16). It may be worthy of note that the proverbial literature here intends to make a clear distinction between a *buz* against man and a *bazah* against Yahweh. He who looks on God's messengers with disrespect exposes himself to the wrath of Yahweh (2 Ch. 36:16). The phrase "to despise the oath" (→ אלה *'ālāh,* Ezk. 16:59; 17:16,18) means to break the covenant with Yahweh. Zedekiah's treaty with Nebuchadnezzar is regarded as "an agreement affirmed in the presence of Yahweh"; [12] thus the expression "my oath which he despised" (17:19) may be explained as a reference to the sacrosanct function of the agreement. The prophet announces Yahweh's reply to Israel, in which he declares that he will deal with them ac-

---

[11] Bertram, 805.
[12] Zimmerli, *BK,* XIII, 375.

cording to what they have done (16:59); Zedekiah is told that he will die in Babylon (17:16). Thus the contempt comes back upon the author of the *bazah*. The "bloody city," Jerusalem, deserves Yahweh's reproof, it despises (*bazah*) his holy things and profanes (→ חלל *chālal*) his sabbaths (Ezk. 22:8). The punitive reply will not be long coming (vv. 13ff.). Moreover, in Mal. 1:6f. *bazah* is the central idea in a fabricated discussion. Here the priests are accused of treating Yahweh's name with contempt (v. 6a). The question in which this particular *bazah* occurs (v. 6b) is followed by the reference to the unclean sacrificial cult which pollutes the altar (v. 7a). Its cleanness is desecrated by the priests considering Yahweh's "table" to be "insignificant" (v. 7b) and ultimately by their considering his food to be "contemptible" (v. 12). This last predicate is again the root *bazah* in the niphal form *nibhzeh*. Thus both speech and counterspeech revolve around a meaning of *bazah*. But the priests themselves will become victims of the very disrespect that ultimately they had shown to Yahweh: "I make you despised (*nibhzim*) and abased (*shephalim*) before all the people" (2:9a). Here also we see that ultimately a *bazah* of man is directed against Yahweh, while a *nibhzeh* is directed against man. The sacral legal relationship is a result of this.

3. *Historico-Theological Function.* In the linguistic usage of the OT, the behavior suggested by the root *bazah* touches mainly on Yahweh's sphere of activity. This is not very clear in the apparent marginal notes of tradition history. The refusal to give Saul a present (1 S. 10:27) was an expression of contempt and "indicates doubt in the judgment of God, which is now degraded." [13] From the moment that he "disdains" (*bazah*) the "youth" (*na'ar*) David (1 S. 17:42), Goliath is the inferior of the two. The same is true of Michal, who remains childless because she despised (2 S. 6:16; 1 Ch. 15:29) him who had humbled himself before Yahweh (2 S. 6:22). Consequently, he who carries out a *bazah* against one chosen by Yahweh is himself condemned to insignificance. It is impossible to avoid this impression entirely even in Gen. 25:34: Esau despises his birthright, the sign that he had been divinely chosen. The sentence at the end of this verse is an interpretation of the previously described event. By his irresponsible behavior toward the choice Jacob offered him, actually Esau despises himself and also Yahweh; therefore he must change places with Jacob. Thus the perspective shifts to the sketch of the one who appears exposed to the disrespect.

III. Man As Object.

1. *Disapproval As Contempt.* The idea of "being confounded" is inherent in *buz* all along. Thus Judah strives to avoid becoming a laughing-stock as a result of his experience with Tamar (Gen. 38:23). It is obvious that the author is interested in showing that "throughout this incident Judah incurs no guilt." [14]

---

[13] Hertzberg, *ATD*, X, 67.
[14] H. Gunkel, *Genesis* (⁷1966), 417.

Jerusalem looks on Assyria with contempt (*buz*) and scorn (*la'agh*) (2 K. 19:21; Isa. 37:22). Conversely, enemies have looked with contempt (*buz*) on the people of Yahweh (Ezk. 36:4f.). However, in the period when the temple of Jerusalem lay in ruins, the vision of the building of a new temple follows a time in which the temple was despised (Zec. 4:10). According to Proverbs, it is legitimate to despise a person who has malicious intentions: "one of perverse mind is despised" (Prov. 12:8); or: "when wickedness comes, contempt comes also" (18:3). In 12:8 *buz* stands in antithesis to *halal*, "to be commended," and in 18:3 it is synonymous with → חרפה *cherpāh*, "disgrace." The latest examples of the roots *buz* (cf. Cant. 8:1,7) and *bazah* (cf. Est. 1:17f.; 3:6; Dnl. 11:21; Neh. 2:19) have no theological relevance whatsoever.

2. *Despising Outsiders*. The prolongation of *buz*, "contempt," is a burden the righteous must bear. Moreover, one who presumably is secure has contempt for one who is unfortunate (Job 12:5). The one who is accused of sin fears the contempt of his family (31:34). As a result of this distress he flees to his God for help (v. 35). One who has been especially chosen by Yahweh is exposed to the ridicule of the world around him, derided by the lips of those who speak in pride (→ גאון *gā'ôn*) and contempt (Ps. 31:19[18]). The psalmist prays that scorn (*cherpah*) and contempt be taken away from the believer (119:22). And yet, "the one who obeys is the one who suffers." [15] Indeed, he thinks that he has endured more than enough disgrace and scorn from the arrogant: only Yahweh can help him (123:3f.). Yahweh's undefinable omnipotence is not ultimately revealed in that he apportions clear judgment in conformity with his unfathomable nature; in fact he even pours contempt upon "princes" (107:40; Job 12:21). The predicate *nibhzeh*, which has already been mentioned above, is applied almost exclusively to men who have been outlawed by the world around them. This seems to be the case in 1 S. 15:9, where it is certain that "worthless" human life also is to be destroyed when the ban is carried out. According to Jer. 22:28, the people will treat Jehoiachin with contempt in complete violation of the law, as a "useless" vessel which no one can use any longer.

A person who has been rejected by Yahweh can be "despised" (*nibhzeh*) by the righteous (Ps. 15:4), for even Yahweh himself despises the "phantoms" of the wicked (73:20). Thus the existence of the "despised" (*nibhzeh*) is characterized by ambiguity. This sort of condition can become reality with or without tangible guilt. Consequently *nibhzeh*, "to be despised," always has reference to Yahweh because in the final analysis he is the one who defines what it means "to be despised." He who does not forget Yahweh's precepts must confess that he is *nibhzeh*, "despised" (Ps. 119:141). In light of this kind of reflection, the person who is weak has the prospect of again being led to such an acknowledgment by Yahweh. The predicate *bazuy*, "despised," is used in a similar way of those who stand outside the community of Yahweh, whether they are guilty of sin or not. Edom's fate is that she will become insignificant: "I will make you

---

[15] Kraus.

small among the nations, despised among men" (Jer. 49:15; Ob. 2). The Preacher considers complete resignation to be the fate of the poor man, that outsider of society: no one, apparently not even God, pays any attention to his wisdom (Eccl. 9:16). Even though he believes God has forsaken him (Ps. 22:2[1]), the person uttering the lament in Ps. 22:7(6) knows that still there is reasonable hope for him. He suffers as a worm and not as a man, he is "despised" (*bazuy*) and scorned by the people. In his loneliness the one who is "despised" (*bazuy*) is scorned for his faith; but still he prays (v. 12[11]).

3. *Contempt and Salvation.* The Servant of Yahweh is almost the archetype of the *nibhzeh* and of the *bazuy,* "the one despised." The predicate *nibhzeh,* "despised," is a key word in the description of his character: "He was despised (*nibhzeh*) and rejected by men, a man of sorrows, and acquainted with grief; and as one from whom men hide their faces he was despised (*nibhzeh*), and we esteemed him not" (Isa. 53:3). Perhaps we should read *nbzhw,*[16] "we despised him," in place of the second *nibhzeh* following 1QIs[a]: then the statement would receive additional importance. The life of the chosen one is plainly exposed to the contempt of all. The expression *libhzoh nephesh* (RSV, "to one deeply despised") in Isa. 49:7 is textually uncertain. De Leeuw wants to translate the phrase *bazah nephesh* "to give one's life."[17] This would mean that the servant voluntarily decided to suffer contempt. It seems better to emend the text to one of the regular participial forms in order to make it agree with the following *metha'ebh,* "the one abhorred." The one who is so despised by all the world still stands immovable in the grace of Yahweh, for *bazah,* "being despised," which comes directly from Yahweh, will never fall upon the chosen one. According to Ps. 22:25(24), Yahweh has not despised or "abhorred" (*shiqqats*) the affliction of the afflicted; he has heard (*shomea'*) the needy and has not despised those that are in bonds (69:34[33]); he has regarded the prayer of the destitute and has not despised his prayer (102:18[17]), for God will not despise a "broken and contrite heart" (51:19[17]).[18]

Görg

---

[16] Cf. *KBL*[3].

[17] De Leeuw, 200.

[18] For additional information concerning terminology related to "scorn," cf. esp. Preuss, 147ff.

בזז bzz; בַּז baz;

שלל šll; שָׁלָל shālāl

Contents: I. Etymology, Distribution in the OT. II. In Laws. III. Taking Spoil in General. IV. In Prophetic Texts. V. To Preserve One's Life As Spoil. VI. The Spoil Speeds, The Prey Hastes.

I. Etymology, Distribution in the OT. To a great extent the two roots *bzz* and *šll* are synonymous and are often used together either in parallelism (Isa. 10:2,6; Jer. 49:32; Ezk. 26:12; 29:19; 38:12,13; 39:10; Dnl. 11:24) or in constructions in which *shalal* stands in an objective relationship to *bazaz* (Dt. 2:35; 3:7; 20:14; Josh. 8:2,27; 11:14; 2 Ch. 20:25; 28:8; Est. 3:13; 8:11). The constructions *bazaz baz (bizzah)* or *shalal shalal* occur frequently: the former in Nu. 31:32; 2 Ch. 25:13; Isa. 10:6; Ezk. 29:19; 38:12f.; and the latter in Isa. 10:6; Ezk. 29:19; 38:12. The verb *bazaz* takes as an object either *shalal*[1] or *baz, bizzah* as an internal object, or cities (e.g., in 2 Ch. 14:13 [Eng. v. 14]), countries (Isa. 24:3), palaces (Am. 3:11), women and children (Nu. 14:3,31; Dt. 1:39). It occurs 36 times in the qal, twice in the niphal, and once in the pual. The verb *shalal* appears 10 times in the qal and twice in the hithpael. As far as the nouns are concerned, *baz* denotes the act of plundering, while *shalal* means the spoil that is taken. *shasah*, "to plunder," is found in parallelism with *bazaz* (Isa. 17:14; 42:22,24; Jer. 30:16; and 9 other times). *'adh* also means "spoil" (Gen. 49:27 and perhaps Isa. 9:5[6]). *bazaz* has cognates with the same meaning in Phoenician,[2] in different Aramaic dialects (even Official Aram.),[3] and in Arabic (*bazza*). *shalal* corresponds to Akk. *šalālu* and perhaps to the Old South Arab. *tll*,[4] both meaning "to plunder" (we cannot be sure whether the Arab. *talla*, "to fall [down], to destroy," is a cognate with these words). The Akk. *šalālu* occurs quite frequently with the noun *šallatu* ("spoil and prisoners of war," "prisoners of war") in the annals, with both personal and material obj. (inhabitants, treasures, etc.). *šālil šallate*, "he who plunders the spoil," appears as a royal epithet in connection with Ashurbanipal.[5]

---

bzz. P. Humbert, "Maher Šalal Haš Baz," *ZAW*, 50 (1932), 90-92; A. Jirku, "Zu 'Eilebeute' in Jes 8,1.3," *ThLZ*, 75 (1950), 118; S. Morenz, "Zu 'Eilebeute,'" *ThLZ*, 74 (1949), 697-99; H. J. Stoebe, "Raub und Beute," *SVT*, 16 (1967), 340-354; E. Vogt, "'Eilig tun' als adverbielles Verb und der Name des Sohnes Isaias in Is. 8,1," *Bibl*, 48 (1967), 63-69.

[1] See above.
[2] *DISO*, 30.
[3] *Ibid.*
[4] ContiRossini, 260.
[5] Seux, 281.

II. In Laws. The law concerning war in Dt. 20 commands that the men of a conquered city be put to death, but "the women and the little ones, the cattle, and everything else in the city, all its spoil (*kol shelalah*), you shall take as booty for yourselves (*tabhoz lakh*); and you shall enjoy the spoil (*shelal*) of your enemies, which Yahweh your God has given you" (v. 14). But if it is a Canaanite city, it is to be completely destroyed by the ban (→ חרם *chāram;* vv. 16-18; cf. Dt. 13:17[16]). In this way a limit is placed on the free disposal of the spoil as given by God.

In connection with a victory over the Midianites, in which Israel captured (*bazaz*) some prisoners and some spoils of war including cattle (*behemah*), property (*miqneh*), and wealth (*chayil:* Nu. 31:9, cf. vv. 11f.), the Israelites are commanded to divide equally that which was taken (*malqoach*), man and beast, between the warriors and the rest of the congregation (31:26f.). Then vv. 31ff. give an account of the division of these spoils.

III. Taking Spoil in General. When the OT speaks of taking spoil, it can use different word combinations, which also give a picture of the scope of this concept. Cattle (*behemah*) and booty (*shalal*) are taken as spoil (*bazaz*): Dt. 2:35; 3:7; Josh. 8:2,27; 11:14; cf. the prisoners and the *shalal,* "spoil," in 2 Ch. 28:8. Gen. 34:29 probably means that women and children were taken as prisoners (*shabhah*) and "all that was in the houses" was taken as spoil (*bazaz*). According to 1 S. 30:20, flocks and herds (*tso'n vebhaqar*) are the spoil (*shalal*) of David (cf. 1 S. 15:21). Josh. 7:21 reckons a mantle among the *shalal,* and the Song of Deborah mentions many-colored garments (RSV "dyed stuffs") as *shalal* (Jgs. 5:30). Jer. 49:32 names camels and *miqneh,* "herds of cattle," as *baz* or *shalal*. Ezk. 26:12 speaks of the spoil (*shalal*) of riches (*chayil*) and of the prey (*bazaz*) of merchandise (*rekhullah*); cf. further 2 Ch. 20:25; cattle, goods, clothing, and precious things. Thus in some passages a distinction is made between prisoners and *shalal* or between cattle and *shalal,* while in other passages cattle are designated as *shalal*. On the other hand, it can be said that the leading classes in Israel make widows their spoil (*shalal*) and the fatherless their prey (*bazaz*), Isa. 10:2. Zec. 2:13(9) says that Israel will become plunder for those who formerly served them. According to Jer. 50:10 Chaldea will be plundered (*shalal*), and her plunderers (*sholel*) will be sated.

Frequently the OT speaks of "dividing the spoil" (*chalaq shalal*), in archaic texts like Jgs. 5:30; Gen. 49:27; Ex. 15:9; Ps. 68:13(12); and also in Josh. 22:8; Isa. 9:2(3); 33:23; 53:12; Zec. 14:1; Prov. 16:19. At the same time, the joy connected with dividing the spoil is also emphasized: Isa. 9:2(3); cf. Ps. 119:162 and the triumphant tone in Zec. 14:1 and Isa. 53:12.

IV. In Prophetic Texts. In prophetic texts, the words derived from the roots *bzz* and *šll* sometimes occur in oracles of judgment and sometimes in oracles of salvation. First, let us notice certain oracles of judgment. Isa. 10:6 says that Assyria comes "to take spoil and to seize plunder" (*lishlol shalal velabhoz baz*). The Babylonians will "plunder (*bazaz*), seize (*laqach*), and carry to Babylon" the prized belongings and treasures of Jerusalem (Jer. 20:5). Yahweh says through Jeremiah, "Your (Judah's) wealth (*chayil*) and all your treasures (*'otsar*) I will give as spoil (*labhaz 'etten*)" (15:13; 17:3). Ezekiel says that Nebuchadrezzar will carry off the wealth of Egypt, despoil its spoil and plunder its plunder (*veshalal shelalah ubhazaz bizzah,* Ezk. 29:19), and something similar concerning Gog (Ezk. 38:12f.). Yahweh will give the silver and gold of Jerusalem (its images) to foreigners for a prey (*baz*) and to the wicked of the earth for a spoil (*shalal*) (Ezk. 7:21; cf. also 25:7; 26:5; and in addition 34:8,22,28: Yahweh's sheep will no longer be a prey [*baz*]).

On the other hand, in some oracles of salvation it says that Israel is indeed a robbed and plundered people (Isa. 42:22,24, *bazaz, shasah*), but will not remain such. "Those who despoil you shall become a spoil, and all who prey on you I will make a prey (*baz*)" (Jer. 30:16). After the fall of Gog, those who dwell in Israel "will despoil (*shalal*) those who despoiled them, and plunder (*bazaz*) those who plundered them" (Ezk. 39:10).

V. To Preserve One's Life As Spoil. A unique expression occurs four times in Jeremiah (21:9; 38:2; 39:18; 45:5): "to preserve one's *nephesh* (life) as *shalal* (spoil)" (RSV "to have one's life as a prize of war"), i.e., barely to escape with one's life.

VI. The Spoil Speeds, The Prey Hastes. The words *maher shalal chash baz,* "the spoil speeds, the prey hastes," occur in Isa. 8:1,3 as the name of a son of Isaiah. This name is supposed to mean that the wealth of Damascus and the spoil of Samaria will soon be carried away by the Assyrians. Jirku wants to derive *maher* from Ugaritic, where *mhr* means "servant, soldier," and to translate the expression in Isa. 8:1,3 "warrior of spoil, hastening to prey." But this translation ruins the parallelism, and therefore the explanation given by Morenz is to be preferred. According to him, we should compare this phrase with an Egyptian expression found frequently in documents of the eighteenth dynasty. Its significance here is the two imperatives *is ḥ3k,* "hasten, despoil," which often, however, are used as a substantive with the meaning "easy, effortless spoil," as in the statement: "His majesty captured him (the rebel) as a prisoner of war, all his people as *is ḥ3k.*" This expression could have infiltrated into the military language at Jerusalem.

Ringgren

בחן *bḥn;* בָּחוֹן *bāchôn*

Contents: I. Meaning, Etymology, Occurrences. II. Semantic Field of "Trying (Testing)" and the Peculiar Meaning of *bḥn.* III. *'ebhen bochan.*

I. Meaning, Etymology, Occurrences. With one exception the root *bḥn* occurs in Hebrew only as a verb, and in the OT, Sirach, and the Qumran texts it means "to try (to put to the test)." Apparently it is not found in Mishnaic Hebrew, [1] but it appears in the Hebrew of the Amoraim, [2] rather frequently in the hiphil with the meaning "to distinguish" (and has largely replaced the Biblical Heb. *hibhdil*), infrequently in the piel with the meaning "to examine, inspect," and late and sporadically–reintroduced from Biblical Hebrew–in the form and with the meaning it had in the OT. Aram. *bḥn* means "to try" (possibly this is Imperial Aram.). [3] It appears in the Targum in the peal and the ithpeal. In Syriac it is found in various stems (and derivatives). The Arab. *mḥn,* I, VIII, means "to try, test." Perhaps there is a connection between *bḥn* and the Biblical Heb. *bḥr* II, "to try" (rare and uncertain). [4] The Aramaic and Arabic etymologies (as possibly also *bḥr* II) are decisive against K. Sethe's also otherwise untenable assumption that the OT root *bḥn* was borrowed from Egyptian; yet it is possible that *bochan,* etc., [5] were derived from Egyptian. It is thus not possible to discern a meaning more primitive than "to try," which is common to all these verbs of the various linguistic areas. In Biblical Hebrew, in addition to the verb (in the qal and niphal), the subst. *bachon,* "assayer," occurs once.

In the LXX, *bḥn* is translated by *dokimázein,* "to put to the test, examine" (12 times), *etázein,* "to examine" (3 times), *exetázein,* "to examine" (twice), *krínein,* "to judge," *diakrínein,* "to separate, judge correctly, give a decision," etc.

II. Semantic Field of "Trying (Testing)" and the Peculiar Meaning of bḥn. The most important verbs having a meaning similar to that of *bḥn* are → חקר *chāqar,* "to search," *nāsāh,* "to test, try," and *tsāraph,* "to smelt, refine, test." *bḥn* appears once in poetic parallelism with *tsaraph,* and once in an expression using *tsaraph* which enlarges on and continues the idea of *bḥn. bḥn* occurs in

---

[1] Middle Hebrew, mhe[1] according to E. Y. Kutscher in *SVT,* 16 (1967), 160.

[2] mhe[2] according to Kutscher.

[3] See *LidzEph,* II (1908), 229/233: 7.

[4] According to M. Wagner, *Die lexikalischen und grammatikalischen Aramaismen im alttestamentlichen Hebräisch. BZAW,* 96 (1966), No. 38, OT Heb. borrowed *bḥr* II from Aram.; cf. *idem, SVT,* 16, 358f.

[5] See III below.

parallelism with *chaqar* twice and with *nasah* once, and it is also connected with *nasah* once when *nasah* further explains the concept intended by *bḥn*. These verbs are distributed in the OT as follows: *bḥn* occurs 28 times, 24 in poetry and 4 in prose (10 times in the Prophets, 8 times in Pss., once in Prov., and 5 times in Job); it has a religious connotation with God as subj. and man as obj. 22 times, and with man as subj. 3 times. *chaqar* appears 26 times, 17 in poetry and 9 in prose (once in Dt., 3 times in the Prophets, 5 times in Prov. and Eccl., and 6 times in Job); it has a religious connotation with God as subj. 5 times. *nasah* is found 36 times, 8 in poetry and 28 in prose (8 times in Dt., 6 times in Pss., twice in Eccl., once in Job); it has a religious connotation with God as subj. 12 times and with man as subj. 11 times. *tsaraph* occurs 20 times, 17 in poetry and 3 in prose (7 times in the Prophets, 8 times in Pss., and once in Prov.); it has a religious connotation (including "to refine, purify") 11 times with God as subject.

The following points can be made on the basis of this survey.

(a) In the religious sense, in sentences in which God is subject and man is object, or vice versa, *bḥn* and *nasah* occur with approximately the same frequency. In the majority of cases, *bḥn* expresses the concept of divine testing and divine knowledge of man, while *nasah* is used almost an equal number of times for divine testing and human defiance. *tsaraph* and *chaqar* (which, however, is used only rarely in the religious sense and will be disregarded in what follows) are found only in the first sense.

(b) *bḥn* and *tsaraph* are used primarily in poetic material. *nasah* appears predominantly in prose; it occurs quite frequently in the Deuteronomic and Deuteronomistic writings.

(c) *bḥn* and *tsaraph* are at home and wholly alive in the realm of common-place objective matters. *nasah* means to test the feasibility of some action (1 S. 17:39; Dt. 28:56), to try a person's physical or spiritual abilities (Dnl. 1:12; 1 K. 10:1), to study things and to experiment with them under different circumstances (Eccl. 7:23). *tsaraph* means "to smelt > to refine > to try or test." On the other hand, with one exception *bḥn* takes only God or man (sometimes this is clarified by the addition of "heart" or "kidneys," as well as "thoughts, ways, words") as an object. It does not occur in any objective practical main or secondary realm which might draw one's attention away from its use in the spiritual or religious realm (its use in Zec. 13:9 is an exception; here it appears in a simile!).

(d) Further observations need to be made concerning the use of these words in the spiritual and religious realm. *tsaraph* (without an exception) and *nasah* (with only one exception) mean to seek to attain knowledge or understanding through trial or temptation. But almost half of the passages that use *bḥn* in the OT do not connect the acquisition of knowledge with any normal activity. They give the impression that one attains knowledge purely intellectually or intuitively. The etymology of *bḥn* (which is discussed above) agrees with this: *bḥn* or a phonetic counterpart (*bḥr* is an exception?) appears in Semitic languages only (still?) with the fully developed meaning "to try (test)," etc. That *bḥn* (as distinguished from *nasah*) means "to test through an action, to lead into temptation" only very rarely, also agrees with this. And this is confirmed even further by the occurrence of *bḥn* (in contrast with *nasah* and *tsaraph*) in poetic parallelism with verbs of knowing (twice) and seeing (3 times), i.e., understanding. And finally it is confirmed in that the Middle Heb. *bḥn* (hiphil) means exclusively "to divide, separate, distinguish" (a purely cognitive act).

Consequently *bḥn* is the most spiritual of all these synonyms; it is used quite specifically of people. This is also apparent from the distribution of *bḥn* in the OT. *bḥn* almost always has a religious connotation in the OT, and out of the synonyms meaning "to try, test," it is the one used most frequently in the Psalms and Job. It has a peculiar significance for Jeremiah, the prophet in whom message and person had become most intimately entwined and for whom this combination had become the greatest problem (it occurs 6 times in Jeremiah in comparison with twice in all other prophets); he had come to know God as the one who "tries the kidneys and the heart" (RSV "the heart and the mind," 11:20; cf. 17:10; 20:12).

Again the author of Ps. 139 is not primarily concerned with the fact that God tests man, but with his unlimited knowledge of man, of which he (the poet) is fully aware. Accordingly he uses *yadha'*, "to know," five times in speaking of God and twice in speaking of himself in this psalm. God possesses and realizes this knowledge in various ways, which is also clear from the different verbs he uses: to experience, to see, to search, to create, to lead (all occurring several times or in several variations). *bḥn*, "to try," occurs only once in this psalm (v. 23), and it might well have become lost in its isolation if it had not been protected by its repeated parallelism with other verbs and, set together with them in the scope of the poem, been a part of the expression of the only prayer in this psalm, a prayer that seems unnecessary like the prayer of every worshipper ("there is no word on my tongue which thou, O Yahweh, dost not know completely," v. 4), and yet is not: May God, who knows everything, try him and know him.

III. 'ebhen bochan. *'ebhen bochan* in Isa. 28:16 (above we suggested that *bochan* comes from a root homonymous with *bḥn*) is often connected symbolically with the *bḥn* presently under consideration, and is taken to mean "touchstone" or "tried stone." Several scholars think that the former is the best interpretation. [6] Indirectly the more recent proposals in support of this view go back to Sethe, [7] although he does not accept this interpretation of the phrase in Isa. 28:16. [8] His explanation must be rejected for the following reasons. (a) One can

---

[6] E.g., Sebastian Schmidt, *Commentarius super ... prophetias Jesaiae ...* (1693), 255f.; J. Cocceius, *Lexicon ... sermoni hebraici ...*, I (1777), 148f.; C. von Orelli, *Die Propheten Jesaja und Jeremia ...* (²1891), 101; Th. O Lambdin, *JAOS,* 73 (1953), 148; *KBL³*.

[7] K. Sethe, *SPAW* (1933), 894-909.

[8] Sethe, 907.

only infer with some degree of probability that ancient man was acquainted with
the touchstone in pre-Hellenistic Egypt; actually the earliest reference to it is in
Greek literature (*básanos, Lydía, líthos;* from the time of Theognis, the end of the
6th century B.C.). (b) In ancient (and even postexilic) Israel the purity of gold
was determined by melting (Prov. 17:3 = 27:21 [standardizing!]; cf. Zec. 13:9),
and for obvious reasons it is unlikely that this method would continue to have
been used after the touchstone test had been discovered. The translation "tried
stone" probably goes back to the Vulgate (*lapidem probatum*), possibly to "the
three" (*líthon dókimon*), but the expressions are not clear. This interpretation
also is wholly unlikely. Building material was not tested, and the assumption that
this expression referred to a stone "tried" for building purposes (so called because its use had "tested" it) is farfetched linguistically and technically. But
'*ebhen bochan* is not "pre-Cambrian . . . slate" (after the Egyptian) [9] either, since
this material is not found in Palestine, and cannot be included among the ashlars
which were imported into Palestine during the OT period. '*ebhen bochan* means
"a stone used in building a fortress" (*bachan, bochan, bachun/bachin*, "fortress"), an interpretation that can be traced back to the Qumran texts (1QS 8:7f.;
1QH 6:26; 7:9), i.e., it means an ashlar (often decorated with illustrations and
pictures) [10] which was used characteristically for building a fortress in the monarchical period. Isa. 28:16 says that God is laying such a stone as a cornerstone
of Zion (fortress, temple, city, mountain? cf. 14:32; 54:11; 1 K. 5:31 [Eng.
v. 17]). This stone has an inscription, which perhaps is to be understood as a
name. Inscriptions were also chiseled on the foundation walls of temples and
palaces in Mesopotamia, mainly on the cornerstones. Occasionally stones were
given names. A Kudurru (a stone inscribed with a record of a gift of land or a
purchase of land) from the time of Marduknadinaḫḫes [11] has the name "He sets
the limits on eternity." But the name of the stone in Zion is: "He who believes
is not in haste," i.e., he lets God do his work in his own good time (cf. Isa. 5:19).

Tsevat

---

[9] So L. Köhler, *ThZ*, 3 (1947), 390-93; *KBL*, 117; see also Sethe, 907.
[10] E.g., *BRL*, 372f.
[11] See L. W. King, *Babylonian Boundary Stones . . .* (1912), VII, A 1-3 = 2,40.

בָּחַר *bāchar*

Contents: I. In the Ancient Near East: 1. Egypt; 2. Mesopotamia. II. Etymology, Derivatives. III. Use in the OT: 1. Secular Meaning; 2. With Yahweh As Subject: Choice of the King; 3. Choice of the Priesthood; 4. "The Place Which Yahweh Chooses"; 5. The Election of the People; 6. Human Choices As Acts of Religious Confession; 7. Summary.

I. In the Ancient Near East.

1. *Egypt.* The Egyp. *śtp*[1] (which occurs in literature from the Middle Kingdom on) means "to choose," i.e., to choose someone or something out of a larger group or to give preference to someone or something above another, e.g., in Sinuhe B, 79, "he allowed me to choose some of his land, some of the choicest portions of that which he possessed." Frequently Egyptian texts also mention the object of the choice: "to be king" or "in order to do something" (e.g., *Urk.*, IV, 361: Hatshepsut, "she whom he [the god] chose to protect Egypt"). "He whom the king has chosen" is a title of honor. "The chosen thing" is the elite, the best. One interesting idea in Egyptian literature is the choice of the king by the god, which the earlier texts express by the verb *mry*, "to love": the pharaoh will be loved by God more than all others are loved by him,[2] an affirmation that appears from the thirteenth dynasty on in connection with the choice of the king or the love of God for the king.[3] From the eighteenth dynasty on, *śtp n*, "chosen by" the deity, occurs as a royal title.

2. *Mesopotamia.* In Mesopotamian literature, the choice of the king is of particular interest. The verb *(w)atû* means "to seek," "to discover," "to choose."[4]

---

bāchar. R. E. Clements, "Deuteronomy and the Jerusalem Cult Tradition," *VT*, 15 (1965), 300-312; K. Galling, *Die Erwählungstraditionen Israels. BZAW*, 48 (1928); K. Koch, "Zur Geschichte der Erwählungsvorstellung in Israel," *ZAW*, 67 (1955), 205-226; E. W. Nicholson, *Deuteronomy and Tradition* (Oxford, 1967), esp. pp. 95-100; L. Perlitt, *Bundestheologie im AT. WMANT*, 36 (1969); G. Quell, "ἐκλέγομαι B. Election in the OT," *TDNT*, IV, 145-168; H. H. Rowley, *The Biblical Doctrine of Election* (London, 1950); J. Schreiner, *Sion-Jerusalem, Jahwes Königssitz* (1963), esp. pp. 51-56; M. Sekine, "Vom Verstehen der Heilsgeschichte," *ZAW*, 75 (1963), 145-154; J. M. P. Smith, "The Chosen People," *AJSL*, 45 (1928/29), 73-82; Th. C. Vriezen, *Die Erwählung Israels nach dem AT. AThANT*, 24 (1953); H. Wildberger, *Jahwes Eigentumsvolk. AThANT*, 37 (1960); G. E. Wright, *The OT Against its Environment* (1950), 46-54.

[1] *WbÄS*, IV, 307f.

[2] E. Blumenthal, "Untersuchungen zum äg. Königtum des MR," *ASAW*, 61/1 (1970), 67ff.; cf. E. Otto, "Bedeutungsnuancen der Verben *mrj* 'lieben' und *mśdj*, 'hassen,'" *MDAI*, 25 (1969), 98-100.

[3] Blumenthal, 74f.; S. Morenz, "Die Erwählung zwischen Gott und König in Ägypten," *Sino-Japonica. Festschrift für A. Wedemeyer* (1956), 118-137.

[4] *CAD*, I/2, 518ff.

When the king is designated as *itūt kun libbi* DN, "the one chosen by the faithful heart of God" (or Sum. *šà-ge pà-da,* "chosen by the heart"),[5] this is connected with the familiar idea that the eyes of the god search for the king to appoint him to his office.[6] Thus *itūt ilāni,* "Chosen One of the gods," alternates with *nīš ēnē ilāni,* "the one to whom the eyes of the gods have been directed." Again, frequently the purpose of the choice is emphasized, e.g., "in order to be shepherd of the land,"[7] "in order to preserve righteousness and justice" (Hammurabi).

Bergman–Ringgren

II. **Etymology, Derivatives.** The Heb. root *bḥr* means a careful choice occasioned by actual needs, and thus a very conscious choice and one that can be examined in light of certain criteria, in contrast perhaps to making a selection (*ra'ah le,* RSV "providing"), to deciding as an act of an especially intimate relationship, or to "taking" (*laqach*) and "determining" (*ho'il*).[8] In my opinion there is only one root *bḥr,* for it can hardly be proved that it is necessary to derive *bachur,* "young man" (< *baḥḥur*),[9] from a separate root. The Akk. *baḥūlātu,* "vassals, troops," which *KBL²* cites as a parallel to *bachur,* is (as *KBL²* correctly states) only distinguished artificially from the usual *ba'ūlātu* in Sargon and Sennacherib and can hardly justify the assumption of an independent root. On the other hand, it is quite possible etymologically to suppose that *bachur* was derived from the normal root *bḥr,* and there would be little difficulty in assuming that this derivation had already occurred in Canaanite. *CAD* and *AHw* also think there is only one verbal root *bḥr* in Hebrew. Also, the assumption of a *bḥr* III[10] cannot be defended, in my opinion, since *bḥr* in 1 S. 20:30 certainly conveys the usual meaning, and we should read *yechubbar,* "to be united to," with the *qere* and several manuscripts in Eccl. 9:4 instead of the nonsensical MT *yebhuchar.*[11]

The Akk. *bêrum* is the most important Semitic parallel to the Heb. *bḥr.* From Old Akkadian on, *bêrum* means "to choose" and "to test" (much rarer), and thus manifests no noteworthy peculiarities. The Late Bab. *beḥēru,* "to choose" (e.g., oxen), together with the ptcp. *bēḥiru,* "official to levy troops," etc.,[12] came into Akkadian from Aramaic.

While it is quite certain that the Akkadian root means "to test," this meaning can hardly be shown for the Hebrew root. The text of Isa. 48:10 is uncertain;

---

[5] Seux, 121f., 434f.

[6] P. Dhorme, *La religion assyro-babylonienne* (Paris, 1910), 150ff.; R. Labat, *Le caractère religieux de la royauté assyro-babylonienne* (Paris, 1939), 45ff.

[7] Seux, 435.

[8] Cf. Quell, 149-152.

[9] *BLe,* §§ 67f., cf. 24q.

[10] See *KBL²* on 1 S. 20:30; Eccl. 9:4; the existence of a root *bḥr* III has been proposed by Dahood.

[11] See *KBL².*

[12] In agreement with *CAD* and *AHw* in opposition to a *be'rum,* "picked soldier," in *ARM,* XV, 193, cited in *KBL².*

and Job 34:4,33; Sir. 4:17 [13] can be translated "lead to a decision" in harmony with a later linguistic development in Hebrew, and does not really exclude the element of choice.

In the following material we shall limit ourselves to a study of the verb in the qal and to the derivative *bachir,* "chosen," which apparently was deliberately differentiated from the pass. ptcp. *bachur* and represents a purely religious idea as perhaps *chasidh,* "pious, godly" (the text of 2 S. 21:6 is uncertain). There is no need to deal with *bachur,* "young man," or *bechuroth (bechurim),* "young age," here. The ideas conveyed by these words are stereotyped because they were derived from the root *bhr* very early. All the passive forms and the noun *mibhchar* mean "choice, select" (the text of Job 36:21 is questionable), even in Prov. 10:20. They contribute nothing to the meaning of the root that could not be deduced from the use of the verb.

III. Use in the OT.

1. *Secular Meaning. bhr* is used remarkably often in the OT in narrating events in the religious sphere, considering that it is a thoroughly secular word– but should such a distinction be made here between secular and religious practices? After all, a careful, well-thought-out choice is necessary in both realms, as when David chooses stones that would be suitable for his sling (1 S. 17:40), or when the carpenter who sets up an image carefully chooses the wood that is essential for it (Isa. 40:20), or when the sons of God choose some of the daughters of men to become their wives because of their beauty (Gen. 6:2), or when the inhabitants of Jerusalem choose trees and gardens to embellish their cult (Isa. 1:29), or when Lot chooses the Jordan valley for his dwelling place (Gen. 13:11), or when the prophets of Baal carefully choose the bull which they wish to offer in order to emphasize their prayer for rain (1 K. 18:25). The careful, well-thought-out choice is the same everywhere, and it would not make sense to distinguish one from the other.

In all these examples the principles determining the choice can be scrutinized, and this seems to be characteristic of *bhr.* At any rate this is also true of the following examples. Moses chooses men to judge the people at all times (Ex. 18:25). Joshua is given the commission to choose warriors that are capable of fighting the Amalekites (Ex. 17:9). Joshua chooses a special regiment of 30,000 men to ambush the soldiers of Ai when they come out of that city (Josh. 8:3), cf. 2 S. 10:9. But it can also be said: when David is threatened by Absalom's rebellion, David's servants are ready to do whatever the king decides (2 S. 15:15). In his situation Job chooses strangling instead of life (Job 7:15; cf. Jer. 8:3). In my opinion the critical passage, 1 S. 20:30, is to be understood in a similar way. Saul does not reprove his son Jonathan merely for being David's partner (thus the LXX), but he says much more significantly that the king's son had made a choice in favor of David which actually brought shame on the king and was in opposition to him, whether Jonathan intended it this way or not.

---

[13] Cf. *KBL²*.

2. *With Yahweh As Subject: Choice of the King.* When we move from this idea to the examples in the OT where Yahweh is the subject of the choosing, then that which Quell has called the rational element, [14] i.e., the scrutiny of the criteria, is simply confirmed. First, as one likes to emphasize with Quell, [15] the prophetic call does not belong here, because Yahweh's prophetic word is characterized by the unexpected and the unforeseen. Therefore, it does not seem very likely to me that Isa. 42:1 means God's servant is chosen as a prophet is chosen. With Westermann, [16] it is much better to think of a *homo politicus,* whose politics, of course, are fundamentally different from politics as it is usually understood. [17] On the other hand, it must be regarded as typical that the root *bḥr* plays a role in some priestly families. The oracle in 1 S. 2:28 probably comes from a rather early period: "I chose it (i.e., the house of your father) out of all the tribes of Israel to be my priest, to go up to my altar, to burn incense, to wear an ephod before me." It is immediately clear that he who is appointed to determine what sacrifices are suitable must himself be carefully chosen, and it is obvious that the one who makes this choice is Yahweh himself.

This example is important for the choice of the king, which I would view in exactly the same way. The king is also an official who is appointed over holy things which he must attend to with great precision and consistency. Since he is the man who leads Yahweh's wars, and since Yahweh himself is present in the camp as the commander-in-chief, the way the war is conducted is under strict rites. That *bḥr* plays a role in very old texts is in harmony with this, for the word vanishes thereafter and does not reappear until we come to the Deuteronomic and Deuteronomistic material and to Haggai. It is restricted to Saul and David with one reference to Absalom (2 S. 16:18), and thus appears in a time when the rites of the Yahweh war were still playing an important role, as the Saul tradition in particular shows. 1 S. 10:24 speaks of Saul's choice (the text of 2 S. 21:6 is questionable). This verse belongs to the narrative in 10:17-27a (27b is uncertain), which has been edited only at the beginning (vv. 18,19a) by the Deuteronomistic historian. Two elements in this narrative point to the sphere of the wars of Yahweh. (a) Saul is chosen by casting lots, which is known otherwise only in the Yahweh war in Josh. 7:16ff. (Casting lots was a way in which Yahweh indicated his choice and was not considered arbitrary by the contemporaries of this author.) (b) After Yahweh chose him to be king (here the people merely acclaim him as king, while 1 S. 11:15 describes the political elevation of the king), Saul created a standing army at Gibeah whose hearts God had touched (10:26), i.e., it is an army understood in a sacral sense. In addition perhaps we should refer to two other points. (c) The conflict described in 1 S. 15 can be understood only if the central issue is not merely the difference between sacrifice and the devoted thing, but also that Saul, as head of the tribes of Israel (v. 17), was explicitly responsible for observing the precepts of the Yahweh war and failed

---

[14] Quell, 152.

[15] *Ibid.,* 156f.

[16] Westermann, *ATD, in loc.*

[17] See below.

in his office by disobeying them. Under these circumstances, Saul's removal from office is actually the proper way to resolve the conflict. (d) In connection with Saul's anointing, Yahweh tells Samuel (9:17) that Saul was supposed to restrain the people ('atsar here does not mean "to rule," as many scholars like to translate it). Since Saul is assigned the task of leading Israel in war against the Philistines in 9:16, and since 9:17 refers back to this, something of a military nature must be intended in v. 17 also. In my opinion, it denotes the military consolidation of the widely divergent tribes of Israel, which could be consolidated only by summoning them to follow Yahweh, their military commander-in-chief.

Summarizing, we may say that the use of bhr in 1 S. 10:24 most easily denotes a careful choice of the official by Yahweh himself, i.e., by the commander-in-chief, for the purpose of fighting the war of Yahweh.

In the biblical tradition, the choice of David has been connected with that of Saul. 2 S. 6:21 puts the following words in the mouth of David: "It was before Yahweh, who chose me above your (i.e., Michal's) father, and above all his house, to appoint me as naghidh (prince) over Israel, the people of Yahweh, that I humbled myself." The connection with the choice of Saul is clear, but the event to which this passage refers is not: when was David chosen in the manner described in 2 S. 6:21? The only real narrative of David's choice is found in 1 S. 16:1-13, and it is almost universally agreed that the interpretation in 2 S. (5:2) 6:21 does not refer to this passage. Rather, 2 S. 6:21 simply expresses positively what 1 S. 15:28 had said negatively: "And Samuel said to him (Saul), Yahweh has torn the kingdom of Israel from you this day, and has given it to a neighbor of yours, who is better than you." 1 S. 25:28 and 2 S. 5:2 explain the sense in which David is Saul's neighbor: after Saul's rejection and before David's flight it was David who conducted the wars of Yahweh and led out and brought in Israel, and not the king. Thus finally, it remains to be asked whether the reason behind 2 S. 16:18, which certainly contains a cajolery of Hushai, is that Absalom (according to the words of Hushai) conducts the war of Yahweh against David, because Absalom had stolen the hearts of the men of Israel under the pretext that he would judge righteously (15:6) and therefore fought against the very David whom he had denounced because he was doing a poor job as judge.

From the time of David on, the word bhr disappears from the language used to describe the raising up of a king. This could be due to an accident in transmitting the tradition. But it is much more likely that this word disappeared because David changed the military arrangement in Israel and with one exception[18] the levy was no longer used. Thus to me it seems impossible to avoid the conclusion that Dt. 17:15a in the Deuteronomic law of the king is the remnant of a very old tradition, to which reference is also made in 1 S. 8:9b and 10:25.[19] In no case does Dt. 17:15a represent a Deuteronomic addition; this motif is too isolated in Deuteronomy for this to be the case, and furthermore the Deuteronomistic history uses bhr in connection with the choice of a king only in 1 K. 8:16 and 11:34. These passages seem to refer to the Deuteronomic law, so that

---

[18] On this see Noth, *History of Israel* (trans. 1958), 194f.
[19] See *ZAW*, 77 (1965), 286ff.

the Deuteronomistic history does not consider any dynasty to have been chosen
by God except the house of Saul and the house of David. To be sure, Jeroboam I
was called (1 K. 11:29ff.); but he brought upon the northern state those sins
which sealed their fate. None of his successors deviated from these sins, and
thus after David nothing more of a fundamental nature could be said about a
divine election. It is clear that *bḥr* is used here in a way different from the way
it is used in the primitive tradition in that the choice of the royal house in the
Deuteronomistic history is made parallel to the choice of Jerusalem. It preserves
no recollection that originally the choice of the king was connected with his
responsibility to conduct the war of Yahweh, but it treats the choice of David
(like the choice of the sanctuary) as a factor in salvation. However, this was not
formulated into a system and a dogma until the Chronicler's history (1 Ch.
28:4ff.; cf. Ps. 78:67-70). Finally we must mention Hag. 2:23. Here in an oracle
of Yahweh the announcement is made that Zerubbabel will be chosen as Yahweh's signet ring. One should not think of leadership in war here, because
Yahweh himself will overthrow the throne of kingdoms and destroy the strength
of the nations. Zerubbabel will be Yahweh's attorney, although the text does not
specify the sense in which this is meant. He may be regarded as carefully tested,
since among other things he advocated the separation of Jerusalem from Samaria
and thus a strong Yahwistic policy.

Consequently, in biblical accounts dealing with the choice of the king *bḥr*
experienced an important change. With regard to king Saul *bḥr* meant quite
simply a proper choice of a commander-in-chief for the sanctity of war. Thus
there is hardly any justification for speaking of a pronounced ideological use of
bḥr[20] unless one wants to see an ideology in the sanctity of war and in the careful
choice of a king to conduct it. The view in 2 S. 6:21 (David) was still fundamentally the same, but this use of *bḥr* stops with David (Absalom). *bḥr* appears as
a primitive concept in Dt. 17:15a, but as a primitive idea it becomes the bearer
of a new idea in the Deuteronomistic scribal circle. Now David and his dynasty
are regarded as the chosen representative of the kingdom, and the original simple
concept of choice receives an ideological component inasmuch as the purpose
of the Deuteronomistic history is to show that Yahweh recognized the choice of
the Davidides until Manasseh brought this dynasty to an end. Thus *bḥr* gets a
meaning that is defined more forcibly in 2 S. 7 than in 6:21. The Chronicler's
statements affirming that Solomon was also chosen (1 Ch. 28:5), which probably
are intended to cast the blame for the division of the kingdom entirely on the
northern kingdom, stand in the Deuteronomistic tradition, although the Chronicler entirely omits the northern kingdom as an element restricting and correcting
the Davidides. While the choice of David is rather peripheral and quite insignificant in comparison with the choice of Jerusalem in the Deuteronomist's view,
the dogma of David is complete in the Chronicler's work, even though neither
of these historical works assigns a present significance to the kingdom. *bḥr*
points not backward but forward in Hag. 2:23 and especially in Isa. 42:1, which

---

20 Contra Quell, 149, 36f.

sees a chosen one whose features are to be surmised rather than specifically comprehended. [21]

3. *Choice of the Priesthood.* Now briefly let us take a look at the choice of the priesthood. We have already mentioned the choice of the Elides above. In view of the development of *bḥr* in the interpretation of the choice of the king, the following observations can be made. In 1 S. 2:27ff. the prevailing viewpoint seems to be that Yahweh carefully chose a family to perform a specific task, and thus it is logical that Yahweh can reject this family if it despises him instead of honoring him (v. 30b). This choice is not absolute, but is determined by a purpose and can be revoked if those chosen deviate from that purpose. In my opinion, this is also the meaning of *bḥr* in Dt. 18:5. However, the situation is different in 21:5, a very casual statement concerning the choice of the Levitical priests. Here the choice includes a privilege that guards the Levitical priests against the claims of other (would-be) priesthoods–it is given a dogmatic character. Of course, the idea of Yahweh's choice is not a central point in the theology of the Deuteronomic and Deuteronomistic writing circle. Therefore the word *bḥr* is not strengthened or even emphasized in this material, but would seem to be simply a reflection of Dt. 18:5. Its use in Nu. 16:5,7; 17:20(5) is certainly different. In these passages the major point of interest is the process of choosing and not so much the priestly qualifications. Therefore, the main idea is the conviction that a religious practice cannot be invented or managed arbitrarily; this reform program was probably thought through carefully first in the Deuteronomic cult formula and is the result of the bitter experiences of the preexilic period with cultic acts.

4. *"The Place Which Yahweh Chooses."* The formula "the *place* which Yahweh has chosen . . . " does not occur in the Deuteronomistic history. The only exception is Josh. 9:27b, but it has no counterevidence since it is part of an addition to the primitive tradition in Josh. 9 (this is not a Deuteronomistic gloss as Noth assumes, [22] since the Deuteronomistic *maqom,* "place," is not used, but part of the later history as Hertzberg thinks). [23] The Deuteronomistic history says either "the city . . . " or "Jerusalem . . . ," and therefore must be omitted in searching for the explanation of the meaning and origin of this formula.

The Deuteronomic formula appears in six variations:

a. The short formula "the place which Yahweh has chosen": Dt. 12:18,26; 14:25; 15:20; 16:7,16; 17:8,10; 18:6; 31:11 (Josh. 9:27).

b. The short formula plus "in one of your tribes": 12:14.

c. The short formula plus "to make his name dwell (*leshakken*) there": 12:11; 14:23; 16:2,6,11; 26:2.

d. The short formula plus "to put (*lasum*) his name there": 12:21; 14:24.

e. The short formula plus "out of all your tribes" plus "to put his name there" plus "to make his habitation there" (*leshikhno*): 12:5.

---

[21] Von Rad, *OT Theol,* II (trans. 1965), 247.

[22] Noth, *Josua²,* *in loc.*

[23] Hertzberg, *ATD,* IX, *in loc.*

As the Massoretic pointing stands, the construction of this last sentence is un-usually involved. It reads: "But to the place which Yahweh your God has chosen out of all your tribes to put his name there–ye turn yourselves to its inhabitant, and thou shalt go thither." *leshikhno* was probably inserted, because *darash* when construed with *'el* always refers to a person (God, other gods, spirits of the dead), and never to a place. Consequently, it does not seem best to suppose that the textual error was made in the punctuation of *leshikhno*. Rather, it seems to be the insertion of *leshikhno thidhreshu,* "ye turn yourselves to its inhabitant," that has changed the emphasis. The context seems to call for an emphasis on the idea that the Israelites are not to make many altars arbitrarily, but are to go to one chosen sanctuary (read *thabho'u,* "you [pl.] shall come," instead of *ubha'tha,* "and thou [sing.] shalt come"), but as the MT now stands the emphasis is on the idea that they are not to go to the sanctuaries of other gods, but to Yahweh's sanctuary. In any case Dt. 12:5 contains the most expanded stage of the formula and need not be considered any further. From an analysis of the other formulas, it does not seem best to regard the short formula as the origin of the Deuteron-omic cult formula, because although there can be no question that it means the central sanctuary everywhere, this does not prove that as such we are forced to conclude that it means *one* sanctuary, as is clear in that it was thought necessary to add "in one of your tribes" in 12:14. [24] The only two forms that can even be considered as the possible original form are d. and e., which expand the short form by adding a final infinitive clause. This clause does not specify the purpose of the choice, as Hulst has correctly seen–it stands naturally in the normal wor-ship. Instead, the author states the basis on which the sanctuary was chosen. To paraphrase, the two forms have the following meaning: one cannot worship Yahweh in every place that has been designated as a place of worship. Rather, Yahweh himself determines the place where he can be worshipped in an accept-able manner. In principle, then, it would be possible for Yahweh to choose more than one place to be worshipped; but the place he has chosen is determined by his having made his name dwell there or having put his name there. Of course, if it is asked where such a place is to be found, most of the sanctuaries are ex-cluded from the very outset. There is no record of this sort of place at Beer-sheba or Tabor, at Gilgal or Mizpah, or at Shiloh or Bethel or Shechem. Yahweh may have appeared at these places, but this does not mean that he has made his name dwell there. Thus the concluding phrase in Dt. 12:5 already contains the program of reform; it does not contain a theology of the name of God, but, as de Vaux has shown, an affirmation of ownership. [25] This represents a strict inter-pretation of the broad statement in Ex. 20:24b: "in every place where I cause my name to be remembered I will come to you and bless you."

But the OT has preserved this kind of affirmation of ownership only with regard to Jerusalem. It is portrayed clearly and entirely apart from Deuteronomic

---

[24] A. R. Hulst in his important review of Vriezen, *Die Erwählung Israels,* in *BiOr,* 19 (1962), 61, holds otherwise; but he does argue that the short formula denotes the central sanctuary.

[25] R. de Vaux, *BZAW,* 105 (1967), 219ff.

influence in the ancient text in Ps. 132:13f. This psalm, which is certainly pre-exilic, [26] represents the Zion theology, in which Yahweh's occupation of Zion is not attributed to the king's will, but to Yahweh's own act. The choice of the king is based on the choice of Zion, so that the power of the king emanates from Zion (Ps. 110:2). This significant theology has so permeated OT thought that in reality Royal Hymns like Pss. 110 and 2 have become Hymns of Yahweh. But the pre-requisite for this was the affirmation of Yahweh's ownership of Zion, which provided the institutional assurance of independence guaranteed in relationship to and by the kingship itself. The document that contains this extremely im-portant conception of throne and altar is Ps. 132, which states:

> For Yahweh has chosen Zion;
> he has desired it for his habitation:
> "This is my resting place for ever;
> here I will dwell, for I have desired it" (vv. 13f.).

Thus, when we survey the whole situation, the following interpretation seems to be demanded. (a) The short formula always simply refers to one of the long forms. (b) The short formula with the inf. *lasum,* which (apart from the distended form in Dt. 12:5) occurs in only two subordinate clauses (12:21; 14:24), is also found in the Deuteronomistic history (1 K. 11:36; 14:21 = 2 Ch. 12:13; 2 K. 21:7), which is not the case with the short formula plus *leshakken*. This seems to in-dicate that there is a significant difference between these two long forms, and that only one of them was acceptable to the Deuteronomistic historian. In light of this, two things are worthy of note. (1) The formula *sum shemo,* "to put his name," is exactly equivalent to the Akk. expression *šakānu šumšu,* which ap-pears in two letters of Abdi-Ḫepa written from Jerusalem in the pre-Israelite period (EA No. 282, lines 60-63; No. 288, lines 5-7). It has the ring of a dis-tinctively Jerusalemite tradition. (2) The same expression is well suited to the desire of the Deuteronomistic historian to proclaim that the son of David built a house for Yahweh's name. By way of contrast the short formula with *leshakken* gives the impression that Yahweh himself provides a dwelling place for his name, because a man-made structure would be superfluous. The temple building must have always called to mind its builder Solomon, whose name undoubtedly con-tinued to be inseparably connected with the division of the kingdom. But the *leshakken,* bypassing Solomon, seems to be connected with king David and the unity of the tribes under one name. (c) The most appropriate introduction to the Deuteronomic cult formula seems to be in the speech in Dt. 12:(8)9-12, which is continued in v. 13 in the singular.

As has already been pointed out, the Deuteronomistic history does not use *maqom,* "place," in connection with this formula. Instead it speaks of the city and its temple. This programmatic statement appears in 1 K. 8:16f.: "I (Yahweh) chose no city in all the tribes of Israel in which to build a house. But I chose 'Jerusalem that my name might be there, and I chose' David to be over my people Israel. Now he (Yahweh) was with the heart of David my father to build

---

[26] Cf. Kraus, *BK, in loc.*

a house for the name of Yahweh, the God of Israel." It is not Zion, but all Jerusalem, that is the place where Yahweh's name would be, and the chosen kingdom was entrusted with the task of building a house to his name. Elsewhere in the Deuteronomistic history the concept of choice is mentioned in only three connections: (a) the dedication of the temple, 1 K. 8:16,44; (b) the so-called division of the kingdom, 1 K. 11:13,32,36; 14:21; (c) king Manasseh and the rejection of the city and the temple, 2 K. 21:7; 23:27. The last two contexts are of particular interest. In the account of the division of the kingdom, the perpetuity of the dynasty of David is not based simply on the choice of David (this is peripheral in 11:34), but on the choice of Jerusalem, as is stated most impressively in 11:36, and then in 11:13,32, which are derived from it. This makes it probable that the Deuteronomistic historian had already taken into consideration the tradition of the City of God (cf. Ps. 101:8) on which Yahweh wished to confer his special protection. For this reason it is that much more terrible and decisive that Rehoboam the Davidide, to whom Yahweh gave the kingdom and whom Yahweh allowed to live in the chosen city, did that which was evil in the eyes of Yahweh. Thus from the very beginning, the Deuteronomistic historian felt it necessary to bring accusations against the Davidic dynasty until the city and the temple were rejected because of the sins of the Davidide Manasseh (2 K. 23:27). While the Deuteronomistic historian spared his people nothing concerning the severity of the judgment, the Chronicler repeats only words that express a positive attitude toward the temple and the city, in spite of 2 K. 23:27 (see 2 Ch. 6:5; 7:12,16; 12:13; 33:7). But Zechariah announces the new choice of Jerusalem (Zec. 1:17; 2:16[12]), which means that he is not willing to admit the abrogation of the divine choice of this city, and therefore here and in Isa. 14:1 'odh is to be translated by "further." But in my view the Deuteronomistic historian and Zechariah think that the choice of Jerusalem can be nullified just as the author of 1 S. 2:28 thinks the choice of the house of Eli can be nullified, because this choice is not based on the city's relationship to God, but Jerusalem was chosen for a particular purpose.

5. *The Election of the People.* Up to this point, the meaning of the word *bhr* throughout has turned out to be "choice" in connection with intelligible, verifiable categories. This also applied to the cult place, which was determined by Yahweh's name having taken up its dwelling there—an occurrence that had its unforgettable mooring in Israel's history. It has been shown that the same thing was true with regard to the choice of the people, and the word *bhr* is not broad enough to cover the range of ideas included in the German word *Erwählung* (English *choice*) or the dogmatic rubric *electio*. [27] Instead *bhr* conveys a relatively narrow portion of this idea when it is used in the OT to speak of Yahweh's choice of Israel to be his people, and the fundamental idea of *bhr* only rarely stands at the center of what is meant by *electio*.

Everywhere that *bhr* occurs in relationship to persons, it denotes choice out

---

[27] So correctly Vriezen, *passim.*

of a group (generally out of the totality of the people), so that the chosen one discharges a function in relationship to the group. Thus throughout, *bḥr* includes the idea of separating, but in the sense that the one separated by *bḥr*, "choosing, selection," stood that much more clearly in the service of the whole. In my opinion the election of the people in the OT is to be treated in a similar way. The horizon of the election of the people of Israel is the peoples of the world, in relationship to which as a whole the "individual" Israel was chosen. *bḥr* as a technical term for the election of the people of Israel stands under the symbol of universalism.

At the very outset, this investigation is faced with a difficulty: As soon as *bḥr* is clearly used to convey the concept of the election of the people of Israel (and this is the case in the Deuteronomic/Deuteronomistic writing circle), it is mentioned so casually and unemphatically that it cannot possibly be a deliberate proclamation there. The important passages where *bḥr* is used in this sense are Dt. 4:37; 7:6f.; 10:14f.; 14:2; and 1 K. 3:8. We read in Dt. 14:1f.: "You are the sons of Yahweh your God; you shall not cut yourselves or make any baldness on your foreheads for the dead. For you are a people holy to Yahweh your God, and Yahweh has chosen you to be a people for his own possession, out of all the peoples that are on the face of the earth." If we compare this passage with the Deuteronomic cult formula, where the concept of choosing something or someone out of a whole also occurs twice (Dt. 12:5,14), we find this idea: Israel, which was chosen as a peculiar people from among and in relationship to the peoples of the world, cannot adopt those kinds of superstitious practices which are described in 14:1. [28] Here again *bḥr* is entirely rational and understandable. Yahweh has worked in behalf of his people so that they would be a peculiar (holy) people. As the people that is distinguished by the unique unalterability of its God, Israel has its role in the circle of nations. It might be said that Israel is Yahweh's witness, although this is not specifically stated before Deutero-Isaiah. In Dt. 14:2 *bḥr* is used only very casually in a subordinate clause, and not as a proclamation. The same is true of its use in 7:1ff. In this passage Israel is commanded to defeat the peoples of Canaan, to utterly destroy them, to make no covenant with them, and to show them no mercy; and then this reason is given: "For you are a people holy to Yahweh your God; Yahweh your God has chosen you to be a people for his own possession, out of all the peoples that are on the face of the earth" (v. 6). This text assumes that Israel was quite willing to come to terms with the Canaanites, to learn from them, and to intermarry with them. It assumes that the Canaanite way of life and religiosity had a great attraction for Israel and the required unyieldingness was felt to be a strange law. If such unyieldingness is required, something important must be at stake, and actually the Deuteronomist sees in the Canaanite religion simply those things which are not sanctioned by God, viz., altars made by men; rites devised by

---

28 Otherwise Vriezen, 51ff., who is influenced too much by the motif of the holy people in his view of the Deuteronomic passages, and thus interprets them in the direction of the Deuteronomic Torah. Furthermore, it seems to me that Vriezen does not take into account sufficiently the contingency of the election in Deuteronomy.

men; this entire embellishment of deities with the spirit of the blessing of grain, oil, and wine, of the womb and of the flock, which Hosea called the spirit of harlotry, and in which there are no standards other than that of securing a blessing. In this sort of religion God does not really have anything to say, but is merely the guarantor of human interests, which are also restricted to everything that can be represented in the *hieros gamos* (sacred marriage). If Israel does not take an inflexible stand against this religion she can never be the people of Yahweh, because he can never be understood as he really is as long as Canaanitism is connected with him. But in this case *bḥr* means that in her struggle against the Canaanite spirit Israel is the people chosen with reference to all peoples, in that all religions have to take their stand in the struggle Israel undertakes paradigmatically and in the final analysis inflexibly.

That which is stated concerning individual regulations in Dt. 14:1f. and 7:1ff. is applied to the entire law in 10:14f. (pl.); it is not necessary to discuss this in detail here. However, 7:7f. is important: "It was not because you were more in number than any other people that Yahweh· set his love upon you and chose you, for you were the fewest of all peoples; but it is because Yahweh loves you, and is keeping the oath which he swore to your fathers, that Yahweh has brought you out with a mighty hand. . . . " The nation of Israel always saw the necessity of viewing the greatness of the nation in light of the greatness of her God. This viewpoint is clearly expressed in this passage. Israel is smaller than all peoples; her God is not that of national power, and the viewpoint of her election is not determined by the number of people that occupy the land. 7:7f. also speak quite positively of the undemonstrable mystery of the love of God for his people, as Rowley has shown so impressively. [29] But it is crucial that the choice of Israel is to be understood not in terms of national might, but of the love with which Yahweh loves his people.

The statement found in Solomon's prayer at Gibeon in 1 K. 3:8 seems to contradict Dt. 7:7f., because at first glance Solomon seems to be speaking of the important chosen people which he must rule. However, the text follows a different line of thought. V. 9 uses the language of international wisdom when it says: "Give thy servant therefore *an understanding heart* to govern thy people, that I may discern between good and evil." [30] Here the king wishes something for all nations representatively, and the people that Yahweh chose stands at the center of the nations.

In all these passages, with the possible exception of Dt. 10:12ff. (which is certainly not very early), it almost goes without saying that *bḥr* is not emphasized. Is the situation any different in Deutero-Isaiah? It seems to me that the point in Deutero-Isaiah is not that this prophet is proclaiming the choice of Israel, but that the catastrophe of the exile confirms this choice. To be sure, the prophet leaves no doubt that he considers the existence of the people as a people obliterated; but to him this fact and the message he has to proclaim are not an occasion for despair, but for witnessing. Yahweh declared that which was going to happen.

---

[29] H. H. Rowley, *The Biblical Doctrine of Election,* chap. 1.
[30] Cf. H. Brunner, "Das hörende Herz," *ThLZ,* 79 (1954), 697ff.

Because that which he had announced came to pass, Yahweh is proved to be the only real God in the lawsuit with the nations, since no god does what Yahweh did, viz., deliver his own people to destruction in order to give those that remain the prospect of truth; or, to state it differently, since Yahweh did not renounce his deity for the sake of saving his people (Isa. 43:8ff.). Thus the extinguished people are a people of hope, because at the very moment they know they are extinguished they are placed in a situation where they can observe the uniqueness of their God, and thus are instructed to proclaim to the nations that Yahweh is the only God because he shows no respect of persons (43:10). Consequently the choice is by no means abrogated (41:8ff.). Formerly Yahweh led up Israel, in the person of Abraham, from a corner of the earth; what would cause him to save his people from Babylon? Indeed, water must flow in the wilderness for the chosen ones (43:20), and the emperor Cyrus is called to burst the bonds of the miserable people who are no more and who have merely the unique God as their only God (45:4). Thus Yahweh will pour water on the thirsty ground and Israel will spring up like fresh grass (44:1ff.). Israel's existence is not gone. On the contrary! Her importance to the world is just arriving.

Thus it is clear that also in Deutero-Isaiah *bḥr* is not a new motif, but one that is well known. It is used paradoxically in the preaching of this prophet to show vividly and clearly that Israel was chosen for the nations, and at the very moment she was destroyed was put in a position where she could enter into a lawsuit with the nations.

We mention Ezk. 20:5 only in passing. Here *bḥr* seems to be used in an entirely absolute sense, but we must always keep in mind that when Yahweh speaks, it is the ruler of the world of Ezk. 1 who speaks and not the God of the ark. However, like Deutero-Isaiah, Ezekiel concentrates almost exclusively on the exiles and proclaims God to the dispersed people as the God of the whole world who does not reject his people, but afflicts them when they are obstinate. Isa. 14:1 is different. It announces a new choice of the people of Israel, which is perhaps analogous to the Deuteronomistic concept of the rejection of Jerusalem and to the new choice of Jerusalem proclaimed by Zechariah. [31]

If one raises the question of the origin of the *bḥr* motif which is assumed as already well known in all these passages, in my opinion it is most natural to look to the influence of the hymnic tradition. This is stated most simply in Ps. 117: "Praise Yahweh, all nations!/ Extol him, all peoples! For great is his steadfast love toward us;/ and the faithfulness of Yahweh endures for ever. Hallelujah!" In this hymn all nations of the earth, the globe, and the heavenly court are called to praise, but the object of praise is what Yahweh had done for and with Israel. A biblical writer can use *bḥr* to convey this idea, and he can do this quite incidentally and without displaying any programmatic concept by using *bḥr* merely to make his readers aware of what he is saying, as is the case in Ps. 33:8-15. The words in Ps. 135:1-4 are addressed to the servants of Yahweh in the outer court. But this much can be said: the election of the people of Israel did not attain the level of a dogmatic topic in the OT under the word *bḥr*. On the

---

[31] Contra Vriezen, 74.

other hand, it is worthy of note that in Isa. 65:9,15,22; Ps. 105:6,43; 106:5; 1 Ch. 16:13 the "sons of Jacob" are called chosen ones (*bechirim*). Like *bachûr* in the sense of "elect, chosen," *bachîr* in these passages actually paved the way for a consciousness of being chosen of God, and it has only little in common with the way *bḥr* is used to describe the choice of the people of Israel, and denotes the members of God's family. It is no longer a question of mission; rather their distinctiveness is derived from the God who chose them. There is a growing consciousness that as a true Israelite one bears the yoke of the kingdom of God.

6. *Human Choices As Acts of Religious Confession.* Nothing certain can be determined about the meaning of *bḥr* in Jgs. 5:8 because of the textual problems in this verse. Thus, it is from Deuteronomy on that *bḥr* first appears as an act of religious confession. Dt. 30:19 admonishes the hearers of the law to choose life, i.e., the author strongly affirmed that Israelites had chosen and still were to choose differently from others. Thus in this passage *bḥr* exhibits a new consciousness, viz., that here the author is primarily concerned with the difference between that which Yahweh wants and that which Israel chooses, and understands Israel's existence as the result of an act of confession. The classical expression of this is found in Josh. 24:15,22 (from the Deuteronomistic historian). In a historical interpretation, the Deuteronomistic historian brings to a level of consciousness something that lay below the surface from the beginning in Israel's faith, viz., that Israel had made a decision to serve Yahweh and now she can and will be affected by this choice.[32] In Jgs. 10:14 this choice comes into conflict with the choice of other gods, i.e., Israel does not fall into the power of other gods, but chooses them, because one cannot serve other gods without denying the uniqueness and exclusiveness of Yahweh. Similarly, 1 S. 8:18(12:13) speaks contemptuously of "the king whom you have chosen." Just as no other god can be put alongside Yahweh if Yahweh is to remain himself, so no other power can be put alongside him which as a worldly power would also guarantee life (1 S. 8:8)–national common sense corrupts religion.

Now a later use of the word *bḥr* agrees with this use of the word. It is more concerned with the aspect of deciding, so that *bḥr* is not so much the carefully weighed choice as the careful activity of choosing itself. Thus the author of Isa. 56:4 can declare that if a eunuch (who was considered to be unworthy to participate in the cult and thus stood on the outer fringe of the Yahweh community) decided (*bḥr*) to do the things that pleased Yahweh, then Yahweh would acknowledge him for what he had done. Conversely, the reproof in 65:12 (cf. 66:4; Prov. 1:29) says that those who are addressed have not decided to do that which pleases Yahweh, but sanction other points of view. And even Yahweh himself can be reported to say that he could not decide in favor of a specific form of fasting which was being practiced, because it was inappropriate at that time, and in place of it he stated the form of fasting on which he had decided (Isa. 58:5f.). In Ps. 25:12 we almost have an ambiguous teaching. This poem says that anyone who wishes to be instructed by Yahweh will be instructed by him concerning the

---

[32] For details cf. Perlitt, 239ff.

way he should choose, i.e., in favor of which he should decide. The choice is and remains an action of the godly. Life and death will be set before him, and tacitly he is made aware of the risk that is involved in choosing life. Here one would do well to compare Ps. 119:30,173, where the worshipper emphasizes that he has chosen the way of faithfulness, the way of Yahweh's precepts. Finally, we must mention Job 34:4,33 which mark the transition to the meaning "to examine," which occurs in Aramaic. These verses state that in a legal case a decision must be made as to what is good and what is bad. In these passages *bḥr* is not quite identical with the Aramaic word meaning "to examine," since the context is not limited to examining the evidence, but also involves passing judgment. Nevertheless, throughout this passage the examination is an aspect of the choosing intended by the word *bḥr,* and thus the transition to this idea is not surprising at all.

7. *Summary.* An investigation of the use of *bḥr* in postexilic Judaism lies outside the scope of the present study. Unfortunately the views expressed in *TDNT* [33] make no attempt to comprehend the religious problem posed in post-biblical Judaism by the word *bḥr* and the concept of election.

Vriezen correctly stated the fundamental concept conveyed by the OT word *bḥr* when he wrote: "In the OT the choice is always the action of God, of his grace, and always contains a mission for man; and only out of this mission can man comprehend the choice of God." [34] However, this general explanation may not be applicable to the term *bechirim,* "chosen ones," which is used of the godly. [35] Instead this seems to be a defensive term which indeed still shows a consciousness of mission, but carries the idea that one must be tested by suffering and that only Yahweh himself can produce in one the sense of being chosen. But this also takes us beyond the use of *bḥr* in the OT. In any case, in the OT *bḥr* is used not to describe that which constitutes the basic relationship between God and his people (this concept is conveyed by the *yadha',* "to know," of Am. 3:1), but to denote that which results from this basic relationship. Thus when Neh. 9:7 says that Yahweh has already chosen Abraham, this fits the situation of the prayer in this context, the purpose of which was to make known in the syncretism of the time of Ezra and Nehemiah that Judah has the mission of maintaining her identity and of resisting the temptation to be assimilated by the nations, as long as election is to mean a mission to the nations.

Seebass

---

[33] *TDNT,* IV, 170-172, 182ff.
[34] Vriezen, 109.
[35] Contra Vriezen, 109.

בָּטַח *bāṭach;* בֶּטַח *beṭach;* בִּטְחָה *biṭchāh;*
בִּטָּחוֹן *biṭṭāchôn;* מִבְטָח *mibhṭāch*

Contents: I. Etymology and Forms. II. Meaning. III. Usage: 1. Security That Is Taken for Granted; 2. False Security; 3. Security in God. IV. Historical Development.

I. Etymology and Forms. The root *bṭḥ* is preserved in Middle Hebrew and in Jewish Aramaic, but it can hardly be traced with certainty in other Semitic languages. The Arab. *baṭaḥa* has an entirely different meaning: "to knock down, throw down." Whether *ba-ti-i-ti* which occurs in EA 145, 56 is really cognate with Heb. *bṭḥ* is at least not so clear that any absolute conclusions can be based on it. So the meaning of *bṭḥ* can be determined only by its usage.

Köhler, to be sure, did attempt to determine the original meaning of *batach*. He compares *'abhattichim,* "watermelons," with Arab. *baṭaḥ,* attested by Musil,[1] which "means a mare which is so pregnant that the offspring can be felt. It is easy to see what the fully pregnant mare and watermelons have in common. Both are 'plump, taut.'" Thus Köhler thinks that the same root lies behind both words and that it means "to be plump, taut" = "to be firm, tight." But it would be just as natural to conclude that it meant "to be swelling, growing," or "to become round." In any case the meaning "to be firm, tight," cannot be inferred with certainty from a comparison of these two words. Thus it is unlikely that this root inferred by Köhler is identical with the root *baṭaḥ,* "to feel secure." The proof Köhler gives for making this identification is that in all cases, "to be firm" is the original meaning of the words that mean "to trust, be confident, rely on." But this is questionable linguistically. Thus if one wishes to trace Heb. *'abhattichim* and Arab. *baṭaḥ* back to the same root, which is still worth considering, he must distinguish it from *bṭḥ* "to feel secure." Indeed, in Hebrew homonymous roots are nothing uncommon.

But perhaps Köhler's conjecture about the existence of a root *baṭaḥ,* "to be plump, taut, swelling, growing," might help solve a *crux interpretum. mabhtichi* in Ps. 22:10 (Eng. v. 9) poses difficulties for commentators: can one expect an infant to trust? But would not the context be clear if this text were translated: "For thou didst take me from the womb, thou didst make me plump (fat) on my mother's breast"? To be sure, the basis for this interpretation is weak. But still

---

bāṭach. J. Blau, "Über homonyme und angeblich homonyme Wurzeln," *VT,* 6 (1956), 244; R. Bultmann, "The OT View of Hope," *TDNT,* II, 521-23; L. Köhler, "Hebräische Vokabeln. 18. אבטחים 19. Die Wurzel בטח," *ZAW,* 55 (1937), 172f.; L. Kopf, "Arabische Etymologien und Parallelen zum Bibelwörterbuch," *VT,* 8 (1958), 161-215, *bṭḥ,* 165-68; A. Weiser, "The Stem בטח," *TDNT,* VI, 191f.

[1] Musil, *Arabia Peträa,* 3, 273.

the context actually demands a concrete act of God on the worshipper from his youth on, and this would consist of God not only taking him from the womb, but also making him grow on his mother's breast. Skoss thinks this should be translated, "who laid me on my mother's breast," [2] and Kopf, "who caused me to lie (protected) on my mother's breast." [3]

G. R. Driver, [4] J. Blau, and especially L. Kopf take the Arab. *baṭaḥa*, "to knock down, throw on the ground," VII "to fall down, to lie stretched out," etc., as the starting-point for the semantic investigation: "but on the basis of the uses of the Hebrew root itself it is possible to demonstrate a transition from the meaning 'to lie' to the meaning 'to rely on, to trust in.'" [5] The use of the verbs *shakhabh*, "to lie down, take rest" (Job 11:18; Hos. 2:20[18]), and *rabhats*, "to lie down" (Isa. 14:30), with *labhetach*, "in safety," also points to this original meaning of *bṭḥ*.

The proper name *mbṭḥyhw* is found in the Lachish Ostracon I, 4; and we encounter *mbṭḥyh*, "Yahweh is (my) confidence," and *mpṭḥyh* in the Elephantine Papyri. [6]

Various words are derived from the root *bṭḥ*: first there is a verb *batach*, which usually appears in the qal and rarely in the hiphil; then there is a noun in the segholate form *betach*, which is usually used adverbially; and there is also another noun with the *mem*-preformative *mibhtach*. We may add to this isolated forms such as *bitchah* (Isa. 30:15), *bittachon* (Isa. 36:4; Eccl. 9:4), and *battuchoth* (Job 12:6). Since the meaning varies in a similar way in all forms, it is appropriate to treat them together.

II. Meaning. The derivatives of the root *bṭḥ* first of all have the meaning "to feel secure, be unconcerned," or, specifying the reason for the security, "to rely on something or someone." However, quite often this general meaning has a negative ring: the thing on which one relies turns out to be deceptive, so that the words derived from the root *bṭḥ* are actually used to indicate a false security, a *securitas*. But these words are also used to convey the idea of complete security in God alone. This ambivalence is significant in understanding the use of the root *bṭḥ*. It was also felt by the translators of the LXX. They rendered *bṭḥ* in the negative sense predominantly by *pepoithénai*, "to trust in, believe in, put confidence in," but when a text used *bṭḥ* to convey the idea of relying on God, they ordinarily used *elpízein*, "to hope." The LXX translation of *bṭḥ* in Ps. 115 is perhaps of particular significance: in v. 8 (LXX 113:16) it is rendered by *pepoithótes*, but in vv. 9,10,11 (LXX 113:17,18,19) by *elpízein;* cf. also Ps. 49:7(6) (LXX 48:7); 135:18 (LXX 134:18); 146:3 (LXX 145:3). Frequently *bṭḥ* is translated by *pepoithénai* in Isaiah and Jeremiah when the reference is to false security.

---

2 Skoss, *Jewish Studies Kohut* (New York, 1935), 552.
3 Kopf, 166.
4 G. R. Driver, *Festschrift Robinson* (1950), 59f.
5 Kopf, 166.
6 *AP*, 295a, 297b; *BMAP*, 187.

III. Usage.

1. *Security That Is Taken for Granted.* In passages where derivatives of
the root *bṭḥ* are used to describe relationships between human beings, frequently
they describe security that is taken for granted, but which also turns out to be disappointed, i.e., a credulous, frivolous, or even arrogant unconcern and security.

The Shechemites were credulous (Gen. 34:25). They felt secure because they
had made a *berith,* "covenant," with Jacob. For this reason the deed of the two
sons of Jacob was even more questionable when they took advantage of this
unconcern! (In this text *betach* refers to *ha'ir,* "the city"; it was not the sons of
Jacob who felt secure, but the inhabitants of the city.) The situation in Laish
(Jgs. 18:7,10,27) is similar. The city is completely unsuspecting and feels secure
(*shoqet ubhoteach*); and for this reason it is taken by surprise when the Danites
attack. Their gullibility is their downfall. But at the same time the biblical writer
censures the Danites for taking advantage of this situation.

Prov. 3:29 explicitly emphasizes that when people take advantage of those
who trust in them, it is a transgression against loyalty and trust: "Do not plan
evil against your neighbor who dwells trustingly beside you." Therefore, it is evil
when Gog devises a scheme to go up against a land that lives in complete unconcern (Ezk. 38:10,11). The reproof in Mic. 2:8 probably has a similar meaning.
Thus *bṭḥ* can denote an unconcern based on a security that is taken for granted,
but which always poses a threat for those who possess it.

The attitude of the Midianites who assumed that they would not be attacked
by the Israelites after they had made a raid on them (Jgs. 8:11) is not so much
the feeling of a security that is taken for granted, but a frivolous attitude.

2. *False Security.* But frequently *bṭḥ* is used to describe a person who thinks
he is secure, but is deceived because the object on which his feeling of security is
based is unreliable. When we take all the passages in which *bṭḥ* is used in this
sense, we get a picture of everything to which the heart of man clings and on
which he believes he can build his life, but which will end in failure.

This includes many different things. First of all, these texts affirm that men
cannot rely on riches: "He who trusts in his riches will fall" (Prov. 11:28; Ps.
49:7[6] and 52:9[7] also declare that it is vain to trust in riches). Thus Job
explicitly denies that he had made gold the basis of his security (31:24). [7]

Nor can one rely on his own house; the evildoer who attempts this will be
frustrated, as Bildad emphasizes twice (Job 8:14; 18:14).

Fortified cities and walls "in which you trust" (Jer. 5:17; Dt. 28:52) or chariots
and horses (Isa. 31:1) are not reliable either, no matter how many they may be.
And although Israel feels secure in the multitude of her warriors, they will not
be able to help (Hos. 10:13). Therefore, the prophet Amos also pronounces an
oracle of woe against those who trust in Samaria (Am. 6:1; we may also mention
Jer. 48:7 [according to the LXX text] and 49:4 here, which censure those who
trust in strongholds and treasures). The psalmist recognizes this untrustworthi-

---

[7] On Jer. 48:7 and 49:4, see below.

ness of all weapons: "For not in my bow do I trust, nor can my sword save me" (Ps. 44:7[6]).

But neither can one rely on man! It is not difficult to understand that this is true of a *boghedh,* a faithless man (Prov. 25:19). But Jer. 17:5 contains a curse against the man who trusts in man and thus makes flesh his strength. One cannot even feel secure in the help of princes (Ps. 146:3). These two ideas appear together in Ps. 118:8f., which contains an emphatic contrast between *bṭh,* "putting confidence in, trusting in," man and princes, and *chasah,* "taking refuge," in God. Quite often the OT states that one cannot rely on Pharaoh or on Egypt, as in the Isaiah narrative in Isa. 36:4,5,6,9 followed by 2 Ch. 32:10; and in Isa. 31:1;[8] Jer. 2:37; 46:25; Ezk. 29:16. Egypt disappoints everyone that has anything to do with her. When Jgs. 9:26 states that the Shechemites put confidence in Gaal, the implication too seems to be that he would disappoint them. A person can even be wrong about his friends; it can be dangerous to rely on them, as the warnings and laments in Jer. 9:3(4); Mic. 7:5; and Ps. 41:10(9) state. Thus, have no confidence in man or in a wild animal (Job 39:11).

Most of all, man must not have confidence in himself. He must not trust in his own strength (Isa. 30:12; Ps. 62:11[10]; Prov. 21:22), or in his own beauty, which is a gift of Yahweh, as the beauty he gave to Jerusalem (Ezk. 16:15), or in himself, for "he who trusts in his own mind is a fool" (Prov. 28:26), or in his own "righteousness" (Ezk. 33:12), or even in his own "wickedness," as the prophet says in his reproach against Babylon (Isa. 47:10).

Again, he who seeks for security in "idols" (*'atsabbim,* Ps. 115:8; 135:18) or who trusts in "images" (Isa. 42:17; Hab. 2:18) or "Bethel" (Jer. 48:13) shall be put to shame.

Jeremiah carries this skepticism still further. Judah believes that the temple is a reliable object of trust. After all, it is the temple of Yahweh (Jer. 7:4,14), and the Nabis (prophets) declared Yahweh's words affirming that the temple was inviolable. But Jeremiah states that Judah is deceived about this, for all these are deceptive words and one cannot rely on them (Jer. 7:4,8; 13:25; 28:15; 29:31).

Thus in these passages *bṭh* means "to rely on a thing of nought," as Isa. 59:4 puts it, and this can only lead to shame. Thus the participle used absolutely has the meaning "credulous, self-confident." It appears in Prov. 14:16 as a characteristic of the "fool": "The fool goes into a rage and feels secure";[9] in Zeph. 2:15 it is used of Nineveh, in Isa. 47:8 of Babylon, in Jer. 49:31 of Hazor, in Ezk. 30:9 of Ethiopia, in Ezk. 39:6 of the islands (coastlands), and in Isa. 32:9-11 of the daughters of Jerusalem. In all these passages it refers to one who "thinks he is secure," but is wrong.

No doubt this should also be borne in mind in explicating Eccl. 9:4. Certainly every living thing has hope. But the word used here is *bittachon,* and the context includes the idea that this "hope" also will be disappointed in the end, for all

---

8 See above.
9 With Ringgren, *ATD,* XVI/1, *in loc.*

life ends in death, as the context states quite clearly. [10] Similarly Job 6:20 states that the kind of hope that the caravans of Tema have will be confounded.

This absolute usage of *bṭḥ* in its clearly negative sense shows first of all that the negative meaning is characteristic of *bṭḥ*. When one has the kind of "self-security or trust" suggested by this sense of *bṭḥ,* it almost always leads into error and will be disappointed or will result in apathy, whether the object of trust is riches or weapons, princes or friends, powers and authorities or man himself, his strength and righteousness. Nor can one rely on ïdols or even on the temple of God. No matter what a man trusts in, he will be confounded!

3. *Security in God.* In contrast to this clear linguistic usage of *bṭḥ* there is another that is even clearer. The community of Yahweh can know for sure that it can rely on him. This certainty is expressed in texts that praise the person who relies on Yahweh. Thus we read in Jer. 17:7 (in contrast to 17:5) [11]: "Blessed (with a → ברוך *bārûkh*) is the man who trusts in Yahweh," and in Prov. 16:20: "Happy (with an → אשרי *'ashrê*) is he who trusts in Yahweh" (see also Ps. 40:5 [4]; 84:13[12]). Similar statements are made concerning the *boteach,* "the one who trusts," and the *botechim,* "those who trust," in Prov. 28:25; 29:25; Ps. 32:10; 125:1; they are refreshed, protected, surrounded by good things, and will not fall (cf. also Prov. 14:26 and Ps. 112:7). Since not only Jer. 17:7 but also Ps. 32:10 and 112:7 belong to the sphere of Wisdom, it is clear that there is a strong interest in Wisdom in these passages.

The recurring admonition, "Trust in the Lord!" can be understood in light of this. It is especially impressive in the antithetical statement in Prov. 3:5: "Trust in Yahweh with all your heart, and do not rely on your own insight." It also appears in the twofold admonition in Ps. 37:3,5: "Trust in Yahweh"; in Prov. 22:19; in the summons to the community in Ps. 4:6(5); 62:9(8); Isa. 26:4; and in the comprehensive summons to Israel, the house of Aaron, and all those who fear the Lord in Ps. 115:9,10,11. We find similar expressions in Ps. 40:4(3) and 9:11(10), the latter of which adds the reason, "for thou hast ïot forsaken those who seek thee," and in Jer. 49:11 and Isa. 50:10, the latter of which says: "Who walks in darkness and has no light, yet trusts in the name of Yahweh and relies upon his God." Thus in distress and darkness also, one is to seek security and support in God.

This admonition is expressed in a most emphatic way in Isaiah when he shows Judah (perhaps again in a critical situation) where her strength really lies: "In returning and rest you could be saved; in quietness and assurance shall be your strength. And you would not" (Isa. 30:15). In another passage (7:9), Isaiah connects the continued existence of the house of David with "faith." In a similar way, here he connects the continued existence of Judah with returning, rest, and quietness, i.e., with that inner security which is hidden in Yahweh and receives power and strength therefrom.

In addition, a number of texts in the OT contain this confession: "I trust in

---

[10] Cf. Hertzberg, *KAT,* XVII/4, and Zimmerli, *ATD,* XVI/1, *in loc.*
[11] See above.

thee, in thy mercy and grace!" This appears in particular in the laments: Ps. 13:6(5); 25:2; 26:1; 28:7; 31:7,15(6,14); 52:10(8); 55:24(23); 56:4,5,12(3,4, 11); 86:2; 143:8; and 71:5. But it is also found in Wisdom Psalms like 91:2; 119:42; occasionally elsewhere, as in 27:3; 33:21; 65:6(5); Isa. 12:2; 26:3; and in the narrative in Isa. 36:7,15. These passages are held together by a common bond, viz., that in time of need, whatever it may be, there is no way for man to survive but to take refuge in Yahweh, to trust in him, and to have confidence in him. This gives these confessions their peculiar strength; the inner power of the worshipper rests on this certainty. The Assyrian intermediaries try to determine this inner certainty when they refer to the other "gods" that were unable to save their worshippers from the Assyrian army. But Yahweh is not one among many gods; he is the only God and therefore man can put his confidence in him.

In comparison with the promise made to the *boteach,* "the one who trusts," and with the admonition to "trust" and the confession of "trust", the simple statement that someone "trusted" or "trusts" in Yahweh is rather rare. 2 K. 18:5 says concerning Hezekiah, "He trusted in Yahweh, the God of Israel." 1 Ch. 5:20 makes a similar statement concerning the Reubenites. Sennacherib sends to Hezekiah and tries to shake his faith in Yahweh (Isa. 37:10), and Jeremiah promises Ebedmelech a divine blessing because he has put his trust in God (Jer. 39:18). Ps. 21:8(7) says that the king trusted in the Lord, and Ps. 22:5,6(4,5) makes a similar affirmation concerning the fathers. It is quite difficult as well to find objective statements in the OT concerning present trust in Yahweh. It is easier to find statements concerning present lack of trust. Thus Zephaniah (3:2) laments that Jerusalem had not trusted in Yahweh, and Ps. 78:22 laments that the fathers had not trusted in him.

Thus the feeling of being secure in God is the only certain support for human life. When Israel lives securely, it is a result of divine guidance: 1 S. 12:11; 1 K. 5:5(4:25); Ps. 78:53. The phrase "to dwell (lie down) securely (in safety)" in particular is found repeatedly in divine promises: Isa. 14:30; Hos. 2:20(18); Dt. 12:10; 33:12,28; Jer. 23:6; 33:16; 32:37; Ezk. 28:26; 34:25,27,28; 38:8,14; 39:26; Lev. 25:18,19; 26:5; Zec. 14:11; Isa. 32:17f. Thus it was especially in the time of Jeremiah, Ezekiel, Deuteronomy, and the Holiness Code that Israel looked forward to a time when she could again "dwell (lie down) securely (in safety)," i.e., when she could live under Yahweh's protection. This kind of security is also the substance of human confidence, as it is stated in Ps. 4:9(8): "Thou alone, O Lord, makest me dwell in safety" (cf. also Ps. 16:9 and Job 24:23?). But it is also the result of a righteous life acceptable to God, as Prov. 1:33 says: "he who listens to me will dwell secure" (so similarly 3:23; 10:9; Job 11:18).

Thus there is an intimate connection between "seeking security in God" and "security" in external and internal life.

By way of contrast, there are only a few passages where *bṭh* is used in a positive sense with relationship to man. A man trusts in his wife (Prov. 31:11); a "righteous man" feels secure (28:1); he who hates suretyship is secure (11:15). The Israelites are not disappointed when they trust in the men in ambush (Jgs. 20:36).

IV. Historical Development. The historical development of the root *bṭḥ* is
hard to determine. This is partly because many passages, e.g., the pertinent
psalms, cannot be dated precisely. Above all it is not clear how this root can have
such a varied connotation that almost always it can have a negative meaning
when applied to man and a positive meaning when applied to God. Weiser refers
to Isa. 30:15 and argues that Isaiah played an important role in the history of
this word; but it is very doubtful whether he really gave so much impetus to its
development. Perhaps it would be more appropriate to emphasize that the root
bṭḥ is intimately connected with Wisdom Literature. This would explain how it
could be used in this material first of all ambivalently in statements concerning
man, and only in a positive sense when it was applied to God. Isaiah, whose
language is strongly influenced by Wisdom terminology, could have used the
form *bitchah* in order to express the peculiar idea of "trust" in God. [12] Afterward there arose a greater and greater distinction between the two usages of
bṭḥ depending on whether a particular passage was speaking of man or of God.
Man may be disappointed by man, but he can know there is security in God's care.

Jepsen

---

[12] See above.

בֶּטֶן *beṭen*

Contents: I. 1. Etymology, Evidence; 2. Meaning. II. Concrete Uses in the OT: 1. Stomach and Consumption; 2. Womb and Reproduction; 3. From Birth (with *min*); 4. Acts of
Prostration; 5. The Inner Man. III. Specific Theological Usages: 1. Life Begins in the Womb;
2. Blessings and Curses; 3. Ezekiel and the Scroll.

I. 1. *Etymology, Evidence.* The word *beṭen* appears primarily in Hebrew
with cognates in Aramaic and Arabic and South Canaanite, the last having been
found as a gloss (*baṭnu*) in the Amarna Letters (232:10; 233:14; 234:9). The
basic meaning seems to be "interior," [1] which would compare quite closely with
the Gk. *koilía* and *gastḗr* (both = "hollow"), the two words used almost exclusively to translate *beṭen* in the LXX. In the Letters from Accho of the Amarna
Tablets, it occurs three times to describe the supplicant's prostration. He bows
down seven times "on his belly and on his back."

---

beṭen. J. Behm, "κοιλία," *TDNT*, III, 786-89; M. Dahood, "Qoheleth and Northwest
Semitic Philology," *Bibl*, 43 (1962), 349-365; *idem*, "Hebrew-Ugaritic Lexicography," *Bibl*,
44 (1963), 301; M. Gilula, "An Egyptian Parallel to Jeremia I 4-5," *VT*, 17 (1967), 114; A. R.
Johnson, *The Vitality of the Individual in the Thought of Ancient Israel* (Cardiff, ²1964),
74f.; Pedersen, *ILC*, I-II, 170ff.

[1] *KBL³*, 119.

2. *Meaning.* In the OT *beten* has the following meanings:

(a) "Belly" or "lower abdomen," either of a man (Jgs. 3:21,22) or a woman, where the belly usually refers to a "pregnant belly" (Hos. 9:11; Cant. 7:3 [Eng. v. 2]). In Job 40:16 we have a reference to the "belly" of Behemoth, the primordial "bull of heaven."

(b) "Stomach" as the central digestive organ (Prov. 13:25; 18:8 = 26:22; Ezk. 3:3).

(c) "Womb" or "procreative organ"–in a woman it appears often in parallelism with the more exclusive term → רחם *rechem,* "womb" (Jer. 1:5; Isa. 46:3; Ps. 22:11[10]; 58:4[3]; Job 3:11; 10:18,19; 31:15). A man can also speak of children as having come from his *beten.* In the idioms *peri biṭni,* "the fruit of my womb," and *bene biṭni,* "the children (lit. sons) of my womb," the *beten* may well be a synecdoche for "body"; the children come from his body, not from his belly (Mic. 6:7; Job 19:17; [2] cf. Ps. 132:11). In Hos. 9:11,16, Ephraim is the personified nation of northern Israel with a *beten.* Deutero-Isaiah speaks of the nation also as having been formed in a *beten* (Isa. 44:2,24; etc.).

(d) "Inner parts" of the body generally (Prov. 22:18), similar to → מעים *mēʿîm.*

(e) "Innermost part" of the upper cosmos, viz., the firmament (Job 38:29), as well as the lower cosmos, Sheol (Jonah 2:3[2]).

(f) "Architectural projection," most likely upon which pillars of a building stood (1 K. 7:20); cf. 1QM 5:13, "sheath" or "curve" on the sickle-shaped sword. [3]

II. Concrete Uses in the OT. Two of the primary contexts in which *beten* appears are those concerned with human consumption and reproduction. The belly is the primary digestive organ and it also functions, especially in the woman, to bring forth young. Birth from the womb is the *terminus a quo* of an individual's life and it is frequently used (hyperbolically to be sure) of the time when certain life-activities began.

1. *Stomach and Consumption.* Words of gossip are like delicious bits of food that go down into the *beten* (Prov. 18:8). Traditional wisdom viewed a sated man as being righteous while the "belly of the wicked suffers want" (Prov. 13:25). It made a difference, however, whether or not the filled belly and the wealth it represented were achieved by greed. We meet this argument in the speeches of Eliphaz and Zophar (Job 15,20), where, in disputing with Job, they point to his poverty as a sign of his wickedness (20:15,20,23). When judgment comes he vomits up what he has consumed (20:15). (Job, of course, has a counterargument in chap. 21: the wicked in fact very much live the good life.) Along similar lines is the account in Jgs. 3:21f. of Ehud plunging the sword into the *beten* of Eglon king of Moab. No doubt there was a feeling of justice when a well-sated ruler was put to the sword, as the narrator spares us few details in

---

[2] See on this Pope, *Job. AB,* XV, 132.
[3] *VT,* 5 (1955), 534; *ThLZ,* 81 (1956), 29f.

his description. Eglon, we are told, was a "very fat man" (v. 17) in whom the sword went into the *beten* up to the handle (v. 22).

2. *Womb and Reproduction*. For the woman, the belly is most happily the "pregnant belly." Rebekah was found to have twins in her *beten* (Gen. 25:24). One of them, Jacob, earned his name "to take by the heel" in the *beten* (Hos. 12:4[3]). Children were called "fruit of the womb" (*peri beten*, Ps. 127:3; Isa. 13:18; etc.). They could be derived from the man's body also. Job refers to *bene bitni*, "the sons of my womb" (Job 19:17), and Yahweh swears an oath to David saying, "One of the sons of your body (*mipperi bhitnekha*) I will set on your throne" (Ps. 132:11). Micah asks rhetorically, "Shall I give . . . the fruit of my body (*peri bhitni*) for the sin of my soul?" (Mic. 6:7).

3. *From Birth (with min)*. In Job 31:18 the idiom *mibbeten* refers to Job's birth. He says hyperbolically, "from my youth I reared him like a father, and from my mother's womb (*mibbeten 'immi*) I guided her." [4] In other words, Job has always been rearing orphans and guiding widows.

4. *Acts of Prostration*. When one lies prostrate on the ground, his "belly" and his "neck" become major contact points. Dahood has correctly translated *nephesh* as "neck" in Ps. 44:26(25), where it appears in parallelism with *beten* to describe an act of prostration: "For our neck (*naphshenu*) is bowed down to the dust, our belly (*bitnenu*) cleaves to the ground." This is corroborated by Egyptian reliefs depicting slaves touching the ground with their necks, [5] and we recall that the Amarna texts used "belly" in a context of prostration. [6] The same is true in Ps. 31:10(9), which reads, *'asheshah bhekha'as 'eni naphshi ubhitni*, "my eye is wasted from grief, my soul and my body also." Here the eye is suffering from weeping and the neck and belly are worn from continual prostration. It is possible, though not necessary, to view the *beten* as the place where the tears originate, following Dahood. [7]

5. *The Inner Man*. The *beten* also represents the "inner man," in which thoughts are stored up and from which they issue forth. Man is advised to keep the words of the wise in his *beten* (LXX *kardía*), having them continually ready for a proper time when they may be spoken (Prov. 22:18). The *ruach*, "spirit," which carries forth these words, is also in the *beten*. Elihu, who has thus far restrained himself from entering the Job dialogue, can do so no longer, as the combination of the spirit (*ruach*) and words (*millim*) in his *beten* will make him burst if he does not release them (Job 32:18f.; cf. Jer. 20:9). In yet another attack upon Job (15:2), Eliphaz speaks disparagingly about *ruach* in *bitno;* a wise man should not be a "bag of hot air." [8] The "breath of man" (*nishmath*

---

4 On the emendation of the text, see Pope, 198, 204.
5 Dahood, *AB*, XVI, 268.
6 See above.
7 Dahood, *AB*, XVII, xxiv.
8 Pope, 108.

'adham) is the lamp of Yahweh which searches the chambers of the heart, *chadhre bhaten* (Prov. 20:27), chambers that get periodic cleansings by means of physical punishment (v. 30). Evil thoughts can also be stored up in the *beten* (Job 15:35), but if a man has spoken well his *beten* is satisfied (Prov. 18:20). Finally, in the psalm of Habakkuk (Hab. 3:16), the *beten* trembles along with the lips as destruction approaches. Usually it is the "bowels" (*me'im*) and "heart" (*lebh*) that manifest inward fear and distress (cf. Jer. 4:19; Lam. 1:20; 2:11; Job 30:27).

III. Specific Theological Usages.

1. *Life Begins in the Womb.* (a) Yahweh creates man and brings him to birth. The womb is where Yahweh's creative activity takes place. The psalmist says, "Thou didst knit me together in my mother's womb" (*bebheten 'immi*, Ps. 139:13). Like many of Yahweh's other mighty works, this too is a mystery (Eccl. 11:5). Yahweh also brings the child to birth; thus in theological contexts *mibbeten* has two meanings: "from within the womb" (Job 1:21; Ps. 22:10[9]) or "from birth" (Jgs. 13:5; Ps. 58:4[3]; 71:6).

(b) Birth, then, being the *terminus a quo* in life, is often viewed both by Yahweh and by man as the beginning of a relationship. Or, on the other hand, it may be the point at which a relationship goes awry. After being taken by Yahweh from the womb, the psalmist says he was kept safe by Yahweh on his mother's breasts (Ps. 22:10f.[9f.]; 71:6). The wicked, by contrast, go astray *merachem*, "from the womb," and speak lies *mibbeten*, "from birth" (Ps. 58:4[3]). Yahweh also calls his chosen men from the womb. Samson is to be a Nazirite *min habbaten*, "from the womb" (RSV "from birth," Jgs. 13:5,7). Calling Jeremiah to be a prophet, Yahweh speaks hyperbolically, saying, "Before (*beterem*) I formed you in the womb (*babbeten*) I knew you, and before (*beterem*) you were born (*tetse' merechem*) I consecrated you" (Jer. 1:5). Similarly, we are often told that some god called Egyptian and Babylonian kings from the womb. [9]

(c) In Deutero-Isaiah the lordship and parental character of Yahweh burst forth, as we get a panoramic view of Yahweh's historical relationship with his servant. Yahweh formed the servant from the womb (*mibbeten*, Isa. 44:2,24; 49:5). It was from the womb that he carried him (46:3) and called him to be his *'ebhedh*, "servant" (49:1; cf. v. 3). Israel was a rebel from the womb (48:8); but as a mother does not forget the *'ulah merachem*, "sucking child," nor lack compassion for the *ben bitnah*, "son of her womb," indeed even if she does, Yahweh will not forget his servant (49:15).

2. *Blessings and Curses.* (a) "Sons are a heritage from Yahweh, the fruit of the womb (*peri habbaten*) a reward" (Ps. 127:3). In Deuteronomy they are a

---

[9] A. Moret, *Du caractère religieux de la royauté pharaonique* (Paris, 1902), 65; R. Labat, *Le caractère religieux de la royauté assyro-babylonienne* (Paris, 1939), 45f.; cf. Gilula, 114.

blessing and their absence is a curse. If the people do good, Yahweh will bless the fruit of the body, the fruit of the ground and the fruit of the cattle (Dt. 7:13; 28:4,11; 30:9). If they do evil, the same will be cursed (Dt. 28:18)–the people will themselves aid in bringing the curse to pass; they are told: "you will (then) eat the fruit of your own bodies" (*peri bitnekha*, v. 53). The prophets are the ones who appropriate the curse. In Hosea, Yahweh speaks to a personified nation, Ephraim, saying there will be "no birth, no pregnancy, no conception" (*milledhah umibbeten umeherayon*, Hos. 9:11). Yet even if they do bear, Yahweh will destroy *machamadde bhitnam*, "the beloved children of their womb" (RSV "their beloved children," v. 16; cf. v. 12). Not only against Israel, but also against Babylon Yahweh will have no mercy on the *peri bheten*, "fruit of the womb" (Isa. 13:18). With Job and Jeremiah, we hear them curse their own birth. Jeremiah wishes he had died in the womb (*rachem*) and thereby caused his mother comparatively less shame than his birth has brought her (Jer. 20:17). Job curses an impersonal cosmos (Job 3:3-11), not God, it is important to note, "because it did not shut the doors of my (mother's) womb" (*dalthe bhitni*). Would that he had died just after being born (vv. 10f.) and been carried from the womb to the grave (10:19). It is also in Job alone that we find a vestige of the common ancient Near Eastern view concerning Mother Earth. Looking to the continuity between birth and death, Job says in 1:21: *'arom yatsathi mibbeten 'immi 'arom 'ashubh shammah*. Job came naked from the womb and he will return there (*shammah*) naked. This is, of course, not the mother's womb to which he will return, but to the womb of Mother Earth.[10] Sirach also speaks of the life cycle as beginning in the mother's womb and ending when one returns to the "mother of all," i.e., Mother Earth (Sir. 40:1).

(b) God also brings curses to the stomach. When one has accumulated unjust wealth, it may very well be sweet in the mouth (Job 20:12), but not satisfying in the *beten*. God's anger will enter the *beten* causing him to vomit it up (vv. 15,23). The stomach is probably also referred to in the curse of Ps. 17:14, although it is coupled with the notion that the children will also be the heirs, thus a double meaning may be intended.

(c) An ancient ordeal is prescribed in Nu. 5:11-31 for a woman suspected of unfaithfulness to her husband. The woman is required to drink water mixed with dirt from the floor, along with written curses that are washed off into the solution. This will enter her body and cause bitter pain. If she does not survive the ordeal, which indicates her guilt, then "her body will swell and her thigh fall away" (*tsabhethah bhitnah venaphelah yerekhah*, v. 27). The *yarekh*, "thigh," is no doubt a euphemistic term. It appears in parallelism with *beten*, "body," and must refer to one of the female reproductive organs. We know that if she survives and is declared clean, she can conceive and have children (v. 28): thus nonsurvival either will result in damage to the female reproductive organs, or, if she has conceived in an extramarital affair, then it could refer to loss of the child.

---

[10] Pope, 16.

3. *Ezekiel and the Scroll.* In the call and commissioning of Ezekiel, Yahweh gives him a scroll to eat with words of judgment written upon it (Ezk. 2:8ff.). In his mouth these words are "sweet as honey" (*kidhbhash lemathoq;* cf. Ps. 119:103). Then they go down into his *beten,* "stomach" (Ezk. 3:3), and since they convey a bitter message, the words make Ezekiel bitter (3:14). Jeremiah also, in a context reflecting upon his call, tells of eating a scroll which was at first very good but later caused him much pain (Jer. 15:16-18). A final parallel occurs in the book of Revelation: a scroll to be eaten is sweet as honey in the mouth but bitter when it enters the stomach (*koilía,* Rev. 10:8-11).

Freedman, Lundbom

בִּין bîn; בִּינָה bînāh; תְּבוּנָה t^ebhûnāh

Contents: I. 1. Etymology; 2. In Ugaritic; 3. Forms in Hebrew. II. Semantic Analysis: 1. In the Qal; 2. In the Hiphil; 3. In the Hithpolel; 4. In the Niphal; 5. *binah;* 6. *tebhunah.* III. Summary. IV. In the Qumran Literature.

I. 1. *Etymology.* The root *byn* is connected with the subst. *bayin,* "interval, space between" (analogous to Arab. *bainun* or *baina,* Old South Arab. *byn,* Ugar. *bn,* and Phoen.),[1] used as a preposition (*ben,* "between"). Consequently the original meaning of *byn* was "to distinguish, separate," a meaning that also appears in different nuances in other Semitic languages: Arab. *bāna,* "to be clear, understandable," II "to make clear, understandable," *bayyinun,* "clear, distinct," Old South Arab. *byn,* "to go away, carry off," Ethiop. *bayyana,* "to distinguish, separate, observe, perceive," Ugar. *bn,* "to understand,"[2] Palmyrene *aphel,* "to elucidate, state precisely,"[3] Biblical Aram. *byn.*[4]

2. *In Ugaritic.* The Ugar. *bn* occurs three times for certain, viz., in *CTA,* 3 [V AB], III, 24, "in order that the earth's masses may understand," where it is in parallelism with *yd',* "to know"; in *CTA,* 3, IV, 59, where it is used in a similar way; and in *CTA,* 4 [II AB], V, 122, "Hear, O victorious Baal, Understand, O rider of the clouds," where it is in parallelism with *šm',* "to hear." The two other examples given in *WUS,* 50 must be interpreted differently.

3. *Forms in Hebrew.* In Hebrew the verb *byn* occurs in the qal, niphal, polel, (*hithbonan*), hithpolel and hiphil; and the substantives *binah,* "understanding,"

---

bîn. See the literature listed under → חכמה *chokhmāh,* "wisdom."

1 *DISO,* 34.
2 *WUS,* 50.
3 *DISO,* 34.
4 See below.

and *tebhunah*, "understanding, knowledge," also come from this root. → חכם *chākham*, "to be wise," and → שׂכל *śākhal*, "to be prudent," are among the synonyms of *byn*, but this is not to imply that *byn* is an exclusively Wisdom word.

II. Semantic Analysis.

1. *In the Qal*. The primary meaning of *byn* in the qal is "to give heed to, to perceive." The "strange woman" looks out of the window and "perceives" a young man (Prov. 7:7). Nehemiah "perceives" the evil that Eliashib has done (Neh. 13:7). Job complains that God passes by him so quickly that he does not see or "perceive" him (Job 9:11). Ezra "observes" (gives attention to) the people and finds that there are no Levites among them (Ezr. 8:15).

From the context in which *byn* appears this verb receives an ideological-theological emphasis. Frequently it is used to convey the idea of giving attention to God's deeds. In Moses' farewell song, the people are summoned to remember (→ זכר *zākhar*) the days of old, and to "consider" the years of past generations, in order that they might come to know how Yahweh chose Israel (Dt. 32:7). The same song says concerning the foolish, apostate people: "If they were wise, they would understand (*sakhal* in the hiphil) this, they would discern their latter end" (→ אחרית *'achʰrîth*, Dt. 32:29). Similarly in Ps. 73:17 the psalmist says that he went into the sanctuary of God "in order to 'perceive' their (i.e., the ungodly people's) end." Both passages declare the inevitable consequences of revolt against God. In the same sense, Ps. 50:22 admonishes those who forget God to "give heed," and to consider the righteous judgment of God lest he rend them. Here *byn* means to "come to an understanding," which would lead to conversion. But the ungodly do not "take heed to" (regard) the works of Yahweh; therefore he will destroy them (Ps. 28:5). The prudent "looks" where he is going, but the *pethi*, "simple," "believes everything" (Prov. 14:15). Ps. 19:13 (Eng. v. 12) is a little different, "Who can 'discern' his errors (*sheghi'oth*)?" Here "errors" is in parallelism with "hidden (faults)," and thus means errors which are not manifest, and which are not immediately perceptible.

Daniel "gives attention to" (or "perceives") the number of years that Jeremiah had predicted (Dnl. 9:2), and derives apocalyptic instruction from this. Similarly, in 9:23 he is called upon to "consider" (qal) the word and to "understand" (hiphil) the vision, and in 10:1 it is stated that he did just this.

byn is connected quite naturally with terms meaning "to hear" and "to see," and in such instances it obviously denotes the act of perceiving. Thus Job speaks of God as his legal partner: "I would learn what he would answer me, and 'perceive' what he would say to me" (Job 23:5). But wherever he looks (*ra'ah, chazah*) he does not "perceive" him (23:8). In another place he says: "My eye has seen all this, my ear has heard and 'understood' it. What you know, I also know" (13:1f.). [5] In Ps. 94:7 the ungodly say: "Yahweh does not see; the God of Jacob does not 'perceive.'" Contrariwise the worshipper in 5:2(1) asks God to give ear to (*ha'azinah*) his words and to "give heed" to his groaning; of course, he is also

---

[5] On the connection of *byn* with *yd'*, see below.

asking for God to intervene here. Two passages in Isaiah, viz., 6:9f. and 32:3f.,
are more illuminating. In 6:9f. the prophet receives the command to preach to
the people, "Hear and hear, but do not 'perceive'; see and see, but do not 'understand' (yd')." The idea is that the external seeing and hearing will not lead to a
deeper understanding of the situation, the heart of the people will become hard
(fat, shamen in the hiphil), so that they see, hear, and understand (byn) nothing
that God might heal them. The prophet's use of the verb shubh may point to the
idea of conversion (but it is also possible to translate: "that they may be healed
again"). Isa. 32:3f. has reference to the Messianic future, when the eyes of those
who see will really see, the ears of those who hear will really hear, and the heart
of the rash will "have good judgment" (lit. "understand to know," yabhin
ladha'ath). Thus the seeing and hearing will result in a knowledge of God.

In the last two passages byn is connected with yd', "to know." This is also
the case in many other passages, and in fact in very different contexts: Job 15:9,
"What do you know that we do not know? What do you 'understand' that is not
clear to us?" Prov. 24:12: God who weighs the heart "perceives" it, he who
keeps watch over the soul knows that which man wants to deny. Job 14:21:
The dead does not know or "perceive" what happens to his children. Isa. 44:18:
Idols see, hear, and "discern" nothing–the same thing is said of the "sons of
God" in Ps. 82:5. The following passages contain ideas that are more clearly
connected with Wisdom ideology: Prov. 2:5: "Then you will 'understand' the
fear of Yahweh and find the knowledge (da'ath) of God"; 19:25: "Reprove a
man of understanding (nabhon), and he will 'gain' knowledge (yabhin da'ath)."

Accordingly, chakham, "to be wise," is frequently used as a synonym of byn,
even and in particular outside the Wisdom Literature strictly speaking. Thus,
e.g., we read in the concluding verse of the book of Hosea (14:10[9]): "Whoever
is wise, let him 'understand' these things; whoever is discerning (nabhon), let him
know (yd') them." The context here shows that the prophet is speaking of the
ways of Yahweh. Similarly Jer. 9:11(12) says, "Who is the man so wise that
he can understand this? To whom has the mouth of Yahweh spoken, that he
may explain why the land is ruined?" Thus ultimately only the word that comes
from Yahweh can give correct understanding. In Ps. 92:7(6) the Wisdom character of the word byn is emphasized by antithetical concepts: "The dull (brutish,
→ בער bā'ar) man cannot know (yadha'), the stupid (→ כסיל kesîl) cannot 'understand' this," viz., the greatness of God's works and the depth of his thoughts.
In Job 42:3 Job confesses that he has spoken out of a lack of knowledge (beli
da'ath), "without understanding," things too wonderful for him, which he did
not know (yd').

byn is also connected with śkl in the hiphil, "to have insight, to understand."
We have already mentioned one example above (Dt. 32:29). Here we may also
refer to Ps. 94:8: "Understand, O dullest (b'r) of the people! Fools (kesil), why
will you not be wise (śkl)?" and Dnl. 12:10: "None of the wicked (rš') shall
'understand'; but those who are wise (maskilim) shall understand." In this last
passage, again the author has reference to apocalyptic understanding.

Several times already we have seen that byn is translated by "understand."
There are several other examples of byn used in this sense: Neh. 8:8: the people

"understood" the book that was read; Job 36:29: no one "understands" the spreading of the clouds; Dnl. 12:8, "I heard, but I did not understand" (here the writer probably has reference to a deeper understanding); with *ki*, "that," in 1 S. 3:8: Eli understands that it is Yahweh who is speaking to Samuel; 2 S. 12:19: because of the behavior of those who were present, David "understood" (RSV "perceived") that the child was dead. Prov. 29:19: a slave will not be improved by discipline, even though he "understands" he will not submit. Job 18:2: "'Understand' (RSV 'Consider'), and then we will speak to each other." Ps. 139:2: God "understands" (RSV "discerns") our thoughts from afar. Ps. 49:21(20): a man without understanding (*lo' yabhin;* cf. v. 13[12], *bal yalin*—should we read *yabhin* here also?) is like the beasts. Prov. 28:5: Evil men do not "understand" what is right (RSV "justice," *mishpat;* cf. also 29:7). Isa. 43:10: "they will 'understand' (come to an understanding) and believe (*he'emin*) me and understand (*yd'*) that I am He."

Thus *byn* takes a number of objects. It is used of human understanding in the sense of wisdom or apocalyptic understanding or simply of man's knowledge of God. And it is also used of divine knowledge. It can denote both the understanding and the deeds resulting from that understanding.

2. *In the Hiphil.* Frequently the hiphil form of *byn* has the same meaning as the qal. Sometimes it means "to give heed" and sometimes "to understand." The idea "to give heed" occurs, e.g., in Ps. 33:15: God "gives heed to" (RSV "observes") the deeds of men; Isa. 40:21: "Have you not known? Have you not heard? ... Have you not 'given heed' to the foundations of the earth?" (the idea is that one should learn from earlier experiences and from God's act of creation); Isa. 57:1: devout men are taken away without anyone noticing or giving heed to it. Four examples of this meaning of the hiphil of *byn* occur in the book of Daniel in passages that have to do with giving heed to the revelation (8:5,17; 9:23; 10:11). Prov. 14:8: the wise man "gives heed" to his way. Neh. 8:12: the people celebrate the Feast of Tabernacles, "because they had 'given heed to' (RSV 'understood') the words that were declared to them." Here the deed which results from the understanding is included in the idea conveyed by *byn*.

When it has the meaning "to understand," *hebhin* is frequently connected with *yd'*, "to know." Thus Mic. 4:12 says: "(The foreign nations) do not know (*yd'*) the thoughts of Yahweh, and they do not 'understand' his plan" (he will destroy them). This combination is quite frequent in the Wisdom Literature, e.g., in Prov. 1:2: "That men may know (*yd'*) wisdom and instruction, 'understand' words of insight (*binah*)" (cf. 1:6, "to understand a *mashal*, 'proverb,' and a *melitsah*, 'figure'"). In Dnl. 1:4 the king commands that the young men be gathered "who were skilful in all wisdom" (*maskilim bekhol chokhmah*), who were endowed with knowledge (*yodhe'e dha'ath*), and who understood learning (*mebhine madda'*)—thus the entire Wisdom terminology! Dnl. 1:17: Daniel understood all visions and dreams; 2:21: Daniel traces his wisdom back to God (God gives *mande'a' leyadh'e bhinah*, "knowledge to those who have understanding"). Thus, in these passages in the book of Daniel we find Wisdom terminology used in the apocalyptic sphere.

hebhin also has this meaning elsewhere. Prov. 8:5 admonishes the *petha'im,* "simple ones," and foolish men (*kesilim*) "to become prudent" and to "understand" discretion (*'ormah*). Neh. 8:3 tells how Ezra read the law to those who could understand. The combination "men, women, and *kol mebhin lishmoa'* (all who could hear with understanding)" in v. 2 seems to suggest that the last phrase refers to the children; the same thing seems to be intended by the expression *kol yodhea' mebhin,* "all who have knowledge and understanding," in Neh. 10:29(28) (cf. also 8:8: the people understood what was read). *mebhin* is also used to denote one who is skilful at doing something, i.e., one who is an expert (cf. the verb in Dnl. 1:17 above): 2 Ch. 34:12, "those who were skilful with instruments of music"; Dnl. 8:23, "experienced in plots (RSV riddles) (*mebhin chidhoth*)"; 1 Ch. 15:22: "he was skilful in (directing music)." All these examples are late; cf. 1 S. 16:18, *yodhea' naggen,* "who is skilful in playing the lyre."

hebhin occurs twice with God as subject: Job 28:23: God "understands" the way to wisdom; 1 Ch. 28:9: Yahweh, who searches the heart, "understands" every plan and thought (*yetser umachashabhoth*).

In conjunction with the original meaning of *byn,* in one passage *hebhin* means "to discern," viz., in 1 K. 3:9, where Solomon asks for understanding to discern between good and evil as a good judge (cf. 3:11).

Finally, as a true causative *hebhin* means "to give understanding," "to cause to understand," "to teach." Of particular interest is Isa. 28:9, where the prophet's audience asks scornfully, "Whom will he teach (*yoreh*) knowledge, and to whom will he impart revelation (*yabhin shemu'ah*)?" Does he think that we are little children? Later v. 19 refers back to this text: when the punishment comes, it will be a terror "to impart revelation." Isa. 40:14 asks, "Whom did he (God) consult to teach him understanding (RSV, for his enlightenment, *yabhin*), and who taught (*lamadh*) him the path of justice, and taught (*lamadh*) him knowledge (*da'ath*), and showed (*yodhia'*) him the way of understanding (*tebhunah*)?" In a series of passages Ps. 119 speaks of gaining understanding in the commandments of God (vv. 34,73,125,130,144,169). Dnl. 8:16 contains a request that the angel Gabriel may cause Daniel to understand a vision, and Dnl. 11:33 speaks of the people who are wise (*maskile 'am*), who will make many understand. Job 6:24 says, "Teach (*horu*) me, and I will be silent, 'make me understand' how I have erred." *hebhin* is used to express the effectiveness of the teacher in 1 Ch. 25:8 (the teacher with his pupils); 2 Ch. 35:3 (the Levites taught all Israel); Ezr. 8:16; Neh. 8:7,9.

3. *In the Hithpolel.* The examples of *byn* in the hithpolel are found almost exclusively outside the Wisdom Literature (the exceptions appear in Job 11:11; 23:15; 26:14; 30:20; 31:1; 32:12; 37:14 without Wisdom character; and in Sir. 3:22; 7:5; 9:5).

This form is used quite generally with the meaning "to consider diligently," "to look at closely." The woman who brought her case before Solomon had "looked at the child more closely" and had discovered that it was not her child (1 K. 3:21). The shades in Sheol "stare at" the king of Babylon (Isa. 14:16). Though one "looks well," he does not find the place of the ungodly (Ps. 37:10).

Job resolved not to "look" upon a virgin (Job 31:1, quoted in Sir. 9:5). Elihu "gave attention" to the friends of Job (32:12). Twice *hithbonan* stands in parallelism with a verb meaning "to see": Isa. 52:15, "That which has not been told them they shall see, and that which they have not heard 'they shall understand,'" and Jer. 2:10, "Send to Kedar and 'examine with care'; see if there has been such a thing"; once with a verb meaning "to hear": Job 37:14, "Hear (*he'ezin*) this, O Job; stop and 'consider' the wondrous works of God"; once with *zakhar*, "to remember": Isa. 43:18: "Remember not the former things, nor 'consider' the things of old" (now Yahweh is doing a new thing!); and three times with *yadha'*, "to know": Job 38:18, "Have you 'looked at' (understood; RSV 'comprehended') the expanse of the earth? Declare, if you know all this" (thus this knowledge is the result of looking); Job 11:11, "For he knows worthless men; he sees iniquity and '(truly) gives heed' to it" (*lo'*, "not," is either to be deleted or is to be interpreted as an archaizing corroborative particle); and Isa. 1:3, "Israel does not know, my people does not 'understand'" (i.e., they cannot correctly evaluate their own situation, and they do not know God). In Job 30:20, Job says to God, "I cry to thee and thou dost not answer me; I stand, and thou dost (not) (read *lo'*) 'heed' me." Ps. 107:43 speaks of giving heed to Yahweh's deeds, and Ps. 119:95 speaks of giving heed to God's words. Job 23:15 says, "when I consider, I am in dread of him." This "giving heed" or "considering" leads to comprehending or understanding: Job 26:14, "the thunder of his power, who can 'understand'?"; Ps. 119:104, "Through thy precepts 'I get understanding'" (cf. v. 100, "I 'understand more' than the aged, for I keep [*natsar*] thy precepts"). Jer. 23:20 and 30:24 announce that there will be a sudden understanding at the "end of the days"; both of these passages have to do with the judgment of Yahweh's fierce anger.

4. *In the Niphal.* There is only one example of the niphal of *byn* as a finite verb in the OT, in Isa. 10:13, where the king of Assyria says: "By the strength of my hand I have done it, and by my wisdom, for I have understanding (*nebhunothi*)." Elsewhere we find only the ptcp. *nabhon*, "intelligent." It is a typical Wisdom word. In 18 of the 22 occurrences of this word in the OT, it is connected intimately or loosely with *chakham*, "wise," or *chokhmah*, "wisdom." Joseph is "a man discreet and wise" '(Gen. 41:33,39); Moses chooses wise and understanding men as heads over Israel (Dt. 1:13); Solomon has a wise and discerning heart (1 K. 3:12); Israel is a wise and understanding people (Dt. 4:6–in this late chapter the law is an indication of the superiority of the people of God as far as wisdom is concerned). Isaiah speaks of people who "are wise in their own eyes, and consider themselves to be 'intelligent'" (Isa. 5:21), and of the time when God will intervene and bring to nought the wisdom of the wise and the discernment of the discerning (29:14). Jeremiah reproves the people because they are foolish (→ אֱוִיל *'evîl*), they know not God, they are stupid children (*banim sekhalim*), they have no understanding, and are skilled only in doing evil (Jer. 4:22). [6]

---

[6] On Hos. 14:10(9), see II.1 above.

But *nabhon* is at home particularly in Proverbs. In 16:21 it is synonymous with *chakham lebh*, "wise of heart"; according to 10:13 he who has understanding speaks wisdom, and here the antithesis of *nabhon* is *chasar lebh*, "him who lacks sense." In 1:5 *nabhon* is in parallelism with *chakham*, "the wise man"; according to 14:33 a man of understanding has wisdom, and here *nabhon* is contrasted with *kesil*, "fool." In several passages *nabhon* is connected with *daʿath*, "knowledge" (14:6; 15:14; 18:15; 19:25). *nabhon* also occurs in Prov. 17:28; Sir. 9:11; and Eccl. 9:11; in the last passage it is connected with *chakham*, "wise," and *yadhaʿ*, "to know."

Finally, *nebhon dabhar* means "prudent in speech" (1 S. 16:18, of David), and *nebhon lachash* means "expert in charms" (Isa. 3:3).

5. *binah. binah*, "insight, understanding," is for the most part, but not exclusively, a Wisdom word. In 19 of the 39 times it occurs in the OT, it is explicitly connected with *chokhmah*, "wisdom," and in 6 other passages (Prov. 3:5; 4:1; 9:6; 23:4; 30:2; and Sir. 6:25) the Wisdom character of this word is assured by the sapiential context in which it occurs.

binah, "understanding," can refer to arts and crafts (2 Ch. 2:12[13], *yodheaʿ binah*, "endued with understanding"; 1 K. 7:14 says, "full of *chokhmah, tebhunah*, and *daʿath*, i.e., wisdom, understanding, and skill"), or to "the times" (evidently referring to diviners and astrologers, 1 Ch. 12:33), or to the office of king (22:12, *sakhel ubhinah*, "discretion and understanding"; 2 Ch. 2:11[12], of Solomon; Isa. 11:2, transferred to the Messianic king: "the spirit of wisdom and understanding"). According to Dt. 4:6, the law is the peculiar wisdom and understanding of Israel. [7] According to Isa. 29:14, Yahweh will bring to nought the wisdom of the wise and the discernment of the discerning by intervening in history—so this text has reference to human discernment altogether. The same is true of Job 38:4, which states that human understanding cannot comprehend God's wonders (cf. also Job 39:26). The inhabitants of the devastated heathen city are a people without discernment (*loʾ ʿam binoth huʾ*), and thus they do not understand the ways of God (Isa. 27:11). In the coming age of salvation those who err and those who murmur will come to understanding and will accept instruction (Isa. 29:24). The meaning of Job 38:36 is dubious: God has put wisdom in *tuchoth*, and given understanding to *sekhvi*—it is possible that this text is referring to divination. [8]

The Wisdom books emphasize how important it is to get (→ קנה *qānāh;* Prov. 4:5,7; 16:16), to seek (23:23), or to learn (4:1; cf. 1:2; 2:3) wisdom and understanding. In Job 28:12,20, the question is asked, "Where shall wisdom or understanding be found?"–God alone knows (v. 23). Thus we read, "The fear of Yahweh is wisdom, and the knowledge of the Holy One is insight" (Prov. 9:10; cf. Job 28:28). Thus it can even be said: "Trust in Yahweh and do not rely on your own insight" (*binah*, Prov. 3:5; cf. 23:4). *binah* also appears in connection with

---

[7] Cf. II.4 above.
[8] See the commentaries.

personified Wisdom in Prov. 7:4: "Say to wisdom, 'You are my sister,' and call insight your intimate friend."

In the book of Daniel *binah* may have a very general meaning, as when it is used of the wisdom and understanding of Daniel (1:20). But there are a number of passages in this book where it has reference to the understanding of visions and auditions (8:5,15,16,17,27; 9:22; 10:1,11,12,14; 12:8,10). Isa. 33:19, which speaks of an incomprehensible (*'en binah*) language, is different.

6. *tebhunah*. *tebhunah*, "understanding," has strong connections with Wisdom thought, just like *binah* (with which it stands in parallelism once, Prov. 2:3). Out of the 42 times *tebhunah* occurs in the OT, it appears 19 times in Proverbs and 4 times in Job; 22 times it is explicitly connected with *chokhmah*, "wisdom."

Frequently *tebhunah* means skill in an occupation. Bezalel's technical skill is described as "the Spirit of God, *chokhmah*, *tebhunah*, and *da'ath*, i.e., ability, intelligence, and knowledge" (Ex. 31:3; 35:31; cf. 36:1). We are told that Hiram was full of wisdom, *tebhunah*, and *da'ath*, i.e., understanding, and skill (1 K. 7:14). Ps. 78:72 extols David's understanding as shepherd of his people. Ezk. 28:4 says that the king of Tyre had gotten wealth for himself by his wisdom and understanding. This may very well have reference to his ability in business, but it sounds more like the writer is degrading him for trusting in his *own* human understanding. The same thing may be said of Hos. 13:2: they have made idols by their own understanding: human technical skill can create no gods at all (cf. Isa. 44:19, the worshippers of idols are without understanding). 1 K. 5:9(4:29) speaks of Solomon's wisdom and understanding. In other respects the Wisdom texts that use *tebhunah* contain the normal statements, especially concerning the necessity of getting wisdom and understanding and of giving heed to instruction (Prov. 2:2f.,11; 5:1), concerning the advantages of understanding (2:11; 24:3), concerning the self-control of a man of understanding (11:12; 14:29; 17:27; cf. also 15:21), and concerning Wisdom's invitation (8:1). *tebhunah* is used in antithesis to *chasar lebh*, "lacking understanding or sense" (11:12; 15:21), *'ivveleth*, "folly" (14:29; 15:21), and *kesil*, "fool" (18:2). Wisdom and understanding are gifts of God (2:6); they are found only with him (Job 12:13, as are *'etsah*, "counsel," and *da'ath*, "knowledge"), and no human wisdom, understanding, or counsel (*'etsah*) can prevail against him (Prov. 21:30).

In contrast to *binah*, *tebhunah* is also used as a divine attribute. Thus, several passages emphasize that God created heaven and earth by wisdom and knowledge (Jer. 10:12; 51:15; Ps. 136:5; Prov. 3:19; cf. also the text in Job 26:12, which contains mythological elements). His understanding is unsearchable (*'en chaqer*, Isa. 40:28) and beyond measure (*'en mispar*, Ps. 147:5).

III. Summary. In light of what has been said above, it is difficult to write a history of the root *byn* or to assign it to specific genres. A great number of examples of the use of this root come from the everyday language of the people. Someone "perceives" or "observes" something, or "gives heed" to it, or "comprehends" it or "understands" it–this is simply stated without any hidden implications. The texts that use *byn* in referring to a person's skill in a craft or an occupation are of particular interest. It goes without saying that several of the examples are to be found in the Wisdom Literature. Both *binah* and *tebhunah* appear as synonyms of → חכמה *chokhmāh,* "wisdom," with all the nuances of meaning of which it is capable. The root *byn* is also used remarkably often in the book of Daniel referring to apocalyptic understanding.

IV. In the Qumran Literature. In the Qumran literature, *binah* (there is no example of *tebhunah*) occurs along with the other Wisdom terminology (*da'ath, chokhmah, sakhal, 'ormah*) in the sense of saving insight, which at the same time arises from the study of the law and is based on revelation, e.g., in the list of virtues in 1QS 4:3, and in the formula "I know (or, we know) these things because of thy understanding" (1QM 10:16; 1QH 1:21; 14:12; 15:12). Man does not have this understanding in himself (1QH 1:23; 2:19; 4:7; cf. 12:33, verb), but it is given to him by God (1QH 2:17; 14:8f.; 4,12). Accordingly, the hiphil of this verb is used to convey the idea of instruction imparted in the community (1QS 3:13; 4:22, 6:15). The ptcp. *mebhonan,* "learned," occurs in the Damascus Document referring to those who were familiar with the book *hagho,* "the Book of Meditation" (CD B 10:6; 13:2; 14:7). Elsewhere in the Qumran literature this verb is used in senses similar to that which it has in the Bible, e.g., "to understand the marvels or works of God" (1QS 11:19; 1QH 7:32; 11:28; 12:27), "to understand all these things" (1QH 17:21), "the foolish of heart (*kesile lebh*) cannot 'understand' these things" (1QH 1:37), "no one understands thy wisdom" (1QH 10:2).

Ringgren

בַּיִת *bayith*

Contents: I. Etymology and Related Expressions in Hebrew. II. In the Ancient Near East: 1. Egypt; 2. Mesopotamia; 3. Asia Minor in the Time of the Hittite Empire; 4. Ugarit; 5. Early Greece. III. Designation for a Building (or Part of a Building): 1. House; 2. Palace; 3. Temple; 4. Room or Hall. IV. Designation for an Abode. V. Designation for "The Inside." VI. Designation for Family, Clan, or Tribe. VII. Designation for Household, Estate, or Wealth. VIII. In Place Names.

I. Etymology and Related Expressions in Hebrew. The primitive Semitic **bait-* is quite prevalent in the Semitic languages. It can be recognized in Akk. *bītu* (Assyr. *bētu*), Ugar. *bt,* Aram. *byt,* Ethiop. *bēt,* Arab. *bait,* Phoen. *bt,* and

---

bayith. A.-G. Barrois, *Manuel d'archéologie biblique,* I (Paris, 1939), 244-285; H. K. Beebe, "Ancient Palestinian Dwellings," *BA,* 31 (1968), 38-58; A. Causse, "La crise de la solidarité de famille et de clan dans l'Ancien Israel," *RHPR,* 10 (1930), 24-60; Dalman, *AuS,* VII, 1-175; E. Ebeling, "Familie," *RLA,* III, 9-14; A. Erman-H. Ranke, *Ägypten und ägyptisches Leben im Altertum* (1923); Fiechter, "Haus," *PW,* VII, 2523-2546; Numa D. Fustel de Coulanges, *The Ancient City* (Eng. ed. 1873), 40-116; K. Galling, "Haus," *BRL,* 266-273; A. Goetze,

(continued on p. 108)

Heb. *bayith*. The word **bait-* was probably a primary noun. It cannot be derived from any known verb. On the contrary, denominative verbs (like Akk. *biātum/bātu* and Arab. *bāta*, both meaning "to spend the night") were derived from the noun **bait-*. Since the uses of Heb. *bayith* were so diverse and varied, it is impossible to state any adequate synonym for it. Here we mention only approximately synonymous words. → אֹהֶל *'ōhel*, "tent," meant more than a movable dwelling. Frequently it has to be translated "home," "dwelling," or "family." It would hardly be possible to show that *bayith* had an earlier original meaning other than "house." If the primitive Semitic word *bait* was used in the period of the cave dwellers, there hardly remains a trace of *bait* in the sense of "cave." Instead, the ordinary Hebrew word for "cave" is *me'arah*. Other Hebrew words denoting dwellings or buildings are *birah*, "castle, palace," *hekhal*, "palace, temple," *chatser*, "settled abode, settlement, village," *moshabh*, "dwelling, dwelling-place," *ma'on*, "refuge, habitation," *miqdash*, "sacred place, sanctuary," and *mishkan*, "dwelling place, tabernacle."

II. In the Ancient Near East.

1. *Egypt*. The determinative sign for the usual Egyptian nouns for house (*pr* and *ḥ.t*) is a rectangle with an opening on the lower side. This sign is similar to the outline of the wall of a one-room house. It is also used as a determinative sign for other synonymous words: *'.t*, "chamber, room, department," *iwnn*, "dwelling place of the gods," *ḥnw*, "interior, residence," *m'ḥ'.t*, "grave, cenotaph," *iwy.t*, "house, sanctuary, ward, district." Egyp. *pr* ("house") meant not only a building, but also a part of a house or (figuratively) a container: a box for ointments, a sheath for a bow or a mirror. As the house par excellence, *pr* meant the palace of the king, [1] which is also called *pr '3*, "great house." In the language of the New Kingdom, these words meant the pharaoh himself. Thus, the OT usually calls him *par'oh*. In addition, *pr* frequently means "temple," [2] and then usually appears with a suffix or a genitive to designate the deity living there. In many cases names of cities originated from this word, as *pr Wsir*, "Busiris," *pr itmw*, "Pithom," etc. *Pr* is also used of the dwelling place of the dead (i.e., the grave), e.g., in the expression *pr.f nfr n nḥḥ*, "his beautiful house of eternity," or *pr (n) ḏ.t*, "house of eternity."

Pr also refers to the inhabitant or occupant of a house, e.g., *pr it.f*, "the family of his father," and also means "household," e.g., *grg pr*, "to establish a house-

"Kleinasien," *HAW*, 3:1:3:3:1 (²1957), 85-95, 118; P. Koschaker, "Familienformen," *ArOr*, 18 (1950), 210-296; *idem*, "Fratriarchat, Hausgemeinschaft und Mutterrecht in Keilschriftrechten," *ZA*, 41 (1933), 1-89; S. Krauss, *Talmudische Archäologie*, I, 19-48; I. Mendelsohn, "The Family in the Ancient Near East," *BA*, 11 (1948), 24-40; A. Merrill, "The House of Keret," *SEÅ*, 33 (1968), 5-17; O. Michel, "οἶκος," *TDNT*, V, 119-136; Pedersen, *ILC*, I-II, 46-60; D. M. Robinson, "Haus," *PW Suppl.*, VII, 224-278; A. van Selms, *Marriage and Family Life in Ugaritic Literature* (London, 1954); Å. Sjöberg, "Zu einigen Verwandtschaftsbezeichnungen im Sumerischen," *Heidelberger Studien zum Alten Orient* (1967), 201-231; W. Robertson Smith, *Kinship and Marriage* (London, 1885); R. de Vaux, *AncIsr*, 19-23.

  [1] *WbÄS*, I, 512f.
  [2] *WbÄS*, I, 513, 7ff.

hold" = to marry, *nb.t pr,* "the lady of the house" = wife. But usually *pr* and *h.t* should not be translated "family," the terms for which are *mhwt* and *ꜣbt;* the determinative sign for both of these is a seated man and a seated woman.

2. *Mesopotamia.* In the earliest Mesopotamian documents, the ideas of "house" and "dwelling" were expressed by Sum. *é, gá,* and *èš.* On the whole, these words denoted the same group of ideas as Akk. *bītu:* "house, dwelling, temple, sanctuary, palace (usually, however, *é-gal*), possession, storehouse, room, vessel, place, region, household, family, property." But the majority of Sumerian documents come from the time in which Akkadian had begun to replace Sumerian as the spoken language. Therefore, it is very difficult to determine whether all these ideas originally inhered in the Sumerian words or arose under the influence of Akk. *bītu.* The Sumerian word for "family, tribe," was *im-ri-a* (or *im-ru-a*), which the Babylonian scribes translate by *kimtu, nišūtu* and *salātu.* Akk. *bītu* means above all "house, dwelling, building," but like Heb. *bayith* it contains many different subordinate ideas: "space, room, place of residence, ship's cabin, container, box, stable, pen, real estate, household, house community, family." In the Akkadian lists of synonyms, the scribes used the word *bītu* to explain many technical terms such as *ašru,* "place, spot, abode," *atmānu,* "holy of holies, sanctuary, temple," *dūru,* "walled place, fortification, citadel," *emāšu,* "an inner room of the temple," *gegunû,* "temple on a terrace," *kissu,* "sanctuary," *kummu,* "holy interior, sanctuary," *kungu,* a type of house, *kūpu,* a building, *māšartu,* "arsenal"? *maštaku,* "chamber, compartment," *miparru/gipāru,* "divine dwelling," *sagû,* a type of temple, *tu'u,* "chamber, niche," and *urāšu,* "interior."

Frequently the word *bītu* occurs as a *nomen regens* (governing noun) in combinations of words. Sometimes a construct expression denotes a building, e.g., *bīt āli,* "town hall," *bīt ili,* "house of God, temple," *bīt kīli,* "prison," *bīt ridûti,* "house of succession, palace of the crown-prince," *bīt šarri,* "royal house," and *bīt ṭuppi,* "tablet house, archive, school." Other construct expressions refer to spaces or rooms: *bīt erši,* "bedroom," *bīt rimki,* "bathhouse or bathroom," and *bīt sinnišāti,* "house for women" in the palace. Occasionally such expressions allude to a container, e.g., *bīt nūri,* "lamp," *bīt qēmi,* "flour sack." Construct phrases with *bītu* are also used to describe different kinds of territory: *bīt dulli,* "field under the plow," *bīt ṭābti,* "salt desert"; or feudal possessions: *bīt narkabti,* "feudal property for chariot warriors" (cf. Ugar. *bt mrkbt,* Heb. *beth markabhoth,* "place of chariots," as a place name, Josh. 19:5; 1 Ch. 4:31), late Bab. *bīt sîsî,* "land for horses," feudal land for horsemen.

A Mesopotamian family (*bītu*) was composed of the *pater familias* (father, *abu*), his wife (or wives, *aššatu*), his sons (*mārū*) and daughters (*mārātu/i*), his unmarried brothers and sisters, his clients (*teḫû*), and his domestic servants (*aštapīru*). Usually a distinction was made between the small family (*bītu, kimtu, qinnu*) and the great family (*illatu, nišūtu*), i.e., the tribe.

3. *Asia Minor in the Time of the Hittite Empire.* The Hittite word that is translated "house" occurs in two primitive forms: *per-* and *parn-.* According

to Laroche, [3] *per-* originally denoted a rock dwelling (i.e., a cave). Outside the old Anatolian languages (Hittite, Luwian, Lycian, Lydian), words from the root **per-/*parn-,* "house, dwelling," are not known. This word is probably not primitive Indo-Germanic, but a word belonging to the old Asia Minor culture. Its similarity with Egyp. *pr* is only apparent.

Friedrich suggests only "house" and "estate" as nuances of this word. [4] But obviously the translation "house" also includes "palace" (*haššuwaš per*) and "temple" (*šiunaš per*). The word *per-/parn-* (often written É) includes all buildings and edifices on a site. Therefore the compound expression *A.ŠÀ* ("fields") and *per-/parn-* denotes the entirety of an estate. [5] The semi-ideographic terms *É tarnuwaš* and *É ḫalentuwaš,* if they are intended to express the spoken forms **tarnuwaš per* and **ḫalentuwaš per,* can be regarded as evidences for *per-/parn-,* "space, room, part of a building." *per-/parn-,* "family," appears in the expression *per iya-/ešša-,* "to establish a family," [6] in the household lists of the Vow of Pudu-ḫepa, and in the census lists of the Hittite court. The Hittite family was composed of the *pater familias* (father, *atta-*), his wife (Sum. *DAM*), his own and his adopted children (Sum. *DUMU.MEŠ*), his dependent relatives, and his domestic servants (Sum. *LÚAMA.A.TU* = Akk. *aštapiru*). The Hittites distinguish between the small family (*per-/parn-*) and the great family or tribe (*ḫaššatar, pankur*).

4. *Ugarit.* In the Ugaritic texts the word *bt,* "house," can be translated in different ways: "house of a deity, temple, sanctuary" (*bt 'l*), "house of a king, palace" (*bt mlk*), "stable" (*bt 'lpm*), "storehouse for war-chariots (?)," (*bt mrkbt;* but cf. Akk. *bīt narkabti* as a feudal property, and the Heb. place name *beth markaboth*). *ḥwt,* "house, dynasty, kingdom," occurs as a synonym of *bt.* This *ḥwt* could be an Egyptian loanword (*ḥ.t*), [7] but it can also be a genuine Semitic word which is evidenced in the Heb. *chavvoth,* "tent-villages" (Nu. 32:41; Dt. 3:14; Josh. 13:30; Jgs. 10:4; 1 K. 4:13; 1 Ch. 2:23). One could also recognize the same word in the proper name *Chavvah,* "Eve." The Israelite narrator would have given it a new meaning and explained it erroneously as "the living one" (Gen. 3:20). Another synonym of *bt* is *šph,* "family, dynasty, ruler's house," which is cognate to the Heb. *mishpachah,* "clan." In two Ugaritic epics, *bt* occupies the center of interest and has still different nuances of meaning. In the Baal Epic it is used of building a house (i.e., temple) for Baal, and in the Keret Epic, of the preservation of the dynasty. [8]

5. *Early Greece.* In the Homeric epics two related words are used to express the idea of "house, dwelling, family," viz., *oíkos* and *oikía. oíkos* was already

[3] E. Laroche, *RHA,* 76 (1965), 52-54.
[4] J. Friedrich, *Heth. Wörterbuch,* 162.
[5] *Heth. Gesetze,* § 44b.
[6] Cf. Ḫatt. III, 6.
[7] See II.1.
[8] Cf. esp. Merrill.

known in the Mycenaean period (13th century B.C.); it clearly appears in the so-called Linear B tablets (written *wo-i-ko-de* = *woikonde*, "homeward"). This word originated from the Indo-European root **ueik-/uik-/uoiko-*,[9] "house, settlement" (cf. Lat. *vicus* and *villa*). In the Homeric epics *oíkos* can be translated by the following words: house, dwelling, cave (of the Cyclops), temple, palace, grave, treasury, treasurehouse, possessions, property, family, household. Other Greek words synonymous with *oíkos* and *oikía* are *dómos*, "house," *dôma*, "house, housetop, roof," *oíkēsis*, "house, dwelling," *oíkēma*, "room, apartment," and *génos*, "descendants, family." The family as described in Homer is very similar to the Semitic and Hittite families. It was composed of a father, his wife, his own and adopted children, dependent relatives, clients, and domestic servants (i.e., male and female slaves).

III. Designation for a Building (or Part of a Building).

1. *House.* Heb. *bayith* is a building (*banah*, "to build," Gen. 33:17; Dt. 20:5; 22:8; 28:30) made of wood (*'etsim*, 1 K. 5:22f.[8f.]) and stone (*'ebhen*, 1 K. 6:7; 7:9; Hab. 2:11; Ps. 118:22), in which a man and his family live (Dt. 6:7; 19:1; 21:12f.). The OT emphasizes that it is vain to build a house without God's blessing (Ps. 127:1; cf. Job 27:18). Amos reproves the building of extravagant houses, and as a punishment for doing so he proclaims that those who build them will not live in them (Am. 5:11; cf. also Zeph. 1:13, and positively as a promise Am. 9:14– which is probably secondary).

2. *Palace.* If the main occupant of the building was the king, the building was called *beth hammelekh*, "the king's house, the palace" (Gen. 12:15; Jer. 39:8). The royal official who had supervision over the palace bore the title *'asher 'al habbayith*, "manager of the palace" (1 K. 4:6; 16:9; 2 K. 15:5; etc.).[10] → הֵיכָל *hêkhāl*, "palace, temple," is a loanword from Sum. *é-gal*, "great house, palace."[11] The same word occurs in the Ugaritic texts as *hkl*.[12] The earlier meaning, "palace," is found in both Akkadian and Ugaritic, but the meaning "temple" seems to be secondary. It arose from the idea that the deity was a king (or a queen) and thus was supposed to live in a palace (cf. 2 S. 7:2ff.).

3. *Temple.* When a building was built to receive the deity or his servants (priests, musicians, etc.), it was called a *beth ha'elohim*, "house of God, temple" (Jgs. 17:5; Dnl. 1:2; etc.). The concept of "temple" is also expressed simply by *beth* before the divine name: *beth yhvh*, "temple of Yahweh" (Ex. 23:19; 34:26; Dt. 23:19[18]; etc., and also on the Arad Ostraca),[13] *beth daghon*, "temple of Dagon" (1 S. 5:2,5; 1 Ch. 10:10), *beth 'ashtaroth*, "temple of Astarte" (1 S. 31:10),

---

9 J. Pokorny, *Indogermanisches Wörterbuch* (1959), 1311.

10 Cf. T. Mettinger, *Solomonic State Officials* (Lund, 1971), 70-110.

11 *KBL³*, 234f.; *AHw*, 191f.

12 *UT*, Glossary, No. 763.

13 See Y. Aharoni, *BA*, 31 (1968), 16f.

beth 'el, "temple of El" (Gen. 12:8),[14] beth ba'al berith, "temple of Baal-berith" (Jgs. 9:4), and beth 'el berith, "temple of El-berith" (9:46). [15]

The temples in Bethel and Dan, which were regarded as the official sanctuaries of the state of Israel, are called beth mamlakhah, "house of the kingdom," "royal sanctuary" (Am. 7:13). The word hekhal is also used in the OT in the sense of "temple." [16]

In Solomon's prayer at the dedication of the temple (1 K. 8; 2 Ch. 6), the king states that even heaven cannot contain God, "how much less this house which I have built" (1 K. 8:27). And yet this house is called Yahweh's dwelling place (8:13), and the king asks Yahweh to open his eyes toward this house where his name is (a Deuteronomistic expression) and to hear the prayers that are uttered there (8:29). This house is called by Yahweh's name (8:43, shimekha niqra' 'al habbayith); here a person acknowledges (hodhah) his name and prays and makes supplication to him (8:33). Thus Yahweh is present in his house in a special way. And yet, several times the king emphasizes that he hears prayers in heaven, where he dwells (8:30,32,34,39,43,49). It is worthy of note that before Solomon began his prayer of dedication, the text states that Yahweh's kabhodh, "glory," filled the house so that the priests could not stand to minister (8:11)–here also the Deuteronomistic historian uses the priestly expression kabhodh. Much more logically, the Chronicler makes this statement after the prayer of dedication (2 Ch. 7:1f.).

In Isa. 56:7, the temple is called a "house of prayer" (beth tephillah).

The Psalms reflect a high regard for the temple. [17] It is holy because God is there (Ps. 93:5). A person comes into Yahweh's house with burnt-offerings (66:5 [4]), and there delights in fat (a sacrificial meal? 36:9[8]). It is Yahweh's chesedh, "steadfast love," that one can find in the temple (5:8[7]). People go to the house of Yahweh in processions (42:5[4]; 55:15[14]), they express their desire for a divine blessing there (118:26), and thus secure the blessing. The psalmist is glad when one says to him, "Let us go to the house of Yahweh" (122:1). A person loves "the habitation (ma'on) of his house" (26:8) because his kabhodh, "glory," dwells there. Psalmists express the desire to dwell (→ ישׁב yāshabh) in Yahweh's house (23:6; 27:4), and those who dwell in his house ever sing his praise (84:5 [4]). The righteous are like green olive trees "in the house of Yahweh" (52:10[8]; 92:14[13])–probably referring to their growth and permanence.

In his Temple Sermon, Jeremiah speaks out against a false temple, thus indicating a high regard for the temple (Jer. 7,26). "Do not trust in these deceptive words: 'This is the temple of Yahweh, the temple of Yahweh, the temple of Yahweh'" (7:4). When the people do not improve their deeds and practice real justice, it is vain to stand before God "in this house" (7:10). The house which is called by Yahweh's name has become a den of robbers (7:11); thus it will not stand if the people continue in their false trust (7:14; cf. 26:6). Thus the temple

[14] Cf. H. Ringgren, Israelite Religion (trans. 1966), 23, and the commentaries.
[15] For additional names for the temple, see under VIII.
[16] See III.2 above.
[17] Cf. Ringgren, The Faith of the Psalmists (1963), chap. 1.

in itself is no guarantee of God's help, but if the people will live according to the will of Yahweh, it will be a sign of his presence and benevolence for ever (7:7).

4. *Room or Hall.* If the "house" (i.e., palace or temple) was very large and was composed of several buildings, each building (and sometimes each room or hall) in the complex could be called a *bayith.* Accordingly, *beth hachoreph,* "winter house," was the term used for the winter residence (i.e., a particular quarter in the palace) of the king (Jer. 36:22; cf. Am. 3:15, which refers to a winter house along with a summer house, and *KAI,* 216.19 [Bar-rākib], which mentions a particular summer house). *beth mishteh hayyayin* (Est. 7:8) was the drinking hall of Ahasuerus. *beth hannashim,* "house of the women" (2:3), meant the harem, and *beth 'abhadhim,* "house of slaves" (Dt. 5:6), the slave quarter or the slave district (this expression is applied to the whole land of Egypt in Dt. 5:6; Ex. 20:2; Dt. 6:12; 7:8; 8:14; etc.).

IV. Designation for an Abode. As a place of residence for the dead, Sheol was regarded as a *bayith* (Job 17:13; 30:23). The grave was called a *beth 'olam,* "eternal home" (Ps. 49:12[11]; Eccl. 12:5)–a similar expression is found in Phoenician and Palmyrene. [18] Moreover, the authors of the OT documents used *bayith* to denote the habitat of moths (Job 27:18), a spider's web (Job 8:14), a bird's nest (Ps. 84:4[3]; 104:17), the human body (Job 4:19), a box containing perfume, a perfume bottle (Isa. 3:20), [19] a holder for the bars of the tabernacle (Ex. 26:29), and a holder for the poles used to carry the table of showbread (Ex. 37:14). The *battim mele'im kol tubh,* "houses full of good tidings," of Dt. 6:11 are clearly to be understood as "treasuries, storehouses."

V. Designation for "The Inside." *bayith* occurs in the following constructions in the sense of "the inside" (in antithesis to *chuts,* "the outside, outer"): *bayethah* (with the *he*-locale: [20] Ex. 28:26; 39:19; etc.), *mibbayith* (Gen. 6:14; 2 K. 6:30), *mibbayethah* (1 K. 6:15), *beth le* (Ezk. 1:27), *mibbayith le* (1 K. 6:16), *lemibbeth le* (Nu. 18:7), and *'el mibbeth le* (2 K. 11:15).

VI. Designation for Family, Clan, or Tribe. *bayith,* "family," includes the *pater familias* (father, → אב *'ābh*), his wife (→ אשה *'ishshāh*), his own and his adopted children ("sons and daughters," *banim ubhanoth*), his dependent relatives, his clients (→ לוי *lēvî,* "Levite"; → גר *gēr,* "sojourner"; → תושב *tôshābh,* "sojourner"), and his menservants and maidservants (*'abhadhim va'amahoth*). The household of Abraham was composed of Abraham, his wife Sarah, his concubine Hagar, his sons Isaac and Ishmael, his dependent relative Lot and his family, his servants (including Eliezer of Damascus: Gen. 15:2), and his trained men (*chanikhav,* 14:14), who are described as *yelidhe bhetho,* "born in his

---

[18] *DISO,* 35; perhaps of Egyptian origin, E. Jenni, *Das Wort 'ôlām im AT* (1953), 79ff.
[19] Otherwise Wildberger, *BK,* X, 143, "amulet."
[20] *GK,* § 90; E. A. Speiser, *IEJ,* 4 (1954), 108-115; *UT,* § 11.1.

house." This social unit (i.e., the household) is also described in legal and cultic contexts. The Sabbath law required the cessation of all work in every household (*bayith*), which included sons, daughters, menservants, maidservants, cattle, and clients (*gerim*, "sojourners," Ex. 20:10). According to the Deuteronomic laws, each man and his family celebrated the established festivals and presented all sacrifices as a group (Dt. 12:7; 14:26; 15:20). As the Passover meal, each *bayith*, "household," was supposed to eat a roasted lamb together (Ex. 12:3f.). According to the Priestly law, an unmarried daughter was to stay in her father's *bayith*, "house" (Nu. 30:4[3]). A married woman was considered to be part of her husband's *bayith* (Nu. 30:11[10]). A childless widow (→ אלמנה *'almānāh*) or a divorcée (*gerushah*) was to return to her father's *bayith* (Nu. 30:10f.[9f.]; cf. also Ruth 1:8-14). In the genealogical hierarchy, the *bayith* was a subdivision of the clan (→ משפחה *mishpāchāh*), which in turn was a subdivision of the tribe (→ שבט *shēbhet*) (Josh. 7:14).

There has long been recognized in the OT a certain solidarity between a man and his house. If a man committed a serious sin, God's punishment fell on him and his house (Josh. 7:1-15, etc.). Similarly, God delivered an innocent man (or an innocent woman) and his (or her) house from punishment (Gen. 7:1; Josh. 2:12; 6:22; 1 K. 17:15). Joshua tells the Israelite assembly at Shechem that he and his house will serve Yahweh (Josh. 24:15; cf. also Acts 16 in the NT).

Units that were smaller than the tribe but larger than single families were also called *bayith: beth 'aharon*, "house of Aaron" (Ps. 115:10,12; 118:3); and *beth makhir*, "house of Machir" (2 S. 9:4). But ordinarily such a unit was called *mishpachah*, "clan" (Nu. 26:6,57), and their members *bene*, "sons of," + a proper name (Ex. 6:19; Nu. 3:20; etc.). Since *bayith* also meant "descendants," the tribe was often called the "house" of its ancestor: *beth levi*, "house of Levi" (Ex. 2:1), *beth yehudhah*, "house of Judah" (2 S. 2:4,7,10,11; 12:8; etc.), *beth 'ephrayim*, "house of Ephraim" (Jgs. 10:9), and *beth binyamin*, "house of Benjamin" (2 S. 3:19; 1 K. 12:23; etc.). Above the tribe in the hierarchy stood the tribal league, which often formed a state. This league was also called a *bayith*. In the period of the judges and of the first three kings of Israel (Saul, David, and Solomon), this league was composed of twelve tribes. It was called *beth yisra'el*, "the house of Israel" (1 S. 7:2,3; 2 S. 1:12; 6:5,15; 12:8; 16:3). Beginning with the reign of Rehoboam we find two leagues: the northern league, which was called *beth yisra'el*, "house of Israel" (1 K. 12:21; etc.), and the southern league, which was called *beth yehudhah*, "house of Judah" (1 K. 12:21,23; 2 K. 19:30; etc.). It is worthy of note that Ezekiel frequently uses *beth yisra'el* as an address (182 times).[21] His term *beth meri*, "rebellious house" (Ezk. 2:5-8; 3:9,26f.; etc.), seems to be a derogatory synonym of "house of Israel" (like *beth 'aven*, "house of iniquity," instead of *beth 'el*, "house of God," in Hos. 4:15).

If the ancestor after whom the house was named was a king, we should translate the word *bayith* "dynasty" (cf. the use of Ugar. *ḥwt* mentioned above).[22] This linguistic usage is found in the expressions *beth sha'ul*, "house of Saul"

---

[21] Cf. G. A. Danell, *Studies in the Name Israel* (Uppsala, 1946), 237f.
[22] See I.4 above.

(2 S. 3:1,6,8,10; 9:1-3; 16:5,8; 19:18[17]); *beth davidh,* "house of David" (1 S. 20:16; 1 K. 12:16; 13:2); *beth 'ach'abh,* "house of Ahab" (2 K. 8:18,27); *beth yehu',* "house of Jehu" (Hos. 1:4); *beth yerobh'am,* "house of Jeroboam" (1 K. 13:34; 14:10; 16:3; 21:22); and *beth ba'sha',* "house of Baasha" (1 K. 16:3,7; 21:22). In the prophecy of Nathan (2 S. 7:4-17 = 1 Ch. 17:3-15), there is a word-play on *bayith.* On the one hand it is used of the temple David wanted to build (2 S. 7:5,13), and on the other, of the dynasty of David which Yahweh promised to establish for ever (2 S. 7:11,16 = 1 Ch. 17:10).

VII. Designation for Household, Estate, or Wealth. The word *bayith* can also mean "what is in the house," i.e., possessions, tools, servants, and cattle. The original tenth commandment of the Decalog prohibits coveting the house of one's neighbor (Ex. 20:17a); the latter addition to this command (v. 17b) explains this as including wife, manservant, maidservant, ox, ass, and "anything that is your neighbor's." After the death of Haman, his whole "house" (i.e., estate) was given to Queen Esther (Est. 8:1). Jacob was concerned about the poor condition of his house (i.e., wealth, Gen. 30:30). Balaam regarded a reward amounting to *melo' bheth,* "a house full," as unacceptable for his task (Nu. 22:18; 24:13). Similarly, a prophet of Judah refused a reward amounting to half of the *bayith* of Jeroboam I (1 K. 13:8). The Egyptian Pharaoh appointed Joseph as overseer of his whole "house" (Gen. 39:4f.; 41:40). The book of Genesis mentions an anonymous official who was the steward of Joseph's house (Gen. 43:16, 19; 44:1,4). The Egyptian title for such an official was *ḥry pr,* "he who is placed over the house." [23]

VIII. In Place Names. Among places names the first element of which is the word *bayith,* we may mention the following:
1. Those in which the second element is a divine name: *beth 'el,* "Bethel" (Gen. 12:8; etc.); *beth ba'al me'on,* "Beth-baal-meon" (Josh. 13:17; shortened to *beth me'on,* "Beth-meon," Jer. 48:23, or *be'on,* "Beon," Nu. 32:3); *beth daghon,* "Beth-dagon" (Josh. 15:41; 19:27); *beth choron,* "Beth-horon" (Josh. 16:5; 18:13; etc.); *beth 'azmaveth,* "Beth-azmaveth" (Ezr. 2:24; Neh. 7:28; 12:29); *beth 'anoth,* "Beth-anath" (Josh. 15:59; 19:38; Jgs. 1:33); and *beth shemesh,* "Beth-shemesh" (Josh. 15:10; etc.);

2. Those in which the second element is a topographical term: *beth ha'arabhah,* "Beth-arabah" (Josh. 15:6,61; 18:18,22); *beth tsur,* "Beth-zur" (Josh. 15:58; etc.); *beth hayeshimoth,* "Beth-jeshimoth" (Nu. 33:49; Josh. 12:3; 13:20; etc.); *beth dibhlathayim,* "Beth-diblathaim" (Jer. 48:22); and *beth ha'emeq* "Beth-emek" (Josh. 19:27);

3. Those in which the second element is a simple substantive: *beth ha'etsel,* "Beth-ezel" (Mic. 1:11); *beth lebha'oth,* "Beth-lebaoth" (Josh. 15:32; 19:6);

---

[23] Cf. Heb. *'al habbayith* under III.2 above; and see J. Vergote, *Joseph en Egypte* (Leuven, 1959), 99, 171.

beth gadher, "Beth-gader" (Josh. 12:13; 1 Ch. 2:51); *beth haggilgal,* "Beth-gilgal" (Neh. 12:29); *beth hakkerem,* "Beth-haccherem" (Jer. 6:1); *beth lechem,* "Bethlehem" (Gen. 35:19; according to some scholars, originally a divine name stood here instead of "Bethlehem"); *beth hammarkabhoth,* "Beth-marcaboth" (Josh. 19:5; 1 Ch. 4:31); *beth tappuach,* "Beth-tappuah" (Josh. 15:53); *beth rechobh,* "Beth-rehob" (Nu. 13:21; Jgs. 18:28; 2 S. 10:6); and *beth hashshittah,* "Beth-shittah" (Jgs. 7:22);

4. Those in which the second element is a proper name or a family name: *beth choghlah,* "Beth-hoglah" (Josh. 15:6; 18:19,21); and *beth yo'abh,* "Beth-joab" (1 Ch. 2:54).

Hoffner

בָּכָה *bākhāh*

Contents: I. 1. Occurrences; 2. Meaning and Usage. II. Secular Weeping: 1. In Connection with Excitement; 2. In Connection with Emotional Grief; 3. Ritual Mourning. III. Religious Weeping: 1. Lament over Individual Distress; 2. In Connection with Popular Laments; 3. In Connection with Acts of Repentance; 4. Out of Awe; 5. In Eschatological Texts; 6. Cultic Wailing over a Deity.

I. 1. *Occurrences.* Since weeping is an act common to mankind, the verb *bkh* occurs in all Semitic languages (it is found in the OT *ca.* 130 times, and appears only in the qal and the piel [Jer. 31:15; Ezk. 8:14]). The substantives *bekheh,* "weeping" (? Ezr. 10:1), *bakhuth,* "weeping" (Gen. 35:8, "oak of weeping"; we should probably read *bakhuth,* "weeping," or *bekhoth,* "to weep," instead of *benoth,* "daughters, maidens," in Lam. 3:51), which occur once apiece in the OT, and *bekhi,* "weeping," which occurs 30 times in the OT, are derived from this root. In Gen. 50:4, *bekhith,* "weeping," is a collective denoting a funeral wake. A synonym of *bkh* is *dm',* "to shed tears" (the verb is found only

---

bākhāh. T. Collins, "The Physiology of Tears in the OT," *CBQ,* 33 (1971), 18-38, 185-197; P. Heinisch, *Die Trauergebräuche bei den Israeliten. BZfr,* 13/7-8 (1931); *idem, Die Totenklage im AT. BZfr,* 13/9-10 (1931); F. F. Hvidberg, *Weeping and Laughter in the OT. A Study of Canaanite-Israelite Religion* (posthumous English ed., 1962); review in *ZAW,* 57 (1939), 150-52; H. Jahnow, *Das hebräische Leichenlied. BZAW,* 36 (1923); E. Lipiński, *La liturgie pénitentielle dans la Bible. LD,* 52 (Paris, 1969); M. Noth, *ZThK,* 47 (1950)= *GSAT* (1957), 188-229; J. L. Palache, "Über das Weinen in der jüd. Religion," *ZDMG,* 70 (1916), 251-56; K. H. Rengstorf, "κλαίω, κλαυθμός," *TDNT,* III, 722-26; H. Ringgren, *Israelite Religion* (trans. 1966); J. Scharbert, *Der Schmerz im AT. BBB,* 8 (1955), 111f.; W. Schmidt, *ZRGG,* 15 (1963), 1-13; W. von Soden, *RGG³,* I, 688f.; G. Stählin, "κόπτω. Mourning in the OT," *TDNT,* III, 836-841; A. J. Wensinck, "Über das Weinen in den monotheistischen Religionen Vorderasiens," *Festschrift für E. Sachau* (1915), 26-35; C. Westermann, "Struktur und Geschichte der Klage im AT," *ZAW,* 66 (1954), 44-80; G. Widengren, *Sakrales Königtum* (1955); E. M. Yamauchi, *JBL,* 84 (1965), 283-290; *JSS,* 11 (1966), 10-15.

in Jer. 13:17; Sir. 12:16; 31:13) with its subst. *dimʿah,* "tear" (which occurs 24 times in the OT); this root is also widely attested in the Semitic languages.

2. *Meaning and Usage.* Like the Gk. *klaíō* and *dakrýō,* and the Lat. *fleo* and *lacrimo,* Heb. *bkh,* "weeping," comes from the mouth and voice, while *dmʿ,* "shedding tears," comes from the eyes[1] (thus Ps. 102:10 [Eng. v. 9] does not mean "I mingle my drink with tears," but "amidst weeping"). Of course, these two ideas can be connected (par.: Isa. 16:9; Jer. 8:23[9:1]; 13:17; 31:16 ["voice/ weeping, eyes/tears"]; Ezk. 24:16; Mal. 2:13; Ps. 126:5f.; Lam. 1:2,16). We encounter *demaʿ* or *dimʿah* more in lyrical texts, esp. in the Pss., Jer., and Lam.; in the Pentateuch and the Historical Books this substantive appears only in 2 K. 20:5. Since *bkh,* "to weep, bewail," has a broader meaning, it is used more frequently than *dmʿ* and can appear alongside a series of similar expressions. [2] Even to the present day, Orientals do not weep quietly, but are quite inclined to loud weeping and lamenting, thus explaining the frequent connection of *bkh,* "weeping," with *qol,* "the voice," in the OT. [3] Also *bkh* is modified by the adv. "bitter" (→ מר *mar*), [4] which expresses more the violent emotion connected with weeping: Isa. 22:4; 33:7; Jer. 31:15; Sir. 38:17; cf. Ezk. 27:31. Verbs meaning "to laugh, to rejoice," are used in antithesis to *bkh* in the OT: Isa. 65:19; Mic. 1:10; Ps. 30:6(5); 126:5f.; Eccl. 3:4; Ezr. 3:13; Bar. 4:11,23.

Using several examples, Collins tries to show that according to the popular and poetic idea, the source of tears was the inner part of man, especially the heart, from which they ascend into the throat and eyes. From a psychosomatic point of view, weeping is an outpouring of physical energy.

II. Secular Weeping.

1. *In Connection with Excitement.* Apart from the weeping of little children (Ex. 2:6; Wisd. 7:3), weeping is an indication of the widest variety of excitement: in Nu. 11:4,10,13,18,20 *bkh* is used to describe the behavior of the murmuring people, and in Jgs. 14:16f. that of the angry wife of Samson. The weeping of those returning from exile (Jer. 31:9; 50:4) refers more to a feeling and anxiety about the future than real mourning. Likewise, Ps. 126:5f. probably reflects the concept of a type of grief which had become proverbial in the statement: "They who sow in tears will reap with joy." We cannot be sure whether cultic wailing for a vegetation deity stands behind this line; [5] in any case, the postexilic poet of this psalm no longer knew of such an ancient background for it. People also weep in connection with the unexpected joy of meeting someone they had not seen before or for a long time: Jacob: Gen. 29:11; 33:4; Joseph: Gen. 42:24; 43:30; 45:2; 46:29; 50:17; Tobias: Tob. 7:6f.; 11:9,13.

---

[1] Collins, 20ff.
[2] See below, II.3.
[3] Cf. Collins, 37f.
[4] Collins, 35.
[5] Hvidberg, 133f.

2. *In Connection with Emotional Grief.* But usually weeping is an expression of emotional grief (of course, this is not to overlook that there is such a thing as feigned weeping: Jer. 41:6; Sir. 12:16), e.g., in cases like the weeping of Hannah who was greatly provoked, 1 S. 1:7,8,10; Israel's weeping because of the distress they were suffering at the hands of a threatening enemy army, 1 S. 11:4; 30:4; weeping because of a coming calamity or a calamity that had already begun, 2 K. 8:11f.; Isa. 15:3,5; 22:4; 33:7; Jer. 8:23(9:1); 9:9(10); 13:17; 14:17; 48:5, 32 = Isa. 16:9; Mic. 1:10; [6] Lam. 1:2,16; 3:51; weeping at a time of bidding farewell, 1 S. 20:41; 2 S. 3:16; Ruth 1:9,14; Tob. 5:16,22; weeping on the occasion of David's flight from Jerusalem, 2 S. 15:23,30; weeping of God's people in exile, Ps. 137:1; Bar. 1:5; 4:11,23; weeping over the temple, Ezr. 3:12; weeping because of suffering and sympathy, Job 2:12; 16:16; 30:25,31; Eccl. 4:1; weeping because of anxiety, Est. 8:3; Tob. 7:17; Rachel's weeping for her children, Jer. 31:15; and weeping over those who despise God's law, Ps. 119:136. We may add to this in particular weeping on the occasion of the death of close friends or relatives: Gen. 23:2; 35:8; 37:34f.; 50:1,3; Nu. 20:29; Dt. 34:8; 2 S. 13:36; 19:2 (1); Jer. 8:23(9:1).

3. *Ritual Mourning.* In times of affliction and suffering of a private and public nature, frequently weeping was only one aspect of stereotyped mourning rites. These are enumerated along with weeping in a number of OT texts: Isa. 15:2-5; 22:12; Ezk. 24:22f.; Joel 2:12f.; Est. 4:1-3. A special case among these rites is the mourning for the dead which was practiced by many peoples of antiquity (→ אבל *'ābhal,* "to mourn"; *saphadh,* "to wail, lament"). [7] Since these rites correspond to a great extent with the natural indication of grief, a magical effect for or against the dead is not likely, at least in the OT. The weeping of relatives and friends was a regular part of the lament over the dead. Professional mourners (Am. 5:16f.; Eccl. 12:5; 2 Ch. 35:25), and especially mourning women (2 S. 1:24; Jer. 9:16,19[17,20]; 49:3; Ezk. 32:16; Ps. 78:64; Job 27:15), were called to weep in times of death. Again, the expression "to weep" in particular is used to describe lamenting over the dead: 2 S. 1:11f.; 3:32-34; Jer. 22:10; 1 Macc. 9:20; Sir. 38:16f. There seems to have been an annual lament over the daughter of Jephthah and king Josiah (Jgs. 11:40; 2 Ch. 35:25). However, the account of the daughter of Jephthah who bewails her virginity contains a problem which can hardly be resolved, viz., whether this text perhaps originally represented a different setting for the lament motif (a wedding custom? a cultic custom?), which has been "historicized" by the story of Jephthah's sacrifice. The more formal the lament, the more one would have to doubt the inner sympathy of the mourner; but usually sympathy was not lacking (cf. Sir. 38:16-23). The poetic transition of the lament to an entire nation by the literary prophets (in particular using the verb "to weep": Jer. 9:9,16f.[10,17f.]; Ezk. 27:31) grew out of the popular lament. The purpose here is not consolation, but emotion.

---

[6] Cf. S. J. Schwantes, *VT,* 14 (1964), 455.
[7] *TDNT,* III, 836-39.

III. Religious Weeping.

1. *Lament over Individual Distress.* Ordinary human weeping has hardly any religious significance. The "lament over distress" has more theological significance and is completely different from the lament over the dead. In his affliction, man weeps before God (Dt. 1:45; 2 K. 20:3 = Isa. 38:3; 2 K. 22:19 = 2 Ch. 34:27; Tob. 3:1) as a means of intensifying his prayer and of arousing God's compassion (Isa. 30:19; Ps. 6:7-9[6-8]; 39:13[12]; 56:9[8]; Sir. 35:17-20). Man knows that he is dependent on God, acknowledges his own destitution, and hopes for grace from the strong and yet compassionate judge (→ *'ābhal*). Thus the consolation of God follows the weeping of those returning home from exile (Jer. 31:9). There is homesickness and trust in God in the tears of the lonely: Ps. 42:4(3); Job 16:20. Moreover, this sort of humble behavior is assumed in the well-known genre, the Individual Lament, even if the word "weeping" does not occur. In a prayer of thanksgiving we read: "he delivered (kept) my eyes from tears" (Ps. 116:8). The narrative in 2 S. 12:15-23 relates a very peculiar set of circumstances: as long as the sick child is alive, David fasts and weeps in order to persuade God to spare the child; but after the lad dies, he stops his acts of penitence and grief. Here the secular lament over the dead is transformed and is replaced by the lament over distress. But it should not be concluded from this that a general change of custom took place.

2. *In Connection with Popular Laments.* Quite similarly, "weeping" also occurs in texts dealing with the collective popular lament, either in connection with a threatening public distress or a public distress which was already a reality: Jgs. 20:23,26; 21:2; weeping is connected with fasting in Zec. 7:3; Bar. 1:5; 1 Macc. 7:36; 2 Macc. 11:6; 13:12; Ps. 80:6 (5, "bread of tears"); Lam. 2:18. Its setting (*Sitz im Leben*) is usually an assembly for public worship. Combined cultic "weeping" is also mentioned in Nu. 25:6; Jgs. 2:4 (here with an etiological explanation of the name "Bochim"). The Israelites weep because of remorse and shame (Jer. 3:21), and thus show their readiness to return to God. The people weep because God will not accept their sacrifice: Mal. 2:13.

3. *In Connection with Acts of Repentance.* In the postexilic period, public confessions of sin are connected with general prayers of petition and lament where "weeping" is mentioned. In conjunction with such acts of repentance, "weeping" is a sign of acknowledgement of sin and of remorse over having broken the covenant: Ezr. 10:1; Neh. 1:4; Joel 2:12-17. Collective penitent weeping is typically biblical, and is just as foreign to Greek texts of lamentation as is the weeping of imploring and hoping in prayer. [8]

4. *Out of Awe.* In addition to all the forms of lament over distress and remorse, there is also a weeping which simply arises from a consciousness of the distance between small, weak man and God. It is the result of being over-

---

[8] *TDNT*, III, 724.

come by the *Mysterium tremendum et fascinosum* (awful and fearful mystery). However, there is hardly any evidence of this religious motif in the OT (? Hos. 12:5[4]; Neh. 8:9), but it does appear in the LXX of Ps. 95:6 (94:6 in LXX): "Let us weep before the Lord, our Maker" (the LXX translator has confused *barakh* with *bakhah*). Furthermore, in harmony with the predominant concept of God in the OT, God is never described as one who weeps in any of its anthropopathic statements. The only terms used to describe his emotional feelings are → עצב *'ātsabh,* "to be grieved"; → כעס *kā'as,* "to be angry"; and → נחם *nācham,* "to be sorry, repent." [9]

5. *In Eschatological Texts.* With the rise of eschatological expectations, we find promises to the righteous that Yahweh will wipe away tears from all faces (Isa. 25:8; cf. 65:19). Apocalyptists prepare themselves to receive visions by fasting and weeping (4 Esd. 5:13,20; 6:35; 2 Bar. 9:2). When the judgment draws near, there will be weeping (2 Bar. 48:41; 52:3), and the sinners especially will weep in the place where they are afflicted (1 En. 96:2; 108:3,5; 2 En. 7:2), an idea which forms a transition to the NT texts dealing with the final judgment. [10]

6. *Cultic Wailing over a Deity.* In the heathen cult drama, it appears that worshippers bewailed the death of different vegetation deities. Ezekiel sees the weeping for Tammuz before the Jerusalem temple (Ezk. 8:14), which he considers to be an abomination.

As has already been mentioned above, representatives of the so-called Myth and Ritual school in particular believe that Jgs. 11:34-40 and Ps. 126:5f. go back to such a custom, and they suppose that there are still slight traces of it lying behind many OT passages. In their syncretistic rites, Israelites also probably wept over Yahweh as a dying and rising god; indeed, the sacral king himself probably represented him in the drama of the official cult. [11] It must be said that advocates of this view have to press their exegesis too far to arrive at such a position. The idea that such foreign customs were adopted by orthodox Israel is methodologically doubtful and purely hypothetical. But we do know, particularly from the reproaches of the prophets, that the Baal cult posed a threat to the Yahweh religion from the very first. It is uncertain whether there was specifically a weeping for Yahweh/Baal.

Hamp

---

[9] Scharbert, 223.

[10] *TDNT,* III, 724f.; on "wailing and gnashing of teeth," cf. *BZ,* N.F. 16 (1972), 121f.

[11] Thus esp. Widengren and more cautiously Hvidberg, cf. p. 136, with basic material concerning "cultic weeping."

בְּכוֹר bᵉkhôr;   בכר bkr;

בְּכֹרָה bᵉkhōrāh;   בִּכּוּרִים bikkûrîm

Contents: I. The Root *bkr:* 1. Meaning; 2. Derivatives. II. 1. *bikkurim;* 2. *bᵉkhôr(ôth)* (of beasts) in the Law. III. "Firstborn": 1. In the Ancient Near East: a. Arabia; b. Mesopotamia in the Bronze Age, and Surrounding Regions; c. Ugarit; d. Egypt; 2. In Israel: a. Terms for "Firstborn"; b. The Concept "Firstborn"; c. The Position of the Firstborn According to the Law: α. Right of Succession; β. In the Cult; d. The Role of the Firstborn and Its Theological Significance in the Narratives.

I. The Root bkr.

1. *Meaning.* The Arab. *bkr* (in different roots) means "to arise, do (something) early" (so similarly in Ethiop.); Syr. *bkr* in the pael, "to be the first, do (something) as the first"; the Middle Heb., Targum, Christian Palestinian, Aram. *bkyr(h),* "early rain"; and the Middle Heb. *bkyr,* "early cultivation." Akk. *bukru,* "son," stands as an exception (it is used mainly in poetic texts and is applied chiefly to the gods and only very rarely to men). In different languages, we find mostly one-syllable substantives for "firstborn" derived from this root (Aram. *bakr,* Heb. *bekhor,* Arab. *bikr,* Ethiop. *bakʷer*).[1] *bakkaru, bakru,* "young camel, young ass," in Akkadian is probably related to this root (cf. Arab. *bakr*).[2] These different terms indicate that the central meaning of the root *bkr* in Hebrew, "firstborn," is the original one. The nuances "early (earliest)" and "offspring, successor," are present in this idea in a similar way and in a close relationship. This original meaning of *bkr* occurs in all these languages (except Akk.), and also in vulgar Aramaic, Ugaritic, and South Arabic.

2. *Derivatives.* Several verb forms are derived from the root *bkr:* the piel, "to bear new fruit" (Middle Heb., "to ripen early," "to bear or give birth for the

bᵉkhôr. A.-G. Barrois, *Manuel d'archéologie biblique,* II (1953), 28-30; I. Benzinger, *Hebräische Archäologie* (³1927), index, p. 416b; L. Delekat, *BHHW,* I, 434; O. Eissfeldt, *Erstlinge und Zehnten im AT. BWANT,* 22 (1917); J. G. Frazer, *Folk-Lore in the OT,* I (1918), 429-566; abridged ed. (1923), 172-204; T. H. Gaster, *IDB,* IV, 148f.; E. S. Hartom, *EMiqr,* II, 123-26, 126-28; J. Hempel, "Ein Vorfrage zum Erstgeburtsopfer," *ZAW,* 54 (1936), 311-13; J. Henninger, "Zum Erstgeborenenrecht bei den Semiten," *Festschrift für W. Caskel* (1968), 162-183; Y. Kaufmann, *The Religion of Israel,* abridged by M. Greenberg (1960), 188f.; J. Klíma, *Untersuchungen zum altbabylonischen Erbrecht* (1940), 15-33; V. H. Kooy, *IDB,* II, 270-72; F. R. Kraus, "Vom altmesopotamischen Erbrecht," *Essays in Oriental Laws of Succession. Studia ... ad iura orientis antiqui pertinentia,* IX (1969), 1-13; *idem,* "Erbrechtliche Terminologie im alten Mesopotamien," *Essays,* 18-57; W. Michaelis, "πρωτότοκος, πρωτοτοκεῖα," *TDNT,* VI, 871-881; J. Morgenstern, *IDB,* II, 270; Pedersen, *ILC,* III-IV, 299-307, 313-322; W. R. Smith, *Lectures on the Religion of the Semites* (²1907, ³1927), 462-65; de Vaux, *AncIsr,* 41f., 53, 380f., 404, 490ff.; A. Wendel, "Erstlinge," *RGG³,* II, 609f.

[1] *AHw,* 137.
[2] *AHw,* 97.

first time"), "to treat (legally) as a firstborn"; the pual, "to belong to Yahweh as a firstborn"; and the hiphil, "to bear or give birth for the first time." A number of nouns come from this same root: *bekhorah*, "position of the firstborn" (the "firstborn" is called *bekhirah*); *bekher*, "young camel"; *bikhrah*, "young she-ass" (in light of the context in Jer. 2:23f. [3] and of Akk. *bakru*, "abundance of asses," it is hardly justifiable to translate *bikhrah* as "female camel"[4]); *bikkurah*, "early fruit"; and *bikkurim*, "firstfruits." In addition, three or four proper names are derived from this root, which are mainly Benjaminite.

II. 1. *bikkurim*. *bikkurim*, "firstfruits," usually has a cultic connotation. It is used generally and ambiguously in Ex. 23:19; 34:26; Nu. 18:13; 28:26; Ezk. 44:30; Neh. 10:36 (Eng. v. 35); 13:31. It is used of the firstfruits of the field, including bread, in Ex. 23:16; 34:22; Lev. 2:14; 23:17,20; 2 K. 4:42; and of plants in Nu. 13:20 (grapes); Nah. 3:12 (figs); Neh. 10:36(35). The relationship of the firstfruits called *bikkurim* to those called →רֵאשִׁית *rē'shîth* and to those called *re'shith bikkurim* (Ex. 23:19; 34:26; Ezk. 44:30), and the specific significance of each of these in the cult, cannot be completely explained by the extensive synonymity of these expressions, especially since *re'shith* can also mean "the best." [5] In what follows, the few passages that use only *re'shith* to denote "first-fruits" will be noted. According to the legislation in Ex. 23 and 34, the firstfruits (probably at the second pilgrimage festival) were to be brought into the sanctuary; but we are not told what was done with them there. The same thing applies to the legislation in P (Lev. and Nu.), except that this material states that the firstfruits are to be brought during the celebration of the Feast of Weeks, [6] and that they are to be given to the priest as a tax. In Deuteronomy, which uses only *re'shith* (18:4; 26:1ff.), there is no technical term for placing the firstfruits in the temple. In 18:4, the firstfruits are purely priestly taxes (cf. Neh. 10:38[37]). Attempts to reconstruct a historical development of the use of firstfruits from these data fail to produce any conclusive results.

2. *bekhor(oth)* (of beasts) in the Law. *bekhor(oth)* means "firstborn" of beasts (in apposition to or in connection with *peter* [*rechem*], "that which first opens [the womb]"). In the law it is given, in a certain sense, a "middle position" between vegetable firstfruits and human firstborn. The pertinent texts frequently deal with the firstborn of beasts in connection with these, and as far as possible from the same point of view. According to Ex. 13:2,12(f.); 22:28(29); 34:19(f.), the male firstborn of clean beasts are to be set apart for God; Ex. 13:15 expressly commands that they be sacrificed. The laws in P are similar to those in Exodus: the firstborn belong to God (Lev. 27:26[f.]; Nu. [3:41]; 8:17; 18:15,17f. [they are to be sacrificed, but usually this is done by the priests]). Unclean beasts are redeemed; Exodus leaves it up to the owner either to redeem an ass or to kill it

---

[3] See Ben Yehuda's *Wörterbuch*, 7620b, n.

[4] *KBL*[3].

[5] See *GesB, s.v.*

[6] Cf. Elliger, *HAT*, 4, 316.

by breaking its neck. But according to Deuteronomy the owner must eat the firstborn in the sanctuary (12:6; 14:23; 15:19f.). 15:19f. explains that they are holy and forbids any profane usufruct. Finally, Dt. 18:4 allots the first (re'shith) fleece that is sheared to the priests.

III. "Firstborn."

1. *In the Ancient Near East.* a. *Arabia.* It seems reasonably certain from the material presented by Henninger that the pre-Islamic Arabs showed no preference for a firstborn son, at least as far as a right of succession was concerned. The Islamic law reflects nothing different from this. Deviations from this norm have been recorded occasionally in Palestine and Transjordan in more recent times, but too rarely and too unimpressively to require a reassessment of this picture. Henninger suggests the possibility "that the law of the firstborn (among the Semites) arose in a culture of seminomads"; [7] however, in making this statement he allows himself to be led essentially by general historical viewpoints.

b. *Mesopotamia in the Bronze Age, and Surrounding Regions.* There is no comprehensive study of the attitude toward the firstborn in ancient Mesopotamia; the works of Klíma and Kraus, which are limited to conditions in Old Babylonia (*ca.* 1800-1600 B.C.), are the most important contributions on this subject. There is no word corresponding to Heb. *bekhor* in ancient Mesopotamia. Sum. *ibila* can mean "firstborn, son who has claim to the inheritance" (this is the oldest meaning), but it does not have to mean this (there is no evidence that Akk. *aplu* means "firstborn" or "firstborn son who has claim to the inheritance"). [8] Moreover, *māru* (or *aḫu*) *rabû,* "greater elder son (brother)," occurs (the Heb. equivalent is found, e.g., in Gen. 27:42), which also means a son who is preferred to receive the right of succession. These two expressions also appear in combination (*aplu rabû*). There is no evidence for a uniform law on the right of succession. The Babylonian collections of laws contain no statutes on this subject, even though the Code of Hammurabi offered ample opportunity for such statutes, as in § 150 or 170ff. However, it is clear from private legal documents that on the whole in the Old Babylonian period the firstborn son enjoyed certain special privileges in matters pertaining to inheritance in southern and middle Babylonia, [9] but not in northern Babylonia. The *ana ittishu* series, a formal juridical collection from the southern Babylonian city of Nippur, takes into account injustices done to the firstborn (6:I:1-8). Here and elsewhere, the Sumerian term used to describe the privileged portion claimed for the firstborn is *síbta,* and the Akkadian term is *elātu.* By way of contrast, in an Old Babylonian letter concerning the northern Babylonian city of Sippar we read that contrary to the assumption of the female recipient, "there is no institution concerning younger and older heirs (*aplūtum ṣeḫertum u rabītum*) in Sippar." [10] There is a well-known document from the

---

[7] Henninger, 182.
[8] Cf. *AHw,* 58; *CAD,* I/2, 173-77.
[9] See, e.g., M. Schorr, *Urkunden des altbabylonischen . . . Rechts* (1913), No. 20.
[10] F. R. Kraus, *Altbabylonische Briefe,* I (1964), No. 92:16f.

city of Mari on the middle Euphrates from the Hammurabi period which explicitly affirms the priority of the firstborn. [11] In Middle Assyrian law, this privileged position is firmly established in legal statutes (Laws B § 1 = O § 3 [*ca.* 1350-1150 B.C.]), and according to evidence found in some documents [12] was actually practiced. The right of the firstborn is also practiced everywhere in the Hurrian city of Nuzi (15th-14th centuries B.C.); [13] however, in wills of those who had died we encounter partial or complete deviations from this legal practice. [14] In contrast to this, in Alalach (in northwest Syria), which was influenced by Hurrians, no trace of the idea of the privilege of the firstborn has been found, notwithstanding assertions to the contrary.

The size of the portion given to the firstborn (his normal inheritance plus a preferential portion) is not the same in the various cuneiform laws; but as far as we now know, usually the firstborn received twice as much as each succeeding son, but sometimes less. [15]

c. *Ugarit.* From the life of the city-state of Ugarit in the middle or latter half of the 13th century B.C. we know the following concerning the privilege of the firstborn. A father leaves his two sons an inheritance divided equally between them, but allots to the older son a field as an additional portion; we do not know the size of the portion given to the elder son in relationship to the entire inheritance. [16] Another document dealing with an inheritance also may have said something about the special position of the elder son in a damaged portion of the tablet. [17] Finally, there is a remote possibility that a third document refers to the privileged position of the firstborn; [18] Nougayrol thinks that this is certain. [19] The conclusions that had been reached about the primacy of the firstborn at Ugarit in the legal documents which were published before 1968 have no foundation. In the documents belonging to the narrative literature, there are only one or two allusions to the position of honor and preference held by the firstborn child! King *Krt* and king *Pbl* strive to marry the "lovely *Hry,* the child of thy firstborn," or perhaps "thy firstborn child" (*šph bkrk*). [20] In a later chapter the god El promises *Krt* many offspring and says in conclusion: *ṣġrthn 'bkrn,* [21] which is usually translated, "I will declare the youngest to be the firstborn." As far as grammar and subject matter are concerned, this is incontestable; but in the portions of the text that have been preserved this interpretation has nothing

---

[11] *ARM,* VIII, 1.

[12] E.g., *AfO,* 20 (1963), 121f.

[13] E.g., E. M. Cassin, *L'adoption à Nuzi* (1938), 285-88.

[14] E.g., C. H. Gordon, *AnOr,* 12 (1935), 171f. (as well as *CAD,* XXI, 140b); E. A. Speiser, *JCS,* 17 (1963), 70.

[15] See Klíma, 29-32.

[16] J. Nougayrol, *Ugaritica,* V (1968), 10f.: RS 17.36.

[17] *Ibid.,* 12: RS 17.38, line 6; but cf. Gen. 43:33.

[18] *Ibid.,* 173: RS 21.230, line 5.

[19] *Ibid.,* 174, n. 1.

[20] *CTA,* 14 [I K], IV, 144.

[21] *CTA,* 15 [III K], III, 16.

to support it. Nor is there any basis for the outlandish explanations of this text that have been suggested. [22]

d. *Egypt.* We know nothing about the position of the firstborn in the Jewish military colony of Elephantine (5th century B.C.). In Hellenistic Egypt the first-born was especially privileged, but there is much about this that is still obscure. [23]

2. *In Israel.* a. *Terms for "Firstborn."* The usual term for firstborn in the OT is *bekhor.* Sometimes *gadhol,* "elder, eldest," means firstborn representatively (e.g., in Gen. 27:1,42; 44:12). *qaton* and *tsaʿir,* "younger, youngest," occur in antithesis to both of these terms. Once *rabh,* "elder," is used in the sense of firstborn, and *tsaʿir* appears in antithesis to it (Gen. 25:23: archaizing; cf. the Akk. *rabū-ṣeḫru*). [24] The Chronicler uses several expressions for the favored position of a son who is not a firstborn, and these occur in explicit contrast to the root *bkr.* These expressions are: *gabhar,* "to become strong" (1 Ch. 5:[1-]2, in dependence on Gen. 27:37); *naghidh,* "prince" (1 Ch. 5:[1-]2); and *roʾsh,* "chief" (1 Ch. 26:10).

b. *The Concept "Firstborn."* In the laws of Exodus and Numbers, especially in texts that treat human and animal firstborn together, and in Ezk. 20:26 the expression *peter (rechem),* "one who opens (the womb)," is used frequently. This phrase defines the firstborn with reference to his mother. However, this definition could not have been the predominant one. Not only did it stand in opposition to the emphatic patriarchal character of the Israelite family, but also it would have seriously damaged the idea and legal custom of primogeniture, especially in the case of contemporary (occasional) polygamy. Israel adhered to laws of primogeniture through the father. The firstborn was called *reʾshith ʾon,* "the first of the (procreative) strength" of the father, also and even particularly in texts that deal with polygamy (Gen. 49:3; Dt. 21:17; cf. Ps. 78:51; 105:36).

c. *The Position of the Firstborn According to the Law.* α. *Right of Succession.* According to Dt. 21:15-17, a father is forbidden to disregard the order of the birth of his sons and to assign the privileged position of the major beneficiary of his possessions to his favorite son who is not the firstborn. This is called "the right of the firstborn" (*mishpat habbekhorah*), which is defined as *"pi shenayim* of all that he (i.e., the testator) has." According to some scholars, e.g., Noth, [25] *pi shenayim* means "two-thirds," i.e., the firstborn received two-thirds of the entire inheritance, and all the other sons received an equal of the other third. Noth's reasons are: (1) the above-mentioned Mari text, [26] which has *shittîn,* "two-thirds," in a situation comparable to that described in Dt. 21:15-17; and

---

[22] A. van Selms, *Marriage and Family Life* (1954), 140f.; J. Gray, *The Krt Text in the Literature of Ras Shamra* (²1964), 60.

[23] P. W. Pestman, in *Essays on Oriental Laws of Succession* (1969), 65-67, 77.

[24] On *peter (rechem)* and *reʾshith ʾon,* see under b.

[25] M. Noth, *Die Ursprünge des alten Israel* (1961), 19f.

[26] III.1.b.

(2) Zec. 13:8. However, this interpretation must be rejected.[27] Actually, *pi shenayim* means "a portion of two, a double portion" (cf. Sir. 12:5). Thus, if there are three parties concerned, the firstborn would receive two-thirds; if there are four parties concerned, he would receive two-fourths, etc. This explanation is supported by a comparison with the pertinent texts from Mesopotamia.[28] It is impossible to be sure whether it is true that the inheritance which the law has in mind applies only to movable possessions, while the other possessions remain in the family undivided, as de Vaux would like to assume;[29] but this is not likely (Dt. 25:5 and Ps. 133:1[30] probably do not have the normal situation in mind). Esau sold this special portion and nothing else (Gen. 25:31-34), just as in Old Babylonia and in Nuzi inheritances are the object of buying and selling among brothers.[31] Esau's rank and position are not affected by this transaction, as chap. 27 shows quite clearly. On the other hand, the Elijah narrative uses the language of the law (*pi shenayim be*) symbolically to affirm and to defend the superiority of Elisha (2 K. 2:9) over the other prophets (vv. 3,5,7, and 15).

In connection with this diversity of opinion as to the size of the inheritance of the firstborn, the alleged intention of the lawgiver to maintain the uniformity of agricultural production as much as possible can have played only a subordinate role at best. To the contrary, the law of the firstborn is nothing but an expression of the exceedingly high esteem in which the first child was held, especially if that child was male. The first is the best. *re'shith* has both of these meanings, and in the expression *re'shith 'on,* "the first of the (procreative) strength," the latter sense is quite clear. Thus, *bekhor* assumes the meaning "excellent" (par. to *'elyon,* "highest," Ps. 89:28[27]), and actually functions as a sign of the elative when *bekhor* appears in the construct with *maveth,* "the firstborn of death" (Job 18:13), and *dallim,* "the firstborn of the poor" (Isa. 14:30).

β. *In the Cult.* It is not only the best that belongs to God, but also the first. It would be presumptuous for man to enjoy something without first giving God his portion. The firstborn of man and beast and the firstfruits of field and garden (see also Lev. 19:23-25) are given to God as his portion by sacral consecration, and therefore can be set free for secular use only by redemption (usually → פדה *pādhāh*), i.e., substitution or ransom (Ex. 13:13,15; 34:20; Lev. 27:26f.; Nu. 3:44-51; 18:15-17; Dt. 14:23-26). The firstborn of nonsacrificial animals and the firstborn of man must be redeemed. (Ezekiel's strange view of the plight of the firstborn in 20:25f. can be understood only in light of the overall context of his speech.) However, in the legislation in the book of Numbers (P), the law concerning the redemption of the firstborn of man is always connected with the appointment of the Levites (Nu. 3:11-13,40f.,44f.; 8:16-18; there is a transitional law in 3:46-48). The religio-phenomenological basis for God's claim on the firstborn is his mighty acts in Israel's history (Nu. 3:13; 8:17; anticipated by Ex.

---

[27] On this Mari text, see G. Boyer, *ARM,* VIII. *Textes juridiques* (1958), 182; linguistically, Noth interprets Zec. 13:8 too narrowly.
[28] III.1.b.
[29] *AncIsr,* 53.
[30] See H. Gunkel, *in loc.*
[31] Schorr, *Urkunden,* 232; E. H. Cassin, *L'adoption,* 230-33.

13:15): when God slew "all the firstborn in the land of Egypt"(!), all the first-born fell to him (cf. Ex. 12:12f.,23). It is true that he spared the firstborn of the Israelites, but this does not mean that he relinquishes his claim on them, but only that he changes its nature.

d. *The Role of the Firstborn and Its Theological Significance in the Narratives.* If civil and sacral law testify to a firmly established position of the firstborn, everything in the narratives is in a state of flux. The stories of Abel and Cain, Jacob and Esau, Joseph (Judah) and Reuben, Ephraim and Manasseh (Moses and Aaron, David and his brothers, Solomon and Adonijah) have some bearing on the subject, and usually refer to a direct or indirect intervention of God. It is not unlikely that the patriarchal narratives want to describe a time in which the firstborn (frequently) enjoyed no privileged position. Frazer wants to find indications of an original ultimogeniture in Israel, [32] but this is little likely. But in their present form, these narratives are written for an audience which considers the laws of the firstborn to have full weight, and which, therefore, is fully aware of the tension between sacred history and present responsibility. The book of Genesis endeavors to present a heightening of this tension, as e.g., in the story of Ephraim and Manasseh in chap. 48, and this not only for aesthetic reasons but at least as much for religious reasons: God's freedom in leading his people in history preserves them from the usual human tendency to crystallize their traditions into an institution as they move from one generation to the next and as they form their society. From the diverse ideas and customs concerning the firstborn which were present in the cultures around Israel (and in the beginning probably also in Israel), the OT chooses that of the privileged position of the firstborn in the law and in the ritual of daily life in preference to the principle of equal prospects for the great lines of history. This principle makes possible a historical presentation of the early period when (in a very natural way) there was no permanent position of leadership or privilege of one tribe above another. This makes it possible for the narrative to bestow on Israel, which was still in the process of being constituted and which was the youngest of the nations, the title of firstborn: "Thus says the Lord, Israel is my firstborn son" (Ex. 4:22; echoed in Jer. 31:8f.). When Jeremiah speaks of the holiness of Israel and of the protection which God gives to his people, in the final analysis he bases this on the idea (again, contrary to all historical reality) that Israel is the first (*re'shith,* RSV "firstfruits") of Yahweh's harvest (Jer. 2:3), and therefore belongs to him and to him alone.

Tsevat

---

[32] Frazer, 429-433, 481-84, abridged ed., 172-75, 202-204.

בָּלָה *bālāh*

Contents: I. Etymology. II. Usage and Meaning: 1. Physical and Physiological; 2. Figurative: a. Deterioration of the Cosmos; b. Transitoriness of Man; 3. Enjoyment; 4. Ambivalence, Analogy to *kālāh*. III. Theology: 1. Relevance Only from the Context; 2. God As Hidden Subject.

I. **Etymology.** The radicals of the Heb. root *blh* form an ordinary Semitic root.[1] Outside the Hebrew language, it appears as a verb and a noun in Akkadian, in the later stages of Babylonian and Assyrian, meaning "to die out (go out of use), waste away (perish), condition of nonexistence."[2] Short forms[3] or later expansions of short forms are used as negatives, (negative) prepositions, and conjunctions in the entire spectrum of Semitic languages. *bal,* "not," *beli,* "not, without," and *bilti,* "not, except," frequently with *be, le,* and *min,* are more closely related etymologically.[4] However, they are of little semantic or theological relevance for the verb and noun forms found in the Bible. The etymology of → בְּלִיַּעַל *beliyyaʿal,* "Belial," is uncertain, and in any case it is considered to have become semantically independent. To be sure, *beli mah (belimah)* stands in parallelism to *tohu* in Job 26:7, but it should probably be interpreted as a preposition with a pronoun. Thus, these terms also are excluded from this discussion.

II. **Usage and Meaning.**

1. *Physical and Physiological.* In the earliest texts in which *blh* occurs, it is used as a verb and as an adjective and means that something that is ordinarily used daily has become worn out, "fragile," by time and use, and can hardly continue to be used even if it is repaired: *mebhuqqaʿim umetsorarim,* "torn and mended" (Josh. 9:4); *metullaʾoth,* "patched" (9:5); *hithbaqqaʿu,* "they are burst" (v. 13). At first sight, the wineskins, saddlebags, clothes, and sandals of the Gibeonites appear to the Israelites to be old (in antithesis to *chadhashim,* "new," v. 13) and scarcely able to be used any longer (vv. 4,5,13). In this context and elsewhere, the LXX usually translates *blh* by some form of *palaióō,* "to make old, become old." In Jer. 38:11f., the subst. **beloyim* or **beloʾim* means "rags, torn clothes."

Therefore, the absence of natural deterioration during the forty years that Israel was in the wilderness is regarded as evidence of the special guidance of

---

bālāh. P. Haupt, "Semitic Verbs derived from Particles," *AJSL,* 22 (1905/1906), 257-261; H. Seesemann, "παλαιός," *TDNT,* V, 717-720.

[1] Cf. *UT,* 19.474; *AHw,* 121.

[2] Cf. *CAD,* II, 63, 70f., 74f.; *AHw,* 100, 121; *UT,* 19, 474.

[3] According to Haupt, 259: the etymological origin of the verb.

[4] Cf. *KBL, s.v.; UT,* 19.466 with additional literature; for usages in the Qumran material, cf. J. A. Fitzmyer, *The Genesis Apocryphon of Qumran Cave I. BietOr,* 18A (²1971), 95f.

God (Dt. 8:4; cf. the LXX *ou katetríbe apó sou,* "did not wear out from thee"; however, LXX[B] is not as literal: *ouk epalaiṓthē,* "did not become old [wear out]"; see also Dt. 29:4 [Eng. v. 5] and the free quotation in Neh. 9:21). In Gen. 18:12, Sarah applies the "coarse term"[5] *blh* to herself as an old, withered woman (cf. "and my lord [husband] is old," Gen. 18:12b; notice here the careful distinction that is made between the idea that Sarah was "old," *blh,* and that Abraham was "old," → זָקֵן, *zāqēn* = *presbýteros* in the LXX of vv. 11a and 12b; the LXX did not translate *belothi* as an inf., but Aquila, *metá tó katatribḗnaí me,* "after I have worn out," and Symmachus *metá tó palaiōthḗnaí me,* "after I have become old," probably did).[6] *labbalah* in Ezk. 23:43 probably means a woman worn out by licentious living (the LXX understands this term as an interrogative particle expecting a negative answer plus a suffix: *ouk en toútois...,* "not in these...?").

In describing the persecutions of the Davidides, 1 Ch. 17:9 reads *lebhallotho,* "shall waste them," instead of *le'annotho,* "shall afflict them," in the parallel passage in 2 S. 7:10. There is a cognate Aramaic form, *yebhalle',* "he shall wear out" (LXX *katatrípsei,* "he shall wear out"; Theodotion *palaiṓsei,* "he shall become old"), which has a similar meaning, in Dnl. 7:25.

2. *Figurative.* a. *Deterioration of the Cosmos.* Israel's enemies are weak and feeble when God opposes them. In the third Servant Song of Deutero-Isaiah, first the prophet may be using the figure of the worn-out garment to describe them, and then (in parallelism) the figure of damage done by moths: Isa. 50:9, *kullam kabbeghedh yibhlu,* "all of them will wear out like a garment." This figure is expanded with parallel expressions in the variations (perhaps postexilic) that follow in this context: the heavens will vanish like smoke, the earth will wear out like a garment (*ha'arets kabbeghedh tibhleh*), they who dwell in it will die like gnats, but God's salvation will be immovable (Isa. 51:6; in 51:8, the figure of the moth eating a garment stands alone).[7] Similarly, in Ps. 102:27(26) the author contrasts God's stability with the heavens and the earth, which are transitory and easily replaceable like a garment. According to most ancient versions (but not the LXX), Job 14:12 states that the dead will awake when the heavens disappear (*bilti*), i.e., never, because it is assumed that they will not disappear.

b. *Transitoriness of Man.* In laments and wisdom texts, *blh* is used to describe the most severe distress of the worshipper (sometimes without the figure of a garment): the bones have wasted away (Ps. 32:3, *balu 'atsamai;* LXX: *epalaiṓthē tá ostá mou*) or have been broken, while the flesh and the skin have wasted away (Lam. 3:4, *billah bhesari ve'ori shibbar 'atsmothai;* cf. also Ps. 49:15[14], which, of course, is critically very difficult). The most general statement of this kind is probably the latest one: Sir. 14:17, "All flesh becomes old like a garment," death alone is eternal law (*kol habbasar kabbeghedh yibhleh vechoq 'olam gevoa' yighva'u*).

---

[5] According to Gunkel, *Genesis* ([7]1966), 198.

[6] Cf. Skinner, *Genesis. ICC* (1951), 301f.

[7] Cf. Westermann, *ATD,* XIX, 187-191.

3. *Enjoyment.* One or two examples stand in contrast to all these meanings. In Isa. 65:22 we find this statement: *uma'aseh yedhehem yebhallu bḥechirai,* "and my chosen ones shall long enjoy the work of their hands." The complaint concerning the wicked in Job 21:13 is similar: *yebhallu bhattobh yemehem,* "they enjoy their days in prosperity." Context and parallelism clearly show that *blh* has a positive sense in these passages: "to enjoy," [8] "to use for oneself," "not to be deprived of success by others." The LXX translators were not aware of this meaning. In Isa. 65:22, they translate *yebhallu* by the common *palaiōsousin,* "they will become old." In Job 21:13, they read *yekhallu,* "they complete (end)," instead of *yebhallu,* because it is often uncertain as to which of these was the original reading of the MT. A similar vacillation occurs in Isa. 10:25, where several Hebrew manuscripts have *takhlitham,* "their end," instead of *tabhlitham,* "their destruction," as Ps. 139:22; Job 28:3 (from *kalah*).

4. *Ambivalence, Analogy to kālāh.* Semantically *blh* seems to be ambivalent between a positive and a negative extreme, just like *kalah.* It is even possible that the very frequent root *klh* had some influence on the very rare root *blh,* which was reassumed only in the later period (with theological overtones). *blh* may have been selected intentionally to replace *klh,* especially in poetic texts, and therefore may have a stronger theological significance than *klh.* This would explain why the LXX translates the various forms of *blh* by some form of *palaióō,* "to become old," in all instances in which the Hebrew text reads some form of *blh* (the only exception is found in Dt. 29:4[5], which uses *katetríbē,* "[they were] worn out," which may have been suggested by the idea of the torn sandals or selected for the sake of variety). By way of contrast, *palaióō* is never used to translate the more than 30 different occurrences of the various forms of *klh.* It seems that the LXX translators did not know how to render the rare word *blh,* and always translated it mechanically and thus poorly (perhaps following the translation of some text, possibly Josh. 9, as precedent).

III. Theology.

1. *Relevance Only from the Context.* The earliest examples of the use of *blh* (and the only ones that are pre-Deuteronomic, Josh. 9:4,5,13; Gen. 18:12) are in and of themselves "natural," "secular," and have theological significance only as they are viewed in connection with certain facts in the life and history of Israel. Josh. 9:4,5,13 have an etiological purpose (cf. Josh. 9:27,21,24). What is at stake in Gen. 18:12 is the being or nonbeing of the people, the reliability of God's promises. The theological idea in Dt. 8:4 and 29:4(5) is intensified by the marvelous events during the period of wilderness wandering and by the parenetic or recitative-liturgical context, [9] but probably without any conscious allusion to Josh. 9.

---

[8] *KBL.*

[9] Cf. N. Lohfink, *Das Hauptgebot. AnBibl,* 20 (1963), 62, 191; E. W. Nicholson, *Deuteronomy and Tradition* (1967), 21.

There is no mechanical or technical idea connected with *blh:* the process this work describes is "obvious," inevitable (Josh. 9; Gen. 18:12); therefore, if the process is reversed, only God can do it (Dt. 8:4; 29:4[5]); man has no power to bring about any change at all.

2. *God As Hidden Subject.* Perhaps the early use of *blh* in a context that, although hardly based on theological considerations, still has to do with divine guidance, along with possible mythical ideas underlying[10] the figure of the worn-out garment which appears much later in the Bible,[11] were the main reasons why *blh* was popular in the prophetic context. The use of *blh* in Isa. 65:22 and Job 21:13 may represent a conscious effort to make concrete a frequently used, but perhaps somewhat faded idea of the anticipated time of salvation (cf. Am. 5:11; Mic. 6:15; Dt. 28:30-33; Isa. 52:8f.), or to give new color to the old complaint about the inexplicable success of the wicked, reveal the time of salvation evocatively as a work of God's power, and connect it with that which had been begun already in times of salvation in the past. In any case, it is impossible to understand how the interpretation of *blh* as mere "lesser value or valuelessness"[12] in Isa. 65:22 and Job 21:13 can be correct.

The intensive forms with transitive meaning and human subject could also be due to this theological coloring which *blh* apparently has received. In the final analysis, disastrous events are not the work of man. God stands behind them, unseen but assumed, to prevent them (1 Ch. 17:9), or to make clear their proper relationship as events of the last time which immediately precede the great transformation (Dnl. 7:25).

Gamberoni

---

10 Cf. Gilg. XI, 244-255, e.g., in *ANET*[3], 96a.
11 Cf. R. Eisler, *Weltenmantel und Himmelszelt*, I (1910), 51ff.
12 Seesemann, 718.

בְּלִיַּעַל *bᵉliyyaʿal*

Contents: I. Etymology, Occurrences. II. 1. As a Term Referring to the Powers of Chaos; 2. In Juridical Contexts; 3. In Connection with the King; 4. In Connection with Cultic Abuses. III. Usage in Late Judaism.

I. Etymology, Occurrences. The etymology of *bᵉliyyaʿal* is uncertain and debated; the ancient versions help define the various nuances of its meaning in

---

bᵉliyyaʿal. W. von Baudissin, "The Original Meaning of 'Belial,'" *ExpT,* 9 (1897/1898), 40-45; G. R. Driver, "Hebrew Notes," *ZAW,* 52 (1934), 51-56; K. Galling, "Belial," *RGG*[3], I, 1025f.; J. E. Hogg, "Belial in the OT," *AJSL,* 44 (1927/1928), 56-58; P. Joüon, "בליעל Bélial," *Bibl,* 5 (1924), 178-183; H. Kosmala, "The Three Nets of Belial," *ASTI,* 4 (1965), 91-

(continued on p. 132)

a general way, but do not illuminate the etymological problem it poses. [1] The attempts to explain this word etymologically fall into three main groups: a. in origin, it was a mythological term or was derived from a mythological name; b. originally it was a Hebrew neologism composed of the negative *beli* + a positive concept (usually expressed by a verbal form); c. it was derived from a root → בלע *bālaʿ*. [2]

a. Some scholars argue that *beliyyaʿal* evolved from the root → בעל *baʿal*, "Baal," by deliberate metathesis and the addition of a diminutive *lamedh*. [3] Nicolsky thinks it is a name for Azazel, composed of *baʿal* + *yaʿal*, "lord of he-goats." [4] Others maintain that it is a derivative of the name of the Akkadian goddess *Belili*. Since this goddess was a deity of the underworld, the Heb. derivative *beliyyaʿal* came to designate the underworld. [5] This interpretation is certainly incorrect, because the character of Belili as a deity of the underworld is extremely doubtful. [6]

b. According to the Rabbinic interpretation, which was later adopted by Jerome, *beliyyaʿal* comes from *beli* + *ʿol*, "yoke," and thus *beliyyaʿal* means those who throw off the yoke of God. [7] However, this explanation has become obsolete. In its place, two other interpretations in particular have become popular. One is that *beliyyaʿal* is a combination of *beli* + some form of the root *ʿalah*, "to go up," and thus means either "that which does not go up," i.e., "that which is not successful," thus "wickedness," etc., [8] or "(the place from which) one does not go up" (or "cannot go up"), and similar explanations which have reference to the underworld and are to be connected with the Akk. expression *māt (erṣet) lā tāri*, "the land from which there is no return." [9] However, most

113; V. Maag, "Bᵉlijaʿal im AT," *ThZ*, 21 (1965), 287-299; N. Nicolsky, *Spuren magischer Formeln in den Psalmen. BZAW*, 46 (1927); Pedersen, *ILC*, I-II; T. Stenhouse, "Baal and Belial," *ZAW*, 33 (1913), 295-305; D. Winton Thomas, "בליעל in the OT," *Biblical and Patristic Studies in Memory of R. P. Casey* (1963), 11-19.

Special literature on III: W. Bousset, *Die Religion des Judentums. HNT*, 21 (³1926); H. W. Huppenbauer, "Belial in den Qumrantexten," *ThZ*, 15 (1959), 81-89; B. Noack, *Satanás und Sotería* (Copenhagen, 1948); P. van den Osten-Sacken, *Gott und Belial. Studien zur Umwelt des NT*, 6 (1969).

[1] Synopses of the translations and paraphrases may be found in Hogg, 56f., and Thomas, 11f.
[2] A synopsis of the usual explanations occurs in Thomas, 15-19.
[3] Stenhouse, 299f.; and Maag, *SchThU*, 20 (1950), 35f., refer to *Baʿal-yam*.
[4] Nicolsky, 86.
[5] Cheyne, *ExpT*, 8 (1896/1897), 423f.; and *EMiqr*, I (1899), 525-27; cf. the extensive discussion in *ExpT*, 8 (1896/1897), and 9 (1897/1898), between Cheyne, von Baudissin, Hommel, and Jensen.
[6] Cf. *WbMyth*, I, 67f.; A. Falkenstein, *Festschrift für W. Caskel* (Leiden, 1968), 96-110.
[7] See Moore, *Judges* (1895), 419; cf. Thomas, 15.
[8] Baudissin, 44; cf. *KBL*³, 128.
[9] According to Cheyne, *loc. cit.*, as a popular etymological reinterpretation of the "mythological" derivative; cf. Nicolsky, 85; *CAD*, IV, 308; and Cross-Freedman, *JBL*, 72 (1953), 22.

modern scholars think it is a combination of *beli* + some form of the root *yaʿal*, which means "to profit, to benefit" (this verb occurs only in the hiphil). Thus, the last element in the word *beliyyaʿal* is usually interpreted as a verb in the qal or as a noun (neither form occurs in the OT), and *beliyyaʿal* is thought to mean "uselessness," "negative actions," "nothingness," etc. [10] These interpretations are supported by similar Hebrew forms (*beli daʿath*, "without knowledge," and *beli shem*, "without name") [11] and by the Ugar. expression *blmlk*, "no-king." [12]

c. In light of the cognate root in Arabic, some scholars argue that *beliyyaʿal* comes from the root *balaʿ*, which in turn can be interpreted in various ways. *balaʿ* III [13] is connected with Arab. *balaġa*, and means either "to entangle, confuse," [14] or "to harm, injure." [15] In view of this, *beliyyaʿal* could be taken as *balaʿ* with an afformative *-l*, which would mean either "entanglement, confusion," or "harm, damage" (perhaps "pest, vermin"). [16] Other critics retain the usual meaning of *balaʿ*, "to swallow," and then take *beliyyaʿal* to mean either "destruction," [17] "(devouring) abyss" = Sheol, [18] or personified "(mythological) enemy." [19]

There is hardly a convincing solution to the etymological problem posed by *beliyyaʿal*. This much can be said, however: it is based on some mythological term whose meaning we are no longer able to recover or on some name, which has been "interpreted" by popular etymology as a negative with the prefix *beli*. The twofold emphasis that comes to be attached to *beliyyaʿal* in the process of this development must be retained: concrete-personal and abstract-conceptual. Some scholars emphasize the abstract too strongly ("uselessness," etc.); others emphasize the personal: *Beliyyaʿal* is a devil figure [20] (lit. "a [being] without value"), a prince of the underworld, [21] or an "idol." [22] But the one side must not be emphasized at the expense of the other, and so in what follows we shall leave the word untranslated.

It is hard to say whether there is a reminiscence of mythological ideas in the frequent use of the phrase "sons of belial." [23] It seems more likely that what we have here is simply another example of the Hebrew idiom using *ben*, "son," with some term in order to indicate an intimate relationship between the person

[10] So the more recent Heb. lexicons, Pedersen, 413f., 539, and many others.
[11] Baudissin, 44.
[12] Galling, 1025.
[13] *KBL*³.
[14] Driver, 52f.
[15] Guillaume, *JTS,* 13 (1962), 321.
[16] See Maag, 287.
[17] Burney, *The Hebrew Text of Kings* (Oxford, 1903), 246f.
[18] Thomas, 18f.
[19] Haldar, *The Book of Nahum* (Uppsala, 1946), 33, 114.
[20] Joüon.
[21] Nicolsky, 85.
[22] Galling, 1025.
[23] Stenhouse, 299.

and the character or activity suggested by that term. [24] In turn, other expressions like *'ish beliyya'al, debhar beliyya'al,* etc., grow out of this one. *beliyya'al* has the article only three times (1 S. 25:25; 2 S. 16:7; 1 K. 21:13). [25] It occurs 27 times in the OT, mainly in the Deuteronomistic history (15 times), only twice in the Prophets, 3 times in the Psalms, and not at all in the Tetrateuch.

II. 1. *As a Term Referring to the Powers of Chaos.* Scholars frequently seek to support the hypothesis that *beliyya'al* is a mythological name or at least has a mythological substratum from Ps. 18:5(4) (= 2 S. 22:5) and 41:9(8). In the former passage, the king in peril of his life is said to be threatened by *nachale bheliyya'al,* "torrents of belial." Here *beliyya'al* appears in parallelism with → מות *māveth* and → שאול *she'ôl* in a group of mythological figures. The "torrents of belial" clearly have an underworld quality and represent both death and the waters of chaos, because in Hebrew thought the underworld and the chaotic abyss are identical. [26] The use of *beliyya'al* in Ps. 41:9(8) is quite similar. The enemies wish that "a belial thing" would come upon the sufferer (here the parallel terms are → שוא *shāv'*, → און *'āven*, and → רעה *rā'āh*). It is immaterial whether this expression has reference to sickness or death; both are manifestations of the power of Sheol. [27] Therefore, since *beliyya'al* is associated with death and chaos, it is easy to understand why it could be used more generally for anything that comes from the powers of chaos, and for the Israelites this is anything that is hostile to God and to society. Maag correctly emphasizes that *beliyya'al* is found primarily in contexts that have to do with the dissolution of the order of social life, [28] although he interprets *beliyya'al* too abstractly as "original evil." [29]

2. *In Juridical Contexts.* From what has already been said, it should not be surprising that the word *beliyya'al* occurs in purely juridical contexts. The continuation of society depends on maintaining the law. Various wrongdoers are called *'anashim bene beliyya'al,* "men who are sons of belial," in Jgs. 19:22; 20:13 (the homosexuals at Gibeah); and 1 K. 21:10,13 (the perjurers in the lawsuit against Naboth; in the last passage this expression occurs twice, the second time as *'anshe habbeliyya'al*). [30] In both instances, the basic social order is violated. Prov. 19:28 must also be understood against a juridical background: *'edh beliyya'al yalits mishpat,* "the belial witness mocks at justice" (*beliyya'al* here stands in parallelism with → רשעים *reshā'îm* and → און *'āven* in the following line). Dt. 15:9 should be interpreted in a similar way. Here the neglect of responsibility to the poor is said to be *dabhar ... beliyya'al,* "a matter (something) that is belial." Finally, *beliyya'al* is used in a weakened sense in a couple of passages

[24] See the list of parallel expressions like *bene 'avlah,* "sons of injustice," etc., in Baudissin, 42f.

[25] See Baudissin, 42; Joüon, 180.

[26] Pedersen, 463f.; Ph. Reymond, *L'eau, sa vie, et sa signification dans l'AT. SVT,* 6 (Leiden, 1958), 212-14.

[27] Pedersen, 466-470; cf. Mowinckel, *Psalmenstudien,* I (1921), 18f.

[28] Maag, 294.

[29] *Ibid.,* 295, 298.

[30] On the syntactical problem in Jgs. 19:22, see Moore, *Judges,* 419.

where it is applied to persons who are hostile to society. In 1 S. 25:17,25, Nabal is described as *ben beliyya'al*, "a son of belial," and *'ish habbeliyya'al*, "man of belial." Surely the writer is thinking not only of his folly, but also of his asocial "behavior."[31] In a similar way, the jealous soldiers of David are called *kol 'ish ra' ubheliyya'al*, "evil and belial-like men" in 1 S. 30:22.[32]

3. *In Connection with the King.* People who undermine the monarchy (one of the sustaining institutions of society) are *bene bheliyya'al*, "sons of belial," or *'ish beliyya'al*, "man of belial": 1 S. 10:27 (Saul's enemies); 2 S. 20:1 (the rebel, Sheba); and 2 Ch. 13:7 (the supporters of Jeroboam I, who are also called *reqim*, "unstable"). On the other hand, the agitator Shimei calls David a "man of blood and a man of belial" (*'ish haddamim ve'ish habbeliyya'al*, 2 S. 16:7). It is evident from Job 34:18 that this is a scandalous accusation: God alone can call the king *beliyya'al* and the nobles → רָשָׁע *rāshā'*, "wicked." Here the royal ideal shines through; a king who is *beliyya'al* is an impossibility. In one of the OT treatises on statecraft ("Fürstenspiegel"), the king says he is free from any *debhar beliyya'al*, "belial thing" (Ps. 101:3). And in a similar poem, which has been handed down as "the last words of David" (2 S. 23:1-7), *beliyya'al* is used as the antithesis to the righteous king (v. 6). The emphasis on → צְדָקָה *tsedhāqāh*, "righteousness," in this passage is characteristic. This idea is "society oriented." It denotes the quality that preserves society, which is attacked by *beliyya'al*.[33] But in Israelite thought, the hostile king who opposes Yahweh and his people is an instrument of the powers of chaos; as a matter of fact, he is often identical with these powers. Therefore, the king of Assyria can also be described as *yo'ets beliyya'al*, "one who makes belial plans" (Nah. 1:11; here this expression is in parallelism with *choshebh ra'ah*, "one who plots evil"). In Nah. 2:1(1:15), he is called *(ben) beliyya'al*, "son of belial" (the MT has only *beliyya'al*, but *ben* probably fell out by haplography).[34]

4. *In Connection with Cultic Abuses.* The cultic life also belongs to the social order which can be threatened by *beliyya'al*.[35] However, the word *beliyya'al* is rarely used in such contexts. The sons of Eli are called *bene bheliyya'al*, "sons of belial," "who do not know the Lord," i.e., who do not respect the cultic rules of the Yahweh worship (1 S. 2:12). Hannah is afraid she will be considered a *bath beliyya'al*, "daughter of belial," when Eli thinks that she came into the house of God drunk (1 S. 1:16). Those who induce Israel to commit the cardinal cultic sin, that of worshipping foreign gods, are *'anashim bene bheliyya'al*, "men who are sons of belial" (Dt. 13:14[13]). But of particular interest are two other passages that probably belong here. Prov. 6:12 speaks of an *'ish 'aven*, "a wicked man," and identifies him with an *'adham beliyya'al* "a belial man," who de-

---

31 Maag, 290f.
32 On this construction, see Joüon, 181f.
33 See Pedersen, 338-345.
34 See Horst, *HAT*, 14, 158.
35 Maag, 294.

ceives those associated with him by means of strange gestures. According to Mowinckel, these gestures are "magical" or "powerful" signs used by the worker of *'aven,* "iniquity," or sorcerer. [36] In this way, he abuses the medium of cultic power. The obscure passage in Prov. 16:27 may have a similar meaning: "An *'ish beliyyaʻal* (a man of belial) digs calamity" (cf. 26:27).

III. Usage in Late Judaism. The Qumran Thanksgiving Psalms in particular provide a bridge from the OT use of *beliyyaʻal* to its use in Late Judaism. Here we find several reminiscences of OT expressions using this word (*nachale bheliyyaʻal, yoʻets beliyyaʻal,* etc., often in connection with the roots → זמם *zāmam,* "to devise plots," or → חשב *chāshabh,* "to devise"). [37] But the personified use of *beliyyaʻal* in the other Qumran texts and in the Pseudepigrapha is more typical for this period. Here "Belial" or "Beliar" (so outside the Qumran texts) is identical with Satan (cf. 2 Cor. 6:15). In the dualistic Qumran theology, he is the prince of this world, the leader of the children of darkness in the war against the children of light, and the tempter. [38] In the Pseudepigrapha (esp. in the Martyrdom of Isa. and XII P.), Beliar is primarily the tempter who lures man into sin by his spirits and rules over sinful man. [39]

Otzen

בלל *bll* → בבל *bābhel*

---

[36] Mowinckel, *Psalmenstudien,* I, 24f.
[37] See Kuhn, *Konkordanz* (1960), 33; and Huppenbauer, 81-84.
[38] Huppenbauer, 84-89; van den Osten-Sacken, 73-78, 116-120; etc.
[39] Bousset, 334f.; Noack, 31-34, 44-49.

| בָּלַע *bālaʻ*; בֶּלַע *belaʻ* |

Contents: I. Etymology, Meaning. II. Linguistic Usage in the OT. III. Specific Theological Significance.

I. Etymology, Meaning. The etymology of the root *blʻ* has not been explained satisfactorily because scholars have been unable to agree as to whether the examples of *blʻ* in the OT must be traced back to and understood in relation-

---

bālaʻ. J. Barth, *Beiträge zur Erklärung des Jesaja* (1885), 4f.; G. R. Driver, "Hebrew Notes," *ZAW,* 52 (1934), 52; H. Guillaume, "A Note on the √ בלע," *JTS,* 13 (1962), 320ff.

ship to one,[1] two,[2] or even three[3] roots. In most cases it is clear that the word under consideration comes from the root *blʿ* meaning "to swallow," which occurs in postbiblical Hebrew and in Aramaic, and has analogies in the other Semitic languages.[4] Therefore, it is etymologically certain that the original meaning of *blʿ* was "to gulp down" or "to swallow," lit. "to snatch with the mouth and to gulp down through the esophagus," which is obviously synonymous with *'kl*, "to eat."

Many scholars assume that there is a second root *blʿ* cognate with Arab. *balaġa* (original meaning = "to reach, attain"), and they attempt to support this with various evidence. The case they try to make is not very convincing, however, because first of all the meaning they assign to this root, "to strike, torment, torture,"[5] is by no means necessary in the OT texts to which they appeal (2 S. 17:16; Isa. 3:12; 9:15 [Eng. v. 16]; 19:3; 28:7; Ps. 35:25; 52:6[4]; 55:10[9]; 107:27; Job 2:3; 10:8; 37:20; Eccl. 10:12), and the other meaning "to communicate, inform,"[6] is excluded in 2 S. 17:16 by the context, and simply has nothing convincing to commend it in Job 37:20, where the text is extremely difficult (cf. Prov. 19:28, where the conjectural reading is *yabbiaʿ*, "pour out").

Still others think that there is a third root *blʿ* connected with *blh* and *bll,* and that it means "to confuse."[7] However, there is no justification for this whatsoever, because there is no compelling reason to connect *blʿ* with *blh* or *bll,* and the meaning "to confuse" is not necessary in the passages that are cited in defense of this view. Thus, the suggestions that there are two or three roots *blʿ* must be rejected.

II. Linguistic Usage in the OT.
The root *blʿ* appears in the OT as a verb in the qal, niphal, piel, pual, and hithpael, and as a substantive.

The basic root means to swallow something (originally something edible). Thus the fundamental meaning of *blʿ* is to swallow a delectable morsel (Isa. 28:4: a first-ripe fig), or some food that has become scarce (Hos. 8:7: grain), eagerly and quickly before anyone else can get to it. It means to swallow food rapidly in connection with certain miraculous events: seven thin ears swallow seven fat ones (Gen. 41:7,24), Aaron's rod swallows the rods of the Egyptian magicians (Ex. 7:12), Yahweh's right hand swallows the earth (Ex. 15:12), a fish swallows the prophet Jonah (Jonah 2:1[1:17]).

blʿ is used in a figurative sense, especially with man as object. Here it means primarily to destroy or to remove men quickly so that they may no longer be found in their place. The company with Korah is swallowed up by the ground (Nu. 16:30,32,34; 26:10; Dt. 11:6; Ps. 106:17), Israel is swallowed up by her enemies (Hos. 8:8; Ps. 124:3), the inhabitants of Jerusalem are swallowed up by

---

[1] *BDB.*

[2] Driver, Guillaume.

[3] Barth; *KBL.*

[4] See *KBL,* 129.

[5] Driver, Guillaume.

[6] *KBL.*

[7] Barth; *KBL.*

Nebuchadnezzar (Jer. 51:34), and the godly are swallowed up (alive) by sinners (Prov. 1:12).

bl' is also used figuratively to convey the idea of a person's downfall, as e.g., when one who has fallen into great distress is said to be swallowed up by the deep (Ps. 69:16[15]), or when one who has become drunk with wine is said to be swallowed up with wine (*nibhle'u min hayyayin*), and thus is confused and staggers (Isa. 28:7). *bl'* is also used figuratively to describe the seizure and expending of wealth and possessions (Job 20:15,18).

In the other conjugations (the intensive binions), *bl'* is used figuratively to express more strongly a destructive effect. However, the emphasis differs from passage to passage, depending on whether the author has in mind the process of eating or consuming, or the end result of this process.

Thus *bl'* can be applied (in the participial form) to the enemies of Israel as those who destroy her (Isa. 49:19), and on a different plane to uprooting someone from his home and carrying him away (Job 8:18, referring to the destruction of the ungodly), to plunging people into adversity or to threatening peoples' lives with destruction (Isa. 9:15[16], associated with the concept of leading people astray; Ps. 35:25, referring to the worshipper being destroyed by his enemies; Lam. 2:16, referring to the daughter of Jerusalem being destroyed by enemies: Eccl. 10:12, referring to a person being destroyed by the lips of a fool; Job 2:3; 10:8, referring to Job being destroyed by Yahweh; see also Job 37:20: perhaps it would be told him [Yahweh] that he [man] would speak when someone says that he would be destroyed), to a violent destruction (Hab. 1:13, of the righteous being destroyed by the wicked), and even to a total annihilation (2 S. 17:16, referring to David and his men being destroyed by Absalom's men; Ps. 21:10[9], referring to Israel's enemies being destroyed by Yahweh). This root is also used to denote squandering a treasure (Prov. 21:20), tearing out a tongue (Ps. 55:10[9]), destroying a heritage (2 S. 20:19f.), devastating a land (Lam. 2:2, 5,8), inverting a tried and tested social structure (Isa. 3:12), frustrating a plan (Isa. 19:3), foiling human wisdom (Ps. 107:27, hithpael: to show that someone is foiled), tearing a covering (Isa. 25:7), and overcoming death (Isa. 25:8).

bl' is also found in an expression which seems to have been common in the OT, viz., *'adh bil'i ruqqi,* lit. "till I swallow my spittle" (Job 7:19), or *kebhalla',* lit. "as a swallowing" (Nu. 4:20), which is an idiom meaning "only for a moment." It also occurs in Arabic.

Finally the subst. *bela',* which occurs only twice in the OT, actually exhibits one of the two main nuances belonging to the root *bl',* since it means that which is swallowed (Jer. 51:44, referring to Bel in Babylon) and destruction (Ps. 52:6 [4], *dibhre bhala',* "words of destruction"; RSV, "words that devour").

III. Specific Theological Significance. It is striking that *bl'* appears especially in contexts that have to do with the elimination and destruction of one who is persecuted without just cause, innocent, righteous, or a godly worshipper. Sometimes it can also be found in passages describing the malicious attempts of external enemies to harm or destroy Israel; in these texts Israel is pictured as helpless or as one who is treated unrighteously. Israel's enemies seek her destruction (Isa.

49:19), they rise up against God's people to swallow them up (Ps. 124:3), the wicked Egyptians attack Israel and the nations like a greedy fisher of peoples (Hab. 1:13), and Nebuchadnezzar plunders the inhabitants of Jerusalem like an insatiable monster and leaves the land empty like an empty vessel (Jer. 51:34). Or it may be used to describe the enemy from within who lies in wait for an individual godly or righteous person, or to portray the evildoer and sinner who loves words of destruction (Ps. 52:6[4]) and strives to destroy the life and posessions of the godly man (Prov. 1:12). It is even used to describe Yahweh, who takes everything away from his righteous servant except his life, as in the case of Job (Job 2:3; 10:8; 37:20).

But *blʿ* is also used to denote the punitive intervention and judgment of Yahweh. If this concept appears only indirectly in the picture of Israel being swallowed up by her enemies in Hos. 8:8, it is clearly expressed in the context referring to the downfall of Judah and Jerusalem in Lam. 2:2,5,8: in his wrath, like an enemy Yahweh has devastated Judah, its land and its strongholds. Also, when the company of Korah is swallowed up by the earth (Nu. 16:30ff.; 26:10; Dt. 11:6; Ps. 106:17), this is explicitly interpreted as Yahweh's punitive response. But the destruction of Yahweh's enemies (Ps. 21:10[9]), the tearing out of the slanderous tongue of the evildoer (Ps. 55:10[9]), and the frustrating of the plans of the Egyptians (Isa. 19:3), are also to be understood as judgments of Yahweh. *blʿ* is also used to describe Yahweh's saving acts, when the picture of the earth being swallowed up by Yahweh's right hand clearly refers to the wondrous destruction of the Egyptians and the salvation of Israel at the Red Sea (Ex. 15:12), and when the coming of the eschatological age of salvation is expressed in concrete terms as the tearing of a covering that protects and restrains the nations, and as the overcoming of death (Isa. 25:7,8).

Schüpphaus

בָּמָה *bāmāh*

Contents: I. 1. Etymology, Occurrences; 2. Meaning. II. 1. The Location of a *bamah;* 2. Archeological Evidence; 3. Appearance of and Furnishings for a *bamah*. III. The Religious and Theological Significance of a *bamah:* 1. Legitimate or Illegitimate Cult Place; 2. The Connection Between the *bamah* and the Cult of the Dead.

I. 1. *Etymology, Occurrences*. The word *bamah*, which may be of pre-Semitic origin, probably comes from the form **bahmat(u)*.[1] With slight variations this

---

bāmāh. W. F. Albright, "The High Place in Ancient Palestine," *SVT*, 4 (1957), 242-258; R. Brinker, *The Influence of Sanctuaries in Early Israel* (Manchester, 1946); D. Conrad, *Studien zum Altargesetz, Ex 20:24-26* (diss., Marburg, 1968); O. Eissfeldt, "Hesekiel Kap. 16 als Geschichtsquelle," *JPOS*, 16 (1936), 286-292=*KlSchr*, II, 101-106; G. Fohrer, *History of Israelite Religion* (trans. 1972); C. C. McCown, "Hebrew High Places and Cult Remains,"

[1] Albright, 245, 256.

(continued on p. 140)

root is found in almost all Semitic languages (Akk. *bāntu, bāmtu,* pl. *bāmāti;* [2] Ugar. *bmt;* [3] Arab. *buhmat*). In Hebrew the spelling *bomah* (1QIsᵃ) was also common along with *bamah;* this could reflect dialectical differences within Hebrew. The Mesha Inscription has *hbmt.* [4]

2. *Meaning.* The cognate word in Akkadian means "back," "center of the body" (of an animal), but also "ridge," "high place" (in the territory). Similarly, Ugar. *bmt* denotes the "back" or "torso" of an animal. Accordingly, *bamah* has the following meanings in the OT: (a) It has the original meaning "back," referring to the back of a man (Dt. 33:29), and figuratively to the back of the clouds (Isa. 14:14; Job 9:8, here read *ʿabh,* "clouds," with several Heb. mss.). [5] (b) In close relationship to this, *bamah* means "ridge," "high ground" (Dt. 32:13; 2 S. 1:19,25; Am. 4:13; Mic. 1:3; 3:12; Isa. 58:14; Ps. 18:34 [Eng. v. 33]). (c) The primary meaning of *bamah* in the OT is "cultic high place" or "cult place" (1 S. 9:12; 1 K. 11:7; 2 Ch. 33:17; Jer. 48:35). It is used in this sense about 80 times in the OT. Here *bamah* has been transferred from the topographical elevation to the cultic area so frequently found on that elevation, but it is likely that *bamah* also refers to the form of the cult place which rises above the surrounding terrain (cf. the explanation of the name *bamah* in Ezk. 20:28f.). [6] (d) *bamah* also means "mound" in the OT, because of the appearance of a mound in relation to the territory around it (Isa. 53:9, read *bomatho* with 1QIsᵃ; [7] Job 27:15, read *bamoth*). [8] As archeological discoveries in the Negeb of Palestine, the Sinai peninsula, and Southern Arabia show, it was common from the fourth century B.C. on to erect stones over the grave of a dead person according to a specific plan, and these stones marked a clear elevation in the area (cf. Josh. 7:26; 8:29; 2 S. 18:17). The twofold meaning of the Arab. *buhmat* = "boulder" and "holy sepulchre," [9] is connected with this meaning of *bamah* and confirms it retrospectively. (e) In addition, *bamah* has the special meaning "stela" (on the Mesha Inscription, [10] and in the LXX of Lev. 26:30; Nu. 21:28; 33:52). Besides the appearance of the elevation, the frequent association of stelae with cult places [11] would seem to have given rise to this meaning of *bamah.*

JBL, 69 (1950), 205-219; T. Oestreicher, *Reichstempel und Ortsheiligtümer in Israel. BFChTh,* 33/3 (1930); H. Ringgren, *Israelite Religion* (trans. 1966); K.-D. Schunk, "Zentralheiligtum, Grenzheiligtum und 'Höhenheiligtum' in Israel," *Numen,* 18 (1971), 132-140; A. Schwarzenbach, *Die geographische Terminologie im Hebräischen des AT* (1954); de Vaux, *AncIsr,* II; L. H. Vincent, "La notion biblique du haut-lieu," *RB,* 55 (1948), 245-278, 438-445; S. Yeivin, "The High-Place at Gibeon," *RHJE,* 1 (1947), 143-47.

[2] *AHw,* 101.

[3] *WUS,* 50.

[4] *KAI,* 181.3.

[5] Cf. G. Fohrer, *KAT,* XVI, 195.

[6] See also below, II.1.

[7] Cf. Albright, 244-46; similarly B. Duhm, *Das Buch Jesaja* (⁵1968), 402.

[8] Cf. S. Iwry, *JBL,* 76 (1957), 225-232.

[9] Cf. Lane, I, 268c.

[10] *KAI,* 181.3; in addition cf. Albright, 248.

[11] Cf. below, II.3.

II. 1. *The Location of a bamah.* A natural elevation was preferred as a location for a *bamah* = "cult place," even in the pre-Israelite period (Nu. 21:28). Similarly, the *bamoth* of the peoples around Israel were built mainly on elevated places (Jer. 48:35; Isa. 15:2). Therefore, it is not surprising that the *bamoth* of the Israelites also, which in many cases were taken over from the Canaanites, were usually located on elevated areas. Thus Samuel goes up to the nearby *bamah* or comes down again from it to the village (1 S. 9:13f.,19,25), and he declares that Saul will meet a band of prophets coming down from a *bamah* (1 S. 10:5). According to 1 K. 11:7 and 2 K. 23:13, Solomon built cult places for the gods Chemosh and Milcom on the Mount of Olives located east of Jerusalem; and in 1 K. 14:23; 2 K. 16:4; and 2 Ch. 28:4, the cult on the *bamoth* and the cult on the hills are mentioned side by side.

But in addition, Israel knew of *bamoth* that were located in valleys or ravines. Thus, in the valley of ben Hinnom near Jerusalem there was a cult place of Topheth (Jer. 7:31; 19:5f.; 32:35), and according to Ezk. 6:3 Yahweh announces to the ravines and the valleys as well as the mountains and hills that he will destroy their *bamoth*.

But even apart from these cult places which were connected with particular sections of the country around a city or village, there were also *bamoth* which were located in a settlement (1 K. 13:32; 2 K. 17:9,29; 23:5,8; 2 Ch. 21:11 [LXX]; 28:25). Generally these cult places were undoubtedly built by men, as archeological excavations demonstrate, [12] and as the frequent connection of *bamah* with verbs meaning "to build" and "to break down" suggests (1 K. 13:32; 2 K. 17:9; 23:8).

As these last two types of *bamoth* show, the translation "high place sanctuary," which frequently occurs, does not give an adequate picture of the real nature of a *bamah*. On the basis of archeological and biblical evidence, it would probably be best to translate *bamah* as "a small elevation for cultic use" [13] or "cult place." Also, it is clear from all the evidence that, generally speaking, from the pre-monarchical period on each village had its own *bamah*.

2. *Archeological Evidence.* The various possibilities for the location and structure of a *bamah* are established and illustrated more precisely by archeological investigations. Thus, an oval platform approximately 8 to 10 meters wide was unearthed at Tell el-Mutesellim (Megiddo). It was made of unhewn stones and furnished with a flight of stairs. This structure, which is preserved up to 1.25 meters above the surrounding area and which had the shape of a great round altar, was clearly used for sacrificial purposes, and was used continually for several centuries beginning with the middle of the third millennium B.C. In Nahariya near Haifa a heap of stones has been uncovered which also is almost circular in shape. It is approximately 6 meters in diameter and apparently comes from the beginning of the second millennium B.C. A similar platform has been discovered in a sanc-

---

[12] See below, II.2.
[13] De Vaux.

tuary at Tell el-Qedah (Hazor) on the Wadi Waqqas dating from the thirteenth
century B.C.

In addition to this evidence there are also two tumuli which were excavated on
a ridge southwest of Jerusalem, and which are to be dated in the eighth to seventh
centuries B.C. They consist of an agglomeration of stones and earth covering
an area measuring about 25 meters in diameter. A person had to climb a flight
of wide steps to go up on it, and it was surrounded by a polygonal wall. The
excavators found no remains of a chamber or a grave underneath the heap of
stones, therefore this also must have been a cult place. Finally, the remains
of the Nabatean "high place sanctuaries" at Petra can also help us determine
the normal location and structures of a *bamah*. There can be little doubt that
they go back to Canaanite and Israelite prototypes or cultic practices. [14] However, the rows of stelae that have been discovered at Tell el-Jazar (Gezer) and
Tell el-Qedah (Hazor) should probably be identified with a typical component
of the bamah, the *matstsebhah*. [15]

3. *Appearance of and Furnishings for a bamah.* In keeping with its character
as a cult place, each *bamah* was furnished with an altar for offering sacrifices,
which was a most important element (2 K. 21:3; 2 Ch. 14:2[3]; Ezk. 6:6). The
altar was either built of stones separate from the *bamah* (2 K. 23:15, LXX; 2 Ch.
34:3f.), or was made by the builders as a portion of the *bamah* itself. This may
explain the Gk. *bōmós* = "platform," "altar," which seems to be cognate with
the Canaanite-Israelite *bamah*. [16]

Besides the altar, the most important furnishings of the *bamah* were a wooden
pole = → אשרה *'ashērāh*, and one or more stone pillars = → מצבה *matstsēbhāh*
(1 K. 14:23; 2 K. 18:4; 23:13f.; 2 Ch. 14:2[3]). Occasionally one or more stone
images (*pasil*) might also be found at a *bamah* as symbolic sculptured forms of
the *matstsebhah* (2 Ch. 33:19; 34:3,7; Jgs. 3:19,26?; the Hazor sanctuary). The
'asherah, which occasionally could be a live tree (Mic. 5:13[14]), was a symbol
of the goddess of fertility. However, two things could be suggested by the
matstsebhoth: first, because of the influence of Canaanite religion, in a number
of cases they symbolized the male deity (2 K. 3:2); and secondly, they were used
as commemorative pillars for one who had died, i.e., as grave stelae (Gen. 35:20;
2 S. 18:18; and Ezk. 43:7, where *pegher* has the same meaning as *matstsebhah* =
"pillar," analogous to Lev. 26:30 and Ugar. *pgr*, [17] and the rows of stelae at
Gezer and Hazor). Both interpretations probably had their origin in the idea
that the *matstsebhah* is a commemorative stela which functions as a testimony
or witness. Just as the *matstsebhah* is a memento of a divine revelation and a sign
of the divine presence, so it is also a witness to one who has died. If the *pesilim*,
"images," are symbolic extensions of the *matstsebhoth*, this interpretation of the
matstsebhoth would help to explain why *pesilim* were built occasionally at the
bamoth.

---

14 Cf. Albright, 257.
15 See below, II.3.
16 Albright, *Archaeology and the Religion of Israel* (⁴1956), 202, n. 24; Ringgren, 177.
17 Following D. Neiman, *JBL*, 67 (1948), 55-60.

Along with smaller cultic vessels like lavers and basins for cultic ablutions, ephod and teraphim, the incense altars (*chammanim*) were another important furnishing of the *bamoth* (Lev. 26:30; 2 Ch. 14:4[5]; 34:4,7; Ezk. 6:4,6; cf. also Hos. 4:13). They were made of stone or clay, and in many cases were set up on the great altar (2 Ch. 34:4).

Finally each *bamah* seems to have had a tent or a smaller or larger room covered with some sort of roof where the sacrificial meals were eaten and where the cultic vessels were stored (cf. Ezk. 16:16; 1 S. 9:22; moreover, when the author of 1 K. 3:5 describes Solomon's nocturnal dream at the *bamah,* he has reference to a building connected with the *bamah* in some way). 1 S. 9:22 calls this room, which had space for about thirty men, a *lishkah* = "hall." However, this would seem to be only one specific term, chosen in a particular case, used for the more general expression *beth (batte) bamoth,* "house (houses) of (on) the high places" (1 K. 12:31; 13:32; 2 K. 17:29,32; 23:19). Albright argues that *beth bamoth* means a "stela temple." [18] In opposition to this, it should be pointed out that the *bamoth* were always open cult places built in the open air (cf. 1 K. 14:23; 2 K. 16:4; 17:10), only a part of which were taken up by the *beth,* "house."

III. The Religious and Theological Significance of a bamah.

1. *Legitimate or Illegitimate Cult Place.* In the Canaanite cult, the *bamah,* along with the temple building, represented a valid and wholly acceptable form of cult place (cf. Nu. 33:52). After the conquest of Canaan, at first the Israelites also had a positive attitude toward the numerous *bamoth* they took over from the Canaanites, although the natural assumption was that now these *bamoth* functioned as cult places for the Yahweh cult. Thus, not only did the Israelites take over the *habbamah haggedholah,* "great high place," of Gibeon from the non-Israelite Gibeonites as a legitimate cult place, but in all probability they even elevated it to the position of a royal sanctuary or central sanctuary under king Saul. [19] Accordingly, even king Solomon offered a great sacrifice to Yahweh and received a revelation of Yahweh at Gibeon after his accession to the throne (1 K. 3:4f.). In a similar way, Samuel assumes as a matter of course that he will participate in a sacrificial meal on the *bamah* in his hometown, and also invites Saul (whom Yahweh had already told him he had chosen to be king) to accompany him (1 S. 9:16-24).

Even after the building of the temple (*hekhal*) in Jerusalem, which as a central sanctuary carries on the tradition of the *hekhal* at Shiloh, and after the establishment of a specific central sanctuary for the northern kingdom of Israel in Samaria and the so-called frontier sanctuaries in the divided kingdoms of Israel and Judah, the *bamoth* continue to be regarded as legitimate cult places. This positive assessment is not changed in the territory of the northern kingdom of Israel by the loss of national independence (2 K. 17:32), but it is conclusively rejected in

[18] Albright, *SVT,* 248, 253.
[19] Cf. K.-D. Schunck, *Benjamin. BZAW,* 86 (1963), 134-37.

the southern kingdom of Judah by king Josiah (2 K. 23:8f.). Since the central sanctuary in Samaria and the temple in Jerusalem were at times given over to foreign gods or to their images and cults (2 K. 10:18-27; 21:7), for centuries the *bamoth,* which were spread out over the whole land, championed the Yahweh religion primarily, in spite of their inclination to support a syncretistic cult.

The predominantly negative estimation of the *bamoth* found in the present form of the OT is due to prophetic criticism of the establishment of these cult places and of the type of cult practiced there, and to the Deuteronomistic movement which advocated the centralization of the cult at Jerusalem. The prophets recognized the great danger of a syncretistic religion and cult practices, which were represented by the presence of an *'asherah,* "sacred pole," and a *matstsebhah,* "pillar," beside an altar of Yahweh. Old Canaanite fertility rites with their immoral practices were kept alive in conjunction with the *'asherah,* and it was not difficult for the people to conclude that the *matstsebhah* represented the deity himself (whether it be → בַּעַל *ba'al,* "Baal," in the earlier period, or Yahweh in the later). Other Canaanite practices like child sacrifice also appeared, which were carried on in these very cultic institutions that Israel had taken over from the Canaanites (Jer. 7:31; 19:5f.; 32:35). Thus for the prophets the *bamah,* as a cultic institution, must have become a general symbol for a place that was detrimental to the pure Yahweh faith and Yahweh cult, and which therefore was to be rejected (Am. 7:9; Hos. 10:8; Jer. 19:3-5). In addition to this prophetic evaluation of the *bamah,* we encounter the view that there was no place where one could worship Yahweh acceptably except the Jerusalem temple, a view that probably was championed by priestly circles in Jerusalem. This idea, which is based on Josiah's reform and the centralization of the cult connected with that reform, was first used by the first redactor of the Book of Kings [20] as a criterion for determining whether the people and the individual kings of the kingdom of Judah conducted themselves as the commands of Yahweh required (1 K. 3:3; 14:23; 15:14; 22:44[43]; 2 K. 12:4[3]; 14:4; 15:4,35a; 16:4; 18:4; 21:3; 23:5, 8,13,15). Then, under considerable prophetic influence, the Deuteronomistic history extended this criterion to cover the northern kingdom of Israel also (2 K. 17:9,11), while the author of Ps. 78, probably living in the sixth century B.C., carries the illegitimacy of the *bamoth* back even into the period of the judges. Later, we find the same picture in the Chronicler's history as we do in Kings (2 Ch. 14:2,4[3,5]; 15:17; 17:6; 20:33; etc.), and yet the Chronicler enhances the evaluation of the *bamah* at Gibeon by connecting it with the → אֹהֶל מוֹעֵד *'ōhel mô'ēdh,* "tent of meeting" (2 Ch. 1:3,13).

2. *The Connection Between the bamah and the Cult of the Dead.* In spite of obscurity in details, it may be regarded as certain that the *bamah* also had some connection with the cult of the dead. For one thing a tumulus could be called *bamah,* and for another thing stelae erected in the *bamah* as a cult place had the function of preserving the memory of a deceased person who had been highly esteemed. Although the OT does not place any evaluation on the tumulus

---

[20] Cf. A. Jepsen, *Die Quellen des Königsbuches* ([2]1956), 60-76.

pro or con (Isa. 53:9, 1QIsᵃ; Job 27:15, conjec.), the burial stelae of the cult places were subjected to the same criticism as the cult places themselves (Ezk. 43:7, where *pegher* means "stela"). [21]

The passage that is frequently cited as a classical example of the connection between the *bamah* and the cult of the dead, Isa. 6:13, [22] is not conclusive. The consonants *bmh* in 1QIsᵃ seem to have reference to a *bamah*, but it is best to point this word *bameh* with Sawyer [23] following the analogy of Isa. 2:22; Mal. 1:6f.; and 3:7f., and to interpret it as introducing a commentary on the foregoing word of God.

Schunck

---

[21] Cf. above, II.3.
[22] Iwry, 225-232; Albright, 254f.
[23] J. Sawyer, *ASTI,* 3 (1964), 111-13.

בֵּן *bēn*

Contents: I. "Son" in the Ancient Near East; 1. Egypt; 2. Mesopotamia; 3. Ugarit. II. *ben* in the Semitic Languages: 1. Occurrences; 2. Etymology. III. Meaning in the OT. IV. Theological Evaluation: 1. In the Human Sphere; 2. Divine Sonship: a. Israel As God's Son; b. The King; c. The Sons of the Gods.

I. "Son" in the Ancient Near East.

1. *Egypt.* The Egyp. *s3* means both "son" and "heir." The idea that the oldest son is the father's heir is ancient and occurs as early as the Pyramid Texts (1538, 1814). In the Middle Kingdom, however, the right of inheritance is frequently transmitted through the female line: thus the son of the oldest daughter

---

bēn. G. Cooke, "The Israelite King as Son of God," *ZAW,* 73 (1961), 202-225; *idem,* "The Sons of (the) God(s)," *ZAW,* 76 (1964), 22-47; F. Dexinger, *Sturz der Göttersöhne oder Engel vor der Sintflut?* (Vienna, 1966); H. Donner, "Adoption oder Legitimation?" *OrAnt,* 8 (1969), 87-119; O. Eissfeldt, "Sohnespflichten im Alten Orient," *Syr,* 43 (1966), 39-47= *KlSchr,* IV, 264-270; F. C. Fensham, "The Son of a Handmaid in Northwest Semitic," *VT,* 19 (1969), 312-321; G. Fohrer, *TDNT,* VIII, 340-354; J. de Fraine, *L'aspect religieux de la royauté israélite.* AnBibl, 3 (Rome, 1954); *idem, Adam und seine Nachkommen* (1962); W. Herrmann, "Die Gottessöhne," *ZRGG,* 12 (1960), 242-251; P. Joüon, "Les unions entre les 'Fils de Dieu' et les 'Filles des hommes,'" *RScR,* 29 (1939), 108-114; H. Junker, "Zur Erklärung von Gen 6,1-4," *Bibl,* 16 (1935), 205-212; A. Phillips, "The Interpretation of 2 Samuel XII 5-6," *VT,* 16 (1966), 242-44; J. R. Porter, "Son or Grandson?" *JTS,* 17 (1966), 54-67; A. Safran, "La conception juive de l'homme," *RTP,* 98 (1964), 193-207; J. Scharbert, "Traditions- und Redaktionsgeschichte von Gn 6,1-4," *BZ,* N.F. 11 (1967), 66-78; W. H. Schmidt, "Anthropologische Begriffe im AT," *EvTh,* 24 (1964), 374-388; A. Vaccari, "De Messia 'Filio Dei' in Vetere Testamento," *VD,* 15 (1935), 48-55, 77-86; J. G. Williams, "The Prophetic 'Father.' A Brief Explanation of the Term 'Sons of the Prophets,'" *JBL,* 85 (1966), 344-48.

receives the inheritance.[1] In general, the son is considered to be his father's successor. In particular, he is responsible for the burial cult of his deceased father: he writes his epitaph and brings him necessary food on the various festival days.[2]

The oldest son is called *sꜣ śmśw* or *sꜣ wr* (*wr* = "great"). *sꜣ tpy* is a particular expression for "firstborn."[3] The king is usually called the son of various deities (*sꜣ imn*, etc.). The expression *sꜣ.f n ḫt.f*, "his own son," places a particular emphasis on physical sonship. The intimate relationship between the pharaoh and the god is expressed by the formula *sꜣ.f mry.f*, "his beloved son."[4] *sꜣ mr.f*, "the son whom he loves," was applied to Horus in particular as the ideal son. The royal title *sꜣ Rʿ*, "son of Re," which is common from the fourth dynasty on, is significant.

Proper names designating those who bear them as "son of a certain man (or woman)" are very common in the first interim period, but they are not used very frequently in the Middle Kingdom.[5] Occasionally we also find "son" with a place name: *sꜣ P*, "son of Buto," etc.[6] Names that designate a person as son of a deity are inconceivable in the Old Kingdom, but they become more and more frequent later.[7] These names commend those who bear them to the special protection of the deity.

2. *Mesopotamia*. Akkadian has two words for "son" (other then *bīnu*):[8] *aplu* (Sum. *ibila*),[9] which originally meant "heir," and *māru* (cf. Aram. *mārē, māryā'*, "lord," and Arab. *imru', almar'u*, "man"–Sum. *dumu*). It distinguishes between a person's own sons and daughters, who are "his own flesh (*nu-nu-ne, širšu*) and blood (*nu-sa-ne, dāmūšu*)," his "seed" (*zēru*, → זרע *zeraʿ*), and adopted sons.[10] Adoption was rather frequent in Mesopotamia.[11] Originally "heir" was identical with "son." In general, from the first Babylonian dynasty on *aplu* means "heir," and thus includes adopted sons and collateral heirs.

Among the Sumerians, if a man did not have a son, his daughter received the inheritance.[12] At a later time only sons received the inheritance, and it was divided equally among them. Occasionally, a Sumerian text will mention that the oldest son (→ בכור *bᵉkhôr*, "firstborn") received a larger portion. Only the son was responsible for carrying on the father's name and family,[13] and therefore sometimes "name," *šumu*, is synonymous with "son." Consequently, the birth of

---

1 Erman-Ranke, *Ägypten und ägyptisches Leben im Altertum* (1923), 183.
2 *Ibid.*, 184.
3 *WbÄS*, III, 409, 3.
4 *Ibid.*, 5.
5 Ranke, *PN*, II, 176.
6 *Ibid.*, I, 281.
7 *Ibid.*, II, 226; and idem, "Ägypter als Götterkinder," *Corolla L. Curtius* (1937), 180ff.
8 See below, II.1.a.
9 However, cf. A. Falkenstein, *Genava*, N.S. 8, 313.
10 *RLA*, III, 10.
11 David, *RLA*, I, 37ff.
12 *CAD*, I/2, 176.
13 Meissner, *BuA*, I, 394.

a son is very desirable, and "the heart of a husband is grieved over a wife who has given birth to a girl, but not a son." [14]

Like Heb. *ben*, *māru* is also used to denote membership in a group or a profession or some other relationship, as e.g., *mār awīlim*, "citizen," *mārū bārûm*, "bārū priest," *mār ālim*, "son (i.e., citizen) of a city," *mār bīti*, "house slave," *mār šiprim*, "son of the message," i.e., "messenger." [15]

Of particular interest are the cases in which a man is designated as son of a deity. Both *apil* and *mār* appear in proper names of this sort: Apil-Shamash, Mār-Shamash, "son of Shamash." [16] The intention of such names is to place the person named under the special protection of the deity. This is quite clear in the name *amēlu mār/apil ilišu*, "the man, son of his god," referring to the particular tutelary god of the man. [17] In a special sense the king is known as son of the deity. [18] Different deities are referred to as father and mother of the king. However, the pertinent texts never state clearly what this sonship means. Some expressions found in them leave the impression that it has reference to a physical birth or begettal; but since one and the same king appears as son of several deities, such statements concerning the king's origin probably should not be taken too literally. [19] Labat believes that these statements have in mind a kind of adoption, but one has to admit with Sjöberg that nothing like this is ever explicitly stated. [20] It is certain that these expressions mean that in some way the king is indebted to a deity for his life.

3. *Ugarit.* Several Ugaritic texts emphasize the importance of having a son as heir. Danel has no son, and entreats El to give him one. [21] The entire Keret Epic is concerned about procuring a woman who can bear Keret a son. An often repeated passage in the Aqhat text describes a son's responsibilities: he is to fulfil the cultic duties for the father, protect him from attack and slander, sustain him when he gets drunk, make his roof leakproof, and wash his clothes. [22]

Bergman–Ringgren

II. ben in the Semitic Languages.

1. *Occurrences.* ben is one of those words that occur most frequently in the Hebrew Bible (4850 times), [23] and that are most characteristic of the Semitic culture. It occurs in most Semitic languages.

---

[14] *Ibid.*, 389f., following *ABRT*, I, 4, 13f.

[15] *AHw*, 615f.

[16] Stamm, *AN*, 260f.

[17] P. Dhorme, *La religion assyro-babylonienne* (Paris, 1910), 198ff.; Seux, 159.

[18] Cf. the examples given in Seux, 42, 159f., and for *dumu*, 392f.

[19] Cf. Å. Sjöberg, *RoB*, 20 (1961), 14-29.

[20] R. Labat, *Le caractère religieux de la royauté assyro-babylonienne* (Paris, 1939), 63f.; Sjöberg, *Orientalia Suecana*, 21 (1972), 87-112.

[21] *CTA*, 17 [II D].

[22] *CTA*, 17, I, 27-34, 45ff.; II, 1-8, 16-23; see A. van Selms, *Marriage and Family Life in Ugaritic Literature* (London, 1954), 100ff.; K. Koch, *ZA*, N.F. 24 (1947), 214ff.; → אָב *'ābh*.

[23] *KBL³*.

a. With the exception of *būnu* (in late Babylonian texts), Bab. and Assyr. *binu(m)* means "son." It is found in Old Akkadian and Late Babylonian poetic texts, and in Neo-Assyrian proper names. It is used for both gods and men. In a Late Babylonian list of synonyms, *bīn bīni* means "grandson."

b. *bn* (pl. *bnm*) is very familiar in Phoenician and Punic texts. [24] In the construct state, the *n* can be assimilated to the first consonant of the following word. [25] Occasionally we encounter the forms *bl* and *bm*. [26] The Aram. form *br* occurs in two Phoenician inscriptions of Zinjirli. [27] Also in the Phoenician-Punic inscriptions *bn bn* means "grandson." [28] As in Hebrew, [29] Phoen.-Pun. *bn* also denotes relationship or membership, e.g., in the expressions *bn' 'm*, "the people," *bn 'dm*, "the men," *bn 'lm*, "the gods," *bn hmlk*, "a royal prince," *bt šmnm št*, "a woman of eighty years," [30] *bn msk ymm* (?), "son of a (small) number of days" (?). [31]

c. The same ambiguity also occurs in Ugaritic. *bn* (pl. *bnm*) and *bt* (pl. *bnt*) mean first of all "son" or "daughter." As a designation of relationship or membership, *bn* is used of an inhabitant of a land or of a city: *bn ʒgrt*, "citizen of Ugarit." We also encounter these expressions: *bn 'mt*, "servant," and *bt 'mt*, "maidservant," [32] *bn ʒlm mt*, "the god Mot," *bn ʒl* and *bn ʒlm*, "gods," *bn qrytm*, "townsman," and *bn tlhnm*, "fellow-boarder." [33] Once we find the expression *bn bn*, "grandson," in Ugaritic. [34]

d. In Aramaic texts *bar*, pl. *banim*, is the normal word for "son." Here also *bar bar* means "grandson." *bar* can also be used for the feminine sex in the sense of "child," e.g., *bari*, "my daughter." [35] We also encounter these forms: *br btny*, "my own son," *bny byth*, "the members of his family," *br byt'*, "royal prince, a member of the royal house," *br '(y)nš*, "someone," and *br hrn*, "a distinguished person." In addition, *bar* can be used to describe a relationship or membership: *bnt mwq' šmš*, "women who come from the East," *bny šyrt'*, "members of a caravan," *bny qryt'*, "the people of the village," and *br šnt 18*, "a wife of 18 years." [36]

---

[24] *KAI*, 1.1 (Aḥīrām); 10.1 (Yeḥawmilk); etc. On this form, cf. J. Friedrich-W. Röllig, *Phönizisch-Punische Grammatik* (Rome, ²1970), § 240.9.

[25] *KAI*, 6.1; 7.3; 8.

[26] Cf. Friedrich-Röllig, §§ 53 and 56b.

[27] *KAI*, 24.1,4,9; 25.3.

[28] *KAI*, 10.1; 14.14; 15; 16; 40.4; 124.1.

[29] Cf. below, III.5, 8, 9.

[30] These examples are given in *DISO*, 37.

[31] *KAI*, 14.3,12f.

[32] Contra *UT*, Glossary, No. 481, "daughter of a handmaid."

[33] Cf. *ibid.*, and *WUS*, 51f.; but on the two passages mentioned last, cf. G. R. Driver, *CML*, 85.

[34] *CTA*, 22 [Rp III], B, 3.

[35] *BMAP*, Papyrus 6, line 3.

[36] These examples are taken from *DISO*, 41ff.

e. Since it was possible, in the case of the Old Arab. form *bin^{un}, for the vowel in context to fall out after an open syllable (e.g., *bi-$bini$-$h\bar{\iota} > bi$-bni-$h\bar{\iota}$), the context form (i)bn, which permeated into Arabic as an exclusive form, arose. [37] The plural of bin seems to have been read by the ablaut ban, [38] and by repeated connection the external plural ending was added to this form in the Arab. banūna and Heb. bānīm. The broken Arab. pl. form 'abnā' is rare; however, it is best not to refer to it as a "rare plural," [39] because usually banūna stands for a small number. In Arabic, too, ibn can denote relationship or membership and a person's age. In modern written Arab. ibn al-balad means "resident in a locality, native," ibn al-ḥarb means "man of war, fighting man," and ibn ḫamsīn sana means "fifty-year-old." [40]

f. Undoubtedly it is due to more than a mere accident that Egyp. bn and its derivatives include the realm of creation and reproduction. Even as early as in the Coffin Texts, bn has the meaning "to copulate, to beget." In its reduplicated form bnbn, the verb means "to erect" (the phallus). In its two meanings "obelisk" and "a certain kind of bread," the subst. bnbn seems to have reference to the phallus. bnnwt means "manhood, courage," bnnt the Chon stamp of Karnak understood as the primeval hill, and bnw the phoenix as a symbol of creation. [41]

2. *Etymology*. The etymology of the words ben and bar has not yet been explained satisfactorily. The pl. banim, which is also used for bar, seems to indicate that bar came from ben by means of a change in sounds, through a transition from n to r. Some scholars think that the Heb. noun ben is to be derived from the root banah, "to build" (which is also used of "building a house" = "establishing a family": Gen. 16:2; 30:3; 1 S. 2:35; 1 K. 11:38; Ruth 4:11), and that the Aram. noun bar is to be derived from the root bara', "to create, bring forth." [42] However, both of these views are doubtful. It is better to assume that ben and bar, like other related forms, are primitive forms and thus are not to be derived from any root.

III. Meaning in the OT. In the OT, ben and bar are used extensively to express family and hereditary relationships. Furthermore, when an intimate relationship between two persons or some connection between two things continually exists, this is frequently described in terms of the father-son formula.

---

[37] Cf. W. Fischer, "Silbenstruktur und Vokalismus im Arabischen," *ZDMG*, 117 (1967), 30-77, esp. p. 43.

[38] W. W. Müller, in a letter to the author.

[39] Lane, I, 262a.

[40] These examples are taken from H. Wehr, *Arab. Wörterbuch für die Schriftsprache der Gegenwart* (³1958), *s.v.*

[41] Cf. W. A. Ward, *ZÄS*, 95 (1968), 66f.; J. Baines, "Bnbn: Mythological and Linguistic Notes," *Or*, 39 (1970), 389-404.

[42] Thus de Fraine, *Adam*, 128, etc.; cf. the explanation of Arab. ibn, "because he is the father's building," in Lane, I, 262a.

1. In the majority of cases, *ben* or *bar* means a son begotten by the father (Gen. 4:17,25f.; Ex. 1:16; Nu. 27:8; Dnl. 5:22). The genitive of the father (Ex. 6:25) or of the mother (Gen. 29:12) can be added to *ben* or *bar* when it has this meaning. In Gen. 5:4, etc., sons and daughters (*banim ubhanoth*) are mentioned side by side. Sons begotten by a young father are figuratively called *bene hanneʿurim*, "sons of youth" (Ps. 127:4), while *ben zequnim*, "son of old age," in Gen. 37:3 means a son begotten in old age. The pl. *banim*, lit. "sons," can mean children of both sexes (Gen 3:16; 21:7; 30:1; Ex. 21:5; Ps. 128:3).

ben hammelekh, "son of the king" (or *bene hammelekh*, "sons of the king"), usually denotes the prince as son of the king (Jgs. 8:18; 2 S. 9:11; 13:4; with *bar:* Ezr. 6:10). However, in Ps. 72:1 *ben melekh* (par. to *melekh*) probably means the king himself, and in 1 K. 22:26 it probably denotes a royal official. [43]

2. *ben* and *bar* can also denote other relationships. Thus brothers are called *bene ʾabhikha*, "your father's sons" (Gen. 49:8), or *ben/bene ʾimmo/ʾimmi*, "son/ sons of his mother/my mother" (43:29; Jgs. 8:19; Ps. 69:9 [Eng. v. 8]; Cant. 1:6). The *bene bhanim*, "sons' sons" or "children's children," in Gen. 45:10; Ex. 34:7; and Jer. 27:7 are the grandchildren. Sometimes *ben* by itself can also mean grandchildren, as in Gen. 31:28; 32:1 (31:55) (Laban and the children of Leah and Rachel); 2 S. 19:25(24) (Saul and Meribbaal); 2 K. 9:20 (Nimshi and Jehu; cf. 9:14); Ezr. 5:1 (Iddo and Zechariah; cf. Zec. 1:1); Neh. 12:23 (Eliashib and Johanan; cf. 12:10f.). In the case of the relationship between Nahor and Laban, however, the tradition in Gen. 29:5 differs from that found in 22:23; 24:24,29.

A nephew is called *ben ʾachiv*, "his brother's son" (Gen. 12:5); daughters-in-law, *neshe bhaneykha*, "your sons' wives" (6:18); and a cousin, *ben dodhi*. The offspring of animals are also called *banim*, without any necessary implication that male descendants exclusively are intended (Gen. 32:16[15]; 49:11; Nu. 15:24; Dt. 22:6f.; Zec. 9:9; Ps. 29:6; Job 4:11; 39:4; Ezr. 6:9). *ben* can also be used in expressions denoting the bough or sprout of a tree (Gen. 49:22: *ben porath*, "a fruitful bough"). The obscure statement in Job 38:32, which refers to the smaller stars in the constellation of the lion, should probably be interpreted in a similar manner.

3. The custom of adding the name of the father, and frequently even the names of other ancestors, appositionally is in harmony with the genealogical concept of the Semites. In this construction *ben* took on a patronymic connotation which saw the individual in an organic, living connection with the family and the tribe. Thus *ben* can be used to convey the idea that a person belongs to a people or to a tribe: the sons of Esau (Dt. 2:4,12,22,29), of Lot (2:9,19), of Hamor the father of Shechem (Gen. 33:19; 34:2), of Seir the Horite (36:20; 2 Ch. 25:11), of Anak (Nu. 13:33; Josh. 15:14; Jgs. 1:20), and of Judah (Joel 4:6[3:6]). The expression *bene yisraʾel*, "sons (children) of Israel," occurs very

---

[43] On the view that *ben hammelekh* means "belonging to the palace of the king," cf. G. Brin, *AION*, 19 (1969), 433-465.

frequently. It denotes the organized community of Israel as a unit, and is not to be understood to imply that the OT authors intended to place emphasis on one specific ancestor of the people.

4. Frequently geographic and national entities are said to be sons of a place or of a land, as in the expressions sons of Bethlehem (Ezr. 2:21; Neh. 7:26; Jer. 6:1), of Jericho (Ezr. 2:34; Neh. 7:37), of Jerusalem (Isa. 51:18; 54:13; 60:4; Jer. 5:7; Joel 4:6[3:6]), of Zion (Isa. 49:22,25; Jer. 30:20; Joel 2:23; Zec. 9:13; Ps. 147:13; 149:2; Lam. 4:2), of Samaria (Ezk. 23:10), of Eden (2 K. 19:12; Isa. 37:12), of Edom (Ps. 137:7), of Ammon (Nu. 21:24; Dt. 2:19; Jgs. 3:13; Isa. 11:14; Jer. 9:25[26]; Ezk. 25:2f.,5,10), of Heth (Gen. 23:3,5,7,10,16,20; 25:10), of Egypt (Ezk. 16:26), of Javan (Zec. 9:13; cf. Joel 4:6[3:6]), of the East (Gen. 29:1; Jgs. 6:3,33; 7:12; 8:10; 1 K. 5:10[4:30]; Isa. 11:14; Jer. 49:28; Ezk. 25:4, 10; Job 1:3), of Noph or Memphis (Jer. 2:16), of Kedar (Isa. 21:17), and of Babylon (Ezk. 23:15,17,23). In Ezr. 2:1, *bene hammedhinah* means "those who belong to the province of Judah." In Dt. 32:14, rams pastured in Bashan are called *bene bhashan*, "sons (children) of Bashan." The tribal name Benjamin, "son of the right hand" (=of the south)=southerner, also belongs here. [44]

bene bhayith, "sons of the house," are servants born in the house (Gen. 15:3; Eccl. 2:7); the *bene 'ammi*, "sons of my people" (Gen. 23:11; Jgs. 14:16), *bene 'ammekha*, "sons of your own people" (Lev. 19:18; Ezk. 3:11; 33:2; 37:18; Dnl. 12:1), *bene 'ammah*, "sons of her people" (Jgs. 14:17), *bene 'amman*, "sons of their people" (Lev. 20:17), and *bene 'ammo*, "the sons of his people" (Nu. 22:5), are "countrymen." On the other hand, the *bene (han)nekhar*, "sons of foreign-ness" (2 S. 22:45f.; Ps. 18:45f.[44f.]; 144:7,11; Ezk. 44:7; Isa. 56:6; 60:10; 61:5; 62:8; sing. *ben [han]nekhar*, "son of foreignness," Gen. 17:12,27; Ex. 12:43; Lev. 22:25; Ezk. 44:9; Neh. 9:2; Isa. 56:3), are foreigners. The men of the tribes of Israel are called *bene shibhte bhene yisra'el*, "the sons of the tribes of the sons of Israel" (Nu. 36:3). The *bene 'erets habberith*, "the sons of the land of the covenant" (Ezk. 30:5), are the relatives of the chosen people.

5. An individual is distinguished from the collective community of which he is a part or from mankind in general by the expressions → בֶּן־אָדָם *ben 'ādhām*, "son of man" (esp. in Ezk.; Ps. 8:5[4]; pl. Dt. 32:8; Eccl. 1:13), *ben 'enosh*, "son of man" (Ps. 144:3), *bene 'anasha'* (Dnl. 2:38; 5:21) or → בְּנֵי אִישׁ *benê 'îsh*, "sons of men" (Ps. 4:3[2]; 49:3[2]; 62:10[9]; Lam. 3:33), *ben mebhish*, "a son causing shame" (Prov. 10:5), *ben maskil* (Prov. 10:5) or *ben mebhin*, "a son acting prudently (wisely)" (Prov. 28:7). A study of Ps. 144:3 (where *'adham* is par. to *ben 'enosh*) shows that *'enosh*, "man," and *ben 'adham*, "son of man," in Ps. 8:5(4) are synonyms, and that there is no intensification from the collective to the individual. [45]

---

44 For a discussion of this name, cf. G. Dossin, "Benjaminites dans les textes de Mari," *Mélanges Dussaud,* II (Paris, 1939), 981-996, esp. p. 982; and H. Tadmor, *JNES,* 17 (1958), 130, n. 12.

45 Contra L. Köhler, *ThZ,* 1 (1945), 77f.; cf. also p. 374.

That which is true of man also applies to animals: *ben baqar,* "son of cattle" (Gen. 18:7; Ex. 29:1; Lev. 1:5: an individual cow), *ben yonah,* "son of a dove" (Lev. 12:6; pl. 1:14: individual doves), and *bene harammakhim,* "sons of mares" (Est. 8:10: individual mares).

6. *ben* is used as an affectionate address to younger students or hearers in Isa. 19:11; 1 S. 3:6,16; 24:17(16); 26:17,21,25; 2 S. 18:22; Prov. 1:8,10; 2:1; 3:1, 11,21; 4:10,20; 5:1; 6:1; 7:1; 19:27; 23:15; Eccl. 12:12; Ps. 34:12(11). A certain degree of subordination is expressed by *ben* in Josh. 7:19; 1 S. 4:16; 25:8; 2 S. 18:22; 2 K. 16:7, where *ben* and → עֶבֶד *'ebhedh,* "servant," can stand in parallelism.

7. *ben* is used in various figurative expressions. Isa. 5:1 uses the phrase *ben shamen,* "son of oil," to emphasize the fertility of a hill. Lucifer, the morning star, is called *ben shachar,* "son of the dawn" (Isa. 14:12). Sparks flying up from a fire are called *bene resheph,* "sons of fire (heat)" (Job 5:7). Arrows are called *bene qasheth,* "sons of the bow" (Job 41:20[28]), or *bene 'ashpatho,* "sons of the quiver" (Lam. 3:13). Zerubbabel and Joshua are honored with the title *bene hayyitshar,* "sons of oil" (Zec. 4:14), because they will be given the messianic leadership in the End Time.

8. *ben* and *bar* are also used to denote membership in certain social and professional groups. Thus *bene haggolah,* "sons of exile," means those who have been carried into exile (Ezr. 4:1; 6:20; 8:35; 2 Ch. 25:13; Aram. Dnl. 2:25, etc.; Ezr. 6:16), *ben chorim,* "son of nobles," freedmen (Eccl. 10:17; cf. Neh. 4:8[14]), *bene 'ebhyon,* the poor (Ps. 72:4), *bene hattoshabhim,* sojourners (Lev. 25:45), and *bene ha'am,* the common people (2 K. 23:6; Jer. 26:23; 2 Ch. 35:5, 7,12f.).

The following expressions refer to professional groups: *ben haraqqachim,* "son of perfumers" = perfumer (Neh. 3:8), and *bene hameshorerim,* singers (Neh. 12:28). An entire group of singers can be denoted by their eponym, so perhaps *bene qorach,* "sons of Korah" (Ps. 42:1; 44:1; 46:1; 47:1; 49:1; 84:1; 87:1; 88:1; in Eng. this expression is printed in the superscriptions over each of these Pss.), and *bene 'asaph,* "sons of Asaph" (2 Ch. 35:15). The priests are called *bene hakkohanim,* "sons of the priests" (Ezr. 2:61; 10:18; Neh. 12:35; 1 Ch. 9:30), or, after their founder or eponym, *bene 'aharon,* "sons of Aaron" (Lev. 1:5,11; 2:2f.,10; 13:2; 21:1; Nu. 10:8; 2 Ch. 35:14), *bene levi,* "sons of Levi" (Dt. 21:5; Ezr. 8:15), and *bene tsadhoq,* "sons of Zadok" (Ezk. 40:46; 44:15; 48:11). The prophets and their disciples are called *bene hannebhi'im,* "sons of the prophets" (1 K. 20:35; 2 K. 2:3,5,7,15; 4:1,38; 5:22; 6:1; 9:1; sing. [!] *ben nabhi',* "a prophet's son," Am. 7:14), and a wise man is called *ben chakhamim,* "son of the wise men" (Isa. 19:11).

ben is used in the same way when a text refers to an animal that belongs to a certain species. In Ps. 114:4 (where *bene tso'n,* "sons of sheep," i.e., "lambs," is par. to *'elim,* "rams"), Ps. 147:9 (where *bene 'orebh,* "sons of a raven," i.e., "young ravens," is par. to *behemah,* "beast[s]"), and Prov. 30:17 (where *'orebhe,* "ravens," is par. to *bene nasher,* "sons of a vulture," i.e., "vultures"), the parallelism shows that the expressions using *ben* do not mean the offspring of these animals, but the sheep species, the raven species, and the vulture species respectively.

9. *ben* or *bar* is also used to classify men individually in different groups according to ethical and moral standards: *bene chayil,* "sons of strength," are the valiant (1 S. 14:52; 18:17; 2 S. 2:7; 1 K. 1:52; 2 K. 2:16; Dt. 3:18; Jgs. 18:2; 21:10; 2 Ch. 17:7); *bene taʿanugh,* "sons of daintiness," dainty sons or "children of delight" (RSV, Mic. 1:16); *bene shachats,* "sons of pride," the proud (beasts, Job 28:8; 41:26[34]); *bene meri,* "sons of rebellion," rebels (Nu. 17:25[10]); *bene* → בְלִיַעַל *beliyyaʿal,* "sons of belial," worthless or base persons (Dt. 13:14 [13]; Jgs. 19:22; 1 S. 2:12; 10:27; 25:17; 1 K. 21:10,13; 2 Ch. 13:7), *bene shaʾon,* "sons of uproar," noisy persons (Jer. 48:45); *bene ʿavlah,* "sons of injustice," wicked or violent persons (2 S. 3:34; 7:10; Hos. 10:9; Ps. 89:23[22]); *bene nabhal gam bene bheli shem,* "sons of a fool, also sons without a name," the wicked and dishonorable brood (Job 30:8); *bene ʿoni,* "sons of affliction," the afflicted (Prov. 31:5); *ben hameratstseach,* "son of murdering," a murderer (2 K. 6:32); and *bene haggedhudh,* "sons of the band (troop)," a band of robbers (2 Ch. 25:13).

Fate or a threatening calamity also affects the people in a community: *bene hattaʿarubhoth,* "sons of pledges," means hostages (2 K. 14:14); *ben temuthah* or *ben maveth,* "son of death," a person who deserves to die (1 S. 20:31; 26:16; 2 S. 12:5; Ps. 79:11; 102:21[20]); *ben gorni,* "son of my threshing floor," one who will be threshed on the threshing floor (Isa. 21:10); and *bin hakkoth,* "son of scourging or smiting," one who deserves to be beaten (Dt. 25:2). The expression *bene shikkulayikh,* "sons of thy childlessness" (Isa. 49:20), is boldly paradoxical.

10. Finally, *ben* and *bar* are used in expressions that indicate a period of time or a person's age: *bin laylah,* "son of the night," means one night old, i.e., something that grew up in a night (Jonah 4:10); *ben shemonath yamim,* "son of eight days," eight days old (Gen. 17:12); *ben chamesh meʾoth shanah,* five hundred years old (5:32); and *seh... ben shanah,* a one-year-old lamb (Ex. 12:5). In the singular this kind of expression is usually connected with a suffix (Lev. 12:6; 23:12; Nu. 6:12,14; 7 [12 times]; Ezk. 46:13), but in the plural it always occurs without a suffix (Lev. 9:3; 23:18f.; Nu. 7 [14 times]; 28f. [15 times]; and Mic. 6:6).

IV. Theological Evaluation.

1. *In the Human Sphere.* a. The value of a son is determined by the value of life, which is the highest good for biblical man. The life of parents is continued in their children. Thus, sons are the first consolation given to the first parents after they lose paradise: life continues (Gen. 4:1f.). P states expressly that Adam

passed on to his first son not only life, but also the likeness and image of God (5:3). Even the judgment brought on man by the flood is not intended to call into question the continuity of human life, because Noah is instructed to take his three sons and their wives with him on the ark (6:18; cf. 7:7; 8:18), and after the flood Noah's sons receive the blessing and the covenant along with him (9:1, 8). The idea that the descendants of the salvation bearer are recipients of the gift of salvation just as fully as the salvation bearer himself, which is made concrete in Israel (cf., e.g., Ex. 12:24; 13:14-16) and in a unique way in the house of David (2 S. 7:12; 1 Ch. 17:11; 2 Ch .13:5), is already prominent in these passages.

b. The life of a father has meaning only insofar as it is continued in his son (Gen. 15:2f.). Therefore, childlessness (Jer. 16:2) or the loss of an only son (Gen. 22:2) is the most painful sacrifice. A son keeps the name of his father from being forgotten (2 S. 18:18). Consequently, the promise (Gen. 16:11; 17:16,19; 18:10; Jgs. 13:3ff.; 2 K. 4:16; 1 Ch. 22:9; Isa. 7:14) and birth (Gen. 16:15; 21:2; 41:50-52; Jgs. 13:24; Ruth 4:13; 1 S. 1:20; 2 K. 4:17; Isa. 8:3; Jer. 20:15) of a son are the most important events in the life of a man and his wife. This is particularly true of the firstborn son (→ בכור bekhôr), "firstborn of man" (Gen. 49:3). Thus, OT writers liked to mention the age of a father at the time of the conception or birth of his first son (Gen. 5:3ff.; 11:10ff.; 21:5). Sons are the greatest pride of parents and especially of the wife. Rachel assails her husband Jacob, saying, "Give me sons, or I shall die" (Gen. 30:1; cf. Ps. 113:9; 127:3f.; 128:3,6). To refuse to allow a father to kiss his children and his grandchildren good-bye is heartless (Gen. 31:28; cf. 32:1[31:55]). It is surprising that a good man could mean more to his wife than ten sons (1 S. 1:8), and that a good daughter-in-law could mean more to her mother-in-law than seven sons (Ruth 4:15). A man of God rebukes Eli because he honors his sons more than Yahweh (1 S. 2:29).

c. This last passage (1 S. 2:29) is the only one in the OT that speaks of a parent "honoring" (verb → כבד kābhēdh) his sons, and here this concept is presented in a negative sense. Ordinarily, it is the parents who are to be honored (Ex. 20:12 par.; Mic. 7:6). The use of the verb kabhedh in these texts connects parents with the sacral sphere, since this verb is used in the Hebrew Bible only with reference to Yahweh or with reference to persons and things that have a sacral character (cf. also the sin of Ham in Gen. 9:22). However, the OT deals soberly with the "human weakness" of parents, as is clear from the principle that the children are not responsible for the sins of the fathers, which certainly cannot be later than Deuteronomy, and probably originated much earlier (Dt. 24:16; 2 Ch. 25:4; Job 21:19; Jer. 31:29f.; Ezk. 18:2). Indeed, this human weakness, or rather inhumanity, can go so far that in times of severe distress parents can even eat their own children (Lev. 26:29; Dt. 28:53-57; 2 K. 6:28f.; Jer. 19:9; but cf. Ezk. 5:10, where the prophet announces just the opposite, viz., that children will eat their own parents).

d. In the more restricted sense, the family of the OT consisted of parents, son and daughter, manservant and maidservant (cf., e.g., Dt. 16:11,14). Parents are responsible for the moral life of their sons and daughters (Ex. 20:10 par.; Job 1:5), and for instructing their sons in particular in the law (Ex. 13:14; Dt. 11:19; Josh. 4:6f.,21f.). To be sure, the OT urges that children be given strict discipline (Prov. 13:24; 19:18; 29:17), for a wise son makes a glad father (10:1); and Dt. 21:18-21 (cf. Prov. 19:26) even describes an extreme case in which parents, by mutual agreement, are to bring a stubborn and rebellious son before the elders of the city to be punished by death. However, the compassionate love of a human father for his son remains the classic symbol for the compassionate paternal love of God (Ps. 103:13; Mal. 3:17; cf. Lk. 15:11-32).

2. *Divine Sonship*. a. *Israel As God's Son*. Frequently Yahweh's relationship to Israel or to the Israelites is represented as a father-son relationship. Thus Yahweh calls Israel "my son" (Ex. 4:23; Hos. 11:1), "my firstborn son" *(beni bhekhori,* Ex. 4:22; *bekhori,* Jer. 31:9), and the Israelites "my sons" (Isa. 45:11), or "my sons and daughters" (43:6); and OT writers refer to the Israelites as "sons" (63:8), "his sons" (Dt. 32:5), or "his sons and daughters" (32:19). Accordingly, Yahweh is called Israel's father (→ אב *'ābh,* 32:6,18; Jer. 3:4). The whole people is addressed with the words *banim 'attem,* "you are sons" (Dt. 14:1), and *bene 'el chai,* "sons of the living God" (Hos. 2:1[1:10]). In prophetic accusations, the people are called "sons" without a suffix (Isa. 1:2), "sons who deal corruptly" (1:4), "rebellious sons" (30:1), "lying sons" (30:9), "faithless sons" (Jer. 3:14,22), "stupid sons" (4:22), and "sons in whom is no faithfulness" (Dt. 32:20). Ephraim is an "unwise son" (Hos. 13:13). On the other hand, *dor baneykha,* "the generation of thy sons (children)," in Ps. 73:15 has reference to the godly.

These expressions convey two ideas. For one thing, they emphasize the distance between Yahweh and Israel and affirm that the people are subordinate to Yahweh. But they also express Yahweh's love for his people, and thus complement the biblical figures of Yahweh as shepherd, husband, and redeemer of his people.

b. *The King*. The passages in which the king is designated as God's son (2 S. 7:14 par.; Ps. 89:27f.[26f.]; 2:7) are disputed. But the possible influence of ancient Near Eastern ideas of sacral kingship on this concept is restricted a priori in that Israel had no place for the idea of a physical begettal of the king by the deity. The king of Israel was not called "son of God" just because he was king or because he acceded to the throne. Rather, the only way he could become the "son of God" and thereby be given a portion of Yahweh's sphere of authority was for Yahweh officially to declare him to be his son. It is incorrect to interpret this expression as a kind of adoption of the king by Yahweh[46] (because the institution of adoption was not known in Israel). It is better to view it as "a mythical element which has been transferred to the realm of metaphor."[47]

---

[46] Cf. esp. M. Noth, "God, King and Nation in the OT," *The Laws of the Pentateuch and Other Essays* (trans. 1966), 145ff.

[47] H. Donner, 114.

The present form of the prophecy of Nathan in 2 S. 7 is the result of complicated literary growth, in which at least three stages can be distinguished. [48] The statement with which we are concerned in this discussion ("I will be his father, and he shall be my son...," vv.14f.) appears to belong to the middle stage. The most logical explanation of the use of this phrase here is that the human father-son relationship is used as a prototype for Yahweh's judging and saving activity with regard to the Davidic dynasty. However, since the OT refers to the Davidic covenant in such an implicit and matter-of-fact way (cf. 2 S. 23:5; 2 Ch. 13:5; 21:7; Ps. 89:4,29,35,40 [3,28,34,39]; Jer. 33:21), the father-son formula takes on the character of a covenant formula. [49]

Ps. 89 should also be understood as an expansion of the fundamental idea in 2 S. 7. It is true that the word *ben* is not used in this psalm with reference to the king. But still this text clearly speaks of Yahweh's relationship to the king in terms of the father-son relationship: for one thing, the king addresses Yahweh as → אָב *'ābh*, "father" (v. 27a[26a]), and for another, Yahweh makes or appoints (*nathan*) the king the firstborn (*bekhor*, v. 28a[27a]; cf. Jer. 1:5: *nabhi' laggoyim nethattikha*, "I appointed you a prophet to the nations"), the *'elyon*, "highest," of the kings of the earth (v. 28b[27b]). Verse 29(28) states explicitly that the divine sonship of the king is rooted in the Davidic covenant (*chesedh*, "steadfast love"; *berith*, "covenant"; cf. vv. 4,35,40[3,34,39]). The designation of the king of Israel as "firstborn" seems to imply that the kings of other nations were also considered to be "sons" of Yahweh. But this text affirms that the king of Israel is much closer to Yahweh than they, not only by calling him *bekhor*, but even more by giving him the title *'elyon*, which only in this passage in the entire OT refers to a man. "This extraordinary statement approaches a deification of the king (cf. Ps. 45:7[6])." [50]

Ps. 2:7, where Yahweh's decree to the king begins with the words, "You are my son, today I have begotten you," brings us almost terrifyingly close to the idea of divine birth. But it is clear from the word "today," which has reference to the enthronement ceremony (cf. v. 6), that the author of this passage cannot have a physical fatherhood in mind either. Since the formula, "you are my son, today I have begotten you," was not restricted to the royal ritual, but was at home in human legal terminology, it would seem to refer less to the adoption of a foreign child than to the recognition of a child born to a slave as the wife's representative. Although there are no examples of this formula, the practice, as is obvious from Hammurabi (CH, §§ 170f.) and the OT (Gen. 30:1-13), was well known.

The author of the oracle of salvation in Isa. 9:5f.(6f.), which is hardly an authentic oracle from Isaiah of Jerusalem, announces the coming of the Messiah upon the throne of David as a royal child and a prince. The parallelism of

---

[48] Cf. esp. L. Rost, *Die Überlieferung von der Thronnachfolge Davids. BWANT*, 3/6 (1926), 47ff.

[49] Cf. N. Poulssen, *König und Tempel im Glaubenszeugnis des ATs. SBM*, 3 (1967), 43f.

[50] H.-J. Kraus, *BK*, XV², 623; cf. also C. R. North, *ZAW*, 50 (1932), 26; G. W. Ahlström, *Psalm 89* (Lund, 1959), 111-13.

"son" and "child" indicates that he has in mind a thoroughly human birth. [51] Nevertheless, this text views birth and accession to the throne in one glance; [52] and in the enthronement described in v. 5aβ(6aβ) on, the king receives the name *'el gibbor* (RSV, "Mighty God"), which brings us to the (likewise postexilic) context of Ps. 45:4(3) (→ גבור *gibbôr,* "mighty"), 7(6) (→ אלהים *'elōhîm,* "God").

It is generally considered to be certain that the Egyptian coronation ritual [53] (of which, admittedly, we have only an incomplete knowledge) had a significant influence on the formulation of the Jerusalem ritual. However, the fundamental differences between the Egyptian and Israelite royal theology must not be overlooked. The idea of a physical divine begettal rooted in myth [54] was clearly transformed into the concept of a divine sonship based on election and covenant. The only OT text that could possibly be used to support the view that the king was called → אלהים *'elōhim,* "God," without qualification, is Ps. 45:7a,8b (6a, 7b). But it is not certain whether *'elohim* is actually to be read as a vocative in these two verses. [55] And even if this were the case, this one instance would hardly be a sufficient basis for the assumption that the Egyptian or Mesopotamian ideas concerning the divine sonship of the king were simply taken over in Israel without modification. [56] It is especially noteworthy that in the three texts that are crucial to this issue (2 S. 7; Pss. 2 and 89), there is no mention of a wife at all, but the whole event involves only God and the king. By way of contrast, Isa. 9:5f.(6f.) and 7:14 speak altogether of human conception and birth. Finally, the theme of Ps. 45 is not the birth, but the marriage, of the king.

c. The Sons of the Gods. The connection of *ben* or *bar* with beings that belong to the divine world is also a matter of dispute. The expressions that continue to be under discussion are: *bene 'elim,* "sons of gods" (Ps. 29:1; 89:7[6]), *bene 'elyon,* "sons of the Most High" (Ps. 82:6), *bene (ha)'elohim,* "sons of God" (Gen. 6:2,4; Job 1:6; 2:1; 38:7), and *bar 'elahin,* "a son of the gods" (Dnl. 3:25). (It is striking that *ben* is never used in construct before *yhvh.*) These phrases are to be seen in connection with the ancient Near Eastern ideas concerning the assembly of the divine or heavenly beings (cf. also Ps. 82:1; 89:6,8 [5,7]). The expression *bene ha'elohim,* "sons of God," in Gen. 6:1-4 has been the object of numerous investigations. [57] There can be no doubt that in this fragment of a mythical narrative the author of the original oral or written tradition was thinking of gods, especially in light of the Ugaritic parallels (where *bn* is often used to denote membership in a group). [58] Many scholars correctly refer to

---

[51] Cf. H. Wildberger, *BK,* X, 377.

[52] G. Fohrer, *Das Buch Jesaja,* I (²1966), 141.

[53] Cf. *RÄR, s.v.* "Krönung" ("Coronation").

[54] On this cf. esp. H. Brunner, *Die Geburt des Gottkönigs. ÄgAbh* (1964).

[55] So recently B. Couroyer, *RB,* 78 (1971), 233-241.

[56] Cf. esp. K.-H. Bernhardt, *Das Problem der altorientalischen Königsideologie im AT. SVT,* 8 (1961).

[57] Cf. the bibliography from 1937 to 1967 in Scharbert.

[58] Cf. II.1.c; III.8.

CTA, 32 [*UT,* 2], 16f., as a classic Ugaritic parallel to the phrase in Gen. 6:1-4:

> The offering which we offer,
> the sacrifice which we sacrifice,
> it ascends to the (father of the *bn ʾl*),
> it ascends to the dwelling of the *bn ʾl,*
> to the assembly of the *bn ʾl.* [59]

Dexinger wants to interpret the *bene ha'elohim,* "sons of God," in Gen. 6:1-4 as heroes, and he appeals to the Ugaritic literature to support his view; but he overlooks that in the Ugaritic material there is evidence only that the singular of *bn ʾl* has this meaning, and not the plural. [60] Another problem is the difference between the way the Israelite narrator (J, but earlier a separate source) [61] and the final redactor of the Pentateuch understood the phrase *bene ha'elohim,* "sons of God." It is highly probable that the earlier narrator was thinking of heavenly beings in the broader sense. This is certainly the case with the final redactor of the Pentateuch, even though the LXX renders *bene ha'elohim* in Gen. 6:2,4 by *hoi huioí toú theoú,* "the sons of God," and not by *ángeloi,* "angels," as it does in Job 1:6; 2:1; 38:7. At any rate, this interpretation [62] came into Jewish tradition and proved to be the springboard for legends about the fall of angels and the origin of demons growing out of them (cf. esp. 1 En. 6–36; Jub. 5:1-10). The view that *bene ha'elohim* has reference to the descendants of Seth, which has been abandoned in more recent times by most scholars, but which has been advocated again by Scharbert, [63] can hardly be defended, because it does not adequately take into account the intentional contrast between the *bene ha'elohim,* "sons of God," and the *benoth ha'adham,* "daughters of men." The idea of a pantheon under the leadership of a supreme god is also clear in the *bene 'elim,* "sons of gods," of Ps. 29:1 (originally this text probably read "Baal" instead of "Yahweh"), and 89:7(6) (where it is in parallelism to *qehal qedhoshim,* "assembly of the holy ones," in v. 6[5], and *sodh qedhoshim,* "council of the holy ones," in v. 8[7]). [64]

In Ps. 82:6, the *bene 'elyon,* "sons of the Most High" (par. to *'elohim,* "gods"), which will be called into account by Yahweh, are not human rulers or judges. Rather, this phrase presupposes the idea that the other nations have their own gods, and that the head of all the gods is *'elyon.* [65] We find the same idea in Dt. 32:8, which states that *'Elyon* fixed the bounds of the peoples "according to the number of the gods" (MT *bene yisra'el,* "sons [children] of Israel"; LXX

---

[59] Cf. the list of other Ugaritic texts on this subject in Dexinger, 31-37.

[60] Cf. the summary in *ibid.,* 37.

[61] Cf. Scharbert, 69-71.

[62] For the history of this interpretation, see Dexinger, 97-101.

[63] Cf. *ibid.,* 106-108.

[64] On the assembly of the gods, cf. H. Gese, *Die Religionen Altsyriens* (1970), 100-102, and esp. the expression *kl dr bn 'lm,* "the whole sphere of the gods," *KAI,* 26A III, 19.

[65] On the idea that *'Elyon* is "the power standing above and before everything," cf. Gese, 116f.

angélōn theoú, "angels of God"; 4Q *bene 'el* [...], "sons of God"). [66] One should be very wary about identifying *'Elyon* too quickly with Yahweh in this passage, [67] even if the original text contains a summons to "all *'elohim"* ("gods," 4Q; LXX *huioí theoú,* "the sons of God") to fall down before Yahweh.

On the other hand, the old idea of the "council of the gods" has lost much of its original color in the book of Job. Here, the *bene (ha)'elohim,* "sons of God" (Job 1:6; 2:1; 38:7) compose the heavenly court of "angels" which are completely subordinate to Yahweh and thus must appear before Yahweh to give an account of their activities to him and to receive his instructions. Of course, the parallelism of *bene 'elohim,* "sons of God," and *kokhebhe bhoqer,* "morning stars" (38:7), would seem to point to an original connection between the *bene 'elohim,* "sons of God," and a pantheon.

The book of Daniel stands in the stream of apocalypticism with its extensive angelology. Therefore, the *bar 'elahin,* "son of the gods" (Dnl. 3:25), is undoubtedly an angel, just like *'ir veqaddish,* "a watcher, a holy one" (4:10,14,20 [13,17,23]), and *sar,* "prince" (10:13,20f.).

H. Haag

---

[66] Cf. P. W. Skehan, *BASOR,* 136 (1954), 12-15; R. Meyer, *Festschrift für W. Rudolph* (1961), 197-209; cf. also M. Tsevat, "God and the Gods in Assembly," *HUCA,* 40/41 (1969/ 1970), 123-137, on this point, pp. 132f.

[67] With Meyer and Tsevat.

בֶּן־אָדָם *ben 'ādhām*

Contents: I. Occurrences and Meaning: 1. In Hebrew; 2. In Aramaic; 3. In Phoenician. II. Theological Significance: 1. In the OT in General; 2. In Ezekiel; 3. In Daniel.

I. Occurrences and Meaning.

1. *In Hebrew.* a. In the Hebrew OT, *ben 'adham* means a single man within the species or race, [1] and therefore as a rule it should be translated simply "man" (not "son of man" or "human being"). Of course, a single man can also be denoted

---

ben 'ādhām. A bibliography of recent studies on the "son of man" problem is given by R. Marlow, "The Son of Man in Recent Journal Literature," *CBQ,* 28 (1966), 20-30; cf. the supplement of J. B. Cortés-F. M. Gatti, *Bibl,* 49 (1968), 458, n. 1; and *TDNT,* VIII, 400f. Here we will list only the most important recent works that are pertinent to the use of this expression in the OT.

A. Bentzen, *Messias, Moses redivivus, Menschensohn* (Zürich, 1948); F. H. Borsch, *The Son of Man in Myth and History* (London, 1967); J. Bowman, "The Background of the Term 'Son of Man,'" *ExpT,* 59 (1947/1948), 283-88; C. H. W. Brekelmans, "The Saints of the Most High and Their Kingdom," *OTS,* 14 (1965), 305-329; J. Y. Campbell, "The Origin

(continued on p. 160)

[1] → אדם *'ādhām* I.1; → בן *bēn* III.5.

by → אדם 'ādhām alone, or by → אִישׁ 'îsh, or by → אֱנוֹשׁ 'enôsh; and at the same time, ben 'adham can also mean "men" in general (Isa. 51:12; Ps. 146:3). While ben 'enosh, "son of man," occurs only once in the OT (Ps. 144:3), ben 'adham appears 152 times (in the sing. and pl. together). But apart from Ezekiel, [2] ben 'adham is found mainly in poetic texts (esp. in Pss., Prov., and Eccl.) and in the majority of cases in parallelism. [3]

The determinative form (ben ha'adham) does not appear in Hebrew in the singular. Only in 1QS 11:20 has a later scribe added a he above the word 'adham, which certainly represents a literal rendering of the Aram. bar nasha'. The pl. bene ha'adham, "sons of man (men)" (instead of the more common bene 'adham) occurs 14 times in the OT, [4] and in Ecclesiastes is used exclusively (Gen. 11:5; 1 K. 8:39; Ps. 33:13; 145:12; Eccl. 1:13; 2:3,8; 3:10,18f.,21; 8:11; 9:3,12).

---

and Meaning of the Term Son of Man," *JTS,* 48 (1947), 145-155; A. Caquot, "Les quatre bêtes et le 'Fils d'Homme,'" *Sem,* 17 (1967), 37-71; C. Colpe, "ὁ υἱὸς τοῦ ἀνθρώπου," *TDNT,* VIII, 400-477; *idem,* "Der Begriff 'Menschensohn' und die Methode der Erforschung messianischer Prototypen," *Kairos,* N.F. 11 (1969), 241-263; J. Coppens, "Le Fils d'Homme daniélique, vizir céleste?" *ETL,* 40 (1964), 72-80; *idem,* "La vision daniélique du Fils d'Homme," *VT,* 19 (1969), 171-182; J. Coppens-L. Dequeker, "Le Fils d'homme et les Saints du Très-Haut en Daniel VII, dans les Apocryphes et dans le NT," *Löwen* (²1961), 55-101 = *ETL,* 37 (1961), 5-51; O. Cullmann, *Christology of the NT* (trans. 1959), 137-192; E. Dhanis, "De Filio Hominis in VT et in Judaismo," *Greg,* 45 (1964), 5-59; J. A. Emerton, "The Origin of the Son of Man Imagery," *JTS,* N.S. 9 (1958), 225-242; A. Feuillet, "Le Fils de l'Homme de Daniel et la tradition biblique," *RB,* 60 (1953), 170-202, 321-346; A. Gelston, "A Sidelight on the 'Son of Man,'" *SJT,* 22 (1969), 189-196; H. Gressmann, *Der Messias* (1929), 341-414; R. Hanhart, "Die Heiligen des Höchsten," *SVT,* 16 (1967), 90-101; A. J. B. Higgins, "Son of Man-Forschung since 'The Teaching of Jesus,'" *NT Essays. Studies in Memory of T. W. Manson* (Manchester, 1959), 119-135; H. L. Jansen, *Die Henochgestalt* (Oslo, 1940); C. H. Kraeling, *Anthropos and the Son of Man. A Study in the Religious Syncretism of the Hellenistic Orient* (New York, 1927), 128-165; *idem,* "Some Babylonian and Iranian Mythology in the Seventh Chapter of Daniel," *Oriental Studies in Honour of C. E. Pavry* (London, 1933), 228-231; H. Kruse, "Compositio Libri Danielis et idea Filii Hominis," *VD,* 37 (1959), 147-161, 193-211; T. W. Manson, "The Son of Man in Daniel, Enoch and the Gospels," *BJRL,* 32 (1949/1950), 171-193; J. Morgenstern, "The 'Son of Man' of Daniel 7,13f. A New Interpretation," *JBL,* 80 (1961), 65-77; *idem, Some Significant Antecedents of Christianity* (Leiden, 1966), 61-80; S. Mowinckel, *He That Cometh* (Oxford, ²1959), 346-450; J. Muilenburg, "The Son of Man in Daniel and the Ethiopic Apocalypse of Enoch," *JBL,* 79 (1960), 197-209; J. Nelis, "Menschensohn," in *BL²,* 1128-1134; M. Noth, "The Holy Ones of the Most High," *The Laws of the Pentateuch and Other Essays* (trans. 1966), 215ff.; P. Parker, "The Meaning of 'Son of Man,'" *JBL,* 60 (1941), 151-57; L. Rost, "Zur Deutung des Menschensohnes in Daniel 7," *Gott und die Götter. Festschrift für E. Fascher* (1959), 41-43; E. Sjöberg, *Der Menschensohn im äthiopischen Henochbuch* (Lund, 1946); *idem,* "בֶּן־אָדָם und בַּר־אֱנָשׁ im Hebräischen und Aramäischen," *AcOr,* 21 (1950/1951), 57-65, 91-107; G. H. P. Thompson, "The Son of Man: The Evidence of the DSS," *ExpT,* 72 (1961), 125; G. Vermès, "The Use of בַּר נָשָׁא/בַּר נָשׁ in Jewish Aramaic," M. Black, *An Aramaic Approach to the Gospels and Acts* (Oxford, ³1967), 310-328; J. L. C. Ylarri, "Los bene ha'elohîm en Gen 6,1-4," *EstBíb,* 28 (1969), 5-31; W. Zimmerli, *Was ist der Mensch? Göttinger Universitätsreden,* 44 (1964). Cf. also the comms. on Ezekiel and Daniel.

2 See II.2.
3 See below.
4 *KBL³,* 14 should be corrected accordingly.

b. *ben 'adham* appears in parallelism with → אֱנוֹשׁ *'enôsh,* "man," in Isa. 51:12; 56:2; Ps. 8:5(4); and Job 25:6; with → אִישׁ *'îsh,* "man," in Nu. 23:19; Jer. 49:18, 33; 50:40; 51:43; Ps. 80:18 (Eng. v. 17); and Job 35:8; with *nedhibhim,* "princes," in Ps. 146:3; and with *gebher,* "man," in Job 16:21 (however, in this verse it would seem better to read *bên,* "between," instead of *ben,* "son"). In Dnl. 8:17, *ben 'adham* is taken over from Ezk. 2:1.

The pl. *bene 'adham,* "sons of man (men)," [5] means single men in the plural, and is often a poetic expression for the human race ("mankind"): Jer. 32:19; Ezk. 31:14; Dnl. 10:16; Joel 1:12; Ps. 11:4; 12:2,9(1,8); 14:2; 31:20(19); 36:8(7); 45:3(2); 53:3(2); 57:5(4); 58:2(1); 66:5; 89:48(47); 107:8,15,21,31; 115:16; Prov. 15:11. Also *bene 'adham* is used frequently in parallelism, viz., with *goyim,* "nations" (Dt. 32:8); *'anashim,* "men" (2 S. 7:14); *'ish,* "man" (Isa. 52:14; Mic. 5:6[7]); *'erets,* "earth" (Ps. 21:11[10]; Prov. 8:31); *bene 'ish,* "sons of man (men)" (Ps. 49:3[2]; 62:10[9]); *'enosh,* "man" (90:3); and *'ishim,* "men" (Prov. 8:4). Accordingly, sometimes *bene 'adham* in a genitive construction is translated "human," e.g., in 2 S. 7:14 ("human stripes") and Dnl. 10:16 ("human hand"). *bene 'ish,* "sons of man (men)," in Ps. 4:3(2) and Lam. 3:33 means the same thing as *bene 'adham,* but the author of Ps. 49:3(2) seems to contrast *bene 'adham* with *bene 'ish* (→ אִישׁ *'îsh*). On the other hand, *bene 'ish 'echadh* (Gen. 42:11,13) means "the sons of one man."

c. In the Qumran literature, *ben 'adham* or *ben ha'adham* is used as a collective term for mankind in 1QH 4:30 or 1QS 11:20(4Q184 4:4?), but never as a title for the figure of the eschatological savior. The phrase *bene 'adham* (1QS 11:6,15; 1QH 2:24; 4:32; 4Q181 1:1; 11QPs^a 24:15; etc.) or *bene 'ish* (1QS 3:13; 4:15,20,26; 1QM 11:14; 4Q184 1:17) means the human race or mankind. Here, as in the OT, [6] the emphasis is on human weakness in the presence of God (cf. 1QS 11:15; 1QH 5:11,15; 6:11; 11:6). *bene ha'adham* in 1QH 1:27 means the same thing (however, in CD B 12:4 it means "some people"; cf. 14:11: *kol ha'adham* = each one). It is worthy of note that the use of *bene 'adham* is limited almost ·exclusively to hymnic passages (1QS 11; 1QH; 11QPs^a 24[= Ps. 155]; 4Q184).

2. *In Aramaic.* In Aramaic, which does not have the word *'adham,* the expression corresponding to Heb. *ben 'adham* is *bar 'enash* (→ אֱנוֹשׁ *'enôsh*). *bar* in Aramaic was not as necessary to convey the idea of a single person as *ben* in Hebrew because *'enash* alone can mean "a man" or "men, mankind." Thus, up to the present time only two examples of *bar 'enash* have been discovered in inscriptions: *KAI,* 224.16 (Sefire, 8th century B.C.), and the Aramaic-Greek bilingual text from Georgia, lines 19f. [7] (2nd century A.D.). In both cases, this expression means "someone." In the Aramaic portions of the OT, the indeterminate form *'enash* means an indefinite person or man (Dnl. 2:10; 5:5; 6:8[7]);

---

5 On the form *bene ha'adham,* see above, a.
6 Cf. below, II.1.
7 *JNES,* 15 (1956), 20, 24.

kol 'enash, "each, every, any, whoever" (3:10; 5:7; 6:13 [12]; Ezr. 6:11; cf. *kol di 'enash*, "whoever," in a tomb inscription discovered at Jerusalem); [8] and the determinative form *'ana(o)sha'*, men in general (Dnl. 4:13f.,22,29f.[16f.,25,32f.]), but *bene 'anasha'* also means exactly the same thing (2:38; 5:21). *bar 'enash* means a single human being as distinguished from a single animal (7:13).

In the Palestinian Targum of the Pentateuch, Heb. *'adham* is usually rendered by *bar nash*, and *ha'adham* by *bar nasha'*. But when *'adham* is understood in a collective sense, it can also be translated by *bene 'anasha'* or *bene nasha'*. In the Targumim to the Prophets and Writings, *ben 'adham* is rendered by *bar nash(a')*. In the Talmudic literature, Gen Rabba and 1QGenAp, *bar nash(a')* and *bene nash* have a wide range of meanings, including "the man," "a man," "someone" (or "no one"), and "people"; in fact, in some contexts *bar nash(a')* is the term for "I." [9]

3. *In Phoenician.* The only Phoenician example of *bn 'dm* = men (par. to gods) that has been discovered thus far appears on the base of a votive stela from Memphis [10] (2nd/1st century B.C.). *bn 'dm* does not occur in Ugaritic literature, and is completely unknown in Akkadian.

II. Theological Significance.

1. *In the OT in General.* Even if the only possible rendering of *ben 'adham* is "man" and the translations "son of man" and "human being" are to be rejected, it cannot be denied that this expression points to the weakness and frailty of man. For in almost all passages where *ben 'adham* occurs, it stands in emphatic contrast to God. Yahweh comes down to see the tower the *bene 'adham* have built (Gen. 11:5). Nathan, to be sure, announces that the offspring of David will be chastened with the stripes of the *bene 'adham;* but he also states that Yahweh will never take his *chesedh*, "steadfast love," from him (2 S. 7:14f.). Yahweh looks down from heaven, his palace, on the *bene 'adham* (Ps. 11:4; 14:2; 33:13; 53:3[2]; Jer. 32:19), to whom he has given the earth for a dwelling place (Ps. 115:16), and who, therefore, are "under heaven" (Eccl. 2:3). He rules with power over the *bene 'adham* (Ps. 66:5), he works his wonders among them (107:8,15, 21,31; cf. 145:12), and they take refuge in the shadow of his wings (36:8[7]). Yahweh defends the godly from the *bene 'adham* (12:2,9[1,8]; 31:20[19]; 57:5 [4]), they are but a breath before him (62:10[9]; cf. 89:48[47]; 90:3), they go down to the Pit (Ezk. 31:14; cf. Eccl. 3:19,21), they are delivered over to misfortune (Eccl. 9:12), and appointed for affliction (1:13; 3:10). When Yahweh destroys Babylon, no *ben 'adham* will dwell there any longer (Jer. 49:18,33; 50:40; 51:43). There is no help in the *ben 'adham* (in contrast to Yahweh, Ps. 146:3). Therefore, Israel trusts in Yahweh and not in the *bene 'adham* (Mic. 5:6[7]). The king himself is only a *ben 'adham,* and depends on Yahweh's help

---

[8] *RB*, 65 (1958), 409.
[9] Vermès.
[10] *KAI*, 48.4.

(Ps. 80:18[17]). In view of the comforts Yahweh gives, Israel does not have to be afraid of the transitory *bene 'adham* (Isa. 51:12).

The *'elim,* "gods," rule high above the *bene 'adham* (Ps. 58:2[1]). When he looks at the firmament, it becomes quite clear to the *ben 'adham* that he is only a little less than God (8:5[4]). According to Ps. 45:3(2), the king is the fairest of the *bene 'adham.* By way of contrast, the *'ebedh,* "servant," is so disfigured that he no longer looks like a *ben 'adham;* this forms a striking contrast to his subsequent exaltation by Yahweh (Isa. 52:14f.). Divine Wisdom addresses herself to the *bene 'adham* (Prov. 8:4,31), and the salvation Yahweh offers calls upon the *ben 'adham* to make a decision (Isa. 56:2). The son of man is weak both physically and morally. The *bene ha'adham* do evil (Eccl. 8:11), which, of course, affects not God, but the *bene 'adham* (Job 35:8). If the stars are not clean in God's sight, how could the *ben 'adham* be (25:6)? The heart of the *bene ha'adham* is full of evil (Eccl. 9:3), but it lies more open before Yahweh than Sheol and Abaddon (Prov. 15:11).

2. *In Ezekiel.* The way Yahweh addresses the exilic prophet Ezekiel as *ben 'adham,* which occurs 93 times in the book of Ezekiel (2:1; etc.; cf. Dnl. 8:17),[11] certainly is to be interpreted as an increased emphasis on the distance separating God and man. As Zimmerli has appropriately observed, "the antithetical word *'el* (God) must be understood by implication" when *ben 'adham* is used in Ezekiel.[12] The strange exclusiveness of this address is to be seen in connection with the one-sided emphasis on divine transcendence which began with Ezekiel, especially as it had come to be associated with apocalypticism. Whether one thinks it best to give Ezekiel the title "father of apocalypticism"[13] or not,[14] it cannot be denied that he is the first to use certain typical apocalyptic techniques (the heaping up of visions, the systematic cultivation of symbolism, initial sketches of an angelology, etc.). There is nothing in the address *ben 'adham* that would lead one to think it has an affectionate ring,[15] for it emphasizes remoteness rather than nearness, and the rule of God rather than the fatherhood of God. In Ezekiel the translation "son of man" should be avoided more than in the rest of the OT, and "man" should be considered the only possible rendering.

3. *In Daniel.* The expression *bar 'enash* in Dnl. 7:13 is of special significance, but more because of the way it is interpreted later than because of its meaning in its present context in Daniel. No additional evidence should be required to see that in this passage also the only acceptable translation is "man." Furthermore, it may be regarded as certain that Dnl. 7 in its present form is not homo-

---

[11] Of the 93 occurrences, we find the expression *ve'attah ben 'adham,* "and thou, son of man," 23 times. On the distinction between these two formulas, cf. C. B. Houk, *JBL,* 88 (1969), 184-190.

[12] W. Zimmerli, *BK,* XIII, 70.

[13] So L. Dürr, *Die Stellung des Propheten Ezechiel in der israelitisch-jüdischen Apokalyptik* (1923); etc.

[14] So G. Fohrer, *Die Hauptprobleme des Buches Ezechiel. BZAW,* 72 (1952), 164, 264.

[15] Dürr, 40.

geneous, but a later expansion and adaptation of an earlier tradition (as is the case also with Dnl. 2), especially since the work of Noth on this subject. [16] This can be seen most clearly in the different meanings intended by the expression "the saints of the Most High." Undoubtedly Noth is correct in arguing that in the earlier stage of this tradition "the saints of the Most High" were understood to be heavenly beings. [17] But in the second stage, they were that portion of the Jewish people who remained true to their faith during the persecution of the Jews by Antiochus IV Epiphanes. [18] The only difficulty is determining which parts of Dnl. 7 belong to this second stage. Although there will always be uncertainties on this point, basically the view of Dequeker seems to point in the right direction.

First of all, vv. 20-22 seem to belong to the later redaction (we cannot here investigate the question of an earlier and a later redactor of this chapter). They speak of the eleventh horn and of the subjugation of the saints until the Ancient of Days comes in judgment, and gives them power and grants them the kingdom. The later redactor is also responsible for v. 24 (the eleventh horn). Noth translates v. 25a this way: "he will speak words against the Most High and grieve the saints of the Most High severely." [19] If we interpret "the saints of the Most High" as heavenly beings (which is improbable), v. 25a certainly cannot fit v. 25b, which states that the saints of the Most High will be given into the power of the insolent king for $3^1/_2$ times. Vv. 26f. belong to the earlier stratum, [20] and it is necessary to attribute only 'am, "people," in v. 27 to the redactor, for it is not correct to translate 'am qaddishe 'elyonim by "band (troop) of the saints of the Most High" on the basis of the Qumran literature, and to understand "the saints" as heavenly beings. [21] In Daniel, 'am never means anything but "people," and the striking parallel between v. 27, "the greatness of the kingdoms under the whole heaven shall be given to the people of the saints of the Most High," and 2:44, "and the sovereignty of this kingdom shall not be left to another people," should make it quite clear that 'am in 7:27 also means an earthly people.

But we must not overlook that the alternation between early and late pieces begins in vv. 8-14. The original description of the vision breaks off in v. 7 and is not resumed until vv. 11b,12. And if the "Ancient of Days" is a later element in v. 22, it must also be late in vv. 9f. The same is true of bar nasha', "son of man," which is never mentioned in the expanded interpretation of the vision. V. 11a would also seem to be secondary. [22] There can be no doubt that vv. 9f.,13f. are to be attributed to the redaction. [23] A whole series of expressions (sholtan, "dominion," malkhu, "kingdom," 'am, "people," pelach, "to serve," and 'alam, "everlasting") shows that v. 14 was modeled after v. 27. Thus, it is natural to

---

[16] Noth, "The Holy Ones of the Most High"; Caquot holds otherwise.
[17] R. Hanhart has denied this, but is incorrect.
[18] So correctly Dequeker, 50-54.
[19] Noth, 224; cf. also Colpe, 424.
[20] Following Dequeker, 31, 53.
[21] Noth, Colpe.
[22] O. Plöger, KAT, XVIII, 104; Dequeker, 26f.
[23] Cf. Colpe, 422f.

conclude that the Ancient of Days (vv. 9f.) and the *bar nasha’*, "son of man," both belong to the later stratum, which anticipates world dominion, not for the angels, but for the godly Jews. Thus *bar nasha’* clearly refers back to the "(people of the) saints (of the Most High)" in vv. 21f.,27, understood as the faithful Israel.

Therefore, we have no reservations about accepting the view that the *bar ’enash* represents the kingdom of the people of Yahweh whose existence is from above, in contrast to the kingdoms that are hostile to Yahweh, represented by the four beasts, which come from below. The vague description "like a man" (*kebhar ’enash*, v. 13) corresponds to the description of the beasts ("like a lion," v. 4; "like a bear," v. 5; "like a leopard," v. 6), and is characteristic of apocalyptic style. It cannot be implied from this that this "man" has a mysterious character. Nor can it be maintained that he "is a heavenly being, i.e., an angel or even God," [24] on the basis of 10:16,18. It is obvious that Dnl. 10 is dependent on Ezk. 1, and therefore, that *’ish* (v. 5) and *’adham* (vv. 16,18) do not mean an angel, but God himself (cf. *kemar’eh ’adham*, "the appearance of a man," in Dnl. 10:18 with *kemar’eh ’adham*, "a likeness as it were of a human form," in Ezk. 1:26). But since the "Ancient of Days" in Dnl. 7:13 is God, the *bar ’enash* cannot be God too, even though it is said that the son of man comes "with the clouds of heaven." The clouds of heaven are not so much a personal attribute of the *bar ’enash* as they are part of the heavenly scenery as a whole.

The biblical and Ugaritic parallels to *‘attiq yomayya’*, "Ancient of Days," as a designation for Yahweh are well known. [25] The *bar ’enash* is brought before him to receive the everlasting dominion. There is another reference to Israel's being brought before Yahweh to receive the kingdom in the account of Saul's election as king in 1 S. 10:20f. (where the same verb *qarabh*, "to bring," is used). However, in 1 S. 10 the kingdom is given to a representative of the kingdom, whereas in Dnl. 7 it is given to the whole people; and in 1 S. 10 the kingdom is ephemeral, whereas in Dnl. 7 it is eternal. Nevertheless in both texts, the kingdom is founded on the ancient kingdom of Yahweh. [26] Thus Dnl. 7:13f. describes a great curve back to the beginnings of Israel. This alone also makes the expression *‘attiq yomayya’*, "Ancient of Days," completely intelligible. This phrase does not simply declare the eternity of Yahweh, but in the distress of persecution expresses the theological belief, which Deutero-Isaiah in particular espoused, that the One who showed himself as Savior in the past will also show himself as Savior in the future; that the One who acted at the first will also act at the last (Isa. 41:4; 43:10,13; 46:4; 48:12; cf. Ps. 102:26-29[25-28]). [27]

H. Haag

---

[24] *Ibid.,* 423; similarly, Coppens in Coppens-Dequeker, 61-67, sees in *bar ’enash* a symbol for the angelic hosts.

[25] → אל *’ēl* II.2.b.

[26] Cf. H. Wildberger, *Jahwes Eigentumsvolk* (Zürich, 1960), esp. pp. 80-95.

[27] On *ben ’adham* in the Pseudepigrapha, see *TDNT,* VIII, 423-29.

בָּנָה bānāh; בִּנְיָה binyāh; בִּנְיָן binyān;
*מִבְנֶה mibhneh; תַּבְנִית tabhnîth

Contents: I. The Root: 1. Etymology and Occurrences; 2. Meaning and Function. II. General Usage: 1. Subjects of Building; 2. Objects of Building; 3. Types of Building Activity; 4. Figurative Usage. III. Theological Usage: 1. God Builds; 2. Refusal to Build; 3. Judgment and Salvation; 4. Sacral Structures. IV. Derivatives: 1. *binyah, binyan*, *mibhneh;* 2. *tabhnith.*

I. The Root.

1. *Etymology and Occurrences.* bnh is a well-known root in the various Semitic languages. It is found in Ugaritic (*bny*), Moabite (the Mesha Stela, line 9), Phoenician, Old Aramaic, Biblical Aramaic, Arabic, etc. The meaning "to build" is connected with the radicals bnh (or bny or bnw) in Akkadian (*banû*)[1] and probably also in Ugaritic.[2] This root also means "create" in Akkadian and Ugaritic. In Hebrew and Biblical Aramaic, the predominant meaning of bnh is "to build" with its wide variety of nuances, all of which can be traced back to this original meaning. bnh is not restricted to certain literary complexes of the OT, although neither *banah* nor any of its derivatives occurs in Lev., Joel, Ob., Jonah, Nah., Est. Including the Biblical Aramaic occurrences of this root, the different verb forms of bnh appear about 390 times in the OT, mostly in the qal (Aram. peal), and less frequently in the niphal (Aram. hithpeel), which should be translated passively ("to be built"). When used in connection with other verbs which convey the idea of making something through a particular type of crafts-

bānāh. W. F. Albright, *The Archaeology of Palestine* (1949, 1963); W. Andrae, *Das Gotteshaus und die Urformen des Bauens im Alten Orient* (1930); *idem*, "Kultbau im Alten Orient," *Mélanges Syriens offerts à M. R. Dussaud*, II (1939), 867-871; M. Avi-Yonah–S. Yeivin–M. Stekelis, *The Antiquities of Israel* (in Heb.), I (Tel Aviv, 1955), *passim*; R. Bach, "Bauen und Pflanzen," *Studien zur Theologie der alttestamentlichen Überlieferung. Festschrift für G. von Rad* (1961), 7-32; A.-G. Barrois, *Manuel d'archéologie biblique*, I-II (Paris, 1939-1953), *passim*; H. K. Beebe, "Ancient Palestinian Dwellings," *BA*, 31 (1968), 38-58; I. Benzinger, *Hebräische Archäologie* ([3]1927), *passim*; G. J. Botterweck–G. Cornfeld, eds., *Die Bibel und ihre Welt* (1969), "Ausgrabungen in Palästina," "Stadtanlage (israelitische)," "Tempel"; Th. A. Busink, *Der Tempel von Jerusalem*, I: *Der Tempel Salomos* (Leiden, 1970); D. Conrad, *Studien zum Altargesetz, Ex 20:24-26* (diss., 1968); Dalman, *AuS*, VII (1942), 1-175; H. J. Franken–C. A. Franken-Battershill, *A Primer of OT Archaeology* (Leiden, 1963); K. M. Kenyon, *Archaeology in the Holy Land* ([3]1970), *passim*; O. Michel, "οἰκοδομέω," *TDNT*, V, 136-144, esp. pp. 137f.; H. H. Nelson–L. Oppenheim–G. E. Wright, "The Significance of the Temple in the Ancient Near East," *BA*, 7 (1944), 41-63, 66-77; M. Noth, *The OT World* (trans. 1966), *passim; idem, BK*, IX/1 (1968), 95-167; N. Poulssen, *König und Tempel im Glaubenszeugnis des ATs. SBM*, 3 (1967); de Vaux, *AncIsr*, II, *passim*; C. Watzinger, *Denkmäler Palästinas*, I (1933); II (1935), *passim*; G. E. Wright, *Biblical Archaeology* (1962); W. Zimmerli, *Ezechiel. BK*, XIII/2 (1969), 980-1249.

[1] *AHw*, 103; *CAD*, II, 83ff.
[2] J. Gray, *The Legacy of Canaan. SVT*, 5 ([2]1965), 189.

manship, frequently the meaning of *banah* is defined much more precisely in the OT. Again and again, *banah* is found in parallelism with '*asah*, "to make," *kun* (hiphil), "to make, prepare," *yasadh* (piel), "to found, establish," *qum* (hiphil), "to erect, build," *chatsabh*, "to hew, hew out," *natah*, "to spread out, pitch (a tent)," *chazaq* (piel and hiphil), "to make strong, repair," '*amadh* (hiphil), "to set up, erect," and other verbs which go into detail even more. *banah* can be used with the accusative of the building material,[3] and thus frequently takes a double accusative. The object of *banah* can be expressed in different ways in Heb., viz., by the infinitive construct plus *le,* by direct prepositional statements, and by paratactic verbal clauses ("he built and dwelt"; cf. Dt. 8:12; 1 K. 12:25). A fairly accurate picture of the various meanings of the root *bnh* can be reconstructed by examining the various contexts in which it occurs. *banah* has a literal meaning in the overwhelming majority of instances in the OT, but it is also used in a figurative sense in a considerable percentage of cases, yet without abandoning the basic idea in the root.

Several nouns can be traced back to the root *bnh*, viz., *binyan* ("structure, building"), *binyah* ("building, temple"), *mibhneh* (the "work," the "building"), which occurs only in Ezekiel, and *tabhnith* ("pattern, copy, figure, representation, ground plan"), which is also used in different contexts, although apparently always in late texts. There are 29 different substantival constructions involving nouns built from the root *bnh* in the OT (including one Aram. expression using **binyan* in Ezr. 5:4). Along with these, we must also add the proper names and place names (e.g., *benayahu*, "Benaiah," *yabhneh*, "Jabneh," etc.), which indicate various nuances of meaning contained in the root *bnh*, both literal and figurative. → בן *bēn,* "son," and → בת *bath,* "daughter," must also be listed among the derivatives of *bnh/bny.*[4]

2. *Meaning and Function. banah* introduces us to the realm of craftsmanship, where material products are made out of different kinds of material. Therefore, *banah* logically requires a personal subject, which can be either individual or collective. In two passages in the Wisdom Literature, the subject is an abstract idea ("Wisdom," *chokhmoth,* Prov. 9:1; 14:1), which is, of course, a personification. When the verb *banah* is used in a literal sense, it can take only external, concrete, solid objects as its object. It should be noted that *banah* describes not only an act performed on a certain object, but also the process of that object's coming into existence. A statement to the effect that a certain object was brought into existence frequently includes implicitly as well the purpose intended in producing that object. Occasionally, of course, this is made specific by the addition of formal or syntactical clauses.[5] In its figurative usages, *banah* frequently functions in personal dimensions and in comparisons and symbols (e.g., in Am. 9:11, which states that the "booth of David that is fallen" will be rebuilt; and in Ps. 89:3 [Eng. v. 2], where the obj. of *banah* is an abstract idea, *chesedh,*

---

[3] See Brockelmann, *Synt.,* on the accusative.

[4] Cf. *KBL*[3] and *WUS*, No. 534.

[5] See above, I.1.

"steadfast love"). The meaning of *banah* is modified by the context, the double accusative, prepositional phrases, and parallel expressions; and these various nuances should be taken into consideration in translating each passage where *banah* occurs. In addition to "build," *banah* may be translated "build up," "rebuild," "finish or improve (a building)," "add to (a building)," "demolish (a building)," "establish," "found," "erect," "strengthen or fortify," "restore," "make or construct," "cast up (a rampart)," etc., ideas all of which grow logically out of the original meaning. These meanings partially limit the broader concept of "building" and describe a particular aspect of the building activity which contributes to the "building." Fundamentally, "building" always has to do with "creating" and "bringing into existence," and it implies the functioning of creative powers. The context also clarifies the means by which the *banah*, "building," takes place. Sometimes we encounter detailed statements about and evidence of specialized "building." *banah* is used in descriptions of secular and sacral buildings, and of the manufacture of larger or smaller individual objects (houses, towers, doors, walls, cities, etc., temples, altars, cult objects, etc.), and in references to technical structures built for military purposes (fortifications, strongholds, walls, etc.). *banah* is used figuratively to denote the "building" of a family, people, dynasty, or individual, and to describe the creation of the world in theological contexts.

II. General Usage.

1. *Subjects of Building.* In conjunction with the transition to sedentary culture and life, at first the Israelite tribes made booths (*'asah sukkah*) and pitched tents (*natah 'ohel*), and then later in place of these dwellings they built houses (*banah bayith*), Gen. 33:17 (J),19 (E). The building (in part, rebuilding) of settlements and cities by individual tribes is repeatedly mentioned in summary notes, Nu. 32:34-38; Jgs. 18:28; 21:23. Occasionally a city is mentioned as the collective subject of building activity (Ashur builds Nineveh, Gen. 10:11). Under compulsory service, "Israel" builds store-cities for Ramses (Ex. 1:11); and the prophet Hosea condemns Israel and Judah collectively in his explanation for announcing doom because their building activity is "against God" (Hos. 8:14; cf. Am. 3:13-15). Within the various divisions of the people, individual classes and groups are called builders (Mic. 3:10). Frequently the building projects of individuals are mentioned separately, especially those of the kings. The buildings of David and Solomon are well known (2 S. 5:9; 1 K. 5–9, passim; Solomon's desire to build, 1 K. 9:19: *chashaq libhnoth*). The OT mentions in detail the building (or improving) of cities and palaces by Israelite and Judean kings. 1 Ch. 7:24 states that Beth-horon and Uzzen-sheerah were built by a woman (Sheerah, the granddaughter of Ephraim, and daughter of one Beriah). It is obvious that buildings were not built by individuals with their own hands. This can be seen very easily in the building program of the "governor Nehemiah" (Neh. 3–4). According to Neh. 3:1 the high-priest Eliashib and his brethren the priests put their hands to the work. Elsewhere it is said that numerous slave laborers (1 K. 5:27-28 [13-14]; 9:20-21) and hired construction workers and artisans (5:20,32 [6,18]; 2 K.

12:12 [11]; 22:6, [*hab*]*bonim*) were available for the construction of buildings in
Israel and Judah. Tyre in particular was famous for its experts in building artistic
buildings (Ezk. 27:4). Strictly speaking, *banah* should be translated "have built"
in this context. Israel knows of early historical or prehistorical building activities.
In the genealogy of Cain handed down by J, the writer states that Cain (or
Enoch?) built a city (Gen. 4:17). Scholars are not agreed as to whether J, when
he took up this note from the Cain traditions that had been handed down to him,
was cautiously trying to criticize the kind of culture represented by Cain. In the
Wisdom Literature, "wisdom" and "folly" are personified and can be the subject
of different activities; cf. wisdom and that of building, Prov. 9:1; 14:1. They are
regarded as human powers, and as such they are treated as subjects in figures or
in comparisons. [6]

2. *Objects of Building.* The range of objects (the lists of "structures") that
are connected with the verb *banah* in the OT is broad, especially if we consider
the indications of various activities associated with building in different contexts,
and these help us define the various ways in which *banah* is used. For detailed
information pertaining to archeology and the history of culture, one should consult the pertinent studies in archeology and special publications. Also, it is not
possible in this article to give a complete list of the objects of the verb *banah*
found in the OT and to discuss each one in detail. And yet, a general survey of
these objects is instructive in an attempt to come to a better understanding of
banah. Statistically, *banah* is connected with the building of cities (or a city)
more than any other single object. Peoples, tribes, kings, and individuals build
cities (Gen. 4:17; 10:11; 11:4,8; Nu. 32; Jgs. 18:28; 21:23; 1 K. 12:25), great
and goodly (Dt. 6:10; Josh. 24:13) and established (Nu. 21:27), together with
their daughter villages (*benotheha,* 1 Ch. 8:12). In the time of Nehemiah the
singers (*hameshorarim*) build for themselves villages (*chatserim*) around Jerusalem (Neh. 12:29). Jerusalem is the *benuyah,* the city that is built; Yahweh
himself is the master builder (Ps. 122:3; 147:2); and therefore, it is regarded as
the "city of the fathers' sepulchres" which is to be rebuilt (Neh. 2:5). Destroyed
cities (ruins, *chorbhoth ʿolam,* "ancient ruins," *hechorabhoth,* "waste places")
will be rebuilt or repaired (Jer. 31:38; Ezk. 36:10,33; Isa. 58:12; 61:4; these
texts use not only *banah,* "to build," but also *yeqomem,* "to raise up," and
chiddesh, "to repair"). Omri buys the hill of Samaria and builds (on) it (i.e., he
builds a city on it, 1 K. 16:24). The OT repeatedly mentions fortifications in connection with the building of a city. It speaks of building *ʿare matsor* (2 Ch. 8:5),
ʿare metsuroth (11:6-10), *ʿare mibhtsar* (Nu. 32:36), and *ʿarim betsuroth,* all of
which mean "fortified cities." Occasionally, the character of the fortification can
be determined only from the context, e.g., when 1 K. 15:17 states that Baasha
built Ramah. In addition to residential cities, the OT also mentions store cities
(Ex. 1:11; 1 K. 9:19: *ʿare* [*ham*]*miskenoth*), cities for chariots, and cities for
horsemen (*ʿare harekhebh; ʿare happarashim;* 1 K. 9:19; 2 Ch. 8:4-7). Some late
texts mention the building of fortresses (2 Ch. 17:12; 27:4, *biraniyyoth*).

---

[6] On this whole issue, cf. *BRL,* 81-83.

A second kind of object of *banah* in the OT is individual buildings directly connected with the layout of a city. The OT gives an amazing amount of detail in describing these buildings. In these descriptions, of course, synonyms of *banah* are used to some extent, and these help us to determine the meaning of this verb more precisely. E.g., 1 K. 16:34 speaks of rebuilding Jericho by laying (*yasadh* in the piel) its foundation and by setting up (*natsabh* in the hiphil) its gates (*delatheha*). The erection or repair of a wall (or the closing up of breaches and holes in it) is an important part of building a city (1 K. 3:1, *chomath yerushalayim sabhibh*, "the wall around Jerusalem"; 2 Ch. 27:3; the wall of Ophel; Ps. 51:20 [18]; 2 Ch. 8:5; 14:6[7]; 32:5; Neh. 2:17; 3:35,38[4:3,6]; Mic. 7:11, *gadher*). *sabhibh,* "round about," in 2 S. 5:9, probably suggests the building of a wall. Gates and bars are parts of a wall (2 Ch. 8:5; 14:6[7]; Neh. 3:1,3,13). While some of the various terms used are synonyms, some of them probably denote different objects (e.g., gates and leaves of a door). Neh. 3:35(4:3) mentions a "stone wall." Towers and battlements (*mighdaloth,* "towers"; *tirath keseph,* "battlement of silver") could be built upon the wall (2 Ch. 32:5; Cant. 8:9-10). The → מגדל *mighdāl,* "tower," is another individual structure in the layout of an ancient city which functioned as a fortification (Gen. 11:4; 2 Ch. 14:6[7]; 26:9). Of course, watchtowers were built (*banah*) in a vineyard (Isa. 5:2), or in a field (2 Ch. 27:4), or even in the wilderness (26:10). In Jerusalem, Solomon built (or completed) a kind of acropolis, which is called *millo'* in Hebrew (1 K. 9:15, 24; 11:27). The OT mentions houses (*bayith, battim*) and palaces (*bayith,* 2 S. 5:9; 1 K. 7:1-2; 10:4; *hekhal,* Hos. 8:14; *'armon,* Jer. 30:18)[7] within the city. Building houses is one of the primary functions of sedentary human life (Gen. 33:17; Dt. 8:12; 20:5; 22:8; 28:30). According to the Deuteronomic law, certain specific rules must be followed in building a *bayith chadhash,* "new house" (it must have a parapet on the roof, Dt. 22:8; the builder is to be protected between the time the house is built and the time it is dedicated [inhabited], 20:5). 1 K. 22:39 indicates that sometimes luxurious houses were built in Israel (Ahab builds a *beth hashshen,* "ivory house"; cf. Am. 3:15). Amos mentions building houses of hewn stone (*batte ghazith,* 5:11; cf. Isa. 9:9 [10]). *banah* is used of building balconies (or upper chambers, Am. 9:6, conjec.) and of constructing an inner wall (*chayits,* Ezk. 13:10).[8] With the exception of building a sacred house (temple, etc.),[9] there are no further distinctions in the meaning of *banah* when it is used in connection with building a house. Nu. 32:16,36 describe the building of sheepfolds (*gedherah*)[10] and houses or cities in conjunction with the beginning of sedentary life. Neh. 2:5 mentions that sepulchres had been built in the city of Jerusalem. The meaning of the *chorabhoth* (RSV "ruins") which kings and counselors built, according to Job 3:14, is disputed; some say this word means "sepulchres," and others that it means "pyramids."

---

[7] Cf. *BRL.*
[8] See *KBL*[2].
[9] See below.
[10] *KBL*[3], "stone sheepfold."

A third type of object connected with *banah* in the OT is special structures for war. We have already mentioned towers, walls, battlements, fortified cities, and strongholds, i.e., constructions within the city. In addition, we should mention siegeworks which were built for the purpose of besieging fortified cities, including the *matsor* (Dt. 20:20, offensive rampart; Zec. 9:3, defensive rampart), the *dayeq (sabhibh),* "bulwark (round about)" (2 K. 25:1; Jer. 52:4; Ezk. 17:17; 21:27[22]; this is described in detail in the account of the symbolic act of Ezekiel in Ezk. 4:2), and the *metsodhim gedholim,* "great siegeworks" (Eccl. 9:14). [11] In order to specify the whereabouts of the dead who are left unburied (unnoticed) after a battle, a *tsiyyun* (sign) was set up (*banah*) beside (*'etslo*) a bone of the deceased, until the grave-diggers performed their duties (Ezk. 39:15). Finally, Ezk. 27:5 makes a part of a ship, viz., the ship's planks (*luach, kol luchothayim*), the object of *banah.* It is important to study the context of this passage carefully in order to understand the techniques of ancient shipbuilding in detail, because this is not described by the verb *banah* alone (27:5-7).

3. *Types of Building Activity.* As has already been pointed out, the OT speaks of those acquainted with building materials, carpenters, and specialists. We can learn the types of building they did from the qal active participle of *banah (boneh* or *bonim),* the verbs used to describe their work, and specific statements concerning their work in various contexts where it is mentioned. Thus, e.g., the builders of Solomon and Hiram hew (*pasal*) stones, obviously to build the palace (1 K. 5:32[18]), but they also prepare (*kun* in the hiphil) timber and stones for the same purpose (*libhnoth habbayith,* "to build the house"). Prior to this process, they select stones they think are suitable for building, and "reject" (*ma'as*) those they consider to be useless (Ps. 118:22). Other *bonim,* "builders," lay foundations (*yissedhu,* Ezr. 3:10), and still others make perfect (*kalelu*) the beauty of what is being built (Ezk. 27:4). On the other hand, in 2 S. 5:11 (1 Ch. 14:1), *charashe 'ets,* "workers in wood = carpenters," *charashe 'ebhen,* "workers in stone = masons," and *charashe qir,* "workers on a wall = masons," are all used as subjects of *vayyibhnu,* "built." Carpenters, stonemasons, *godherim,* "masons," *chotsebhe ha'ebhen,* "stonecutters," *'ose hammela'khah,* "workmen" (2 K. 12:12f.[11f.]; 22:6), and *choresh nechosheth,* "worker in bronze" (1 K. 7:14), appear in parallelism to *bonim,* "builders," in the OT. We may conclude from this that the verb *banah* can also be used in speaking of specialized building. Therefore, one proverb states that a house is built by *chokhmah,* "wisdom," and *tebhunah,* "understanding" (Prov. 24:3; cf. 9:1; 14:1; here wisdom and understanding are described as building instruments). According to 1 K. 7:14, workers in metal must have "wisdom," "understanding," and *da'ath,* "knowledge, skill," although in this passage these terms are not directly connected with *banah.*

The OT mentions several building materials, including stones (Neh. 3:35[4:3]), bricks and hewn stones (1 K. 15:22; Am. 5:11; Isa. 9:9[10]), and in particular

---

11 See the comms. *in loc.,* conjec. *metsurim.*

different kinds of wood (1 K. 15:22), especially cedar (2 S. 5:11; Ezk. 27:5; Jer. 22:14-15), cypress, and oak (Ezk. 27:5-7). On the other hand, Dt. 20:20 contains a prohibition against using the wood of fruit trees for building purposes. The OT also refers to ivory (1 K. 22:39; Ezk. 27:6), silver (Cant. 8:9), bronze and "costly stone" (1 K. 7:9,14ff., here only mentioned in the context, and not directly connected with *banah*) as building materials. It follows from this that still other "building materials" might be listed, and that those mentioned in connection with the verb *banah* represent only a portion of them. It is curious that no building tools are mentioned in connection with *banah* in the OT (with the exception of 1 K. 6:7). However, several passages in the OT contain detailed statements about different structures, e.g., 1 K. 7 (halls, pillars, capitals, etc.), Cant. 4:4 (tower with stone ledges or layers of stone), [12] and Jer. 22:14-15 (spacious, breezy upper rooms). This further indicates that *banah* in the OT is used to denote entirely different kinds of structures, including general building, special building, and even manufacturing artistic embellishments. But at the same time, it is impossible to draw conclusions from the absence of *banah* in specific contexts that deal with the phenomenology of building. E.g., the context of 1 K. 7 is very broad. This chapter contains some very specific statements about the building of Solomon's palace (using entirely different verbs!), and yet in vv. 1-2 these are all subsumed under the principal term *banah*.

4. *Figurative Usage.* Just as building procedures are used as parables, symbols, or figures, so *banah* can have a figurative meaning. The ideas suggested by *banah* are so versatile that this verb can be used to describe situations in areas that have nothing to do with building. The hopes false prophets arouse in their hearers are like the irresponsible work of a builder who uses whitewash to make it appear that a wall made without cement is strong and durable (Ezk. 13:10). In a symbolic act, Ezekiel portrays the siege of Jerusalem (he builds a wall symbolically, Ezk. 4:2). Yahweh tells Jeremiah that he is to be a fortified city, an iron pillar, and bronze walls (Jer. 1:18), thus transferring a picture from the realm of building to a historical function! Yahweh sets Jeremiah over (ʿal) the nations in order to break down and destroy, but also to plant and to build (*libhnoth*). The text here compares not the existence, but the activity, of the prophet with that of a master builder (Jer. 1:10; cf. 18:9). [13] There is a time to build up and a time to break down; everything has its time (Eccl. 3:3). In the descriptive songs of Canticles, prominent parts of the body are compared with building structures (Cant. 4:4, "your neck is *kemighdal davidh ... banuy lethalpiyyoth,* like the tower of David, built for an arsenal"; cf. 8:9). Under specific conditions (adopting the oath *chay yhvh,* "as Yahweh lives"), the nations around Israel shall be built up in the midst of the people of Israel (Jer. 12:16, *venibhnu bethokh ʿammi,* "then they shall be built up in the midst of my people"). The idea of a tribe or a nation "being built up" by its descendants should also be mentioned here (Gen. 16:2; 30:3, *banah* in the niphal; Ruth 4:11: Leah and

---

[12] See *KBL²*.
[13] See R. Bach, *Festschrift für G. von Rad* (1961), 7-32.

Rachel built up [banu] the *beth yisra'el,* "house of Israel"). "To build up a (his) brother's house" is a technical term in the Deuteronomic Levirate law (Dt. 25:9). The expression *banah bayith,* "build a house," is used by Nathan in the dynastic promise to David (2 S. 7). It is not hard to understand why the figurative use of *banah* plays an important role in conveying theological ideas. [14]

III. Theological Usage.

1. *God Builds.* In the OT God also clearly appears as subject of *banah* activities which are quite concrete and extensive, e.g., in J's creation theology (Gen. 2:22, "and Yahweh built the rib... into a woman"), in doxological contexts, as in the Amos tradition (Am. 9:6, Yahweh builds his upper chambers in the heavens, and founds his vault upon the earth; cf. Ps. 104:2-3), and in theological statements concerning salvation which are modeled on creation theology (Ps. 78:69, Yahweh built his sanctuary like the high heavens, like the earth, which he has founded for ever; cf. Isa. 66:1-2). In this connection we should also mention Ps. 89:3(2), which states that Yahweh's steadfast love was established for ever, and his faithfulness is firm as the heavens. Yahweh is regarded as the master builder of Jerusalem (*boneh yerushalayim*) and of his sanctuary (Ps. 78:69; 147:2), even though it is assumed that men actually built them (Jer. 32:31). Also, he will again build up Zion which is lying in ruins (Ps. 102:15-17[14-16]). The fortified city of Jerusalem is a subject of rejoicing for pilgrims (122:1-3). Yahweh promotes and restrains the building of the temple (2 S. 7:5,7,13; 1 Ch. 17:4,6,12). Actually, no house can be built unless Yahweh builds it; the builders labor in vain without Yahweh (Ps. 127:1). Structures that men build are at Yahweh's disposal (Dt. 6:10; Josh. 24:13), and he gives them to whomever he will. Buildings made for war (ramparts) are of no profit to a warrior without Yahweh's will (Ezk. 17:17; but see 21:27[22]). According to this very strongly deterministic theological world view, God has the power not only to build, but also to break down. This motif, which is especially important in Jeremiah (45:4), is expanded even more by the figure of planting and uprooting (Jer. 1:10; 18:9; 24:6; 42:10; Mal. 1:4). If God tears down, no one can rebuild without his help (Job 12:14). Several passages that have already been mentioned show that this meaning of *banah* is transferred to the realm of history (Jer. 31:4: "again I will build you, and you shall be built, *bethulath yisra'el,* O virgin Israel!" Jer. 31:28; 33:7; Ezk. 36:36). This is particularly clear in the dynastic promises, where the symbolic character of *banah* is demonstrated by the figurative use of *bayith,* "house" (=descendants, seed, dynasty, 2 S. 7:11,27; Ps. 89:5[4] [with *zera',* "seed," and *kisse',* "throne"]; 1 Ch. 17:10,25; rebuilding the fallen *sukkath davidh,* "booth of David," Am. 9:11; the dynastic promise to Jeroboam I, 1 K. 11:38; the promise of a *bayith ne'eman,* "sure house," to the faithful and loyal priest who was to be raised up in place of Eli, 1 S. 2:35). A man's good fortune is understood as "being built up" by God (Job 22:23, "if you return to *shaddai,*

---

[14] See III.

the Almighty, you will be built up"). The godly can pray against the wicked and
evildoers: May Yahweh break them down and build them up no more (Ps. 28:5).
The knowledge that *gam nibhnu 'ose rish'ah,* "those who do evil are built up,"
is hard to bear (Mal. 3:15).

2. *Refusal to Build.* The Rechabites, who were considered to be particularly
loyal worshippers of Yahweh (2 K. 10), refuse the distinctive blessings of the
civilized land, including the building of houses, because of a nomadic ideal (Jer.
35:7-9). Qoheleth decries the disadvantages of civilization (in the course of which
he says, *banithi li battim,* "I build houses"), which he considers vain and un-
profitable (Eccl. 2:4,11). Jeremiah censures Jehoiakim for his desire for luxury
which manifested itself in the lavish building program on his palace, because it
involved treating the poor with injustice and unrighteousness (Jer. 22:13-15).
The fact that Jehoiakim "builds his house by unrighteousness" is indicative of
the instability of his entire governmental system. About a hundred years before
Jeremiah, Micah announced that the upper classes in Jerusalem would be overthrown because they built Zion *bedhamim,* "with blood," and Jerusalem *be'avlah,*
"with wrong" (Mic. 3:10; cf. Hab. 2:12). If the social problem (forced labor)
is raised in these prophetic passages, the injustices they depict are the occasion
of basic declarations. In the final analysis, the strength and durability of a building depends on doing the will of Yahweh, i.e., on practicing justice and righteousness. The OT can tell of hybrid building (presumably for one's own honor, Gen.
11:4). Hosea laments that Israel and Judah had forgotten Yahweh their Maker
and built palaces and cities (Hos. 8:14). Sometimes the announced disaster is
that Yahweh will destroy that which has been built.

3. *Judgment and Salvation.* The OT speaks of Yahweh causing buildings to be
torn down as a judgment or curse. It also states that the wicked will build houses,
but shall not dwell in them (Zeph. 1:13; Dt. 28:30). Furthermore, OT oracles of
judgment include the announcement that a certain city shall not be built again
(Dt. 13:17[16]; Ezk. 26:14; Josh. 6:26 [1 K. 16:34, the rebuilding of Jericho
was possible only at the price of child sacrifice]; Isa. 25:2). Man's determination
to build cannot stand against God's determination to punish sinners (e.g., Edom
in Mal. 1:4).

Conversely, the positive assurance that certain people will dwell securely (build
and dwell) must be regarded as a gift of salvation (Ezk. 28:26; Ps. 69:36[35];
Isa. 44:26; 65:21-22). Jeremiah's instructions in his letter to the Babylonian
exiles to build houses, plant gardens, and establish families are intended as a
hopeful and salutary sign of God's faithfulness (Jer. 29:5f.,28). The time of
salvation is characterized by energetic building or rebuilding activity. All the
nuances of meaning of *banah,* including the figurative, appear in descriptions
of the time of salvation. Yahweh is the one responsible for this gift of salvation
(Ezk. 36:10,33,36; 28:26; Jer. 30:18; 31:38[-40]), although he may use human
powers to accomplish it, e.g., Cyrus (Isa. 44:28) or foreigners (60:10). The OT
speaks of the rebuilding of Jerusalem, cities (Ps. 69:36[35]; Isa. 58:12; 61:4),
walls (Mic. 7:11; Ps. 51:20[18]; Neh. 2:5,17-20; 3:1), vineyards and fields, but

especially the temple (Isa. 44:28; Ezr. 1:2[-5]; Ps. 102:15-17[14-16]; Hag. 1; Zec. 1:16; 6:12f.,15; 8:9). The rebuilding (*banah*) of Israel as the *beth yisra'el*, "house of Israel," or the *bethulath yisra'el*, "virgin Israel," as a historical power (Jer. 24:6; 31:4,28; 33:7; Am. 9:14f.), and the reestablishment of the Davidic dynasty (Am. 9:11), lie on the horizon of Israel's expectation of salvation. Thus, fundamentally the activity suggested by *banah* is used to describe the world restored according to the will of God.

4. *Sacral Structures*. Throughout the OT there are references to cult places, altars, temples, and sanctuaries as objects built by man, which either are ordained or at least instigated by Yahweh, or represent man's response to a divine act. The earliest history refers to the building of an altar (*mizbeach*, Gen. 8:20, Noah). In the patriarchal narratives handed down by J and E, the patriarchs build altars in different places in Palestine (or on the mountain of God) (Gen. 12:7, Abraham at Shechem; 12:8, Abraham at Bethel; 13:18, Abraham at Mamre-Hebron; 22:9, Abraham on Mt. Moriah; 26:25, Isaac at Beer-sheba; 35:7, Jacob at Bethel). The technical term for this in these narratives is *vayyibhen sham NN mizbeach leyhvh*, "and so-and-so built there an altar to Yahweh." The old Gideon tradition also knows of this custom of building an altar at a site where God had appeared (Jgs. 6:24). In the account of Gideon's conflict with Canaanitism, Gideon is charged to destroy the altar of Baal and to build an altar of Yahweh (*bamma'arakhah*, "in the right order," RSV "with stones laid in due order," Jgs. 6:26,28). The Book of the Covenant (as well as Dt.) contains instructions as to how an altar should be built. If it is an altar of stone (in contrast to an altar of earth, Ex. 20:24), then only unhewn stones are to be used (Ex. 20:25; Dt. 27:5f.). The OT contains accounts of several prominent figures building altars, e.g., Moses after the battle with the Amalekites (Ex. 17:15, E) and in connection with the making of the covenant on the mountain of God (Ex. 24:4, E, which mentions the building of an altar and of 12 *matstsebhoth*, "pillars," according to the number of the tribes), Joshua on Mt. Ebal (Josh. 8:30), the Transjordanian tribes as a witness to their fidelity to Yahweh (Josh. 22:10f.,16,19,23,26-29), Samuel at Ramah (1 S. 7:17), Saul (1 S. 14:35, possibly in connection with the great stone which had been rolled [*galal*] nearby, v. 33), David at the threshing floor of Araunah (2 S. 24:18 with *qum* in the hiphil, "rear, raise up"; 24:21,25 with *banah*, "build") in response to the command of the prophet Gad for the purpose of averting the plague that was spreading among the people (cf. 1 Ch. 21:22,26), Solomon (1 K. 9:25; 2 Ch. 8:12), Elijah on Mt. Carmel (1 K. 18:32, with the stones he built an altar *beshem yhvh*, "in the name of Yahweh"), Manasseh (2 Ch. 33:16, *qere*), and Jeshua ben Jozadak and Zerubbabel ben Shealtiel (Ezr. 3:2; v. 3 with *kun* in the hiphil, "set"). According to the Balaam-Balak tradition of E, it is necessary to build seven altars to prepare for the divine revelation (Nu. 23:1,14,29). Also in one of the appendices of the book of Judges (Jgs. 21:4), the people of Israel build an altar so that they might establish contact with God in a time of oppression (cf. 1 S. 14:35).

The OT speaks of the building of different cult places, altars, and cult objects which were used in the worship of other gods. These practices were condemned especially in the Deuteronomistic and Chronicler's historical works, and in the Prophetic literature (2 K. 17:9,10-12). Ex. 32:5 occupies a remarkable inter-mediate position. [15] The context condemns Aaron's action, but Ex. 32:5 seems to refer to the building of a legitimate altar. Also in 1 K. 3:2 the "cult on the high places" which Solomon and the people under him practiced is justified be-cause the temple had not yet been built (cf. 3:3; is v. 3 an addition by a later scribe?). [16] The OT does not look with approval at Solomon's building of a → במה *bāmāh,* "high place," for the Moabite god Chemosh and the Ammonite god Molech or Milcom (1 K. 11:7; see also 2 K. 23:13). The OT mentions the build-ing of *bamoth,* "high places," in connection with → מצבות *matstsēbhôth,* "pillars," and → אשרים *'ᵃshērîm,* "Asherim," in the time of Rehoboam (1 K. 14:23). This text also has in mind local phenomena, probably in connection with pillars and Asherim in particular, when it says, "on every high hill" and "under every green tree." Ahab built (*banah*) a Baal temple (*bayith,* "house") in Samaria, in which he erected (*qum* in the hiphil) an altar for (*le*) Baal (1 K. 16:32,33). The kind of altar the priest Uriah built before the Jerusalem temple, at the command of and according to the pattern given by king Ahaz while he was visiting Tiglath-pileser III in Damascus, is not entirely clear (2 K. 16:11). But in light of 2 K. 16:14 and 2 Ch. 28:16-27 (esp. v. 23), it is likely that it was regarded as an ille-gitimate altar. Manasseh in particular went to great extremes in building up the idolatrous cult, according to the Deuteronomistic history (2 K. 21:3-5; 2 Ch. 33:3-5,15,19, which use *banah* in connection with *bamoth,* "high places," *mizbechoth,* "altars," for "all the host of heaven" in the two outer courts of the temple, as well as *qum* in the hiphil, "to erect, set up," *'asah,* "to make," and *sim* in the hiphil, "to put," in connection with altars for Baal, Asherim, *pesilim,* "images," etc.). Jeremiah and Ezekiel lament the apostasy of Jerusalem and Judah from faith in Yahweh by the building of the *bamoth hattopheth,* "high places of Topheth" (Jer. 7:31), the *bamoth habba'al,* "high places of Baal" (Jer. 19:5; 32:35), a *gabh,* i.e., a mound on the base of the altar, perhaps for the purpose of cultic prostitution, [17] and a *ramah,* a "lofty place" (Ezk. 16:24f.).

One must not overlook that the building of the temple (*banah* with *bayith,* "house," *miqdash,* "sanctuary," and *hekhal,* "temple") has a far-reaching the-ological significance in the OT. This is clear in the account of the building of Solomon's temple and in the record of the erection of the second temple after the exile. According to the sources, *banah* is used far more extensively in con-nection with the building of Solomon's temple (the Deuteronomistic and Chron-icler's histories) than with the building of the second temple (the Chronicler and the postexilic prophets). In spite of the difficulty of determining the internal relationships of the so-called Prophecy of Nathan (2 S. 7:5,7,11,13) either by the traditio-historical method or by analyzing the subject matter, it is clear that the central point in this complex and (as it seems) in the whole tradition of the

---

[15] Cf. Noth, *ATD,* V, *in loc.*

[16] See Noth, *BK,* IX/1, 49.

[17] See *KBL².*

building of the Solomonic temple lies in the ambiguity of the *bayith* (some-times meaning "temple," and sometimes "offspring," i.e., dynasty) that is to be built. David's desire to build a temple for Yahweh or for his ark is rejected because of his military activities (1 K. 5:17[3]; 1 Ch. 22:8), and instead of this David is promised that his *zera'*, "seed," would build the house of God (2 S. 7:13). 1 K. 5:17,19(3,5) explicitly refer to this. Even if 2 S. 7:13 is secondary, the idea of a promise as the theological basis is firmly rooted in the tradition of the building of the temple. David's desire is rejected because Yahweh alone may choose the time, place, and person for the building of the temple (1 K. 8:16-20). Like the Deuteronomistic history, Chronicles has unqualified interest in this the-ological foundation. David charges Solomon to build the temple (1 Ch. 22:6) ac-cording to the special promise of God, which is given to Solomon in conjunction with the gift of discretion and understanding, success in building, and Yahweh's presence to help him through David's mediation (stated in the jussive, 22:9-12). According to 1 Ch. 28:10 (cf. vv. 2-6), the assumption lying behind the building of the temple is God's choice (→ בחר *bāchar*), and encouragement and comfort are intimately connected with God's promise. David even intercedes for Solomon (that he might have a *lebhabh shalem,* "whole heart," 1 Ch. 29:19). Solomon defends the greatness of the work of building the temple on the ground of the absolute greatness of his God (2 Ch. 2:4,8[5,9]), although the fundamental the-ological problem remains that it is impossible to build a house for the God of Israel (already emphasized in D at 1 K. 8:27), and that no one should be so bold as to build the temple since the heaven of heavens cannot contain Yahweh (2 Ch. 2:5[6]; 6:18). The special workers and special building materials are represented as provided by God (2 Ch. 2:6f.[7f.]). The successful completion of the building of the temple is interpreted as proof that Yahweh has kept (*qum* in the hiphil) his word. The temple that has been built is the center of the entire cult community, the focal point for members of the community who are sojourning far away, to-ward which they face when they pray (1 K. 8:44,48; 2 Ch. 6:34,38). God appears to Solomon when he dedicates the temple ("as he had appeared to him at Gibeon"), consecrates it, and declares it to be the perpetual dwelling place for His name, eyes, and heart (1 K. 9:3; 2 Ch. 7:12,16).

In the tradition of the building of the temple there are numerous detailed statements describing the way the temple was built, but we will not be able to deal with these individually here. The reader is given an astonishing amount of information concerning the measurements (1 K. 6:2-4), materials, building methods, individual building elements and structures (e.g., walls, wings, outer courts, internal features, taking into consideration only terms connected with *banah,* "to build"!), and special workers and their tasks (which are clarified by words that are used in parallelism with *banah,* e.g., *pasal,* "to hew out," *kun,* "to prepare," *'asah,* "to make," *'achaz,* "to grasp, take hold of," *yasadh,* "to found, establish," etc., 1 K. 5:31f.[17f.]; 6f.; and par. in 2 Ch. 3f.). Several dif-ferent kinds of tools are also mentioned in connection with *banah* in this one passage (1 K. 6:7, hammer, chisel, iron tool). *banah* occurs an unusually large number of times in these chapters, and has a variety of technical meanings depending on the different specialized ways it is used in connection with the building of the temple, its various parts, and its substructures. [18]

In the tradition of the Chronicler, a so-called "edict of Cyrus" lies behind the rebuilding of the temple. But following the theology of Deutero-Isaiah, the Chronicler declares that God charged Cyrus to build the Jerusalem temple (*vehu' phaqadh 'alay libhnoth lo bhayith*, "and he has charged me to build him a house," 2 Ch. 36:23; Ezr. 1:2-4; 6:3-5 [this last text is in Aramaic]). A special divine stimulus was necessary to motivate the returning exiles to begin the work of rebuilding the temple (*he'ir ruach la'aloth libhnoth*, "[God] had stirred up [their] spirit to go up to rebuild," Ezr. 1:5). According to Ezr. 4:3, the Samaritans were forbidden to help in the work of building the sanctuary. The difficulties and postponements resulting from this are attributed to the opposition of the Samaritans in this text, but in Hag. 1:2 they are attributed to the widespread belief of the Jews that the time to build the temple had not yet come. In this context also, the reader learns a great number of details about the materials, dimensions, building methods, etc., connected with the rebuilding of the Jerusalem temple (Hag. 1:8; Ezr. 6:3-5; 4–6). The theological significance of this second temple is strongly emphasized by Zechariah when he announces that the building of the temple will be undertaken by a messianic figure, the *tsemach*, "branch," who is both priest and king (Zec. 6:12f.). This figure cannot be Cyrus. Zec. 6:15, which states that those who are far off shall come and help to build the sanctuary, is connected with Ezr. 1:5. The repeatedly mentioned prophetic encouragement and support that must accompany the building of the temple during its various stages, e.g., between laying the foundation and rebuilding (Zec. 8:9; Ezr. 5:2), is worthy of note. We have already mentioned that the rebuilding of the temple, the city, and the fortification is an expression of God's salvation. [19]

IV. Derivatives. Some of the Hebrew nouns built from the root *bnh* should also be translated as nouns in English. Although there are nouns derived from this very root in Ugaritic in Syria-Palestine at a relatively early period, [20] the Hebrew derivatives to be treated here appear without exception in late literary contexts of the OT.

1. *binyah, binyan, *mibhneh. binyah, binyan,* and **mibhneh* are found exclusively in the block of traditional material ascribed to Ezekiel that deals with the program of building the temple, in chaps. 40–48, or more particularly in chaps. 40–42. *mibhneh* occurs only in the construct in the expression *kemibhneh 'ir*, "like the structure of a city," and means a group composed of several buildings but looking like a single building when taken as a whole. [21] Similarly, a Phoe-

---

[18] On this whole issue, see *BRL!*

[19] See III.3. In addition to the comms., see K. Galling, *Studien zur Geschichte Israels im persischen Zeitalter* (1964), esp. chaps. 2, "Die Proklamation des Kyros in Esra 1," and 6, "Serubbabel und der Hohepriester beim Wiederaufbau des Tempels in Jerusalem."

[20] Cf. *WUS*, No. 534.

[21] Fohrer-Galling, *HAT, in loc.,* "layout of the city"; Zimmerli, *BK, in loc.,* "city-like structure."

nician inscription uses the phrase *mbnt ḥṣr bt 'lm*, [22] which seems to have reference to the general impression that related structural units make on the observer. *binyah* in Ezk. 41:13 (which is also a hapax legomenon) means one part of a building alongside others, which belongs to the whole structure as an individual part. [23] The same thing applies to *binyan*, which occurs seven times in Ezk. 40–42. In 40:5 it is used of a wall, which is also called *chomah* in the same verse. However, *binyan* is not used to emphasize the function of the wall as a protection or boundary, but the wall as a product of the building process with a certain height and breadth.

In 41:12 (twice) and 41:15, the same noun is used of a certain exceptionally large building located west of the temple yard; but it is not described in further detail. [24] The *binyan* mentioned in 41:12,15 in describing various structures in the temple complex is used in 42:1,5,10 as a fixed reference point to describe the location of other buildings in the area. [25] Thus *binyah* and *binyan* mean individual buildings in a complex of buildings (*mibhneh*) located in a prescribed area. It seems that the only derivative of the root *bnh* in Biblical Aramaic, *binyana'* (determinative), has the same meaning (Ezr. 5:4). To be sure, Aram. *binyana'* certainly means the temple, but this is to be understood in the sense the Samaritan governor had in mind when he questioned Zerubbabel and Jeshua, namely, as an individual building located in the building that is supposed to be a temple (*bayith*, "house"). The Samaritan governor does not make this distinction (using *bayith* in Ezr. 5:3, and then *banayin* in 5:4) primarily to cast disdainful disparagement on that which he found the Jews doing. Instead, he uses these terms primarily to distinguish an individual building which is part of the building complex, but which is not yet a temple with all the chambers and buildings that go together to compose it.

2. *tabhnith*. The meaning of *tabhnith* is much more difficult to ascertain than the derivatives discussed in IV.1 above. [26] P's Sinai tradition preserves the account of Moses receiving detailed instructions from Yahweh on the mountain of God concerning the building of the sanctuary, the individual pieces of furniture for the cult, and the cult service. Yahweh shows Moses the pattern of God's holy tabernacle and all its furniture (Ex. 25:9 [twice], 40). Here *tabhnith* means "pattern, model." It may well be that P fills in the details of the description of what Moses was supposed to have seen from the details of the Jerusalem temple as he knew it (it makes little difference whether this was the first or second temple for the interpretation of this context), and thus *tabhnith* could be understood as "building" in the true sense. At the same time, it is also true that in this whole narrative P separates *tabhnith* from the Jerusalem temple, transfers it to the theophanic, visionary aspect of the Sinai event, and now intends it to

---

[22] *KAI*, 60.2; cf. 65.1.

[23] Cf. Zimmerli, *BK, in loc.*

[24] Cf. Zimmerli, *BK*, XIII, 1038-1043; Fohrer-Galling, *HAT*, 13, 232f., 264.

[25] Cf. K. Elliger, "Die grossen Tempelsakristeien im Verfassungsentwurf des Ezechiel (42,1ff.)," *Geschichte und AT. Festschrift für A. Alt. BHTh*, 16 (1953), 79-103.

[26] Cf. the eight different meanings given to this word in *KBL*².

be understood as "first copy," "prototype," or even "pattern." *tabhnith* seems to be used with its most primitive meaning in Ps. 144:12 (structure of a temple or palace) and Josh. 22:28: a structure of the altar of Yahweh which our fathers made (*'asah*). Josh. 22:28 is to be found in those passages in the book of Joshua that are closely connected with the thought of P. [27] Of course, the author might have intended that *tabhnith* be taken in the sense of "likeness" or "copy" in this passage in the narrative, since the altar here was not used as such, but was looked upon as a witness (a memorial); however, the preceding verses clearly speak of the building of an altar. On the other hand, *tabhnith* must be translated "copy" (RSV "pattern") in 2 K. 16:10, although "instruction in building" would not be incorrect. *tabhnith* means "ground plan" in 1 Ch. 28 in the account of the instructions David gave his son Solomon for building the temple and its furniture (vv. 11,12,19), while *tabhnith hammerkabhah* in v. 18 probably should be translated "pattern" or "structure of the chariot." [28] To be sure, here also *tabhnith* appears in a text that has to do more with the intention to build a chariot than with information about the structure of the chariot after it has been built. Perhaps it would be best to translate this passage as follows: "...also for the chariot (which they were planning) to build...," thus placing *tabhnith* in the same category as the other furnishings described in this chapter. The formula *vethabhnith kol 'asher hayah bharuach 'immo le,* "and the plan of all that he had in mind for," in v. 12 is worthy of note. This certainly refers not to a plan or model which David was given in a vision, but rather to the well-formulated design and clear idea David had for the construction of the temple complex. [29] 28:19 says that ultimately these ideas came from Yahweh.

tabhnith is found several times in connection with sacral art in Dt. 4, which is a late chapter. The Israelites are forbidden to make any kind of image of their God, whether it be in the form of a man or of some kind of beast (4:16,17,18). The context here tends to interpret *tabhnith* in the sense of "graven image," but first of all it means merely the likeness of some sort of living creature. This passage says nothing about how such an image might have been made or the material that might have been used to make it. Dt. 4 does not condemn the act of making an image, but making it to serve as a *pesel,* "idol," or a *semel,* "image," since such is a "graven image." Deutero-Isaiah describes in detail the way such images were made as they were shaped into the *tabhnith 'ish,* "figure of a man" (Isa. 44:13).

After entering through a door in the wall into the outer court of the temple, Ezekiel sees all kinds of images (*kol tabhnith...*) of creeping things and beasts portrayed (*mechuqqeh*) upon the wall, and the performance of a cultic ceremony before them (Ezk. 8:10). In this passage, *tabhnith* means the representation of the relief or the pictures portrayed on the wall, and here in Ezekiel it again has the specific sense of "graven image." *tabhnith* means the same thing in Ps. 106:20, where Ex. 32 is interpreted in the sense of idolatry (*tabhnith shor,* "image of an ox").

---

[27] Noth, *HAT,* 7, 133-35.
[28] Cf. Rudolph, *HAT,* 21, 188.
[29] Contra *ibid.*

Finally, twice Ezekiel uses *tabhnith* in the sense of "such a thing as," "something like" (a man's hand). In 8:3 he uses this word to describe the grip with which Yahweh had seized a lock of his head ("and he put forth the form of a hand"), and in 10:8 he wants to convey the idea that the cherubim which he had seen in a theophany have "such a thing as (something like) a man's hand." These two passages are trying to express realities of the divine sphere which transcend human conception. In order to emphasize that God and the cherubim work "personally" in human life, Ezekiel describes their activity as the work of a hand. Their functions may be compared with the functions of a hand. It is a hand, and yet not really a hand, but a *tabhnith yadh*, "form of a hand." The indefinite character that *tabhnith* deliberately establishes in this context develops naturally from the original sense attaching to the root *bnh/bny*, viz., "structure," "image," "pattern."

Wagner

בַּעַל *ba'al*

Contents: I. 1. Etymology and Secular Use; 2. Use as A Divine Name in the Ancient Near East. II. The Canaanite Baal Outside the OT: 1. Forms and Character; 2. Consort; 3. Mythology; 4. Cult. III. Baal in the OT: 1. Names and Forms; 2. Historical Outline; 3. Overall Picture; 4. Indirect Statements; 5. Theological and Religious Significance.

I. 1. *Etymology and Secular Use.* The common Semitic word *ba'lu*[1] means "lord," and with the following genitive frequently "owner." A few examples may be mentioned: Akk. *bēlī*, "my lord," Ugar. *b'ly*, "my lord"; Akk. *bēl bīti*, "owner of the house," *bēl eqli*, "owner of the field," *bēl ṣēni*, "owner of

ba'al. W. F. Albright in *Festschrift für A. Bertholet* (1950), 1-14; *idem, Yahweh and the Gods of Canaan* (London, 1968), 108ff.; H. Bacht, A. Baumstark, T. Klauser, F. Nötscher, *RAC*, I (1950), 1063-1113; W. W. Baudissin, *RE*, II (³1897), 323-340; *idem, Adonis und Esmun* (1911), esp. pp. 24ff.; *idem, Kyrios als Gottesname im Judentum*, I-IV (1929), 389ff.; H. Bauer, *ZAW*, 51 (1933), 86ff.; L. Bronner, *The Stories of Elijah and Elisha as Polemics against Baal Worship* (Leiden, 1968); E. Dhorme, *AnSt*, 6 (1956), 57-61; H. J. W. Drijvers, *Ba'al Shamin, de Heer van de Hemel* (1971); R. Dussaud, *Les découvertes de Ras Shamra (Ugarit) et l'AT* (Paris, ²1941), esp. pp. 97ff., 115ff.; O. Eissfeldt, *Baal Zaphon, Zeus Kasios und der Durchzug der Israeliten durchs Meer* (1932); *idem, KlSchr*, I (1962), 1-12; II (1963), 171-198; IV (1968), 53-57; H. Gese, *RdM*, 10/2 (1970), 3-232, esp. pp. 119ff. (see the Index, 472f.); J. Gray, *The Legacy of Canaan. SVT*, 5 (²1965), esp. pp. 20ff., 163ff.; H. Gressmann, *BZAW*, 33 (1918), 191-216; N. C. Habel, *Yahweh versus Baal* (New York, 1964); R. Hillmann, *Wasser und Berg. Kosmische Verbindungslinien zwischen dem kanaanäischen Wettergott und Jahwe* (1965); M. Höfner, *WbMyth*, I (1965), 429f., 431, 480f.; J. Hoftijzer, *Religio Aramaica* (Leiden, 1968, see Index); O. Kaiser, *Die mythische Bedeutung des Meeres in*

[1] Cf. *KBL*³, 137.

(continued on p. 182)

sheep"; Phoen. *bʿl bqr*, "owner of a herd of cattle," *bʿl ṣʾn*, "owner of sheep"; Aram. *bʿly rkb*, "owner of a war-chariot," *bʿl ksp*, "owner of silver"; Heb. *baʿal hashshor*, "owner of the ox" (Ex. 21:28), *baʿal habbor*, "owner of the pit" (Ex. 21:34), and *baʿal habbayith*, "owner of the house" (Ex. 22:7 [Eng. v. 8]). In this sense *baʿal* is also used in the plural of respect, of an individual owner (Ex. 21:29; Isa. 1:3).

The husband is "owner" of his wife, and therefore *bʿl* also means "husband" (e.g., in *PRU*, II, No. 77; *DISO*, 40 under 2c; Gen. 20:3; 21:3,22; Dt. 22:22; 24:4; etc.). Moreover, he is "lord of the house," "head of the family" (Akk. *bēl bīti;* Ugar. *bʿl bt*), and the king is "lord" [2] over lands, cities, and subjects. [3] In another sense, *bʿl* can indicate that a person participates in a community. Thus *bʿl* is used of a member of the city aristocracy (*DISO*, 40 under 2d; Jgs. 9:2; 20:5; 1 S. 23:11f.; 2 S. 21:12; etc.) and of a partner in a covenant, Akk. *bēl adê* or Heb. *baʿal berith* (Gen. 14:13). *bʿl* is even more idiomatic in expressions that describe an activity or a characteristic, e.g., in Akk. *bēl birki*, "runner," *bēl dāmi*, "murderer," or Ugar. *bʿl ḥẓ*, "the archer," [4] *bʿl knp*, "the winged one," [5] *bʿl qrnm wḏnb*, "one having horns and tail," [6] and the Hebrew expressions corresponding with them, as *baʿale chitstsim*, "archers" (Gen. 49:23), *baʿal kanaph*, "bird" (Prov. 1:17; cf. Eccl. 10:20), and *baʿal haqqeranayim*, "having two horns" (Dnl. 8:6,20).

2. *Use As a Divine Name in the Ancient Near East.* In the appellative sense *bēlum* is used very early in Mesopotamia as an epithet for different gods, at first probably in a genitive construction where the word in the genitive indicates the domain or object controlled ("lord of..."), and soon also as an absolute epithet ("the lord"). [7] Then *bēlum* occurs regularly with this meaning. Thus, the moon-god Sin is the *Bēl-Ḥarrān* (=*bʿl ḥrn*, *KAI*, 218), "lord of Harrān"; see also

---

Ägypten, Ugarit und Israel. BZAW, 78 (²1962); A. S. Kapelrud, *Baal in the Ras Shamra Texts* (Copenhagen, 1952); H. Klengel, *JCS*, 19 (1965), 87-93; J. Kühlewein, *ThAT*, I, 327ff.; J. C. de Moor, *The Seasonal Pattern in the Ugaritic Myth of Baʿlu. AOAT*, 16 (1971); *idem, New Year with Canaanites and Israelites*, 2 vols. (1972); M. J. Mulder, *Baʿal in het OT* ('s-Gravenhage, 1962); *idem, Kanaänitische Goden in het OT* (Den Haag, 1965), 25-36; U. Oldenburg, *The Conflict between 'El and Baʿal in Canaanite Religion* (Leiden, 1969); G. Östborn, *Yahweh and Baal in the Book of Hosea and Related Documents. LUÅ*, 51/6 (Lund, 1956); M. H. Pope-W. Röllig, *WbMyth*, I (1965), 253-273; H. D. Preuss, *Verspottung fremder Religionen im AT. BWANT*, 5/12 (1971); E. Rössler, *Jahwe und die Götter im Pentateuch und im dtr. Geschichtswerk* (1966); H. H. Rowley, *BJRL*, 39 (1956/57) 200-233; *idem, BJRL*, 42 (1960), 190-219; W. H. Schmidt, *Königtum Gottes in Ugarit und Israel. BZAW*, 80 (²1966); *idem, ZRGG*, 15 (1963), 1-13; R. Stadelmann, *Syrisch-palästinensische Gottheiten in Ägypten* (1967), 15ff., 32ff.; J. Starcky, *Palmyre* (Paris, 1952), 85-106; R. de Vaux, *BMB*, 5 (1941), 7-20; *idem,* in *Ugaritica*, VI (1969), 501-517.

[2] *CAD*, II, 194.

[3] E.g., Ugaritic, *CTA*, 1 [VI AB], IV, 6; 2 [III AB], I, 17; 6 [I AB], VI, 57; 15 [III K], IV, 28; *PRU*, V, No. 60:11,13,15,19.

[4] *PRU*, II, No. 1, v. 3; see Gaster, *Myth, Legend and Custom* (New York, 1969), 671.

[5] *CTA*, 36, 6.

[6] *Ugaritica*, V, chap. III, No. 1, v. 20; see De Moor, *UF*, 2 (1970), 350.

[7] See Tallqvist, *Akk. Götterepitheta* (1938), 40ff.; *CAD*, II, 193f.

Ugaritic, *CTA,* 24 [NK], 41f., *hll bʿl gml,* "Hilāl, lord of the (shepherd's) crook";
KAI, 24.16, *rkbʾl bʿl bt,* "Rākib-El, lord of the house"; and *KAI,* 145.5, *ḥṭr myskr... bʿl ḥrdt,* "H-M..., lord of terror." [8]

The practice of calling a god simply "lord" without feeling any desire or necessity of adding other titles probably originated from the religious hesitation to utter the actual divine name of the deity (→ אדון *ʾādhôn*). It is impossible to determine where and when this first took place. [9]

In Old Assyrian texts *Bēlum* appears as the name of a specific deity. [10] His character cannot be defined more precisely, but he is clearly distinguished from Adad and Ashur. Perhaps he is to be identified with Enlil. [11] From the Kassite Period on, Bēl as "the Lord" par excellence means in Babylonia the national god Marduk, who probably took this title over from Enlil. In certain cases, both of these gods exhibit certain features of a storm-god, and yet they are never able to supplant the true storm-gods. [12] The name of Bēl also appears later in non-Akkadian sources. [13]

The divine name *bʿl* also occurs in Amorite proper names from Mari, Tell al-Rimah, and Chagar Bazar. [14] However, it is not entirely certain that *bʿl* had already become a proper name for the storm-god here. In light of expressions like *dIM bēl Kallassu* and *dIM bēl Ḥalab,* both of which were found at Mari, it might be regarded as unlikely that the ideogram of the storm-god was already read as *bʿl* at that time. However, this argument is not conclusive, because *Ugaritica,* V, chap. I, No. 18, 4 reads *dIM be-el* ḫur. sag *Ḥa-zi* for the simple *bʿl ṣpn* of the alphabetic version. Further, it should be observed that the storm-god of Ḥalab in Ugarit is not called **hd (hdd/ʿdd) bʿl ḫlb,* but simply *bʿl ḫlb.* Finally, the Ugaritic texts themselves show that the home of Baal's father was in Tuttul in northern Mesopotamia. [15] Thus, it is quite possible that the Amorites of northern Mesopotamia and northern Syria called the storm-god *baʿlum* as early as the eighteenth century B.C.

In the seventeenth century B.C. *bʿl* is found several times in Egypt as an element in Asiatic proper names, [16] but again it is uncertain whether it was applied to the storm-god. From the fourteenth century B.C. on, however, the storm-god was worshiped in Egypt also under the proper name *bʿl.* Even earlier, possibly beginning in the eighteenth century B.C., the Asiatic storm-god was identified with

---

[8] For examples in Old Arabic see, e.g., Ryckmans, *Les religions arabes préislamiques* (Louvain, ²1951), 46; Höfner, 493f.

[9] In any case, the name Baal is not to be found in an Egyptian cylinder seal of the Old Kingdom from Byblos, as thought by P. Montet, *Byblos et l'Egypte, Texte* (Paris, 1928), 62ff.; *Le drame d'Avaris* (Paris, 1941), 25. Contra, see Goedicke, *MDAI,* 19 (1963), 1-6; Albright, *BASOR,* 176 (1964), 44f.; 179 (1965), 39.

[10] H. Hirsch, *BAfO,* 13/14 (1961), 22ff.

[11] Cf. R. Frankena, *Tākultu* (Leiden, 1954), 87.

[12] See Edzard, *WbMyth,* I, 135ff.

[13] *KBL³,* 126; *KAI,* 264; Hoftijzer, 26ff., 55.

[14] Huffmon, *APNM,* 100, 174f.; Walker, *Iraq,* 32 (1970), 27ff.; Loretz, *AOAT,* 3, 19.

[15] See below.

[16] Yeivin, *JEA,* 45 (1959), 16ff.; Helck, *ÄgAbh,* 5 (1962), 81; Stadelmann, 13.

the Egyptian god Seth, but there is no clear identification of Baal and Seth until the Ramessid period. [17]

In the fifteenth century B.C., the name of Baal appears sporadically in proper names of the Alalakh IV stratum (Alalakh Tablets 132, 3; 207, 26;[18] short names which probably contain the name of the god). The Amarna Letters from the fourteenth century B.C. show a rather uniform distribution of proper names containing the component *b'l* over the whole of Syria and Palestine.[19] Here it should be noted that sometimes the syllabic writing of the name *b'l* is used interchangeably with the ideogram of the storm-god (*dIM*). In the Amarna Letters the same ideogram is also used for the storm-gods Haddu and Teshshub. However, in light of Egyptian parallels, it is absolutely certain that EA 147, 13-15 (Tyre) is describing Baal's thunder (thus we should read *ki-ma dba'la* in line 14). [20]

In Ugarit, *dIM* should usually be read *ba'lu,* but sometimes it should be taken as *haddu.* [21] *dU* stands alongside *dIM* for *ba'lu* and *ba'lūma* (pl. of respect, corresponding to secular usage). [22] Here, of course, *ba'lu* always means the storm-god.

It is hard to imagine that the Egyptians, the Amarna scribes, the Ugaritic scribes, and perhaps also the Amorites, and later the Phoenicians, the Punic scribes, and the Israelites[23] would have called the storm-god simply *b'l,* if this had not been clearly understood as his proper name, but could have been interpreted as an epithet which was not intelligible without more precise definition. Thus, no later than the middle of the second millennium B.C. on, when Western Semitic peoples used *b'l* or *b'lm* in an absolute sense, they were thinking of a single god Baal, who could probably assume different forms and certainly existed in many local settings, but in general represented the same concept of deity.

However, when *b'l* is not used in an absolute sense, but is connected with a genitive that defines it more precisely, it is frequently hard to decide whether *b'l* should be understood as a proper name or as an appellative honorific title of another god. The former possibility should not be dismissed too hastily, because other divine names were also frequently connected with genitives (some Ugar. examples are: *'trt ṣrm, 'ttrt ḫr, 'ttrt šd, ršp gn,* and *ršp ṣbȝ*). Thus, it is just as legitimate to translate *b'l X* "Baal of X" as it is to translate it "lord of X." Furthermore, it has been convincingly demonstrated that *b'l* followed by a genitive frequently means simply the storm-god Baal. In the Ugaritic texts, *b'l (mrym) ṣpn* is used interchangeably with *b'l(m)* and *hd* (Haddu) quite regularly. Since this god was the national god of Ugarit, *b'l ȝgrt,* which sometimes appears outside the literary texts, probably should also be interpreted simply as a local manifestation of the great god.

---

[17] Gressmann, 198ff.; Helck, *ÄgAbh,* 5 (1962), 482ff.; Stadelmann, 15ff., 32ff.; Zandee, *ZÄS,* 90 (1963), 144ff.; Te Velde, *Seth, God of Confusion* (Leiden, 1967), 109ff.

[18] Cf. *WO,* 5 (1969/70), 64, and *UF,* 1 (1969), 39, n. 26.

[19] Gressmann, 195; Rainey, *AOAT,* 8, 88.

[20] See also *CTA,* 4 [II AB], VII, 29-32; with *AOAT,* 16, 159, 162.

[21] Gröndahl, *PNU,* 116f., 132f.

[22] See above, and Rainey, *IEJ,* 19 (1969), 108f.; De Moor, *UF,* 2 (1970), 219, 226; for Israel, see below.

[23] See below.

Similarly, in the Phoenician inscription in *KAI*, 26, *b'l* is obviously identical
with *b'l krntryš*. The juxtaposition of *KAI*, 78.2, *l'dn lb'l šmm wlrbt ltnt pn b'l*,
KAI, 105.1, *l'dn lb'l ḥmn wlrbt ltnt pn b'l* (cf. *KAI*, 79.1f.; 85.1f.; 86.1f., etc.),
RES, 330, 1, *l'dn lb'l 'dr wlrbt ltynt pn b'l*, and *KAI*, 137.1, *l'dn lb'l wltnt
pn b'l*, shows that no great distinction can have been made between *b'l šmm*,
b'l ḥmn, *b'l 'dr*, and simple *b'l*. If it is legitimate to compare these with *KAI*,
14.18, *bt lb'l ṣdn wbt l'štrt šm b'l*, as seems natural, then the Baal of Sidon
could be added to these examples. In this connection, it should also be mentioned that in some Neo-Punic inscriptions vows are made *lb'l*, "to Baal," without any additional specification, although it is certain that *b'l* means *b'l ḥmn* in
North Africa. [24]

Nevertheless, frequently different Baals are mentioned side by side: so e.g.,
in *KAI*, 24.15f., *b'l ṣmd* is mentioned with *b'l ḥmn;* in *KAI*, 78.2-4, *b'l šmn*
with *b'l ḥmn* and *b'l mgnm;* in *KAI*, 162.1, *b'l ḥmn* with *bl 'dr* (=*b'l 'dr*);
in Borger, IV 10, *dBa-al-sa-me-me* with *dBa-al-ma-la-ge-e* and *dBa-al-ṣa-pu-
nu;* [25] and in *RES*, 329, *b'l 'dn* with *b'l ḥmn*. At first glance, this seems to
contradict the material cited above. Generally speaking, though, these terms
reflect distinctions which may have been important on a local level, but most of
which on the whole are rather unimportant, as will be shown below under II.1.
However, one cannot exclude the possibility that other gods are hidden underneath names of this type, i.e., *b'l* can function as an epithet. *KAI*, 47.1, *lmlqrt b'l
ṣr* shows how difficult it can be to determine the meaning of *b'l* in some contexts. Should this be translated "Melkart, lord of Tyre," or "Melkart, Baal of
Tyre?" Undoubtedly, Melkart was distinguished from other Baals, [26] but as we
have seen, this is not decisive. We also know that Baal was worshipped as the
storm-god in Tyre (EA 147, 13-15; [27] cf. 1 K. 16:31f.; 18:16ff.). Like Baal,
Melkart was married to Astarte, and like Baal, he was a dying and rising god. [28]
Unfortunately, this does not solve the problem, because Josephus (*Contra Apion.*
i.18[118]) speaks of a temple of Zeus (= Baal) and of a temple of Heracles (=
Melkart) at Tyre; and Cicero also (*De nat. deor.* iii.16) distinguishes between a
Tyrian Zeus (= Baal) and a Heracles that was worshipped at Tyre.

II. The Canaanite Baal Outside the OT.

1. *Forms and Character*. When the Egyptian sources make explicit references
to Baal, [29] they are not very instructive, and yet they show clearly that Baal was
regarded as the god of the storm. He is a war-god who wields the *ktp*-weapon,
like Baal in the Ugaritic myth. [30] Anat and Astarte are mentioned as consorts

---

24 *RES*, 303, 326, 1545.
25 Borger, *BAfO*, 9 (1956), 69.
26 *Ibid.*: IV, 10, 14.
27 See above.
28 Lipiński, *CRRA*, 17, 30ff.
29 See above, I.2.
30 *CTA*, 6 [I AB], V, 3.

of Seth/Baal. Moreover, the passage in EA 147, 13-15 [31] also designates Baal as the god of thunder.

Other than this, outside the OT, [32] we find the term Baal used only in expressions that qualify it more precisely, e.g., in *b'l 'dr*, **b'l bq'h*, *b'l ḥmn*, *b'l ḥlb*, **b'l krml*, *b'l krntryš*, **b'l mrqd*, *b'l pn 'rṣ*, *b'l ṣdn*, *b'l ṣmd*, *b'l ṣpn*, *b'l šd*, and *b'l šmm* (we have disregarded orthographic variations; the names with asterisks beside them have not yet been found in Semitic sources). Frequently we know so little about a certain Baal that it is impossible to determine his character more precisely. But in cases where more information is available, the characteristics of a storm-god are attached to *b'l* repeatedly (this is true of *b'l bq'h*, *b'l ḥlb*, *b'l krml*, *b'l ṣpn*, and *b'l šmm*). As the giver of rain, *b'l* is responsible for the growth of vegetation (this is seen in *b'l bq'h*, *b'l ḥmn*, *b'l krntryš*, *b'l ṣpn*, *b'l šd*, and *b'l šmm*). Therefore, he was also repeatedly identified with Zeus and Jupiter (this is the case with *b'l 'dr*, *b'l bq'h*, *b'l ḥmn*, *b'l krml*, *b'l mrqd*, *b'l ṣpn*, *b'l šd*, and *b'l šmm*). The consort of these Baals is always a goddess of love and fertility (this applies specifically to *b'l 'dr*, *b'l bq'h*, *b'l ḥmn*, *b'l ḥlb*, *b'l ṣdn*, *b'l ṣpn*, *b'l šd*, and *b'l šmm*). His symbol is the bull (this can be shown explicitly for *b'l bq'h*, *b'l ḥlb*, *b'l krntryš*, *b'l ṣpn*, and *b'l šmm*). Some of his names can be traced back directly to Ugaritic mythology (*b'l mrqd*, *b'l pn 'rṣ*, *b'l ṣmd*, *b'l ṣpn*, and *b'l šmm*).

Finally, it should be made clear that these "local" forms of the storm-god were worshipped far beyond the borders of their original home. E.g., the storm-god of Ḥalab was also held in high esteem outside the country of Yamhad which was ruled from Ḥalab. The same is also true of *b'l ṣpn*, whose cult extended from Antioch in northern Syria to Egypt, and from Marseilles to Jordan. Such a widespread veneration would scarcely have been possible if these Baals had been regarded as foreign gods. Rather, we are compelled to suppose that they were popular representatives of a single well-defined god figure. The many "local" representations of Baal worship could be compared with those of the Roman Catholic Mary worship. Just as one can speak of Notre Dame (Our Lady) of Paris, or of Lourdes, or of the North, one can also speak of the lord of Ṣapān, or of Sidon, or of Ugarit, even though one has in mind merely variations of a single figure.

From the Ugaritic texts, *b'l ṣpn* is by far the best known of all the Baals. His dwelling place was on Jebel el-Aqra' (1759 meters above sea level), about 40 kilometers north of Ugarit. The Semites called this mountain Ṣapānu (later → צפון tsāphôn), and the non-Semites called it Ḥazi (later Kasios). Sanctuaries of *b'l ṣpn* were established round about the Mediterranean Sea, e.g., at the port of *Prw-nfr* at Memphis under the eighteenth Egyptian dynasty.

Because of its extraordinary location, from the very first Mt. Ṣapānu was an ideal point of orientation for sailors. Its name could very well have meant "observation post." This could explain the unusual popularity of *b'l ṣpn* in the

---

[31] See above.
[32] See below, III.

port cities. However, he was also worshipped in Jordan,[33] and it is certainly
not too bold to assume that there was a time when all of Canaan was guided
spiritually by this mountain, so that *tsaphon* came to be synonymous with the
"North" in Palestine.

In Ugarit *b'l ṣpn* was plainly and undoubtedly the national god. Nevertheless,
usually the "canonical" lists of gods from Ugarit put him in fourth place, after
ʾlḃb, the god of the fathers, *ʾl*, father of the gods and head of the pantheon,
and *dgn,* the father of Baal. And yet, in other lists Baal is promoted in Ugaritic
thought at the expense of these older gods,[34] so that his father Dagan, who no
longer played any role in the Ugaritic religion, was often "forgotten."

The real name of the Ugaritic Baal was Haddu (= Hadad, Adad), but this
name was used only in the sacred texts. Even as early as the Old Babylonian
period Baal had been represented as the son of Dagan under the name Adad.[35]
Thus it is not a peculiarity of Ugaritic religion when it frequently calls Baal-
Had *bn dgn,* "son of Dagan." According to *Ugaritica,* V, chap. III, Nos. 7,15
this Dagan was the god of Tuttul in northern Mesopotamia, which is confirmed
by the Mari and Terqa texts. It is likely that Baal-Had infiltrated into the Old
Amorite pantheon of Ugarit from that region at a relatively late time. This was
explained theologically by the assumption of a marriage between him and Anat,
the daughter of El.[36]

The late acceptance of Baal into the Ugaritic pantheon is perhaps reflected in
the peculiar tension between Baal and the family of El, which is mentioned
repeatedly. El supports his son Yam in his plot against Baal[37] and does not give
Baal any opportunity to defend himself when the messengers of Yam demand
his extradition.[38] Baal is successful in persuading El to give him permission to
build a palace only with the greatest effort.[39] When Baal dies through the in-
strumentality of Mot, another of El's favorite sons,[40] El indeed mourns, but he
does not intervene; his consort and his sons rejoice over the death of Baal.[41]
On several occasions Baal has to defeat the sons of El and Aṯirat.[42] In another
myth,[43] again it is El who creates the monsters who mortally wound Baal. Sometimes even Anat and ʿAṯtart could turn against Baal's best interests.[44]

Undoubtedly, at Ugarit *b'l ṣpn* is above all the storm-god. He rules over
clouds, winds, thunder, lightning, rain, dew, and snow. In these semiarid regions,
all life was dependent on a sufficient amount of precipitation. Therefore, Baal
is the "Almighty" (*'lʒyn*), the "Exalted One" (*'ly*), the "Sovereign, Lord of the

---

[33] Eissfeldt, *Baal Zaphon,* 9f.
[34] De Moor, *UF,* 2 (1970), 217ff.
[35] Dossin, *CRRA,* 3, 129.
[36] De Moor, *AOAT,* 16, 111.
[37] *CTA,* 1 [VI AB], IV; 2 [III AB], III, see *AOAT,* 16, 116ff.
[38] *CTA,* 2 [III AB], I.
[39] *CTA,* 3 [V AB], E-F; 4 [II AB], I-V.
[40] *CTA,* 5 [I* AB], VI.
[41] *CTA,* 6 [I AB], I, 39-41.
[42] *CTA,* 2 [III AB], IV; 6 [I AB], V, 1, VI, 16ff.; cf. 4 [II AB], II, 24-26.
[43] *CTA,* 12 [BH].
[44] *CTA,* 2 [III AB], 40, IV, 28, and in the legend of Aqhat.

Earth" (*zbl b'l 'rṣ*), the king above whom no other can stand, [45] the one who gives substance to all living creatures. [46] When his sweet rain revives field and seed, the heads of the peasant farmers are lifted up. [47] When his return to the earth is announced, men begin to dream of streams of oil and honey, [48] the symbols of abundance. But when he withdraws and the parched land cannot be plowed [49] or the vegetation withers, [50] this naturally gives rise to despair. [51] It is no wonder that a myth was created here to attempt to explain the change of the seasons. [52]

Baal is also a war-god, "the Mightiest of Heroes" (*'l'y qrdm*). He fights against monsters like *ltn* [53] (cf. Leviathan in Isa. 27:1), *tnn* (Tunnanu = Tannin), [54] and *'klm*, [55] conquers dangerous enemies like Yam [56] and Mot, [57] and defeats many cities. [58] His equally violent lover, Anat, frequently helps him in battle. [59]

As is often true in the history of religion, the warring aspect was connected with that of sexual love. Several texts from Ugarit deal with the amorous affairs of the lovers Baal and Anat. [60] However, it is not Baal who gives men children, but El, "the father of men" (*'b 'dm*), even if it is at Baal's intercession. [61]

Even though Baal is represented at Ugarit in basically anthropomorphic terms, sometimes he also has intercourse with a cow. [62] This should not lead one to conclude that the people of Ugarit sanctioned bestiality, [63] but rather that Baal, as a potent fertility-god, could assume the form of a bull. But Baal is never explicitly called a "bull," which is probably due to his inability to displace the old bull-god El completely from his role as procreator (*bny bnwt*). [64]

2. *Consort.* In the late period of Ugarit's history Anat came to be associated with Astarte more and more so that the two of them together formed a pair of goddesses. [65] Thus, it is not surprising that elsewhere Astarte or both these love-

---

[45] *CTA*, 3 [V AB], E, 41; 4 [II AB], IV, 44, VII, 49f.

[46] *CTA*, 4 [II AB], VII, 50-52.

[47] *CTA*, 16 [II K], III; cf. *AOAT*, 16, 99.

[48] *CTA*, 6 [I AB], III.

[49] *CTA*, 6 [I AB], IV, 25-29.

[50] *CTA*, 19 [I D], I, 18, 30f., 61ff.; cf. 12 [BH], II, 44.

[51] *CTA*, 19 [I D], I, 34ff.

[52] See below, II.3.

[53] *CTA*, 5 [I* AB], I, 1-3.

[54] *PRU*, II, No. 1, v. 1.

[55] *CTA*, 12 [BH].

[56] *CTA*, 2 [III AB], IV; 4 [II AB], VII, 2-5.

[57] *CTA*, 6 [I AB], VI, 16ff.

[58] *CTA*, 4 [II AB], VII, 6ff.

[59] E.g., *CTA*, 3 [V AB], D, 34ff.; 10 [IV AB], II, 23-25; see Kapelrud, *The Violent Goddess* (Oslo, 1969), 48ff.

[60] See below, II.2.

[61] *CTA*, 15 [III K], II; 17 [II D], I.

[62] *CTA*, 5 [I* AB], V, 18ff; cf. *CTA*, 10-11 [IV AB]; *PRU*, V, No. 124.

[63] See *AOAT*, 16, 188, n. 17.

[64] See *UF*, 2 (1970), 313, and *CTA*, 23 [SS]. On the mythology and cult of *b'l ṣpn*, see further below, II.3-4.

[65] Gese, 161f.; De Moor, *UF*, 2, 228.

goddesses appear as consorts of Baal. Later they were united in the one figure Atargatis or succeeded by other fertility-goddesses like Tinnit, Baʻalat, Belti, Aphrodite, and Venus, but sometimes also by a more maternal figure like Asherah (→ אֲשֵׁרָה *ʼaš̌ērāh*), Hera, or Juno. Thus, it is no longer possible to contend that Baal had more than one consort (perhaps consisting of two persons); to the present time no arguments to this effect have proved valid. [66]

It is certain that Anat (*btlt*), Tinnit (*Virgo Caelestis*), and Atargatis (*Virgo*) were regarded as virginal deities. This probably does not mean that they were *virgines intactae* (i.e., that they had never had sexual relations), but only that they had never brought a divine child into the world, [67] which is related to their being considered hermaphroditic beings. [68]

These names of Baal's partners are hard to understand: Ugar. *ʻttrt šm bʻl*, Phoen. *ʻštrt šm bʻl*, Phoen. *sml bʻl*, and Pun. *tnt pn bʻl*. However, the meanings *sml* ("likeness") and *pn* ("face") are clear in and of themselves. Frequently, the name (*šm*) of a deity is to be understood as his external visible being, his "appearance" (→ שֵׁם *šēm*). Therefore, perhaps *sml*, *pn* and *šm* should be interpreted in the sense of "alter ego," "better half" (cf. *keneghdo*, "fit for him," in Gen. 2:18,20). [69]

3. *Mythology.* We find myths about Baal only in Ugaritic, Hittite, and Egyptian tradition. But if a single idea of deity lay behind the local Baals whose manifestations differed more or less from place to place, [70] one might expect local variations of these mythological narratives, but not a completely different mythology, among the Canaanite worshippers of Baal. [71]

The most extensive mythological series from Ugarit consists of six tablets written by a certain Ilimilku. [72] *CTA*, 7 and 8, and *Ugaritica*, V, chap. III, Nos. 3-4 contain somewhat divergent fragments of the same myth. There is practically unanimous agreement among scholars concerning the order of the tablets in *CTA*, 4-6, but there is wide disagreement as to the order and relationship of the fragments *CTA*, 1-3. According to a recent theory, [73] the tablets should be read in the following order: 3-1-2-4-5-6. In this case, the myth can be seen to relate in chronological sequence how the course of the normal climatic, agrarian, and cultic year of the people of Ugarit came to be determined by the experiences and deeds of Baal. [74] Therefore, we find here the mythological patterns of the seasons (symbolized by the succession of Baal-Yam-Baal-Môt/ʻAṭṭar-Baal to

---

[66] *AOAT*, 16, 81f.

[67] *UF*, 1 (1969), 182, 224.

[68] On Anat/Astarte, see *UF*, 1, 171; *AOAT*, 16, 132, 193; on Tinnit, see Albright, *Yahweh and the Gods of Canaan*, 112f.

[69] Other views are given in part in W. Herrmann, *MIO*, 15 (1969), 22f.; but see also Dölger, *Antike und Christentum*, I (1929), 93.

[70] See above, I.2; II.1.

[71] Cf. *AOAT*, 16, 52ff.

[72] *CTA*, 1-6 [VI AB, III AB, V AB; II AB, I* AB, I AB].

[73] De Moor, *AOAT*, 16.

[74] For other views, see *AOAT*, 16, 9ff.

the throne), of the highlights in the life of the peasant and fisherman, of the most important festivals and rites, and, of course, of the origin of the cult center. The narrative was probably recited at the Autumn New Year Festival. [75]

Another myth (which, unfortunately, is fragmentary) [76] relates how Anat goes out in search for Baal while he is chasing wild cows in the region around Lake Huleh. Overwhelmed by her beauty, Baal promises her wonderful ecstatic love. But since Anat herself cannot give birth to a child, [77] she enters into a wild cow, she and Baal have sexual relations, and she gives birth to a bull. [78]

According to CTA, 12 [BH], Baal makes two slave-goddesses pregnant at their entreaty, and then in the desert they give birth to monsters that are similar to wild bulls. Baal chases them, but he is wounded and lies in the mire sick with fever for "seven, yea eight" years. The earth dries up during his absence until his relatives finally find him. [79]

A fragment in the Hittite language from Boghazköy [80] contains a Canaanite myth in which Asherah (→ אשרה 'ašērāh) tried to seduce the storm-god.

4. *Cult.* For a description of the Baal cult, Ugarit again furnishes the greatest amount of material. At the present time, four great festivals for Baal are more or less discernible. The most important was the New Year Festival in the Autumn. [81] It was celebrated during the first seven days of the month, *rʾš yn* ("the first of the wine," September-October). The king organized sacrificial meals to honor Baal in Ugarit and on Mt. Ṣapān. Baal's return from the under-world and his enthronement on Mt. Ṣapān were probably celebrated. At the same time it was the vintage festival in which new wine was drunk in large quantities. On the first day of the festival, the king offered sacrifices on the roof of the temple where tabernacles had been erected (cf. Jer. 32:29; Neh. 8:10). On the same day, a bunch of grapes was offered to El. According to CTA, 3 [V AB], A, 9-17, Baal drank the new wine out of a holy cup, which no woman was allowed to witness. This ritual of drinking wine probably took place in those cult associations of Baal worshippers called *mrzḥ*. [82]

As in the Assyrian New Year Ritual in KAR, No. 214, [83] many gods are invited to drink with Baal-Had in the ritual in *Ugaritica,* V, chap. III, No. 2. This agrees with other Ugaritic texts which state that on this occasion much wine

---

[75] See below. For another, very incomplete version of the Yam episode from Egypt, see Stadelmann, 127ff.

[76] CTA, 10 [IV AB].

[77] See above, II.2.

[78] Other fragments of the same type may be found in CTA, 11, RS 22.225 and perhaps in PRU, V, No. 124; similar narratives concerning Baal and Anat were known in Egypt, Stadelmann, 131ff.

[79] For fragments of additional Baal myths from Ugarit, see AOAT, 16, 6f.

[80] ANET³, 519.

[81] On this festival, see De Moor, *New Year with Canaanites and Israelites.*

[82] For Ugarit: O. Eissfeldt, *Ugaritica,* VI, 187ff.; Miller, AnOr, 48 (1972), 37ff.; for Sidon: KAI, 60.1; for Marseilles: KAI, 69.16; for Palmyra: Hoftijzer, 28f.

[83] Cf. Frankena, *Tākultu,* 23ff.

was distributed among the gods; provisions were also given to men and even to the dead. Wine, bread, and meat for the sacral meals were taken from the annual taxes. At the meals people were crowned with garlands, and sang, played, and danced before Baal.

There are other events which seem to have taken place during the New Year Festival, although we cannot be certain about this. The great Baal myth was probably read. There was a holy marriage between El, Aṯirat, and Rḥmy (perhaps Anat), which presumably was represented in the cult by the king, the queen, and a priestess. The festival was also regarded as the official beginning of the preparation of purple. There was a four-day ritual battle of Anat with the concluding rite of the "rain maiden," probably performed by a princess.

Presumably other Canaanites also celebrated the Autumn New Year Festival with Baal-Had.[84] To some extent this also lies behind the Israelite Feast of Harvest or of Tabernacles (chagh ha'asiph, → סכה sukkāh). Azitawadda calls it zbḥ ymm, "Festival of the Yearly Sacrifice,"[85] which is very similar to the terminology in 1 S. 1:21; 2:19 (cf. the annual fees and the alleged drunkenness of Hannah); and 20:6 (note that this feast lasted several days beginning with the New Moon, as in Ugarit).

The other three festivals of Baal can be reconstructed only in very vague outlines. They are: the Festival of the Dedication of the Temple about the time of the spring equinox, which possibly corresponded to the beginning of the civil year;[86] the Festival of Mourning for Baal a month later, presumably with a rite of the first sheaf, sacrifices on Ṣapān, and a procession of Anat-Astarte;[87] and the Festival of the Destruction of Môt in June, presumably with a rite of the last sheaf.[88] Other than referring to numerous establishments of temples, stelae, and votive offerings, the other Canaanite sources furnish only very little material that would help in describing the Baal cult. Azitawadda offered sacrifices not only on the New Year, but also at the time of plowing and at the time of harvest.[89] Also the sacrificial texts from Ugarit,[90] Marseilles (b'l ṣpn),[91] and Carthage (perhaps b'l ḥmn)[92] offer information about types of sacrifices, materials used in sacrifices, and fees paid to the priests. Human sacrifice to Baal is unknown at Ugarit. Greek and Latin authors refer to human sacrifice, however, to b'l ḥmn, among others, and yet according to the Punic inscriptions he was satisfied with substitute sacrifices of animals.[93]

According to sources in the OT, late classical antiquity, and early Christianity, many obscene rites took place in the cult of the Baals and their partners. There

---

[84] Cf., e.g., *KAI*, 214.21f.
[85] *KAI*, 26 A III.1, C IV.4; see *AOAT*, 16, 59, n. 45.
[86] *AOAT*, 16, 61f., 155.
[87] *AOAT*, 16, 195f., 200f.
[88] *AOAT*, 16, 212ff.
[89] *KAI*, 26 A III.1f., C IV.5.
[90] Enumerated in *UF*, 2, 188f.
[91] *KAI*, 69.
[92] *KAI*, 74, 75; *CIS*, I, 168-170, 3916, 3917.
[93] *KAI*, II, 76f.; Gese, 174f.; Teixidor, *Syr*, 46 (1969), 321.

is little trace of this in the Ugaritic material. If we disregard the ritual described in *CTA,* 23 [SS], which deals with the holy wedding of El, the only other evidence of obscene rites at Ugarit is found in the mythological love scenes between Baal and Anat. [94] But since certain scenes of the myth were acted out symbolically in the Ugaritic cult, this might be assumed here as well. In any case, it is certain that (quite differently than in Israel) the queens, princesses, and other women (*ʒnšt,* "amiable maidens") actively participated in the Ugaritic cult, which suggests, but does not prove the conjecture that sacral prostitution was practiced in this cult.

De Moor

III. Baal in the OT.

1. *Names and Forms.* As a divine name, *ba'al* occurs 76 times in the OT: 58 times in the singular (always with the article) and 18 times in the plural. For a long time scholars have thought that Baal with the article was only an appellative to denote different local numina whose real names were otherwise unknown. However, the discoveries at Ras Shamra and other places [95] have shown that Baal can be the proper name of a specific deity. *ba'al* with the article belongs to the category of common nouns and adjectives which can be regarded as proper names when referring to a specific individual. [96]

It is doubtful whether the pl. *habbe'alim* (Jgs. 2:11; 3:7; 8:33; 10:6,10; 1 S. 7:4; 12:10; 1 K. 18:18; Jer. 2:23; 9:13[14]; Hos. 2:15,19[13,17]; 11:2; 2 Ch. 17:3; 24:7; 28:2; 33:3; 34:4), which occasionally also appears in secular usage, [97] should be regarded as a "plural of respect" (as at Ugarit). [98] To be sure, *ba'al* and *be'alim* are frequently used indiscriminately (cf. Jgs. 2:11 with 2:13; 2:13 with 10:6; 1 S. 7:4; and 12:10; Jgs. 8:33a with 8:33b; 1 K. 18:18 with 18:19ff.; Hos. 2:10,18[8,16] with 2:15,19[13,17]; 2 Ch. 23:17 with 24:7; and 2 K. 21:3 with 2 Ch. 33:3), but the "lovers" of Hos. 2 and "the strangers" of Jer. 2:25 (cf. 2:23) show clearly that *habbe'alim* was understood to mean several manifestations, although evidently it was believed they were more or less similar to the one Baal. [99] Also opposing the idea that *habbe'alim* is to be taken as a plural of respect is that this word often appears in stereotyped Deuteronomistic formulas which express a negative attitude toward it, e.g., *'abhadh 'eth habbe'alim,* "to serve the Baals" (Jgs. 2:11; 3:7; 10:6; 1 S. 12:10), and *halakh 'achare habbe'alim,* "to follow (lit. go after) the Baals." And, elsewhere the OT authors have shown anything but respect for Baal. In Jer. 11:13 (cf. 3:24; Hos. 9:10) *ba'al* is replaced by *bosheth,* "shame," [100] and the same is true of

---

[94] See above.

[95] See above.

[96] Brockelmann, *Synt.,* § 21c.

[97] See above, I.1.

[98] See above, I.2; cf. *GK* § 124i.

[99] See above, II.1.

[100] Probably not in the Lachish Ostraca, *KAI,* 196.6, as Michaud, *Sur la pierre et l'argile* (Neuchâtel/Paris, 1958), 101, proposes.

proper names in the books of Samuel that originally were compound names using *baʿal*, e.g., *ʾeshbaʿal*, "Eshbaal" (1 Ch. 8:33; 9:39)=*ʾish-bosheth*, "Ishbosheth" (2 S. 2:8,10,12,15; 3:8,14f.; 4:5,8,12); *yerubbaʿal*, "Jerubbaal" (Jgs. 6:32; 7:1; 8:29,35; 9:1ff.; 1 S. 12:11)=*yerubbesheth*, "Jerubbesheth" (2 S. 11:21); *meri(b[bh])baʿal*, "Merib-baal" (1 Ch. 8:34; 9:40)=*mephibhosheth*, "Mephibosheth" (2 S. 4:4; 9:6ff.; 16:1,4; 19:25f.,31[24f.,30]; 21:7f.). [101]

Here it should be emphasized at the start that the OT writers show a basic aversion to idols in general (cf., e.g., Jer. 10:1ff., or Isa. 44:6ff.). Moreover, we must take into consideration an *interpretatio israelitica*. [102] It was not the intention of the biblical writers to teach their readers in detail concerning the character or the peculiarities of Canaanite religion. In addition, they were inclined to speak of Baal and his worship in pejorative terms. This is clear not only from the transformation of *baʿal* into *bosheth*, "shame," but also from the various titles used for Baal-peor in the OT: Baal-peor (Baal of Peor) (Nu. 25:3; Dt. 4:3; Hos. 9:10; Ps. 106:28), Peor (Nu. 25:18; 31:16; Josh. 22:17), *bosheth*, "shame," and **ʾohabh*, "object of love" (Hos. 9:10; cf. *shiqquts*, "detestable"), which clearly emphasizes the religious aversion of the different writers. [103]

This brings out the importance of carefully distinguishing between earlier and later witnesses. Thus, old narratives can be incorporated into a later redaction (e.g., the Deuteronomistic history), as in the case in the book of Judges. [104] Parallel pericopes in the books of Kings and Chronicles also contain differences (cf., e.g., 2 K. 21:3 with 2 Ch. 33:3). Furthermore, the books of Chronicles contain midrashic notes which come from the pen of later scribal authors, e.g., in 2 Ch. 17:3; 24:7 (cf. 2 K. 12:8[7]); 28:2 (cf. 2 K. 16:3); and 34:4 (cf. 2 K. 23:5f.). The use of the feminine article with Baal in different texts of the LXX (2 K. 21:3; Jer. 2:8; 12:16; etc.) and in the NT (Rom. 11:4) indicates that there was a growing aversion to using the name Baal in the later period. Baal's name was replaced by *hē aischýnē*, "the shame." [105] Perhaps prophets like Hosea (2:18f.[16f.]) and Jeremiah (11:13) provided the stimulus for these titles of Baal as well as for those which are pejorative.

"Baal" occurs much more frequently in the singular than in the plural (Jgs. 2:13; 6:25ff.; 1 K. 16:31f.; 18:19ff.; 19:18; 22:54[53]; 2 K. 3:2; 10:18ff.; 11:18; 17:16; 21:3; 23:4f.; Jer. 2:8; 7:9; 11:13,17; 12:16; 19:5; 23:13,27; 32:29,35; Hos. 2:10[8]; 13:1; Zeph. 1:4; 2 Ch. 23:17). It is clear from many of these passages that *habbaʿal* here cannot be regarded as an appellative of different Canaanite gods, but only as the name of a specific god with which Israel came into contact from the period of the settlement in Canaan to the exile. [106] The OT does not reveal whether another unknown divine name lies hidden behind the name "Baal," e.g., Hadad. [107] However, it does confirm the impression made

---

[101] Cf. Mulder, *VT*, 18 (1968), 113f.
[102] Mulder, *NedThT*, 24 (1969), 414.
[103] Cf. Mulder, *Baʿal*, 133.
[104] See above.
[105] Dillmann, *MKPAW* (1882), 601ff.; Mulder, *Baʿal*, 174ff.
[106] Y. Kaufmann, *The Religion of Israel* (Chicago, 1960), 133ff., holds otherwise.
[107] See above, II.1; Dussaud, *RHR*, 113, 5ff.

by the Ugaritic texts that it has in mind Baal par excellence, the god of storm
and fertility, who appears in different local manifestations and nuances.

These local manifestations are revealed in the names of Baal that contain
geographical or other elements. Baal-peor, Baal-berith, and Baal-zebub are titles
of the god Baal worth special attention. *Baal-peor* (Nu. 25:3,5,E; Dt. 4:3; Hos.
9:10; Ps. 106:28) was worshipped on the mountain of Peor in Moab east of the
Dead Sea. According to Nu. 25, his cult was characterized by sacral prostitution
and by eating a sacrificial meal, by means of which an intimate relationship was
established between the god and his worshippers (*tsamadh* in the niphal, "to
yoke," Nu. 25:3,5; Ps. 106:28, or *nazar* in the niphal, "to consecrate oneself,"
Hos. 9:10). This Baal was worshipped in a sanctuary, as is clear from the expression *beth pe'or,* "house (temple) of Peor" (Dt. 3:29; 4:46; 34:6; Josh. 13:20). [108]
The location of this sanctuary has not yet been determined. [109]

Baal-berith (Jgs. 8:33; 9:4) is the god of Shechem. Jgs. 9:46 speaks of El-
berith, but it is questionable whether this god is to be identified with Baal-berith
or whether we are to assume that there were two gods with two temples in
Shechem. [110] The precise meaning of the name Baal-berith ("Baal of the Covenant") has not been explained satisfactorily enough for us to be able to understand the function of this Baal in Shechem, [111] or even to be able to explain his
significance in the history of Israelite religion. [112] It may be regarded as certain
that the account in Jgs. 8:33, which says that this Baal was a Canaanite god, is
reliable. This is supported by Jgs. 9:27, which speaks of a thanksgiving festival
in the sanctuary of the god after the grape gathering. [113] Thus Baal-berith was
certainly also a god of vegetation and a local manifestation of the Baal par
excellence.

Baal-zebub is mentioned as the god of the Philistine city of Ekron (2 K. 1:2f.,
6,16). The only discernible function of this deity is that of giving advice and
help in cases of illness or injury. Baal-zebub ("lord of the flies") is probably
a deliberate distortion of *b'l zbl* or *zbl b'l*. [114]

In addition to these three titles of Baal, the name "Baal" frequently occurs in
geographical names: [115] Baal-gad, Baal-hamon, Baal-hazor, Baal-hermon, Baal-
meon, Baal-perazim, Baal-shalishah, Baal-tamar, Baal-zaphon, [116] Bamoth-baal,
(Gur) Baal, [117] and Kiriath-baal. As far as history of religion is concerned, very

---

[108] For other titles of this Baal, see above.

[109] Noth, *ZAW,* 60 (1944), 19ff.; Henke, *ZDPV,* 75 (1959), 160ff.; Wolff, *BK,* XIV/1, 213f.

[110] Cf. Mulder, *Ba'al,* 136f.; contra, Clements, *JSS,* 13 (1968), 26, n. 3.

[111] The different hypotheses are critically evaluated in Clements, 21ff.

[112] However, see Nielsen, *Shechem. A Traditio-Historical Investigation* (Copenhagen,
²1959).

[113] See above, II.4.

[114] This title occurs in the Ugaritic material, see above, II.1.; for other views see Mulder,
Ba'al, 141ff.; Gaston, *ThZ,* 18 (1962), 247ff.; Fensham, *ZAW,* 79 (1967), 361ff.; and → רבה
dibbāh.

[115] This is discussed in detail in Mulder, *Ba'al,* 144ff.

[116] See also Cazelles, *RB,* 62 (1955), 332ff.

[117] See Lipiński, *RSO,* 44 (1969), 83ff.

little is to be learned from these place names; but this list shows how widespread
the Baal cult was in Palestine.

2. *Historical Outline.* According to Nu. 25, [118] there was a conflict between
Yahweh and Baal even before the settlement in Canaan. But it is worthy of note
that the OT never refers to a struggle between Yahweh and El, the head of the
Canaanite pantheon. This is probably connected with the fact that El was often
identified with Yahweh, especially in the book of Genesis (→ אֵל *'ēl*). [119] Parallels
have frequently been drawn between the tension between El and Baal in the
Ugaritic texts [120] and that between Yahweh and Baal in the OT, and some have
even concluded that Yahweh was identical with El. [121] However, many of the
questions encountered here still need clarification.

By the time of the period of the judges, Yahweh and Baal are presumed to
be in conflict (Jgs. 6:25ff., E). During the night, Gideon destroyed an altar of
Baal and the → אֲשֵׁרָה *'ashērāh*, "Asherah," that was standing beside it. He also
built an altar to Yahweh, his God. Afterward his father had to protect him
from the threat of the people of the city. He said, "If Baal is a god, let him contend for himself."

Later, a greater conflict between Yahweh and Baal took place under the
Omrides (1 K. 18:16ff.). This narrative is anticipated by the note in 1 K. 16:31f.
that Omri's son, Ahab, took for wife Jezebel, the daughter of Ethbaal, king of
the Sidonians, and at the same time began to serve Baal. He erected an altar
for Baal in the house of Baal which he had built in Samaria. According to
Josephus (*Ant.* viii.13.1[317]), this text has reference to the Baal of the city of
Tyre, and, in connection with the description of the divine judgment on Carmel,
it has often been assumed that this god was Melkart. But for one thing, it is uncertain whether Melkart can be identified with the Baal of Tyre, [122] and moreover, it cannot be inferred from the account in 1 K. 18 that the Baal of Carmel
was the city-god of Tyre. Undoubtedly certain elements in the description of the
scene on Carmel would seem to correspond to the ritual of Melkart, [123] but the
Baal of Carmel is never identified with Melkart-Hercules in any *interpretatio
graeca* of this god. Also, nothing in the text points to a "modified funeral pile
ritual." [124] Finally, in a theological evaluation, 1 K. 21:25f. shows that the OT
writer regarded the actions of Ahab as a continuation of the cult "of the Amorites, whom Yahweh had cast out before the people of Israel." The author's
purpose is not to depict the Baal of Carmel as a foreign element in a real sense.
He regards this Baal as a local manifestation of the storm-god that had been well
known since ancient times. [125]

---

[118] Cf. Rössler, 94ff.

[119] Eissfeldt, *KlSchr,* III, 386ff.; Weidmann, *FRLANT,* 94 (1968) with literature.

[120] See above, II.1.

[121] Oldenburg, 164ff.

[122] See above, I.2.

[123] De Vaux, *BMB,* 7ff.

[124] Galling, *Geschichte und AT* (1953), 109, contra de Vaux.

[125] See Alt, *KlSchr,* II, 135ff.; Galling, 105ff.; following Eissfeldt, *ZAW,* 57 (1939), 20ff.,
Baalshamēm; a synopsis of other views is given by Rowley, *BJRL,* 194.

But the events on Carmel by no means brought Baal worship to an end. 1 K. 22:54(53) and 2 K. 3:2 tell how Ahab's sons worshipped Baal, and 2 K. 10:18ff. describes Jehu's extermination of Baal worship from the northern kingdom. But in the meantime the Baal cult blossomed out again in Judah as a result of the support of Athaliah, the wife of Joram and daughter of Ahab. 2 K. 11:18 states that the people of the land broke into the Baal temple at Jerusalem, tore down his image, and killed his priests. The erection of altars for Baal is mentioned among the "abominable practices" of Manasseh enumerated in 2 K. 21:2ff. Finally, Josiah's reform would seem to have brought the Baal cult to an end in Judah (2 K. 23:4ff.; cf. 2 Ch. 34:4). By abolishing all decentralized cult places, where foreign cults always had good chances of surviving, he was successful in preventing at least an official apostasy into Baalism.

The appearance of prophets offered a great deal of support to this reform movement. Jeremiah had a direct influence on it. But also the earlier work of Hosea in the northern kingdom was not without influence in the attempt at restoration in the time of Josiah. The danger of a syncretism of the Canaanite vegetation religion with the Yahweh religion was by no means imaginary in that time. [126] Although Hosea used the word *ba'al* itself only a few times, he continually reproved the Baal religion of the northern kingdom which was posing as a type of Yahwism. His words are often taken from the Baal cult or the Baal mythology, and his marriage (Hos. 1 and 3) is not merely a likeness of Yahweh's love for his people, but it also gives us insight into the situation of the people who had yielded to the Baal cult.

Many hypotheses have been proposed to explain Yahweh's command to Hosea to take "a wife of harlotry and children of harlotry" (Hos. 1:2). Is this an example of a general fertility rite common in the Baal cult described by Lucian (*De Dea Syra* 6) and Herodotus (*Hist.* i.199; cf. also Dt. 23:18f.[17f.]; Prov. 7:13ff.; and esp. Jgs. 11:34ff., the "bewailing of virginity"), [127] or is this a unique command, intended to emphasize the prophet's task? Against the background of other statements in the OT (e.g., Hos. 4:13ff.), Rost has called the custom of young women offering themselves for sale to strangers and thus being called "women of harlotry" an initiation rite. [128] However, other scholars have denied that this custom was widespread in Israel. [129]

Like Jeremiah and Zephaniah, other prophets censured the Baal cult without always having to use the name of Baal explicitly. Ezekiel condemns Jerusalem's infidelity in harsh words (cf. Ezk. 16; 23; etc.), but he does not mention Baal a single time by name, not even when he speaks of Jerusalem's idolatry (he does refer to Tammuz in Ezk. 8:14). After the exile, "the names of the Baals were removed from Israel's mouth" (Hos. 2:19[17]). But it is questionable whether the Baal cult entirely vanished, especially if "the abomination that makes des-

---

[126] On this, cf. also G. W. Ahlström, *Aspects of Syncretism in Israelite Religion* (Lund, 1963).

[127] In addition cf., e.g., Wolff, *BK,* XIV/1, 13ff., 107ff.

[128] Rost, *Festschrift A. Bertholet* (1950), 451ff.

[129] Rudolph, *ZAW,* 75 (1963), 65ff.

olate" of Dnl. 9:27; 11:31; and 12:11 is interpreted to mean that a cult object was erected for Baal-shamem in the Jerusalem temple. [130]

3. *Overall Picture.* If we now consider the overall picture that can be drawn from direct statements concerning the god Baal as presented in the OT, first of all it is clear that the OT never speaks of a pantheon of Baal. The goddesses → אשרה *ᵃsherāh,* "Asherah" (Jgs. 3:7; 1 K. 18:19; cf. 1 K. 16:33; 2 K. 23:4) and → עשתרות *ʿashtārôth,* "Ashtaroth" (Jgs. 2:13; 10:6; 1 S. 7:3f.; 12:10) probably are intimately associated with this god, [131] although some scholars believe that *habbeʿalim vehaʿashtaroth,* "the Baals and the Ashtaroth," together mean simply "gods and goddesses," like Akk. *ilāni u ištarāti.* [132]

Once child sacrifice is attributed to Baal rather than to Molech (Jer. 19:5). [133] As far as the Baal cult is concerned, we are told that altars (in Ophrah, Jgs. 6:25ff.; on Carmel, 1 K. 18:26; in Samaria, 16:32; in Jerusalem, 2 K. 11:18) and temples (in Shechem, Jgs. 9:4; in Samaria, 1 K. 16:32; in Jerusalem, 2 K. 11:18) were built to him. Sometimes the cult place was fortified (Jgs. 6:26), or was built on a → במה *bāmāh,* "high place" (Jer. 19:5; 32:35; cf. Nu. 22:41; Josh. 13:17). Sometimes incense is offered to Baal on rooftops (Jer. 32:29). [134] Certain geographical names indicate that the Baal cult was practiced near or on mountains.

According to the OT, Baal had many worshippers as early as the period of the judges (Jgs. 6:25ff.; 8:33; 9:4; etc.), but he also had many worshippers later, as the statement that only 7000 people had not bowed the knee to Baal (1 K. 19:18) impressively emphasizes. The personnel of the Baal cult consisted of priests (2 K. 10:19; 11:18; cf. *hakkemarim* in Zeph. 1:4) and/or prophets (1 K. 18:19ff.; 2 K. 10:19), who sacrificed, performed cultic dances, [135] became ecstatic, [136] and "prophesied" (Jer. 2:8; 23:13). Finally, the king could sacrifice to Baal (2 K. 10:25).

In addition to altars, the Baal cult also had → מצבות *matstsēbhôth,* "pillars" (2 K. 3:2; 10:26f.), and images (11:18; Hos. 11:2; 13:2; cf. the golden calves mentioned in Ex. 32:1ff.; 1 K. 12:28ff.; the bull was a symbol of Baal). [137] An *ᵃsherah* stood beside the altar (Jgs. 6:25; cf. 1 K. 16:32f.; 2 K. 17:16; 2 Ch. 33:3). → חמנים *chammānîm,* "incense altars," could stand on the altar (2 Ch. 34:4). Scholars frequently identify these with small, slender limestone altars which have been found several times in excavations, and understand them as decorative altars placed at the corners of a great altar of burnt-offering. [138]

---

130 So Eissfeldt, *ZAW,* 57 (1939), 24.
131 See above, II.2.
132 Caquot, *Syr,* 35 (1958), 57.
133 See above, II.4, and Mulder, *Baʿal,* 75ff.
134 See above, II.4.
135 Cf. Baal Markod, *RAC,* I, 1077f.
136 Cf. the Mari prophets and the Wen-Amon narrative, *ANET,* 25ff.
137 See above, II.1, and also Noth, *BK,* IX/1, 283ff.
138 Galling, *RGG³,* I, 254; and with caution, Haran, *VT,* 10 (1960), 118ff.

The OT uses different words to denote cultic actions: → עבד 'ābhadh, "to serve" (Jgs. 2:11,13; 3:7; 1 K. 16:31; 22:54[53]; etc.); → השתחוה hishtach*vāh, "to bow down" (1 K. 16:31; 22:54[53]); → כרע kāra', "to bow the knee," and/or → נשק nāshaq, "to kiss" (an image or a matstsebhah, "pillar"; 1 K. 19:18; Hos. 13:2).

The verb → זנה zānāh, "to play the harlot," occurs frequently in the immediate context of descriptions of the Baal cult (Jgs. 8:33, and esp. in Hosea: 1:2; 2:7[5]; 3:3; 4:10ff.; 5:3; 9:1; cf. zenunim, "harlotry," 1:2; 2:6[4]; 4:12; 5:4; and zenuth, "harlotry," 4:11; 6:10). It is possible that this refers to sacral prostitution. [139] The OT presents no evidence that there was also a "holy marriage" among the Canaanites which was acted out cultically. [140] Sometimes incense was offered to Baal (2 K. 23:5; 2 Ch. 28:4; Jer. 7:9; 11:13,17; cf. Hos. 2:15[13]; 11:2; on roofs, Jer. 32:29), people inquired of him by means of the oracle (2 K. 1:2ff.), and swore by him (Zeph. 1:4), an action that could have the character of a confession of faith (Jer. 12:16). The OT mentions solemn processions for Baal (Hos. 2:15[13]; cf. Dt. 4:3; Jer. 2:23; 9:13[14]: halakh → אחרי 'ach*rê habbe'alim, "to follow [lit. go after] the Baals"). Canaanites and also Israelites called on the name of Baal (1 K. 18:24ff.; Hos. 2:19[17]). They offered bloody and non-bloody sacrifices (1 K. 18:23; 2 K. 10:24; Hos. 11:2; and 2 K. 23:5; Jer. 7:9; 11:13,17), bulls (Jgs. 6:25; 1 K. 18:23ff.), but also children (Jer. 19:5) to him. They ate sacrificial meals which were designed to bring about an intimate relationship between Baal and his followers (Nu. 25:3ff.; Ps. 106:28; Hos. 9:10). Festival assemblies are mentioned in Jgs. 9:27 and 2 K. 10:19f. [141] Possibly a special kind of garment (2 K. 10:22) or other valuables (Hos. 2:10,15[8,13]) were worn in the cult.

According to the OT, Baal is primarily a fertility-god, as, e.g., 1 K. 18 and Hos. 2 indicate. The greatest gift Baal can give is rain, [142] as well as everything that is necessary for life (Hos. 2). The OT knows that the mountain tops are the dwelling place of this deity, [143] and also that Baal is a god of heaven, since it frequently mentions him in connection with the host of heaven, the sun, the moon, and the symbols of the zodiac (2 K. 17:16; 21:3; 23:4f.; cf. Jer. 32:29). It is doubtful whether this justifies the view that he should be identified with Baal-shamem. [144] Perhaps it may be concluded from the scene of the divine judgment on Carmel that Baal's adherents on this occasion believed that he disappeared in the summer and they expected him to return in the autumn [145] (1 K. 18:27; [146] cf. also Hos. 6:1ff.). [147]

---

[139] See above, III.2.
[140] See above, II.4.
[141] For festivals in Ugarit, see above, II.4.
[142] On 1 K. 18, cf. De Moor, AOAT, 16, 95.
[143] See above.
[144] Eissfeldt.
[145] See above, II.1 and 3.
[146] Colpe, AOAT, 1, 23ff.
[147] On this passage, cf. Wolff, BK, XIV/1, 150.

4. *Indirect Statements*. These direct statements about the Baal cult are supported by indirect statements concerning it: the latter show just how great the impact of the Canaanite religion was on Israel. This applies not only to Israel's literary and ideological borrowing from Canaanite culture, which was far superior to the nomadic standards of the wandering Israelites, but also to the many not unimportant theological concepts of the Israelite community. Among the literary borrowings we can mention, e.g., those texts in which Yahweh was praised with epithets similar to those which were applied to Baal in the Canaanite epics. [148] Like Baal in the Ugaritic texts, Yahweh rides upon the clouds (*rkb ʿrpt;* cf. Ps. 68:5[4]; and also 104:3; Dt. 33:26), and makes himself known in the tempest and the storm (Ps. 29; 18:14[12]; 46:7[6]; 77:19[18]; 97:4; 104:7; etc.). If this literal agreement in the wording proves clearly that Israel applied Baal's character to Yahweh, the case for this becomes even stronger when Israel adopts complete mythological ideas from Baalism: just as Baal fights against the *ltn*, the *btn brḥ*, *btn ʿqltn*, and *tnn,* [149] Yahweh fights against Leviathan (→ לִוְיָתָן *livyathan*), the *nachash bariach*, "the fleeing serpent," *nachash ʿaqallathon*, "the twisting serpent," and *hattannin*, "the dragon," in Isa. 27:1 (cf. Ps. 74:14; 104:26; and also Job 3:8; 40:25[41:1]). It is quite possible that to some extent psalms like Pss. 29 and 68 are songs originally written for Baal and later transferred to Yahweh. The examples can be multiplied easily.

There are other examples of Israel borrowing Canaanite ideology and theology. Thus, Israel inherited at least the form of Yahweh's kingdom from the Canaanites, [150] no matter how much the content of this concept was unique in Israelite religion.

The extent to which these lines of thought should be followed in detail must remain undecided here. Frequently it is impossible to say precisely whether certain elements are to be traced back to Baal, El, or some other deity. In general it may be said that Yahweh took over many characteristics of El, but strongly resisted an integration of Baal into Yahweh's domain, in spite of several individual elements that Yahweh borrowed from Baal. [151] Certain elements stood in the way of achieving an identification of Baal and Yahweh, e.g., the yearly dying and rising of Baal.

5. *Theological and Religious Significance*. It is clear from what has been said that the theological significance of the Canaanite storm- and fertility-god, his cult and his mythology, for Yahwism must have been unusually great. Behind the local differentiations in his name and character, he was the Canaanite god par excellence, with whom the nomadic tribes of Israel who confessed Yahweh came into contact from their emigration from Egypt till after the exile (cf., e.g., Zec. 12:11). In Palestine, a nomadic culture from the wilderness came into conflict with a rural culture which had already been settled for a long time in the land. Without intending to idealize the wilderness period for Israel, the prophets

---

[148] See above, II.1; and also Gray, Hillmann, Kaiser, and Schmidt.
[149] See above, II.1.
[150] Schmidt; cf. also Maag, *SVT*, 7 (1960), 129ff.; *NedThT*, 21 (1966), 176f.
[151] Cf. Maag, *NedThT*, 21, 180ff.

frequently saw clearly the difference between a religion of the wilderness and a religion in a civilized land (cf., e.g., Hos. 2:16f.[14f.]; Ezk. 20:10ff.; Jer. 35), which was related to the conflict between Yahweh and Baal. [152] However, the important differences between the worshippers of Yahweh who immigrated from the wilderness and the settled agricultural worshippers of Baal could not prevent Israel from borrowing from the very first both secular and religious customs and practices, which were assimilated rather quickly from the settled population in Canaan. [153] This led to a struggle between Yahweh and Baal, in which Israel began to view elements of the Baal religion polemically. Baal's ability to be assimilated or to appear under different names could lead to the idea of a Baal polytheism. Later OT writers did not fail to take advantage of this idea by speaking contemptuously of *habbe'alim,* "the Baals," false deities or idols, in order to emphasize the unity of Yahweh by way of contrast. The word *ba'al* itself, which formerly could also be applied to Yahweh (*be'alyah,* "Bealiah," 1 Ch. 12:6[5]), [154] came to have such an evil sound that at a later period it was not only avoided, but was even replaced by other words. [155] Hos. 2:18f.(16f.) indicates that this epithet ("Baal") evidently was preferred in the Baalized Yahweh cult.

Since the Baal cult was synchronized with the cyclical events of nature, which had great significance for the agricultural population of Canaan, its fertility rites (sacral prostitution) appeared obscene to the worshippers of Yahweh and their myths deifications of nature. Therefore, these religious customs of the Baal religion were condemned by the prophets, and the worshippers of Yahweh were forbidden to take part in any aspect of this religion. Elijah and his colleagues found it easy to ridicule Baal and his worshippers, because they saw the one distinction between Baal and Yahweh that affected everything else: according to the Israelite view, Yahweh was the only sovereign over the whole cosmos, which was his special creation; but even according to Baal's own worshippers, Baal was lord only over a part of the cosmos, which he merely preserved. To be sure, at Ugarit Baal was called the "Almighty," and "the king above which no other can stand"; [156] but the worshippers of Baal themselves considered this to be a pious exaggeration. According to the theology of Ugarit, the Great King El stood above his vassal Baal; [157] and Baal was humiliated and defeated by other gods, like Yam and Môt, precisely because they had more power over the other spheres of creation than he did. The Canaanites could explain the change from one season to another and differences between good and bad years only by believing that sometimes Baal was weak, sick, or even dead. This was a basic assumption of their religion. But such ideas were foreign to monotheistic Yahwism.

Mulder

---

[152] Cf. the description of the nomadic pole and its historical understanding with that of the sedentary Canaanite pole and its naturistic understanding in Maag, *NedThT,* 21, 165ff.

[153] Cf. the Feast of Tabernacles, above, II.4.

[154] See Noth, *IPN,* 121.

[155] See above, III.1.

[156] See above, II.1.

[157] See *AOAT,* 16, 121.

בער b‘r; בַּעַר ba‘ar; בָּעִיר bā‘îr

Contents: I. The Roots. II. "To Burn." III. "To Exterminate." IV. "To Feed On, Graze." V. "To Be Stupid."

I. The Roots. The words that contain the consonants *b‘r* present a very confused picture with regard to both etymology and meaning. There are at least three different roots containing these consonants: (a) One means "to burn" (cf. the Jewish Aram., Christian Palestinian *b‘r*, "to burn," Ugar. *b‘r*, perhaps "to burn," [1] the Phoen. root meaning "to burn" [?] in the dubious example in *CIS*, I, 86, A 6, Moabite *mb‘r*, "altar," [2] and perhaps also Arab. *baḡara*, "to have an unquenchable thirst," and *waḡa/ira*, "to be hot, angry"). (b) Another means "to exterminate, feed on or graze" (also in Jewish Aram.; cf. Syr. *b‘r*, "to ascertain, attain," pael "to search thoroughly, gather, glean, destroy"). (c) Still another means "to be stupid," which is derived from *ba‘ir*, "beast, cattle" (cf. Arab. *ba‘ara*, "to drop dung," *ba‘ir*, "camel," Syr. *be‘îrā*, "camel," Old South Arab. *b‘r*, "beast," esp. "camel," Ethiop. *bě‘ěrā*, "beast, ox"). The Ugaritic examples are not clear. Driver records only the meaning "to burn," [3] Aistleitner gives only "to exterminate," but in the causative conjugations "to drive on, urge, incite," [4] while Gordon thinks *b‘r* has "several meanings": "to devastate" [5] (cf. Isa. 5:5), "to reject, disappoint," [6] "to lead, guide," [7] and "to drive away" (an enemy, RS 24.247). [8]

II. "To Burn." *b‘r* with the meaning "to burn" is found in some tradition complexes that are rather easy to define. Purely concrete examples are rare, but cf. Jgs. 15:14.

In the first place, *b‘r* appears in descriptions of theophanies. The bush in which Yahweh reveals himself to Moses burns (*b‘r*), but is not consumed (again *b‘r*) by the fire (Ex. 3:2f.). [9] In the Prologue of Deuteronomy three times it is

---

b‘r. D. N. Freedman, "The Burning Bush," *Bibl*, 50 (1969), 245f.; J. L'Hour, "Une législation criminelle dans le Deutéronome," *Bibl*, 44 (1963), 1-28; R. P. Merendino, *Das deuteronomische Gesetz. BBB*, 31 (1969).

[1] But see below.
[2] W. L. Reed–F. V. Winnett, *BASOR*, 172 (1963), 1-9.
[3] Driver, *CML*, 163.
[4] Aistleitner, *WUS*, No. 559.
[5] *UT*, 2114, 9.
[6] *UT*, 2065, 21.
[7] *CTA*, 14 [I K], 101, 190; *UT*, 1002, 52; does the twofold meaning "to lead" and "to shine" occur in *CTA*, 4 [II AB], IV, 16?
[8] See *UT*, Glossary, No. 495.
[9] On this, cf. Freedman.

stated that Mt. Horeb "burned with fire" (bo‘er ba’esh) in connection with the revelation of Yahweh (Dt. 4:11; 5:23; 9:15). Also, in Ps. 18 Yahweh appears in smoke and fire and "with burning (RSV glowing) coals" (gechalim ba‘aru, v. 9 [Eng. v. 8]; cf. ba‘aru gachale ’esh, "coals of fire burned [RSV flamed forth]," 2 S. 22:13; Ps. 18 otherwise, → ג‎ּ‎ח‎ל‎ ghl).

Secondly, b‘r frequently appears in connection with the wrath of God, in Isa. 30:27 in a description that is like a theophany: "the name of Yahweh comes from far, burning with his anger" (bo‘er ’appo; → א‎ַ‎ף‎ ’aph). The same section also says that "the breath (neshamah) of Yahweh is like a stream of brimstone, which sets his fireplace (→ ת‎ּ‎פ‎ת‎ tōpheth) on fire" (bo‘arah bah, Isa. 30:33). Thus, this passage emphasizes the burning power of the divine wrath. b‘r also occurs in connection with wrath in Isa. 42:25; Jer. 4:4 (chemah, "wrath"); 7:20 (’aph vechemah, "anger and wrath"); 21:12 (chemah, "wrath"); 44:6 (chemah ve’aph, "wrath and anger"); Ps. 2:12 (’aph, "anger"); 89:47 (46) (chemah, "wrath"); and Est. 1:12. Several of these passages emphasize that no one can quench this burning (Jer. 4:4; 7:20; 21:12). → ק‎ִ‎נ‎ְ‎א‎ה‎ qin’āh, "jealousy," can also be used as the subject of this verb (Ps. 79:5). Similarly, the day (→ י‎ו‎ם‎ yôm) of Yahweh is "burning" (Mal. 3:19 [4:1]).

Thirdly, b‘r is used with "fire," which is depicted as God's instrument to punish the wicked. The anger of Yahweh was kindled (charah) against the murmuring people in the wilderness, "and the fire of Yahweh burned (ba‘ar) among them, and consumed some outlying parts of the camp" (Nu. 11:1); so the name of that place was called Taberah (tabh‘erah) (this explanation is probably secondary, and is possibly a derivation from b‘r, "to remove, consume," or ba‘r, "dung"). This section is quite similar to descriptions of theophanies. Elsewhere, too, b‘r appears in connection with Yahweh's judgment by fire, e.g., in Isa. 1:31: the strong and his work shall burn together, with none to quench them; Isa. 9:17(18): wickedness (rish‘ah) burns like a fire, and consumes every herb (figure for destruction); Isa. 10:17: the Holy One of Israel will become a flame, which will burn and devour his thorns and briers; Ps. 106:18, referring to the fire that destroyed Dathan and Abiram.

As an expression of an intense emotion, b‘r is used not only with anger, but also with sorrow and agony. Thus the author of Ps. 39:4(3) says, "my heart became hot (cham) within me; as I mused the fire burned (b‘r)," to express his emotional grief. [10] And Jeremiah confesses that when he wanted to be silent and not to proclaim the word of God, a fire was kindled in his heart which he could not suppress (Jer. 20:9).

Usually the piel form of b‘r has a more literal meaning: Ex. 35:3 (the Israelites are not to kindle a fire on the sabbath day); Lev. 6:5(12) (the priest is to keep a fire burning on the altar, cf. Neh. 10:35[34]; Isa. 40:16); Jer. 7:18 (the Jews kindle sacrificial fire to the queen of heaven); Isa. 44:15 (wood serves as kindling); Ezk. 39:9 (the Israelites are to burn the weapons of their enemies). The pual forms also have a more literal meaning, as in the reference to the fire

---

[10] Cf. Berger, UF, 2 (1970), 8.

burning in the brazier in Jer. 36:22 (cf. 2 Ch. 4:20; 13:11, which refer to lamps burning). Sometimes this form is also used of the fire of divine punishment (Ezk. 21:4[20:48]; cf. Isa. 50:11). The hiphil form of *b‘r* also usually has a literal meaning: Ex. 22:5(6) (he who has kindled a fire in the field shall make full restitution); Jgs. 15:5 (Samson sets fire to the torches and burns up the grain-fields of the Philistines); Ezk. 5:2 (Ezekiel is to burn a third part of his hair which he had cut off); and 2 Ch. 28:3 (Ahaz burns his children in the fire; → מלך *melekh*). The only passage in the OT where the hiphil is used of the fire of divine punishment is Nah. 2:14(13).

III. "To Exterminate." Perhaps the passage in which *b‘r* most clearly means "to exterminate" is 1 K. 14:10, where the prophet Ahijah announces Yahweh's judgment against Jeroboam I in this way: "I will bring evil (*ra‘ah*) upon the house of Jeroboam, and will cut off (*karath* in the hiphil) from Jeroboam every male, both great and small (RSV, both bond and free in Israel), and will utterly consume (*b‘r*) the house of Jeroboam, as a man burns up dung until it is all gone." Elijah proclaims a shorter variation of this against Ahab in 1 K. 21:21 (cf. also 1 K. 16:3, which uses the hiphil of *b‘r*). In 1 K. 21:21, again *ra‘ah*, "evil," and *karath*, "to cut off," are used in parallelism with *b‘r*. *b‘r* has a similar meaning in 2 S. 4:11: David will "exterminate from the land" (RSV, destroy from the earth) the men who killed Ish-bosheth. Here we may also mention the use of *b‘r* in 1 K. 22:47(46) (with the coll. obj. *qadhesh*, "male cult prostitutes"); 2 K. 23:24 (with the objs. "mediums and wizards"); 2 Ch. 19:3 (with the obj. "the Asherahs"); Dt. 26:13f. (with the obj. "the tithe" as a holy gift); and perhaps also Isa. 4:4 (*ruach ba‘er* exterminates uncleanness and murder; this Heb. phrase can hardly mean "the spirit of burning"); [11] and Nu. 24:22 (Kain falls to *ba‘er*, and is taken into captivity).

A group of casuistic laws in Deuteronomy is of very special interest. In these laws the punishment is positively characterized by the words, "you shall exterminate (RSV purge) the evil from your midst." [12] The oldest sections in this group (Dt. 19:11-13; 21:18-21; 22:22; and 24:7) deal with the crimes of murder, stubbornness of a son, adultery, and kidnapping, and have a counterpart in the *moth yumath* ("shall be put to death") series in Ex. 21:12-17. [13] The precept in Dt. 22:22 has been expanded by additional precepts for specific cases (vv. 13-21, 23f.; the *bi‘arta* formula is missing in vv. 25-27). In addition to these, we also find this phrase in Dt. 19:16-19 in connection with a false witness; and in 21:1-9 this formula is used of an unknown murderer, but like 19:11-13 the object of *b‘r* is not "the evil," but "innocent blood." In 17:8-13 this expression is used in connection with disregard for a priestly decision in a difficult case; here the precept is understood in a very general way and is hardly old. Finally, this formula is used in some laws concerning idolatry: Dt. 13:2-6(1-5), (7-12[6-11]) (13-17[12-16], without the formula); and 17:2-7. The basic idea is clearly the

---

[11] See Wildberger, *BK*, X, 151, 159.
[12] L'Hour.
[13] Merendino, 336.

purification of the tribal or national community: the evildoer must be rejected. Of course, this idea is still completely relevant in regulations concerning idolatry.

This expression is probably based on an ancient formula for excommunication, which von Rad compares with the use of *karath*, "to cut off," in H and P ("that man shall be cut off from among his people," Lev. 17:4,9,14; 18:29; 19:8; 20:17; 22:3; 23:29 [H]; Nu. 9:13; 15:30,31; 19:13,20; Lev. 7:20,21,25,27 [P]). [14] But it should be observed that the *karath* formula expresses the punishment itself, whereas the *ba'ar* formula (in the texts presently under discussion) comes after the announcement of punishment. *karath* is used to express the idea of excommunication, while *ba'ar* is used to express the idea of purifying the community. The same thought is found in Jgs. 20:13 (the evildoers in Gibeah are to be put to death and thus the evil will be exterminated), and in the examples mentioned above in 1 K. 22:47(46); 2 K. 23:24; and 2 Ch. 19:3.

IV. "To Feed On, Graze." *b'r* quite explicitly means "to feed on, graze" in the law in Ex. 22:4(5): when a man causes a field or vineyard to be grazed over (*b'r* in the hiphil), or lets his beast (*ba'ir*) loose, and it feeds (*b'r* in the piel) in another man's field, he shall make restitution. *b'r* seems to have a similar meaning in three passages in Isaiah where many exegetes have interpreted it to mean "burn down" [15] or "destroy." [16] In Isa. 3:14 and 5:5, the object of *b'r* is clearly Israel represented as a vineyard, and thus only the meaning "graze, feed on," fits. Isa. 6:13 has to do with the destruction of Israel represented under the figure of a fallen tree; here also "graze, feed on," fits better than "burn down."

V. "To Be Stupid." *ba'ir* means "beast, cattle," and is quite concrete and commonplace (Gen. 45:17; Ex. 22:4[5]; Nu.20:4,8,11; Ps. 78:48). The verb *b'r* in the sense of "stupid" is related to this noun. It occurs five times in Wisdom contexts. An *'ish ba'ar* (RSV "dull man") knows (*yadha'*) nothing, a stupid man (*kesil*) understands (→ בין *bîn*) nothing (Ps. 92:7 [6]). He who hates reproof (*tokhachath*) is *ba'ar*, "stupid"; he who loves *musar*, "discipline," loves *da'ath*, "knowledge" (Prov.12:1). Like the wise, the fool (*kesil*) and the stupid (*ba'ar*) must die and perish (Ps. 49:11[10]). In these passages, *ba'ar* is certainly part of the vocabulary of Wisdom as a word meaning "the unwise." Two passages affirm that the *ba'ar*, "stupid fellow," does not have *human* intelligence, viz., Prov. 30:2, "I am *ba'ar me'ish*, too stupid to be a man, and I do not have *binath 'adham*, the understanding of a man"; and Ps. 73:22, "I am *ba'ar*, stupid, without knowledge (*lo' 'edha'*), I have become a beast (*behemoth*) toward thee." Thus, such a person is like a stupid animal.

Several times the verb *b'r* means "to be stupid" (3 times in the qal, and 4 times in the niphal). In Jer. 10:8, the worship of idols is described as foolish (*ksl*) and stupid (*b'r*). In Ps. 94:8, the stupid (*b'r*, RSV "dull") and the foolish (*kesil*) are invited to gain insight and understanding–this is addressed to those people who

---

[14] Von Rad, *OT Theol,* I (trans. 1962), 264, n. 182.
[15] *KBL.*
[16] *GesB.*

are not willing to acknowledge the omniscience of Yahweh. In Jer. 10:14 (=51:17), the worshippers of idols are described as stupid creatures (*nibhʿar*) without knowledge (*middaʿath*). Jer. 10:21 speaks of stupid (*nibhʿar*) shepherds, i.e., leaders of the people who have not inquired of (→ דרש *dārash*) Yahweh. Isa. 19:11 says that the Egyptians are foolish (→ אויל *ʾevîl*), and their counselors give stupid (*nibhʿar*) counsel. Finally, Ezk. 21:36(31) states that in his wrath Yahweh will deliver the Ammonites to *ʾanashim boʿarim*, i.e., to barbaric and savage men (cf. the LXX *andrōn barbárōn*).

Ringgren

בצע *bṣʿ*; בֶּצַע *betsaʿ*

Contents: I. 1. Etymology; 2. Occurrences; 3. Meaning. II. To Be Cut Off=To Die. III. The Theological Criticism of Profitmaking.

I. 1. *Etymology*. The root *bṣʿ* does not appear in Akkadian. The reference to such a root in *GesB*, which is traced back to P. Haupt, is due to a wrong reading. *bṣʿ* is found in Arabic as *baḍaʿa*, "to cut (e.g., meat in pieces), hew in pieces, cut up, dismember, dissect." The verb *bḍʿ* occurs in Old South Arabic with the limited meaning "to cut off (the head or the lifecord)=to behead, kill."[1] The noun *bḍʿ*, "division, divided piece of land=region, territory,"[2] lies within the scope of the meaning of this verb. The place name *bḍʿtm* seems to correspond to the modern Baḍʿa,[3] and, like the prep. *bbḍʿ*, "near,"[4] and "according to,"[5] presumably belongs to the root *bḍʿ*. Ethiop. *bäḍʿa* (with the variant *bäṣʿa*), meaning "to decide, evaluate," and then specifically "to set something aside for God=to consecrate," is derived from the original meaning "to cut, cut off." This root should also be compared with the Tigré *bäṣʿa*, "to make a promise,"[6] and (in close relationship to the root) *bĕṣʿat*, "(leather) cloth," while Leslau's note[7] that the Amharic *bäṭṭa*, Geʿez *bäṭḥa*, "make an incision," is "related to Hebrew *bṣʿ*,"[8] seems rather doubtful.

The dispute over whether the verb *bṣʿ* is found in Ugaritic can be regarded as resolved in light of the publication of the uncertain text *CTA*, 5, I, 20f. To be sure, C. Virolleaud, H. Bauer, T. H. Gaster, H. L. Ginsberg, G. R. Driver, A.

---

[1] E.g., *CIH*, 353, 13; 397, 11; 407, 25; *RES*, 3943, 2; and Ja 586, 22; 631, 31; 649, 11,18, 35,37; 665, 35.

[2] E.g., *RES*, 3945, 6; 3607, 2; Ja 555, 3.

[3] Cf. H. von Wissmann, *SBAW*, 246 (1964), 351.

[4] Gl 1693, 11.

[5] Gl 1150, 4.

[6] Littmann-Höfner, *Wörterbuch der Tigrē-Sprache* (1962), 301.

[7] Leslau, *Hebrew Cognates in Amharic* (Wiesbaden, 1959), 35.

[8] So already Dillmann, *Lexicon Linguae Aethiopicae* (1865), 544.

Jirku, J. Aistleitner, and W. F. Albright read *hm šbʿ ydt ybṣʿ* in lines 20/21, and then arrive at the translation, "behold, seven pieces are apportioned," or the like. However, the photograph of this tablet [9] and its transcription [10] reveal that there is a space between *ydty* and *bṣʿ*, which may have contained a word divider, but which in any case clearly establishes the word division. Therefore, as C. H. Gordon suggested first in his *Ugaritic Manual* (1955), this text must be read, *hm šbʿ ydty bṣʿ*, and translated, "behold, my seven pieces (I will eat) out of the dish." Thus, in spite of Aistleitner's claim, [11] the root *bṣʿ* is not found in Ugaritic. Also, the Egyp. root *wdʿ*, "to divide, separate," and then: "to separate parties to a dispute = to judge," is certainly cognate with the Semitic root *bdʿ*. [12] On the other hand, the supposed connection between this root and a Chado-Hamitic root written *ʾbvsʌ, and meaning "to break in pieces," [13] is doubtful. Cushite cognates are also uncertain.

No conclusion can be drawn concerning the specific meaning of the verb in Nabatean from the two occurrences of *bṣʿ* in Nabatean in the Papyrus Fragments A 5 and B 7. [14] In A 5 the reading is not entirely certain. Starcky thinks the meaning is, "to quarrel (about the price)" or "to divide (the contested amount)." [15] In B 7, the poor condition of the fragment makes it impossible to determine the context in which the verb stands. In line 6 of the Neo-Punic inscription in *KAI*, 119 from Leptis Magna, we find the phrase *wbṣʿm nʿmm*, which perhaps means "cheerful contributions," and a little later *nbṣʿ* or *mbṣʿ*, which possibly means "giving a contribution." The inscription is destroyed at the end of the line, and so it is impossible to reconstruct the complete continuity of thought with certainty. [16] With proper caution, it may be argued that the root *bṣʿ* occurs in Neo-Punic, and that its meaning has evolved from "cut off, make a profit," to "give a contribution," and thus *bṣʿ* is understood throughout in a positive sense.

2. *Occurrences.* Altogether, the Heb. root *bṣʿ* occurs 39 times in the OT. The noun form *betsaʿ* occurs in the majority of cases, while the verb appears in the qal only ten times and in the piel only six. If one considers the distribution of these occurrences in the biblical books, one will discover that a good two-thirds are found in the prophetic literature.

3. *Meaning.* The original meaning of the verb is "to cut off," and presumably it was used at an early period as a technical term in the manufacture of carpets [17] with reference to the weaver "cutting off" a ready-woven piece of material from the thrum. It is not difficult to see how this gave rise to the figurative meaning "to cut off the lifecord" on the one hand, and "to cut off a piece, i.e., to take

---

[9] *CTA*, Plate XI.
[10] *CTA*, Fig. 18.
[11] Aistleitner, *WUS*, No. 562.
[12] Cf. W. W. Müller, *Mus*, 74 (1961), 201; and W. A. Ward, *ZÄS*, 95 (1969), 65f.
[13] Cf. *Jazyki Afríki* (Moscow, 1966), 28.
[14] Cf. J. Starcky, *RB*, 61 (1954), 161-181.
[15] *Ibid.*, 170.
[16] On the possible reconstructions of this sentence, cf. *KAI*, II, 125f.
[17] Dalman, *AuS*, V, 123f.

one's cut, profit," on the other. The meaning of the noun is limited almost entirely to this latter idea. In almost all the passages in the OT where it occurs, *betsaʿ* means "a piece that is cut off, (illegal) profit or gain."

II. To Be Cut Off = To Die. The OT refers to death as a "being cut off," e.g., in Ps. 88:6 (Eng. v. 5), where the poet says that Yahweh remembers the dead no more because they are cut off from his hand (*nighzaru;* cf. also Isa. 53:8; Ezk. 37:11; Lam. 3:54), or in Job 21:21, where death is compared with the number of a person's months being cut off (*chutstsatsu*).

The most figurative passage in which *bṣʿ* (piel) appears with the meaning "to die" is Isa. 38:12. Begrich clarifies the meaning of this verb when he writes: "The life of the singer has been woven to the end. Yahweh has rolled it up, and does the last thing which the weaver has to do with a piece of woven cloth, i.e., he cuts the last thread." [18] This use of *bṣʿ* as a technical term of the weaving profession also occurs in Middle Hebrew, as Kutscher has shown. [19] Therefore, in the other passages where *bṣʿ*, "to cut off," appears with the meaning "to die," the figure of weaving can also be assumed, even if other figures like that of the cutting off of tent cords were considered.

Thus, in the oracles against foreign nations in Jer. 46–51, these words are addressed to Babylon in 51:13: "Your end has come, the ell of your being cut off" (*'ammath bitsʿekh;* the text is not to be contested!). In Job 6:9, Job expresses the wish "that God would let loose (*yatter*) his hand and cut me off (*vibhatstseʿeni*)"; and in a similar way, a gloss in Job 27:8 says that God cuts off a person's life (read *pi yebhatstsaʿ*), i.e., he puts an end to his life.

III. The Theological Criticism of Profitmaking. The story of Jacob's use of craftiness in order to gain abundant flocks (Gen. 30:25-43) shows that the OT is not fundamentally opposed to making profit and gaining riches and possessions as a result of striving to get gain. Sir. 42:5 emphasizes that there is no need for a merchant to be ashamed of his profit.

The noun *betsaʿ* originally had a neutral connotation. Of course, it is true that there are no passages in the OT that use *betsaʿ* in the sense of a positive striving for gain, but all the examples of *betsaʿ* that do not speak of gain in the material sense reveal that originally the root *bṣʿ* did not convey a negative idea exclusively. Thus, Judah asks his brothers: "What would we have (what profit, *mah betsaʿ*, would it be to us) if we slay our brother?" (Gen. 37:26), and the worshipper in Ps. 30:10(9) asks God, "What profit (*mah betsaʿ*) is my blood to thee?" Similarly, the use of *betsaʿ* in Job 22:3 and Mal. 3:14 shows that *betsaʿ*, "profitmaking," in and of itself is not illegal according to OT thought.

In the account of the new method for administering justice which Moses introduced upon the advice of his father-in-law in Ex. 18:13-27, the qualifications for the men who were to be chosen for this work are that they must fear

---

[18] J. Begrich, *Der Psalm des Hiskia* (1926), 31.
[19] E. Y. Kutscher, *Tarbiz,* 16 (1944/45), 45.

God, be trustworthy, and hate (unjust) gain (*soneʾe bhatsaʿ*, Ex. 18:21, E), which are considered to be indispensable virtues of a judge. The context makes it clear that here *betsaʿ* means unjust gain, and thus a bribe. The same meaning appears in 1 S. 8:3, where the sons of Samuel, Joel and Abijah, are described much like the sons of Eli, viz., they did not walk in the footsteps of their fathers, but went after their own gain (*vayyattu ʾachare habbatsaʿ*). The meaning of *betsaʿ* is explained in the parallel lines that follow: "they took bribes and perverted justice." Here, as in Ex. 18:21, the immoral practice of trying to aid justice by requiring baksheesh is described as wicked greed.

The late insertion in Isa. 33:15b contains the answer to the question, "On what conditions can one have a part in the kingdom of God?" This answer emphasizes even stronger that the godly not only despises the profit of oppression (*moʾes bebhetsaʿ maʿashaqqoth*), but even shakes his hands, lest they hold a bribe.

In the announcement of judgment in Isa. 56:9-12, the leaders of the people are condemned because they are interested only in their own profit; each one pursues his own (unjust) gain (*ʾish lebhitsʿo*, 56:11b). 57:17 must also be interpreted in this way if the traditional text is correct: God was angry with Israel because of the iniquity of their striving after unjust gain (*baʿavon bitsʿo*). [20] Jer. 6:13 (which is identical with 8:10) also condemns the greed of the entire people: "every one is greedy for (unjust) gain" (*kullo botseaʿ batsaʿ*), and the parallel stich explains: "every one deals falsely."

The oracle concerning King Jehoiakim in Jer. 22:13-19 describes the typical Oriental despot, who is concerned only with his own profit (*ʿal bitsʿekha*, v. 17), and thus does not hesitate to oppress, extort, or even murder under cover of the law.

Ezekiel also denounces greed. In Ezk. 22:12f., the sinful Israelites are reproved because they defraud their neighbors by force. Yahweh claps his hands together to call attention to the dishonest gain and murders that were taking place in the midst of the people. In 22:27, the officials are condemned because they get gain by bloodshed and murder. Finally, in 33:31 the exiles are reproved because of their greed. To be sure, the people come to the prophet and hear him, but they do not obey his words; their heart is set on lying and getting gain. "As the motive for getting gain, greed is regarded as protection from harm," [21] Hab. 2:9. "Like the bird who builds his nest as high as possible, thinking that in this way he can protect himself from all danger, so the world power intends to protect itself from danger, and thus from God and his punishment, by getting all 'gain'...." [22] In Ps. 119:36, the worshipper prays: "Incline my heart to thy testimonies, and not to gain!"

Finally, the Wisdom Literature warns that pursuit after gain destroys one's life, but promises that he who hates gain and bribes will have life (Prov. 1:19; 15:27; 28:16).

D. Kellermann

---

[20] Duhm reads, "the iniquity of his covetousness," but cf. Torrey, 436!

[21] Elliger, *ATD*, 45.

[22] *Ibid.*

בָּקָר bāqār

Contents: I. 1. Etymology and Semitic Dialects; 2. Occurrences in the OT; 3. Words for "Ox"; 4. Expressions Using *baqar;* 5. The LXX. II. 1. *baqar* As a Domestic and Gregarious Animal; 2. *baqar* As a Work Animal; 3. Meat and Sour Milk; 4. *baqar* in Commerce, Law, and Treaties; 5. *baqar* As Booty; 6. *baqar* in Figures for Peace. III. 1. *baqar* As a Sacrificial Animal; 2. Images and Representations of a *baqar*.

I. 1. *Etymology and Semitic Dialects.* The etymology of *baqar* cannot be determined precisely. It is unlikely that it is a derivative of *bqr* I piel, "to investigate, pay heed to."[1] *baqar* is found mainly in West Semitic dialects.

a. In a Mari letter,[2] it is reported: "The soldiers and the cattle (*buqāru*) are in good condition," i.e., the soldiers and their supply of meat are in good order. No other examples from Mari are known.[3]

b. There is no example of *buqāru* in Assyrian; but cf. *b/pug/qurru.*[4] *bugurra* appears in *KAR,* 154, verso 11 as a sacrifice, and in *SVAT,* 13, 34 verso 1 with the determinative UZU as sacrificial meat of an ox[5] or a sheep.[6] There is probably no relationship between *baqar* and Assyr. *bakkaru,* "young camel," "young ass," cf. Heb. *bekher.* The Akkadian word that corresponds to Heb. *baqar* is *lītu(m)* II, later *littu* I, "cow."[7]

c. In Northwest Semitic dialects, *bqr* does not appear in Ugaritic, Moabite, or Amurritic. Phoen. *bqr*[8] occurs in the Kilamuwa Inscription (825 B.C.)[9] along with sheep–flock of sheep, cattle (*'lp*)–herd of cattle (*bqr*), linen–byssus, as wealth and possessions. The reading of the example of Inscription II from

bāqār. F. S. Bodenheimer, *The Animals of Palestine* (Jerusalem, 1935); *idem, haḥai be'artsōth hammiqrā',* II, 355-362; Dalman, *AuS,* VI (1939), 168-178; Index, 380; K. Elliger, *HAT,* 4 (1966), Index; J. Feliks, *The Animal World of the Bible* (Tel Aviv, 1962); M.-L. Henry, *Das Tier im religiösen Bewusstsein des alttestamentlichen Menschen. SgV,* 220/221 (1958); H. Kraemer, *PW Supplement,* VII, cols. 1161, 1163, 1164, 1165, 1170; O. Michel, *TDNT,* IV, 760-62; W. Pangritz, *Das Tier in der Bibel* (1963); R. Pinney, *The Animals in the Bible* (Philadelphia, 1964).

1 Cf. M. Wagner, *Die lexikalischen und grammatikalischen Aramaismen im alttestamentlichen Hebräisch. BZAW,* 96 (1966), No. 45.
2 *ARM,* II, No. 131, 39.
3 *AHw,* 139a; *CAD,* II, 323, *buqāru;* but cf. *būlum, AHw,* 137, and *ṣēnum.*
4 *AHw,* 136: piece of meat; *CAD,* II, 307: an edible organ of a sacrificial animal.
5 Von Soden.
6 *CAD.*
7 *AHw,* 557f.
8 *DISO,* 41.
9 *KAI,* I, 24, 121; II, 30-34.

Larnax Lapethos [10] is disputed: some read *smdt bqr,* "a yoke of oxen," [11] while others read, *[k]tbt wsmrt bqr,* "[the tablet of bronze] which I ... wrote and fastened on the wall." Middle Hebrew has the words *bāqār,* "cattle," *baqrūt,* "cattle-shed, stable," and *baqqār,* "cowboy."

d. *bqr* and its derivatives are found in Western and Eastern Aramaic, and *baqara,* "herdsman," "herd of cattle," [12] and *baqra,* "herd," "paddock," [13] occur in Mandean.

e. In Southwest Semitic dialects, we may compare Arab. *baqar,* pl. *buqūr, abāqir,* "ox," "cow," *ubqūr,* "cow," "ox," and perhaps *baqqār,* "breeder of oxen." [14] In the Old South Arab. Inscriptions, *bqr* appears often among the spoils: children, cattle (*b'r*) (camels, oxen [*bqrm*], asses, small livestock). [15]

2. *Occurrences in the OT.* baqar occurs in the OT 183 times: Gen., 17 times; Ex., 9; Lev., 12; Nu., 50; Dt., 10; Jgs., 1; 1-2 S., 19; 1-2 K., 14; Isa., 5; Jer., 4; Ezk., 6; Hos., Joel, Am., Jonah, Hab., and Pss., 1 each; Job, 4; Eccl. and Neh., 1 each; and 1-2 Ch., 24. 61 examples come from the Priestly source, and 12 go back to J. The examples in Ezk. are related to P, while those in Am., Job, and Eccl. come from a Wisdom background. Only 8 certain examples are found in the Prophets.

3. *Words for "Cattle."* The following Hebrew words have essentially the same meaning as *baqar* (183 times): *behemah,* 188 times; *miqneh,* 76; *'eghel,* 35; *'eghlah,* 12; *par,* 131; and *shor,* 79. *baqar* is defined more precisely in the OT by *zakhar,* "male," 4 times, and once each by *tobh,* "good," and *neqebhah,* "female."

4. *Expressions Using baqar.* a. *tso'n ubhaqar,* "sheep and oxen (or cattle)," or "flocks and herds," appears as a stereotyped expression in the OT 32 times in the absolute, and 12 times in construct expressions or divided only by numerals or related terms. In lists of men and animals, groups of animals, or even groups of sacrifices, this expression occurs in the singular in contrast to the plural forms around it, and in construct forms (cf. 1 S. 15:9; Jer. 31:12; 2 Ch. 32:29; 1 S. 15:21; 30:20) it is treated as a syntactical unit. In the list in Ex. 10:9, which contains pairs of opposites, *tso'n,* "flocks," is set in contrast to *baqar,* "herds." Thus, the first redactor of P unites *kebhes,* "lamb," and *'ez,* "goat," under *tso'n* (Lev. 1:10), [16] and makes *tso'n* a separate species from *baqar.* The

---

[10] *RES,* 1211, line 13.
[11] Friedrich, *Phönizisch-punische Grammatik* (Rome, 1951), 21.
[12] *MdD,* 49.
[13] Lidzbarski, *Ginza,* 431.
[14] Cf. also *LidzEph,* II, 350.
[15] *RES,* 3945, 19=649, 40f. *bqr* is also used of a sacrificial tax or fee in *CIH,* 540, 43, 89; 541, 124, etc.
[16] Cf. Elliger, *HAT,* 4, *in loc.*

expression *tso'n ubhaqar* is found 13 times in Genesis, while the same phrase in reversed order, *baqar vetso'n,* "cattle (or oxen) and sheep" or "herds and flocks" (which appears a total of 25 times in the OT), is found only 8 times in P, but it occurs 7 times in Deuteronomy, [17] which is worthy of note. This phrase in reversed order appears above all in regulations concerning sacrifice (cf. also the 4 examples in Ch.), because the most valuable material is always mentioned first in lists of sacrifices.

b. The sequence *par[im] ben baqar,* "young bull," *'ayil,* "ram," *kebhes,* "lamb," is rigidly followed in Nu. 7:15-87 and in the sacrificial calendar in 28:11–29:17. The construct form *par ben baqar,* "young bull" (which occurs 30 times in the OT) appears exclusively in P and Ezekiel. In the phrase *ben baqar, ben* can be understood as a determinative [18] to convey the idea that what follows belongs to a certain species or class. [19]

c. In the expression *miqneh bhaqar* (RSV "flocks and herds," or "herds and flocks," Gen. 26:14; 47:17; Eccl. 2:7; 2 Ch. 32:29), *baqar* represents the uninterchangeable generic character, and *miqneh* assumes the collective function; the situation is different in Nu. 7:88.

5. *The LXX. baqar* is translated by the following words in the LXX: *boukólion,* "herd of cattle," 13 times; *boús,* "ox, cow," 101; *dámalis,* "heifer, young cow," 12; *ktênos,* "domesticated animal," and *moschárion,* "little calf," twice each; and *móschos,* "calf, young bull," 33.

II. 1. *baqar As a Domestic and Gregarious Animal.* Like all other cattle, *baqar* constitutes part of the possessions and wealth of the family and the tribe. The *baqar* appeared in Palestine first in the Late Stone Age, [20] and is like the lean Arabic ox, which produced only a small amount of milk and meat. This animal was driven in herds. It consists of three breeds, to which the humpback ox also belongs. *baqar* appears for the first time in the OT as a possession of Abraham and Lot.

baqar is depicted as a material possession along with other animals and with *'abhadhim,* "menservants" (Gen. 12:16; 13:5 with *'ohalim,* "tents"; 20:14; 32:8 [7]; Eccl. 2:7), with animals and *'abhuddah,* "servants" (Gen. 26:14; Job 1:3), and with silver and gold (Gen. 24:35; 13:5). For Sarah's sake, the pharaoh dealt well with (*hetibh*) Abraham, who was rich in herds, "sheep, oxen, he-asses, menservants, maidservants, she-asses, and camels" (Gen. 12:16; this is a literary addition of the Yahwist, whose intention is to prepare the reader for the consequence in Gen. 13). [21] Lot's wealth is designated by connecting "flocks and

---

17 See above.
18 Oberhuber, *VT,* 3 (1953), 2-45: on this point, p. 34.
19 *GK,* § 128v, paragraph 2.
20 Cf. Bodenheimer, *Animal Life,* 36f.; Thomsen, *Reallexikon,* XI, 142.
21 R. Kilian, *Die vorpriesterlichen Abrahams-Überlieferungen. BBB,* 24 (1966), 13.

herds" with *'ohel,* "tents," a combination that occurs only in Gen. 13:5 in the OT. Jacob returns to Palestine with herds giving suck (*baqar 'aloth,* 33:13). In ancient times, wealth was reckoned not in terms of money, arable land, or possession of houses, but in terms of cattle (cf. 12:16; 26:14; 30:43; 46:32; Dt. 3:19; 1 S. 25:2; Job 1:3). In lists of animals indicating a person's possessions, usually *tso'n,* "sheep," are mentioned first, and then *baqar,* "cattle." This provides another explanation for the reversal of these two terms in the priestly regulations, which were not concerned with the number of livestock a person had, but with the value of sacrificial animals. *tsemedh,* "a pair," was used as a standard term in computing the number of a person's livestock. The domestic servants which are necessary to work and to tend the animals are mentioned after the animals (Gen. 12:16; 26:14), because slaves are regarded not as legal individuals, but as legal objects and assets.

Gen. 24:35 (J) and Job 42:12 do not regard possessions and wealth as human achievements, but as blessings of Yahweh. Thus a list of possessions including *baqar* can also occur in an oracle of doom (Isa. 7:21), or one can confiscate another person's property (2 S. 12:2-4).

When Joseph expresses his desire that his family be near him (Gen. 45:10), he has in mind all the possessions of his family and household. Since the existence of his family is at stake, Joseph tells the pharaoh not only about his father and his brothers, but also about *tso'nam ubheqaram,* "their flocks and herds," and all that they possess (47:1). The existence and environment of a family and of an individual are affected when the cattle or the flocks are in danger. Thus, the pharaoh attempts to restrain the Israelites by making them leave their *tso'n ubhaqar,* "flocks and herds," behind while they go to serve Yahweh (Ex. 10:24); but Moses demands that he release them with all their possessions (12:32). According to Jonah 3:7, the king of Nineveh decrees an official repentance, in which the cattle are included, because they are part of the household and community of fate of the Ninevites, and therefore must participate in the process of fasting and repentance. In an oracle of doom in Jer. 5:14-17, the prophet speaks of the total destruction of the land, its inhabitants and its produce, including its flocks and herds (v. 17), because they are necessary to the continuation of life and of the household. In 3:24, a later glossator seems to have interpreted the "acquired property" (RSV, "all for which our fathers labored," *yeghia'*) as "their flocks and their herds, their sons and their daughters."

2. baqar As a Work Animal. In agriculture, the ox is the most important work animal. Elisha plowed with twelve yoke of oxen, which he abandoned when he met Elijah in order to follow him (1 K. 19:19,21). According to 1 S. 11:5, Saul was coming from the field behind the oxen (*baqar*). Job 1:14 tells of Job's servants plowing with oxen (*baqar choreshoth*).

Thus Dt. 21:3 explicitly states that only an ox (RSV "heifer") which has not been pulled in the yoke and which has never been worked can be offered as an atonement for murder and thus as a restoration to acceptance in the cult. The neck of the ox (heifer) was broken in this unique act of atonement. Thus, we are not dealing here with a sacrifice, but, in light of the way the animal was slaughtered and of the place where it was slaughtered, with a "magical process for removing a sin."[22]

The Ark Narrative preserves the tradition that oxen pulled the cart carrying the ark of the covenant, but the oxen put it in danger (*shamat*, RSV "stumbled"; cf. 1 Ch. 13:9). Therefore, *baqar*, "oxen," were not as suitable for pulling a cart as *paroth 'aloth*, "milch cows," which did not get off the road (cf. 1 S. 6:7, 10,12).

3. *Meat and Sour Milk*. However, the value of a cow depended not only on its ability to work, but also on its production of meat and milk. To the three travellers who came to his tent, Abraham served *ben baqar*, "a calf," meal, flat cakes, soft butter, and milk, to show his hospitality (Gen. 18:7). In this original narrative, the young calf is described as especially tender and good (*rakh vatobh*). *baqar* appears along with natural produce and meal as a part of the royal meal that was eaten when David was exalted by his mighty men as king over Israel in Hebron (1 Ch. 12:41[40]).

The significance of this sort of meal, which is composed of *baqar* in particular, is also shown in 1 K. 1:9: *baqar*, "oxen," together with *tso'n*, "sheep," and *meri'*, "fatlings," are used for a communal meal which Adonijah, as David's successor, must proclaim. At Solomon's court, the daily consumption of ten fat oxen (*baqar beri'im*) and twenty pasture-fed cattle (*baqar re'i*) was common (5:3[4:23]). However, we do not have more precise information about this. Probably these numbers simply indicate the huge size of Solomon's royal household.

In Joel 1:18, *baqar* is not part of the luxury of a rich royal household, but, like the grain of the granary and the seed of the field, a vital necessity for man. Therefore, the fact that the livestock are perplexed by the distress is a sign of the imminent day of judgment over Israel. In this text, → בהמה *behēmāh*, "beasts," is used in parallelism with the herds of *baqar*, and flocks of *tso'n*, "sheep," which are mentioned afterward. In this antithesis, again *baqar* can only mean the species "cow" or "ox," which was put in jeopardy especially because of the dryness of the pastures. When Moses complains to Yahweh because the Israelites do not have meat to eat in the wilderness (Nu. 11:22, J), he receives the promise of divine help which will "more than satisfy" their craving. Thus the narrative expresses the idea that a miracle of the "divine hand" will take place and even Moses himself will be astonished.

Dt. 14:4 explicitly allows the Israelites to eat beef, which indicates that a *baqar*, "ox, cow," can be slaughtered in a purely secular sense, and its meat can be used to provide nourishment. This is confirmed by similar examples in 1 K. 19:21 and in the accusation in Isa. 22:13. In addition to the meat, the *chem'ath baqar*, "curds from the herd" (Dt. 32:14), and the *shephoth baqar*, "cheese from the herd" (2 S. 17:29), were also eaten. The herds of Bashan (Dt. 32:14) were regarded as especially fat and fine domestic animals. Not only do OT writers know of cattle in the pastures (cf. Joel 1:18), but also of fattening cattle in stalls (cf. Hab. 3:17).

---

22 G. von Rad, *ATD*, VIII, 97.

4. *baqar in Commerce, Law, and Treaties.* The importance of cattle in commerce, law, and treaties is clear when Joseph exchanges bread for cattle in the time of the famine (Gen. 47:17). David in particular sets a royal official over the herds of cattle (*baqar*, 1 Ch. 27:29). David bought *baqar*, "oxen," from Araunah for silver (2 S. 24:24).

In harmony with this, a particularly high restitution is required for stealing an animal because of its high value, and, of course, also as a punishment for a deliberate violation of the law: five oxen for one ox (Ex. 21:37[22:1]).

Finally, *baqar*, "oxen," are also used in connection with making a covenant or a treaty, as, e.g., when Abraham made a covenant with Abimelech and gave him *tso'n ubhaqar*, "sheep and oxen" (Gen. 21:27; cf. also 15:8ff.). Saul symbolically cuts an ox (*baqar*) in pieces in order to bind the tribes to put forth a united effort (1 S. 11:7).

5. *baqar As Booty.* baqar is mentioned frequently in the OT as a part of the booty (→ בזז *bāzaz*) taken by a conquering army, and with two exceptions (Nu. 31:28 and Job 1:14) always follows *tso'n*, "sheep" (Nu. 31:33,38,44; 1 S. 14:32; Gen. 34:28; 1 S. 30:20). In such contexts, twice it appears in connection with *chamorim*, "asses" (Nu. 31:28; Gen. 34:28); once each with *ha'adham*, "persons" (Nu. 31:28), and *'athonoth*, "asses" (Job 1:14), and once with a collective idea, viz., *'eth 'asher ba'ir ... bassadheh*, "whatever was in the city and in the field" (Gen. 34:28). Here also *baqar* is to be understood as a species in contrast to *'adham*, "man," and *tso'n*, "sheep." The twofold appearance of *baqar* in 1 S. 14:32 is worthy of note. First of all, *baqar* is used in the general sense to refer to a species, and is not defined more precisely with regard to sex, age, or quality. Then the *bene bhaqar*, lit. "sons of cattle" (RSV "calves"), are mentioned, which are distinguished from the general species "cattle or oxen" by referring to age, "young cow or ox." *baqar* also occurs in the sense of the species "cattle or oxen" in connection with the ban or devoted thing (15:9,14,15,21; 27:9).

6. *baqar in Figures for Peace.* In Isa. 11:7, the restoration of peace between man and beast is illustrated by the figure of the peaceable coexistence of animals. The lion shall eat straw like the ox (cf. Isa. 65:25). The strained relationships between men and animals which presently exist will be overcome and the original situation in Paradise will be restored.

III. 1. *baqar As a Sacrificial Animal.* baqar plays a special role as a sacrificial animal in the laws concerning sacrifice. The condition and suitability of the sacrificial animals are important to priest and layman alike.

a. The expression *baqar tamim*, "ox (cow) without blemish," is used 16 times in the OT (always in the priestly regulations) to describe the quality essential to a sacrificial animal. The ideas included in this phrase are described in detail in Lev. 22:17-25: → תמים *tāmîm*, "complete, whole, entire," is a technical term in sacrificial language (1:3,10; 3:1,6,9; 4:3,23,28,32; etc.).[23] This "completeness, wholeness," is defined by the exclusion of six defects in the animal in 22:22 (cf. 21:18-20). Under these provisions, *baqar* is used as a sacrificial animal mainly in three types of sacrifices.

It is used in the burnt-offering (*'olah:* Lev. 1:3; 23:18; Nu. 15:3,8,24; 28:11, 19,27; 29:2,8,13; Dt. 12:6; Nu. 7:15,21,27,33,39,45,51,57,63,69,75,81,87; 2 S. 24:22; Ps. 66:15; 1 Ch. 21:23), in which the whole ox was burned.

It is used in sacrifices involving a communal meal (*zebhach,* "sacrifice," *zebhach shelamim,* "peace offering": Lev. 22:21; 3:1; Nu. 15:3,8; Dt. 12:6; 16:2; 1 S. 15:15; 16:2; 1 K. 8:63; 19:21; 2 Ch. 7:5; 15:11; Nu. 22:40; 1 K. 19:20; 2 Ch. 18:2), in which the animal was divided up between Yahweh, the priests, and those offering the sacrifice; cf. the sacrifice of oxen with a communal meal in Lev. 3:1-5, and the sacrifice of sheep with a communal meal in 3:6-11. Whereas the ox offered for a burnt-offering can only be a male (hence the addition of *zakhar,* "male," in 1:3; 22:19), the regulations pertaining to a sacrifice involving a communal meal also allow a female animal to be offered (*neqebhah,* "female," 3:1).

baqar lechatta'th is a sacrifice in the form of "an ox (RSV young bull) for a sin-offering" (Lev. 4:3,14; 9:2; Nu. 8:8; Lev. 16:3; Nu. 15:24; Ezk. 45:18), which in particular atones for sins (committed unwittingly) against the commandments (*mitsvah*) with a blood rite.

In P, *qorban,* "offering," includes the burnt-offering and the sacrifice involving a communal meal.[24] The *qorban baqar,* "offering from the herd," is sacrificed in particular to atone for the sins of the high priest and of the people. In the burnt-offering, the animal is chosen (*laqach,* lit. "taken") from the species *baqar* to be a *qorban,* and is brought to be slaughtered (*shachat*) before the door of the tent of meeting (Lev. 1:3).

b. A stereotyped series of sacrifices seems to have been developed corresponding to the sacrificial calendar (Nu. 28f.). In this series, *baqar,* as a valuable animal, is always mentioned in first place. The content of Nu. 28f. presupposes texts from the exilic and postexilic periods, and must be dated after 15:1-16. This collection of cultic and ritual regulations concerning the addition of cereal-offerings and drink-offerings (Nu. 15), with a parallel expression *'ishsheh layhvh 'olah 'o zebhach (shelamim),* "an offering by fire to Yahweh for a burnt-offering or for a sacrifice (or for a peace-offering)" (15:3,8), goes beyond Lev. 1-7, because it contains regulations not only for animal- and cereal-offerings, but also for drink-offerings. "The scale of values of the sacrificial animals rises from the (male) sheep, via the ram to the bull...."[25] But even in earlier lists of sacrifices, *baqar* is mentioned at the beginning (cf. Lev. 1:2, redactor). In a construct expression typical of the law of centralization of the cult, Dt. 12:6 speaks of *bekhoroth baqar,* "the firstlings of the herd." A comparison with the lists

---

23 Cf. Elliger, 299, n. 6.
24 Cf. *ibid.,* 34, n. 2.
25 Noth, *Numbers. OTL* (trans. 1968), 114.

of sacrifices used for the sin-offering (Lev. 4:3,14; 9:2; 16:3) shows that in the main offerings oxen (RSV "young bulls") were used as sacrificial animals, and that (after a sheep and a ram) a *par ben baqar*, "young bull," was regarded as the most valuable sacrificial animal. In opposition to Lev. 4:22-35, the first P redactor [26] has also expanded the law with a new regulation concerning the sin-offering of the *qahal*, "congregation." In doing this, in keeping with sacrificial procedure, he replaced "young bull" (*par*), "originally probably any young male animal," [27] with *se'ir 'izzim*, "goat," and, as in 16:3 and 23:18, assigned it to the species *baqar*.

c. In this process of expanding earlier regulations, the expression *par ben baqar*, "young bull of the species ox (or cattle)" (Lev. 4:3,14; 16:3; 23:18; Nu. 7 [12 times]; Ezk. 43:19,23,25; etc.) came to be used in legal language as a technical term for the main sacrificial animal. P probably intentionally avoided the related term *'eghel*, "calf," because of the criticism of the cult places Dan and Bethel: Lev. 9:3 does mention the young bull (*'eghel*), but this comes from an earlier stratum. However, in the literary expansion in 9:2, this has been corrected by the addition of *ben baqar*, so that when all is said and done the young bull is not used at all in P. Ezekiel and supplementary laws like Nu. 15:24 are oriented toward this legal language. In the context of the legislation concerning the centralization of the cult, *baqar* takes on a theologico-historical relevance in Dt. 16:2, for in connection with *zabhach pesach*, "you shall offer the passover," it indicates that an official community festival at the central cult place arose out of the passover as a family festival. *zabhach*, "to offer, sacrifice," is usually connected with *ben baqar*, "calf," i.e., a special relationship or communion was supposed to have been expressed by the slaughter of the ox or young bull and the meal that was connected with it. Thus, e.g., according to Nu. 22:40, Balak tried to establish a fateful communion with Balaam by sacrificing oxen and sheep.

2. *Images and Representations of a baqar.* According to 1 K. 7:44 (par. 2 Ch. 4:15), 25 (2 Ch. 4:3); and 2 K. 16:17, the bronze sea was carried by twelve oxen. Ornaments with lions and oxen were set in the frames of the ten stands of bronze (1 K. 7:29). The captain of Nebuchadnezzar's guard had these representations broken in pieces when the Babylonians destroyed the temple (Jer. 52:20). [28]

Beck

---

[26] Elliger: Po[1].

[27] Elliger, 69.

[28] On the significance of the ox in the history of religion and in art, cf. the synopsis under → שׁוֹר *shôr*, "ox."

בֹּקֶר bōqer

Contents: I. In the Ancient Near East: 1. Egypt; 2. Mesopotamia. II. Etymology: 1. The Root; 2. Derivation. III. Occurrences: 1. In Extrabiblical Literature; 2. In the OT; 3. Syntax. IV. Meanings: 1. Daybreak; 2. Tomorrow (Morning); 3. Day. V. "Help in the Morning."

I. In the Ancient Near East.

1. *Egypt.* The usual Egyptian word for "morning" is *dwȝ(w)* or *dwȝ(y).t.*[1] Another word is *bkȝ*, which occurs less frequently.[2] Often the time intended is defined more precisely, as, e.g., in the expression *tp-dwȝ(y).t*, which possibly means "the beginning of the morning," and which is translated "dawn" or "early morning." But also, like *dwȝ(y).t* alone, this phrase usually refers to the sunrise. Therefore, it does not seem to be used for the purpose of emphasizing the time just before the rising of the sun. It is interesting to connect *dwȝ(y).t* with the verb *dwȝ*, "to praise, extol,"[3] which, if there is a relationship between these two words, means lit. "to praise in the morning."

The religious life of the Egyptians is in many ways oriented to the rising sun. Even in prehistoric time it is possible to trace the practice of burying a corpse with the face toward the east, which agrees completely with the custom in the Old Kingdom.[4] Thus, East is the holy direction and morning the holy time, which is confirmed again and again by the sun theology, which gradually became more and more predominant.

Usually a temple was built with its long sides in an east-west direction (at least, this was the ideal). This indicates that the Egyptians put a great deal of stock in the east and in the morning. A special "morning house" played an important role in the morning ritual.[5] The purification and adorning of the king/priest took place in the morning house.

The morning service occupies a special place in the daily temple ritual.[6] As the first of three daily rituals, it represented the wholly predominant divine ser-

---

bōqer. C. Barth, "Theophanie," *EvTh,* 28 (1968), 521-533; M. Bič, "Der Prophet Amos–ein Haepatoscopus," *VT,* 1 (1951), 293-96; L. Delekat, "Zum hebr. Wörterbuch," *VT,* 14 (1964), 7-9; H. R. Stroes, "Does the day begin in the evening or morning?" *VT,* 16 (1966), 460-475; J. Ziegler, "Die Hilfe Gottes 'am Morgen,'" *Festschrift F. Nötscher. BBB,* 1 (1950), 281-88.

[1] *WbÄS,* V, 422.
[2] *WbÄS,* I, 481; see below.
[3] *WbÄS,* V, 426.
[4] *RÄR,* 564ff.
[5] H. Kees, *RT,* 36 (1914), 1ff.; A. M. Blackman, *JEA,* 5 (1918), 148ff.
[6] A. Moret, *Le rituel du culte divin journalier en Egypte* (Paris, 1902); M. Alliot, *Le culte d'Horus à Edfou* (Cairo, 1949), chap. 2.

vice which had come to be representative of the great festival rituals. In this morning service, there is a special morning address of the deity, which was used as early as the Pyramid Texts, and gradually grew into a litany: "In peace. May thy awakening be peaceful. Thou shalt awake in peace. Etc." [7] The main elements of this morning ritual are these: opening of the naos, awakening of the deity, bathing, clothing, and feeding of the deity. Originally, this was probably a morning service of the pharaoh in the royal palace. To be sure, the rising of the sun did not play a role in this ritual, but sometimes solar elements appear.

Egyptian literature emphasizes especially that the morning, with its revival of the whole of nature, is the natural time to begin the sun's rotation. Thus, a favorite theme in this material is the rejoicing of newly revived nature, which is well known especially in the great Hymn to Aten. [8] Assmann deals in detail with the cultic function of the Songs of the Sun appearing in "narrative" form. [9] This hymn form primarily appears to be cultic, and not to have been used until a late time in funerary contexts. Since it often bears the title *dwꜣ*, "praise, exaltation," this could be a bridge between *dwꜣ*, "to praise," and *dwꜣ*, "morning."

Bergman

2. *Mesopotamia.* The Akk. *šēru*, "morning," is related etymologically to → שׁחר *shachar*, "dawn," and is antithetical to *līlātu* or *tamḫātu*, "evening," in some contexts, and to *urru*, "day," in others. The morning is mentioned in connection with "becoming bright" (*namāru*), [10] and with the rising of the sun (*ina šēri kīma ᵈŠamaš aṣê*, "in the morning with the rising of the sun"). The hymns to the Sun repeatedly testify to the cheerful mood in the sunrise, though without using the word "morning," as, e.g., in these statements: "At the sight of thee, all princes rejoice, the Igigu exult altogether"; [11] "Thy glory has covered the mountains that stand out clearly, the lands are full of thy brilliance altogether"; [12] "As soon as the glare of fire shines at thy rising, the stars of heaven are hidden, in heaven thou alone art glorious, none among the gods can compare with thee." [13]

In the (late) New Year Ritual of Anu from Uruk, [14] there is a morning service for the supreme god. The gods gather together before him, and the supreme god is bathed and fed. This ritual clearly reflects the morning service in the royal palace. [15]

Ringgren

---

[7] Cf. also A. Erman, "Hymnen an das Diadem der Pharaonen," *APAW* (1911), 15ff.; A. Barucq, *L'expression de la louange divine* (Cairo, 1962), 86ff.

[8] *AOT²*, 15ff.

[9] J. Assmann, *Liturgische Lieder an den Sonnengott*, I (1969), see Register (Index) B *s.v.* "Epiphanie" and "Sonnenaufgang."

[10] *AHw*, 769, with examples.

[11] *SAHG*, 240.

[12] *SAHG*, 241.

[13] *SAHG*, 248.

[14] Thureau-Dangin, *Rituels accadiens* (1921), 89ff.

[15] A. L. Oppenheim, *Ancient Mesopotamia* (1964), 193.

II. Etymology.

1. *The Root. bqr* is a common Semitic root, but there is no clarity about the "original meaning" and its relationship to the different "derived" or "figurative" meanings. According to Palache and Seeligmann,[16] the original meaning is to be perceived in Arab. *baqara,* "to split, open." The use of *bqr* as a technical term for inspecting a sacrifice could be connected with this meaning; cf. the Middle Hebrew, Jewish Aramaic, "to examine (the intestines of sacrificial animals)"; Mowinckel on *bqr* in the piel in 2 K. 16:15; Ps. 27:4;[17] and the Nabatean *mbqr'* (a priestly title; cf. also *mbqr,* the overseer of the community, in 1QS and CD).[18] In any case, this helps explain the oft recurring meaning, "to examine, investigate," cf. the Biblical Aramaic, Syriac, "to bore through, search after"; Mandean, "to split, test"; Ethiop. *baqala,* "to examine, punish"; and Heb. *baqar* in the piel, "to examine" (Lev. 13:36); "care for (RSV search, seek)" (Ezk. 34:11f.); "to consider, reflect" (Prov. 20:25; Sir. 11:7). The Akk. *b/paqāru,* "to claim, demand," stands somewhat by itself; cf. Bab. *b/paqrū,* "(claim of) vindication," which might help explain the difficult *biqqoreth* in Lev. 19:20.[19] Both the common Semitic → בקר *bāqār,* "cattle," and presumably also *boqer,* "morning," which occurs only in Hebrew, are derivatives of *bqr,* although the semantic relationship is obscure in both cases.

2. *Derivation.* a. The meaning of *boqer* might be explained by establishing a connection between the idea of "splitting," "opening," or "boring through," and "breaking through, piercing" (sc. of light), i.e., "daybreak" = "morning."[20] The related roots *bqʻ,* "to split" (Heb., Middle Heb., Jewish Aram.; Ugar. *bqʻ*; the intransitive Moabite *bqʻ,* cf. the Mesha Inscription, line 15,[21] *mbqʻ hšḥrt,* of the breaking of the dawn; Isa. 58:8, *yibbaqaʻ kashshachar ʼorekha,* "your light shall break forth like the dawn"; and Arab. *baqiʻa,* "to be contrasted, distinguish"), and *pqʻ,* "to split" (Middle Heb., Jewish Aram., Christian Palestinian, Syr., Mandean; and the intransitive Arab. *faqaʼa/faqaʻa*), support this derivation. On the other hand, that this interpretation assumes an intransitive meaning of *bqr,* which this verb never has in Hebrew, speaks against this derivation. In this case, *boqer* could have attained the supposed "proper" meaning "daybreak" only under the influence of related roots which have an intransitive meaning. Negatively speaking, it is also significant that, disregarding Hebrew, none of the Semitic languages developed a noun from the root *bqr* corresponding to *boqer.*[22]

Levy is indulging in semasiological fantasy when he contends that *bqr/bwqr* comes from the root word *bqr,* "to search for, examine" (sc. objects becoming

16 *See KBL*[3].
17 Mowinckel, *Psalmenstudien* (1961), I, 146.
18 See *KBL*[3].
19 Cf. *KBL*[3], 145b.
20 So *GesB, KBL, KBL*[3].
21 *KAI,* 181.
22 On the Arab. *bukrat,* see below, c.

perceptible by the breaking daylight); cf. *shachar,* "early," from the root *shachar,* "to seek"; and *'erebh,* "evening," from the root *'arabh,* "to mix." [23]

b. On the basis of the cultic meaning of *bqr* ("to undertake the examination of a sacrifice"), [24] Bič has suggested that originally *boqer* might have meant the act of examining entrails in the morning; later it came to be used for the time that this act was done. [25] But there is no evidence that such an act was performed each morning, and the textual foundations for this derivation of *boqer* are too meager.

c. *GesB* and *KBL*[3] have discussed the possibility of a semantic relationship between *boqer* and the common Semitic root → בכר *bākhar.* The idea of firstborn or firstfruit is almost universally associated with this root and its derivatives. [26] However, presumably Syr. *bkr* and Arab. *bakara* have preserved the original meaning, "to be/do early"; [27] with this agrees Arab. *bukra(t),* "morning" (Modern Syr. also "tomorrow," *cras*), *bākir,* "matutinal," etc. [28] But if *boqer* in the sense of "early" > "morning," is cognate with *bkr,* then of course it is necessary to explain the "defective" way it is spelled, i.e., with a *qoph*. In the absence of emphatic sounds (as in *teth, tsadhe, tav,* etc.), this cannot be explained as a consonantal dissimilation from *kaph* to *qoph* (or vice versa). However, the *qoph* could very well have come into use without a conscious relationship to the root *bqr*.

d. The Egyp. *bk3,* "morning," presents another possible root from which *boqer* could have been derived. [29] The reason *boqer* has no cognates outside Hebrew could be that it is an Egyptian loanword unknown in the other Semitic languages. [30] If this is the correct explanation, the sound and manner of writing *boqer* are still big problems.

III. Occurrences.

1. *In Extrabiblical Literature.* Thus far, *boqer* has been found only one time in extrabiblical Hebrew. In the marginal inscription of the Lachish Ostracon No. 4, [31] we find the words *ky 'm . btsbt* [.] *hbqr.* This incomplete sentence can be restored at best by conjectures. If the word *tsbt* (root *sbb*) means something like "course" (it could also perhaps mean "change, turn"), then the sender of

---

[23] J. Levy, *WTM,* I (1924).
[24] See above, 1.
[25] M. Bič, 295.
[26] See *KBL*[3], 125b.
[27] See *GesB*.
[28] Cf. Blachère-Chouémi, II, 770f.
[29] See *KBL*[3], 145a; on the other hand, Calice, *Grundlagen der äg.-semit. Wortvergleichung* (1956), 61f., argues that *bk3* is cognate with the Heb. and Aram. *bkr,* "to be early," and *bqr* with Arab. *baqara,* "to split."
[30] But cf. W. Baumgartner in *KBL*[1], XXIX.
[31] *KAI,* 194.9.

the letter promises to do something specific "in the morning" ("when morning comes again,"[32] or "in the course of the morning").[33] There is no exact analogy to this expression in the OT.

2. *In the OT. boqer* is found in the OT 213 times.[34] The different number given in *KBL*[3] (*ca.* 200 times) is partly because the authors of this work regarded the expression *babboqer babboqer,* "morning by morning, every morning," which occurs 13 times in the OT, as only one occurrence. *boqer* is distributed in the OT as follows: Pentateuch 80 times (Gen. 19; Ex. 36; Lev. 9; Nu. 12; and Dt. 4); Former Prophets 52; Latter Prophets 32 (Isa. 11; Jer. 2; Ezk. 10; Minor Prophets 9); and the Kethubhim or Writings 49 (Ps. 18; Job 7). Thematic reasons explain the relatively frequent occurrence of *boqer* in Exodus (it occurs 10 times in Ex. 16 alone!). These statistics show a uniform distribution of *boqer* in the OT, and thus do not permit any conclusions with regard to the age of its literary use.

3. *Syntax.* a. *boqer* is used 17 times without the article, without a preposition, and without a preceding *nomen regens* (governing noun) (Gen. 1:5,8,13,19,23, 31; Ex. 16:7; Nu. 16:5; Dt. 28:67b; 2 S. 23:4; Hos. 7:6; Ps. 5:4 [Eng. v. 3] [twice]; 55:18[17]; Job 24:17; 38:12); it is in these very passages that the interpretation is often difficult.[35]

b. *boqer* often appears with a preposition. In almost half the times *boqer* occurs in the OT, it is used with *be,* "in," and the article (*babboqer* is found 105 times, including the 13 occurrences of the expression *babboqer babboqer,* "morning by morning, every morning"). The prep. *'adh,* "until," with *boqer* follows in second place (*'adh boqer* appears 16 times; *'adh habboqer,* 12; cf. also *'adh 'or habboqer,* "until the light of the morning," 6). The prep. *le,* "to," usually occurs before the singular (*labboqer,* 18 times), and less frequently before the plural (*labbeqarim,* 5 times, determinate in Isa. 33:2; Ps. 73:14; 101:8; Lam. 3:23, indeterminate in Job 7:18). *min,* "from," is seldom used with *boqer* (*mehabboqer,* 3 times; and *min habboqer, min boqer,* and *mibboqer* once each). One should also note *liphnoth (hab)boqer,* "at the turn of the morning" (RSV, "when the morning appeared," Ex. 14:27; Jgs. 19:26; Ps. 46:6[5]); *beterem boqer,* "before morning" (Isa. 17:14); *me'az (me'or,* "from the light of," should probably be read) *habboqer,* "from time of morning" (RSV, "from early morning," Ruth 2:7); *be'or habboqer,* "when the morning dawns" (Mic. 2:1); and *bihyoth habboqer,* "when the morning came" (RSV, "on the morning of," Ex. 19:16).

---

[32] *KAI.*

[33] Cf. *ANET*[2], 322b: "[but I will send] tomorrow morning."

[34] G. Lisowsky, *Konkordanz zum AT,* 276f.

[35] See below, IV.1,2. In order to explain *boqer* in Ps. 5:4b(3b), *KBL*[3], 145a, referring to Mowinckel, proposes a *bqr* I, "sacrifice for omens"; but such a noun does not occur elsewhere; cf. Bič.

Expressions like *mibboqer la'erebh,* "from morning to evening" (RSV, "be-tween morning and evening," Job 4:20); *min habboqer 'adh ha'arebh,* "from morning till evening" (Ex. 18:13f.); *me'erebh 'adh boqer,* "from evening to morn-ing" (27:21; Lev. 24:3; Nu. 9:21); and *mehabboqer ve'adh hatstsohorayim,* "from morning until noon" (1 K. 18:26; cf. the Mesha Inscription, line 15, *mbq' hšḥrt 'd hshrym*),[36] are important in understanding the use of prepositions before *boqer.*

c. *boqer* appears with a preceding substantive that functions as a governing noun in the expressions *'or habboqer,* "light of morning (morning light)" (cf. *'adh 'or habboqer*);[37] *ke'or boqer,* "like the morning light" (2 S. 23:4; in *be'or habboqer* in Mic. 2:1, *'or* is probably an inf.);[38] *kokhebhe bhoqer,* "morning stars" (Job 38:7); *ka'anan boqer,* "morning cloud" (Hos. 6:4); *'ashmoreth hab-boqer,* "morning watch" (Ex. 14:24; 1 S. 11:11); *motsa'e bhoqer,* "the outgoings of the morning" (Ps. 65:9[8]); *mar'eh habboqer,* "the vision of the morning" (Dnl. 8:26); *'olath/'oloth habboqer,* "morning sacrifice(s)" (4 times); and *min-chath habboqer,* "morning oblation" (twice; cf. 2 K. 3:20).

d. As a subject, *boqer* occurs only in the expressions *boqer hayah,* "morning came (RSV, it was morning)" (Ex. 10:13); *'athah bhoqer,* "morning has come (comes)" (Isa. 21:12); and *habboqer 'or,* "the morning was light" (Gen. 44:3); and as an object only in Job 38:12 (Dt. 28:67b is doubtful).

e. A favorite motif especially of the narrative parts of the OT is the expres-sion "to rise/set out early," in which *boqer* regularly appears (→ השכים *hishkîm babboqer* is found 29 times; cf. also Isa. 5:11; Prov. 27:14; Job 1:5; *qum bab-boqer* occurs 7 times).

IV. Meanings. In order to determine the various meanings of *boqer,* it is best to begin with the two certain meanings, viz., "morning," i.e., time of the sunrise, and "tomorrow morning."

1. *Daybreak.* a. It is clear from statements found in certain poetic texts that *boqer* does not mean so much a period of time as a moment of time. It means "daybreak,"[39] i.e., the moment when the darkness and the dawn (*nesheph,* 1 S. 30:17; *ba'aloth hashshachar,* Jonah 4:7; possibly also *liphnoth habboqer*) no longer rule, but the *light* (→ אור *'ôr*). *habboqer hayah,* "it became (RSV was) morning" (Ex. 10:13; cf. Gen. 1:5ff.), means the same thing as *habboqer 'or,* "the morning became (RSV was) light" (Gen. 44:3). In the phrase *'or hab-boqer,*[40] *'or* should generally be understood[41] as an infinitive, i.e., as an event,

---

36 *KAI,* 181.
37 See above, b.
38 See below, IV.1.a.
39 See *KBL*3, 1.
40 See above, III.3.c.
41 *KBL*3 on *'or:* only Mic. 2:1.

and thus is not to be translated "light," but "become bright." Temporally, this "becoming light" coincides with the rising of the sun, cf. *babboqer kizroach hashshemesh,* "in the morning, as soon as the sun is up" (Jgs. 9:33), and *ke'or boqer yizrach shamesh boqer lo' 'abhoth,* "he dawns on them like the morning light, like the sun shining forth upon a cloudless morning" (2 S. 23:4). In this sense, the sunrise may be designated as a synonym of *boqer,* cf. Gen. 32:32(31); Ex. 22:2(3); 2 K. 3:22; Jonah 4:8; Ps. 104:22. Light (→ אור *'ôr*) as such is not identical with the sun (cf. Gen. 1:3f.), though it emanates from the sun, which in that respect can be called *'or* (Job 31:26; Hab. 3:4; Ps. 136:7), or *me'or,* "luminary" (Gen. 1:14-16; Ps. 74:16). In some instances, *'or* can denote daybreak instead of *boqer* (Zeph. 3:5; Job 24:14; Jgs. 19:26; Neh. 8:3). Whether *boqer* in this sense means the moment of daybreak can only be inferred from the context.

b. The use of prepositions before *boqer* [42] plays an important role in determining its meaning, but of course, not always a decisive one. *babboqer* usually means (e.g., in the expression *hishkim babboqer,* "to rise early") "in the morning" = at daybreak, but often (esp. in *babboqer babboqer,* "morning by morning, every morning") this understanding seems too narrow. [43] Also, in most cases *labboqer* means "in the morning" = at daybreak (Am. 4:4; 5:8; Ps. 30:6[5]; 59:17[16]; Ezr. 3:3; Ps. 49:15[14] [the text here is corrupt]; in Jer. 21:12, Rudolph reads *labbeqarim,* "continually"); but sometimes it could also mean "*till* daybreak" (Zeph. 3:3; Ps. 130:6). [44] *liphnoth habboqer,* literally "at the turn of the morning" (RSV, "when the morning appears") means the brief period of time immediately *before* daybreak, thus "toward morning" [45] (cf. *liphnoth 'erebh,* "at the turn of the evening" [RSV, "when evening comes on"], Gen. 24:63; Dt. 23:12[11]). *mehabboqer* means "(only) toward morning" in 2 S. 2:27, [46] but in 1 K. 18:26 it means "*from* daybreak on" (like *mibboqer* in Job 4:20 and *min habboqer* in Ex. 18:13f.), viz., till noon (*'adh hatstsohorayim*) or till sundown (*la'erebh, 'adh ha'erebh, 'adh 'erebh;* on *'erebh* as the moment of sundown, cf. Dt. 16:6). Also *beterem boqer* means "*before* day" (Isa. 17:14). Greatest caution is necessary where *'adh* occurs before *boqer* or *habboqer.* The prep. *'adh* means "to," "even to," frequently including the goal or purpose. [47] Thus, as a rule *'adh boqer, 'adh habboqer,* and *'adh 'or habboqer* mean "even to daybreak," including daybreak, but there are cases where daybreak is clearly excluded, because the context obviously has in mind only the duration of the night (e.g., Ex. 12:22; Lev. 6:2[9]; Jgs. 16:2; 2 K. 10:8,9). [48]

2. *Tomorrow (Morning).* a. If *boqer* with the meaning "daybreak" is somehow related to the preceding night, then Heb. also knows a use of the word

---

[42] Cf. the survey under II.3.b.
[43] See below, 2.b.; 3.b.
[44] For another meaning, see below, 3.b.
[45] Delekat, 8.
[46] *KBL:* "Not before morning."
[47] See *GesB.*
[48] Note further 3.b!

which clearly refers to the preceding day. Even in this case, *boqer* means primarily a specific *moment*, viz., the dawn of the next day, thus "tomorrow morning"; but then it can also mean a *period* of time, viz., the next morning, which can sometimes mean the whole next day, thus "tomorrow." Of the passages mentioned under III.3.a, certainly Ex. 16:7 ("tomorrow you will see") and Nu. 16:5 ("tomorrow Yahweh will show") come into question as possibly having this meaning, and probably also Ps. 5:4a and b (3a,b). [49] In Hos. 7:6, the traditional translation, "in the morning," is to be retained, [50] because here the contrast is clearly between night and day (not between yesterday and tomorrow). [51]

b. Also in several cases where *boqer* is used with the prepositions *be, le,* and *'adh,* we must reckon with the possibility that it might mean "tomorrow" or "tomorrow morning." [52] It seems quite certain that in the expression *hishkim babboqer,* [53] *babboqer* means "in the *early* morning," and not "on the *next* morning": [54] taken alone, *hishkim* and *qum* mean simply "to set out"/"to rise," whereas "early," which is the thrust of this phrase, is brought out clearly by *boqer.* If the writer wishes to express the idea "tomorrow," then this is added (cf. 1 S. 5:4, *vayyashkimu bhabboqer mimmochorath,* "but when they rose early on the next morning"). On the other hand, *babboqer* in Ex. 7:15; 34:2a; and 1 S. 9:19 (like *boqer* in Ex. 16:7 and Nu. 16:5) probably means "tomorrow morning." Delekat has not shown any convincing reasons for interpreting *babboqer* "tomorrow" in Ps. 90:14 and 143:8. [55] Moreover, the context of Isa. 17:11; Ezk. 24:18; and 33:22 [56] does not demand that *babboqer* be translated "on the following day." [57]

The meaning of *labboqer* diverges from its usual sense in Ex. 34:25 and Dt. 16:4: in these two texts, *GesB* translates it "until the following day," and *KBL*[3], "until the next morning." But in these passages, *labboqer* does not include merely daybreak, but the entire morning or day following (in distinction from or in antithesis to the previous day). Ex. 34:2aα with its *vehyeh nakhon labboqer,* "be ready for the coming morning," [58] also belongs here. *labboqer* in Am. 4:4 has a distributive meaning ("every morning"). [59]

When *'adh boqer* and *'adh habboqer* are found in contrast to the previous day, they can also mean "until the next morning" or "until tomorrow"; cf. Ex. 12:10; 16:19f.,23f.; 23:18; 29:34; Lev. 7:15; 19:13; but *not* Nu. 9:15,21; etc.

---

[49] Cf. *GesB* and Delekat, 7, against *KBL* and *KBL*[3], who want to understand the "dissimilative" *boqer* only in Nu. 16:5 in the sense "tomorrow."

[50] With H. W. Wolff, *BK,* XIV/1, *in loc.,* and W. Rudolph, *KAT,* XIII, *in loc.*

[51] On Ps. 5:4(3), see further under IV.

[52] See *GesB.*

[53] See above, III.3.e.; IV.2.a.

[54] So *GesB* and *KBL*[3], 4!

[55] Delekat, 8.

[56] Cf. W. Zimmerli, *BK,* XIII/2, *in loc.*

[57] Delekat, 7.

[58] G. von Rad, *ATD, in loc.;* cf. C. Barth, *EvTh,* 530f.

[59] See below, 3.b.

c. There can be no doubt that in numerous passages *boqer* is intimately re-lated to the *next* day as viewed from the day before. Therefore, it is in order to compare *boqer* with the word normally used for "tomorrow," viz., *machar* or *mimmochorath. boqer* and *machar* were never really synonyms. The differ-ence between them seems to be that *machar* generally meant the entire day that followed, while *boqer* meant specifically the beginning of that day. Generally speaking, noon (*tsohorayim*) was regarded as the time after which *boqer* no longer applied (Ps. 55:18[17]; Jer. 20:16; Ex. 16:21; 1 K. 18:26; cf. the Mesha Inscription, line 15). [60]

d. In connection with the meaning "tomorrow," we must consider the possibil-ity of whether *boqer* can mean the same thing as "early," "soon," or "speedily" in certain contexts. Martin Luther translated *sabbeʿenu bhabboqer chasdekha* in Ps. 90:14, "Satisfy us early with thy grace." John Calvin renders *babboqer* in Ps. 143:8, *tempestive vel celeriter* (promptly or swiftly). Similarly, the Roman Psalterium of 1945 translates *babboqer* in Ps. 90:14 and 143:8 by *cito* ("speed-ily"); [61] and Delekat points out that these two psalms are concerned not with help in the morning, but with help *by this time tomorrow,* thus with *quick* help–as soon as possible. [62] Nevertheless, Ziegler is certainly right when he protests against translating *babboqer* by *cito* ("speedily"). This mere "paraphrased ren-dering" does not agree with the sense of this word in the context any more than Delekat's translation, "tomorrow morning," which presupposes an antithesis and tension between "today" and "tomorrow" which is not present in the text at all. [63]

3. *Day.* a. However, Delekat has rightly emphasized a separate, though secondary, meaning of *boqer*. In some cases (esp., it seems, in poetic speech), this word can mean the *whole day* from morning till evening. [64] When *boqer* and *laylah,* "night," are contrasted with each other (*ʾathah bhoqer vegham laylah,* "morning comes, and also the night," Isa. 21:12; *lehaggidh babboqer chasdekha veʾemunathekha balleloth,* "to declare thy steadfast love in the morn-ing, and thy faithfulness by night," Ps. 92:3[2]), this corresponds exactly with the antithetical pairs of words, *ʾor–choshekh,* "light–darkness," and *yom–laylah,* "day-night" (Gen. 1:5,14); cf. the contrasting terms *boqer–tsalmaveth,* "morn-ing–deep darkness" (Am. 5:8; Job 24:17), and *ʾor–tsalmaveth,* "light–deep dark-ness" (Job 12:22). The *pars pro toto* use of *boqer* for the entire period of daylight is easily explained from the close relationship between *boqer* and *ʾor,* "light." [65]

b. A different question is whether *boqer* can also mean "day" in expressions that must be understood as distributive, as *babboqer babboqer, labboqer lab-boqer,* and *labbeqarim* (*KBL*[3]: "each/every morning," "morning by morning"). [66]

---

[60] *KAI,* 181.

[61] Ziegler, 282.

[62] Delekat, 7f.

[63] On Ziegler's explanation, see below, V.

[64] The evening itself being excluded (Delekat, 8).

[65] See above, 1.a.

[66] See above, III.3.b.

Delekat thinks this is the meaning of *boqer* in Isa. 28:19; 50:4 (*babboqer bab-boqer*); 33:2; Ps. 73:14; 101:8; Job 7:18; Lam. 3:23 (*labbeqarim*); and even in Jer. 21:12 and Am. 4:4 (*labboqer*, "each day"). [67] He wants to find the narrower sense ("each morning") only in those passages where reference is made explicitly to the morning time (Ezk. 46:13-15; 1 Ch. 9:27; 23:30; 2 Ch. 13:11). Then in the poetic passages, the meaning of this expression would be "day after day afresh (anew)," perhaps an equivalent to the more prosaic phrases *yom yom, yom beyom*, etc., "day by day," in which sometimes (!) the following night is included. It is impossible to deny completely the validity of this position, but in dealing with each respective passage involved, it must be asked whether the rendering of *boqer* by "day" does not represent a paraphrase (which may be basically correct). [68]

V. "Help in the Morning." Ziegler has pointed out that in the OT the morning is the "proper time for divine help." [69] This concept does not belong in the realm of the philological "meanings" [70] of *boqer*. Ziegler's thesis, which thus far has been fundamentally opposed only by Delekat, [71] was anticipated by H. Gunkel and F. Nötscher. Referring to Ps. 46:6(5); 90:14; and 143:8, Gunkel speaks of the morning as a "time of good fortune." In 1947, Nötscher spoke of the morning as a "time of good fortune and of God's favorable hearing of a request." [72] In order to understand this thesis, it is important to note that it is not an attempt to interpret the *meaning* of *boqer* in a new way, but to explain its *use* in certain contexts where it is repeated quite frequently in a specific way. The idea that God helps "in the morning" is "clothed either in the form of a statement of faith or of a prayer of confidence in the Psalms and in Psalm-like songs of the OT...." [73] In particular, the passages cited in support of this view are: Ps. 46:6(5) (*liphnoth boqer*, "at the turn of the morning," RSV "right early"); Lam. 3:23; Isa. 33:2 (*labbeqarim*, lit. "to the mornings," RSV "every morning"); Ps. 90:14; 143:8 (*babboqer*, "in the morning"); 88:14(13) (*ubhab-boqer*, "and in the morning"); 5:4(3) (*boqer*, lit. "morning," RSV "in the morning"); 59:17(16) (*labboqer*, lit. "to the morning," RSV "in the morning"); 30:6 (5) (*velabboqer*, lit. "and to the morning," RSV "with the morning"); as well as 2 S. 23:4; Zeph. 3:5; etc. According to Ziegler, it is not the accused sleeping in the temple [74] or the morning sacrifice, [75] but the expectation of the help of God "in the morning" (whose form, content, and motivation is attested only in the OT) that explains the use of *boqer* in these passages.

---

[67] Cf. T. H. Robinson, *HAT*, 14, *in loc.;* H. W. Wolff, *BK*, XIV/2, *in loc.*

[68] Cf. Ziegler, 282, on the rendering of *boqer* by *cito*, "speedily," *omni tempore*, "at all times," and *cotidie*, "daily, every day."

[69] Ziegler, 282.

[70] Cf. Delekat, 9.

[71] *Ibid.*

[72] Cf. also J. Lindblom on Ps. 17:15 in *ZAW*, 59 (1942/1943), 12f.

[73] Ziegler, 281.

[74] H. Schmidt, *BZAW*, 49 (1928) and *HAT*, 15 (1934); cf. Delekat, 9: priestly incubation.

[75] Cf. B. Duhm, *KHC*, XIV (²1922).

It is to Ziegler's undiminished credit that he has called attention to the special use of *boqer* in the Psalms. But we must express reservations about various details in his position.

1. He has combined many heterogeneous elements under the concept "help of God." And yet, only Ps. 46:6(5) (cf. also possibly Ex. 14:30; 2 Ch. 20:17) actually uses the word "help" explicitly. In contradistinction to this, Ps. 5:4a(3a); 143:8; and 90:14 (reading *hashmiʿenu,* "let us hear," instead of *sabbeʿenu,* "satisfy us"?) have to do with Yahweh's favorable *hearing* of the worshipper's request (a priestly salvation oracle?): Ps. 5:4b(3b) and 88:14(13) speak of *prayer* and a *cry* for help in the morning, and Ps. 59:17(16) of *thanksgiving* in the morning. Again, the faithfulness and compassion of Yahweh which are really new and which are to be requested anew "every morning" in Lam. 3:22f. and Isa. 33:2 are something entirely different. Under these circumstances, it is hardly possible to speak of a clearly outlined "concept" or of an idea common to all the passages cited on the "help of God." [76]

2. Also the precise time intended by the expression "in the morning" in the passages cited is not clear. *liphnoth boqer,* "at the turn of the morning" (RSV "right early") in Ps. 46:6(5) does not mean "over night," [77] nor does it coincide temporally with the "morning," i.e., with daybreak. Whether the two occurrences of *boqer* in Ps. 5:4(3) mean "in the morning" or "tomorrow morning," [78] and whether the *ʾeʿerokh lekha* (RSV, "I prepare a sacrifice for thee") in Ps. 5:4b(3b) refers to a morning sacrifice or not, [79] is debatable, to say the least. One must also question whether *labbeqarim* in Lam. 3:23 and Isa. 33:2 refers as specifically to the *breaking* of each new day, [80] as Ziegler thinks. Of course, the expression *babboqer,* "in the morning," stands in Ps. 90:14; 143:8; and 88:14(13), but the different nuances of meaning that are possible for the word *boqer* [81] make it impossible to speak of a homogeneous "concept" even in these texts.

3. But the threefold explanation Ziegler proposes for the phenomenon of the expectation of help "in the morning" is particularly problematic. Undoubtedly there is a biblical (and human!) *symbolism* for sunrise and sunset, morning and evening, day and night, and light and darkness, and this symbolism is certainly connected with real experiences of Israel (and of man!) in its world. Nevertheless, to deduce the time of God's help from events and experiences of nature is far from OT thought. [82] Connecting the time of God's help with the hour of judgment common in Israel causes further difficulties. Certainly the language of the OT is influenced in many respects by Israel's legal life. But a conscious or even

---

[76] Cf. Delekat, 9.

[77] Cf. Delekat, 8.

[78] See above, IV.2.a.

[79] Cf. Delekat, 9, n. 1.

[80] See above, IV.2.b.

[81] See above, 1. on Ps. 88:14(13).

[82] Cf. G. von Rad, "The Theological Problem of the OT Doctrine of Creation," *Problem of the Hexateuch and Other Essays* (trans. 1966), 131-163.

merely actual analogy of ideas concerning civil legal terminology and the revelation of Yahweh in the temple (salvation oracle) seems doubtful. [83] On the other hand, there is great merit in Ziegler's suggestion of a connection between Israel's historical experiences and the help of God "in the morning." There is much that favors the idea that Ps. 46:6(5) has in mind the liberation of Jerusalem in 701 B.C. (2 K.19:35; Isa. 37:36), and perhaps also the miracle at the Red Sea (Ex. 14:30). However, in both instances the help occurred before dawn (*liphnoth boqer*), and what happens in the morning (*babboqer*) is only the subjective recognition of the help (2 K. 19:35 = Isa. 37:36). But even if a connection between the Exodus tradition and the Zion tradition could actually be established here, this still would not justify the conclusion that all or even some of the texts cited really contain the motif of the expectation of salvation. The other examples cited in favor of the motif of help "in the morning" (1 S. 11:1-13; 2 Ch. 20:1-30; 2 K. 3:9-20) fail to prove the point, because the crucial passages (1 S. 11:9 and 2 Ch. 20:16) use not *babboqer* but the vague *machar*, "tomorrow" (Ziegler: "tomorrow morning"!), and in both passages help comes around noon, whereas in 2 K. 3:20 it comes at night. Finally, the motif of help "in the morning" grounded in historical experiences is *missing* right where it could have been included most easily (in the traditions of the "wars of Yahweh"), so that from this aspect also, Ziegler's explanation of these passages in the Psalms is unlikely.

If Ziegler's explanation of the phenomenon of the expectation of help "in the morning" is not acceptable, then it is imperative that we seek for a better explanation. H. Schmidt's view that these passages have in mind the accused "sleeping in the temple" awaiting a morning ordeal, and Delekat's suggestion that they reflect the "requirements of the oracle technique," [84] do not solve the whole complex problem. If a solution is ever found, it will come only as the result of a more precise understanding of the Jerusalem temple cult in the preexilic and postexilic periods. Three things need to be borne in mind if one undertakes an urgently needed new study of this problem.

a. In OT literature, there is no example of a figurative or spiritual use of *boqer* in the sense of good fortune, salvation, help, etc. The earliest examples of such a use are found in the earlier Middle Hebrew. [85]

b. In the OT, therefore, salvation is expected "toward morning," "in the morning," "tomorrow (morning)," or "every morning," not because these times of day by their own virtue were thought to be times of salvation. Morning acquires the quality of the different, new, and future only in context, i.e., in contrast to the night or to (dark) today.

c. The different, new, and future thing that is expected "toward morning," etc., is not directly the content of salvation and help. It was primarily the new presence of Yahweh in a theophany and in an oracle which made the morning the time more than any other when the oppressed and "Israel" expected help.

Barth

---

[83] Cf. Delekat, 9.
[84] *Ibid.*
[85] Cf. Levy, *WTM*, I, *s.v.* בוקר/בקר

בָּקַשׁ biqqēsh; בַּקָּשָׁה baqqāshāh

Contents: I. The Root: 1. Etymology and Occurrences; 2. Meaning and Related Words. II. General Use: 1. Seeking in the Literal Sense; 2. Seeking in the Figurative Sense; 3. Seeking As a Legal Term. III. Theological Use: 1. Seeking God; 2. God Seeks. IV. The Derivative baqqashah.

I. The Root.

1. *Etymology and Occurrences. bqš* is a Semitic root apparently used primarily in the Syrian-Palestinian region, which appears in Ugaritic.[1] It is found in the OT over 220 times. It also occurs in Phoenician,[2] and is used in the Qumran literature and in postbiblical Hebrew texts. In all these language areas, except possibly the Qumran writings that are known thus far, *bqš* means "to seek" in the literal sense of the word. Beyond this, in the OT and in Middle Hebrew texts important expansions and figures are connected with this root. In the Qumran texts (thus far), from the first a less literal and more figurative use of *bqš* seems to be favored. In the overwhelming majority of OT examples of *bqš*, it is found in the piel, and the pual as the passive of the piel appears in only three passages. The late book of Esther and one passage in Ezra use an Aramaized form derived from *bqš*, which has a nominal function (*baqqashah*), and means "request," "desire," "wish," "entreaty." Even though *bqš* is not found in several OT books (Joel, Ob., Jonah, Mic., Hab., Hag.), and appears only once in others (e.g., in Proto-Isa., Job, Lev.), it can be said that this root is widely dispersed in the OT. Both earlier and later OT literary contexts know and use this root. The same thing can also be said for the different speech forms of the OT. There is no genre in which *bqš* is preferred.

2. *Meaning and Related Words.* The literal meaning of *biqqesh* is "to seek," an activity that assumes a personal entity (in Prov. 18:15, "ear" functions as *pars pro toto*) as subject and persons or things as object. This activity has in view the finding of an object which really exists or which is thought to exist, which is not close at hand to the subject at the time of seeking, but is desired most earnestly and initiates the seeking. *biqqesh* has to do with satisfying this desire. What is sought may temporarily be absent; it may be intentionally hidden

---

biqqēsh. O. García de La Fuente, "David busco el rostro de Yahweh (2 Sam 21,1)," *Aug,* 8 (1968), 477-540; H. Greeven, "ζητέω, ζήτησις, ἐκζητέω, ἐπιζητέω," *TDNT,* II, 892-96; J. Reindl, *Das Angesicht Gottes im Sprachgebrauch des AT. ErfThSt,* 23 (1970), esp. pp. 164-174, and the appropriate notes; C. Westermann, "Die Begriffe für Fragen und Suchen im AT," *KuD,* 6 (1960), 2-30.

[1] *WUS* (³1967), No. 572, possibly also used as a proper name in the expression *bn bqš,* cf. No. 571.
[2] *KAI,* 14.5, the Sarcophagus Inscription of 'Eshmun'azar.

or it may never have been found before. "Seeking" in the OT and elsewhere must be understood as a conscious act with a specific goal in mind, and sometimes it must be accompanied by a great deal of effort (Prov. 2:4, as in prospecting for silver), shrewdness, and imagination. The meaning of *biqqesh* varies according to the degree of intensity and the difference in the mode of seeking ("to seek out," "search," "search for," "seek," "wish," "long for," "desire," "demand or ask," etc.). Along with material things and objects, seeking can also take abstract objects, e.g., conflict (Jgs. 14:4), falsehood (Ps. 4:3 [Eng. v. 2]), evil (1 K. 20:7), good (Neh. 2:10), faithfulness (Jer. 5:1), wisdom (Prov. 14:6; 15:14), understanding (Dnl. 8:15), life (Prov. 29:10), peace (Ps. 34:15[14]), the word of God (Am. 8:12), the name of God (Ps. 83:17[16]), a vision (Ezk. 7:26). Frequently the object of *biqqesh* is an additional activity of one's own, which is expressed by the infinitive construct of another verb plus *le,* as e.g., in 1 S. 14:4, *biqqesh yonathan la'abhor,* "Jonathan sought to go over." In this syntactical construction, *biqqesh* assumes the meaning "to want to," "strive," "intend," "pursue a goal," or "plan." Occasionally this idea is also expressed by an *'asher* clause (Dnl. 1:8) or by a verbal noun (9:3, *lebhaqqesh tephillah,* "seeking by prayer").

In all these cases, *biqqesh* takes on the character of an auxiliary verb, which gives the activity expressed by it a voluntary and final color. It is also easy to understand how the transition from a literal to a figurative understanding of "seeking" is possible through the abstract objects and the auxiliary function of *biqqesh.* Sometimes the verb form used with *biqqesh* implies another activity which is not specified more precisely, but whose meaning is clarified from the context. Jer. 5:1 does not mean that *'emunah,* "faithfulness," will be sought and found, but that it should be practiced and done. Quite frequently, this abbreviated mode of speaking is used to express the idea of "killing" or "wanting to kill" in the phrase *biqqesh ('eth) nephesh* (+ suf.) ("to seek the soul, the life, of someone," i.e., "to make an attempt on someone's life"), e.g., in Ex. 4:19; 1 S. 23:15; Jer. 19:9. This construction must be understood positively, in the sense of furthering life, in only one passage, Prov. 29:10. In addition to this abbreviated speech form, the idea of "wanting to kill" is also expressed by the direct mode of speaking with *biqqesh* and the infinitive construct of *muth* (hiphil) or *haragh* plus *le* (Jer. 26:21; Ex. 2:15; 4:24). Sometimes, this character of *biqqesh* implying another activity is expressed by a prepositional phrase (using *'el, min,* or *le*). In 2 S. 3:17, the elders of Israel do not seek David merely to meet with him, but for the purpose of making him king, or better still, to have him as a king over them (*heyithem mebhaqeshim 'eth davidh lemelekh 'alekhem,* "you have been seeking David as king over you"). The young roaring lions ask for their food from God (*me'el,* Ps. 104:21). Legal elements come into play in this expansion of the meaning of *biqqesh* to "wish," "ask for," or "demand." This occurs very clearly in the statement about "seeking the blood of a man" (*halo' 'abhaqqesh 'eth damo miyyedhekhem,* "shall I not now require his blood at your hand?" 2 S. 4:11), where *biqqesh* can assume the sense of "avenge, take revenge on." "Seek" and "wish" can also be used in the sense of "wishing that something would happen to someone." In certain passages, it can even be asked whether an applicative element might not be involved, e.g., in 1 S. 24:10(9); Ps. 122:9. In the cultic sphere, *biqqesh* is found in expressions and formulas that require the meaning "ask," "pray," "implore" (Ps. 27:8; Ex. 33:7). In general, the phrase "seek the face of God" has in mind a cultic activity, without clarifying the manner in which it was performed.

When one considers terms that appear in context with or words that are used in parallelism to *biqqesh,* and thus help in defining its meaning, it becomes apparent that there is a remarkable variability in the use of this word. Words appearing in parallelism to *biqqesh* include → דרשׁ *dārash,* "to seek," → רדף *rādhaph,* "to pursue," → שׁאל *shā'al,* "to ask," → פקד *pāqadh,* "to visit," → בחר *bāchar,* "to choose," etc.; and terms that appear in context with *biqqesh* are → ידע *yādha',* "to know," → ראה *rā'āh,* "to see," → צפה *tsāphāh,* "to look out, watch," → שׁמר *shāmar,* "to keep," → דבר *dibbēr,* "to speak," → הגה *hāghāh,* "to utter, meditate," → אהב *'āhabh,* "to love," etc. To a much greater extent than has been observed with regard to other verbs, the function and meaning of *biqqesh* is determined by the object it takes in any given context. The many different objects *biqqesh* takes in various contexts give rise to the transition from the original meaning "to seek" to other meanings, as e.g., in Isa. 40:20, "to choose" wood to cut; Est. 4:8, "to entreat for someone"; and Zec. 11:16, "to care for." Of course, most of the figurative meanings of this verb can be traced back to the original meaning and explained on the basis of this meaning.

II. General Use.

1. *Seeking in the Literal Sense.* Only Eccl. 3:6 mentions "seeking" in and of itself as a pure function which, together with other functions (e.g., "planting" and "plucking up"), defines human existence; its purpose is to illustrate that all human activities are bound to time and determined by kairos.[3] The general and proper use of *biqqesh* is modified by its function in each context, as in German or English or any other language. An unnamed man asks Joseph, "What are you seeking?" and Joseph replies, "I am seeking my brothers" (Gen. 37:15,16; first the impf., then the participial form). The objects of "seeking" in the OT are understandably quite diversified: lost asses (1 S. 9:3; impv. form, indicating that one person can motivate another to seek something by means of an order or a command; 10:2,14), runaway slaves (1 K. 2:40), Elijah, who had gone up by a whirlwind into heaven (2 K. 2:16f.), water (Isa. 41:17), bread (or livelihood, Ps. 37:25; Lam. 1:11,19), grazing places (1 Ch. 4:39, for the flocks), records proving that people belonged to certain families (Neh. 7:64; Ezr. 2:62), Levites who were needed for the dedication of the city wall (Neh. 12:27), Saul, who was to be made king after the lot had fallen upon him (1 S. 10:21), the expert, the musician (16:16, *'ish yodhea',* RSV, "a man who is skilful"), the medium at Endor (28:7), and comforters in time of calamity (Nah. 3:7). *biqqesh* takes on the precise meaning of "searching out" in the passage that tells how a beautiful

---

[3] K. Galling, *HAT,* 18 (²1969), 93f.; W. Zimmerli, *ATD,* XVI, 169.

maiden was to be sought to perform special services for the aging David (1 K. 1:2f.; in essence, the meaning of *biqqesh* in Est. 2:2 is no different). Here, *biqqesh* can be translated simply "choose."

Frequently the process of "seeking" implies additional actions which are already inherently present in the meaning of "seeking." Seeking after the culprit who had destroyed the altar of Baal and the Asherah implies that he will be punished (Jgs. 6:29). Saul's purpose in seeking for David is to seize and eliminate his rival (1 S. 23:14; 24:3[2]; 26:2; 27:1, "search for," "lie in wait for"; 27:4, "pursue"). The acts that are involved when the OT speaks of finding what is being sought help define the concept of "seeking." This is the case, e.g., when the Philistines seek David (2 S. 5:17; 1 Ch. 14:8). Here even military intentions are described by the verb "seek." Occasionally, this intention which is inherent in the action of seeking is defined more precisely by a parallel verb, e.g., by *radhaph* ("to chase," "pursue"; Josh. 2:22; Jgs. 4:22; 1 S. 23:25; 26:20). The radius of the function of *biqqesh* as its meaning expanded, e.g., in the expression "seeking an inheritance (a *nachalah*)" in Jgs. 18:1, is determined very clearly by the object. Here, "seeking" includes all actions from military conflict between the Danites and the pre-Israelite inhabitants of the land, to settlement, to the securing of the Danites in their new territory. The same is true of Naomi's state-ment about "seeking a resting place for Ruth" in Ruth 3:1. Quite apart from the fact that presumably Naomi is using a legal term, the "seeking" here also includes all individual acts leading to the legal enfranchisement of Ruth in the Bethlehem society. The peculiar tendency of *biqqesh* to widen its connotations far beyond the basic meaning is something that occurs in various realms, as in relationships between two people who love each other (Cant. 3:1f.; 5:6; 6:1, "I sought him whom my soul loves"; cf. Hos. 2:9[7]), in the royal court (Prov. 29:26, "seek the face of the ruler," viz., for the unexpressed purpose of uttering petitions or requests or of obtaining favor), or in the broad sphere of religion. [4] The OT uses only persons as subjects of *biqqesh*. They may be individuals or groups (Saul, David, families, tribes, people, etc.), or even God. Prov. 18:15 (where *'ozen* is subj.) only appears to be an exception. [5] The reference to hearing as a function of "seeking" in this passage is interesting.

The three occurrences of *bqš* in the pual first of all convey the passive mean-ing, "to be sought." Jer. 50:20 says, "the sin of Israel and Judah will be sought" (*yebhuqqash*), but it shall no longer be found because Yahweh has forgiven it. According to Ezk. 26:21, the judgment over Tyre is so complete that this de-stroyed city will be sought (*thebhuqeshi*) in vain. In both passages (but with greater probability in Jer. 50:20), the passive can also be understood as repre-senting an indefinite active with the meaning, "one will seek." The context of Est. 2:23 demands that "seek" be interpreted more precisely as "examine, in-vestigate," and thus in this passage also as a passive (*vayebhuqqash haddabhar*, RSV, "when the affair was investigated").

---

[4] See below.
[5] See above.

2. *Seeking in the Figurative Sense.* Of the various possible ways of using *biq-qesh* in a figurative sense, the constructions with an infinitive construct of another verb followed by *le* after some form of *bqš* compose a relatively large group. Furthermore, if the infinitive construct plus *le* syntactically denotes intention to do something, [6] this is strengthened even more by adding *biqqesh*. The instances in which OT writers express a negative intention (shortening life) are notably more numerous. This is frequently the case with *biqqesh* + the inf. const. of *muth* in the hiphil with *le* (Ex. 4:24 [J] and Jer. 26:21, without *le*) and of *haragh*,[7] "to seek to put to death," and sometimes with *biqqesh* plus *lehakkoth*, "to seek to smite" (1 S. 19:10; 2 S. 21:2), *lehashmidh*, "to seek to destroy" (Zec. 12:9; Est. 3:6), and *lishloach yadh be*, "to seek to lay hands on" (Est. 2:21; 6:2; 4QpPs37 2:17f.). This negative aspect also appears in the expression "he sought (*biqqesh*) to draw you away from Yahweh" (Dt. 13:11[10]). The few passages in which this particular construction is used to express a positive intention can be enumerated quickly. They include the use of *biqqesh* with the inf. const. of *halakh*, "to seek to go" (1 K. 11:22; Zec. 6:7), *'abhar*, "to seek to go over" (1 S. 14:4), *bo'*, "to seek to come" (1 S. 23:10; 4QpNah 1:2), *matsa'*, "to seek to find" (Eccl. 12:10: the Preacher's conscious endeavors to find the right word), *bakhah*, "to seek (a place) to weep" (Gen. 43:30: Joseph's desire to have an opportunity to weep because of his emotions which were aroused by the meeting with his brothers), *shama'*, "to seek to hear" (1 K. 10:24; 2 Ch. 9:23: the official démarche of seeking a ruler [*biqqesh 'eth pene shelomoh*, "sought the face of Solomon"] in order to hear his wisdom), and *yadha'*, "to seek to know" (1QS 5:11: seeking and inquiring concerning the precepts in order to know the hidden matters). It has already been suggested that a strong element of intention is present in this construction, which gives to the activity being described the character of desire and of resolute will and action beyond mere intention. [8]

The negative intention, viz., to kill another person, is also expressed by the shortened phrase *biqqesh ('eth) nephesh*, lit., "to seek the soul (life)," which occurs 30 times in the OT. Almost half these occurrences are found in Jeremiah (e.g., Jer. 11:21; 19:7; 44:30). This phrase also appears rather frequently in the Psalter (Ps. 35:4; 38:13[12]; 40:15[14]; 54:5[3]; 63:10[9]; 70:3[2]; 86:14). Of course, it occurs in both earlier and later literary contexts (Ex. 4:19; Ps. 38:13 [12]; 1QH 2:21). In the Psalter this expression occurs almost exclusively in the Individual Laments. Of the psalms where this phrase occurs, only Ps. 63 contains elements of trust and thanksgiving along with those of lament, which has led some scholars to speak of this psalm as an Individual Song of Thanksgiving. Nevertheless, this would not be outside the context of lamentation, trust, and thanksgiving for help shown. This fact justifies the view that this expression typically belongs in the Individual Lament. In Jeremiah (with the exception of Jer. 4:30) and in some psalms, the participial construction *mebhaqeshe (mebhaqeshim 'eth) naphshi* (and other suffixes), "those seeking my soul (life)," occurs. It follows

---

[6] Cf. Brockelmann, *Synt.* § 47.
[7] See above.
[8] See above, I.2.

from the context and immediate parallel expressions that in this form *biqqesh* denotes the personified effort to take the life of someone else, an enemy or a mortal foe. Along with this shortened form, we also find the long form *biqqesh 'eth nephesh leqachtah,* "to seek someone's life to take it away" (1 K. 19:10,14; cf. Ps. 40:15[14] with *lispothah,* "to seek to snatch away," and Ps. 63:10[9], where *hemmah lesho'ah,* "they in vain [?]" precedes this expression). It is difficult to say which form is more original.

Of the various possible ways of using *biqqesh* in a figurative sense, the constructions with an abstract as object of the verb, mentioned above, [9] must be noted. Jeremiah condemns Israel's efforts to rebel against Yahweh and to run after foreign gods under the figure of seeking after lovers (Jer. 2:33). Here also, *biqqesh* does not mean simply "seeking," but implies the fulfilment of "love" (=apostasy) after the lovers are found, as the wording of this passage shows. [10] In this connection, attention should be called to the expressions "seek good" and "seek evil (or my evil or hurt)" (Ps. 122:9; 71:13,24; 1 S. 24:10[9]; 25:26; 1 K. 20:7; Est. 9:2), where an applicatory element is at work alongside the active. In connection with the general judgment which comes upon the land, Baruch desires "great things" (*gedholoth*) for himself, but Jeremiah can promise him only that Yahweh will spare his life (Jer. 45:5, using *biqqesh* in the sense of "wish," "desire"), which again also includes actions to guarantee his well-being (in contrast with Est. 2:15, "to desire nothing," *lo' bhiqeshah dabhar*). In 1 Ch. 21:3, *biqqesh* must be translated "require." In addition to the figurative meanings mentioned under I.2. above (near the end), we may also mention Dnl. 1:8, where a form of *biqqesh* together with an *'asher* clause must mean "to seek permission": "Daniel sought permission from the chief of the court officials not to defile himself." [11] In the inquiries he makes concerning their wisdom and understanding, the king finds Daniel and his friends ten times more intelligent than all his own professionals in this field (Dnl. 1:20). The context here shows that *biqqesh* contains the element of examination and comparison, which corresponds to the concluding expression using *matsa',* "to find." [12] But also, *biqqesh* has a figurative meaning in the expression *biqqesh dabhar mehem,* "he sought a matter of them," which is used to denote the king's examination of their intelligence. → בקשׁ בּינה, *biqqesh bînāh,* "to seek to understand," in Dnl. 8:15 can be translated, "to meditate about the meaning (of a vision)." Prov. 23:35 uses *biqqesh* plus *yasaph* in the hiphil and *'odh,* "I will seek another drink," to describe the dissipation of one who drinks wine. [13] This further confirms in detail the quite significant changes to which *biqqesh* can be subjected by contextual relationships, where its meaning can be altered by the object or the infinitive which is dependent on *biqqesh,* or by idiomatic peculiarities. Semantically, this root must always have been open to such figurative meanings and modifications.

---

[9] See above, I.2.

[10] Cf. the statements made above under II.1. on Jgs. 18:1 and Ruth 3:1, as well as *baqqesh shalom,* "seek peace," in Ps. 34:15(14).

[11] Cf. Jerusalem Bible, German edition.

[12] Cf. the Legal Terminology; see below, II.3.

[13] Cf. Ringgren, *ATD,* XVI, 95f., and other comms. *in loc.*

But the other thesis that all figures go back to the original meaning "to seek" and can be explained in light of this meaning is equally true.

3. *Seeking As a Legal Term.* There are some contexts in the OT where *biqqesh* can be interpreted in no other way than as a legal term. In these passages, "seek" must be understood in the sense of "require." One of the earliest illustrations of this meaning is to be found in the story of David's rise, where David avenges the assassination of Esh-baal, the son of Saul, on his murderers: "shall I not now require his blood at your hand!?" (2 S. 4:11). This legal idea is also found in the commission of Yahweh to the prophet Ezekiel, when Yahweh put him under obligation (legally) by requiring at his hand the blood of the sinner who has fallen under judgment if the prophet failed to warn him (Ezk. 3:18,20; 33:8: *vedhamo miyyadhekha 'abhaqqesh*, "but his blood I will require at your hand"). The corrupt passage in 1 S. 20:16 (today frequently reconstructed on the basis of the LXX) also seems to deal with rendering an account. It is found in the context of the account concerning the sworn friendship between David and Jonathan. The situation described here assumes the character of a legal contract when reference is made to David's oath to Jonathan (v. 17). Demands for compensation, such as that mentioned, e.g., in Gen. 31:39 (E, perhaps even before this in J), belong in the same context of legal ideas. In the discussion between Jacob and Laban, Jacob explains that while he was serving Laban he accepted the responsibility for everything in the flock which had been stolen or torn by wild beasts ("of my hand you required it," *miyyadhi tebhaqeshennah*). In the story of Joseph, there is a reference to the law of surety (Gen. 43:9). Judah offers himself as surety to his father Israel for Benjamin, whom he wants to take with him to Joseph in Egypt: "of my hand you shall require him, if I do not bring him back to you...." Mention should also be made of the use of *biqqesh* in a demand for something that someone claims is due him or for something that someone claims legally. The claim to the priesthood by the Levites (Korah) and the opposition to this claim by Moses (Nu. 16:10 [P], *ubhiqqashtem gam kehunnah*, "and would you seek the priesthood also?") lead us into the field of cultic law. Also, *biqqesh* plus the prep. *min* is used to describe the exaction of interest (Neh. 5:12). Nehemiah himself waived his claim (*lo' bhiqqashti*, "I did not demand") to the revenue (RSV "food allowance") of the governor (Neh. 5:18). Finally, this legal idea can also be used in the realm of natural law in OT poetry to describe that which is required by a creature for his existence (Ps. 104:21); the young lions roaring for their prey claim their food (that is due them) from God (*ulebhaqqesh me'el 'okhlam*). In this connection, the construction with *biqqesh* plus the prep. *min* is typical. Reference has already been made above [14] to Ruth 3:1. Here *biqqesh*, together with words related to it, is a very comprehensive (complex) legal term including different acts which, to be sure, are related to each other. Further, it must be asked whether the pual construction in Est. 2:23 (*vayebhuqqash haddabhar*, "when the affair was investigated") should be reckoned as legal terminology. However this may be decided, in this particular passage the critical

---

[14] See above, II.1.

expression must be translated, "the case was investigated," and the result of this investigation seems to have been expressed by the niphal of *matsa'* (*yimmatse'* or *lo' yimmatse'*, "it was found" or "it was not found"). Possibly the second of the three examples of the pual of *biqqesh* (Jer. 50:20) also points in the same direction. Here we find *yebhuqqash 'eth 'avon yisra'el* with the negative statement *ve'enennu*, RSV, "iniquity shall be sought in Israel, and there shall be none." The next line, which is in parallelism with this and reads *ve'eth chatto'th yehudhah*, "and sin in Judah," is dependent on the same pual form. Then the result of this investigation is expressed by *lo'* with *matsa'*, "and none shall be found." Beyond this, Jer. 50:20 points to the theological use of *biqqesh*.[15] It is conceivable that the maxim in Prov. 29:26, "many seek the face (RSV favor) of a ruler," represents a legal formula (cf. 1 K. 10:24; 2 Ch. 9:23). Thus, it must be taken into account that ideas originally belonging to the legal realm came to be employed in connection with the theological use of *biqqesh* (e.g., in referring to the sin of Israel, or in demanding that which belongs to the God of Israel). Finally, it should also be kept in mind that in all the passages that speak of making an attempt on someone's life, whether it be in a shorter or more expanded or more direct manner of speaking, the effort to gain a legal retribution may be expressed. E.g., those who sought the life of Moses (Ex. 4:19) did so on the basis of his violation of the law (2:11-15). It follows clearly from all this that *biqqesh* occupies a fixed position in the legal terminology of the OT.

III. Theological Use. The functions of "seeking" are obviously also connected with God in the OT, whether God is the object or the subject of the act of seeking, i.e., *biqqesh* is used theologically. Here also there is evidence for a movement from the literal to the figurative connotation. If it was significant that *biqqesh* stood in parallelism with *darash* in general usage, this must certainly be kept in mind in trying to understand the theological use of this root. Only a detailed investigation can show whether a particular shade of meaning demands that these roots be distinguished from one another.[16] Very frequently a promiscuous use is to be observed.

1. *Seeking God.* The OT uses different formulas for expressing the idea of "seeking God." The simplest is *biqqesh ('eth) yhvh*, "to seek Yahweh" (Ex. 33:7), or even shorter, a form of *biqqesh* plus a pronominal suffix referring to Yahweh, e.g., *mebhaqeshekha*, "(all) who seek thee" (Ps. 40:17[16]). The name of Yahweh (83:17[16]), the word of Yahweh (Am. 8:12), and even the Torah (Mal. 2:7) can take the place of Yahweh as the object of "seek." The OT also speaks rather frequently of "seeking the face of God," *biqqesh 'eth pene yhvh* (2 S. 21:1), and once again it is possible to have an even shorter expression using *panim* with a suffix instead of in construct (Hos. 5:15; Ps. 27:8). It is difficult to say which of these two formulas is more original, whether it be the shorter indirect phrase "seeking God" or the longer direct phrase using *panim*, "seeking the face of God." The latter is more descriptive and immediately understand-

---

[15] See III.
[16] Cf. Reindl and Westermann.

able. In the secular realm, it is used in referring to the king, "seek the face of the king" (Prov. 29:26; cf. 1 K. 10:24; 2 Ch. 9:23), evidently meaning to "obtain the favor of the king." This is hardly to be interpreted in a spiritual and figurative sense, but assumes the personal movement of the one seeking toward the one being sought. To be sure, these few passages do not explicitly state that the audience did this in a fixed ceremony, and yet this can be inferred from a general knowledge of court ceremonial in the ancient Near East and in the OT. Without maintaining that the religious usage is dependent on the secular, it may be assumed for mutual understanding that the same idea is at work in both realms.

From the standpoint of the history of religion, it may be conjectured that the idea of seeking the statue of a deity in the sanctuary stands behind the direct formula with *panim*, "face," in theological usage. Such an interpretation is excluded in the OT because of the prohibition against making idols. The Israelite does not seek an image of God in the sanctuary; rather, he is fully convinced of the invisible presence of Yahweh, whether it be in the future, the past, or the present. The phrase "seeking the face of a deity" always refers to a comprehensible cultic rite at the holy places (temple, sanctuary), where it would have been possible to "seek God" directly or mediately. The oldest examples of this longer, direct formula appear in 2 S. 21:1 and Hos. 5:15, as well as in the Psalms (24:6; 27:8; assuming that these Psalms are to be regarded as preexilic). Furthermore, there are several examples of the short form, "seek God," which (in the context in which they now occur) must have a cultic rite in mind. This leads to the obvious conclusion that it is necessary to begin with the cultic rite in order to understand this phrase, but at the same time it is impossible to say which of the two forms of this phrase is original rather than the other. The short form also occurs in Hos. 5:6, where it clearly has reference to a cultic act; the situation is similar in Ex. 33:7 (J or E?). Of course, to locate this phrase in a "cultic rite" is too general, and in some passages in the OT more precise statements can be made about its setting. [17] Hos. 5:6 explicitly mentions "going with flocks and herds" "to seek Yahweh," and thus refers to a cultic act which is connected with a sacrificial act (cf. 2 Ch. 11:16; 15:15). Zec. 8:21-22 (cf. also v. 23) also has in mind seeking Yahweh in the Jerusalem sanctuary. The setting of the Individual Lament in Ps. 27:7-14 (assuming that these verses do not belong with vv. 1-6) presupposes Yahweh's presence in the temple (a lament with cultic instruction), and thus Ps. 27:8 also has in mind an event in the divine worship which is denoted by the phrase, "seek God's face." The hymn found in 1 Ch. 16 calls those who praise God "those who seek God" (vv. 10,11). The imperative of "seek" is normally used as a summons to worship (v. 11, which uses *darash* and *biqqesh*). In the summons to conversion and the description of repentance, that which is done or that which will be done positively, etc., is called "seeking God" (Dt. 4:29; Hos. 3:5; 5:15; 7:10; Jer. 50:4; 2 Ch. 7:14; 15:4; cf. Jer. 29:13). A cultic rite certainly cannot be excluded a priori in Hos. 3:5 (cf. v. 4!) and Jer. 50:4; and perhaps also in the two passages in the Chronicler's history (on 2 Ch. 15:4, cf.

---

[17] Cf. Reindl, n. 439, whose schematization must be understood as one possible suggestion; other interpretations are also possible.

v. 3), even though these texts use the idea of conversion to express an internalizing of man's relationship to God. The much discussed phenomenon of the
criticism of the cult in ancient Israel (e.g., by the prophets) does not necessarily
have to be understood in the sense of a rejection of the cult.

The meeting at the "Tent of Meeting" mentioned in Ex. 33:7 is also to be
understood as a "cultic rite," a revelatory event. Here, to be sure, it is presented
in connection with Moses, but it seems to include an interrogation of Yahweh
which is possible for the Israelites as mediated by Moses. The expression "seek
the face of Yahweh" in 2 S. 21:1 should probably also be interpreted in the same
way. Here David inquires of Yahweh. Elsewhere in the OT, the idiom used to
express this concept is → שָׁאַל *shā'al bayhvh,* "to inquire of Yahweh" (1 S. 23:2,4;
etc.), which sometimes was done with the help of an ephod (1 S. 30:7,8), and
sometimes (in an inquiry through an oracle) with the help of a cultic ceremonial
act. An inquiry through mediums and wizards was regarded as an abuse of this
practice (Lev. 19:31). In the announcement concerning the future in Mal. 3:1,
the promise is made that Yahweh will come to his temple. At that time it will be
possible to have a (cultic) meeting with him (*yabho' 'el hekhalo ha'adhon 'asher
'attem mebhaqeshim,* "and the Lord whom you seek will come to his temple")
after a process of refining and purifying shall have restored the right offering.
Perhaps seeking torah from the priest, who, as "the messenger of Yahweh
Sebaoth," keeps knowledge on his lips and instruction in his mouth, can also
be regarded as a "cultic rite." Ps. 24:1-5, including v. 6, also speaks of imparting
and seeking torah: "So it happens to the generation which seeks him (*doreshav*),
and which seeks your face, O (God of) Jacob" (following the Jerusalem Bible).
It is not clear whether the desperate and futile efforts *lebhaqqesh 'eth debhar
yhvh,* "to seek the word of Yahweh," of Am. 8:12 should also be understood in
an institutional sense (v. 11 already mentions hungering and thirsting after the
word of God or "hearing the words of God"). Seeking God in Isa. 45:19 is not
to be interpreted institutionally. Fundamentally, this passage has reference to
God's being revealed through his acts in creation and history (cf. v. 18). Here
biqqesh has the sense of "seeking after a revelation," of "knowing God in his
deed." The same questions arise in connection with the same formulas, "seeking
God," or "seeking the face of God," when they are used to refer to the phenomenon of petition, prayer, intercession, as e.g., in David's intercession for the ailing
son of Bathsheba (2 S. 12:16, with the prep. *be'adh,* "on behalf of"), which is
accompanied by fasting. Similarly, in Ezr. 8:21-23 the prayer that God might
grant much success to the project of his people is strongly supported by fasting
(*biqqesh me'elohim,* "to seek from God"; RSV, "to beseech God"). Here also a
"rite performed in the worship service" is not to be excluded a priori. Prayer and
fasting are also intimately related in Dnl. 9:3. It is questionable as to whether a
"private" prayer is conceivable here. Other examples in which *biqqesh + min* is
used before a term for "God" or a divine name in reference to prayer appear
in Ps. 27:4 and 2 Ch. 20:4 (twice, once with *min* and once without it). *min* can
also be replaced by an objective genitive, as in Mal. 2:15, *mebhaqqesh zera'
'elohim,* "waiting for the offspring of God" (this verse is difficult in other respects
as well). Neh. 2:4; Est. 4:8; and 7:7 also show that in the secular realm *biqqesh,*

with or without *min,* can mean "to ask, make a request." In addition, the expression containing *biqqesh* in Est. 4:8 means "to entreat for the people" (*'al 'ammah*). The hearing of prayer is expressed by *matsa',* "to find," in Isa. 65:1, as in general the concept of the successful accomplishment of *biqqesh,* "to seek," is to find (*matsa'*) the goal of the action expressed by *biqqesh* (cf. Dt. 4:29; Jer. 29:13). If Hos. 5:6,15 point to an expansion of the concept of "seeking God" beyond the realm of divine worship and the institutional sense to an internalizing and deepening of godliness which must be proved true above all by fulfilling ethical responsibilities, Zeph. 2:3 (where *biqqesh* is found 3 times!) seems to express this idea even more clearly. In this passage, "seeking God" stands in parallelism with seeking *tsedheq,* "righteousness," and *'anavah,* "humility," and with doing *mishpat yhvh,* "the judgment (RSV commands) of Yahweh" (cf. Dt. 4:29; Jer. 29:13; Isa. 51:1).

Finally, attention must be called to a group of examples in which a participial construction meaning "seekers of Yahweh" (or a construction using a finite verb meaning "those who seek Yahweh") is found. Here one is moving even farther away from the original meaning of *biqqesh,* since the expression "seekers of Yahweh" here means members of the ancient covenant people, Israelites, or perhaps godly Israelites. Such an interpretation is possible, e.g., in Zeph. 1:6: "those who do not seek Yahweh, but have turned away from him, who bow down to the host of heaven, etc.," are members of the people of God who have fallen into judgment. The phrase *mebhaqeshe yhvh,* "seekers of Yahweh" (or *kol mebhaqeshekha,* "all who seek thee," or something similar) appears in a positive sense in the Psalms (Ps. 40:17 [16]; 69:7 [6]; 70:5 [4]; 105:3-4; 1 Ch. 16:10-11) and elsewhere, e.g., Isa. 51:1; 2 Ch. 11:16; Ezr. 8:22 (perhaps also Hos. 3:5). *mebhaqeshe yhvh,* "those who seek Yahweh," are contrasted with *'anshe ra',* "evil men," in the antithetic *parallelismus membrorum* of a wisdom maxim (Prov. 28:5, in the collection of proverbs made by the "men of Hezekiah," which possibly originated about the middle of the monarchical period). This raises the question of whether the contrast should be understood as one between two groups in Israel, or whether it should be interpreted more generally as a contrast between those who follow God and those who deny him. It would seem best to opt for a more general understanding, which was adapted to the Israelite Yahwistic situation.

It is possible to interpret "seeking God" and "seeking the face of God" in different ways in the OT. This would demand that a distinction be made as well between the various kinds of "cultic rites" associated with *biqqesh.* But the formal expressions can expand their meaning, and thus move away from their original connotation to a more general understanding of the "seekers of God" as Israelites. However, the connection between these later meanings and the original cultic situation is still perceptible in the more general use of this root. [18]

2. *God Seeks.* The number of examples in which God appears as subject of "seeking" is disproportionately smaller. Nevertheless, this concept is not absent

---

[18] Cf. Reindl.

from the OT. The "seeking which God does" is expressed in quite different ways. In the Saul tradition, especially the tradition concerning Saul's rejection, "Yahweh seeks out for himself (*lo*) a man after his own heart," and appoints him *"naghidh* (prince) over his people" (1 S. 13:14, here *biqqesh* = "to choose, designate"). The auxiliary use of *biqqesh* followed by the infinitive construct of a different verb and then *le* to denote intention is also found with God as subject, e.g., in Zec. 12:9: "I desire (*'abhaqqesh*) to destroy all nations that come against Jerusalem." In a prayer to Yahweh in Ps. 119:176, the worshipper asks Yahweh to seek (visit) him (he feels that he is lost). In showing the sin of the covenant people who had fallen under God's judgment, in a severe reprimand in which the hearers are reminded of their various crimes in detail, Ezekiel declares to Yahweh that he had found no one who could prevent the judgment by building a dam against the people's sins and by interceding for the people (*lephanay*, "before me," Ezk. 22:30, *va'abhaqqesh mehem 'ish ... velo' matsa'thi*, "and I sought for a man among them, ... but I found none"). This idea plays the same role in Jer. 5:1ff., except that this passage summons those who hear the announcement of judgment to go and search for a man who *'oseh mishpat mebhaqqesh 'emunah*, "does justice and seeks truth," while according to Ezekiel Yahweh himself had searched for such a person in vain. [19]

In Josh. 22:23, a late passage written by P, [20] in a controversy between Transjordanian and Cisjordanian tribes (over an altar which the former had built), the tribes east of Jordan suggest that Yahweh "investigate" the affair (*yhvh hu' yebhaqqesh*, "may Yahweh seek," RSV, "may the Lord himself take vengeance"), search for any unlawful action, and (if necessary) take appropriate measures. Job's lament in 10:6 also speaks of a divine investigation (*biqqesh* + *le*, and in the parallel line *darash* + *le*) for the purpose of establishing iniquity and sin. These thoughts bring to mind Ps. 139, except that in this passage other verbs are used to describe the same kind of situation (→ חקר *chāqar*, "to search," *bachan*, "to examine, test, try," and *ra'ah*, "to see"). In Eccl. 3:15, *biqqesh* appears in a maxim which affirms that all phenomena are determined by God, and thus he is able also to seek that which has "disappeared." [21] Once *biqqesh* is also used in the sense of God's requirements (expectations) (Isa. 1:12, "who seeks this [i.e., the sacrificial cult] of your hand?" Yahweh expects something different!). In the statements in Ezekiel on the theme of the shepherd and his sheep (chap. 34, which is not homogeneous), [22] the prophet delivers a Woe Oracle against the "shepherds" (cf. Zec. 11:16). In this connection, reference is made to the shepherd's responsibility of seeking his sheep which are lost (have gone astray, vv. 4,6; in v. 6 *biqqesh* is found in parallelism with *darash*). In contrast to this, Yahweh himself will perform the responsibilities of a shepherd and in doing so, along with many other acts, he will seek the lost (v. 16). Here, perhaps, a few passages may be mentioned in which the saving deed of God is represented

---

[19] Cf. Zimmerli, *BK*, XIII/1, *in loc.*
[20] Cf. Noth, *HAT*, 7, *in loc.*
[21] Cf. Zimmerli, *ATD*, XVI, 168, 173, 174; Galling, *HAT*, 18, 93-95; but cf. for a different view the Jerusalem Bible: "God cares for (*yebhaqqesh*) the persecuted."
[22] See the comms.!

by depicting God as summoning the godly to seek for his adversary, his accuser, or his affliction in order to establish that they no longer exist because God has removed them (Jer. 50:20; Isa. 41:12; Ps. 37:36). Finally, reference should be made to Eccl. 7:29 and 8:17. These two passages seem to be intimately related. Eccl. 7:29 states that God created man *yashar*, "upright," but that man has "sought" (*biqqesh*) many "devices" (*chishshebhonoth*), i.e., he has become engrossed in deliberations, calculations, and complications, which are in conflict with his nature as a created being. Nevertheless, his lot is *lebhaqqesh*, "to seek," but he is limited in that *lo' yukhal limtso'*, "he cannot find out," he cannot fathom, because everything is the work of God (8:17), fixed and determined by him. In this context, *biqqesh* means "to investigate," "to fathom," as a human function, which again and again enables man to succeed in spite of his basic nature, but which again and again is transcended by God through his determinations.

Even though the number of passages that ascribe a *biqqesh* event to God is small, they present a wide variety of divine activities: choosing, seeking salvation, determining and investigating, demanding, expecting, requiring, going after the lost like a shepherd; even the deliberate element of a completion of an action, expressed by *biqqesh*, is present. Of course, the main emphasis in the theological use of *biqqesh* lies in the realm of the relationships between man and God, where God is depicted as the goal of seeking.

IV. The Derivative baqqashah. *baqqashah*, which appears seven times in Esther and once in Ezra (Est. 5:3,6,7,8; 7:2,3; 9:12; Ezr. 7:6), is formally an (Aram.) pael infinitive with very strong noun characteristics. In all eight passages, this infinitive has a suffix attached to it. Several times *she'elah* stands in parallelism to *baqqashah*, which means "petition," "wish," "desire," "longing," "request." In Esther, *she'elah* is always used in the same expressions as *baqqashah* both in content and in form. The expressions in which it is found are so stereotyped that one would be justified in concluding that it is part of a fixed form in the ceremonial of the court, which also was the setting for *baqqashah*. Sometimes it means the petition (the request, etc.) of a subject or a subordinate to the king, his superior, to grant a specific wish, which could also be completely rejected. Such a request could be made only on specific occasions (by particular audiences).[23] Ezr. 7:6 confirms this interpretation of *baqqashah*. The term is used in connection with *nathan* ("to give") and *'asah* ("to do") when one is speaking or thinking of the expectations of the one making the request. The one in a position to grant a request (at least in Esther) enables a person to make a request by asking: *mah baqqashathekh*, "What is your request?" It is no longer possible to decide whether *baqqashah* (perhaps together with *she'elah*) means the irrecusable petition which, according to Herodotus (ix.110,111), was possible at the royal banquet.[24] At all events, in the OT this word is found exclusively in literary contexts that have their setting in the Persian period. The textual form of Ezra and Esther is late.   *Wagner*

---

23 Cf. the comms., esp. Bardtke, *KAT*, XVII/5, 337f. and *passim;* Ringgren, *ATD*, XVI, 391f. and *passim;* Würthwein, *HAT*, 18, 185 and *passim*.

24 Bardtke has called attention to this custom related by Herodotus.

בָּרָא *bārā'*

Contents: I. In the Ancient Near East: 1. Egypt; 2. Mesopotamia. II. 1. Etymology; 2. Occurrences; 3. LXX. III. Meaning. IV. Theological Usage: 1. Of Cosmic Powers; 2. In the Historical Realm; 3. Of Individual Persons; 4. Other Theological Uses. V. In the Qumran Literature.

I. In the Ancient Near East.

1. *Egypt.* The Egyptian terminology for creation is very plentiful and variegated. Statements concerning the creation and origin of the world are intertwined in a remarkable way, and wholly concrete acts are connected with events that are understood abstractly. Thus, expressions for all sorts of handicrafts alternate with concepts of origin through emanation and birth. Moreover, the idea of a creation by the word is common.

The two most important common Egyptian verbs for creation are *iry* and *ḳmꜣ*, which are usually translated "to make" or "to create." They often stand side by side, e.g., Ptah is described as "the one who made (*iry*) that which is, the one who created (*ḳmꜣ*) that which exists." The verb *iry* covers the entire range of meaning from "manufacture, produce" to a divine "creation"; it also means "to beget": *ir-św*, "his (the king's) begetter." *ḳmꜣ* can also denote the creation itself, [1] and also is used synonymously with *iry*. Light, fire, seasons, etc., appear as objects of this verb, and *ḳmꜣ-św*, "his begetter," occurs. The use of *iry* and *ḳmꜣ* as synonyms in the Book of the Dead 15 A is typical: Re is "lord of the heavens, lord of the earth, who made the things which are above (the stars) and the things which are below (men?), . . . who made the countries and created (*ḳmꜣ*) man, who made the sea and created (*ḳmꜣ*) the Nile, who made the water and gave life to that which dwells therein, who established the mountains, who formed man and beast." "Heaven, earth, and everything which is between them," [2] the underworld, gods and men, plants and animals, are objects of the creative *iry;*

---

bārā'. F. Böhl, "ברא, *bārā*, als Terminus der Weltschöpfung im alttestamentlichen Sprachgebrauch," *Alttestamentl. Studien. R. Kittel zum 60. Geburtstag. BWANT,* 13 (1913), 42-60; H. Braun, "ποιέω," *TDNT,* VI, 458-484; E. Dantinne, "Création et séparation," *Mus,* 74 (1961), 441-451; W. Foerster, "κτίζω," *TDNT,* III, 1000-1035; P. Humbert, "Emploi et portée du verbe bârâ (créer) dans l'AT," *ThZ,* 3 (1947), 401-422; *idem, Opuscules d'un hébraïsant, Mémoires de l'université de Neuchâtel,* 26 (1958), 146-165; J. Körner, "Die Bedeutung der Wurzel bārā im AT," *OLZ,* 64 (1969), 533-540; J. van der Ploeg, "Le sens du verbe hébreu ברא bārā," *Mus,* 59 (1946), 143-157; N. H. Ridderbos, "Genesis 1₁ und ₂," *OTS,* 12 (1958), 219-223; W. H. Schmidt, *Die Schöpfungsgeschichte der Priesterschrift. WMANT,* 17 (²1967), 130f., 164-67, 182-85; C. Westermann, *BK,* I (1967), 120, 136-39.

On I. 1.: S. Morenz, *Egyptian Religion* (trans. 1973), 159ff.; M. Sandman-Holmberg, *The God Ptah* (Lund, 1946), 31ff.; S. Sauneron-J. Yoyotte, *La naissance du monde selon l'Egypte ancienne. Sources orientales,* 1 (Paris, 1959), 17ff.; J. Zandee, *De hymnen aan Amon van Papyrus Leiden I 350* (Leiden, 1947).

[1] Zandee, 38.
[2] E. Chassinat, *Le temple d'Edfou,* I (1892), 133, 8.

this also applies to the creator himself in a paradigmatic way.[3] An interesting combination of internal and external creation appears in the expression, "that which the heart created (km³) and the hands made."[4] It should be observed that km³ can also mean "to forge or refine metal," and thus could be listed among verbs used to describe the work of artisans.

Other common Egyptian verbs used to denote creation are š³ʿ and šhpr. š³ʿ, "to begin," is usually construed with another verb: Horus, who first created all things (š³ʿ km³; R. Lepsius, *Denkmäler* [1849ff.], IV, 53a). Thoth is "the one who by his command originated that which is."[5] The creator-god is also called š³ʿ hpr, "the one who first brought into being." A favorite way of expressing continuous creation in Egyptian was by using šhpr, "to form, bring into being, cause to arise."[6]

Other verbs of creation denote the activities of artisans; but the concrete meaning is insignificant for the most part in comparison with the general meaning "to create." Thus we find, e.g., (a) nby,[7] "to form, establish," which originally denotes the smelting of metals, and is often used of Ptah;[8] it takes as an object gods, kings, heaven and earth, and limbs of men;[9] (b) kd, lit. "to fashion pots, build," used especially with living creatures; it takes gods, men, and animals as objects (the potter par excellence is Khnum); (c) hmw, "to make," used especially of the carpenter, e.g., Amun, "who has made himself" (Leiden Papyrus I, 350; II, 26), Ptah, "who made the earth according to the plans of his heart" (Berlin Papyrus 3048, III, 1).[10] Later, in the same hymn (VII, 6-8), Ptah is praised as the one "who formed (nby) the gods and men and all animals, who made (iry) all lands, beaches, and the great ocean in his name 'Maker of the Earth' (hmw t³)."

But creation is also understood as an emanation from the original god. Sometimes this is expressed by the general term šhpr, "to bring into being, cause to arise," and sometimes by wtt, "to beget,"[11] and mśy, "to bring forth, give birth to."[12] The emanation concept received its classic shape and continuation in the genealogy of the Heliopolitan gods: "It was indeed their children who brought into being a number of types of creatures in this world in the form of children and grandchildren."[13] The original god is even wtt św ds.f, "the one who has begotten himself."[14] It is important to note how closely the expressions for creation and begettal are related to each other.

---

[3] Zandee, 38.

[4] Examples appear in *WbÄS*, V, 36, 2.

[5] Chassinat, *Edfou*, II, 16, 4f.

[6] *WbÄS*, IV, 240ff. See esp. the well-developed hpr theology of the Bremner-Rhind Papyrus 26, 21ff. and 28, 20ff.; translated in Sauneron-Yoyotte, 48ff.

[7] *WbÄS*, II, 241.

[8] Sandman-Holmberg, 46f.

[9] Zandee, 38.

[10] On Ptah as an artisan, see Sandman-Holmberg, 45ff.

[11] *WbÄS*, I, 381ff.

[12] *WbÄS*, II, 137f.; Morenz, 162f.

[13] The Bremner-Rhind Papyrus 29, 5f., Sauneron-Yoyotte, 48ff.

[14] *WbÄS*, I, 381, 15.

The idea of creation by the word [15] is found in the so-called Teaching of the Gods from Memphis. [16] The creative words of Ptah are "conceived in the heart and commanded with the tongue" (lines 56f.). A particular example of this teaching from Heliopolis states that the divine pair Hu ("utterance") and Sia ("understanding") are products of the creation of Atum. [17] It should be observed that the ideas of creation by the word are often closely related to statements of an entirely different type.

Bergman

2. *Mesopotamia*. The common Akkadian word for "create," *banû*, [18] also means "to build" (e.g., a house, a city), [19] "to set up, make" (e.g., a stela, an image, a boat), [20] and "to beget" (esp. in the ptcp., *abu banûa*, "my father and begetter"). [21] It is used with gods as subject in various cosmogonic contexts in the sense of "create." The expression "to create with the hands" (e.g., EnEl V, 135, "the earth which your hands created") [22] is especially instructive. The opposite of *banû* is *abātu*, "to destroy," as is clear from EnEl IV, 22: Marduk obtains the power to create and to destroy by his word. *banû* is used several times of the creation of the world in EnEl, e.g., III, 121, "May everything which I create be unchangeable"; IV, 45,47, Marduk creates the wind; IV, 136; VI, 2, with *nikiltu*, "artistic work," as obj.; IV, 145, with the heaven as obj.; VI, 7, with man as obj. In the cosmogonic introduction to the well-known exorcism against toothache, [23] it says: "After Anu had created (*ibnû*) heaven, heaven had created the earth, the earth had created the rivers, the rivers had created the trenches, and the trenches had created the mire, the mire created the worm." Gods and abstract ideas like wisdom, strife, adjuration, and righteousness, also occur as objects of *banû*. [24] *bānû*, "creator," appears several times as a divine epithet, [25] e.g., in *bān kalâmi*, "creator of all," *bānû kibrāti*, "creator of the regions of the world," *bān šamê u erṣeti*, "creator of the heaven and of the earth," *bānû nišê*, "creator of man," but also *bānû kīnāti*, "creator of righteousness," *bānû tērēti*, "creator of omens," and *bānû nīmēqi*, "creator of wisdom." Ashur is even called *bānû ramānišu*, "he who created himself."

But other verbs are also used in EnEl in connection with the creation, e.g., *epēšu*, "to make" (with the obj. man, VII, 90; regions of the world, VII, 89; and the storm, I, 126), *bašāmu D*, "to form" (with the obj. the dwelling place of the gods, V, 1) and *izuzzu Š*, "to set up, bring into being" (with the obj. dragons, etc., I, 141; man, VI, 5; and the stars, V, 2,4).

Ringgren

[15] Morenz, 163ff.
[16] *ANET*, 4ff.; Sauneron-Yoyotte, 62ff.
[17] *RÄR*, 318f., 715.
[18] *AHw*, 103; *CAD*, II, 83ff.
[19] *CAD*, II, 85f.
[20] *CAD*, II, 86f.
[21] *CAD*, II, 94f.
[22] Cf. *ANET³*, 502.
[23] CT 17, 50; *AOT*, 133f.
[24] *CAD*, II, 88f.
[25] *CAD*, II, 94f.; Tallqvist, *Akk. Götterepitheta* (1938), 68ff.

II. 1. *Etymology.* As yet, the root *br'* has not been found in the older Semitic languages outside the OT. Possibly it is related to the Old South Arab. root *br'* "to build," *mbr'*, "building," cf. Soq. "to bring forth, give birth to"; [26] the Pun. root *br'* seems to mean "a sculptor." [27] As far as its meaning is concerned, this root is more closely connected with the use of the common Semitic root *bny*, "to build." However, from the viewpoint of the history of language, *bny* is hardly to be derived from a postulated common Semitic root *br'*. [28] The Heb. root *br'* probably has the original meaning "to separate, divide." [29]

2. *Occurrences.* *bara'* occurs 49 times in the OT, and that primarily in texts dating clearly from the exilic period or later: Deutero-Isaiah (17 times), Genesis P (10), Trito-Isaiah (3), Ezekiel (3), Malachi (once), and Ecclesiastes (once). The majority of examples of the occurrence of this word in the Psalms also belong to the same period (Ps. 51:12 [Eng. v. 10]; 102:19[18]; 104:30; 148:5). Its occurrences in Gen. 5:1; Ex. 34:10; Isa. 4:5; Jer. 31:22; and Am. 4:13 are to be ascribed to redactional work in the late exilic or the postexilic period. Its appearance in Dt. 4:32 is Deuteronomistic. The only passages using *bara'* that can even be considered as preexilic are Nu. 16:30 (twice) and Ps. 89:13,48(12,47), [30] and even in these texts the preexilic date is disputed. [31] Therefore, it can be regarded as certain that *bara'* was introduced into OT literature as a theological idea for the first time in the exilic period. Its prior history is unknown. The exilic authors who introduced it into the OT may have taken up an old word and given it a new character. The occurrences of *bara'* in Deutero-Isaiah, Trito-Isaiah, and the Psalms could favor the assumption that this word originated in the cultic language, [32] but there are no certain indications of this. The absence of *bara'* in Job and to a great extent in the Wisdom Literature is striking.   *Bernhardt*

3. *LXX.* The LXX translates *bara'* by *ktízein*, "to create," 17 times (6 times in the Pss., 4 times in Deutero-Isa., twice in Ezk., and once each in Dt., Jer., Am., Mal., and Eccl.), *poieín*, "to make," 15 times (9 times in Gen., 5 times in Deutero-Isa., and once in Trito-Isa.), *árchein*, "to begin," *gennán*, "to beget," *deiknýein*, "to show," *deiknýnai*, "to show" (once each), *gínesthai*, "to become," *katadeiknýnai*, "to show clearly, make known, establish" (3 times each), and *kataskeuázein*, "to build, create" (twice). In Genesis, *bara'* is rendered by *árchein, gínesthai* (3 times), and *poieín* (9 times), in spite of the fact that more

---

[26] *KBL³*.

[27] *DISO,* 43: "engraver."

[28] So J. Barth, *ZA,* 3 (1888), 57; cf. Körner, 534f.

[29] Dantinne; cf. the derivation from an original biradical root *br* in G. J. Botterweck, *Der Triliterismus im Semit. BBB,* 3 (1952), 64f.

[30] By no means can Dt. 4:32; Jer. 31:22; or Am. 4:13 be considered as preexilic, as Körner, 535, again recently has supposed.

[31] See comms. *in loc.*

[32] Böhl; Humbert, *Opuscules,* 161f.

frequently *poieín* is the Greek equivalent of Heb. *'asah* [33] and does not denote the work of God exclusively. By way of contrast, *ktízein* is not found in Genesis. In later translations that followed the translation of the Pentateuch, *bara'* seems to have been rendered more by *ktízein* when it was used of divine creation. [34] The Hexaplaric translations choose *ktízein* as a technical term.

Botterweck

III. Meaning. The scope of the use of the verb *bara'* is greatly limited. It is used exclusively to denote divine creation and appears predominantly in the qal in the OT (38 times), and less frequently in the niphal (10 times). The rare nominal form *berî'āh*, "a creation, created thing," occurs once (Nu. 16:30). As a special theological term, *bara'* is used to express clearly the incomparability of the creative work of God in contrast to all secondary products and likenesses made from already existing material by man. However, in poetic texts *bara'* is used in parallelism with → עשׂה *'āśāh*, "to do, make" (Isa. 41:20; 43:1,7; 45:7,12,18; Am. 4:13), → יצר *yātsar*, "to form" (Isa. 43:1,7; 45:7,18; Am. 4:13), → כון *kûn*, "to establish" (Isa. 45:18), → יסד *yāsadh*, "to found" (Ps. 89:12[11]), and → חדשׁ *chādhash*, "to renew" (51:12[10]), and to a certain extent this results in a levelling of its meaning.

IV. Theological Usage.

1. *Of Cosmic Powers.* The theological concern connected with the introduction of *bara'*, as a designation for God's creative work, into the language of the account of creation in Gen. 1:1–2:4a is especially clear. In this section, the Priestly redaction has interpreted an earlier tradition by making additions and changes in that tradition. [35] However, the text of this earlier tradition used *'asah*, "to make," for the formation of the individual elements of creation by God. Sometimes, P placed a corresponding command of God before this mechanical description of the events of creation, which was done in the earlier tradition only in v. 26 in the account of the creation of man. But in this redactional process, the descriptions of creation using *'asah* in the earlier tradition lost their autonomy and became mere illustrations of the act connected with the creative word. Moreover, P introduced *bara'* into particularly important passages and thus implicitly prevented a misunderstanding of *'asah* in the earlier narrative. This occurred at the beginning of the account of the creation of the animal world (1:21) and in the description of the creation of man (1:27). The creation of man was particularly important to the Priestly redactor. Thus, he uses *bara'* three times in v. 27 alone (cf. also 5:2 and 6:7). Finally, in his initial superscription (1:1) and in his comprehensive concluding remark (2:3,4), P used *bara'* explicitly to refer to creation as a whole, and thus superimposed his view of the

---

[33] Cf. *TDNT*, VI, 459.
[34] Cf. *TDNT*, III, 1027.
[35] For details, see Schmidt, 160ff.

nonpareil character of the creative work of God on the entire pericope. It must be emphasized that P did not concern *bara'* with some figurative idea. This verb does not denote an act that somehow can be described, but simply states that, unconditionally, without further intervention, through God's command something comes into being that had not existed before. "He commanded and they were created" (Ps. 148:5).

Outside of P, *bara'* is used only relatively rarely of the creation of cosmic powers. Usually, appropriate examples of this are found in contexts that praise the majesty of the Creator God (Isa. 40:26,28; Am. 4:13; Ps. 89:13[12]; 148:5), while others are related to the creation of man (Dt. 4:32; Isa. 45:12; and also Ps. 89:48[47]). Between these two groups lie Isa. 42:5 and 45:18, where (as in P) the creation of man is represented as the most important work of creation. Accordingly, Isa. 45:12 states that Yahweh "made" (*'asah*) the earth, but "created" (*bara'*) man.

2. *In the Historical Realm.* In Deutero-Isaiah in particular, *bara'* also takes historical powers and events as its object. Theologically, this extension of the use of this verb is very significant, because it is based on the view that Yahweh's activity in history obtains the quality of the nonpareil work of the Creator God. In this connection, of course, Deutero-Isaiah does not connect his theology of creation with a general theology of history, but with the old theology of election. Thus, indeed, mankind as a whole is the creation of God (Isa. 45:12); and yet, among the nations that have arisen during the course of history, Israel alone is said to have been created by Yahweh (43:1,7,15). The same thought appears in Mal. 2:10. (Basically this view is already anticipated in the Pentateuchal sources J and P by the genealogical connection between creation and the history of Israel, which points to Israel.) By being connected with the theology of election, the historically oriented *bara'* in Deutero-Isaiah takes on a soteriological character.[36] *bara'* no longer denotes an act of Yahweh merely in remote primitive time, but also in the immediately imminent future. Thus, the change of fortune for the exiles is interpreted as a new creative act of Yahweh: *'attah nibhre'u velo' me'az,* "they are created now, not long ago" (48:7). This new creation also extends to natural powers, as the wonderful transformation of the wilderness into a fruitful wooded land shows (41:18ff., *bara'* is found in v. 20). The use of *bara'* in 54:16 shows the extent to which Deutero-Isaiah understands the creative work of God as an act of salvation for Israel: enemy powers can find no fault in the newly established Jerusalem, the new creation, since in the final analysis those who make weapons and those who fight have also been "created" by Yahweh.

A similar linguistic use of *bara'* is also found outside Deutero-Isaiah. Thus, *'am nibhra'* in Ps. 102:19(18) can only mean "a newly created people," in parallelism with *dhor 'acharon,* "a generation to come." In postexilic prophetic texts, the creative act of God in the historical realm expressed by *bara'* is trans-

---

36 Cf. von Rad, *OT Theol,* II (trans. 1965). 238ff.

ferred to the End Time (Isa. 4:5; possibly also the difficult passage in Jer. 31:22).[37] In Trito-Isaiah, it includes the new creation of the whole cosmos (65:17f.).

bara' appears in only two passages having to do with the prehistory of Israel (Ex. 34:10; Nu. 16:30). Here also, that which Yahweh creates has the character of the wonderful, of the entirely new. Ex. 34:10 ("marvels such as have not yet been created") is concerned with the whole issue of the history of election in general, while Nu. 16:30 (*bara' beri'ah*, lit., "to create a creation," RSV, "to create something new") is limited to a single divine intervention, viz., to the opening of the ground to swallow up the opponents of Moses. This connection of the verb *bara'* with an act of divine punishment is unique.

3. *Of Individual Persons.* The dissociation of the idea of creation from primordial times also made it possible for wisdom thought to discern a direct work of the creator (*bore'*) in each individual (Eccl. 12:1). This concept is found in the sense of a *creatio continua* (continual creation) of all creatures in Ps. 104:30. In the corrupted passage in Ps. 89:48(47), *bara'* seems to express the important idea that the vanity (transitoriness? שׁוא *shāv'*) of man is founded on his creation by God.

In Ezekiel, *bara'* is used to refer to individual foreigners. *yom hibbara'akha,* "the day that you were created," seems to mean the day of the birth of the prince of Tyre (Ezk. 28:13,15). 21:35(30) shows that this refers not only to the physical event, but in a general way to the creation of men or human communities in a certain time and place.

4. *Other Theological Uses.* a. The intimate relationship between creation and expectation of salvation in Deutero-Isaiah sometimes results in the use of *bara'* to refer to specific manifestations of future salvation. According to Isa. 45:8, Yahweh "creates" the condition in which *yesha'*, "salvation," and *tsedha-qah,* "righteousness," thrive in rich abundance. Similarly, the hymns of thanksgiving on the lips of those who before had mourned are also Yahweh's creation (Isa. 57:19).

b. The role *bara'* plays in Isa. 45:7 is unique. When the prophet emphasizes that Yahweh creates light and peace as well as darkness and evil, probably his intention is to reject the dualism that was so widespread in the Persian Period.[38] In any case, the emphasis in this passage is on Yahweh's creation of darkness and evil, for only these two ideas are connected with the important word *bara'*, while light and peace are simply objects of *yatsar*, "form," and *'asah*, "make."

c. Ps. 51:12(10) goes beyond the creation of salvation and corruption. Here the worshipper prays ("unmatched in boldness")[39] that God might "create" in him a clean heart. This passage also understands man as alone the work of God in harmony with the view of God as Creator.

Bernhardt

---

[37] See comms. *in loc.*

[38] Cf. König, *Jesaja* (1926), 386f.; Fohrer, *Jesaja,* III (1964), 85f.

[39] Kraus, *BK,* XV, 388.

V. In the Qumran Literature. In the Qumran material, the concept of creation appears mainly in contexts having to do with the predetermination of human destiny. In the War Scroll, it is stated that God created the earth with all its natural phenomena and man (1QM 10:12); in doing this, he obviously determined the location of each phenomenon. The first column of the Hodayoth affirms that God created the earth by his power (1QH 1:13; cf. 13:8, where *hakhin*, "thou hast established through wisdom," stands in parallelism with "thou createdst") and that he knew the works of men before he created them (1QH 1:7). Similarly, he created "a spirit in the tongue" and knows its words in advance (1QH 1:27). In the Hodayoth, it is also stated that God created the just (*tsaddiq*) and the wicked (*rasha'*) (1QH 4:38), and another passage, which, unfortunately, is broken, seems to say that he created the wicked for a specific purpose (15:17). This agrees with the statement in the catechetical part of the Manual of Discipline which says that God created (*bara'*) man to rule over the earth and allotted (*sim*) unto him two spirits (1QS 3:17,18); but it can also say that he created (*bara'*) the two spirits (3:25).

Thus *bara'* expresses above all the idea that everything basically has its origin in the will of the creator and has been predetermined by him. In the Damascus Document, *beri'ah*, "creation," is almost identical with "nature": The rule "one man, one woman," is the "foundation of creation" (*yesodh habberi'ah*, CD 4:21; cf. also 12:15).

1QH 13:11f., *libhro' chadhashoth*, "by creating things that are new," and 1QS 4:25 (which, however, reads *'asoth chadhashah*, "until the new creation") possibly refer to a new creation of the world. [40]

Ringgren

---

[40] See E. Sjöberg, *StTh*, 4 (1950), 44ff.; 9 (1955), 135ff.

בָּרַח **bārach;** בָּרִיחַ **bārîach;** בְּרִיחַ **bᵉrîach**

Contents: I. General Use. II. In the OT: 1. The Verb; 2. The Adj. *bārîach;* 3. *bᵉriach*, "bar."

I. General Use. In Middle and more often in Late Akkadian we find a verb *barāḫu*, [1] the subst. *barīḫu* (a shiny or translucent stone [?]), [2] *burāḫu*, "shining, radiant," which appears exclusively in proper names, [3] and (also only in proper

---

bārach. K. Aartun, "Beiträge zum ugaritischen Lexikon," *WO*, 4 (1967), 282-84; G. R. Driver, "Proverbs XIX.26," *ThZ*, 11 (1955), 373f.; C. H. Gordon, "The Authenticity of the Phoenician Text from Parahyba," *Or*, 37 (1968), 75-80; C. Rabin, "BARIᴬH," *JTS*, 47 (1946), 38-41.

[1] *CAD*, II, 101; *AHw*, 105.

[2] *CAD*, II, 110.

[3] *CAD*, II, 326; cf. *AHw*, 139.

names) the adj. *barḫu* with the same meaning. [4] The etymological and semantic relationships of these words are not clear. It is usually assumed that the meaning of the root is "to shine, radiate." [5] A verb *brḥ* is known in Phoenician-Punic in the G stem (basic stem), [6] possibly also in the causative stem, [7] and in a deverbal nominal form *brḥt*. [8] Depending on the context, Donner-Röllig interpret this root to mean "to flee," [9] or "to lose" or "loss," [10] while Gordon's proposal, "to control, rule over," is attractive because it seems to fit all the passages where this root occurs. [11] For the Ugaritic root, Gordon suggests three homophonous roots, [12] which seem parallel to the biblical texts. [13] In *RA*, 63 (1969), 84, lines 8f., *ba-ar-ḫu* is clearly identified with Akk. *nu'û*, "stupid, barbaric," but this may be simply an approximate explanation of this word. Examples of this root in Arabic (*baraḥa*, "to leave, set out," *barḥ*, "grief, sorrow"), which are more abundant and more widespread, have been cited in support of certain meanings of this root in the biblical texts. [14]

II. In the OT. In the OT we find the verb *barach*, and the nouns *bariach* and *beriach*. Because of the obscure etymological and semantic relationships of these words it is impossible to seek or assume that a common root lies behind them. Instead, we must deal with each of these three words in succession.

1. *The Verb*. The verb *barach* can be used in the hiphil to denote the expulsion or banishment of men (1 Ch. 8:13; Neh. 13:28) or the flight of animals (Job 41:20 [Eng. v. 28]). But in the great majority of cases, this verb appears in some form of the qal. To be sure, it means "to flee" in these instances, but it hardly refers to flight from a threatening battle or an acute danger, but rather to evasion of and escape from continuing, unpleasant, dangerous situations, e.g., tensions and tragedies within the tribe. It has this meaning when it is used of Hagar (Gen. 16:6,8), Jacob (27:43), David and Saul (1 S. 20:1; 21:11[10] [cf. Ps. 57:1 = Eng. superscription]; 23:6; 27:4; 2 S. 4:3), and David and his undutiful sons (2 S. 13:34; 15:14; 19:10[9]; 1 K. 2:7 [cf. Ps. 3:1 = Eng. superscription], 39). Sometimes it is used of the political exile of important men (1 K. 11:17,23, 40; 12:2; cf. Neh. 13:10) or of a flight in panic (Jer. 4:29; 26:21; 39:4; 52:7). In Jer. 26:21, *barach* is followed by *vayyabho'*, "and came" (RSV "and es-

---

[4] *CAD*, II, 110; cf. *AHw*, 107.

[5] Cf. *CAD*, II, 110; *AHw*, 105, with reference to Syr. *barraḥ*, "to make transparent, clear," or *etbarraḥ*, "to shine."

[6] The Aḥiram Inscription, *KAI*, 1, 2; on the debated inscription from Parahyba, cf. Gordon, 76; L. Delekat, *Phönizier in Amerika. BBB*, 32 (1969), 7ff.

[7] The Table of Curses from Carthage, *KAI*, 89.4.

[8] *Ibid., KAI*, 89.6.

[9] *KAI*, 1, 2.

[10] *KAI*, 89.4, 6.

[11] *KAI*, 89.4, 6; contra *DISO*, 43: "to flee."

[12] *UT*, 19, 514-16, "to flee," "evil," "bar."

[13] Cf. Aartun, 282-84, who, however, accepts only the meaning "fugitive."

[14] Esp. Aartun, 282ff.

caped"), and in Jer. 39:4 and 52:7, by *vayyetse'u*, "and went out" (cf. 2 S. 13:37f.). This verb in combination with an infinitive with a preposition in Dnl. 10:7 means "disappear" (*vayyibhrechu behechabhe'*, RSV, "and they fled to hide themselves"; cf. Neh. 6:11). The word may point to the idea of "secrecy," but this concept seems to come more from the circumstances described in the text than from the word itself (e.g., in Gen. 31:20-27).[15] Expressions like *berach lekha*, "Away with you!" sometimes with another imperative of motion before it (e.g., in Gen. 27:43; Am. 7:12), may simply be a fuller way of saying *lekh lekha*, "You go!"[16] In Nu. 24:11, *barach* intensifies the authoritative tone, "Be off with you!" and thus Balaam replies with the plain statement, *hineni holekh*, "Look, I am going" (Nu. 24:14).

barach can also mean the act of fleeing, and thus be translated "to be in flight." Therefore, it can stand before, after, or between verbs of flight, motion, or escape (Jgs. 9:21; 1 S. 19:12); cf. Isa. 22:3: "they have taken to flight (*nadhedhu*) . . . ," therefore *merachoq barachu*, "they fled far away." (The *min* is not to be corrected, but indicates the point of view of those who remained behind, or of the speaker.) In Isa. 52:11f., the dramatic ideas of the first exodus in the Priestly Code (Ex. 12:11), Deuteronomy (Dt. 16:3), and the old Pentateuchal strata (Ex. 12:31-36) are excluded from the new exodus. In spite of this, *barach*, which is used for the first exodus in Ex. 14:5 (J), reappears in connection with the new exodus in Isa. 48:20. Probably this is because the latter text wishes to emphasize the incredible and the miraculous nature of the deliverance more strongly than the elements of hastening and fleeing.

When the OT mentions "fleeing," naturally it usually speaks of one fleeing *from* someone (*liphne*), but it can also speak of one fleeing *to* someone whom he wishes to join because he espouses his cause (1 S. 22:20, *vayyibhrach 'achare dhavidh*, "and he fled after David"). Thus, as has already been pointed out, sometimes the OT emphasizes that the purpose or result of *barach*, "fleeing," is deliverance (1 S. 19:18, *vayyimmalet*, "and he escaped").

It is hardly correct to translate *yabhriach* in Prov. 19:26 simply by "flee" or "put to flight." G. R. Driver thinks this word is cognate with the Arabic form of the same root and suggests that it be rendered, "make life difficult" or "thoroughly disgust."[17] In the book of Jonah, *barach* means the earnest attempt of the prophet to evade God's commission (Jonah 1:3,10; 4:2; cf. Hos. 12:13[12]; Job 27:22). Job uses the verb *barach* in complaining about the transitoriness, the brevity, the "too early end" of life (Job 9:25; 14:2). On the other hand, the scoundrel cannot escape (*barach*) from his fate (Job 20:24; 27:22). Thus, under certain circumstances, it can convey the idea of inescapability if a divine decree is added to or implied in the thought. When an OT text goes beyond the physical meaning of *barach*, in general there is somewhat of a confessional element in the verb, perhaps not least because it is more select and solemn than → נדד *nādhadh* and → נוס *nûs*, which occur more frequently.

---

15 This has been emphasized by Rabin, 40, but rather too strongly.
16 Cf. Brockelmann, *Synt.*, §§ 107f.
17 G. R. Driver, *ThZ*, 373f.

2. *The Adj. bārîach.* Perhaps a nominal form in Isa. 27:1, which has not yet been explained satisfactorily, should be connected with the verb *barach,* viz., *bariach,* in the statement, *'al livyathan nachash bariach ve'al livyathan nachash 'aqallathon,* RSV, "Leviathan the fleeing serpent, Leviathan the twisting serpent." The point of interest here is the meaning of *bariach* as an adjective in apposition to Leviathan in the first stich. There is a passage in the Ugaritic cycle of Baal and 'Anat which is parallel to this text, and which has almost the same structure:[18] in this passage, *ltn* is not repeated in the second stich, and thus Isa. 27:1 has in mind one or the only Leviathan.[19] In both stichoi of the Ugaritic text, *bṯn* (=*pethen,* "venomous serpent") stands in apposition to *ltn.* The meaning of the difficult *bariach* in Isa. 27:1 is still debated. *KBL³,* 149, and recently Aartun, think it should be translated "fleeting" (from *barach*="to flee") and (possibly because of the relationship of meaning and the context) "swift." There is some support for this in the (secondary clarifying and facilitating?) reading *bwrḥ* in 1QIsᵃ. Rabin (41) allows himself to be led by alleged common Semitic original meanings, and thinks that *bariach* might mean "convulsive" or "tortuous" (thus forming a parallelism with the second apposition, *nachash 'aqallathon,* "twisting serpent"), or "slippery," in agreement with the two common Semitic original meanings of the verb *barach,* "to twist" and "to be hairless, smooth, bright."[20] Gordon[21] and Aistleitner[22] argue that *bariach* should be translated "evil" because of the Arabic root.[23] Isa. 15:5 seems to be speaking of fugitives. Here again, 1QIsᵃ apparently has a participle, this time with a suffix and mater lectionis (*brḥvh*).[24] In Job 26:13, presumably *bariach* means a constellation; there is no parallel to it in this verse to provide additional help in determining its meaning.[25] Is the expression in Isa. 27:1 and Job 26:13 a stereotyped *epitheton ornans* (embellishing epithet), whose meaning had already been forgotten in the prebiblical tradition?

3. *berîach, "bar."* In the Priestly stratum of the Pentateuch, *beriach* is a technical term denoting a small part of the wilderness sanctuary, viz., a horizontal transom which held the vertical boards together (Ex. 26:26-29; 36:31-34; cf. 35:11; 39:33; 40:18; Nu. 3:36; 4:31).[26] This function of the *beriach* is expressed twice in the OT paronomastically by verb forms that are considered to be normal for denominatives: "to bar, bolt" (Ex. 26:28, *mabhriach;* 36:33, *libhroach*). But apart from any context of this kind, the hiphil form *vayyabhrichu* in 1 Ch. 12:16(15) (RSV, "and [they] put to flight") seems to have a similar character and meaning.[27] Without any special theological emphasis, *beriach* also

---

[18] *UT,* 67:1:1-2.
[19] Cf. below on Job 26:13.
[20] Cf. above on the Assyr.-Bab. and Syr.
[21] Gordon, *UT,* 19, 515.
[22] Aistleitner, *WUS,* 577.
[23] Cf. Aartun, 283.
[24] Cf. *BHS.*
[25] Cf. the determinative for star used with Akk. *barāḫu, CAD,* II, 101; *AHw,* 105.
[26] See Galling, *HAT,* 3, 135.
[27] Cf. Rudolph, *HAT,* 21, 105; Myers, *AB,* XII, 92.

means a bar on the gate of fortified cities, [28] and synecdochically the entire fortification (cf., e.g., Am. 1:5; 1 K. 4:13; and possibly Isa. 43:14). [29] In Prov. 18:19,
beriach is used figuratively to convey the idea of the impregnable (i.e., implac-
able) stubbornness of a brother who has been grievously offended. Anticipating
a possible reversal of the normal order of the cosmos, *beriach* is used figuratively
in Job 38:10, which speaks of God setting "bars and (wings of) gates" as in-
surmountable boundaries for the sea. The underworld also has bars, which make
it impossible for one to return from there (Jonah 2:7[6]). [30]

Gamberoni

[28] Cf. the concordances.

[29] However, cf. Dahood, *Sacra Pagina,* I (1959), 275.

[30] Cf. *UT,* 1001: rev 8 and 19, 516: *brḥ 'rṣ;* H. Gunkel, *Schöpfung und Chaos* ([2]1921), 36,
38; M. Dahood, "Ugaritic Lexicography," *Mélanges Eugène Tisserant,* I = *Studi e Testi,* 231
(Rome, 1964), 85; *idem, Ugaritic-Hebrew Philology. BietOr,* 17 (1965), 28.

בְּרִית *berîth*

Contents: I. Etymology. II. Meaning. III. Semantic Range: 1. Commitment; 2. Friendship,
Peace, and Benevolence; 3. Establishing a Covenant; 4. Violation of the Covenant. IV. 1. Covenantal Ceremony; 2. Function. V. Covenant and Law: 1. Sitz im Leben (Life Setting);
2. Affinities with Ancient Near Eastern Treaties; 3. Scene of the Covenant. VI. The Covenants with Abraham and David; The Royal Grant. VII. The Covenant and the Origin of
the Apodictic Law. VIII. Covenant Theology. IX. The Covenant in Prophecy. X. The
Origin of the Covenant Concept.

I. Etymology. The etymology of *berith* is not altogether clear. The derivations that have been suggested are these:

1. *berith* is a fem. noun from *brh,* "to eat, dine" (2 S. 3:35; 12:17; 13:5,6,10;
Ps. 69:22 [Eng. v. 21]; Lam. 4:10), and refers to the festive meal accompanying the covenantal ceremony. [1] With this one could compare the Gk. *spondē*

---

berîth. K. Baltzer, *Covenant Formulary* (trans. 1970); J. Begrich, "Berit," *ZAW,* 60
(1944), 1-11; E. Bikerman, "Couper une alliance," *Archives d'histoire du droit oriental,*
5 (1950), 133-156; H. C. Brichto, *The Problem of "Curse" in the Hebrew Bible* (Philadelphia,
1963), 22-76; F. C. Fensham, "Malediction and Benediction in Ancient Near Eastern Vassal-
Treaties and the OT," *ZAW,* 74 (1962), 1-9; G. Fohrer, "Altes Testament—'Amphiktyonie'
und 'Bund,'" *ThLZ,* 91 (1966), 801-816, 893-904; R. Frankena, "The Vassal Treaties of
Esarhaddon and the Dating of Deuteronomy," *OTS,* 14 (1965), 122-154; J. C. Greenfield,
"Stylistic Aspects of the Sefire Treaty Inscriptions," *AcOr,* 29 (1965), 1-18; J. Harvey, "Le
'Rîb Pattern', réquisitoire prophétique sur la rupture de l'alliance," *Bibl,* 43 (1962), 172-196;
D. R. Hillers, *Treaty Curses and the OT Prophets. BietOr,* 16 (1964); H. B. Huffmon, "The
Covenant Lawsuit in the Prophets," *JBL,* 78 (1959), 285-295; A. Jepsen, "Berith. Ein Beitrag

[1] E.g., E. Meyer, *KBL;* L. Köhler, *JSS,* 1 (1956), 4-7.

(continued on p. 254)

(=libation) for "covenant," which reflects the ceremony performed when concluding the covenant. The noun form would then be similar to *shebhith*, which comes from *šbh*. The formal analogy could even be carried further by comparing the form *biryah*, "food" (from *brh*, 2 S. 13:5,7,10) with *shibhyah*, "captives" (from *šbh*). However, *brh* is not the normal verb for "eating." Rather, it is associated with recuperation or convalescence, so that this proposed etymology is quite dubious.

2. *berith* is identical with Akk. *birīt*, "between, among," and corresponds to the Heb. prep. *ben*, which indeed occurs in connection with *berith* (cf. *berith*... *ben... ubhen*, "covenant between X and Y").[2] This equation is based on the assumption that the prep. *birīt* has been developed into an adverb and then into a noun, an assumption that cannot be accepted without reservations. The main difficulty, however, is the coupling of *berith*, "between," with the overlapping prep. *ben*, which results in a tautology.

---

zur Theologie der Exilszeit," *Verbannung und Heimkehr. Festschrift für W. Rudolph* (1961), 161-179; V. Korošec, *Hethitische Staatsverträge. LRSt,* 60 (1931); E. Kutsch, "Gesetz und Gnade," *ZAW,* 79 (1967), 18-35; *idem,* "Sehen und Bestimmen. Die Etymologie von ברית," *Festschrift für K. Galling* (1970), 165-178; O. Loretz, "ברית-Band-Bund," *VT,* 16 (1966), 239-241; D. J. McCarthy, *Treaty and Covenant. AnBibl,* 21 (Rome, 1963); G. Mendenhall, "Covenant Forms in Israelite Tradition," *BA,* 17 (1954), 50-76; W. L. Moran, "The Ancient Near Eastern Background of the Love of God in Deuteronomy," *CBQ,* 25 (1963), 77-87; *idem,* "A Note on the Treaty Terminology of the Sefire Stelas," *JNES,* 22 (1963), 173-76; M. Noth, "Das alttestamentliche Bundschliessen im Lichte eines Mari-Textes," *GSAT* (1957), 142-154; Pedersen, *ILC,* I-II, 265-310; L. Perlitt, *Bundestheologie im AT. WMANT,* 36 (1969); Š. Porúbčan, *Il patto nuovo in Isaia 40–66. AnBibl,* 8 (1958); G. Quell, "διαθήκη," *TDNT,* II, 106-129; J. A. Soggin, "Akkadisch TAR Berîti und hebr. כרת ברית," *VT,* 18 (1968), 210-15; B. Volkwein, "Masoretisches *'edut, 'edwot, 'edot*—'Zeugnis' oder 'Bundesbestimmungen'?" *BZ,* 13 (1969), 18-40; M. Weinfeld, *Deuteronomy and the Deuteronomic School* (Oxford, 1972); *idem,* "The Covenant of Grant in the OT and in the Ancient Near East," *JAOS,* 90 (1970), 184-203; *idem,* "עצת הזקנים לרחבעם," *Lešonenu,* 36 (1971-1972), 3-13; *idem,* הברית והחסד," *Lešonenu,* 36 (1972), 85-105; *idem, JAOS,* 93 (1973), 190-99.
Texts: H. Bengtson, *Die Staatsverträge des Altertums,* II-III (1962-1969); R. Borger, *Die Inschriften Asarhaddons. BAfO,* 9 (1956), 107-109; E. Cavaignac, "Daddassa-Dattasa," *RHA,* 10 (1933), 65ff.; E. Ebeling, *Bruchstücke eines politischen Propagandagedichtes aus einer assyr. Kanzlei. Epos auf Tukulti-Ninurta I. MAOG,* 12/2 (1938); J. A. Fitzmyer, *The Aramaic Inscriptions of Sefire. BietOr,* 19 (1967); J. Friedrich, *Staatsverträge des Hatti-Reiches in hethitischer Sprache. MVÄG,* 31/1 (1926); 34/1 (1930); *idem,* "Der hethitische Soldateneid," *ZA,* N.F. 1 (1924), 161-192; A. Goetze, *Madduwattaš. MVÄG,* 32/1 (1927); C. E. Jean, *ARM,* II. *Lettres diverses* (1950), No. 37; J. Kohler-A. Ungnad, *Assyrische Rechtsurkunden* (1913); J. N. Postgate, *Neo-Assyrian Royal Grants and Decrees. Studia Pohl,* Ser. maior 1 (1969); E. von Schuler, *Hethitische Dienstanweisungen. BAfO,* 10 (1957); Thureau-Dangin, *SAK,* 10ff., 36ff.; L. Waterman, *Royal Correspondence of the Assyrian Empire* (Ann Arbor, 1930-1936), Nos. 1105, 1239; E. F. Weidner, *Politische Dokumente aus Kleinasien. Die Staatsverträge in akk. Sprache aus dem Archiv von Boghazköi. BoSt,* 1/8-9 (1923); *idem,* "Der Staatsvertrag Aššurnirâris VI. von Assyrien mit Mati'ilu von Bît-Agusi," *AfO,* 8 (1932/33), 17-34; D. J. Wiseman, *The Vassal-Treaties of Esarhaddon. Iraq,* 20 (1958), 1-99; *idem, The Alalakh Tablets* (1953); *idem,* "Abban and Alalaḫ," *JCS,* 12 (1958), 124-29.

[2] See M. Noth, *GSAT,* 142-154.

3. Most recently E. Kutsch suggested the derivation of *berith* from *brh* II, "to look for, choose" (cf. Akk. *barû*, "to look"). According to Kutsch, the meaning of this verb developed into "determining" or "fixing." The main evidence for this etymology comes from the word *ḥzh/ḥzwt*, which is parallel to *berith* in Isa. 28:15,18. The verbs *ḥzh* and *r'h* have indeed the meaning of "selecting" or "determining" (cf. Gen. 22:8; Ex. 18:21), but the connection between "selecting," "determining," and "pledging," which *berith* actually implies,[3] is not self-evident.

4. The most plausible solution seems to be the one that associates *berith* with Akk. *birītu*,[4] "clasp," "fetter" (cf. the Talmudic *byryt*). This is supported by the Akkadian and Hittite terms for treaty: Akk. *riksu*, Hitt. *išḫiul*, both meaning "bond." The concept of a *binding* settlement also stands behind Arab. *'aqd*, Lat. *vinculum fidei*, "bond of faith," *contractus*, "contract," and is likewise reflected in German *Bund*. This etymology might support the reading *ma'asoreth habberith* in Ezk. 20:37 ("I will make you enter into the *bond* of the covenant"), suggested long ago. The Greek terms for covenant, *synthḗkē*, *harmonía* (*Iliad* xxii.255), *synthēsía* (ii.339), and *synēmosýnē* (xxii.261), also express the idea of binding/putting together. The "bond" metaphor explains the use of "strengthening" or "fastening" to convey the idea of the "validity" or "reliability" of the treaty. Thus we find in Akk. *dunnunu riksāte*, "to fasten the bonds" (=to validate the treaty), or *riksu dannu*, "strong persistent bond" (=a valid and reliable treaty), and similarly in Aram. *lethaqqaphah 'esar*, "strengthen the bond" (Dnl. 6:8). The Greek term for annulling the pact is *lýein*, "to loosen," which also points to the understanding of the treaty as a bond.

II. Meaning. The original meaning of the Heb. *berith* (as well as of Akk. *riksu* and Hitt. *išḫiul*) is not "agreement or settlement between two parties," as is commonly argued. *berith* implies first and foremost the notion of "imposition," "liability," or "obligation," as might be learned from the "bond" etymology discussed above. Thus we find that the *berith* is commanded (*tsivvah beritho*, "he has commanded his covenant," Ps. 111:9; Jgs. 2:20), which certainly cannot be said about a mutual agreement. As will be shown below, *berith* is synonymous with law and commandment (cf., e.g., Dt. 4:13; 33:9; Isa. 24:5; Ps. 50:16; 103:18), and the covenant at Sinai in Ex. 24 is in its essence an imposition of laws and obligations upon the people (vv. 3-8).

The same applies to the Akk. *riksu* and Hitt. *išḫiul*. The formulas *riksa irkus* in Akkadian and *išḫiul išḫiya* in Hittite occur in connection with a set of commandments imposed by the king on his officials, his soldiers or citizens, as well as his vassals.[5] A *berith* of this kind with soldiers[6] is to be found in 2 K. 11:4. Jehoiada gathers the centurions, "cuts a covenant *to them*, and makes them swear"

---

[3] See below.
[4] So *CAD*, II, 254f.; however, *AHw*, 129f., has *bi/ertum*.
[5] Von Schuler, 5f.; *ABL*, 1105; Weidner, *AfO*, 17, 257ff.
[6] Cf. the "Hittite soldier's oath," *ANET²*, 353ff.

(*vayikhroth lahem berith vayyashba' 'otham*), which is undoubtedly an oath of allegiance in connection with the revolutionary task they are to undertake. The expression *karath berith le* in contrast to *karath berith 'eth*[7] indeed implies the imposition of terms upon the vassal or the subordinated (cf. Josh. 9:15; 1 S. 11:1-2). This mostly involves a promise by the master or suzerain to take his vassal under protection, as this is expressed, e.g., in Dt. 7:1-2, where we read in v. 2, *lo' thikhroth lahem berith velo' techonnem,* RSV, "you shall make no covenant with them, and show no mercy to them," which actually means "do not grant them gracious terms."

berith as a commitment has to be confirmed by an oath (→ אלה *'ālāh;* → שבועה *shᵉbhû'āh*): Gen. 21:22ff.; 26:26ff.; Dt. 29:9ff.(10ff.); Josh. 9:15-20; 2 K. 11:4; Ezk. 16:8; 17:13ff.; which included most probably a conditional imprecation: "May thus and thus happen to me if I violate the obligation." The oath gives the obligation its binding validity, and therefore we find in the Bible as well as in the Mesopotamian and Greek sources the pair of expressions: *berith ve'alah,* "covenant and oath" (Gen. 26:28; Dt. 29:11,13,20[12,14,21]; Ezk. 16:59; 17:18) in Hebrew, *riksu u māmītu/riksāte u māmīte* in the Akkadian of the second millennium B.C., *adê māmīte* in the Neo-Assyrian period, and *hórkos kaí synthḗkē,* "oath and covenant," or *hórkos kaí spondḗ,* "oath and libation," in Greek. This hendiadystic term, first attested in the Hittite treaties, has been most probably crystallized in the middle of the second millennium B.C., in the wake of the establishment of political relations on an international scale between the ancient Near Eastern states. Though originally these two terms express two different concepts, *commitment* on the one hand and *oath* on the other, in course of time they merged, and one could use either of them in order to express the idea of pact. Thus, e.g., instead of "cutting a covenant" (*karath berith*), one could use "cutting an oath" (*karath 'alah,* Dt. 29:11[12]),[8] and instead of "entering a covenant" (*'abhar/ba' babberith*), one could say "entering an oath" (*'abhar/ba' be'alah,* Dt. 29:11[12]; Neh. 10:30[29]). Similarly, in Greek, for establishing a covenant one can use *spondás témnein,* "to cut the covenant" (lit., "libations"), or *hórkia témnein,* "to cut the oaths."

The common term for covenant in Gk. is *synthḗkē.* The LXX, however, for theological reasons, renders *berith* with *diathḗkē,* which rather means "will" or "testament," which in a sense renders the original meaning of *berith.*

III. Semantic Range. The terms for "covenant" in the ancient Near East as well as in the Greek and Roman world (which most likely borrowed their political formulas from the East)[9] are distributed according to two semantic fields: *oath and commitment* on the one hand, *love and friendship* on the other. As has been shown above, the basic terms for "covenant" in Heb. (*'alah,* "oath," *berith,* "covenant"), Akk. (*riksu, māmītu*), Hitt. (*išḫiul* and *lingai*), and Gk. (*synthḗkē, hórkos*) express pledge and commitment, which actually create the covenant.

---

[7] Begrich, 5.

[8] Cf. the Phoen. *krt 'lt, KAI,* 27.8.

[9] Weinfeld, *JAOS,* 93, 190ff.

On the other hand, any settlement between two parties is conditioned by good will or some kind of mutual understanding which enables the conclusion of an agreement, and this is why covenantal relations were expressed by terms like "grace," "brotherhood," "peace," "love," "friendship," etc.

1. *Commitment.* Besides *berith,* "covenant," and *'alah,* "oath," → עדות *'ēdhûth,* "testimony" (and the pl. *'edhoth/'edhevoth*) is used to indicate "covenant." This can clearly be seen by the parallel terms *luchoth ha'edhuth,* "tables of the testimony," and *luchoth habberith,* "tables of the covenant"; and *'aron habberith,* "ark of the covenant," and *'aron ha'edhuth,* "ark of the testimony." *'edhuth* has its counterpart in the Akk. *adū* (pl. *adê*) and Old Aram. *'dn* (emphatic *'dy',* Sefire Treaty). These occur always in the plural and in this respect resemble Heb. *'edhoth/'edhevoth,* which go mostly together with *chuqqim,* "statutes," and *mishpatim,* "judgments," and are therefore to be translated "stipulations," which seems to be also the correct rendering of Akk. *adê* and Aram. *'dn.* The distinction between *'edhuth* and *'edhoth/'edhevoth* is not altogether clear. The Deuteronomistic literature uses *'edhoth/'edhevoth,* whereas the Priestly literature prefers *'edhuth.*

Other synonyms for *berith* in its obligatory sense are: a. → דבר *dābhār,* "word," cf. Hag. 2:5: *haddabhar 'asher karatti,* "the word that I cut," i.e., the promise that I made; Dt. 9:5: *lema'an haqim 'eth haddabhar 'asher nishba',* "that he may confirm the word which he swore" (cf. 8:18: *lema'an haqim 'eth beritho 'asher nishba',* "that he may confirm his covenant which he swore"); Hos. 10:4: *dibberu dhebharim,* "they utter words," i.e., they make agreements;[10] and Ps. 105:8 (where *dabhar* appears in parallelism with *berith*); cf. also 1 S. 20:23. The Akk. *awātu/amātu,* Sum. *enim,* and Hitt. *memiyaš* also denote "covenant" or "covenant stipulations," as does Gk. *hrĕtrē (Odyssey* xiv. 393).

b. → עצה *'ētsāh,* "counsel," and → סוד *sôdh,* "counsel," cf. Isa. 30:1;[11] Hos. 10:6; Zec. 6:13 (*'atsath shalom,* "peaceful counsel" [RSV "understanding"], which is equal to *berith shalom,* "peaceful covenant"); Ps. 25:14 (where *sodh* appears in parallelism with *berith*); cf. *'st hyḥd* in 1QS.

c. *chozeh/chazuth,* "agreement," in Isa. 28:15,18. [12]

d. → תורה *tôrāh,* "law," cf. Hos. 8:1, *'abheru bherithi ve'al torathi pasha'u,* "they have broken my covenant, and transgressed my law"; Isa. 24:5; Mal. 2:8; Ps. 78:10; and 2 K. 22–23 (cf. *lehaqim 'eth dibhre habberith hazzo'th hakkethubhim 'al hassepher hazzeh,* "to perform the words of this *covenant* that were written in this book," 23:3, with *lema'an haqim 'eth dibhre hattorah hakkethubhim 'al hassepher,* "that he might establish the words of the *law* which were written in the book," in 23:24).

---

[10] Weinfeld, *Lešonenu,* 36, 8f.
[11] And see below on *nesekh,* "drink offering, libation."
[12] See above, I.3.

e. *piqudhim*, "expenses," *mishpat*, "judgment," *choq*, "statute," *mitsvah*, "commandment," *'imrah*, "word," along with *torah*, "law," *dabhar*, "word," and *'edhuth*, "testimony," which express the word of God and his command (Lev. 24:8 [cf. v. 9]; Dt. 33:9; 1 K. 11:11; 2 K. 17:13; Isa. 24:5; Ps. 50:16; 103:18; 105:10). That an ancient source like Dt. 33:9f. mentions in one breath *berith*, "covenant," *'imrah*, "word," *mishpat*, "ordinance," and *torah*, "law," indicates that the synonyms under discussion are of old stock. As has been demonstrated above, *berith* in its original sense is indeed close to "command" and "obligation."

f. *linsokh massekhah*, "pour libation," in Isa. 30:1 is the equivalent of the Greek term for covenant making: *spondás spéndein*, [13] and actually parallels making a pact (with Egypt): *'asah 'etsah*.

g. *'amanah*, "firm covenant" (Neh. 10:1[9:38]; 11:23), *'emunah*, "faithfulness" (Ps. 89:25,34,50[24,33,49]; 98:3; etc.), and *'emeth*, "faithfulness" (Mic. 7:20; Ps. 132:11; 146:6, and esp. in *chesedh ve'emeth*, "steadfast love and faithfulness"), which have their counterpart in Akk. *kittu*, [14] Gk. *pístis* (connoting "treaty"), and Lat. *fides/foedus*. The Akkadian equivalent for *'amanah* seems to be *dannatu*, "valid document." The Heb. verb → אמן *'āmēn* as well as Akk. *danānu* signify strength and persistence (cf. *bayith ne'eman*, "sure house," in 1 S. 2:35; 25:28; *makkoth ne'emanoth*, "lasting afflictions," and *cholayim ne'emanim*, "lasting sicknesses," in Dt. 28:59; which should be compared with Akk. *miḥiṣtu dannat*="persistent blow") and hence validity and reliability, [15] cf., e.g., *tsir 'emunim* in Prov. 13:17 with *našparu dannu*, "reliable messenger." [16]

h. *mesharim*, "uprightness," in Dnl. 11:6 (*la'asoth mesharim*, RSV "to make peace"), which is correctly translated in the LXX, *poiĕsasthai synthĕkas*, "to make a treaty." In the Mari documents, *išariš dabābu*, "to speak with uprightness," is synonymous with "making a treaty." [17]

2. *Friendship, Peace, and Benevolence.* The aspect of friendship is expressed by the following synonyms of *berith*: a. → חסד *chesedh*, "steadfast love" Dt. 7:9, 12; 2 S. 7:15; 22:51; 1 K. 3:6; Ps. 89:25,50[24,49]; Isa. 54:10; 55:3; etc.), [18] used mostly in connection with the Abrahamic and Davidic covenants, which belong to the type of the covenantal grant. [19] It is equivalent to Akk. *damiqtu/dēqtu*, which, together with *ṭābtu*, [20] is used as a covenantal term. [21] This term appears in Akkadian and Hebrew very often in the plural: *chasadhim* (=Akk. *damqāte*), Isa. 55:3; 63:7; Ps. 89:50(49); etc.

---

13 See above.
14 Cf. Moran, *JNES*, 22.
15 Weinfeld, *Lešonenu*, 10f.
16 *VAB*, IV, 276, 17f.
17 Weinfeld, *Lešonenu*, 11.
18 Cf. Glueck, 10ff., 16ff.
19 See below, VI.
20 See below.
21 Moran, *JNES*, 22.

b. *tobhah/tobhoth*, "good" (1 S. 25:30; 2 S. 2:6; 7:28);[22] cf. the Akk. *ṭābtu/ ṭābuttu*, and the Aram. *ṭbt'*.[23]

c. → שָׁלוֹם *shālôm*, "peace" (Josh. 9:15; Nu. 25:12; 1 K. 5:26[12]; etc.); cf. Akk. *sulummû* and *salīmu*, Gk. *eirḗnē*, and Lat. *pax*.

d. *'achavah*, "brotherhood" (Zec. 11:14), corresponding to Akk. *aḫḫūtu*, and *berith 'achim*, "covenant of brotherhood," in Am. 1:9; cf. Gk. *symmachía* and Lat. *societas*.

These expressions are often combined into pairs, which is characteristic of covenantal terminology of all periods and all civilizations. Thus, *chesedh ve'emeth*, "loyalty and truth," which appears in a covenantal context (Gen. 24:49; 2 S. 2:6; Mic. 7:20), equals Akk. *kittu ṭābuttu/damiqtu*, which also implies covenant; *habberith vehachesedh*, "covenant and steadfast love" (Dt. 7:9, 12; 1 K. 8:23; etc.), is identical with *'dy' vṭbt'* in the Aramaic Sefire Treaty and *adê ṭābtu* in Akkadian; *berith shalom*, "covenant of peace" (Nu. 25:12; Isa. 54:10; Jer. 33:9; Ezk. 34:25; 37:26), equals Akk. *riksu u salāmu* of the second millennium B.C. and *âde salīme* of the first millennium; *shalom vetobhah*, "peace and prosperity" (Dt. 23:7[6]; Jer. 33:9),[24] equals Assyr. *ṭūbtu u sulummû*. To the same category belong the Gk. expressions *philía kaí symmachía*, "friendship and alliance," *synthḗkē kaí symmachía*, "treaty and alliance, *philía kaí euergesía*, "friendship and kindness," and *hórkos kaí eirḗnē*, "oath and peace."[25]

3. *Establishing a Covenant.* The most common expression for concluding a covenant is *karath berith*, "cut a covenant." The same idiom is seen in Aram. *gzr 'dy'*,[26] Phoen. *krt 'lt 'lm* (cf. the incantation from Arslan Tash),[27] and Gk. *hórkia témnein*, "to cut oaths." It seems that this idiom derives from the ceremony accompanying the covenant, viz., cutting an animal, which was common in the West.[28] However, it is equally possible that "to cut" is figurative for "decide, decree," as in Akk. *parāsu*, "to decide," Aram. *gzr*, Lat. *decidere*, German *entscheiden*, etc. The particles used with *karath berith* are *le*, *'im*, *'eth*, and *'al*. *karath berith le*, "to cut a covenant to," is used of a superior, particularly a conqueror, prescribing terms to an inferior (Ex. 23:32; 34:12,15; Dt. 7:2; Josh. 9:6,7,11,15,16; Jgs. 2:2; 1 S. 11:1), or granting rights and privileges (Isa. 55:3; etc.), and also of one making the inferior party swear or commit itself (Josh. 24:25; 2 S. 5:3; Hos. 2:20[18]). (*karath berith le'lohim*, "to cut a covenant to God," in Ezr. 10:3 and 2 Ch. 29:10 is a late and irregular usage.) However, the same idea might be expressed sometimes by *karath berith 'eth* (cf. Gen.

22 See Weinfeld, *Lešonenu*, 10f.
23 Moran, *JNES*, 22.
24 See D. R. Hillers, *BASOR*, 173 (1964), 46.
25 See Bengtson, Indices.
26 Sefireh I A,7.
27 *KAI*, 27.9.
28 See below, IV.1.

15:18; 2 K. 11:17; 17:35; 23:3; Jer. 34:8). *karath berith 'im*, "to cut a covenant with," implies an agreement of mutual character (Gen. 26:28; Dt. 5:2; 1 S. 22:8). *karath berith le... 'im...* (cf. Hos. 2:20[18]) involves a mutual pact between two parties sponsored or imposed by a third mostly superior party. *karath berith 'al*, "to make a covenant upon" (Ps. 83:4[3]), means to set terms (make an agreement) against somebody.

Not only does one "cut" a *berith*, but also a *dabhar*, "word, promise" (Hag. 2:5), *'alah*, "oath" (Dt. 29:13[14]), and *'amanah*, "firm covenant" (Neh. 10:1 [9:38]), which are synonyms of *berith*. In two instances, *karath* without an object is enough to express the concept of concluding a covenant (1 S. 11:2; 22:8).

Other terms expressing the concluding of a covenant are: (a) *sam berith/ 'edhuth*, "to set (establish) a covenant/a testimony" (2 S. 23:5; Ps. 83:6[5]), which is attested in the Aramaic Sefire Treaty I A,7 (*sm 'dy'*), and is equivalent to Akk. *adê šakānu;* (b) *nathan berith*, "to give a covenant" (Gen. 9:12; 17:2; Nu. 25:12), which is equivalent to Akk. *riksa nadānu*[29] and Gk. *hórkon didónai*, "to give an oath"; (c) *'arakh berith*, "to arrange (set in order) a covenant" (2 S. 23:5), which is equivalent to Akk. *riksa rakāsu* (*'arakh* in the context of sacrifice and war is also expressed in Akk. by *rakāsu*); (d) *heqim berith*, "to erect (raise, establish) a covenant" (Gen. 6:18; 9:9,11; 17:7,10,19; Ex. 6:4; Lev. 26:9; Dt. 8:18; 2 K. 23:3; Jer. 34:18; in later passages *he'emidh berith*, "to establish [appoint] a covenant," Ps. 105:10; and *lishmor 'eth beritho le'omdhah*, "and that by keeping his covenant it might stand," Ezk. 17:14), which has its parallel in Greek, e.g., in the expression *stḗsai philían kaí symmachían*, "to establish friendship and alliance," to make a covenant (1 Macc. 8:17).

The verbs *heqim*, "to erect," *nathan*, "to give," and *sim*, "to set," which are used with *berith*, imply the notion of "establish" or "institute"; cf. *heqim/ nathan/sim* in connection with appointing a judge, a king, a prophet, etc., and likewise Akk. *šakānu, nadānu. heqim*, like *qiyyem*, the piel of *qum* (cf. Ps. 119:106; Est. 9:21ff.), has two meanings, viz., "to establish" and "to fulfill" (for *qiyyem* in the sense of "establishing," cf. Ruth 4:7, and in the sense of "fulfilling," Ps. 119:106; Est. 9:21f.; and for *heqim* in the sense of "fulfilling," cf. Nu. 23:19; Dt. 8:18; 9:5; 1 S. 1:23; 3:12; 1 K. 2:4; Jer. 29:10; 33:14; 34:18); but whereas in *qiyyem* the idea of "fulfilling" is prevalent, in *heqim* the idea of "establishing" is dominant.

Another expression for establishing a covenant is *ba'/hebhi' babberith/be'alah*, "to enter into a covenant (oath)" (1 S. 20:8; Jer. 34:10; Ezk. 16:8; 17:13; 20:37; Neh. 10:30[29]; 2 Ch. 15:12); cf. *'abhar babberith* in Dt. 29:11(12); Assyr. *ina adê erēbu*, Gk. *eisérchesthai eis tás spondás*, "to enter into the libations,"[30] and Lat. *in amicitiam venire*. The standard verbs for "keeping" and "observing" a covenant are *natsar/shamar*, "to keep" (Gen. 17:9,10; Ex. 19:5; Dt. 33:9; Ps. 25:10; 78:10; 103:18), and *zakhar*, "to remember" (Gen. 9:15; Ex. 2:24; 6:5; Lev. 26:42; Ezk. 16:60; Am. 1:9), the same verbs that are used in the covenantal context in the Akk. expressions *adê/ṭābtu naṣāru* or *adê/ṭābtu ḫasāsu*, and in

---

[29] Cf., e.g., *PRU*, IV, 43, 47.
[30] Thucydides v.36.2.

Aram. *nṣr tbt'*.[31] In connection with the patriarchal covenants, a particular usage of this phrase is to be discerned, viz., *shamar habberith vehachesedh le,* "to keep the covenant and the steadfast love to (for)" (Dt. 7:9,12; 1 K. 3:6; 8:23; cf. *natsar chesedh le,* "to keep steadfast love to [for]," in Ex. 34:7), and *zakhar berith le,* "to remember a covenant to (for)" (Ex. 32:13; Lev. 26:45; Ps. 106:45), which has to be understood in the sense of "keeping/remembering in favor of" the descendants of the patriarchs.[32]

Other expressions for the observance of the covenant are *hecheziq babberith,* "to hold fast the covenant" (Isa. 56:4,6), and *ne'eman babberith,* "to be true to (persistent and strong in) the covenant" (Ps. 78:37).

The covenant has to be observed faithfully and sincerely. This is why the covenant terminology is replete with expressions such as: "with the whole heart and with the whole soul" (2 K. 23:3, *bekhol lebh ubhekhol nephesh;* cf. Dt. 6:5), and "to be sincere," expressions encountered in the Hittite and Assyrian treaties: *ina kul libbi, ina gummurti libbi, ina kitti ša libbi,* etc. These expressions found their way into Greek-Hellenistic treaties, where we find such expressions as: *metá pásēs dé prothymías kaí eunoías,* "with all readiness and favor,"[33] *kardía plērei,* "with whole (full) heart," *ek psychḗs,* "from (with) the soul" (1 Macc. 8:11ff.). Though the latter terms might have been influenced by Hebrew usage, as by *belebh shalem* or *bekhol lebh ubhekhol nephesh,* the fact that the same expressions are attested in treaty vocabulary from the Hittite empire onward does not allow us to deny completely their authenticity.

4. *Violation of the Covenant.* The most common term for violating the covenant is *hephar* (→ פרר *pārar*) *berith,* "to break a covenant" (Gen. 17:14; Lev. 26:15,44; Dt. 31:16,20; Jgs. 2:1; 1 K. 15:19; Isa. 24:5; 33:8; Jer. 11:10; 14:21; 31:32; 33:20,21; Ezk. 17:15,16,19; etc.), equivalent in meaning to Akk. *māmīta paraṣu* and Lat. *foedus frangere/rumpere.* The term for violation in the Greek-Hellenistic treaties is *spondás lýein,* "to loosen the treaty"; the LXX rendering of *hephar* is *diaskedázein,* "to scatter, disband." Another term for violating a covenant is *'abhar berith,* "to transgress or trespass a covenant" (Dt. 17:2; Josh. 7:11,15; 23:16; Jgs. 2:20; 2 K. 18:12; Hos. 6:7; 8:1); *'abhar* is equivalent to Akk. *etēqu* and Gk. *parabaínein.* The phrase *'abhar berith* is characteristic of the Deuteronomistic literature, whereas *hephar berith* is preferred by the Priestly literature. Close to *'abhar berith* is the expression *pasha' 'al,* "transgress against" (Hos. 8:1), which reminds us of Akk. *ana adê ḫaṭû,* "to sin against." Another common term for violating a covenant is *'azabh berith,* "to forsake a covenant" (Dt. 29:24[25]; 1 K. 19:10,14; Jer. 22:9; Dnl. 11:30), which is equivalent to Akk. *riksa wuššuru.*[34] Other less common expressions are *shiqqer babberith/be'emunah,* "to be false to a covenant/faithfulness" (Ps. 44:18[17]; 89:34 [33]), which is attested in the Sefire Treaty III, 7, *šqr b'dy';* and *shaqar le,*

---

[31] *KAI,* 266.8.
[32] Weinfeld, *JAOS,* 90, 187f.; 93, 193f.
[33] Bengtson, III, 528.20 = Polybius vii.9.1.
[34] *PRU,* IV, 36, 24.

"to deal falsely with," which is found in a covenantal passage in Gen. 21:23 (*'im tishqor li ulenini ulenekhdi*, "that you will not deal falsely with me, my offspring, or my posterity"), and in the Sefire inscriptions (III, 4) (cf. also in connection with the Davidic covenant, *'im ledhavidh 'akhazzebh*, "I will not lie to David," Ps. 89:36[35]). To this category also belongs *'asah mirmah*, "to make fraudulent alliances" (Dnl. 11:23), which is paralleled by *'bd mrmt* in the Sefire Treaty III, 22. In the Greco-Roman treaties, we find indeed clauses about deceit and treachery, e.g., *adólōs kaí aprophasístōs*, "guilelessly and honestly," *mḗte dólō ponērō*, "without evil deceit" (= the Lat. *sine dolo malo*), etc. Other terms expressing scorn and negligence of a covenant are: *ma'as/bazah berith*, "to despise a covenant" (2 K. 17:15; cf. Isa. 33:8, *ma'as 'edhim*[?], "testimonies (= treaties) are despised"; Ezk. 16:59; 17:18), which is paralleled by Akk. *adê šêṭu; shakhach berith*, "to forget a covenant" (Dt. 4:23,31; Prov. 2:17), which is also attested in the Assyrian literature in the expression *adê mašû;*[35] *chilel berith*, "to profane a covenant" (Mal. 2:10; Ps. 89:35[34]), *shicheth berith*, "to corrupt (violate) a covenant" (Mal. 2:8), *ni'er berith*, "to desecrate (?) (abhor, renounce) a covenant" (Ps. 89:40[39]), and *kipper* (Isa. 28:18), which, like Assyr. *pasāsu* (cf. *pašāšu*), means "to annul" (originally "to rub or graze" the face of the document, cf. *vekhapharta ... bakkopher*, "and cover [it] ... with pitch," in Gen. 6:14). Other, less explicit terms are *shubh min*, "to turn back from" (*'emeth lo' yashubh mimmennah*, "a sure oath from which he will not turn back," Ps. 132:11), which parallels the Neo-Assyr. *tūrtu turru*[36] and *ana kutallu târu*, "to turn back" (= withdraw) in the Hittite treaties,[37] and *shanah*, "to change" (Ps. 89:35[34], *lo' 'achallel berithi umotsa' sephathai lo' 'ashanneh*, "I will not violate my covenant, or alter the word that went forth from my lips"), which is equivalent to Akk. *enû* occurring in treaty contexts.

IV. 1. *Covenantal Ceremony.* Though it is mainly the oath that validates the covenant, the covenantal pledge is most often accompanied by a ceremony. In Gen. 15[38] and Jer. 34, we hear about cutting animals into pieces and passing between them, a ceremony that makes palpable the punishment befalling the one who will violate the pact (cf. esp. Jer. 34:18-20). This reminds us of another covenantal rite, viz., "touching the throat" (*napišta lapātu*), which is attested in the Mesopotamian sources (EnEl VI, 98), and which also comes to exemplify the punishment of the trespasser. Cutting the animals, however, is not as purely symbolic an act as it appears. In Gen. 15; Ex. 24; Ps. 50; the documents from Mari and Alalakh, and Greek sources, the animals brought at the scene of the covenant are considered sacrificial, and therefore are subordinate to a fixed ritual procedure. In Gen. 15, three animals (a calf, a goat, and a ram, each three years old) are offered (cf. 1 S. 1:24 in the Qumran fragment and LXX).[39] Sacri-

35 *BAss*, 2 (1894), 629, 10.
36 Wiseman, *Vassal-Treaties*, 77f.; Borger, *ZA*, 54 (1961), *in loc.*
37 Weidner, *Polit. Dok.*, 42, 26; *PRU*, IV, 55, 19.
38 On this see N. Lohfink, *Die Landverheissung als Eid. SBS*, 28 (1967).
39 See Loewenstamm, *VT*, 18 (1968), 500ff.

fices in Greece and covenantal sacrifices in particular are likewise three in number (*tríttys*), most frequently a ram, a goat, and a boar, all three years of age. [40] From the Mari documents we learn that the king's officials were anxious to perform the covenantal ceremony according to the standard rites. Thus, e.g., we hear from the representative of King Zimrilim that at a covenant occasion which he had to supervise, he was offered a goat and a puppy for the covenantal ceremony, but he insisted on sacrificing or killing a donkey, which seemed to be the more legitimate rite. [41] The same is reflected in the Greek covenantal documents where the parties declare that the sacrifices were done *epichṓrion,* "according to the local custom," which seems to be equivalent to *hórkos nómimos,* "lawful oath." In the Alalakh documents, the animal brought at the covenant occasion is explicitly called "sacrificial." [42]

In Ex. 24 also, the covenantal ceremony is accompanied by sacrifices (*'oloth ushelamim,* "burnt offerings and peace offerings"), but these are not cut in pieces in order to pass between them in Gen. 15 and Jer. 34; only the blood is used for the ceremony. Moses divides the blood of the slaughtered animals in two: one half is thrown upon the altar and the other upon the people, i.e., their representatives (Ex. 24:6-8). The blood ceremony in connection with a covenant is also attested in Zec. 9:11, and mentioned in Herodotus (iii.8) in reference to the Arab tribes. Another ceremonial act that comes to ratify the covenant is a solemn meal (Gen. 26:30; 31:54; Ex. 24:11; 2 S. 3:20). Apparently, salt played a significant role at this meal, and this is why the covenant is sometimes called *berith melach,* "a covenant of salt" (Lev. 2:13; Nu. 18:19; 2 Ch. 13:5; cf. also in a Neo-Bab. letter: "all the persons who have tasted the salt of the Jakin tribe," [43] and *foedus salitum,* "covenant of salt," in Lat.). Other ceremonies accompanying the pledge were:

a. Libations, which gave rise to the Greek term for covenant, *spondḗ,* and (as we have seen) are reflected also in Isa. 30:1 (*nesokh massekhah,* lit., "to pour out a libation," RSV, "make a league").

b. The use of oil and water at the ceremony. [44]

c. Touching the breast, in the Assyrian sources, [45] and putting the hand under the thigh, in Israel (Gen. 24:2,9; 47:29; in connection with dealing *chesedh ve'emeth,* "loyally and truly"), or simply giving the hand (cf. Ezk. 17:18).

d. The exchange of clothes by the parties (1 S. 18:3f.).

The covenant is sometimes accompanied by an external sign or token which

---

[40] Stengel, *Griech. Kultusaltertümer* ([3]1928), 119, 137.
[41] *ARM,* II, 37.
[42] Weinfeld, *JAOS,* 90, 196f.
[43] *ABL,* 747 rev. 6.
[44] Wiseman, *Vassal-Treaties,* 154-56; EnEl VI, 98; Borger, *Asarhaddon,* 43, 51.
[45] Wiseman, *loc. cit.;* Borger, 43, 5.

may remind the parties of their obligation, such as erecting a monument (Gen. 31:45f.; Josh. 24:26f. [cf. the raising of the *stḗlai*, "stelae," at the conclusion of the covenant in the Gk. sources]), which is called *'edh(ah)*, "a witness" or testimony. In other instances, we hear about a physical change in the body as a token for the covenant (cf. 1 S. 11:2). In Israel, circumcision was considered as the "sign of the covenant" (*'oth berith*) of God with Abraham (Gen. 17:11). The expression *'oth berith* is especially characteristic of P, who also explains the Sabbath (Ex. 31:16f.) and the "rainbow" (Gen. 9:17) as "signs of the covenant." The Sabbath, the rainbow, and circumcision are, in fact, the three great covenants established by God at the three critical stages of the history of mankind: the creation (Gen. 1:1; 2:3; Ex. 31:16f.), the reestablishment of mankind after the flood (Gen. 9:1-17), and the birth of the Hebrew nation (Gen. 17).

2. *Function.* Covenants are established between individuals (Gen. 21:22f.; 26:23ff.; 31:44ff.; 47:29 [*chesedh ve'emeth*, "loyally and truly"]; 1 S. 18:3; 23:18), between states and their representatives (1 K. 5:26[12]; 15:19; 20:34; cf. also 2 S. 3:13,21), between kings and their subjects (2 S. 5:3; 2 K. 11:17), between the (military) leader and his soldiers (2 K. 11:4), [46] and between husband and wife (Ezk. 16:8; Mal. 2:14; Prov. 2:17). [47] On the figurative level, we find a covenant between men and animals (Job 5:23; 40:28[41:4]; cf. Hos. 2:20[18]), and also a covenant with death (Isa. 28:15,18).

In certain instances, the covenant is sponsored by a third party, i.e., through mediation, cf. the Gk. *brabeutḗs*, "judge, arbitrator, umpire." Mediation of the covenant is especially characteristic of the covenant with God, where the man of God (priest, prophet, etc.) serves as a mediator. Thus, Moses (Ex. 24) and Joshua (Josh. 24) mediate the covenant between God and Israel; but we find also Jehoiada the priest fulfilling the same function (2 K. 11:17). The latter serves as a mediator in a double covenant: the covenant between God and the king/people on the one hand, and between the king and the people on the other (apparently because the king was still a minor). Another covenant of this kind is the one mentioned in Hos. 2:20(18), where God is to establish a covenant between the people and the beasts of the earth, etc. [48] The people conclude a covenant with their king. Thus, David concluded a covenant with the people when they made him king (2 S. 3:21; 5:3). The same is reported of other kings (2 K. 11:17). Zedekiah made a covenant with the people to proclaim a liberation of the slaves (Jer. 34:8ff.). When the Book of the Law was found under Josiah, the king made a *berith* with the people that they should observe the laws (2 K. 23:3). A similar scene takes place in the assembly at Shechem (Josh. 24:25). [49]

The covenant mostly has "eternal validity": *ledhoroth*, "throughout their generations," *'adh 'olam*, "for ever," *berith 'olam*, "everlasting covenant"; cf. *adi dāriti* and *ūmē ṣāti* in the Akkadian legal documents, and the formulas in

---

[46] Cf. above, II.
[47] Cf. Begrich, 3; on the covenant with God, see below.
[48] Cf. H. W. Wolff, "Jahwe als Bundesmittler," *VT*, 6 (1956), 316-320.
[49] Pedersen, 306f.

the Greek treaties: *eis tón hapánta chrónon, eis tón aiŏna chrónon,* "for all time," etc. This is especially salient in the divine covenants (Gen. 9:12; 17:7; Ex. 31:16; 2 S. 7:16,25,29), but is also found in secular covenants, e.g., in 1 S. 20:15. However, as may be learned from the ancient Near Eastern and Greco-Roman legal documents, covenants were mostly renewed either because of a break of the previous relationship (cf. the renewal of the covenant with God in Ex. 34; 2 K. 11:17; 23:1-3), or as a regular annual arrangement. [50]

The covenant has to be recorded either on stone (but sometimes on metal tablets), on clay (particularly in Mesopotamia), or on a scroll (leather or papyrus). For the stone tablet, Biblical Hebrew uses *luach* (=*le'u* in Akk.), cf. *luchoth habberith,* "tables (tablets) of the covenant," while *sepher* connotes every kind of written document (cf. *sepher habberith,* "book of the covenant," in Ex. 24:7). Breaking the covenant tablets means annulment of the covenant (cf. Akk. *ṭuppam ḥepû*), and this explains why Moses broke the tablets in Ex. 32.

V. Covenant and Law.

1. *Sitz im Leben (Life Setting).* As already indicated above, the covenant at Sinai was mainly the instrument by means of which a set of legal ordinances was imposed on the people. The nature of this covenant and the way it was implemented have been discussed by several scholars. Mowinckel [51] investigated the *Sitz im Leben,* i.e., the provenance, of the Sinai covenant, and came to the conclusion that it reflects an annual celebration including a theophany and a proclamation of the law. His arguments were mainly based on Ps. 50:5ff. and Ps. 81, where theophany is combined with covenant making and decalogue formulas (cf. Ps. 81:10f.[9f.]; 50:7,18f.).

Mowinckel has been followed by Alt, [52] who, investigating the "life setting" of the genuine Israelite law, argued that the so-called apodictic law [53] had been recited at the Feast of Tabernacles at the beginning of the year of release (cf. Dt. 31:10-13). In his opinion, this periodic convocation bound the congregation sacredly and is reflected in the Sinai covenant.

Von Rad [54] went a step further. He raised the question of the significance of the peculiar structure of the book of Deuteronomy: history (chaps. 1–11), laws (12:1–26:15), mutual obligations (26:16-19), and blessings and curses (chaps. 27–29). He correctly observed that such a strange combination of elements could not be an invention of scribes, but must have had its roots in a certain reality. He suggested, therefore, that this structure, and similarly the structure of the Sinai covenant: history (Ex. 19:4-6), law (20:1–23:19), promises and threats (23:20-33), conclusion of the covenant (24:1-11), reflect the procedure of a covenant ceremony which opened with a recital of history, proceeded with the

---

[50] Cf., e.g., *Baghdader Mitteilungen,* 2 (1963), 59 IV 19, and for the classical sources Thucydides v.18.9.

[51] Mowinckel, *Le Décalogue* (1927).

[52] A. Alt, *Die Ursprünge des israelitischen Rechts* (1934).

[53] See below.

[54] G. von Rad, *Problem of the Hexateuch* (trans. 1966), 1-78.

proclamation of the law (accompanied by a sworn obligation), and ended with blessings and curses. Since according to Dt. 27 (cf. Josh. 8:30-35) the Blessings and the Curses had to be recited between Mt. Gerizim and Mt. Ebal, which are located at the site of Shechem, he pointed toward Shechem as the scene of the periodic covenant renewal in ancient Israel. This suggestion looks quite plausible, though one must admit that the periodic covenant festival is still obscure, and there is no evidence about its factual implementation. It is true that Dt. 31:9-13 provides for an assembly every seven years for the purpose of reading from the Book of the Law, but nothing is found in this passage about a covenant celebration.

2. *Affinities with Ancient Near Eastern Treaties.* However, although no real evidence about a covenant festival has been found thus far, the very observation made by von Rad that the literary structure of the book of Deuteronomy and of Ex. 19–24 reflects a covenantal procedure has been confirmed by later investigations. It became clear that the covenant form, as presented in these texts and especially in Deuteronomy, had been in use for centuries in the ancient Near East. In 1954, Mendenhall compared for the first time the structure of Israel's covenant with God with that of the Hittite treaties of the fourteenth and thirteenth centuries B.C. [55] He found that the Hittite treaty (whose form and structure had already been carefully analyzed by Korošec) [56] has a structure identical with that of the biblical covenant. The basic common elements are: 1. Titulature. 2. Historical introduction, which served as a motivation for the vassal's loyalty. 3. Stipulations of the treaty. 4. A list of divine witnesses. 5. Blessings and curses. 6. Recital of the treaty and the deposit of its tablets. Indeed, the Sinai covenant described in Ex. 19–24 has a similar structure, although it is not completely identical. [57] Thus, the divine address in chap. 19 opens with a historical introduction stressing the grace of God with the people and their election (vv. 4-6); then follows the law (20:1–23:19); thereafter comes a series of promises and threats (23:20-33); and finally the ratification of the covenant by means of a cultic ceremony and the recital of the covenant document (24:3-8).

We must admit that the analogy is not a complete one, since what we have in Ex. 19–24 is not a treaty such as is found in the Hittite documents, but rather a narrative about concluding a covenant. Nevertheless, it is clear that that narrative is organized and arranged in line with the treaty pattern. Much clearer is the treaty pattern of the book of Deuteronomy. This book, which is considered by its author as one organic literary creation (cf. the expression, *sepher hattorah hazzeh,* "the Book of this Law") and represents the covenant of the plains of Moab, follows the classic pattern of the treaty in the ancient Near East. Unlike the Sinai covenant in Exodus, which has no list of Blessings and Curses, Deuteronomy (like the treaties, esp. of the first millennium B.C.) has an elaborated series of Blessings and Curses, and likewise provides for witnesses to the covenant:

---

[55] Mendenhall, *BA,* 50-76.
[56] V. Korošec, *Hethitische Staatsverträge.*
[57] Cf. also Baltzer, McCarthy, etc.

"heaven and earth" (4:26; 30:19; 31:25f.), which are missing altogether in the previous sources of the Pentateuch. Deuteronomy also makes explicit reference to the deposit of the tablets of the covenant and the Book of the Law in the divine ark (10:1-5; 31:25f.). The ark (→ ארון 'ārôn), as is well known, had been considered as the footstool of the Deity in ancient Israel (the cherubim constituting the throne), and indeed, it is at the feet of the gods that the treaty documents had to be kept according to the Hittite legal tradition. In Deuteronomy, as in the Hittite treaties, we find a command to recite the law periodically before the public (31:9-13); and, as in the Hittite treaties, so also Deuteronomy demands that the treaty be read before the king or by him (17:18f.). [58]

The historical prologue in Deuteronomy (chaps. 1–11) recalls to a great extent the historical prologue in the Hittite state treaties. In this section, the Hittite suzerain recounts the development of the relationship between him and the vassal. Here, e.g., we read about the commitments and the promises of the overlord to the vassal's ancestors. This theme is broadly described in Deuteronomy's recurring references to the promise made to the patriarchs (4:37f.; 7:8; 9:5). On the other hand, the historical prologue dwells upon the rebelliousness of the vassal's ancestors and its consequences, a feature also brought to expression in the historical introduction of Deuteronomy, which deals amply with the rebelliousness of the wilderness generation.

The historical prologue in the Hittite treaty frequently refers to the land given to the vassal by the suzerain, and to its boundaries, a theme that is fully elaborated in Deuteronomy (Dt. 3:8ff.). Similar in fashion to the Hittite sovereign, who urges the vassal to take possession of the given land—"See I gave you the Zippasla mountain land, occupy it" [59]—God says in Deuteronomy: "I have given the land before you, go occupy it" (1:8,21). In this context, the Hittite king warns the vassal not to trespass beyond the set boundaries. Thus, e.g., Mursilis II says to Manapa-Dattas: "Behold I have given you the Seḥa river-land . . ., but unto Mashuiluwas I have given the land Mira . . ., whereas unto Targasnallis I have given the land Ḥapalla." [60] In the historical prologue of Deuteronomy, we hear similarly: "Behold I have set the land before you" (1:8), "I have given Mt. Seir unto Esau" (2:5), and "I have given Ar to the sons of Lot" (2:9). The purpose of these reminders is to justify the command forbidding the trespass of the fixed borders of these nations.

The analogies are mostly drawn from the Hittite treaties, as these have been preserved in fairly large number and in relatively good condition. However, the few treaties known to us from the first millennium B.C., as the Aramaic treaty from Sefireh, the treaty of Ashurnirari V with Mati'ilu of Bit-Agusi, and the treaty of Esarhaddon with his eastern vassals, do not differ principally from the Hittite treaties; in fact, it seems that there was a continuity in the treaty pattern for approximately 800 years. This might explain why a late book like Deuteronomy preserves elements that also occur in the Hittite treaties from the fourteenth

---

58 Cf. Weinfeld, *Deuteronomy*, 64, n. 3.
59 Madduwatas, *MVÄG*, 32 (1927), recto 17, 19, 46.
60 *MVÄG*, 31 (1926), No. 3 § 3; 34/1 (1930), No. 4 §§ 10f.

and thirteenth centuries B.C. In spite of this continuity in pattern, however, careful analysis reveals certain significant differences between the treaties of the second millennium and those of the first. This applies to the political treaties in the ancient Near East as well as to the theological covenants in Israel. While the Hittite treaties and the Sinaitic covenant have a very short list of curses, those of the first millennium and the covenant in Deuteronomy have long lists of curses. Furthermore, Dt. 28 has preserved a series of curses which has an exact parallel in a Neo-Assyrian treaty, viz., the treaty of Esarhaddon with his eastern vassals regarding the coronation of his son Ashurbanipal (concluded in 672 B.C.). In this treaty, which was published in 1958, we find a series of curses identical in content and order with the curses in Dt. 28. [61] An investigation of those curses has shown that their origin has to be sought in Assyria, since their order can be explained by the hierarchy of the Assyrian pantheon, whereas the order in Deuteronomy has no satisfactory explanation. [62] It is legitimate, then, to suppose that a series of Assyrian treaty curses has been incorporated into the sections of curses in Deuteronomy. It has been rightly conjectured [63] that in his formulation of the covenant, the author of Deuteronomy imitated the Assyrian treaty documents. By this imitation, he undoubtedly intended to make it clear that the pledge of loyalty to the Assyrian emperor had now been replaced by the pledge to Yahweh, a shift that has to be understood against the background of Josiah's liberation from Assyrian domination.

The shift of fealty, as it were, from one suzerain to another also explains some other similarities between the Neo-Assyrian treaties and the covenant in Deuteronomy. Thus, e.g., we find a striking similarity between the laws of sedition in Dt. 13 and the warnings against sedition in the treaties of the first millennium B.C., especially those of Esarhaddon with his vassals. Like the vassal treaties of Esarhaddon, Dt. 13 warns against a prophet inciting to rebel or against any member of the family seducing to break faith with the overlord. In the Aramaic treaty from Sefire, we find among the clauses against sedition a clause concerning a rebellious city, which, like Dt. 13, commands that it be destroyed by the sword. The commands are almost identical in wording in both sources: *vhn qryh h' nkh tkvh bḥrb,* "and if it is a city, you must strike it with a sword," in the Sefire Treaty, and *hakkeh thakkeh 'eth yoshebhe ha'ir hahi' lephi charebh,* "you shall surely put the inhabitants of that city to the sword," in Dt. 13:16(15).

The exhortations in Deuteronomy to keep loyalty to God are very close in form and style to the exhortations in the political treaties. As has been shown by Moran, the concept of the "love of God" in Deuteronomy actually expresses loyalty, and it is in this sense that "love" occurs in the political documents of the ancient Near East. Deuteronomy abounds with terms originating in the diplomatic vocabulary of the ancient Near East. Such expressions as "hearken to the voice of," "be perfect with," "go after," "serve," "fear" (revere), "put

[61] Cf. Wiseman, *Vassal-Treaties,* lines 419-430 with Dt. 28:27-33.
[62] Weinfeld, *Bibl,* 46 (1965), 417-427.
[63] Frankena, 152f.

the words on one's heart," "not turn to the right hand or to the left," etc., are found in the diplomatic letters and state treaties of the second and first millenniums B.C., and are especially prominent in the vassal treaties of Esarhaddon, which are contemporaneous with Deuteronomy. The exhortation occurring in Dt. 6:5 (cf. the covenant of Josiah in 2 K. 23:3,25), to "love God with all the heart, with all the soul, and with all the might," seems to have its origin in the loyalty oaths of the vassal to his suzerain. Thus, the Hittite overlord demands that his vassals serve him with their armies, horses, and chariots, and with all the heart or soul, and that they love the suzerain as they love themselves. Similar exhortations are found both in the Assyrian and in the Greek treaties.[64] The same postulate actually lies behind the above-mentioned scriptures, where *me'odh* has to be understood in the sense of "strength" and "might," as in the LXX (*dýnamis*). *me'odh,* "might," like *koach/chayil,* implies here physical strength as well as material resources (= money), and therefore includes also money/property, as the Aramaic translators render it.

3. *Scene of the Covenant.* The scene of the Josianic covenant in 2 K. 23:1-3 and the scene of the covenant in Dt. 29:9-14(10-15) are presented in a manner that is very close to the descriptions of the treaty ceremonies in the Neo-Assyrian documents. Thus, we read in Dt. 29:9ff.(10ff.): "You stand this day all of you before the Lord . . ., all the men of Israel, your little ones, your wives, . . . that you may enter into the sworn covenant. . . . Nor is it with you only that I make this sworn covenant, but with him who is not here with us . . . as well as with him who stands here this day" (cf. Dt. 5:2-4). A similar declaration is found in the Esarhaddon treaty: "You swear that you, *while you stand at this place* of the swearing . . . wholeheartedly . . . that you will teach (the oath) to your sons *who shall be* after the treaty" (lines 385-390), and similarly: "The treaty with Ramatia . . . *with his sons, . . . his grandsons, . . . young and old, . . . with all of you . . . who will exist in the days to come after the treaty"* (lines 1-7). This section about the perpetual validity of the covenant occurs twice each in the Esarhaddon treaty and in the Deuteronomic covenant, viz., before the stipulations and after them.

At the end of Dt. 29, we read: "And the generation to come, . . . and the foreigner, . . . will say: 'Why has the Lord done thus to the land?' . . . and they will answer: 'It is because they forsook the covenant of the Lord'" (vv. 21-24 [22-25]). This theme of self-condemnation is also encountered in the Neo-Assyrian texts in connection with a breach of the treaty. Thus we read in the annals of Ashurbanipal: "The people of Arabia asked one another, saying: 'Why is it that such evil has befallen Arabia?', and they answered: 'Because we did not observe the valid covenant sworn to the god of Ashur'" (Rassam Cylinder IX, 68-72).

The difference between the Deuteronomic covenant which reflects the treaty pattern of the first millennium B.C., and the earlier covenants reflecting the pattern of the second millennium, may be clearly seen when one compares the covenant ceremonies in Genesis and Exodus with that of Deuteronomy. The

---

[64] Weinfeld, *Lešonenu,* 88f.

patriarchal covenants, secular and religious alike (Gen. 15:9ff.; 21:22ff.; 26:26ff.; 31:44ff.), and the Sinaitic covenant (Ex. 24:1-11), are validated by sacrifices and holy meals, and the same is true of the covenants of the third and second millenniums B.C. Thus, in the stela of Eannatum of Lagash from the third millennium B.C., which describes the concluding of a treaty with the Ummaites, we hear about sacrificing or consuming a calf;[65] in the Mari letters, we find a reference to the killing of an ass at the conclusion of the covenant,[66] and in the Alalakh documents, to cutting the throat of a sheep,[67] an act specifically said to be sacrificial. In the Deuteronomic covenant, and in the contemporary Assyrian and Aramaic treaty documents, it is the oath that validates the covenant, and no mention is made of a sacrifice or a meal (cf. esp. Dt. 29:9ff.[10ff]). Even when a ceremonial act is performed, like the beheading of a ram, it is then explicitly stated that this is no sacrifice, but comes to dramatize the punishment of the party who would violate the treaty (Treaty of Ashurnirari V with Mati'ilu of Bit-Agusi).[68]

VI. The Covenants with Abraham and David; The Royal Grant. Aside from the covenant between Yahweh and Israel described in Exodus and Deuteronomy, two covenants of a different type are found in the Bible. These are the covenant with Abraham (Gen. 15; 17) and the covenant with David (2 S. 7, where *chesedh* = *berith*;[69] cf. Ps. 89), which are concerned with the gift of the land and the gift of the kingdom (dynasty) respectively. In contradistinction to the Mosaic covenants, which are of an obligatory type, the covenants with Abraham and David belong to the promissory type. God swears to Abraham to give the land to his descendants, and similarly promises to David to establish his dynasty without imposing any obligations on them. Although their loyalty to God is presupposed, it does not occur as a condition for keeping the promise. On the contrary, the Davidic promise, as formulated in the vision of Nathan (2 S. 7), contains a clause in which the unconditional nature of the gift is explicitly stated: "I will establish the throne of his kingdom for ever.... When he commits iniquity, I will chasten him, ... but I will not take my steadfast love from him" (2 S. 7:13-15). By the same token, the covenant with the patriarchs is considered as valid for ever ('adh 'olam). Even when Israel sins and is to be severely punished, God intervenes to help because he "will not break his covenant" (Lev. 26:44).

Just as the obligatory covenant in Israel is modelled on the suzerain-vassal type of treaty, so the promissory covenant is modelled on the royal grant. Like the royal grants in the ancient Near East, so also the covenants with Abraham and David are gifts bestowed upon individuals who distinguished themselves in loyally serving their masters. Abraham is promised the land because he

---

[65] *SAK*, 16f., verso I, 37-40.
[66] *ARM*, II, 37, 6-11.
[67] Wiseman, *JCS*, 126, n. 41.
[68] Weidner, *AfO*, 24ff.; cf. the covenant in Jer. 34.
[69] See above, III.2.

obeyed God and followed his mandate (Gen. 26:5; cf. 22:16-18), and similarly
David was given the grace of kingship because he served God in truth, righteousness, and loyalty (1 K. 3:6; 9:4; 11:4,6; 14:8; 15:3). The terminology employed
in this context is very close to that used in the Assyrian grants. Thus in the grant
of Ashurbanipal to his servant, we read: "[Balṭāya] ..., whose heart is whole
to his master, stood before me with truthfulness, walked in perfection in my
palace, ... and kept the charge of my kingship (*iṣṣur maṣṣarti*). ... I took
thought of his kindness and decreed (therefore) his gi[f]t." Identical formulations
are to be found in connection with the promises to Abraham and David. With
regard to Abraham, it is said that "he kept my charge" (lit. "my watch," *shamar
mishmarti*) (Gen. 26:5), "walked before God" (24:40; 48:15), and is expected
"to be perfect" (17:1). David's loyalty to God is couched in phrases that are
even closer to the Assyrian grant terminology, as, "he walked before God in
faithfulness, in righteousness, and in uprightness of heart" (1 K. 3:6), "he followed God with all his heart" (1 K. 14:8), etc.

Land and "house" (=dynasty), the subjects of the Abraham and Davidic
covenants, are the most prominent gifts of the suzerain in the Hittite and Syro-
Palestinian provenance; and like the Hittite grants, the grant of the land to
Abraham and the grant of the "house" to David are unconditional. Thus, we
hear the Hittite king saying to his vassal: "After you, your son and grandson
will possess it; nobody will take it away from them. If one of your descendants
sins, the king will prosecute him, ... but nobody will take away either *his house
or his land* in order to give it to a descendant of somebody else." The same
concept lies behind the promise of the "house" to David and his descendants
in 2 S. 7:8-16.

A Hittite grant typologically similar to the grant of the dynasty to David is
found in the decree of Hattusilis concerning Middannamuwas, his chief scribe:
"Middannamuwas was a man of grace (*kaniššanza UKU-aš*) to my father,... and
my brother Muwatallis was (kindly) disposed to him, promoted him (*kanešta*),
and gave him Hattusas. My grace (*aššul*) was also shown to him.... I committed
myself for the sons of Middannamuwas,... and you will keep... and so shall
the sons of my Sun and the grandsons of my Sun keep. And as my Sun, Hattusilis,
and Puduḫepas, the great queen, were kindly disposed (*kanešta*) toward the sons
of Middanamuwas, so shall be my sons and grandsons.... And they shall not
abandon the grace (*aššulan anda lē daliịanzi*) of my Sun. The grace and their
positions shall not be removed." [70]

Like the Heb. *tobhah/chesedh*, Akk. *ṭābtu/damiqtu*, and Aram. *ṭbt'*, the Hitt.
aššul and *kannešuụar* connote kindness and covenantal relationship. As in the
case of David, so in the Hittite grant, the promise is to be "kept" (*shamar*) for
the future generations of the devoted servant, i.e., "the man of grace" (cf.
chasidhekha, "thy faithful one," in Ps. 89:20[19]). The most striking parallel to
the promise of David is the last sentence: "they shall not abandon the grace....
Their positions shall not be removed." Hitt. (*anda*) *daliịa* is equivalent to Akk.

---

[70] Goetze, *Ḫattušiliš* (1925, ²1967), 40-44.

ezēbu and Heb. *'azabh,* which is often employed in connection with *chesedh/ chesedh ve'emeth,* "steadfast love/steadfast love and truth," while *ueḫ,* "turn away" (remove), is equivalent to Heb. *sur,* which appears in 2 S. 7 in a phrase similar to that of the Hittite grant: *vechasdi lo' yasur mimmennu,* "but my steadfast love will not depart from him" (v. 15).

Similar imagery is found in the Assyrian grants, e.g., in the above-quoted text: "I am Ashurbanipal, ... who does good (*ēpiš ṭābti*), ... who always responds graciously to the officials who serve him, and returns kindness (*gimilli dumqi*) to the reverent (*pāliḫi*), who keeps his royal command (*nāṣir amāt šarrūtišu*) ... PN, a man of kindness and favor (*bēl ṭābti bēl dēqti*), who from the succession to the exercise of kingship served wholeheartedly his master. I took thought of his kindness and decreed his gift. ... Any future prince from among the kings my sons ... do good and kindness (*ṭābtu damiqtu ēpuš*) to them and their seed. They are friends and allies (*bēl ṭābti bēl dēqti*) of the king, their master." [71]

The gift comes, then, as a reward for the "good and kindness" shown by the official to his master, the king, and is considered itself as "good and kindness" (*ṭābtu damiqtu*). Like the Assyrian king who, prompted by the kindness of his servant, promises "good and kindness" (*ṭābtu damiqtu*) to his descendants, so does Yahweh to the offspring of Abraham: "Know therefore that ... your God ... keeps covenant and steadfast love (*shomer habberith vehachesedh*) with those who love him and keep his commandments (*le'ohabhav uleshomere mitsvothav*), to a thousand generations" (Dt. 7:9). Although this verse is taken from Deuteronomy, which is relatively late, its basic formula goes back to more ancient sources like Ex. 20:6 (cf. Dt. 5:10): "the God who shows steadfast love (*'oseh chesedh,* cf. Akk. *ēpiš ṭābti* above) to thousands of those *who love me and keep my commandments,*" and also, "who keeps steadfast love (*notser chesedh*) for thousands" (Ex. 34:7). [72]

The kindness (*chesedh*) of God to David is likewise extended to the future generations, as may be seen from 2 S. 7:15; 22:51; 1 K. 3:6; 8:23; Ps. 89:34f. (33f.). Furthermore, just as the official of Ashurbanipal is called *bēl ṭābti bēl damiqti,* "friend and ally" (lit., "man of kindness and favor"), so Abraham and David are called "the lovers" and "friends of God." The promises to Abraham and David, which originally were unconditional, were understood as conditional only in a later stage of Israelite history. The exile of Northern Israel appeared to refute the claim of the eternity of the Abrahamic covenant, and therefore a reinterpretation of the covenant was necessary, which was done by adding the condition, i.e., that the covenant is eternal only if the donee keeps his loyalty to the donor. It is true that even in the older sources the loyalty of the sons of the patriarchs is presupposed (cf. Gen. 18:19), but this is never considered as the condition for national existence, as it is in Deuteronomy and the Deuteronomistic literature.

---

[71] Postgate, *Neo-Assyrian Grants,* 27ff. (No. 9).
[72] Cf. J. Scharbert, "Formgeschichte und Exegese von Ex 34,6f.," *Bibl,* 38 (1957), 130-150.

VII. The Covenant and the Origin of the Apodictic Law. Though Israel's law codes (esp. the Deuteronomic) are patterned after the model of the vassal treaty, it is clear that law as such belongs to the judicial sphere of human activity, and not to the political sphere, which is the area the vassal treaties represent. It is little wonder, then, that in spite of the undisputed relation between law and covenant in ancient Israel (the Bible itself does not conceive of a law code without a covenant at its base), the question about the origin of the apodictic law [73] is still open to discussion. The main problem is the origin of the apodictic style, and more precisely the legal sayings formulated in the 2nd person (sing. or pl.): "do" or "do not." This kind of legal style is not attested in any of the ancient Near Eastern legal codes, and therefore scholars look for the origin of this style in other areas. Thus, e.g., the observation was made by Gerstenberger [74] that since the apodictic (or, as he calls it, the prohibitive) style (we would rather call it the imperative style) is prevalent in the Wisdom Literature and in a series of old family laws, [75] its origin should be sought in the clan ethos, i.e., in the patriarchal milieu. [76] Others insist on treaty stipulation (formulated in the 2nd person) as the origin of apodictic law, while others cling to the view of Mowinckel, Alt, and von Rad that its origin was in the cultic festival, where law was recited. However, an entire literary genre especially preserved in the Hittite culture has been disregarded by scholars dealing with this complicated problem, viz., the various so-called Instructions of the Hittite empire. These were promulgated for political officials, border commanders, [77] military personnel, [78] and temple officials. [79] They are formulated mostly in the 2nd person (sing. and pl.) and, what is equally important, they are called *išḫiul*, "covenant." From the point of view of type and structure, they are identical with "treaties." [80] Like the political treaties, these "Instructions" become valid by the oath accompanying them. In fact, along with the instructions dictated by the king's authority, we find a declaration of allegiance proclaimed by the officials themselves. [81] Fealty oaths of this kind are also found in later Neo-Assyrian and Neo-Babylonian documents in the political [82] and civil-professional sphere. [83]

These documents are characterized by the dialogue form, i.e., the command of the superior formulated as an address in the 2nd person: "You will keep, etc.," and the declaration of acceptance by the inferior party in the 1st person

---

[73] See above, V.1.
[74] Gerstenberger, *Verkündigung und Forschung*, 14 (1969), 28-44.
[75] Cf. Elliger, *ZAW*, 67 (1955), 1-25.
[76] W. Richter, *Recht und Ethos. StANT*, 15 (1966).
[77] Cf. von Schuler.
[78] Alp, *Belleten*, 11 (1947), 388ff.
[79] Sturtevant-Bechtel, *A Hittite Chrestomathy* (Philadelphia, 1935), 127ff.; *ANET²*, 207ff.
[80] Von Schuler, *Historia*, Einzelschriften, 7 (1964), 45ff.
[81] Von Schuler, *Or*, 25 (1956), 209ff.; Otten, *MDOG*, 94 (1963), 3ff.
[82] Cf. *ABL*, 1105, 1239.
[83] Cf. *ABL*, 33; see D. B. Weisberg, *Guild Structure and Political Allegiance in Early Achaemenid Mesopotamia* (New Haven, 1967).

plural: "We shall keep, etc." [84] The same dialogue pattern is found in an oath made by craftsmen from the early part of the reign of Cyrus. [85]

We find a similar pattern in God's covenant with Israel in conjunction with the law imposed upon them. After Moses recites the law at Mt. Sinai, the people declare: "all the words [86] which the Lord has spoken we will do" (Ex. 24:3; cf. v. 7 and 19:8). The dialogue is also reflected in Dt. 26:17-19 at the conclusion of the Deuteronomic law and before the ceremony between Mt. Ebal and Mt. Gerizim (Dt. 27). Indeed, the recital of the curses and the "Amen" response of the people at this ceremony remind us of the "Hittite soldiers' oath" where the soldiers proclaim "So be it" after each curse recited by the officiating priest. [87]

The analogy with the Hittite "Instructions" may be strengthened by certain parallels in content. Several laws in the Covenant Code, which is chronologically the closest biblical law code to the Hittite treaties, are identical with the instructions given to the Hittite commanders by their king: "Whatever is right, that shall you do.... He who has a complaint must judge it and set him right..." [88] (cf. Ex. 23:1ff.; Lev. 19:15; Dt. 16:18); "A sojourner who dwells in the land..., supply him..." [89] (cf. Ex. 22:20f.[21f.]); "Do not delay (the offerings)" [90] (cf. Ex. 22:28[29]). The Hittite "temple instructions," which are very similar in content to the Priestly laws in the Bible, [91] are also styled in the 2nd person (sing. or pl.) like the biblical laws.

Legal ordinances imposed upon the people and sanctioned by a covenant with the local god are known to us from the third millennium B.C. Urukagina, the prince of Lagash (24th century B.C.) made a "bond" (kešda = covenant) with the god Ningirsu on the legal reform measures promulgated by him. In fact, all the Babylonian law codes are given divine authority. Like the treaties, they have Blessings and Curses at their end, and are inscribed on stelae put in the temple. [92]

Thus, in Israel law and covenant are bound together from the beginning, and the 2nd person address, so prevalent in the Israelite law, can be explained only against the background of the dialogue relationship described above. The pattern of the vassal treaty, which dominates the structure of Deuteronomy, seems to have been superimposed later, and is not inherent in the law itself.

Though the covenant of Moses seems to have given eternal authority to Israelite law, it nevertheless had to be renewed from time to time. Joshua is said to have promulgated the law at the covenant in Shechem (Josh. 24:25). Josiah makes the people commit themselves in a covenant "to keep the commandments

---

[84] E.g., von Schuler, *Dienstanweisungen*, 8-9, § 1f.; *ABL*, 1239 in contrast to 1105; Wiseman, *Vassal-Treaties*, 1-493 in contrast to 494-512.

[85] Weisberg, *Guild Structure*, 5ff.

[86] On *dabhar*, "word," as a covenantal term, see above, III.1.a.

[87] *ANET²*, 353f.

[88] Von Schuler, *Dienstanweisungen*, 48, 28ff.

[89] *Ibid.*, 48, 36.

[90] Sturtevant-Bechtel, *Chrestomathy*, 164, 18.

[91] E.g., J. Milgrom, *JAOS*, 90 (1970), 204ff.

[92] Cf. above, IV.2.

of the Lord" (2 K. 23:1-3). Nehemiah cuts an *'amanah,* "a firm covenant," with the people (Neh. 10:1[9:38]), which is a pledge "to walk in God's law which was given by Moses" (Neh. 10:30[29]), and by the same token the Qumran sect enters the oath "to do what is good, . . . as he (God) commanded by the hand of Moses" (1QS 1:2f.), which is accompanied by a ceremony of Blessings and Curses like that found in Dt. 27. It may be assumed that the covenant had to be renewed only after a break or violation of the old covenant, but it is equally possible that in ancient Israel (i.e., of the First Temple) the renewal of the covenant was done periodically, either yearly (Mowinckel) or every seven years (Dt. 31:9-12, Alt). The annual renewal of the covenant in Qumran is not to be seen as the continuation of an old custom. Instead, this belongs to the laws of associations in the Hellenistic period.[93] However, the very phenomenon of a communal pledge to keep a defined body of rules and laws goes back to older times,[94] although it was especially fostered in the Persian (cf. the *'amanah,* "firm covenant," of Nehemiah) and Hellenistic periods, when the cult was no longer the responsibility of the state, but was given into the hands of various sects and associations.[95]

VIII. Covenant Theology. Long before the parallels between the Israelite covenant and the ancient Near Eastern treaty had been brought to light, W. Eichrodt recognized the importance of the covenant idea in the religion of Israel. He saw in the Sinai covenant a point of departure for understanding Israel's religion. Basic phenomena in Israelite religion like the kingship of God, revelation, liberation from myth, personal attitudes toward God, etc., are to be explained against the background of the covenant, according to Eichrodt.

The discovery of the treaty pattern in the ancient Near East strengthened this hypothesis to a certain extent. The new developments in covenant research brought into broad relief especially the idea of the kingship of God. It now becomes clear that God as king of Israel is not an idea born during the period of the monarchy, as scholars used to think, but on the contrary, is one of the most genuine and most ancient doctrines in Israel. In the period of the judges, the tribes resisted an earthly kingship because of the prevailing belief that God is the real king of Israel, and that the proclamation of an earthly king would constitute betrayal. This is clearly expressed in Gideon's reply to the offer of kingship by the people (Jgs. 8:22f.), but is more salient in Samuel's denunciation of the request for a king (1 S. 8:6f.; 10:17ff.; 12:17). Earthly kingship in Israel was finally accepted, but this was the result of a compromise. David's kingship was conceived as granted to him by the great suzerain (2 S. 7).[96] Thus, the king and the people alike were considered as vassals of God, the real overlord (1 S. 12:14,24f.; 2 K. 11:17).

---

[93] Cf. e.g., W. Erichsen, *Die Satzungen einer ägyptischen Kultgenossenschaft aus der Ptolemäerzeit* (1959).

[94] See above.

[95] See, e.g., E. Ziebarth, *Das griechische Vereinswesen* (1896); M. San Nicolò, *Ägyptisches Vereinswesen zur Zeit der Ptolemäer und Römer,* I (1913); II (1915).

[96] See above.

It seems that this suzerain-vassal psychology has its roots in the political reality of the period of the judges. As is well known, Syria-Palestine in the second half of the second millennium B.C. was dominated by two great political powers in turn, viz., the Egyptians and the Hittites. The king of Egypt and the king of the Hittites respectively were overlords of the petty kingdoms in the area. The land and kingdom of these petty states were conceived as feudal grants bestowed on them by the great suzerain, in exchange for which these states were obliged to be loyal to their master. Israel's concepts of its relationship to God followed similar lines. The Israelites believed that they owed their land and the royal dynasty to their suzerain, God. Furthermore, as the relationship between the suzerain and the vassal had to be based on a written document, i.e., a treaty, so the relationship between God and Israel should be expressed in written form. It is not surprising, therefore, that tablets of the covenant played such an important role in the religion of Israel. As already noted, the tablets had to be deposited in the sanctuary at the feet of the deity, a procedure known to us from the Hittite treaties. Moreover, it appears that, as in the judicial sphere, the written document expresses the validity of the relationship. When the covenant is no longer in force, the document must be destroyed. Thus, the worship of the golden calf, which signifies the breaking of the covenant, is followed by the breaking of the tablets by Moses, the mediator of the covenant (Ex. 32). Indeed, the expression for cancelling a contract in the Babylonian legal literature is "break the tablet" (*ṭuppam ḫepû*). Following the judicial pattern, the renewal of the relationship had to be effected by writing new tablets, which explains why new ones had to be written after the sin of the golden calf, and accounts for the repetition of the Ritual Decalog in Ex. 34:19-25 (cf. 23:10-19). Renewal of a covenant with a vassal, after a break in relationship, by means of writing new tablets is actually attested in Hittite political documents.

IX. The Covenant in Prophecy. 1. A new look at the covenant is apt to explain basic phenomena in Israel's prophetic literature. The admonitory speeches of the prophets are often stylized in the form of a *lawsuit* (Isa. 1:2ff.; Jer. 2:4ff.; Hos. 4:1ff.; Mic. 6:1ff.). God sues the people of Israel in the presence of witnesses such as heaven and earth and mountains (Isa. 1:2; Mic. 6:1f.), witnesses that appear also in the ancient Near Eastern treaties and in the Deuteronomic covenant. Political strifes in the ancient Near East provide parallels to prophetic denunciations. E.g., before going out to battle with the Babylonian king Kashtiliash, the Assyrian king Tukulti-Ninurta accuses him of betraying and violating the treaty between them, and as proof he loudly reads the treaty before the god Shamash. In a similar way, the prophetic lawsuit represents the accusation of God before coming to destroy Israel for violating the covenant. This is clearly expressed in Am. 4:6-11, where a series of curses, similar to those in Lev. 26, is proclaimed in the nature of a warning, before the final judgment or encounter (cf. v. 12, "Prepare to meet your God, O Israel"). [97]

---

[97] See W. Brueggemann, *VT*, 15 (1965), 1-15; otherwise Wolff, *BK, in loc.*

The maledictions in Israelite prophecy remind us of the curses in ancient Near Eastern treaties. Thus, the calamities predicted in the prose sermons of Jeremiah have parallels in the contemporary treaty literature. The most prominent of these are: (1) corpses are devoured by the birds of heaven and the beasts of the earth; (2) joyful sounds are removed; (3) exile; (4) the land is made desolate and becomes a habitation for animals; (5) the dead are dishonored; (6) children are eaten by their parents; (7) people drink poisonous water and eat wormwood; and (8) the sound of the millstones ceases and the light of the oven (or of the candle) goes out. [98]

The purpose of the treaty curses was to portray calamities that would befall the vassal if he violated the treaty. This was usually done by literary similes and a dramatic enactment of the punishment that would befall the transgressor. Both devices were employed by the prophets. As in the treaties, so in the prophetic literature, the similes are drawn from various spheres of life, as is indicated, e.g., in Am. 2:13; 3:12; 5:19; 9:9. The dramatization of the punishment is also very close in form and content to the dramatic enactment in the treaties. Thus, e.g., we read in the Sefire Treaty: "As this calf is cleft, so may Mati'ilu and his nobles be cleft," [99] which, of course, reminds us of Jer. 34:18: "And the men who transgressed my covenant . . . , I will make like the calf which they cut in two and passed between its parts." [100]

2. Elsewhere in the earlier, preexilic prophets, *berith* is explicitly mentioned only rarely. [101] Amos knows the concept of election, but does not mention the covenant. Hosea prefers the marriage motif, and yet he does speak of transgressing (*'abhar*) the covenant twice (Hos. 6:7; 8:1). Micah, Nahum, Zephaniah, and Habakkuk never mention the covenant. The following examples in Isaiah should be cited: Isa. 24:5; 28:15,18; 33:8.

The covenant idea is first given greater importance in Jeremiah. He speaks of the covenant that Yahweh had concluded with the fathers (Jer. 34:13; cf. 11:8), and censures the people because they had broken (*parar*) the covenant and served other gods (11:10; cf. 31:32). In his intercession for the people, he refers to the covenant: "Remember (*zakhar*) and do not break (*parar*) thy covenant with us" (14:21). But he also knows of a new covenant which Yahweh will conclude with Israel in place of the covenant they had broken (31:31ff.). To be sure, this will consist of doing the *torah*, "law," but will differ from the old covenant in that people will know and perform the will of God out of inner motivation. Forgiveness of sins is the basis of this new covenant (v. 34).

In the allegory in Ezk. 16, the prophet Ezekiel speaks of the covenant which Yahweh had made with the young Israel (16:8), but which Israel had broken (v. 59). But now Yahweh will make a new covenant (vv. 60,62), not because of Israel's faithfulness (v. 61), but because Yahweh himself will remember (*zakhar*)

---

98 Weinfeld, *Deuteronomy*, 138ff.
99 *KAI*, 222 A.40.
100 For additional parallels, cf. Rudolph, *HAT*, 12, 205.
101 J. Lindblom, *Prophecy in Ancient Israel* (Oxford, 1962), 329f.

278   בְּרִית berîth

the covenant (v. 60). Elsewhere, also, he promises a new covenant (37:26), which will be a covenant of peace (34:25; 37:26), and an everlasting covenant (16:60; 37:26; cf. also Isa. 61:8).

Deutero-Isaiah speaks twice of the Servant of Yahweh as a *berith 'olam,* "everlasting covenant," once of the renewing of the Davidic covenant (Isa. 55:3), and once of Yahweh's covenant of peace (*berith shelomi,* 54:10, with reference to the covenant with Noah).

X. The Origin of the Covenant Concept. The idea of a covenant between a deity and a people is unknown to us from other religions and cultures. It is not impossible that some of the other ancient peoples also had covenants with their gods. Moab, e.g., is called "the people of Chemosh" (Nu. 21:29), as Israel is called "the people of Yahweh" (Jgs. 5:11; etc.), and both may have had identical relationships with their gods. A covenant of the people of Ashur with Ishtar might be implied in an Assyrian text. [102] It seems, however, that the covenantal idea was a special feature of the religion of Israel, the only one to demand exclusive loyalty and to preclude the possibility of dual or multiple loyalties such as were permitted in other religions, where the believer was bound in diverse relationships to many gods. The stipulation in political treaties demanding exclusive fealty to one king corresponds strikingly with the religious belief in one single, exclusive deity.

The prophets, especially Hosea, Jeremiah, and Ezekiel, expressed the idea of exclusive loyalty by describing the relationship between God and Israel as one between a husband and wife, which itself is also considered covenantal. [103] Although the idea of marital love between God and Israel is not explicitly mentioned in the Pentateuch, it seems to exist there in a latent form. Following other gods is warned against with the statement, "For I the Lord your God am a jealous God" (Ex. 20:5; Dt. 5:9; cf. Ex. 34:14; Josh. 24:19). The root → קנא *qānā',* "to be jealous," is, in fact, used in Nu. 5:14 in the technical sense of a husband who is jealous over his wife. Similarly, the verb used in the Pentateuch for disloyalty is → זנה *zānāh,* "to play the harlot, to whore" (*'achare,* "after"). Furthermore, the formula expressing the covenantal relationship between God and Israel, "I will be your God, and you shall be my people" (Lev. 26:12; Dt. 29:12[13]; etc.), is a legal formula taken from the sphere of marriage, as attested in various legal documents from the ancient Near East (cf. Hos. 2:4[2]). The relationship of the vassal to his suzerain, and that of the wife to her husband, leave no place for double loyalty, and therefore are perfect metaphors for loyalty in a monotheistic religion.

The concept of the kingship of God in Israel seems also to have contributed to the concept of Israel as the vassal of God. It is true that the idea of the kingship of God was prevalent throughout the ancient Near East. Nevertheless, there is an important difference between the Israelite notion of divine kingship and the corresponding idea in other nations. Israel adopted the idea of the kingship of

---

[102] *BAss,* 2 (1894), 628-29, iii, 6-10.
[103] See above, and esp. Ezk. 16:8.

God long before establishing the human institution of kingship. Consequently, for hundreds of years the only kingship recognized and institutionalized in Israel was the kingship of God. During the period of the judges, Yahweh was actually the king of Israel (cf. Jgs. 8:23; 1 S. 8:7; 10:19), and was not, as in the other religions of the ancient Near East, the image of the earthly king.

Weinfeld

בָּרַךְ brk; בְּרָכָה berākhāh

Contents: I. Etymology and Distribution: 1. Word-Formations in Hebrew and Their Occurrences in the OT; 2. In Other Semitic Languages. II. *brk* in the Sense of "Bless," etc., in the OT: 1. The *barukh*-Formula; 2. The Piel; 3. *brk* in Other Conjugations; 4. The Noun. III. *brk* = "To Bless," etc.: 1. In Hebrew Inscriptions; 2. In the Qumran Literature; 3. In the LXX. IV. The Blessing in OT Theology.

I. Etymology and Distribution.

1. *Word-Formations in Hebrew and Their Occurrences in the OT*. The Hebrew lexicons distinguish between two roots: *brk* I, which is attested by the qal meaning "to kneel" (Ps. 95:6; 2 Ch. 6:13), the hiphil meaning "to make (camels) kneel" (Gen. 24:11), and the noun *berekh*, "knee" (sing. only in Isa.

---

brk. 1. General Literature on "Blessing": F. Asensio, "Trayectoria historico-teológica de la 'Bendición' bíblica de Yahveh en labios del hombre," *Greg*, 48 (1967), 253-283; J. P. Audet, "Esquisse historique du genre littéraire de la 'bénédiction' juive et de l'Eucharistie' chrétienne," *RB*, 65 (1958), 371-399; H. W. Beyer, "εὐλογέω," *TDNT*, II, 754-765; E. J. Bickerman, "Bénédiction et prière," *RB*, 69 (1962), 524-532; E. F. F. Bishop, "εὐλογητός," I. *Goldziher Memorial*, I (Budapest, 1948), 82-88; Sheldon H. Blank, "Some Observations Concerning Biblical Prayer," *HUCA*, 32 (1961), 75-90; A. Charbel, "*Todah* como 'sacrifício de Acção de Graças,'" *Atualidades Bíblicas* [em memoria de J. J. Pedreira de Castro], ed. J. Salvador (Petrópolis, 1971), 105-114, esp. pp. 107-09; J. Chelhod, "La baraka chez les Arabes," *RHR*, 148 (1955), 68-88; M. Cohen, "Genou, famille, force dans le monde chamito-sémitique," *Mémorial H. Basset* (Paris, 1928), 203-210; F. C. Fensham, "Malediction and Benediction in Ancient Near Eastern Vassal-Treaties and the OT," *ZAW*, 74 (1962), 1-9; M. Fraenkel, "Berakah 'Segen,'" *Das Neue Israel*, 19 (1966), 177-79; W. Gross, "Jakob, der Mann des Segens," *Bibl*, 49 (1968), 321-344; J. Guillet, "Le langage spontané de la bénédiction dans l'AT," *RScR*, 57 (1969), 163-204; W. J. Harrelson, in *IDB*, I, 446-48; J. Hempel, "Die israelitischen Anschauungen von Segen und Fluch im Lichte altorientalischer Parallelen," *ZDMG*, 79 (1925), 20-110 = *BZAW*, 81 (1961), 30-113; *idem*, in *RGG²*, V, 388-393; C. Z. Hirschberg, in *EMiqr*, II, 354-361; F. Horst, "Segen und Segenshandlungen in der Bibel," *EvTh*, 7 (1947/1948), 23-37; now in *idem, Gottes Recht. ThB*, 12 (1961), 188-202; *idem*, in *RGG³*, V, 1649-1651; P. van Imschoot in *BL²* (1968), 1568f.; E. Jenni, *Das hebräische Pi'el* (Zürich, 1968), esp. pp. 216f.; H. Junker, "Segen als heilsgeschichtliches Motivwort im AT," *Sacra Pagina*, ed. J. Coppens, *et al.*, I. *BETL*, 12-13 (Paris, 1959), 548-558; C. A. Keller-G. Wehmeier, in *THAT*, I (1971), 353-376; B. Landsberger, "Das 'gute Wort,'" *MAOG*, 4 (1928/1929), 294-321; J. Marcus, in *Universal Jewish Encyclopedia*, II, 391-93; S. Mowinckel,

(continued on p. 280)

45:23; the dual occurs 24 times from J to the Chronicler); and *brk* II, for which
the lexicons list the following derivatives and meanings: the qal pass. ptcp.
barukh, "blessed," "praised" (17 times in the Pss., only 6 times in the Prophets,
and elsewhere 48 times from J to the Chronicler), the niphal, "to be blessed, to
bless oneself" (Gen. 12:3; 18:18; 28:14), the piel, "to bless, greet, praise" (Gen.
from J to P 59 times; Pss. 52 times; Dt. 28 times; 1 and 2 Ch. 18 times; Nu.
14 times; 1 and 2 S. 14 times; elsewhere 48 times; this form does not occur in
Ezk., Cant., and Dnl.), the pual, "to be blessed" (13 times from J to the Chronicler; this form does not appear in the Prophets), the hithpael, "to bless oneself,
bless one another" (Gen. 22:18; 26:4; Dt. 29:18 [Eng. v. 19]; Isa. 65:16 [twice];
Jer. 4:2; Ps. 72:17), and the noun *berakhah,* "blessing, praise" (71 times from J
to the Chronicler; in Isa. 1–39 only in 19:24; elsewhere in the Prophets 10 times
from Ezk. on). The proper names *barukh,* "Baruch" (besides Neh. 3:20; 10:7[6];
and 11:5, only in Jer.), *barakh'el,* "Barachel" (Job 32:2,6), *berakhah,* "Beracah"
(1 Ch.12:3), *berekhya(hu),* "Berechiah" (for 6 different persons), and *yebherekh-
yahu,* "Jeberechiah" (Isa. 8:2), are formed from this root. To these must be
added the noun *berēkhāh,* which the lexicons render by "pool, water reservoir,
basin," etc. (2 S. 2:13; 4:12; 1 K. 22:38; 2 K. 18:17; 20:20; Isa. 7:3; 22:9,11;
36:2; Nah. 2:9[8]; Cant. 7:5[4]; Eccl. 2:6; Neh. 2:14; 3:15f.), but whose relationship to *brk* I or to *brk* II is debated.

In the Aramaic portions of the OT, *brk* I is attested by the noun *berakh,*
"knee" (Dnl. 6:11[10]), with the subordinate form *'arkhubbah,* "knee" (5:6),
and the peal ptcp. *barekh,* "kneeling down" (6:11[10]), while *brk* II is attested by
the pass. ptcp. *berikh,* "blessed" (3:28), and the pael *barikh* or *barekh,* "to bless"

Segen und Fluch in Israels Kult und Psalmendichtung. Psalmenstudien, V (Kristiania, 1924);
idem, The Psalms in Israel's Worship (trans. 1962), cf. Index *s.v.* 'blessing'; *idem, Religion
und Kultus* (1953), 64-66; H. Mowvley, "The Concept and Content of 'Blessing' in the OT,"
BT, 16 (1965), 74-80; H.-P. Müller, *Ursprünge und Strukturen alttestamentlicher Eschatologie. BZAW,* 109 (1969), 129-171; A. Murtonen, "The Use and Meaning of the Words *lebārēk*
and *berākhāh* in the OT," *VT,* 9 (1959), 158-177, 330; Pedersen, *ILC,* I-II, 182-212; D.
Piccard, "Réflexions sur l'interprétation chrétienne de trois récits de la Genèse," *Hommage
à W. Vischer* (Montpellier, 1960), 181-190, esp. p. 188; J. Plassmann, *The Signification of
Berākā* (Paris, 1913); J. M. Robinson, "Heilsgeschichte und Lichtungsgeschichte," *EvTh,* 22
(1962), 113-141, esp. pp. 118-134; J. Scharbert, *Solidarität in Segen und Fluch im AT und
in seiner Umwelt. BBB,* 14 (1958); *idem,* "'Fluchen' und 'Segnen' im AT," *Bibl,* 39 (1958),
1-26; *idem, Heilsmittler im AT und im Alten Orient. QuaestDisp,* 23/24 (1964); *idem,* in
LThK, IX (1964), 590-92; *idem,* in Bauer, *Bibeltheol. Wb.* (³1967), 1240-49; H. Schmidt,
"Grüsse und Glückwünsche im Psalter," *ThStKr,* 103 (1931), 141-150; W. Schottroff, *Der
altisraelit. Fluchspruch. WMANT,* 30 (1969), 163-198; S. Smith, "Note on Blessings," *PEQ,*
81 (1949), 57; A. Stuiber in *RAC,* VI, 900-08; W. Sibley Towner, "'Blessed be YHWH' and
'Blessed art Thou, YHWH': The Modulation of a Biblical Formula," *CBQ,* 30/3 (1968), 386-
399; D. Vetter, *Jahwes Mitsein–ein Ausdruck des Segens. ArbT,* 45 (1971); F. Vigouroux, *DB,*
I, 1580-83; K.-H. Walkenhorst, *Der Sinai im liturgischen Verständnis der deuteronomistischen
und priesterlichen Tradition. BBB,* 33 (1969), 160-170; G. Wehmeier, *Der Segen im AT.
Theol. Diss.,* 6 (Basel, 1970); C. Westermann, "Frage nach dem Segen," *ZZ,* 11 (1957), 244-
253; *idem, Der Segen in der Bibel und im Handeln der Kirche* (1968); *idem,* in *BHHW,* III,
1758; *idem,* in *EKL,* III, 917-920.
     2. On Gen. 12:1-3 par.: L. Diez Merino, *La vocación de Abraham* (Rome, 1970); J. Hempel,

(continued on p. 281)

(2:19f.; 4:31[34]). No noun for "pool," etc., occurs in the Aramaic portions of the OT. Scholars are not agreed as to whether *brk* I and II etymologically go back to the same root. [1]

2. *In Other Semitic Languages.* The other Semitic languages do not give additional help. Here, approximately the same three basic meanings, "knee," "blessing," and "water place," can be ascertained for the consonants *brk*. In Akkadian only the noun *birku* or *burku*, "knee," occurs; the meanings "womb," "genitals," and "virility" (*ša lā išû birkē* = "the one who is impotent") are only expansions of the basic meaning or euphemisms. [2] The Akk. *karābu*, which the lexicons render "to pray, bless, greet, consecrate," [3] agrees in meaning with *brk* II, "to bless." The nouns *karābum* and *ikribum*, "prayer, consecration, bless-

---

"Die Wurzeln des Missionswillens im Glauben des AT," *ZAW*, 66 (1954), 244-272, esp. pp. 252f.; J. Hoftijzer, *Die Verheissungen an die drei Erzväter* (Leiden, 1956); R. Kilian, *Die vorpriesterlichen Abrahams-Überlieferungen. BBB*, 24 (1966), 1-15; R. Mosis, "Gen 12,1-4," in J. Schreiner, *Die alttestamentlichen Lesungen*, A/1 (1971), 73-83; J. Muilenburg, "Abraham and the Nations," *In*, 19 (1965), 387-398; R. Rendtorff, "Gen 8,21 und die Urgeschichte des Jahwisten," *KuD*, 7 (1961), 69-78; J. Scharbert, *Heilsmittler*, 77-81; J. Schreiner, "Segen für die Völker," *BZ*, N.F. 6 (1962), 1-31; O. H. Steck, "Genesis 12,1-3 und die Urgeschichte des Jahwisten," *Probleme biblischer Theologie. Festschrift für G. von Rad*, ed. H. W. Wolff (1971), 525-554; H. W. Wolff, "Das Kerygma des Jahwisten," *EvTh*, 24 (1964), 73-98; now in *ThB*, 22 (1964), 345-373.

3. On Gen. 49 and Dt. 33: C. Armerding, "The Last Words of Moses," *BS*, 114 (1957), 225-234; C. M. Carmichael, "Some Sayings in Genesis 49," *JBL*, 88 (1969), 435-444; J. Coppens, "La bénédiction de Jacob," *SVT*, 6 (1958), 97-115; P. C. Craigie, "The Conquest and Early Hebrew Poetry," *TynB*, 20 (1969), 76-94; F. M. Cross, Jr.-D. N. Freedman, "The Blessing of Moses," *JBL*, 67 (1948), 191-210; J. A. Emerton, "Some Difficult Words in Genesis 49," *Words and Meanings. Festschrift D. Winton Thomas*, ed. P. R. Ackroyd and B. Lindars (Cambridge, 1968), 81-93; T. H. Gaster, "An Ancient Eulogy on Israel," *JBL*, 66 (1947), 53-62; E. M. Good, "The 'Blessing' on Judah," *JBL*, 82 (1963), 427-432; A. H. J. Gunneweg, "Über den Sitz im Leben der sog. Stammessprüche," *ZAW*, 76 (1964), 245-255; H.-J. Kittel, *Die Stammessprüche Israels* (diss., Berlin, 1959); I. L. Seeligmann, "A Psalm from Pre-Regal Times," *VT*, 14 (1964), 75-92; E. Sellin, "Zu dem Judaspruch im Jacobsegen und im Mose-segen," *ZAW*, 60 (1944), 57-67; R. Tournay, "Le Psaume et les bénédictions de Moïse," *RB*, 65 (1958), 181-213; B. Vawter, "The Canaanite Background of Gen 49," *CBQ*, 17 (1955), 1-18; H.-J. Zobel, *Stammesspruch und Geschichte. BZAW*, 95 (1965); *idem*, "Die Stammessprüche des Mose-Segens," *Klio*, 46 (1965), 83-92.

4. On Lev. 26:3-13 and Dt. 28:1-14: D. J. McCarthy, *Treaty and Covenant. AnBibl*, 21 (Rome, 1963), 120-130; E. Mørstad, "Overveielser til Dtn 28," *NTT*, 60 (1959), 224-232; *idem, Wenn du der Stimme des Herrn, deines Gottes, gehorchen wirst* (Oslo, 1960); J. G. Plöger, *Literarkritische, formgeschichtliche und stilkritische Untersuchungen zum Deuteronomium. BBB*, 26 (1967), 130-217; G. Seitz, *Redaktionsgeschichtliche Studien zum Deuteronomium. BWANT*, 93 (1971), 254-302.

5. On Nu. 6:22-27: J. Elbogen, *Der jüdische Gottesdienst in seiner geschichtlichen Entwicklung* (³1931), 67-72; M. R. Lehmann, "'Yom Kippur' in Qumran," *RevQ*, 3 (1961), 117-124, esp. p. 120; L. J. Liebreich, "The Songs of Ascent and the Priestly Blessing," *JBL*, 74 (1955), 33-36; J. G. Plöger, "Num 6,22-27," J. Schreiner, *Die alttestamentlichen Lesungen*, B/1 (1969), 95-106; H. Ringgren, "Den aronitiska välsignelsen," *Talenta quinque. Festschrift E. Gulin* (Helsinki, 1953), 35-45.

[1] On the various attempts to explain the etymology of *brk*, cf. Wehmeier, 8-17.
[2] *AHw*, 129, 140; *CAD*, II, 255, 330.
[3] *AHw*, 445f.; *CAD*, VIII, 192-98.

ing," [4] are formed from this root. Whereas earlier scholars explained *karābu* as a metathesis of *brk*, more recent critics are skeptical of this hypothesis and suppose that there was a separate root *krb*, especially since such a root occurs in Old South Arabic ("to consecrate, sacrifice"). [5]

In Ugaritic, *brk* is found once meaning "to kneel," 8 times meaning "knee," once meaning "pool," and 13 times meaning "to bless" with the nuances, "to give the power of the gods (to a man), leave, commend someone to a deity for a blessing" (*brk l*). *brk* with the meaning "to bless" frequently appears with the verb *mrr* = "to be strong, give power." [6]

In Phoenician-Punic only the verb *brk*, "to bless," is attested; the noun *brkh*, "blessing," in *KAI*, 147.3 is uncertain. The verb occurs in the following sentence patterns: (a) *A* (always a deity) *brk/ybrk* (*B*), "*A* blesses (*B*)." Here the verb is usually in the piel, except that in Punic it certainly also appears in the qal and must be translated "to bless" in the sense of granting happiness, vitality, success, etc.; in numerous consecratory inscriptions, this phrase is the concluding formula. (b) *bhym mlqrt šrš ybrk*, "May Melqart bless my successor with life." [7] (c) *A* (a person) *brk B l C* (deity), "*A* commends B to a deity for blessing." [8] (d) *A* (gods) *ybrk' mṣ'y*, "may the gods bless my way," i.e., may they cause my enterprise to succeed. [9] (e) In some consecratory inscriptions we find *ym n'm wbrk;* here we must read *weḇārūk*, and translate, "a pleasant and blessed/successful/favorable (for enterprises) day." (f) The beginning of the Karatepe Inscription, [10] *'nk 'ztwd hbrk b'l*, is uncertain; *KAI* translates, "I am 'ZTWD, one blessed by Baal," which would correspond to Heb. *berukh yhvh*. (g) All other texts in which the qal or pual passive participle could be read are uncertain. [11] There is no example of a formula corresponding to the Heb. *barukh PN*, "Blessed be So-and-so."

In Aramaic texts we encounter the following forms and expressions: peal ptcp.: (a) *bryk PN*, "Blessed be So-and-so"; (b) *bryk PN qdm 'lh'*, "Blessed be So-and-so by the deity"; (c) *bryk PN l'lh'*, "May So-and-so be commended to the deity for a blessing." These expressions appear on tomb inscriptions and graffiti from Egypt in which the survivors of the deceased wish a gracious judgment of death on the deceased before the gods of the next world, and in Nabataean and Palmyrenian consecratory inscriptions. In the consecratory inscription from Hatra, two additional expressions occur: (d) *bryk 'lh'*, "the one blessed of God," [12] and (e) *dkyr wbryk PN qdm 'lh'*, "May So-and-so be remembered and blessed by the god So-and-so." [13] This last expression shows

---

[4] *AHw*, 369f., 445; *CAD*, VII, 62-66; VIII, 192.
[5] Cf. Wehmeier, 14f.; Keller-Wehmeier, 353.
[6] Cf. Wehmeier, 18-26; J. Aistleitner, *WUS*, 58f.; *UT*, 376; Schottroff, 178f.
[7] A. M. Honeyman, *Mus*, 51 (1938), 285-298, line 3.
[8] *KAI*, 50.2f.
[9] Plautus *Poenulus* 931, corrected.
[10] *KAI*, 26 A I.1.
[11] Cf. Wehmeier, 26-47; Schottroff, 179-182; *KAI*, III, p. 5; *DISO*, 44.
[12] *KAI*, 243.2.
[13] *KAI*, 244 and 246.

that the "blessing" is understood as a laudatory commendation before (*qdm*) or to (*l*) the deity. (f) In letters, we find the greeting formula with the pael, *A brk B (l'lh'),* "A blesses B before the deity," or rather, "A commends B, lauding (the deity for the blessing)" (at the beginning of the Hermopolis Papyri I-V; perhaps also on the Elephantine Ostracon 70, conc. 3; however, here Vinnikov reads *brktk* as a noun, and translates, "thy blessing is incumbent on Yaho and Khnum"). [14] (g) A papyrus in the Demotic script contains the formula *ybrk'k' 'lh' PN,* "May the god So-and-so bless thee (or, the god So-and-so is blessing thee?)." [15] (h) In an ostracon from Assuan, the noun *brkh* appears in the formula *A brkh šlḥ l B,* "A sends B blessing/greeting." Other expressions like *'lh' ybrk PN,* "the deity blesses So-and-so," "a fountain (spring) blesses = dispenses (*tbrk*) life-giving power," *bryk šmh l PN,* "Blessed is the name of the deity So-and-so," or *bryk 'lh',* "blessed be the deity So-and-so" (only in Palmyrenian), appear first in post-Christian texts. [16] In pre-Christian Hebrew inscriptions, the noun *brkh* = "pool" occurs (the Siloam inscription). [17]

Thus, in the Northwest Semitic texts, the favorite subject of the verb *brk* is a deity. If man is its subject, in most cases the "blessing" means a laudatory commendation to the deity to bless someone, or merely a greeting formula. According to the context of these texts, the content of the blessing is long life, descendants, prosperity, success, and power. The passive participle of the basic form connotes the possession of powers to bestow happiness and promote life, or (when *l* and *qdm* are used with reference to the deity) the suitability of the blessing from the deity indicated by the commendation. Consequently, apparently the Northwest Semites always understood the deity as a true giver of blessing even when they do not explicitly mention him. [18] Thus far, the deity as object of *brk* has been found only in Palmyra in pre-Christian times.

In Old South Arabic, *brkt* and *mbrk,* "cistern, water reservoir," and *brk,* "to bless" (with the deity as subj.) have been found, but this root has not yet been found with the meaning "knee." The Ethiopic lexicons list among the derivatives of the root *brk* the meanings "to bless, blessing," and "to kneel, knee." The Arabic dictionaries list under *brk* (without distinguishing between different roots) *baraka,* "to kneel" (only of camels), "to rain continuously"; 2: "to utter a blessing"; 3: "to bless, make happy, pray for someone"; 5: "to be blessed, happy, to wish one luck, to ask for a blessing"; 6: "to be praised" (God as subj.), "to be blessed, happy"; 8: "to investigate (inquire into) something eagerly," "to pour out much water" (of clouds); 10: "to be blessed, regard someone as blessed, obtain a blessing"; *barkun,* "a herd of resting camels"; *birkun* or *birkatun,* "pool"; *barakatun,* "blessing, happiness, abundance, fruitfulness," etc. In the Koran, God appears almost exclusively as subject of the verb; [19] but in popular

[14] J. N. Vinnikov, *Pales. Sbornik,* 4 (1959), 222.

[15] R. A. Bowman, *JNES,* 3 (1944), 219-231, col. VII, 3-6.

[16] Aramaic examples may be found in Wehmeier, 49-65; Schottroff, 182-88; Vinnikov, 221f.; *DISO,* 44; *KAI,* III, p. 30.

[17] *KAI,* 189.5.

[18] Cf. Wehmeier, 66.

[19] Cf. Bishop.

Arabic belief, the "blessing" was regarded as an impersonal power that produces fertility and prosperity, and is mediated to the tribe by the father or tribal chief, or to men in their own neighborhood by a holy person, without specifically mentioning God as its source or author. [20] The relationships Arabic lexicographers try to establish between the meanings "herd of kneeling camels," "pool," and "blessing" are based on popular etymology and should not be taken seriously by the scholar.

II. brk in the Sense of "Bless," etc., in the OT.

1. *The barukh-Formula.* Like the *'arur*-formula in connection with → ארר *'ārar* (II.1), the *barukh*-formula plays a special role in the use of the root *brk*. The pass. ptcp. *barukh* is the only form of the qal attested in the OT; it is used in the *barukh*-formula in a way analogous to the way *'arur* is used in the *'arur*-formula, and yet there are important differences. The short formula, *barukh 'attah/'attem,* "Blessed are you," or *barukh PN,* "Blessed is So-and-so," without additions, is found only in later texts, while earlier texts have additions, resulting in the following patterns:

a. *barukh PN 'asher* ... (verb in the perf.), "Blessed be So-and-so who ... " : with a man as subject only in 1 S. 25:33 (Abigail and her discretion), with God as subject in Gen. 14:20; 24:27 (J); Ex. 18:10 (E); 1 S. 25:32,39; 2 S. 18:28; 1 K. 1:48; 5:21 (7); 8:15, 56; Ruth 4:14; Ezr. 7:27; 2 Ch. 2:11(12); Ps. 66:20; 124:6 (using *she* instead of *'asher*); Dnl. 3:28 (Aram. *di*); in Ps. 28:6 and 31:22 (21), *ki* corresponds to the relative pronoun *'asher* (cf. c).

b. *barukh PN leyhvh,* etc., "Blessed be So-and-so by Yahweh," etc.: Gen. 14:19; Jgs. 17:2; 1 S. 15:13; Ruth 3:10; Ps. 115:15.

c. *barukh PN leyhvh 'asher/ki* ... , "May So-and-so be blessed by Yahweh, who/because ... " (verb in the perf.; *'asher* or *ki* refers to the subj. of the nominal sentence): 1 S. 23:21 (*ki*); 2 S. 2:5; Ruth 2:20 (*'asher*). A person always utters this formula in grateful reaction to a good deed which has been done for him by the individual for whom he is invoking the blessing expressed in the formula, or which has been done for a third party with whom the speaker enjoys congenial or friendly relations. The utterance of the formula is an acknowledgment of the solidarity that exists between the speaker and the person for whom the formula is intended, or at least, as in the cases where the formula is put in the mouth of a non-Israelite and is intended for the God of Israel (Ex. 18:10; 1 K. 5:21[7] = 2 Ch. 2:11[12]), respectful appreciation and grateful praise. This statement also applies to Jgs. 17:2: the mother utters the *barukh*-formula for the benefit of her son, because she is thankful that her son told her how her money disappeared, and in this way she cancels the curse that otherwise would have come upon her own son without her suspecting it (cf. → אלה *'ālāh,* "to swear,"

---

[20] Chelhod.

II.1). Thus, she reestablishes the solidarity with him who was destroyed by the curse against the thief, and commends him to Yahweh (*leyhvh*). Like the '*arur*-formula, originally this formula did not have a cultic life setting; it was brought into this setting later (→ ארר '*ārar,* "to curse," II.1). In most cases the formulation is in the 3rd person; but it appears in the 2nd person singular in special familiar addresses to an individual, and in the 2nd person plural in addresses to several persons. No basic difference can be ascertained between these formulations.

d. The reason for a blessing can also be indicated by the participle. We find expressions such as those in Dt. 33:20 (*barukh marchibh gadh,* "Blessed be he who enlarges Gad"); Gen. 27:29; Nu. 24:9 (both in J), where indeed *barukh* comes after the subject (*mebharakhekha barukh,* "they who bless you will be [may they be] blessed, par. to the '*arur*-formula). In this case also, the formula has to do with persons, referred to in the 3rd person, to whom those who are addressed, people with whom the speaker feels himself intimately connected, show or demonstrate good will, solidarity, etc. Here, however, the statement is no longer an immediate reaction to a good deed in the past, but a promise to those who demonstrate their good will, solidarity, or friendship to future Israel or one of its members.

e. But also, the shortened formula *barukh PN,* "Blessed be So-and-so," is not used of just anyone, as in greeting strangers, but only of people to whom one is particularly indebted (1 S. 26:25), or with whom one is connected socially or by the same faith (Dt. 33:20; Ps. 118:26). Then this formula implies an acknowledgment of associations with or sanctions of such persons.

When Yahweh uses the formula *barukh 'ammi,* "Blessed be my people," with reference to Egypt and Assyria in Isa. 19:25, he is saying that one day his intimate relationships with men given through the covenant will also be extended to Assyria and Egypt, and he will acknowledge them as his own people just as he now acknowledges Israel. In the earlier period, the shortened formula in the sense of an acknowledgment of special solidarity with a kinsman or fellow tribesman or fellow believer seems to have been pushed into the background, so that the one speaking the blessing did not name the one being blessed directly, but designated the God they both worshipped as the God of the person being blessed, "*barukh yhvh* (Blessed be Yahweh), the God of Shem" (Gen. 9:26). In this way, not only does Shem's father contrast him with the accursed Canaan, but he also distinguishes him from Japheth, on whom he also pronounces a word of blessing (but without using *brk*!).

Since the short formula implied acknowledgment of an intimate relationship with the person named therein, it was also suited to express acknowledgment of Israel's covenant God. Thus we find the phrase *barukh yhvh,* "Blessed be Yahweh," etc., frequently expanded by an epithet of Yahweh, by an expression for "everlasting," etc. (1 Ch. 16:36; Ps. 41:14[13]; 68:20,36[19,35]; 72:18; 89:53 [52]; 106:48; 135:21; 144:1). Occasionally the 2nd person pronoun, '*attah,* "thou," is inserted between *barukh* and *yhvh,* "Blessed art (be) thou, O Yahweh"

(1 Ch. 29:10; Ps. 119:12). In such expressions, the divine name can be replaced by "my rock" (2 S. 22:47), "the glory of Yahweh" (Ezk. 3:12?), or "his glorious name" (Ps. 72:19: in an additional *barukh*-formula alongside *barukh yhvh*). All these examples are found in relatively late and always cultic texts, in which God is praised not for a specific reason, but in the liturgy or in the daily prayer of the godly. Except for the disputed text in Ezk. 3:12, these "benedictions" also always appear in texts in which Yahweh is praised and his saving deeds to Israel or to the individual worshipper are mentioned, even if the reason for the blessing is missing in the formula. Therefore, the original life setting, viz., the grateful praise for good deeds that have been received, seems to have given way to another setting. Here there is an important distinction between the *barukh*-formula and the *'ashre*-formula, which has an entirely different life setting (→ אשרי *'ashrê*). Later the *barukh*-formula can be completely depleted of any religious connotation, e.g., when people rejoice because they have feathered their nest by unjust deeds (Zec. 11:5).

f. In the examples cited thus far, a statement is to be assumed as the mode of the nominal sentence, and not a wish. Such a statement can also be expressed informally; then *barukh* is followed by the imperfect (*yihyeh:* Gen. 27:33, "he will be blessed"; *tihyeh:* Dt. 7:14, "you shall be blessed"). But three times *barukh* is also used in a wish, and then the word order is reversed: *yehi PN barukh,* "May So-and-so be blessed" (1 K. 10:9 with Yahweh as subj.; Prov. 5:18 with the wife as subj.; and Ruth 2:19 with a third party with whom the speaker feels an intimate relationship as subj.). This word order, but without an imperfect of *hayah,* "to be," corresponds to the nominal phrase *PN barukh,* "So-and-so shall be blessed," in 1 K. 2:45; here, however, the subject of the nominal phrase is identical with the speaker of the formula (Solomon), because by uttering this blessing he desires to put himself at a distance from someone who had been cursed and apparently to guard himself against the curse resting on that person. Because of the context and the word order, it is likely that here also a wish is to be assumed: "But may King Solomon be *barukh* (blessed)." Then Gen. 27:29 and Nu. 24:9 (cf. d) probably also should be translated as a wish: "Those who curse you, may they be cursed, and those who bless you, may they be *barukh* (blessed)."

Even if the *barukh*-phrases are also to be understood as statements, still they should not be interpreted a priori as powerful words that work magic when people are the subject, as is usually done.[21] Appeal cannot be made to Gen. 27:33 in support of this view, because the formula is not used in this passage, but it is merely stated that Jacob shall still be blessed because Isaac had already eaten the meal he had prepared. That the oldest texts refer to God (*le*) or mention God explicitly, and are used as praise or as a declaration of grateful solidarity rather than an incantation, speaks against the magical character of the *barukh*-formulas.

---

[21] Mowinckel, Pedersen, Hempel, and for the earlier texts, Westermann.

g. If the utterance of the *barukh*-formula is occasioned by a good deed that someone has experienced or by a declaration of anticipated solidarity, it can also be used as an announcement of recompense for a praiseworthy behavior (Jer. 17:7: "*barukh* [Blessed] is the man who trusts in Yahweh"), and, along with the '*arur*-formula, as a sanction for laws, as in Dt. 28:3-6. This text is very similar to the corresponding curse sanction (→ ארר '*ārar*, II.1.). The *barukh*-declarations concerning "you" in "your coming in" and "your going out" (v. 6) serve as a framework around the *barukh*-declarations concerning "your" earthly possessions (the fruit of the body, the fruit of the ground, and the fruit of the beasts, v. 4), and the basket and the kneading-trough (v. 5). Here both people and their possessions are regarded as *barukh,* "blessed," but still in the future and on the condition of fidelity to Yahweh's covenant law.

h. As in the Phoenician texts mentioned above under I.2.e., a day could be said to be *barukh,* "blessed," in the OT. But we find this kind of *barukh*-formula only in a negative wish, "Let the day (of one's birth) not be blessed" (*'al yehi bharukh,* par. to "Cursed be the day," Jer. 20:14). The *barukh*-formula can also be used to show special appreciation for a commendable quality in a man (as discretion: 1 S. 25:33, here it is used with a *barukh*-statement addressed to the person himself).

i. Finally, the passive participle in the construct state can refer to a person on whom Yahweh has bestowed kindness in a special way, so that he has become successful and prosperous. This is expressed by the phrase *berukh yhvh,* "blessed (one) of Yahweh," which appears as an address in the vocative (Gen. 24:31), and as a statement in the indicative, "you are *berukh(e) yhvh,* a blessed one (blessed ones) of Yahweh" (Gen. 26:29; Isa. 65:23). From this form-critical analysis, the following conclusions can be drawn with regard to the semantics of the pass. ptcp. *barukh:* God, men, things or property, human qualities, and days can be called *barukh,* "blessed." It is not clear that the OT traditionists use the participle in basically different senses. The examples cited under categories a-c seem to be less concerned with a blessing in the sense that the usual translation "blessed" would suggest, and more with an extolling, grateful praise which both God and man can bestow.[22] Then, the *leyhvh,* "by Yahweh," in b and c indicates that the extolling before Yahweh was a commendation extolling the person named, evidently for the purpose of inciting Yahweh to bless him in an appropriate way. Accordingly, in most cases it would seem best to translate the expressions in a-c this way: "So-and-so (who/because he did thus and so) is (gratefully) praised/is to be (gratefully) praised, is extolled and commended/is to be extolled and commended (by Yahweh)." Naturally, this applies in particular to the short formula discussed under e, used with reference to Yahweh, his name, or his glory, which has always been translated, "Yahweh is praised," etc. This is the way the examples cited under h should also be translated. But the translation, "Praised is . . . ," also gives a good sense in the passages listed under

---

22 Charbel.

g: "He who is faithful to the law, the godly man, will be praised (as a happy man)" by his fellows "in the city and in the field," "when he comes in and when he goes out," in contrast to the lawbreaker, against whom all kinds of curses and invectives will be uttered. The same thing applies to the "fruit of his body, of his ground, and of his beasts," and to his "basket and kneading-trough," because all are astonished by the way they have increased and been abundantly filled. Here, of course, the meaning "blessed" comes in unobtrusively. As a purely verbal adjective, *barukh* is not to be understood as "one who enjoys a blessing." [23]

The meaning "blessed" is also predominant in the other expressions using the pass. ptcp. *barukh;* however, the idea that the person under consideration deserves appreciation, honor, and praise is clear throughout, just as (conversely) the thought that he is fortunate and enjoys respect and prosperity, and thus enjoys the "blessing," is prevalent in the passages cited under a-c, e, and h. But it is particularly clear that the *barukh*-formula, when it is not reduced to empty talk as in Zec. 11:5, is always a manifestation of an intimate relationship with the one for whom it is intended, or an acknowledgment of communion with him; thus it has to do with God's relationship to his people and his worshippers, but especially with Israel's relationship to her God. As an acknowledgment, it became a fixed element in the cult, perhaps beginning in the late monarchical period. There is no certain basis in the OT for Schottroff's view that this formula had its origin in the nomadic society of the Negeb or Sinai. The Aramaic-Nabatean texts he cites in support of this thesis are essentially later than the oldest relevant OT texts. But the occurrence of this formula in J, the earlier strata of D, and Ruth points to Jerusalem as the place of origin. Then it would be conceivable that its occurrence in the OT and among the nomads or semi-nomads in the Negeb region is not accidental, but is due to the close connections between the tribe of Judah and its southern neighbors.

2. *The Piel.* The conjugation in which the root *brk* appears most frequently is the piel. In the OT we find statements using this conjugation with God, other celestial beings (only in Gen. 32:27,30[26,29]; Ps. 103:20f.), people, groups of people, other creatures or things (only in Ps. 103:22; Job 31:20) as subject, and with God, people, nations, beasts, and things as object. Generally speaking, the sentence structure is the same: *A brk B be,* "A blessed B with," followed by a statement about the goods being given, or by the name of the one who charged A to speak. However, there are marked nuances of meaning depending on the subject and object. It is possible to distinguish the following sentence patterns:

a. *A* (superior) *brk B* (inferior), "A blessed B": (α) In the patriarchal narratives, *brk* is used to denote the blessing of the children by the head of the family. Here this phrase can always be translated, "A blesses (blessed) B": in J: Gen. 27 (13 times); 49:28; also 24:60, where the brothers and sisters represent their late father; in E: 32:1(31:55); 48:9,15,20; and in P: 28:1,6. In 24:60; 28:1,6; and

---

23 Wehmeier, 130f.

32:1(31:55), the blessing is connected with bidding farewell to one's children who are leaving on a long journey, but in the other passages, with the approaching death of the father. In 27:27, the blessing is said to be made "before Yahweh," giving it a special importance and solemnity and indicating that it is sanctioned by God. Such a blessing is irrevocable, even if it is obtained surreptitiously (v. 33). The double accusative in *A brk B berakhah*, "A blessed B with a blessing," lies behind the formulation in Gen. 27:41 and 49:28: "A blessed B with a (special, suitable) blessing." Even if formal blessings are announced only in 24:60; 27:29f.; 48:15f.,20; and 49:3-27, and are mentioned in rites (kissing, laying on of hands) only in 27:27; 32:1(31:55); 48:10,17, here *brk* in the piel apparently always means uttering the blessing formula in connection with special rites. But the *barukh*-formula is not used this way because it has another life setting, viz., the promise of numerous descendants and their success in war, of dominion over others, of prosperity, fruitfulness of the fields, honor, etc. To be sure, in 27:28; 48:15,20; and 49:25, God is mentioned, but this is due to the difference in formulation of J or E, and not to ancient traditional wording. Evidently the old benedictions taken over by the narrators did not mention God. The benedictory word of the father, especially if he was the father of a tribe or tribes, was effective as such, because the tribal father, by virtue of his own relationship with the God of the tribe, possessed within himself the power and authority to declare a word that could impart a blessing. David blesses "his house," i.e., his family (2 S. 6:20 = 1 Ch. 16:43). In 2 S. 13:25, the blessing is a substitute for the personal appearance of the father at his son's feast.

(β) Only rarely do the charismatic leaders in the early period of Israel's history "bless" the people or the army. According to P, occasionally Moses and Aaron bless the people (Lev. 9:23). Only the Deuteronomist gives more precise information about a blessing of Moses when he introduces the "Blessing of Moses" in Dt. 33:1 in this way: "This is the blessing with which (double acc.) Moses blessed the Israelites." This is followed by a rehearsal of Yahweh's mighty acts in vv. 2-5, and then a collection of tribal oracles, which are mixed with petitions to Yahweh for blessing and two *barukh*-formulas for individual tribes (vv. 20,24). Here the setting and form of the blessing follow the pattern of the blessing of a dying patriarch (cf. v. 1 with Gen. 27:7; cf. Gen. 48:9–49:33). Josh. 22:6f. says that Joshua blessed the Transjordanian tribes when they left to return to their own territory, which probably simply means that he sent them away with good wishes.

(γ) Occasionally persons in high position bless individual faithful subjects. In Josh. 14:13 and 2 S. 19:40(39) (in conjunction with a kiss), the blessing is pronounced in connection with bidding farewell. In Ex. 39:43 (P), Moses blesses the workmen who made the holy vessels, with gratitude and appreciation for their excellent work.

(δ) As to kings, David (2 S. 6:18 = 1 Ch. 16:2) and Solomon (1 K. 8:14,55 = 2 Ch. 6:3) bless the assembled people on special cultic occasions (the transfer of the ark, the dedication of the temple). David blesses "with (*be*, RSV in) the name of Yahweh." In 1 K. 8 par., the blessing is a solemn liturgical act consisting of gestures, doxology, rehearsal of Yahweh's saving acts, petition, and parenesis. 2 Ch. 31:8 states that Hezekiah and the "princes," at the conclusion of the collection which was destined to make possible the reform of the cult, "blessed Yahweh and his people," which probably means that by means of the *barukh*-formula they thanked Yahweh and the people for the generous collection.

(ε) J and E report that the non-Israelite mantic, Balaam, had the reputation of being able to bless and to curse. According to Nu. 22:6, he whom he blesses is blessed and he whom he curses is cursed (→ ארר *'ārar*). But instead of cursing Israel, as the Moabite king expects, he blesses Israel (Nu. 23:11,20,25; 24:1,10; Josh. 24:10). Balaam does this cursing or blessing in liturgical forms: he has altars built on a high place, and sacrifices offered on them; he withdraws into solitude and waits for divine instructions. Then he formulates oracles that recall the patriarchal oracles of blessing (Nu. 23:7-10,20-24; 24:4-9,17-24), and extols both the mighty deeds Yahweh had performed in behalf of his people and Israel's future victory and good fortune. Actually, the blessing here consists of the proclamation by a seer of words that are favorable to Israel. [24] In J and E, the seer knows that he cannot produce a blessing or a curse through a magical word, but that God merely gives him a glimpse into the past and future of Israel. Here, therefore, in reality "to bless" means "to announce good fortune," etc.

(ζ) 1 S. 2:20 is the only passage that speaks of a priest blessing an individual worshipper. Here also, the wording of the blessing is given: "Yahweh give you children by this woman. . . . " Thus, "to bless" means to wish that someone would receive what he desired. According to Lev. 9:22f., on special cultic occasions Aaron (alone or with Moses) blessed the assembled people with uplifted hands. According to 2 Ch. 30:27, Yahweh heard the priests and the Levites under Hezekiah when they "arose and blessed the people" at the conclusion of the Covenant Renewal Festival. In Ps. 118:26, the priests bless the arriving pilgrims by speaking the *barukh*-formula over them. According to Nu. 6:23, the priests are summoned to bless the Israelites, and this is followed by the appropriate wording resembling ritual instructions (vv. 24-26). This blessing is described in v. 27 as "putting the name of Yahweh on the Israelites," which is followed by the promise that then Yahweh will indeed bless. Here, "to bless" means to commend the people, assembled in the cult, to Yahweh's blessing. Thus, to be sure, because of this promise the priests are certain that Yahweh will bestow blessing at their word, but they also know that their word of blessing is not magical. When Dt. 10:8; 21:5; 1 Ch. 23:13; and Sir. 45:15 say that Yahweh chose the tribe of Levi or Aaron "to bless with (*be*) the name of Yahweh," one certainly thinks of similar blessing formulas like Nu. 6:24-26. In the great liturgy of cursing and blessing at Gerizim in Dt. 27 (cf. Josh. 8:33), the priests and half the tribes have the responsibility of "blessing the people," while the Levites

---

[24] Cf. D. Vetter, *Seherspruch und Segensschilderung. Calwer Theol. Mon., 4* (1974).

and the other half of the tribes are to utter curses on those who despise the covenant law. Whereas *'arur*-formulas are used for the curses, there are no corresponding blessing-formulas, but one of course thinks of analogous *barukh*-formulas.

It is very difficult to determine when the cultic priestly blessing was introduced. It probably originated when the king delegated the main role in the cult to the priest, perhaps in the middle of the monarchical period. It probably never was understood as a word that released magical power, but consisted of a prayer to Yahweh for blessing upon the people, as in Nu. 6:23-27 or in the *barukh*-formula, as in Ps. 118:26.

b. The pattern *A brk B,* "A blessed B," is also used in relationships between equals. Such relationships are assumed by J in the ptcp. *mebharekhekha,* "those who bless you," in Gen. 12:3; 27:29; and Nu. 24:9. This participle refers to persons or tribes who are on friendly terms with the patriarchs and their descendants, and who demonstrate a solidarity and appreciation for them by uttering the *barukh*-formula in their behalf or by wishing them well. Gen. 14:19 (whose original source is disputed) and 48:20 (E) indicate the structure of this kind of "blessing." Melchizedek uses a double *barukh*-formula in blessing Abraham: first he extols and commends Abram to El Elyon, and then he praises El Elyon because he delivered Abram from his enemies. According to Gen. 48:20, Ephraim and Manasseh will be so overloaded with blessings that in the future, when someone wants to bless someone else, he will say: "God make you as Ephraim and Manasseh." In 2 S. 8:10 = 1 Ch. 18:10, the blessing consists of the king of Hamath congratulating David for his victory. In 1 S. 13:10; 2 K. 4:29; and 10:15, *brk* in the piel simply means "to greet, to salute." These passages do not state how the greeting was worded, but it may have been in the form of a wish as in Ruth 2:4, where Boaz greets his servants by saying, "Yahweh be with you," and they reply to his greeting by saying, "Yahweh bless you." In Ps. 129:8, the content of the benedictory greeting is stated this way, "The blessing of Yahweh be upon you." Thus, in all these cases, "to bless" means to greet someone by expressing the wish, "Yahweh bless you," etc. It is difficult to determine whether *brk* in the piel means "to bless," "to greet in a friendly way," or "to extol," in Ps. 62:5(4) and Prov. 27:14. According to Sir. 31(34):23, the lips of men "bless" a well-bred man; this probably means that they extol him, speak of him appreciatively, etc.

c. In the pattern *A brk B,* "A blessed B," B can be identical with A, and then the statement means, "A boasts about himself" (*naphsho*). This is the case in Ps. 49:19(18) and perhaps also in 10:3, although an object is missing in this passage and the MT is uncertain.

d. The pattern *A* (inferior) *brk B* (superior) appears relatively rarely. According to Gen. 47:7,10 (E), Jacob "blesses" Pharaoh at the beginning and at the end of their interview. Here, "to bless" certainly has in mind a wish for blessing directed to God. The same seems to be the case in 2 S. 14:22, which speaks of Joab blessing David. When a debtor "blesses" his generous creditor (Dt. 24:13), and a grateful subject his benevolent king (Ps. 72:15), this certainly means that he gratefully prays that he will receive a blessing. According to 1 K. 8:66, at the conclusion of the liturgy the people utter an intercessory prayer that blessing might be given to the king (cf. Ps. 20; 61:7ff.[6ff.]; 63:12[11]), and according to Ex. 12:32 (J), the pharaoh even asks Israel to bless him when they assemble for worship. In 2 S. 21:3, apparently David expects something similar from the Gibeonites when their demand is satisfied by blood revenge, when he says, "Then pray for the heritage of Yahweh." According to 1 K. 1:47, after the anointing of Solomon, the "king's servants" come to the aged David in order to "bless" him. But what they do is to express the wish that God will make Solomon greater than David. Thus, they bless the old king by asking God to bless his son. The honor that comes upon the father, David, is that he has a son who excels him. According to Prov. 30:11, children also can bless their parents, but here *brk* in the piel is used in the negative in parallel with "curse the father," thus, "do not bless the mother."

e. Interesting observations can be made with regard to the various uses of the pattern *A brk yhvh,* "A blessed Yahweh." In Pre-Deuteronomic texts, it is found only in Gen. 24:48 (J), where Abraham's servant says that he "blessed" Yahweh, who (*'asher*) had led him on the way. The relative clause stating the reason for this blessing suggests that *brk* in the piel means to apply the *barukh*-formula to Yahweh out of gratitude. *brk* is used by the Deuteronomist in a similar way in Dt. 8:10 and Josh. 22:33. In Josh. 22:33, the explicit reason for uttering the *barukh*-formula can be deduced from the context, viz., the settlement of the dispute with the tribes east of the Jordan. There is a relative clause stating the reason for a blessing in Dt. 8:10; but it no longer belongs to the old life setting of the *barukh*-formula, since it does not state a single reason, but assumes Israel's continuous gratitude for the gift of the land. Here the grateful praise of Yahweh took place regularly in the cult at appointed harvest festivals. Elsewhere in the narrative literature, this pattern occurs only in the Chronicler's work and in the corresponding Aramaic literary pattern, *A brk* (in the pael) *leyhvh,* "A blessed Yahweh," in Daniel: 1 Ch. 29:10,20 (here once, perhaps under Aram. influence, *leyhvh* appears along with the usual acc. obj.); 2 Ch. 20:26; 31:8;[25] Neh. 8:6; 9:5; Dnl. 2:19f.; 4:31(34). In Daniel the reason given for praising Yahweh is historical, but in the Chronicler's work it is cultic. Isa. 66:3 reproves those who "bless a monster (= an idol)," i.e., those who render it cultic praise. The construction with a relative clause stating the reason also occurs in Ps. 16:7: "I will (gratefully) praise Yahweh (here, certainly meaning to utter the *barukh*-formula), who gave me counsel." Elsewhere, *brk* in the piel in praises to Yahweh is always found in songs that were composed for the cult or were adapted for cultic use, in appeals to oneself (Ps. 103:1f.; 104:1,35), in appeals to others (Jgs. 5:2,9; Ps. 66:8; 68:27[26]; 96:2; 100:4; 134:1f.; 135:19f.; 145:10,21), and in promises (Ps. 26:12; 34:2[1]; 63:5[4]; 115:18). In all these cases, *brk* appears in formal expressions without any historical reference. Thus the meaning "to praise Yah-

---

25 See above, a.δ.

weh" for *brk* in the piel belongs to the postexilic cultic language, whereas in the earlier period it was used only sporadically in cases where the old *barukh*-formula with the statement of the reason for the blessing was normally employed (Gen. 24:48). Apart from the euphemisms discussed under i, *brk* in the piel with God as object is found in the Wisdom Literature only in Sir. 35(32):13; 39:35; 50:22; and 51:12, where the wise appeal to themselves and others to praise Yahweh for his creative wisdom. This linguistic usage has not found any acceptance in the OT prophetic literature. Thus, the idea that one could "bless" God was not always evident. In the time of the Yahwist, it was customary to "bless" Yahweh only when a particular situation called for some demonstration of gratitude to him; later this became customary in cultic situations. Finally, statements like "I/we will praise Yahweh," "Praise Yahweh," etc., became purely liturgical formulas, and no one was actually expected to utter such an assertion or appeal from the heart, but merely was to recite the *barukh*-formula. Indeed, these formulas existed only for their own sake, and not to praise Yahweh; they became merely formulas of benedictions, which were equivalent to the purely formal expression, *barukh yhvh,* "Blessed be Yahweh."

f. The OT speaks only very rarely of a man blessing an object, objects blessing a man or God, and celestial beings blessing God. According to 1 S. 9:13, Samuel must "bless the sacrifice" before those who are invited begin to eat. This probably means that he asked God to bless those who participated in the sacrificial meal or that he praised God. When Job 31:20 says that "the loins" of a poor man bless the beneficent Job, the "loins" surely represent the whole person. Only in Ps. 103:20ff. are Yahweh's "works," angels, and heavenly host summoned to praise him. Here, the liturgical formula *barakhu yhvh,* "Bless Yahweh," is simply transferred to extra-human creatures.

When we combine the suggestions that have been made under sections a through f, we see that *brk* in the piel always means to express solemn words that show the appreciation, gratitude, respect, joint relationship, or good will of the speaker, thus promoting respect for the one being blessed and, when a man is the object of *brk,* the wish that he might receive happiness, success, and increase of earthly possessions. Only in the oldest tradition strata of the patriarchal narratives do we find traces of magical thinking, where words spoken by a tribal father are thought to have power in themselves to produce or to increase the desired earthly possessions. [26] Elsewhere, *brk* in the piel with people or things as object and people as subject seems always to be understood as a commendation or petition to God to grant success to the person being blessed. When God is the object, *brk* in the piel should always be rendered "praise," etc. When persons are the object, it can be translated "greet," "congratulate," "thank," "extol," but in most cases "bless," depending on the context. With the exception of the few passages where the speaker utters a blessing hypocritically, *brk* in the piel is always a manifestation of solidarity, an acknowledgment of communion with the one who is named as the object. This is also to be noted in texts where

---

[26] Westermann.

God is the object, whose intention is not to show the subservience of the creature and the sovereignty of God, but to express gratitude and the grateful manifestation for the intimate relationship with the God of Israel.

This is also the case when God is the subject and people and things are objects of the blessing.

g. With regard to the use of the pattern *yhvh brk PN*, "Yahweh blessed So-and-so," it is worthy of note that the idea that God utters a blessing formula appears very rarely and mostly in late texts, and that none of the promises to the patriarchs in Genesis or to David and Solomon in D is called a "blessing"; the blessing is always simply held in prospect *in* the promise.

In certain preexilic texts, a divine utterance is not mentioned in connection with *brk*. But the "blessing" that Jacob requests of the mysterious "man" at the Jabbok is certainly an uttering of words, probably accompanied by certain gestures (Gen. 32:27,30[26,29]). A blessing formula, viz., the *barukh*-formula, follows the statement "whom Yahweh blessed," in Isa. 19:25. Ps. 109:28 probably has reference to a benedictory utterance of God in contrast to the curse of a human opponent (here *brk* occurs in contrast to *qll* in the piel without an obj.). P knows a blessing of God with accompanying words in Gen. 1:22,28; 5:2; and 9:1, where God blesses living creatures or man, and in 35:9 and 48:3, where Jacob is blessed, and indeed he presents it in stereotyped formulas like, "Be fruitful and multiply," or, "I will make you fruitful and multiply your seed," etc. But in 17:16,20; 22:17 (revised by P); 25:11; 26:24 (revised by P?); 28:3; Nu. 6:24,27, the context does not indicate divine words of blessing; all these passages have in mind an immediate gift of fertility, wealth, respect, etc. This also seems to be the case with all other traditionists of the OT, in whose works "bless" can always be translated in the sense of "giving vitality, prosperity, abundance, or fertility": J (Gen. 12:2; 26:12; 49:25); E (Gen. 48:16); the Book of the Covenant (Ex. 20:24); Deuteronomy (1:11; 7:13; 14:24; 15:4,6; 26:15; 28:8; 30:16); D (Jgs. 13:24; 2 S. 6:11f.; 7:29); Ruth (2:4); the Chronicler's work (1 Ch. 4:10; 13:14; 17:27; 26:5; 2 Ch. 31:10); the Prophets (only in Isa. 51:2; 61:9); and Psalms (5:13[12]; 28:9; 45:3[2]; 67:2,7[1,6]; 107:38; 115:12f.; 147:13). *brk* in the piel has the same meaning in Hag. 2:19 and Ps. 115:12 without an object. The recipients of blessings in these texts are the people of Israel, their tribal fathers, or individual Israelites. Except for the tribal fathers (in J, E, and Isa. 51:2), whom Yahweh blesses out of pure grace, it is always assumed or (as in Ex. 20:24 and Dt.) demanded that the person being blessed or Israel deserves the blessing because of fidelity to Yahweh and his law. P recognizes all mankind, in fact all creatures, as recipients of the divine blessing. J says that God also blesses non-Israelites when they receive an Israelite or a tribal father of Israel and treat him well; then he blesses "because of (*bighlal*) So-and-so" (Gen. 30:27, 30; 39:5); in general, he blesses all who bless the elect and their "seed" (12:3). Alluding to Gen. 12:3, Sir. 44:21 says that God assured Abraham by an oath that he would "bless the nations through his prosperity." Occasionally the constructions *brk be*="to bless with/in something" (Gen. 24:1: *bekhol*="in all things, in every respect"; Ps. 29:11: *beshalom*="with salvation"), *brk me'odh*, "to bless greatly" (Gen. 24:35), *brk ʿadh koh,* "to bless to such an extent" (Josh. 17:14), and with the double accusative, and *brk PN berakhoth/berakhah,* "to bless with the abundance of blessing/with blessing" (Gen. 49:25; Dt. 12:7; 33:1), indicate that the blessing of God consists of giving vitality and possessions, etc. In Deuteronomy alone are there commonly to be found such expressions as "to bless in (*be*) the work of your hands," "in (*be*) all that your hands undertake," and "in (*be*) all your produce": Dt. 12:7; 15:10,18; 16:15; 23:21(20); 24:19. Only Ex. 20:24; Ps. 128:5; and 134:3 mention a sanctuary as a preferable place for Yahweh's blessing to be given. Foreign gods are never "blessed" in the OT. At the same time, it is worthy of note that Yahweh is hardly ever blessed in the prophets, except in Isa. 19:25; 51:2; and 61:9.

h. Only rarely does the OT say that God blesses things or animals. In J once, apparently, Yahweh blesses the fields (Gen. 27:27), unless the double accusative in this passage should be translated, "the field with which Yahweh blessed him." In Gen. 1:22, God blesses the animals with the multiplication formula common to P. [27] In Gen. 2:3 and Ex. 20:11, he blesses the sabbath, which probably means that through it he mediates the divine blessing to the person who keeps it. According to Job 1:10 and 42:12, God blessed Job's work, and the last part of his life after his misfortune (→ אחרית *ʾachᵃrîth,* "end"). He also blesses the habitation or abode of the righteous (Jer. 31:23; Prov. 3:33), that which grows in the fields (Ps. 65:11[10]), and the provisions (Ps. 132:15). As a positive sanction for his law, God promises that he will bless the bread and water (Ex. 23:25: Book of the Covenant), the fruit of the body and of the ground (Dt. 7:13), the ground (26:15), and the substance (33:11) of him who observes it, i.e., generally speaking, "all the work of your hands" (28:12). Except for Gen. 27:27 and Ex. 23:25, hardly one of these texts originated earlier than the time of Deuteronomy. Thus, the idea that God blesses things, possessions, or days was hardly known in the earlier period, and was only a little more familiar later. Since *brk* in the piel is found especially in connection with laws, it may have originated in general from legal sanctions.

i. The expression *A brk ʾelohim (vamelekh),* "A blessed God (and the king)," in Job 1:5,11; 2:5,9; and 1 K. 21:10,13, is a euphemism. Here *brk* replaces → קלל *qālal* in the piel, "to curse," which denotes a blasphemy or a degrading by contemptuous speech, and sounded so scandalous to the narrators when God was the object that they sought to paraphrase it euphemistically. Therefore, *brk* in the piel is precisely the opposite of *qll* in the piel, which can denote cursing and showing contempt either by words or by acts.

3. *brk in Other Conjugations.* Besides the qal and piel, *brk* occurs in the niphal, pual, and hithpael in the OT.

a. The pual of *brk* is the passive of the piel. The life setting of the *barukh*-formula is reflected in Jgs. 5:24, which means that Jael is to be praised with this

---

[27] See above, g.

formula and extolled with an honorary rite. [28] Similarly, according to Ps. 113:2 and Job 1:21, Yahweh's name deserves to be praised with the *barukh*-formula. These last two passages appear in the form of a wish (*yehi,* "may," "would that"). To be sure, this wish has already become stereotyped like the corresponding piel expression, *barekhu yhvh,* "Bless Yahweh." Nu. 22:6 assumes the benediction of a mantic endowed with special powers to bless and to curse: "he whom you bless (with a word bringing/promising good fortune) is blessed" (*mebhorakh*). Thus, the pual denotes the effect of a word of blessing, which results in real blessing when it is uttered by someone who is particularly empowered with the ability to utter blessings. Therefore, the meanings "to be remembered in a word of blessing" and "to be given auspicious power" run into one another.

The pual corresponds to the piel with God as subject when the former denotes persons or things that have been blessed. When such constructions are used, the only passages that specifically mention Yahweh as author of the blessing are Dt. 33:13 ("His land is blessed by Yahweh"); 2 S. 7:29 (similarly 1 Ch. 17:27); and Ps. 37:22. But there can be no doubt that he is understood as author of the blessing when the OT says that the upright and the God-fearer (Ps. 112:2; 128:4), "he who has a bountiful eye, who shares his bread with the poor" (Prov. 22:9), "will be blessed" (*yebhorakh*). In Ps. 128, vv. 2f. define what is meant by "being blessed" in v. 4: it will be well with him who is blessed, he eats the fruit of his labor, has a fruitful wife and a large number of children around his table. Thus, the pual denotes experiencing auspicious powers, which come from Yahweh upon the godly or the chosen ones (David).

b. The hithpael is found in the following contexts: Dt. 29:18(19) speaks of someone (here, to be sure, someone who is unlawful and arrogant) who says, "It is well with me, I am safe," etc. Consequently, here the meaning must be, "to consider oneself lucky, to believe oneself to be blessed, to pride oneself in being blessed," etc. Isa. 65:16 is to be understood in a similar way. Here the hithpael of *brk* stands in parallelism with *nishba' be'lohim*="to swear by naming the name of God." Thus, *hithbarekh be'lohim* must mean, "to consider oneself lucky/to believe oneself to be blessed, with reference to God," which can mean concretely, "to regard oneself as *berukh yhvh,* blessed by Yahweh, to pride oneself in being blessed by Yahweh." In Gen. 22:18; 26:4; Jer. 4:2 (where *bhekha,* "in you," should probably be read instead of *bho,* "in him"); and Ps. 72:17, the hithpael is also construed with *be,* but refers to the person mentioned or addressed earlier in the text (patriarch, Israel, king). In Ps. 72:17, the parallel line says, "All nations will call him happy," *ye'ashsheruhu,* → אשרי *'ashrê*). Thus, the expression *yithbarekhu bho* also refers appreciatively to the king: all nations will pride themselves in being blessed with reference to the king of Israel, they will pride themselves in participating in the blessing of the king. The same idea must be intended in Gen. 22:18 and 26:4: the other nations will pride themselves in participating in the blessing of Abraham or Isaac and their descendants. Here there is a declaration of solidarity with Israel and its tribal fathers or its king.

---

[28] Wehmeier, 175f.

c. Similarly, *be* is construed with the niphal in Gen. 12:3; 18:18; and 28:14, but the meaning is disputed. [29] The pass. ("will be blessed/will come to know blessing, through So-and-so": Junker and almost the entire tradition with the old translations), middle ("to obtain a blessing through So-and-so": Schreiner), and reflexive meanings ("to wish for oneself a blessing with reference to So-and-so," or "with reference to the good fortune of So-and-so": until now, Scharbert, *et al.*) have been proposed. These interpretations do not contradict each other, when it is considered that in each case *brk* in the niphal denotes a declaration of solidarity with So-and-so, and on this basis the nations can depend on the blessing of Yahweh. On analogy with the hithpael construction, it is possible to capture the meaning of all three interpretations by translating the expression something like this: " . . . then all the nations of the earth shall confer on themselves blessing under your name/with reference to you." If the traditionists had intended the passive idea, "will be blessed/will obtain blessing," they probably would have chosen the pual. [30]

4. *The Noun.* The range of meaning of the noun is approximately the same as that of the verb forms, and appears in the following syntactical constructions:

a. *berakhah* as subject: "Blessing" can be subject of a nominal phrase and of a phrase with the copula *hayah*, "to be." If it is the "blessing of Yahweh" which is "in (*be*) everything" (RSV "upon all") that belongs to a man (Gen. 39:5), is "upon" (*'al*) someone (Ps. 3:9[8]), or "comes upon" someone (129:8: *'el*, unless *'al* is to be read here also), or if it is simply a "blessing" (without Yahweh being specifically mentioned) that is "in" (*be*) something (Isa. 65:8), usually the word "blessing" is used to denote the power coming from Yahweh that brings good fortune and prosperity to man. It can be regarded as a possession of the godly ("your blessing") which, by good works, can be brought "to full measure" (*tšlm*, RSV "may be complete," Sir. 7:32). With this meaning, a blessing "makes rich" (Prov. 10:22); it "comes upon" the one who honors his father (Sir. 3:8f.). But it is also "in everything that a man has" (*bekhol 'asher yesh lo*, Gen. 39:5). According to Sir. 39:22, God's blessing "flows out in profusion like the Nile" over all creation. Sir. 50:20 says that "the blessing of Yahweh was on (*be*) the lips" of the high priest, Simon. The first thing that comes to mind here, perhaps, is the Aaronite blessing in Nu. 6:23-27, but one also thinks of the benedictory power that comes forth from Yahweh upon the people.

It seems that Prov. 10:6 and 11:26 should be understood in a similar way. On the one hand, the "blessings" here are the words of blessing that men utter "on the head (*lero'sh*) of the righteous" or "of him who offers his grain for sale," and on the other, they are powers released by such utterances, produced by God and bringing good fortune to those who are blessed. In the same sense, "the blessing of him who was about to perish comes upon (*'al*)" the one who helps him (Job 29:13), and "the blessing of good things (*birkath tobh*) upon" righteous

---

[29] For a discussion, cf. Wehmeier, 177-79; Schreiner, "Segen für die Völker"; Junker.
[30] So correctly Wehmeier, 178.

judges (Prov. 24:25). "The blessing of the upright" that "helps a city" (Prov. 11:11) is certainly not merely the benedictory word, but also the benedictory power released by it. To be sure, in Dt. 28:2 "these blessings" (*habberakhoth ha'elleh*) which "come upon you and overtake you" are first of all the following *barukh*-formulas, but they are also benedictory powers released by them, which bring good fortune on Israel. *berakhah* can have various shades of meaning within the framework of this ambiguous concept involving benedictory word and benedictory power. Thus, the benedictory words of a tribal father and the full blessings (*berakhoth*) released thereby "are mightier" (*gabheru 'al*) than the normal "bounties desired on the mountains and hills" (Gen. 49:26). Also, a father can concentrate the fulness of the benedictory power at his disposal in one benedictory word to an only son, as a result of which the other children are subordinated to this child; such a "singular blessing" is irrevocable and indivisible when it is expressed and released (Gen. 27:37f.) "before Yahweh" (27:7). In almost all these passages, it is best to translate *berakhah* by the ambiguous word "blessing," but the plural in Gen. 49:26 should probably be rendered "full blessings," or something similar.

b. *berakhah* as object: The same ambiguity is to be observed when *berakhah* is object. When men are the subject in the expression *A berakh B berakhah*, "A blessed B with a blessing" (Gen. 27:41; 49:28; Dt. 33:1), the context shows that the benedictory word is intended, but even then a word that also releases the auspicious power. In Gen. 49:25, the author emphasizes the full blessings that cause the heavens to give rain, the subterranean water to sustain the arable land, and the "breasts and womb" to bear and suckle children. In all four passages, this expression should be translated, "A blessed B with a blessing . . ." or "with the full blessings of. . . ." A person or tribe can be "full of the blessing of Yahweh" (Dt. 33:23). "The blessing and the curse" that Joshua read in conjunction with "all the words of the Torah" (Josh. 8:34) probably are simply the blessing and curse sanctions formulated at the conclusion of the legal corpus. But when Yahweh "commands" (*tsivvah*) his blessing "for you" (Lev. 25:21), or "in your barns and in everything that your hand undertakes" (Dt. 28:8), or on a place (Ps. 133:3), again we must think of power emanating from Yahweh. When the worshipper gives the priest the prescribed dues, "he causes a blessing to rest on his house" (*haniach 'el bethekha*, Ezk. 44:30), and when a worshipper participates in the cult, "he receives a blessing from Yahweh" (*nasa' bherakhah me'eth yhvh*, Ps. 24:5). Yahweh "pours out (*yatsaq*) his blessing on your offspring" (Isa. 44:3); wherever he goes, "he leaves a blessing behind him" (*hish'ir 'acharav*, Joel 2:14), and he "meets the godly with goodly blessings" (*yiqdam birekhoth tobh*, Ps. 21:4[3]). On Israel's head, "he makes the blessing rest (*nḥḥ*), and acknowledges him with blessing" (Sir. 44:23).

Expressions in which *berakhah* is used with *nathan*, "to give," *laqach*, "to take," and *hebhi'*, "to bring," are ambiguous. Moses "sets the blessing before Israel" (*nathan liphne*, Dt. 11:26f.; 30:1,19); he does this by reciting to them the blessing and cursing sanctions of the law, and thus by giving his people the choice of putting into force blessing or curse by their response. According to

Dt. 11:29, Israel is "to set the blessing on Mt. Gerizim and the curse on Mt. Ebal" (*nathan 'al har*). The formula and the power it contains are one. But in Ex. 32:29, the Levites have "a blessing bestowed on them," not through a word, but through their zealous deed. In Gen. 28:4, Isaac anticipates that God will give to his son Jacob "the blessing of Abraham," which does not mean the formula of the Abraham blessing, but the prosperity of Abraham. Dt. 12:15 and 16:16f. also have in mind earthly possessions when they refer to Israel eating meat and grain in the sanctuary "according to the blessing that Yahweh gives you." A blessing can also be a specific gift, e.g., a spring, as in Josh. 15:19 and Jgs. 1:15.

Esau is afraid that he will bring a curse upon himself instead of a blessing (*hebhi' 'al*, Gen. 27:12); by "blessing" he has in mind both his father's words of blessing and the powers released by them. On the other hand, in 1 S. 25:27 Abigail brings a "blessing" for David in the form of food; she brings a "gift of greeting."

If a blessing can be given and brought, it can also be "received" or "taken away" (*laqach*). Thus, the "blessing" which Naaman offers Elisha (2 K. 5:15), or which Jacob offers Esau (Gen. 33:11), is very formidable; it consists of money and clothes or of cattle. On the other hand, the blessing that Jacob took away from Esau (27:35f., where *'atsal*, "to reserve," is used with *berakhah* along with *laqach*) is first of all the father's benedictory word and only secondarily the auspicious power that is found therein. If curses or blessings "come" and "are taken away" according to whether a person "loves" (→ אהב *'āhabh*, "to love," → חפץ *chāphēts*, "to delight in") one or the other, then imprecatory or benedictory words and the power they contain are identical (Ps. 109:17). The same thing applies to expressions like "Yahweh turned the curse into a blessing for you" (Dt. 23:6[5]; Neh. 13:2), and "Yahweh curses (*'rr*) your blessings" (Mal. 2:2). These have reference both to the sanctions of cursing and blessing in the law (Lev. 26; Dt. 28) and to the powers of good fortune or bad fortune that they set in motion. But in Mal. 3:10, "to pour down the blessing" means that the clouds pour out the fructifying rain. The meaning of 2 K. 18:31 = Isa. 36:16 is not clear: perhaps *'asu 'itti bherakhah* should be translated simply, "Make peace with me."

c. Other uses of the noun: A man who blesses others with abundant gifts is a *nephesh berakhah*, "a person who dispenses blessings" (RSV, "a liberal man," Prov. 11:25). A region characterized by fertility is an *'dn brkh*, "an Eden fructified by blessing" (RSV, "a garden of blessing," Sir. 40:27), and a rain that brings fertility is a "shower of (bringing) blessing" (Ezk. 34:26). A faithful man is "great in fulness of blessing" (*rabh berakhoth*, Prov. 28:20). In these cases, the blessed power coming from Yahweh and its effect, prosperity and fertility, are the same. The same idea applies to *berakhah* in 2 S. 7:29; Sir. 4:13; 44:23. The *barukh*-formula or similar expressions refer to the liturgical praise of God when Yahweh is "exalted above all *berakhah* (blessing)" (Neh. 9:5), or when a place is called the "Valley of *berakhah* (Beracah)," "for there they blessed Yahweh" (2 Ch. 20:26). Prov. 10:7 probably has in mind the *barukh*-formula used by a godly person: "The mention (*zekher*) of the righteous took place for (the purpose of) blessing" (*libhrakhah*). Ps. 37:26 seems to mean the same thing: the godly are "for a blessing" (*libhrakhah* without a verb). In the pattern *A yihyeh berakhah*, "A will be a blessing," this meaning is already found in the Yahwist (Gen. 12:2), but after this it does not come to the surface again until Isa. 19:24 and Zec. 8:13. Ps. 21:7(6) means the same thing when it says that God makes (*shith*) the king "a blessing." In these passages, it is not clear, of course, whether the person or group under consideration is subject of the *barukh*-formula (as Isa. 19:24 would seem to indicate), or whether he serves as an example in benedictory words or praises (after the analogy of the curse in Jer. 29:22). The text and meaning of Ps. 84:7(6) are quite uncertain.

III. brk = "To Bless," etc.

1. *In Hebrew Inscriptions.* In pre-Christian Hebrew inscriptions, *brk* II is found in only one ostracon from Samaria, where it appears twice. [31] But probably the proper name Baruch should be read here. In addition, recently the *barukh*-formula has apparently been discovered in a tomb inscription from the monarchical period, in the vicinity of Hebron: *brk 'ryhw lyhvh*, "may Uriah be praised by Yahweh." [32]

2. *In the Qumran Literature.* In the Qumran material the OT meanings of *brk* are retained to some extent, but a peculiar linguistic usage stands out.

a. A certain archaism is noticeable in the use of the *barukh*-formula at Qumran in comparison with the late texts of the OT. It appears in the combination of the formula for God and for man (cf. Gen. 14:19f.): "Blessed be the God of Israel ... and blessed be all those who serve him" (1QM 13:2f.), and in the reappearance of the old statements that give the reason for a blessing, with the verb in the perfect: "Blessed be God ..., who (*'asher*) did thus and so" (1QH 11:27; 16:8; fragm. 4,15; 1Q34 2:3); "Blessed be God, because (*ki*) he ..." (1QM 18:6; 1QH 5:20; 10:14; 11:32). In this material, of course, the act of God in the speaker's behalf is no longer regarded as even directly affecting him. This formula also appears with other ways of expressing the reason syntactically, viz., with *be* ("because of his holy plan," 1QM 13:2), with a participle ("who hast opened unto knowledge," 1QS 11:15; "who keeps favor/the covenant," 1QM 14:4,8; cf. also 11QPs^a 19:7; 26:13), with special attributes ("the God of mercy," 1QH 11:29; "my Lord, great in counsel," 1QH 16:8). The *barukh*-formula is used in the Qumran literature in a way it is never used in the OT, namely, with reference to Zion: "Blessed ... be thy memory, O Zion" (11QPs^a 20:2).

b. As far as the verb is concerned, the hiphil with priests as subject and some sort of food as object is new in the Qumran material. It should probably

---

[31] *KAI*, 188.1f.
[32] Cf. W. G. Dever, *Kadmoniot*, 4 (1971), 90-92.

be translated, "speak the blessing over bread/wine, give thanks for bread/wine" (1QS 6:5f., and accordingly the ptcp. in 1QSam 2:19). The piel is used in the Qumran literature like it is in the OT. However, only priests and the "Teacher" (*maskil*) bless the congregation, the individual members, and the "Prince." In all the pertinent texts, this has reference to the blessing formula similar to the Aaronite blessing in which God's blessing is invoked (1QS 2:1; 1QSa 2:21; 1QSb 1:1; 5:20). In the Qumran material *brk* in the piel with God as object also means "to praise": 1QS 1:19; 6:3,8; 7:1; 1QM 13:7; 14:3f.; 18:6; 1QH 1:31; 2:30; 14:9; fragm. 4,17; 10,8; 22,7; 38,2; 1Q16 8:2. Occasionally the verb is construed with *be* = "because" (1QS 10:16). The expression with the double accusative, *berekh 'el terumath sephathayim,* "to bless God with the offering of the lips" (1QS 9:26; 10:6,14), and the twofold *barukh*-formula for God and the godly following the summons to "bless" God (1QM 13:1ff.), are new in the Qumran literature. Here, then, *brk* means "to praise (God)" and "to bless (men)." Thus, no difference in meaning is to be observed when *brk* takes God as object or when it takes man as object. Also, in the Qumran material, for the most part God "blesses" the godly directly by giving him auspicious powers: 1QS 2:2; 1QSb 1:3; 3:25; 4Q177 1:1–4:10. However, a new concept in the Qumran literature is that God "blesses by the hand (*beyadh*) of the *maskil* (Teacher)" (1QSb 3:28; 4:23). The hithpael is found only in 1QS 2:13, with the same meaning that it has in Dt. 29:18(19): "to pride oneself (unlawfully) in the blessing (of God)."

The noun is used of the word of blessing (1QSb 1:1; 3:22), or the praise of God (1QH 17:20), or the blessing of God in the sense of fertility, good fortune, and prosperity; in the latter sense it appears in the singular (1QM 1:9; 12:3,12; 17:7; 19:4) and plural (1QS 4:7; 1QH fragm. 21,4; 1QSb 1:5; 4:23). 1QS 2:1-4 contains a whole ritual of blessing for the liturgical blessing over the members of the community.

3. *In the LXX.* The LXX translates *brk* II in the piel by *eulogeín,* "to bless." Exceptions to this are found in Ps. 10:3 = LXX 9:24 (*eneulogeísthai,* "to bless"); Dt. 10:8 and 1 Ch. 23:13 (*epeúchesthai,* "to wish, pray for, exult"); Ps. 100(99):4 (*aineín,* "to praise"); Isa. 66:3 (*blásphēmos,* "blasphemer" = *mebharekh 'aven*), and the euphemism in Job 1:5 (*kaká enenóēsan prós theón,* "they conceived evil things against God") and 2:9 (*légein ti hrēma eis kýrion,* "to speak some word unto the Lord"). The passive form of *eulogeín* is used to translate the pual except in Prov. 22:9 (where we find *diatraphḗsetai,* "will be sustained, supported").

For the niphal of *brk,* the LXX has *eneulogeísthai,* "to bless"; and for the hithpael it alternates between *eulogeísthai* and *eneulogeísthai,* except in Dt. 29:18 (19), which has *epiphēmísetai,* "to maintain, affirm." With the exception of Prov. 10:7 (where *libhrakhah* is translated by *met' enkōmíōn,* "with praises"), the LXX always translates the Heb. noun *berakhah* by *eulogía,* "blessing." The Heb. ptcp. *barukh* is rendered alternately by the Gk. ptcp. *eulogēménos* and the adj. *eulogētós;* the latter is preferred when God is blessed. As an exception, the statement, "let that day not be blessed," in Jer. 20:14 is rendered *mḗ éstō epeuktḗ,* "let (that day) not be longed for." The consistent translation of *brk* by some form of *eulog-* shows that the LXX translators apparently interpreted *brk* as "a praising, blessing, congratulating," as a speaking in which a person declares something good or praiseworthy that someone else has done, or promises something good to a person or a thing, viz., happiness and success.

The linguistic usage in the deutero-canonical books (Apocrypha) also confirms this meaning. In this material the expression corresponding to the Heb. *barukh*-formula is *eulogēménon PN* or *eulogētós (esti) PN,* "Blessed is (be) So-and-so." The latter is preferred when God is blessed (Tob. 3:11; 8:5,15ff.; 11:14; 13:18; Jth. 13:17; 1 Macc. 4:30; 2 Macc. 1:17; 15:34; Song Three frequently); but it is also used of angels (Tob. 11:14, along with God) and of men (13:14; Jth. 13:18). The former is generally used when men and angels are blessed (Tob. 11:17; Jth. 13:18; 14:7; 15:10), and of God apparently only when the writer desires to vary his terminology to avoid monotony (Jth. 13:18; 2 Macc. 1:17). But the manuscripts frequently confuse these two forms. It is interesting that the old expansion with a statement giving the reason for the blessing in the past is also found in this material, introduced by *hóti,* "because," in Tob. 8:16f.; 11:14; and by *hós,* "who," in Jth. 13:18; Tob. 13:18; 2 Macc. 1:17; Song Three 3f. The dative expansion *tṓ theṓ,* "by God," occurs in Jth. 13:18. The verb *eulogeín* has the same meaning as Heb. *brk* in the piel. A father "blesses" his children before he dies (1 Macc. 2:69), when he bids them farewell (Tob. 10:11), and at a wedding (Tob. 9:6; 11:17). In Tob. 9:6, where Tobias "blesses" his bride, the text could also mean "praise." There is no example of a man "blessing" his wife or bride in the MT. In Jth. 15:9-12, where extolling praise is given to the heroine, *eulogeín* certainly means "to extol."

In the Apocrypha also, when God is object of *brk,* the verb always means "praise" (Tob. 4:19; 8:15; 11:15f.; 12:6,17f.,20,22; 13:7,15,18; 14:2,6f.,15; 1 Macc. 13:47; 2 Macc. 3:30; 8:27; 11:9; 15:29,34). Frequently a formal eulogy is connected with these expressions. The statement about praising "toward heaven" (1 Macc. 4:24,55) and the use of the dative *tṓ kyríō* instead of the accusative (2 Macc. 10:38) are unique. Once, hidden providence is object of "praise" (2 Macc. 12:41). The passive of *brk* is very rare in the Apocrypha, occurring only in Tob. 4:12 (the patriarchs were blessed in their children) and Wisd. 14:7 (in contrast to the wood of graven images, which is cursed, the wood of the ark is blessed).

The noun *eulogía* occurs rarely in the deutero-canonical texts: Tob. 8:15 (God is praised *en pásē eulogía,* "in every blessing"); 9:6 (God gives "the blessing of heaven"); 11:17 (the bride and groom enter the house *en eulogía kaí chará,* "with blessing and joy"); Wisd. 15:19 (the heathen even worship animals that do not have *tón toú theoú épainon kaí tḗn eulogían autoú,* "the praise of God and his blessing"). These last passages show how close "praise," "congratulation," and "blessing" are.

IV. The Blessing in OT Theology. Whereas several Hebrew roots are equivalent in meaning to Eng. "curse" (→ אלה *'ālāh,* → ארר *'ārar, za'am, qabhabh* or *naqabh,* and → קלל *qālal*), [33] we find what we call "blessing" only in the root *brk,* and yet semantically "blessing" does not exhaust the meaning of *brk,* which includes the concepts of greeting, congratulating, thanking, and praising. Disregarding the meanings "knee" and "pool," perhaps we may outline the theological connections in which *brk* appears as follows:

1. Just as the curse was intended to destroy a man's solidarity with others when he grossly transgressed the basic ethical norms of his clan, religious community, or people, or to prevent his resisting powerful enemies, so the blessing is intended to strengthen *solidarity* with individuals and groups with whom he has or seeks particularly close social, racial, and religious relationships, to whom he owes special thanks, or whose works for his own community or for friends he appreciates. This solidarity was demonstrated by expressing congratulations, by uttering stereotyped formulas of blessing and appreciation (among which the *barukh*-formula was the most common), and by commending someone to God by extolling him and praying that God might bless him. The greeting is also a demonstration of solidarity, and therefore uses *brk.*

2. Like the curse, the blessing is rooted in *magical thought,* in the concept of the efficacious power of a solemn word uttered in stereotyped formulas. But there are only a few traces of this in the OT, above all in the pre-Yahwistic words of blessing spoken by a tribal father or a tribal mother (Gen. 24:60; 49:8-12). By the time the Yahwist incorporated these words into his work in light of his theological view of history, the blessing (like the curse) had lost its magical connotation. In the OT the blessing is almost always attributed to God or closely connected with him. The godly man knew that the only kind of benedictory wishes he could utter were those which God alone could bring to reality. Since a blessing can be brought to reality by God alone, and since it denotes an attachment with or a strengthening of solidarity, it is necessary that the person uttering the blessing be in fellowship with God, seek it, or be worthy of it. Therefore, the blessing (like the curse) is revocable, and can be changed into a curse.

Gen. 27:34-40 is not incompatible with this statement. In this text, one must keep in mind that the Yahwist, merely on the basis of his own contemporary historical situation in which "Jacob" actually prevailed over "Esau," took over the tradition of a blessing of Isaac and molded it into a narrative. Thus, it would have been wholly impossible for him to have even considered that the surreptitious blessing could be revoked. The logical flow of the narrative also prevented any possibility of a revocation. It dealt with the blessing of the firstborn, to whom his brothers were subordinate. This kind of blessing is indivisible. Moreover, it was uttered "before Yahweh," i.e., with God as witness, and therefore has sacral sanction. A revocation of this blessing would have been possible only if Jacob had been cursed. It would not have been possible for the father, Isaac, to abandon all solidarity with Jacob, which would have resulted in a curse on

---

[33] Cf. J. Scharbert, *Bibl* (1958).

him. Consequently, the surreptitious blessing had to remain in force, in keeping with the axiom "Quod dixi, dixi" (What I have spoken, I have spoken). Thus the blessing of Isaac was regarded as indivisible and irrevocable, not because of the magical ideas of the Yahwist or his source, but because of the special situation being described and the purpose that the Yahwist had in mind in this narrative.

The close connection between word and power comes from the ancient mooring of the idea of "blessing" in magical thought. When people are object of the verb, *brk* almost always denotes the uttering of words and formulas which (when the proper stipulations are given and when the words are expressed in a legitimate manner) release a power that brings happiness, prosperity, success, respect, fertility, etc., to the person being blessed, and even beyond his family restores all the blessings that establish friendly relations with the one being blessed. Therefore, in the noun and verb forms of *brk,* benedictory word and auspicious power are inseparably connected, and the *barukh* of the one praised with words is the same as the *barukh* which, as proof of the effect of those words (which indicated the use of the *barukh*-formula), is brought to reality by beneficial powers.

3. The blessing has several life settings (usually analogous to the settings of the curse), which can change in the course of time.

a. The oldest and most persistent setting is the association in house and family. Fathers or family heads bless their children, especially at a wedding (Gen. 24:60; Tob. 7:13), before a journey (Gen. 28:6; 32:1[31:55]), and when they are nearing death (Gen. 27; 49). But also the father of the family and his domestic servants bless one another (Ruth 2:4). This setting of the family is assumed in the patriarchal narratives, mentioned in the narrative literature up into the Maccabean period, and also found in the Wisdom Literature (Sir. 3:9). Thus, it was in use throughout the OT period.

b. One of the oldest settings for the curse was the law. It served as a deterrent to theft, receiving stolen goods, and embezzlement, and as a guarantee for a witness or an oath (→ אלה *'ālāh;* → ארר *'ārar*). There is no analogy to this for the blessing, e.g., to motivate to honesty someone who finds something, or to truthfulness one who bears witness. The only relationship that the blessing has to the law is in the sanctions for legal corpora (Lev. 26; Dt. 28). Occasionally in ancient Near Eastern international treaties, benedictory wishes for partners who are faithful to the treaty appear along with curses for potential violators of the treaty;[34] but in contrast to curses, which became commonplace, they are very rare, and when they do occur they are brief and general, whereas the curses are very extensive and drastic. Also, in Lev. 26 and Dt. 28 the blessing formulas are brief and vague compared with the curse, and there are no blessing formulas corresponding to curse formulas in Dt. 27. Thus the blessing seems to be a later

---

[34] Cf. Fensham; McCarthy, *Treaty and Covenant;* K. Baltzer, *Covenant Formulary* (trans. 1970), esp. pp. 14-16; → ברית *berîth.*

insertion in the legal sanctions. Fulfilment of a treaty and keeping of a law were considered normal and undeserving of special reward. Promises of blessing were probably added to H in Lev. 26 and to Deuteronomy in Dt. 28 when the regulations collected in these complexes were no longer respected as unquestionably binding and means had to be devised to persuade people to observe them. This also seems to have been the main reason why the blessing played no role at all in the preexilic prophets, whereas they did utter curses (although rarely). They considered the ethical and religious demands that they proclaimed so self-evident that they saw no reason to promise blessings to those who practiced them. This attitude changed when the exilic and postexilic prophets came to feel that they must convince the people, and so began to hold out before them Yahweh's blessing.

c. The "blessing" was the most appropriate means of expressing gratitude and respect to a man or to God. Thus the *barukh*-formula was particularly suited for people who had rendered a special service to themselves, a friend, or their own people, or who had given help in time of distress or danger. In this connection it was obviously appropriate to mention the meritorious deed as a reason for the blessing, and to commend to Yahweh the person being blessed. In any case, the expansions of the *barukh*-formula by *leyhvh* and by an *'asher*- or a *ki*-clause giving the reason belong to the oldest tradition. Later the formula was modified and shortened, and thus became a cult formula used to praise Yahweh. But the use of the *barukh*-formula in Dnl., Jth., Tob., Macc., and Qumran shows that the ancient pattern of this formula was rediscovered in the late OT period as a possible means of showing appreciation for particular works and merits of a person, or expressing gratitude to God for saving a person or the nation from a present distress.

d. The original life setting of the *barukh*-formula with God as subject is not the cult either, but expressions of gratitude in response to God's gracious deeds in the present. The same thing is true of the piel of *brk* with God as object. This could have been possible only if the predominant meaning of *brk* in the piel was not "bless," but "extol, praise, give thanks." Therefore, the verb with God as object was used only when one wanted to give thanks for a saving, helping deed. It was only later, perhaps shortly before the exile, that *brk* in the piel and the noun *berakhah* came to be used in the sense of praising God in the cult. At that time, the correct expressions for this formula were used, but without manifesting any real gratitude for concrete help from God in a time of distress. In this period also, of course, expressions and formulas with *brk,* the "benediction," and an acknowledgment of communion with and gratitude to God, continue to be used. However, now they are used not to show thanks for actual help or salvation experienced by an individual or the community, but to show gratitude and appreciation for creation, God's gracious providence, and the grace that he continuously imparted to Israel.

In any case, a certain development in the idea that God blesses can be ascertained. From the very beginning it seems to have been thought unnecessary for God to speak a word or a formula to set in motion a blessing on man and possessions. He simply brought about the blessing directly. It is not until later, especially in P, that one thinks of blessing formulas used by God to release auspicious powers. The kind of clear distinction Westermann makes between God's saving deeds and God's blessings [35] is hardly feasible. God blesses the patriarchs, the people of Israel, and David and his dynasty by enabling them to "possess the gate of their enemies" (Gen. 22:17; 24:60), by making the tribe or the dynasty and the throne continue (2 S. 7:29), by causing the enemies of the people who are faithful to the covenant to be defeated (Dt. 28:7), and by giving the people peace so that they can lie down without being afraid of enemy invasions (Lev. 26:6). This is a blessing that not only guarantees powers of nature and life interwoven with the continuous providence of God (as we find in the majority of appropriate OT examples), but also helps to control extraordinary historical situations.

e. The importance that the theology of Israelite history attributes to the blessing shows that it has something to do with history, and not merely with nature and creation, as Westermann thinks. The theology of history has become a constant setting for uttering blessings.

The tribes in the pre-monarchical period traced their regulations, claims, and peculiarities back to a blessing or a curse that had been uttered or received by the tribal father. Blessing or curse remains an inheritance of the tribe as long as that tribe acknowledges the regulations established by the fathers and the god of the tribal father. [36] Most of the tribal oracles found in Gen. 49 and Dt. 33 originated in this clan thinking of the tribes and were handed down individually. As several of these tribes came to be intimately associated with each other, grew together completely as the proto-Israelite tribes at the end of the period of the judges, and became stronger and stronger at the beginning of the monarchy, such tribal oracles were combined in collections such as we find in Gen. 49 and Dt. 33, but also the tribal sayings, which at one time applied only to a specific league, were inserted into genealogical systems, so that all participating tribes came to be regarded as standing under the blessing of Abraham, Isaac and Jacob. In addition to this, new blessing oracles originated, such as those found in Nu. 23 and 24, which came to be applied to all Israel.

Then, the Yahwist interpreted not only the history of the tribes and of the people of Israel, but also the history of all mankind, from the viewpoint of blessing and curse. Accordingly, he placed primeval history, containing the curses in Gen. 3:17 and 4:11f., before his history of the patriarchs. Thus he views the whole history of mankind and the history of Israel as placed under curse and blessing as formative powers; and yet the blessing, as God's gift to Israel and to all nations (who are viewed as intimately associated with Israel), predominates over the curse. The turning point for the Yahwist is the promise

[35] Westermann, *Der Segen in der Bibel* ... (1968), 19-22.
[36] Scharbert, *BBB,* 14 (1958).

to Abraham in Gen. 12:2f., by means of which the power of the curse brought about by sin is broken. [37]

The Elohist tradition, which of course contains no primeval history, also sees the blessing as a power in Israel's history emanating from the tribal fathers, pregnant with salvation. Whether this tradition also knows the inclusion of the nations in the blessing given to Israel depends on whether one attributes Gen. 22:18 and 26:4 to it or to a later redactor. In any case Jer. 4:2 and Ps. 72:17 adopted the idea that other nations could share in the blessing given to Israel if they acknowledged Israel or its king as bearer of the blessing.

The Deuteronomist does not say anything explicit about a blessing of the tribal fathers, but he is thinking of this when he speaks of the sworn promise of Yahweh to the fathers (Dt. 1:8; etc.), and when he traces back to the God of the fathers the blessing that had already become a reality to Israel (Dt. 1:11). But the blessing resting on the dynasty of David and the benedictory sanction resting on the covenant law are more important for him (Dt. 28). These two kinds of blessing had been Israel's guarantee that Yahweh would not forsake his people, and in the period of distress after 587 B.C. gave them hope that after they returned to Yahweh and his law, they would again receive a blessing in place of the curse they were experiencing.

P sees all animated creation and all mankind standing under a blessing of the Creator (Gen. 1:22,28; 5:2; 9:1), but for Israel and her history he sees a special blessing at work, in competition with the curse of Lev. 26, which depends on fidelity to the law and is bestowed on the people by the priests in the cult (Nu. 6:23-27). According to P, no other people can participate in this special blessing to Israel. The final redactor of the Pentateuch combined and harmonized these different views of blessing and curse, and thus handed down to Judaism and Christianity belief in curse and blessing as powers emanating from God and put in force by human behavior in relationship to the divine law, powers that finally determine the destiny of all mankind, the nations, and the individual.

f. Since blessing comes from God, the blessing of the people also has a cultic life setting. With regard to the great men of God in the pre-monarchical period, the OT says only that they blessed the people in connection with specific contemporary situations. [38] We encounter a cultic blessing for the first time in connection with David and Solomon, but here also it does not yet seem to have been in general use, but is practiced only in connection with specific cultic celebrations (the transfer of the ark, the dedication of the temple). [39] At the conclusion of these celebrations the people also bless the king. It was not until about the middle of the monarchical period that the blessing of the assembled people came to be limited to the priests, and became a regular part of the liturgy. [40]

---

[37] Cf. Wolff, *ThB*, 22; and Steck; the latter takes the position suggested here in opposition to Rendtorff, who thinks that the turning point is to be found in Gen. 8:21.

[38] See above, II.2.a.β.

[39] See above, II.2.a.δ.

[40] See above, II.2.a.ζ.

g. To be sure, the blessing of things (food) is testified in 1 S. 9:13, but in the OT as a whole it is rare, and denotes a "benediction" by God rather than thanksgiving for food. In any case, thanksgiving for food is attested in postbiblical Judaism and in the NT. When legal sanctions and isolated passages elsewhere in the OT speak of blessings on fields, cattle, and the "work of one's hands," the idea is that benedictory powers are released on them because of people that have been blessed. The same may be said of the blessing of the sabbath in P (Gen. 2:3).

Scharbert

בָּרַר *bārar;*   בַּר *bar;* בֹּר *bōr;* בֹּרִית *bōrîth*

Contents: I. Etymology and Use in Ancient Near Eastern Literature. II. Use in the OT: 1. The Verb; 2. The Adjective; 3. The Substantives; 4. Summary; Religio-Ethical Meaning. III. Homonymous Words: 1. *brr* II; 2. Grain; 3. Open Field.

I. Etymology and Use in Ancient Near Eastern Literature. It is most likely that *brr* goes back to a root that originally meant "to be free."[1] According to Lane, the Arab. *br'*, "to be free, be pure" (e.g., of illness, of bad character), is very well attested.[2] Possibly *brr*, "to be good, devout," also belongs here. On the other hand, the meaning "to separate, select," which is found in the OT, at Qumran, and especially in Middle Hebrew and Aramaic,[3] seems to be secondary. In Akkadian, the adj. *barru* already has the meaning "pure" (of metal); similarly, the verb *barāru* means "to glitter."[4] The cognate Ugaritic root also demonstrates the antiquity of the meaning "to be pure, to glitter."[5] Old South Arab. *brr* (causative) means "to purify," and Ethiop. *berūr* means "silver."[6]

II. Use in the OT.

1. *The Verb.* In the OT, the verb in the qal means "to separate" in Ezk. 20:38 (pejorative: "the rebels I am separating [RSV, I will purge] from among you," *barothi mikkem*). Here we may mention *boru*, "select, choose," in 1 S. 17:8, unless the MT *beru* is correct and is to be derived from a root *brh*, "to

---

bārar. F. Hauck-R. Meyer, "καθαρός," *TDNT,* III, 413-423; W. Paschen, *Rein und Unrein. StANT,* 24 (1970); for further literature, see under → טהר *ṭāhēr,* "to be clean, pure."

[1] *GesB,* 119.
[2] Lane, I, 178f.
[3] Levy, *WTM; Chald. Wb.*
[4] *AHw,* 106f.
[5] *WUS,* No. 593; for No. 594, *UT* reads "clear, pure."
[6] Cf. *KBL³.*

decide, determine" (the same root lying behind → בְּרִית bᵉrîth, "covenant"). [7]
hibbaru (niphal) occurs in Isa. 52:11: "purify yourselves," or "separate yourselves" (LXX aphorísthēte). Jer. 4:11 has in mind the cleansing of grain: [8] "a
hot wind, ... not to winnow or cleanse" (lehabhar, hiphil inf.). The piel appears
in Dnl. 11:35: "to refine (litsroph) and to cleanse (lebharer) them and to make
them white (lalben)." The same three verbs occur in the hithpael in Dnl. 12:10.
In 2 S. 22:27 we find the wordplay, "with the pure thou dost show thyself pure"
('im nabhar tittabhar, niphal and hithpael). According to Blau, the latter is a
t-form of the hiphil; [9] in the parallel passage, Ps. 18:27 (Eng. v. 26), the correct
form, tithbarar (hithpael), occurs. It is unnecessary to view this as a variation
from the root gbr. [10] In Eccl. 3:18 we find a qal infinitive with a suffix (lebharam
ha'elohim, "that God is testing them"). KBL³, 155, gives the meaning "select
(?).". Ginsberg's conjecture, "separate from," is hardly convincing. The context
favors the translation "test, examine" ("may God test them in this way"); this
can be connected with the other meanings, "separate, purify"; elsewhere the
meaning "test, examine," is very well attested for the Arab. root bwr. [11] Thus
KBL³, 111, assumes a special root bwr, "to test, examine," as a cognate of brr,
following Driver. [12] It also refers to Eccl. 9:1 as another instance of the same
root meaning "to explore," following Margoliouth. In light of this, the MT of
Eccl. 3:18 and 9:1 can stand as it is.

The ptcp. barur (Aram., Syr. bryr) is clearly attested. Its usage points to the
meaning "separate," [13] which supports the translation "select, choose" (LXX
eklektós, "chosen, select") (Neh. 5:18; 1 Ch. 7:40; 9:22; 16:41; it also appears
in the Qumran literature: CD B 10:4, 'anashim berurim, "chosen men"; and in
Aramaic: Jerusalem Targum on Dt. 1:23, gwbryn bryryn, and on Dt. 29:12[13],
'wm' bryr'). The meaning in Zeph. 3:9 tends toward "pure": saphah bherurah,
"pure lips" (cf. Isa. 6:5, "unclean lips"); cf. also Job 33:3: "my lips speak purely
(that which is pure)" (in KBL³, 148, these two passages are listed separate from
brr, p. 155, without any valid reason).

2. *The Adjective.* The adj. *bar* always means "pure": Ps. 19:9(8): "The
commandment of Yahweh is pure" (barah); Ps. 24:4: "Clean (neqi) hands and
a pure (ubhar) heart"; Ps. 73:1: "Those who are pure in heart" (lebhare lebhabh);
Job 11:4: "I am pure" (ubhar hayithi; in 33:9 we find the synonymous phrase
zakh 'ani, "I am clean"); Sir. 40:21: "a pure voice" (lšwn brh). Prov. 14:4 is
disputed. [14] Presumably "pure crib" means "empty crib" ('ebhus bar), or one
can read 'ephes bar, "no grain." Cant. 6:9 says that the bride is barah leyoladhtah.

---

[7] Cf. the lexicons and J. Pedersen, *Der Eid bei den Semiten* (1914), 44f.

[8] *BLe*, § 443dⁱ.

[9] Blau, *VT*, 7 (1957), 387.

[10] So still *KBL³*; cf. G. Schmuttermayr, *Ps 18 und 2 Sam 22. StANT*, 25 (1971), 100, n. 10.

[11] Lane, I, 274; Brockelmann, *VG*, 272 Aa: double ʿayin and ʿayin vav/yodh verbs are
often confused.

[12] Driver, *JBL*, 55 (1936), 108.

[13] See above, Ezk. 20:38.

[14] See the comms.

The commentaries usually translate this, "selected, chosen (to her that bore her)." But since elsewhere only *barur* is attested with the meaning "selected," [15] it is probably best to suppose that here also the meaning of *bar* is "pure." [16] In the following verse (10) we find the phrase, "pure (clear, bright) as the sun," which also occurs in Ugar. *km špš dbrt* ("like the sun that is pure"), Akk. *kīma šamši zaki,* [17] and the Jerusalem Targum on Ex. 22:2(3): *bryr kšmš'*.

3. *The Substantives.* The abstract substantive *bor* means "purity." It appears in the formulas *bor kappekha,* "purity of your hands" (Job 22:30), and *bor yadhai,* "purity of my hands" (Ps. 18:21,25[20,24]; v. 21[20] is par. to 2 S. 22:21, while 2 S. 22:25 has *bori,* "my purity," which as opposed to Ps. 18:25 [24] is probably not original). *bor,* "lye" (a cleansing agent made out of the ashes of the soap plant), in Isa. 1:25 and Job 9:30 is different, and presumably represents a later development. *borith* in Jer. 2:22 and Mal. 3:2 has approximately the same meaning.

4. *Summary; Religio-Ethical Meaning.* The root *brr* (and its derivatives) occurs 35 times in the OT. No progressive development in the meanings "to be pure, to separate, test or examine" can be ascertained in the OT. This root does not appear at all in the Pentateuch, and, apart from the inserted song in 2 S. 22, the only place it is found in the Deuteronomistic history is in the dubious text in 1 S. 17:8 mentioned earlier. This may be inconsequential, since the concept of "purify" hardly plays any role in historical accounts. The Elohistic statement in Gen. 20:5, "In the integrity (*tom*) of my heart and the purity of my hands (*niqyon kappai*) I have done this," uses other roots. Thus Isa. 1:25 seems to be the oldest text in the OT that uses the root *brr,* and here it already denotes the cleansing agent *bor* (the conjec. trans. "in the furnace" is unnecessary). But an early date is also to be assigned to Ps. 18 = 2 S. 22. [18]

The statements about the purity of the heart or of the hands are of religio-ethical importance. The washing of hands was originally a ceremony in the rite of atonement, [19] as seen from Job 9:30 (*vahazikkothi bebhor kappai,* "and cleanse my hands with lye"); Jer. 2:22 (*tarbi lekh borith,* "you use much soap"); Dt. 21:6 (*yirchatsu 'eth yedhehem,* "they shall wash their hands"); the stereotyped phrase, "I wash my hands in innocence" (Ps. 26:6; 73:13); and Isa. 1:16 (*rachatsu hizzakku,* "wash yourselves, make yourselves clean"). But these and other passages also show that from the external rite there arose a purely figurative mode of expression, so that Jer. 4:14 can even speak of washing the heart (*kabbesi libbekh*); cf. Prov. 20:9, *zikkithi libbi,* "I have made my heart clean." In Ps. 73:13 *'erchats beniqqayon kappai,* "I washed my hands in innocence," stands in parallelism with *zikkithi lebhabhi,* "I kept my heart clean," and v. 1

---

[15] See above.

[16] Zorell, *Lex. Hebr.,* 126, calls attention to Arab. *barr,* "pure, holy," and translates "only beloved."

[17] *WUS,* 593.

[18] Schmuttermayr, 17-24.

[19] Paschen, 70.

refers to the *bare lebhabh*, "pure in heart." "Purity of hands (or heart)" certainly is to be understood only ethically and comprehensively. "Heart" has to do more with the intention, and "hand" with the ethical deed. But these two terms are not clearly distinguished, and in the "liturgy of the gate" in Ps. 24:4, "clean hands" is wholly parallel to "a pure heart." External purification rites without ethical conversion cannot remove guilt (Jer. 2:22). The most frequently used expression for Levitical purification and purity is → טהר *ṭāhēr*, "to be clean, pure." *zakhakh*, "to be bright, pure, clean," is much rarer. But frequently these words also mean "pure" in the general and moral sense, e.g., in Ps. 51:12(10) *lebh tahor*, "clean heart"; Job 17:9, *tahar yadhayim*, "clean hands"; and Prov. 22:11, *tehar lebh*, "purity of heart." Ps. 19:9(8) states that the commandment of Yahweh is pure (*barah*); 18:31(30), that his word (RSV promise) is pure (or true, *tseruphah*); and 12:7(6), that his words (RSV promises) are pure (*tehoroth*); see also the other parallel expressions in Ps. 19:8-10(7-9) and 51:4,9(2,7), where the cultic terminology is given a moral connotation, being used of the forgiveness of sins. Paschen has discussed the approximate synonyms to *brr*. [20]

But in spite of the extensive use of *taher*, later circles, especially among the Wisdom teachers, seem to have used rather the noncultic root *brr* for moral purity. In the Qumran texts, where *brr* and its derivatives appear so far 12 times, this root is used only of ethical purity. "Purity of hands" is mentioned in 1QS 9:15, *kebhor kappav*, "the purity of his hand"; 1QH 16:10, *lehabher kappai*, "to cleanse my hands"; 11QPsª 21:17 (=Sir. 51:20), *kpy hbrwty;* cf. in addition 1QS 1:12, "to purify their understanding" (*lebharer daʿtam*); 4:20, "God will cleanse" (*yebharer ʾel*). The monastic community at Qumran attached a great deal of importance to ritual purifications, but at the same time they emphasized the inner purity of heart, as is indicated, e.g., in 1QS 5:13, "they are not pure (*loʾ yittaharu*) unless they are converted from their malice." The root *taher* is used frequently for Levitical purity, just as in the OT, but it is also used of ethical purity, especially in 1QH. [21]

The absolute purity of God's words and laws agrees with the idea that he requites man according to the (ethical) purity of his hands (Job 22:30; Ps. 18:21, 25,27[20,24,26]=2 S. 22:21,25,27). [22]

III. Homonymous Words.

1. *brr II.* GesB and KBL³ list a *brr* II, meaning "to sharpen" (an arrow), and refer to the Arab. *barā*, "to sharpen." They appeal to Schwarzlose, [23] but he gives as possible meanings, "to cut, pare" (Ḥariri 54,1). The OT texts that come into question here are Jer. 51:11, "Sharpen the arrows" (*habheru hachitstsim*), and Isa. 49:2, "he made me a sharp arrow" (*lechets barur*). But in

---

20 Paschen, 19-26.

21 See K. G. Kuhn, *Konkordanz zu den Qumrantexten* (1960).

22 Paschen, 68-81, deals with the understanding of "purity" in the deed-reward view of the cult lyrical traditions.

23 F. W. Schwarzlose, *Die Waffen der alten Araber* (1886), 295.

view of the meaning "to smooth, polish, purify," or "smooth, polished," it is unnecessary to assume a different root. According to 1QM 5:14, the hilt of the sword is *qeren berurah,* "of smooth, polished (?) horn." On the basis of the meaning "to sharpen," Paschen conjectures that originally the root *brr* was an onomatopoeic word meaning "to rub, grate, pare, scrape," which later came to mean "to make smooth, bright, pure"; then the original idea would appear even in *bor* and *borith,* "lye," since these substances produce foam in the process of rubbing or scraping.[24] All this, of course, is merely hypothetical.

2. *Grain.* Further the subst. *bar* III = "grain," Arab. *burr,* is well attested in the OT:[25] Gen. 41:35,49; 42:3,25; Jer. 23:28; Joel 2:24; Am. 5:11; 8:5f.; Ps. 65:14(13); 72:16; Prov. 11:26 (the meaning of Prov. 14:4 is uncertain).[26] The derivation from *bar,* "pure," is evident to the extent that it denotes purified, i.e., winnowed, grain. However, in Ps. 65:14(13) and 72:16 it is used of grain standing in the field, and thus its etymology is no longer in view.

3. *Open Field.* The only passage in which *bar* IV = "the open field" occurs is Job 39:4. In Arabic, *barr* means the mainland, and the verb *bwr* means "to be uncultivated."[27] In Middle Hebrew, Aramaic, and Syriac, the verb *būr,* "to be uncultivated, desolate," and the subst. *bar* are found often,[28] and thus we are to assume that *bar* in Job 39:4 is an Aramaism.[29] *chevath bara',* "the beasts of the field," appears frequently in Daniel.[30] But it is still questionable whether "open land" is to be connected with the root *br',* "to cut down trees, root out." *GesB,* which assumes that the original meaning of *brr* was "to be free," derives *bar* IV from this root.

Hamp

---

[24] Paschen, 20.
[25] Cf. *KBL*[3], 146.
[26] See above, "pure.'
[27] Lane, I, 274.
[28] Cf. Levy, *WTM,* and *KBL*[3], 146.
[29] M. Wagner, *Die lexikal. und grammatikal. Aramaismen im alttestamentlichen Hebräisch. BZAW,* 96 (1966), No. 47.
[30] *KBL*[2], 1059.

בשׂר **bśr;** בְּשׂוֹרָה **beśôrāh**

Contents: I. Etymology, Occurrences, Usage in the Ancient Near East. II. Secular Usage:
1. Good News in General; 2. With *tobh;* 3. Sad News. III. Theologico-Religious Meaning:
1. Proclamation of Yahweh's Saving Deeds; 2. The Messenger of Joy; 3. Intensification in
Trito-Isaiah.

I. Etymology, Occurrences, Usage in the Ancient Near East. In the OT
the root *bśr* occurs 30 times in all: 14 times as a verb in the piel, once as a verb
in the hithpael, 9 times as a substantival participle, and 6 times as a noun. Since
the Hebrew knows only the intensive form, it seems likely from the start that
a survey of the actual usage of this root in OT contexts will yield only a semantic
analysis, and not an etymological conclusion.

This root is well attested in the ancient Near East. Even if we encounter varying s-sounds, comparative Semitic grammar shows that this is normal.[1] Akkadian
has the forms *bussuru/passuru* and *bussurtu* meaning "to bring a message (news)"
and "message (news)" respectively.[2] In itself, this word is neutral; consequently,
the noun can be defined more precisely by adding other terms, as in the expressions *bussurat lumnim,* "bad news," and *bussurat dumqim,* "good news," or
bussurat ḥadê, "joyful news."[3] In the majority of cases, both the noun and the
verb forms denote a good message or good news. By way of comparison, Arab.
baššara, Old South Arab. *'bśr,*[4] Ethiop. *absara,* and Jewish Aram. *bsr* always
mean "to bring good news." In Ugaritic, the verb *bśr* means "to bring glad
tidings," and in the t-form "to receive it," while the noun *bśrt* means "glad
tidings." These occurrences appear in three passages: *CTA,* 10 [IV AB], III,
34f., where Anat brings Baal the joyful news of the birth of a bull calf, causing
him to rejoice (*śmḥ*); *CTA,* 19 [I D], II, 37, in a broken context which evidently
has to do with news of victory; and *CTA,* 4 [II AB], V, 26f., where Anat brings
Baal the news that a house is going to be built for him.

---

bśr. M. Burrows, "The Origin of the Term 'Gospel,'" *JBL,* 44 (1925), 21-33; G. Dalman,
The Words of Jesus (trans. 1909); K. Elliger, *BK,* XI, 33-35; G. Friedrich, "εὐαγγελίζομαι,"
TDNT, II, 707-710; G. Godu, "Evangile," *DACL,* V/1 (1922), 852-923; D. J. McCarthy, "Vox
bśr praeparat vocem 'evangelium,'" *VD,* 42 (1964), 26-33; J. Scharbert, *Heilsmittler im AT
und im Alten Orient. QuaestDisp,* 23/24 (1964); U. Stiehl, *Einführung in die allgemeine
Semantik* (1970); C. Westermann, *The Praise of God in the Psalms* (trans. 1966); P. Zondervan,
"Het Woord 'Evangelium,'" *Theologisch Tijdschrift,* 43 (1914), 178-213.

[1] Brockelmann, *VG,* 50.
[2] *CAD,* II, 346f.; *AHw,* 142.
[3] For examples, see *CAD.*
[4] ContiRossini, 119.

II. Secular Usage.

1. *Good News in General.* In the OT we find *bśr* and its derivatives in three literary strata. We encounter the nontheological usage especially in the books of Samuel and Kings. The use of this word in the episode of the news about Absalom's death is significant for determining the biblical meaning. It does not lack a certain dialectic, and for this very reason is instructive. The messengers and David, who awaits their arrival, have entirely different ideas about the content of the message: the messengers saw in the death of the insurgent Absalom the opportune occasion for their message, but David, as Absalom's father, hoped that the message would be that Absalom was still alive. Both parties, the messengers (2 S. 18:19,20) and David (18:25,26), speak of "joyful" tidings that are brought or expected by using various forms of *bissar, mebhasser,* and *besorah.* [5] We find the same thing when news of the death of Saul is brought to the land of the Philistines (1 S. 31:9 = 1 Ch. 10:9) and to David (2 S. 4:10); and in connection with the discovery of the flight of the Syrians (2 K. 7:9). David's lament over Saul and Jonathan has the verb *bśr* in the piel in the first stich of 2 S. 1:20, but its parallelism with *samach,* "to rejoice," and *'alaz,* "to exult," makes it clear that the Philistines must have regarded the news as a joyful message. *bśr* is also used in parallelism with *samach* when news of the birth of Jeremiah is brought to his father (Jer. 20:15). Here undoubtedly *bśr* means "news of a joyful event."

2. *With tobh.* In two passages in the OT, *tobh(ah),* "good," modifies the root *bśr:* once it modifies the noun (2 S. 18:27), and once the verb (1 K. 1:42). In both cases this may be because the person to whom the message was carried was under great psychical tension: David anticipated from Ahimaaz, a "good man," the kind of news he wanted to hear; in the midst of the celebration of his self-appointment to the throne, Adonijah became very anxious when he heard an echo of the surprising proclamation of Solomon as king, and he hoped to hear from Jonathan, a "worthy man," words of reassurance. Thus the reason for the addition of *tobh* in these texts is to emphasize that the recipients of the tidings were hoping for "glad" tidings, and not to clarify the meaning of the root. Twice the noun *besorah* means "reward given to a messenger" (2 S. 4:10; 18:22). This also assumes that *bśr* means basically "glad" tidings.

3. *Sad News.* In one passage *mebhasser* is used of a messenger who brings to Eli the priest the sad news of Israel's defeat and of the death of his sons (1 S. 4:17). Does this singular negative use of the root *bśr* justify the conclusion (assumed in *KBL²*) that *bśr* is a neutral word in Hebrew, and must be modified by "glad" or "sad" or something similar to convey the idea of glad or sad tidings? Or are we to agree with Friedrich when he assumes that the original meaning of this root is "glad" tidings? [6] In our opinion Friedrich is correct, because the use

[5] On 2 S. 18:27, see below.
[6] *TDNT,* II, 707.

of this root in extrabiblical literature also reveals the tendency to connect the root *bśr* with "glad" tidings, as Ugaritic in particular shows. The actual use of *bśr* in Biblical Hebrew starts at this semantic stage and further develops it. The exception in 1 S. 4:17 can be interpreted as a levelling down, and does not compel us to postulate that the original meaning in Hebrew was neutral. [7]

III. Theologico-Religious Meaning.

1. *Proclamation of Yahweh's Saving Deeds.* Only the verb and the substantival participle of *bśr* are used in a theologico-religious sense in the OT. Thus we will leave *besorah* out of our discussion from now on. The religious use of *bśr* is found in two rather strictly definable strata, the Psalms and the Prophets.

The use of *bśr* in Ps. 68:12 (Eng. v. 11), which speaks of "female messengers of victory in great number," represents a definite transition from secular news of victory to news of victory in the sphere of salvation history grounded in Yahweh. The text here is not undisputed, but recent commentaries and translations leave it as it stands. [8] The female messengers of victory are probably to be understood on analogy with the women who sang of the victories of Saul and David in 1 S. 18:7f. Ps. 68:12(11) does not have in mind news of victory carried to a specific audience, but a joyful announcement of Yahweh's saving deeds, the "declarative praise" of God. [9] It is only a step from this to the meaning that *bśr* assumes in certain cultic texts (Ps. 40:10[9] and 96:2 = 1 Ch. 16:23). In the cult, *bśr* does not have to do with reporting news, but with joyfully proclaiming Yahweh's great deeds as confession and in order to awaken religious joy.

2. *The Messenger of Joy.* This figure takes on new color in the dramatic sketch of the *mebhasser* who runs on the mountains to Jerusalem as a messenger of joy when Assyria falls (Nah. 2:1[1:15]). Deutero-Isaiah has the same figure, and the more he connects it with basic promises of salvation, the more expressive it becomes. Isa. 52:7 deals not only with the exodus from Babylon (52:11f.), but also with the tidings that in conjunction with this exodus God's royal dominion has begun. In the first stich we find the substantival participle in the absolute meaning "messenger of glad tidings"; then the second stich is in synthetic parallelism, ending with the declaration of the sovereignty of God: here we encounter the significant words *shalom,* "peace," *tobh,* "good," and *yeshuʿah,* "salvation." In this parallel stich, the participle of *bśr* is not substantival, but appears once with the obj. *tobh,* "good," between two *mashmiaʿ* ("publish") clauses in which the objects are *shalom,* "peace," and *yeshuʿah,* "salvation," respectively. The addition, *tobh,* is not adverbial and is not to be interpreted as a clarification of the particular nuance of *bśr;* instead, it is the second element in a threefold series of terms: peace, good, salvation. Similarly, the participle

---

[7] But cf. McCarthy, 32.

[8] Weiser, Kraus, Deissler, *Zürcherbibel, Echterbibel,* etc.

[9] Westermann, 31f.

of *bśr* appears in the absolute in Isa. 40:9 (twice) meaning "female messenger of peace," and in 41:27 meaning "messenger of joy." In Deutero-Isaiah *mebhasser* always refers to Yahweh's victory and the beginning of salvation. [10]

3. *Intensification in Trito-Isaiah.* In Trito-Isaiah we probably have the highest intensification of the meaning of *bśr*. First of all, this root is used in the sense of a proclamation of the praise of God by benevolent multitudes from Sheba, etc. (Isa. 60:6). In Isa. 61:1, it is more than a proclamation, but also more than a prophetic prognosis of the future. In his own interpretation of his mission, the prophet sees as his primary task *lebhasser 'anavim,* "bringing good tidings to the afflicted." Here the verb is absolute, and can denote only a saving message for the oppressed and poor, not a neutral message. The proclamation of a word of salvation, and thus of a joyful message of God, is a primary element in the work of the prophet along with healing, liberating, comforting, saving, etc., and is itself a saving event. The event-character of what is said in this entire pericope is clear to the extent that the proclamation of the prophet must be understood as an "announcement ... which also gives rise to that which is proclaimed." [11] Thus *bśr* acquires an active note. With the announcement of glad tidings, the fulfilment begins; Yahweh himself is present and active in his word.

The height attained in Trito-Isaiah would be complete if we could find in *bśr* the basis for the NT key word *euangélion,* "gospel" (to say something about the later history of this word). Unfortunately, the noun *besorah* is not used in Isa. 61:1, and we do not know which intermediate Aramaic word Jesus used when he spoke of the "good news of the kingdom" (Mt. 4:23). [12] However, in light of the quotation of Isa. 61:1 in Lk. 4:18f. and its adaptation to Jesus there, it is probably not far wrong to regard the translation of *bśr* by the Gk. deponent verb *euangelízesthai* in the LXX as the basis for the key word *euangélion.* [13]

In summary, it can be said that the theologico-religious usage of *bśr* confirms to a great extent the established secular sense of "bringing glad tidings" and develops this in relation to the message of salvation.

Schilling (†)

---

[10] Cf. McCarthy; Elliger, 37f.
[11] Scharbert, 202.
[12] Cf. *DBS,* 5, 1621; Dalman, 95.
[13] *TDNT,* 710.

בָּשָׂר *bāśār*

Contents: I. 1. Etymology; 2. Occurrences, Usage; 3. Meanings. II. Religio-Cultic Usage: 1. Of Animals; 2. Of Man. III. Use in Anthropological Sense: 1. Man's Nature; 2. As a Term Used to Denote Relationship; 3. Nature and Importance. IV. Use in Theological Sense (God and *basar*).

I. 1. *Etymology*. The Heb. *basar*, "flesh," has cognates in most of the Semitic languages. To be sure, Arab. *bašar* means "hide" (*bašarat*, "cattle"),[1] but in Phoenician and in most of the Aramaic dialects, the meaning "flesh" for *bśr* is well attested[2] (Jewish Aram. *biśrā'* or *bisrā'*, Syr. *besrā*, also Mandean). The connection of *basar*, "flesh," with Akk. *bišru*, "small child, toddler,"[3] and Pun. *bśr*, "child, descendant,"[4] is disputed. In Ugaritic, *bšr*, "flesh, body," occurs[5] (more frequently, however, *šʔr*, → שְׁאָר *sheʔār*, "residue, remnant"). In Ethiopic we find *bāsōr* as a loanword,[6] and in Old South Arabic *bśr*, "flesh" (also *kl bśrn*, "all flesh" = man).[7] There is no connection between *basar* and the verb → בשׂר *bśr*, except that they are homonymous.

2. *Occurrences, Usage*. The noun *basar*, whose main meanings are "flesh" and "body," and which also occurs once in the plural (Prov. 14:30), is found in the OT about 270 times (3 times in Biblical Aram.: Dnl. 2:11; 4:9 [Eng. v. 12]; 7:5). It appears in all OT writings except Josh., Am., and Mal., occurring most frequently in the Pentateuch (138 times, 61 of these in Lev. alone), Ezk. (24

---

bāśār. F. Baumgärtel-E. Schweizer, "σάρξ. B. Flesh in the OT," *TDNT*, VII, 105-110; N. P. Bratsiotis, Ἀνθρωπολογία τῆς Παλαιᾶς Διαθήκης, I (Athens, 1967), 52-59, 61-93; H. Goeke, *Das Menschenbild der individuellen Klagelieder* (Bonn, 1971), 204-231; J. L. Helberg, "A Communication on the Semasiological Meaning of Basar," *OuTWP* (1959), 23-28; A. R. Hulst, "Kol-bāśār in der priesterlichen Fluterzählung," *OTS*, 12 (1958), 28-68; H. Huppenbauer, "בשׂר 'Fleisch' in den Texten von Qumran (Höhle I)," *ThZ*, 13 (1957), 298-300; D. Lys, *Bâsâr. La chair dans l'AT* (Paris, 1967); R. Meyer-E. Schweizer, "σάρξ. C. Flesh in Judaism. D. Historical Summary," *TDNT*, VII, 110-124; E. R. Murphy, "Bśr in the Qumrân Literature and *Sarks* in the Epistle to the Romans," *Sacra Pagina*, II (Paris, 1959), 60-76; J. Pryke, "'Spirit' and 'Flesh' in the Qumran Documents and Some NT Texts," *RevQ*, 5 (1964/65), 345-360; W. Reiser, "Die Verwandtschaftsformel in Gen 2,23," *ThZ*, 16 (1960), 1-4; A. Sand, "Der Begriff 'Fleisch' in den paulinischen Hauptbriefen," *Bibl. Untersuchungen*, 2 (1967), 221-237; O. Sander, "Leib-Seele-Dualismus im AT?" *ZAW*, 77 (1965), 329-332; J. Scharbert, *Fleisch, Geist und Seele im Pentateuch. SBS*, 19 (1966); O. Schilling, *Geist und Materie in biblischer Sicht. SBS*, 25 (1967); R. de Vaux, *AncIsr;* C. Westermann, "Leib und Seele in der Bibel," *Zeitwende*, 38 (1967), 440-47.

[1] *KBL³*.
[2] *DISO*, 45.
[3] *AHw*, 131a; *CAD*, II, 270a.
[4] J. Hoftijzer, *VT*, 8 (1958), 288-292; *DISO*, 45.
[5] *WUS*, 60.
[6] Leslau, *Contributions*, 13.
[7] ContiRossini, 119f.

times), Job (18), Isa. (17), Ps. (16), and Jer. (10). [8] Since this word appears with the meaning "flesh" and "body" in all parts of the OT literature (including Sir.) and in the Qumran texts, it would be fruitless to attempt any sort of chronological analysis of its use.

The texts in which *basar* appears show that it was used not only of people, but also of animals. In addition to its primary meanings, this word exhibits a variety of secondary meanings. The OT examples can be divided into secular, religio-cultic, and theological spheres.

3. *Meanings.* The examples of the use of *basar* in the secular realm can be subdivided into the following primary and secondary meanings.

a. "Flesh," used synonymously with → שאר *she'ēr* (Mic. 3:3), and in distinction from → עצם *'etsem,* "bone" (Job 10:11), עור *'ôr,* "skin" (Job 10:11), → דם *dām,* "blood" (Isa. 49:26), etc.: 1. Flesh of living people (2 K. 5:10; healthy, 2 K. 5:14; cf. Job 33:25; rotting, evanescent, Nu. 12:12; Job 33:21; Prov. 5:11; Job 19:20; Zec. 14:12; Isa. 17:4; Ps. 109:24; returning to its former healthy state, Ex. 4:7; cf. 2 K. 5:14). 2. Flesh of animals (Gen. 41:2,3,4,18,19).

b. Flesh as food: 1. Animal flesh as food for people (Nu. 11:4,13,18,21,33; Isa. 22:13; raw, 1 S. 2:15; roasted, Isa. 44:16,19), as food for predatory dogs (Ex. 22:30[31]); 2. Human flesh as food for wild animals (Gen. 40:19; 1 S. 17:44; 2 K. 9:36; Ezk. 39:17f.); 3. Human flesh as food for people, either hyperbolically to illustrate extreme distress (Lev. 26:29; cf. Dt. 28:53,55; Jer. 19:9), or figuratively of the exploitation of the poor by the powerful (Mic. 3:3), of the abuse of a human flock by a harsh shepherd (Zec. 11:16), of a human flock that has come to be without a shepherd and whose sheep are devouring one another (Zec. 11:9), of the enemies of Israel who are to devour one another (Isa. 49:26), of allies devouring one another in a civil war (Isa. 9:19[20]), of the fool who "eats his own flesh" (Eccl. 4:5), and also in the sense of "destroying" (Ps. 27:2) or "slandering" someone (Job 19:22).

c. "Body," the physical in its entirety, as a synonym of → גויה *geviyyāh, gaph,* but also of → נבלה *nebhēlāh,* and in distinction from *she'er,* "flesh" (Prov. 5:11): 1. of living people (Ex. 30:32; Lev. 16:4; Nu. 19:7; Ezk. 11:19; cf. 36:26; Job 6:12; healthy, Dnl. 1:15; Prov. 14:30; diseased, Job 7:5; Prov. 5:11; cf. also Ps. 38:4[3]; 63:2[1]); 2. of dead people, i.e., corpse, and thus parallel to *nebhelah,* "body" (Ps. 79:2), and to *ramuth,* "carcass" (Ezk. 32:5), of a dead boy (2 K. 4:34); 3. of living (Job 41:15[23]) or dead animals (Lev. 17:11; cf. v. 14).

d. Fleshly parts of the body in conjunction with other parts of the body: frequently in connection with *'etsem,* "bone," and *'or,* "skin" (both are used with *basar* in Lam. 3:4); also with *kesel,* "loin" (Ps. 38:8[7]), *mishman,* "fat" (Isa. 17:4), *gidh,* "sinew" (Ezk. 37:6,8; Job 10:11), *se'arah,* "hair" (Job 4:15),

---

[8] Cf. the statistics in Lys, 15-19.

dam, "blood" (Isa. 49:26; Ezk. 39:17f.; cf. the later expression, *basar vedham,* "flesh and blood," Sir. 14:18), *berekh,* "knee" (Ps. 109:24), *reghel,* "foot," *'ayin,* "eye," *lashon,* "tongue," *peh,* "mouth" (Zec. 14:12), etc.

e. For the supposed original meaning "skin," one could cite Ps. 102:6[5]; 119:120; Job 4:15; and Ex. 4:7; and yet in all these passages *basar* could also be translated "flesh." However, this is not the case in other passages, where these two words stand side by side and are clearly to be distinguished (Lev. 13:2ff.; Job 10:11; 19:20; etc.).

f. Euphemistically for "pubic region," "genitals" (Ex. 28:42; cf. Lev. 6:3[10]; 16:4), "penis" (Lev. 15:2,3,7; Ezk. 16:26; 23:20), "vagina" (Lev. 15:19), etc.

g. A term used to indicate relationship. It is used as a basic element in the so-called relationship formula[9] in Gen. 2:23 (*'etsem me'atsamai ubhasar mibbesari,* "bone of my bones and flesh of my flesh"), and thus in the sense of "my own kins-man (relative)" (Gen. 29:14; 2 S. 19:13f.[12f.]; cf. Jgs. 9:2; 2 S. 5:1; 1 Ch. 11:1; it has the same meaning also without *'etsem* in Neh. 5:5, or with *she'er,* "flesh," in Lev. 18:6; 25:49; *basar* is used alone to denote "my own brother" in Gen. 37:27), and is expanded to mean "relative" (Isa. 58:7).

h. *kol basar,* "all flesh," which occurs about 40 times in the OT, has the fol-lowing meanings: 1. "the whole body" of a human being (Lev. 13:3; Nu. 8:7) or an animal (Lev. 4:11; cf. 17:14); 2. "all living creatures," including people and animals (Gen. 6:17; 9:11,15ff.; Nu. 18:15; Ps. 136:25; Dnl. 4:9[12]; Sir. 40:8); 3. "all men," "all mankind" (Isa. 40:5f.; 49:26; Jer. 25:31; 45:5; Ezk. 21:4,10 [20:48; 21:4]; Joel 3:1[2:28]; Zec. 2:17[13]; Ps. 65:3[2]; 145:21; Job 12:10; 34:15; Sir. 1:10; 14:17); 4. "every man" (Isa. 66:16,23f.; Jer. 12:12), "any man" (Dt. 5:26); 5. "all animals," the entire animal world (Gen. 6:19; 7:15f.,21; 8:17; Sir. 13:16; 17:4).

i. "Man," like → אדם *'ādhām,* "man," or → נפש *nephesh,* lit. "soul" (Lev. 13:18,24; Ps. 56:5[4]; cf. Ps. 38:8[7]; Dnl. 2:11).

j. "Fleshly" (Ezk. 11:19; 36:26; Job 10:4; 2 Ch. 32:8), perhaps as an abstract, "corporeality" (Prov. 14:30).

II. Religio-Cultic Usage. In numerous passages, *basar* is used in a religio-cultic context, in various laws, admonitions, etc., sometimes referring to the *basar* of animals and sometimes to the *basar* of man. These passages, most of which are in P, deal first of all with laws concerning food, sacrifices, etc., second-ly with laws concerning purity, sanctification, and clothing, and thirdly with circumcision.

---

[9] Reiser.

1. *Of Animals.* a. Basically the OT allows the eating of animal flesh (cf. Gen. 9:3). However, ordinarily it was eaten only on solemn occasions, when one was showing hospitality to guests, and especially at sacrificial celebrations. Usually the "raw flesh (meat)" (*basar ... chai*, 1 S. 2:15) of a cow (Ex. 29:14; Nu. 18:17f.; 1 K. 19:21), sheep (Ex. 29:32; Nu. 18:17f.; Dt. 16:2), or goat (Lev. 16:27; Nu. 18:17f.) was roasted (Ex. 12:8; 1 S. 2:15) or boiled (1 S. 2:13). The eating of flesh was accompanied by the eating of bread (Isa. 44:19), etc., and the drinking of wine (22:13). Ezk. 11:3,7,11; 24:10 contain a proverbial saying: "It (Jerusalem) is the pot, we are the flesh."

b. In his covenant with Noah after the flood, God gave man for food "everything that moves and lives" (Gen. 9:3; cf. 1:29), but with the crucial limitation that he is not to eat *basar benaphsho dhamo*, "flesh with its life, that is, its blood" (9:4). This general prohibition against eating blood significantly brings blood (→ דם *dām*) into very intimate connection with "soul" (→ נפשׁ *nephesh*), but clearly distinguishes between *nephesh* and *basar*. It requires unconditionally that when a person wants to eat flesh, he let the blood flow out or be poured out on the ground when the animal is slaughtered (this is explicitly stated in Lev. 17:13; Dt. 12:16,24). This is frequently repeated and newly formulated in the Pentateuch, not only in an effort to emphasize, but also to explain and confirm. Thus at the beginning of the Holiness Code, the reason for the prohibition limiting the eating of flesh is stated this way: "For the *nephesh* (life) of the flesh is in the blood, and I have given it for you upon the altar to make atonement for your souls" (Lev. 17:11). The blood belongs to Yahweh and is reserved for him alone; he receives it as sacrificial blood, and in this way effects vicarious atonement for each cult participant, who otherwise would have to die because of his sin. In order to avoid any misunderstanding, this duty is also binding on the stranger among the people (v. 12), and applies to all "flesh," even that of wild game which was not offered in sacrifice (v. 13). Finally, the universal character of the prohibition against eating blood is emphasized strongly by the twice repeated reason given to support it: *ki nephesh kol basar damo ... hu'*, "for the life of all flesh, it ... is its blood" (v. 14). The same reason (but expressed more concisely) is also found in Dt. 12:23 with an ethical and humane color. Thus, instead of the blunt threat of destruction (Lev. 17:10,14), we encounter an appeal directed more to internal responsibility: "Only be sure that you do not eat the blood" (Dt. 12:23), connected with the promise that it will go well with those who seek Yahweh's pleasure (v. 25). But the tendency to balance the prohibition against eating blood with the permission to eat as much flesh as one desires (12:23; cf. 12:15,20ff.,27) is also noteworthy: "as much as you desire, according to the blessing of Yahweh your God which he has given you" (12:15).

c. In particular the OT food laws prohibited the eating of flesh: 1. of all unclean animals (cf. the lists in Lev. 11 and Dt. 14:3-21); 2. of any clean animal that dies or is torn by wild animals (Ex. 22:30[31]; cf. Lev. 11:39f.; 17:15f.; and Dt. 14:21, which states that the Israelites can give or sell its flesh to an alien or foreigner); 3. of an ox that is stoned because it gored someone to death (Ex.

21:28); and 4. of flesh that comes into contact with something unclean (Lev. 7:19). A decisive religio-ethical character can also be seen in these food laws in the respective positive urgent admonition to maintain purity, which also appears in a summons to holiness. Sometimes this summons is uttered by Yahweh himself (Ex. 22:30[31]; Lev. 11:43ff.; 22:8f.), and sometimes it is uttered in his name (Dt. 14:21). Yahweh's holiness, to which appeal is made again and again as a basis for the food laws, is also the motive for every charge to individual purity and holiness. Along with this, the frequent emphasis on one's relationship to Yahweh (Lev. 11:44; Dt. 14:21), on the personal attitude of every member of the people of God toward Yahweh and his commandments expressed in obedience and fidelity (Ex. 22:30[31]; cf. Lev. 11:43ff.; 22:8f.; Dt. 14:21), as a motivation for observing good laws, is noteworthy. Frequently when the OT designates flesh as unclean, it refers to a kind of flesh that plays a certain role in heathen cults. Thus OT food laws had a part in defining the distinction between Israelites and heathen, and these took on greater religio-ethical significance from the time of the exile on. Thus a postexilic prophet censures idolaters who eat forbidden flesh in connection with an idolatrous cult (Isa. 66:17; cf. 65:4). Ezekiel also insists before Yahweh that he has conscientiously observed the food laws: "I have never eaten what died of itself or was torn by beasts, nor has foul flesh come into my mouth" (Ezk. 4:14). Daniel and his fellow believers at the heathen court in Babylon refuse to eat the king's food, in order to remain faithful to the law and not defile themselves (Dnl. 1:8ff.). It is impossible to determine whether the "king's food" (*path bagh hammelekh*, Dnl. 1:8; cf. Jth. 12:1; Tob. 1:12; 2 Macc. 5:27–7:40) also means flesh sacrificed to idols; in general, it is striking that OT law contains no explicit prohibition against eating such flesh or against eating the flesh of animals killed by heathen. Possibly the general food laws of the OT also cover such cases.

Dnl. 10:2f. tells about a three-week "mourning fast" (→ אכל *'ābhal*) during which Daniel ate no flesh, in preparation for receiving a revelation. Evident in such passages is the tendency always present in the OT to try to attain a direct relationship to God by means of true asceticism. Standing in the foreground here is the idea that fasting (which is frequently mentioned in the OT, → צום *tsûm;* → ענה *'ānāh*) as a religio-ethical act can lead to the suppression of the appetite, because eating a large quantity of food (and flesh is included in this, cf. Jgs. 6:19) disturbs the inner relationship with God and imperils fidelity to him (cf. Isa. 22:13; Prov. 23:20). To be sure, according to Dt. 12:15ff. each one may slaughter and eat flesh anywhere and "as much as he desires," according to the blessing that Yahweh has given him, although even here certain restrictions are imposed (Dt. 12:16,23). But the narratives in Ex. 16 (cf. vv. 3,8,12) and Nu. 11 (cf. the frequent use of *basar* in vv. 4,13,18,21,33) also indicate that the inordinate desire for flesh (cf. esp. Nu. 11:18ff.), and not simply the people's hunger, lay behind Israel's murmuring and rebellion against Yahweh (so also Nu. 11:20). A similar example is found in 1 S. 2:12ff., where the sons of Eli demanded raw flesh from those who offered sacrifice in order that they might roast it and enjoy it, and thus blasphemed God because of their desire for flesh.

d. In cultic life, the flesh of animals served as "sacrificial flesh" (*besar haq-qorban,* Ezk. 40:43), which was regarded as "holy flesh" (*besar qodhesh,* Jer. 11:15; Hag. 2:12). Generally speaking, the flesh of all clean domestic animals and some clean birds could be sacrificed. Depending on the kind of sacrifice being offered, the animal was called a *par,* "bull," or *se'ir,* "goat," *hachatta'th,* "for the sin-offering" (Lev. 16:27); *'el hammillu'im,* "the ram of ordination" (Ex. 29:31); and its flesh *besar hammillu'im,* "the flesh for the ordination" (29:34), *besar zebhach todhath shelamim,* "the flesh of the sacrifice of peace-offerings for thanksgiving" (Lev. 7:15), *besar zebhach hashshelamim,* "the flesh of the sacrifice of peace-offerings" (7:21), or simply *besar hazzabhach,* "the flesh of the sacrifice" (7:17). There were certain kinds of sacrificial flesh which no one was allowed to eat; instead, it was to be burned outside the camp: the sin-offering (Ex. 29:14; Lev. 4:11f.; 8:17; 9:11; 16:27), and the "red heifer" whose ashes were used in the preparation of the water of purification (Nu. 19:5). The flesh that was left over from the sacrificial meal was burned either after the first day (Ex. 29:34; Lev. 7:15; 8:32) or on the third day (Lev. 7:17), because by that time it was considered to be unclean (*piggul,* "an abomination," 7:18). The flesh that came in contact with something unclean had also to be burned (7:19).

However, in other cases the sacrificial flesh was eaten, sometimes only by the priesthood, and sometimes by the laymen as well. Thus the priests alone were allowed to eat the sacrificial flesh of the ram of ordination (Ex. 29:31), and only in the sacrificial meal at the door of the *'ohel mo'edh,* "tent of meeting" (29:32; Lev. 8:31), after it had been boiled "in a holy place" (Ex. 29:31). Also, the priests alone were allowed to eat of the sacrificial flesh that they offered for the common people as a sin-offering, which was considered to be "most holy" (*qodhesh qodhashim,* Lev. 6:22[29]), so that any one who touched it was "holy" (6:20[27]). Furthermore, 1 S. 2:13 mentions "the custom of the priests with that which the people sacrificed." The flesh of all clean firstlings (→ בכור *bᵉkhôr*) that was offered in the sanctuary (Nu. 18:15f.), and that which was given freely of the firstborn of men and unclean animals (18:15,18), was also regarded as the custom of the priest. After the priest had received his portion of the *shelamim* (peace)-offering, the layman offering the sacrifice and his kinsmen were allowed to eat his portion in the sacrificial meal if it was clean (Lev. 7:19), for this flesh was *basar mizzebhach hashshelamim,* "the flesh of the sacrifice of the peace-offerings," which belonged to the Lord (7:20f.). Further, on the first night of the passover, the flesh of the paschal lamb, which had been roasted in the fire, was eaten (Ex. 12:8), and one had to be careful not to break any of its bones (12:46). It is also worthy of note that Dt. 12 gives the layman more privileges by allowing him to eat sacrificial flesh (v. 27), although it requires him not to forget the Levite (v. 19). Jgs. 6:19ff. tells how a banquet with boiled flesh which Gideon prepared was changed into a burnt-offering, and 1 S. 2:12ff. gives an account of the misuse of priestly prerogatives with regard to sacrificial flesh by the sons of Eli.

Some of the above-mentioned passages, especially those which designate the sacrificial meal as "holy flesh" belonging to Yahweh, and the demands for purity on the part of those participating in the sacrifice that are dependent on these passages, point to the religio-ethical value of sacrifice. Sacrifice is a means Yahweh uses to allow his people to demonstrate and promote their morally binding covenant communion with him. [10] The prophets do not oppose sacrifice as such, but its superficial use in the cult, where only the ritual is performed and the religio-ethical basis of this cultic reality is despised in their time. They emphasize the true meaning of sacrifice in the OT and its religio-ethical value. Thus Hosea condemns Israel's sacrifices, which in his day are merely a matter of slaughtering animals and eating their flesh, and do not conform to the will of the covenant God, because the inner motivation is missing. Jeremiah also opposes the false idea that the people can draw near to Yahweh by eating animal flesh, while their deeds prevent them from drawing near to him. Thus with a certain irony, he quotes Yahweh as calling to his people: "Add your burnt-offerings to your sacrifices, and eat the flesh" (Jer. 7:21). The eating of the flesh of the burnt-offering (which actually was not supposed to be eaten) reveals the hypocrisy of the one offering the sacrifice, because ostensibly everything he is doing is for Yahweh, when in reality it is done without him and therefore brings about his displeasure. Further, in Jer. 11:15 (cf. already Isa. 1:10ff.) Yahweh asks what his beloved was seeking in his house and whether "holy flesh" could avert her doom. In Ps. 50:13 Yahweh asks a similar question, which also points to the true meaning of the sacrificial cult in the OT: "Do I eat the flesh of bulls?" Here he condemns the false idea that he needs sacrificial flesh.

2. *Of Man.* In religio-cultic life, human *basar* is also used in the sense of "body."

a. A large number of the passages that use *basar* in this way mention laws of purity and holiness. [11] Thus, when some sort of skin disease appears on "the skin of his (a person's) body" (*be'or besaro*), the priest pronounces him "unclean" (→ טמא *ṭāmē'*, Lev. 13:2ff.,10f.,14ff.,18,24,43) or "clean" (→ טהור *ṭāhôr*). In the sexual realm, a man is unclean when he has a discharge from his *basar* (RSV, "body"; 15:2,3,7), [12] and a woman is unclean during her menstrual period (15:19). Other laws direct various people to wash (→ רחץ *rāchats*) their bodies in water: this is the case with the high priest before putting on holy garments (16:4) or his festival robes (16:24), the man who lets the goat go to Azazel (16:26), those who burn the skin, flesh, and dung of the animal offered for a sin-offering (16:27f.) or of the red heifer (Nu. 19:7f.), anyone who comes in contact with unclean animals (Lev. 22:6), a person who eats meat of animals that died of themselves or that were torn (17:16), and one who has recovered from a skin disease (14:9), emitted a discharge (15:13) or semen (15:16).

The Levites are supposed to shave their whole "body" (Nu. 8:7); the anointing oil for the priests is not to be poured upon the "body" of a layman

---

[10] Cf. further H.-J. Kraus, *Worship in Israel* (trans. 1966), 112ff.; and de Vaux, II, 447ff.
[11] De Vaux, II, 460ff.
[12] See above, I.3.f.; otherwise Scharbert, 49.

(Ex. 30:32). Both priests (Lev. 21:5) and laymen (19:28) were forbidden to make cuttings in the flesh. Further, according to Ex. 28:42 the priests must cover "the flesh of their nakedness" (*besar 'ervah*), i.e., their pubic region, with linen breeches when they go into the most holy place or when they approach the altar, "lest they bring guilt upon themselves and die" (v. 43). Lev. 6:3(10) and 16:4 contain similar laws concerning the clothing of the priest when he offers the burnt-offering, and of the high priest on the day of atonement, but in these passages *basar* alone is used. In order to humble himself before Yahweh, a person put sackcloth (→ שַׂק *śaq*) upon his naked body (*'al basar*, 1 K. 21:27; 2 K. 6:30). The religio-ethical element can hardly be denied also in the laws of purification for the human body. In these laws one can recognize a means of separating Israel from her secular or heathen environment, and of indicating her relationship to Yahweh. They also serve as preparations for an inner purity and holiness to which Yahweh calls his covenant people (Lev. 19:2; cf. 11:44f.; 20:7,26; 21:8; etc.).

b. The use of *basar* in connection with the circumcision (→ מול *mûl*) of the foreskin in Gen. 17:11,14,23-25; Lev. 12:3 (*besar ha'orlah*, "the flesh of the foreskin," where *basar* probably means "penis") on the one hand, and in Ezk. 44:7,9 (*'erel basar*, "uncircumcised flesh") on the other, is striking since *basar* is never used in this way anywhere else in the OT. In Gen. 17:10ff., the circumcision of the *besar ha'orlah* is traced back to Yahweh's covenant with Abraham, but is said to be perpetuated in his descendants. Thus this act of circumcision, which was also practiced in the heathen nations around Israel, was given a new pronounced religious meaning, which Yahweh himself defines in the following way, *vehayah le'oth berith beni ubhenekhem*, "and it shall be a sign of the covenant between me and you" (17:11). Thus the circumcision of the *besar ha'orlah* as a covenant responsibility is a crucial sign (→ אות *'ôth*) of the separation of Abraham and his descendants from the heathen world around them, and also of their reception into covenant communion with Yahweh. Thus circumcision is a sign of the covenant (*'oth berith*, 17:11), which makes the covenant of Yahweh visible in the *basar* of the individual participants in the covenant (17:13; cf. Sir. 44:20). [13] It also excludes all "uncircumcised flesh" (*'erel basar*, Ezk. 44:7,9) from this Yahweh covenant or from the covenant people (Gen. 17:14), and the uncircumcised *besar ha'orlah* is the sign that a man is a heathen. In Ezk. 44:7,9, *'erel basar*, "uncircumcised flesh," is supplemented by *'erel lebh*, "uncircumcised heart" (cf. Dt. 10:16; Jer. 4:4; 9:25f.), which indicates that circumcision is not only an external sign of the covenant, restricted to the body, but has in mind the whole man, body and soul, and requires inner motives. In this connection, reference can be made to Ezk. 16:26; 23:20 (here *basar* = "penis"), which speak of Israel's (*'ishshah*, "woman, wife") violation of the covenant and disloyalty to Yahweh (*'ish*, "man, husband") in a figurative sense as harlotry with foreign men who have *gidhle bhasar*, "large penises."

---

[13] See also the excellent observations made by Scharbert, 50f., 55.

III. Use in Anthropological Sense.

1. *Man's Nature. basar* is probably the most comprehensive, most important, and most frequently used anthropological term for the external, fleshly aspect of man's nature, and when used in this sense it can be translated by the two main meanings of this word, "flesh" or "body," depending on the context.

a. Usually *basar* denotes the form of man in its entirety, i.e., the physical, consisting chiefly of flesh, which is recognized throughout the OT as the work of God's hands (Isa. 45:11f.; 64:7[8]; Ps. 119:73; 138:8; Job 10:8ff.; 31:15; etc.). However, it is worthy of note that *basar* is not explicitly mentioned in the account of the creation of man (Gen. 2:7), although *basar* occurs elsewhere in Gen. 2 in its two main senses (vv. 21,23f.); instead, the author uses *neshamah,* "breath," and *nephesh,* "soul." And yet, *basar* appears in other passages alluding to Gen. 2:7 (thus Job 34:14f.). The disparate anthropological statements in the OT affirm that the human body is clothed with *'or,* "skin," and *basar,* knit together with → עצם *'etsem,* "bones," and *gidh,* "sinews" (Job 10:11), and perfused with → דם *dām,* "blood." Further, God has provided it with a *lebh,* "heart" (Ps. 33:15), *kelayoth,* "kidneys" (Ps. 139:13), etc., and especially with a *nephesh* (Jer. 38:16), so that the whole man is a *nephesh chayyah,* "living soul," as long as the → רוח *rûach,* "spirit," given by the *neshamah,* "breath," of God dwells in the *basar* (cf. Job 34:14f.).

b. In its most important meaning, "body," frequently *basar* also denotes the whole external being of man. Thus, e.g., Job asks, "Is my body (*basar*) made of bronze?" (Job 6:12); and when he thinks of his misfortune, a shuddering seizes his body (*basar,* 21:6). One psalmist laments over his physical weakness: "My *basar* (body) is failing and has become thin" (Ps. 109:24), and another says that because of the anger of God there is no soundness in his "body" (38:4,8[3,7]). The Preacher declares: "Much study is a weariness of the flesh" (Eccl. 12:12). *'akhal,* "to devour" (Isa. 9:19[20]; 49:26; Zec. 11:9; Ps. 27:2), and *sabha',* "to be satisfied" (Job 19:22), are used with *basar* to denote the destruction of the whole outer existence of man. We encounter a clear distinction between the physical and the spiritual in passages where *basar* is used for the outer man, and *lebh,* "heart," for the inner. But instances of this sort have in mind the whole man with his twofold, psychosomatic nature. Thus the words of the wise must be kept in the heart (*lebh*), because they are healing to the whole body (*basar,* Prov. 4:20ff.), just as a tranquil heart is healing to the body (14:30). The Preacher says that one must remove vexation from his heart and thus put away pain from his body (Eccl. 11:10). He also warns against bringing guilt on the body through the mouth (5:5[6]; in v. 1[2] *peh,* "mouth," appears in parallelism with *lebh,* "heart").

The equally clear distinction that is made between *basar* and *nephesh,* "soul," is quite remarkable, especially in those texts where both ideas are also used to denote the external or the internal, spiritual aspect of man. Here again, man is viewed as a whole, including his external and his internal being. The psalmist's

nephesh, "soul," thirsts for God, and his *basar,* "flesh, body," faints for him
(Ps. 63:2[1]); his *nephesh* longs, yea faints, for the courts of Yahweh, his heart
and *basar* sing for joy to the living God (Ps. 84:3[2]); his heart is glad, his soul
(→ כבוד *kābhôdh,* "glory")[14] rejoices, and his *basar* dwells secure (Ps. 16:9).
Thus the whole man is devoted to Yahweh, body and soul. The clear distinction
between *basar* and *nephesh* can probably be assured in Job 14:22 (the specific
exegesis of which is disputed), as well as in 13:14 and 12:10, where moreover
kol chai, "every living thing," stands in parallelism with *kol besar 'ish,* "all
mankind," and *nephesh* with *ruach,* "spirit." Undoubtedly the probably proverbial expression, *minnephesh ve'adh basar,* RSV, "both soul and body" (Isa.
10:18, "wholly"),[15] also testifies to this distinction, which seems to have been
ingrained in the consciousness of the people at that time. It is impossible to
miss the distinction intended in these passages, and yet we are not to think of
it as a dualism of soul and body in the Platonic sense. Rather, *basar* and *nephesh*
are to be understood as different aspects of man's existence as a twofold entity.
It is precisely this emphatic anthropological wholeness that is decisive for the
twofold nature of the human being. It excludes any view of a dichotomy between
basar and *nephesh,* "soul," as irreconcilably opposed to each other, and reveals
the mutual organic psychosomatic relationship between them. Thus it also gives
to the concept of personality a compact uniformity, which is expressed by a
distinct consciousness of unity. On this point one should also keep in mind the
passages mentioned above where *basar* is also prominent as an expression of
the spiritual, and exerts spiritual activity, which is characteristic elsewhere of
nephesh or of *lebh,* "heart."

2. *As a Term Used to Denote Relationship.* In this connection we must
mention the frequently emphasized similarity of all men, which is based on the
fact that all men have something in common. Thus the OT refers in particular
to the common creator of all men (Isa. 64:7[8]; etc.), or to the descent of all
men from the first human being (Wisd. 7:1ff.; → אדם *'ādhām*), to man's common
origin (Job 33:6), existence, death (34:15; Wisd. 7:5f.), birth (Job 31:15), to the
common nature of all men (10:10ff.; Ps. 33:15); etc. Generally speaking, all
these things that men have in common can be denoted by *basar,* which, as the
physical aspect of man, represents his tangible reality in an emphatic way, and
makes clear the similarity of human nature dependent on this, as well as the
relationship of men to one another as a collective idea, conditioned by the
fleshly.

a. Thus *basar* appears in the sense of "man" as a synonym of → אדם *'ādhām,*
with a neutral meaning in Lev. 13:18,24; and with a negative connotation in
Ps. 56:5(4); Dnl. 2:11 (Aram.); cf. Gen. 6:3; Jer. 17:5; Ps. 78:38.[16]

---

[14] Cf. F. Nötscher, *VT,* 2 (1952), 358ff.
[15] Cf. the unlikely interpretation, "from the throat to the genitals," suggested by Sander.
[16] See below.

b. Further, the frequent expression *kol basar,* lit. "all flesh," is instructive, especially when it has the meaning "all mankind," "every man," "any man." [17] Moreover, this expression calls to mind *kol nephesh,* "every soul," or *kol nephesh chayyah,* "every living soul," *kol neshamah,* "everything that breathes," *kol chai,* "all life, every living thing," but it has a different nuance of meaning (cf. Gen. 9:15f.), and usually does not occur in the positive sense. Since the negative qualities of human nature are connected with *basar* in the OT, *kol basar* normally appears in a derogatory sense. Consequently, men (all of whom are indeed *basar*), in their existential situation and in their general relationship to each other, are placed before God and in sharp contrast to him. Wherever *kol basar* appears as an idiom (thus with the exception of Lev. 4:11; 13:3; Nu. 8:7; etc.), the idea that the *basar* that all men share in common is used to denote their distinction from God and to emphasize their distance from him lies behind it more or less clearly. As the almighty Creator and Lord, majestically from above God alone rules, judges, and passes judgment on *kol basar,* "all flesh," as his creation. [18]

c. Sometimes *kol basar* also includes the animals subordinate to man, and then it means the whole creation. [19] Even Gen. 1 (cf. vv. 24ff., where the animals are created on the same day as man) and 2 (cf. vv. 19f., where animals are formed "out of the ground" or "from the earth," just as man is in v. 7) indicate a certain relationship between man and animals, which has to do with the external, the fleshly. At the same time, not only in Gen. 1:26f.,28 and 2:19f., but also in 6:19ff., animals stand below man. Thus the flood narrative states that man's behavior also brings divine punishment on the animals (6:12), and that God's decision concerning the fate of man also affects the animals: "I have determined to make an end of all flesh; for the earth is filled with violence through them (i.e., men); behold, I will destroy them with the earth (6:13). But the animals are also included in the expression *kol basar* in Yahweh's covenant of salvation with Noah, where, significantly, *kol basar* is used in connection with *kol nephesh chayyah,* "every living soul (RSV creature)" (9:11,15ff.).

d. *kol basar* is used a few times in the flood narrative to refer to animals alone. In these cases, it is explicitly distinguished from man (Gen. 7:21), and it appears with *min,* "from" (6:19; 7:15f.; 8:17), in order to indicate that species of animals not mentioned are excluded.

e. The relationship shared by all men in that they all are *basar* is specifically applied to the blood relationship through the so-called relationship formula. [20] In this formula, which, in light of the text as it now stands, goes back to Gen.

---

[17] See above, I.3.h.
[18] For further elaboration, see below.
[19] See above, I.3.h.
[20] See above, I.3.g.

2:23, *basar* is again used in a neutral sense, because here the main emphasis is placed on the relationship itself. Thus *'adham* (man? Adam?), after he has been made aware that his nature is different from that of the animals, and after he has declared that they have a subordinate position to man by giving names to the various species, states as → אִישׁ *'ish* (man) the concrete and predominant unity with the *'ishshah* (woman) that God took from him, a unity based on *basar,* and their common nature which is obvious at first glance: *zo'th happa'am 'etsem me'atsamai ubhasar mibbesari,* "This at last is bone of my bones and flesh of my flesh" (Gen. 2:23). This striking formula is also used in the OT to emphasize an existing blood relationship and to stress the responsibilities that this implies. [21]

f. *basar* → אחד *'echādh,* "one flesh," in Gen. 2:24 is a special case. One can find here a reference to monogamy (cf. Mal. 2:14ff.; Prov. 2:17), but also an allusion to the consummation of marriage: that which was *basar 'echadh* before the creation of the *'ishshah,* "woman" (Gen. 2:21f.), is again united into *basar 'echadh* through the consummation of marriage (2:24), and the *basar 'echadh* attested thereby bears undeniable witness to its complete unity. Perhaps an attempt to interpret the relationship formula can also be seen here.

3. *Nature and Importance.* a. The twofold appraisal of man presented above clearly sets in relief the relevant anthropological statements, which in turn make it possible to work out more completely the OT teaching on the nature and importance of man, as well as his situation before God. The characteristics, then, of *basar* are its creatureliness, its absolute dependence on God, its earthly nature, and its weakness, inadequacy, and transitoriness. If God, "in whose hand is the soul of every living thing and the breath of all mankind" (Job 12:10), "should take back his spirit and gather to himself his breath" (34:14), "all flesh would perish together" (34:15), "in which is the breath of life" (Gen. 6:17), and men, "who are dust" (3:19; cf. Ps. 103:14), "since they are but flesh, a wind that passes and comes not again" (Ps. 78:39), "will return to dust" (Job 34:15; cf. Gen. 3:19). Thus all men must die, because they are "flesh" and "dust." Then "the dust returns to the earth as it was, and the spirit returns to God who gave it" (Eccl. 12:7). Yahweh has so ordained it (Gen. 6:3; cf. 3:19). *basar* "passes away" (→ בלה *bālāh,* Lam. 3:4), "wastes away" (→ כלה *kālāh,* Job 33:21; Prov. 5:11), "dissolves, rots" (*maqaq,* Zec. 14:12), is not "bronze" (*nachush,* Job 6:12), is overcome by weariness (Eccl. 12:12), "becomes gaunt" (*kachash,* Ps. 109:24), and its "fat" (*mishman*) grows lean (*razah,* Isa. 17:4). All these characteristic features of *basar,* which denote its nature, fate, and importance, define its situation before God. The metaphor in Isa. 40:6f. especially makes this clear: "All flesh is grass, and all its beauty is like the flower of the field. The grass withers, the flower fades, when the breath of Yahweh blows upon it" (cf. Ps. 103:15f.). [22] And yet, it must be observed that not only is there a reference to the sadness of the fate of *kol basar* in this passage, but also a gentle breeze of recognition, even of

---

[21] See above.
[22] See Bratsiotis, 68ff., 73ff.

appreciation for *basar*, blows through it lightly, because in connection with all the transitoriness of *basar*, it also refers to its simple and natural beauty and adornment (*chesedh*, v. 17).

b. Many statements allow an ethical evaluation of *basar*, which also appear "as ethically susceptible" and "inclining toward sin." [23] Eccl. 2:3; 5:5(6); and 11:10 must be taken into consideration in making such an evaluation. In these passages, *basar* appears to be inclined toward moral excesses, and thus susceptible to sin. Gen. 6:12, which attributes the corruption of the earth to the general corruption of all flesh, points in a different direction. V. 13 connects the foregoing evaluation of *kol basar*, "all flesh," with the announcement of God's resolution: "I have determined (resolved) to make an end of all flesh (the LXX has characteristically *pántes ánthrōpoi*, all men); for the earth is filled with violence through them (i.e., men)." Thus *kol basar* (and not *kol nephesh*, "every soul") shows itself to be unworthy and sinful before God, not only because it has fallen into sin, but also because it is the cause of corruption in the surrounding world. The continually problematic passage, Gen. 6:3, where Yahweh appoints a specific length for man's life in view of his depravity, is very important. Here Yahweh says: *lo' yadhon ruchi bha'adham le'olam beshaggam hu' bhasar*, "My spirit shall not abide in man for ever, for he is flesh." Whether this means that God wants to protect his spirit "against being exposed to too much danger through the flesh" [24] cannot be said with certainty. But it cannot be denied that in this passage sin is intimately connected with *basar*, and that it is also used to denote the ethical aspect of man, in spite of the cosmic dualism between *ruach yhvh*, "the spirit of Yahweh," and *basar* (which is here par. to *'adham*, "man"). Moreover, it can be maintained with certainty that *basar* as a designation of man (so esp. in Ps. 56:5[4]; 78:39; as well as *kol basar*), [25] and especially as an antithesis to God (so Jer. 17:5; Job 10:4; 2 Ch. 32:8), [26] not only emphasizes all the characteristics of *basar* that have been mentioned, but also reflects its ethical inadequacy and inclination to sin as well as its physical nature.

The positive attitude toward *basar* in Ezk. 36:26 (cf. 11:19), where Yahweh promises to give a "new heart" and a "new spirit" to the true Israel, and to take out of their flesh (*basar*) the "stony heart" and give them a "fleshly heart" (*lebh basar*), is an exception. Here *lebh chadhash*, "new heart," is equated with *lebh basar*, "fleshly heart," in contrast to *lebh ha'ebhen*, "stony heart." Consequently, this passage represents a significant step in the direction of bridging the gulf between *ruach* and *basar*, because it places them side by side, not as opposites, but as positive powers, or one might say as allies. To be sure, all this will take place in the future. And yet the ethical dimension of *basar* is also illuminated by the statement made here.

---

[23] Scharbert, 77.

[24] So Scharbert, 80.

[25] See above.

[26] In addition, see IV.

IV. Use in Theological Sense (God and basar). It is significant for the OT concept of God that, in spite of the frequent use of anthropomorphisms in the OT, God is never referred to as being *basar* as in the case of *nephesh*, "soul." Rather, the OT emphasizes that God is not *basar*, and sharply distinguishes him from all *basar*. Whenever *basar* is connected with God, it simply emphasizes the immense distance and difference of flesh from God, the complete dependence of flesh on God, and the striking antithesis between flesh and God. This serves to bring out the nature and characteristics of God, especially his superiority, eternity, omnipotence, goodness, holiness, providence, etc., in short, everything that stands in contrast to the nature and characteristics of man. In the OT, this contrast is expressed in particular by the word *ruach*, "spirit." While man is characterized as *basar* to distinguish him from God, generally speaking God is characterized as *ruach*. In addition to Gen. 6:3, which has already been mentioned, Isa. 31:3 should also be cited: "The Egyptians are men, and not God; and their horses are flesh, and not spirit." Not only does this statement contrast *'adham*, "man," with *'el*, "God," and *basar* with *ruach*, but it also places these opposites in parallelism with one another, so that *'adham–lo' 'el*, "men–not God," is synonymous with *basar–lo' ruach*, "flesh–not spirit." In this sense, Job asks God in Job 10:4: "Hast thou eyes of flesh? Dost thou see as man sees?" (cf. the LXX rendering of *basar* by *brotós*, "mortal man"). Here *ra'ah 'enosh*, "man sees," which stands in parallelism with *'ene bhasar*, "eyes of flesh," is the opposite of divine seeing. Similarly, in 2 Ch. 32:8 the "arm of flesh" stands in contrast to "Yahweh our God will help us." In Jer. 17:5 ("the man who trusts in man and makes flesh his arm, whose heart turns away from Yahweh"), *'adham* and *basar* form the antithesis to *yhvh*. Similarly Ps. 56:5(4) characterizes man as flesh, and contrasts *'elohim*, "God," with *basar* (cf. also Dnl. 2:11).

Except in Ezk. 10:12, where *kol basar* is used in a figurative sense to describe the form of the cherubim, *basar* never refers to a heavenly being. And God has absolutely no need of *basar* for food. Thus he asks those bringing sacrifices: "Do I eat the flesh of bulls, or drink the blood of goats?" (Ps. 50:13). Indeed, his angel (→ מלאך *mal'ākh*) completely refuses the meal Gideon has prepared for him including flesh, and changes the flesh that was offered into a burnt-offering (Jgs. 6:19ff.). In a figurative sense, the OT avoids attributing to Yahweh enjoyment of flesh (Dt. 32:42).

The OT frequently affirms Yahweh's superiority over all flesh. Yahweh declares that he is the God of all flesh (Jer. 32:27), and his people are to honor him as such. At the same time, his dominion also includes the *ruach*, "spirit," dwelling in *basar* (Nu. 16:22; 27:16, *yhvh 'elohe haruchoth lekhol basar*, "Yahweh, the God of the spirits of all flesh"; the LXX, which reads *vekhol basar*, "and of all flesh," emphasizes even more the dualism between mortal flesh and life-giving spirit). God, the exalted and omnipotent creator, lets his spirit abide in *basar*, which he has formed (Job 10:11), [27] as long as he wishes (Gen. 6:3), [28] and thereby gives man life. And when he "in whose hand is the spirit of all

---

[27] See above, III.1.a.
[28] See above.

human flesh" (Job 12:10) takes back his spirit, all flesh must die (34:15). Likewise, he can call the dead to life, for he can cause "flesh" to come upon their dry bones and put his spirit in them again, so that they will be alive again (Ezk. 37:1ff.–used symbolically of the revival of the people). He also has control over health and disease, and the physical condition of *basar* in general (Ex. 4:7; 2 K. 4:34; 5:10,14; Ps. 38:4[3]; Job 2:5; 33:25; Lam. 3:4; etc.); he determines the fate of *kol basar,* "all flesh" (Gen. 6:12f.,17; 7:21).

In his exalted goodness, which also manifests itself as omnipotent providence, God is the one "who gives food to all flesh" (Ps. 136:25). Thus he sees to it that the rebellious Israelites are given food (flesh and manna) in the wilderness (Ex. 16:8,12; cf. Nu. 11:4,13,18,21,33), and has the ravens bring flesh to his prophet (1 K. 17:6).

To God "all flesh comes" (Ps. 65:3[2]), and "all flesh shall bless his holy name for ever and ever" (Ps. 145:21). Likewise, the godly man sings for joy to him with his "body" (Ps. 84:3[2]), or faints (longs) for him (Ps. 63:2), and the upright is convinced that he also will see God "without his flesh" (Job 19:26). [29]

As the perfect and holy one, God cannot bear the corruption of "all flesh," and he determines to destroy *kol basar* (Gen. 6:13). On the whole, because of man's sin, God limited their life-span to 120 years, "for they are flesh" (6:3). In this light the frequently attested OT belief that everyone who sees God must die (Ex. 19:21; 20:19; Lev. 16:2; Nu. 4:20; Dt. 5:24ff.; 18:16; Jgs. 6:22f.; 13:22; Isa. 6:5; etc.) is to be understood. "For who is a mortal man (RSV, who is there of all flesh, *kol basar*), that has heard the voice of the living God speaking out of the midst of fire, as we have, and has still lived?" (Dt. 5:26). It is in the same light that we are to understand the covering of the nakedness (*basar*) of the priesthood when they come before Yahweh, "lest they bring guilt upon themselves and die" (Ex. 28:42f.; cf. Lev. 6:3 [10]; 16:4), and also the fact that OT authors use *kol basar* in particular contexts that contrast man with the exalted and holy God. Thus, "Be silent, all flesh, before Yahweh; for he has roused himself from his holy dwelling" (Zec. 2:17[13]). Also, "the body (flesh)" of the godly "trembles for fear of him (God)" (Ps. 119:120), and in connection with a vision, "the hair of one's body (flesh) stands up" (Job 4:15).

When Yahweh "enters into judgment with all flesh, he delivers the wicked to the sword" (Jer. 25:31), "for by fire will Yahweh execute judgment, and by his sword, upon all flesh" (Isa. 66:16). Whereas the community of those faithful to God (*kol basar*) will come again and again to worship him (66:23b), the dead bodies of the wicked "shall be an abhorrence to all flesh" (66:24b). When he "brings evil upon all flesh" (Jer. 45:5), "no flesh has peace" (12:12), for "his sword shall devour flesh" (Dt. 32:42). Yahweh summons all birds to a gruesome sacrificial meal on the mountains of Israel with the cry: "You shall eat flesh, ... you shall eat the flesh of the mighty" (Ezk. 39:17f.). Yahweh's vengeful sword against Jerusalem and Ammon (Ezk. 21) is no less frightening. Using the figure of a forest fire, first of all he affirms that all flesh will see that he has kindled it. Then he declares: "Because I will cut off from you both righteous and wicked,

---

[29] The interpretation of this verse is disputed; see the comms.

therefore my sword shall go out of its sheath against all flesh from south to north; and all flesh shall know that I Yahweh..." (vv. 9f.[4f.]). Also, the "flesh" of all the nations that wage war against Jerusalem "shall rot" (Zec. 14:12), and Yahweh affirms, "I will make your oppressors eat their own flesh, ... then all flesh shall know that I am the Lord your Savior, and your Redeemer" (Isa. 49:26).

But the OT also speaks of Yahweh pardoning *basar*. He does not let *kol basar* perish in the flood (Gen. 6:19; 7:15f.; 8:17), in order that afterward he may make an everlasting covenant with *kol basar* that was saved, so that never again shall "all flesh" be cut off by the waters of a flood (9:11; cf. vv. 15ff.). Likewise he puts the sign of his covenant with Abraham in the *basar* of every male covenant member (17:11,14,23ff.). And Ps. 78:38f. explains the history of salvation: "Yet he, being compassionate, forgave their iniquity, and did not destroy them; he restrained his anger often. ... He remembered that they were but flesh." Further, Yahweh declares through the prophets that he will give a "fleshly heart" to the true Israel (Ezk. 11:19; 36:26), and "that the glory of Yahweh shall be revealed and 'all flesh' shall see it together, for the mouth of Yahweh has spoken" (Isa. 40:5). But this announcement in particular appears to be the high point of the divine pardon: "It shall come to pass afterward, that I will pour out my spirit on 'all flesh'; your sons and your daughters shall prophesy" (Joel 3:1[2:28]).

N. P. Bratsiotis

בַּת *bath*

Contents: I. 1. Occurrences: a. *bath* By Itself; b. In Proper Names; 2. Meaning in the OT. II. Position and Evaluation of a Daughter: 1. In Comparison with a Son; 2. Parental Authority to Dispose of a Daughter; 3. Individual Rights of a Daughter; 4. Danger; 5. Laws in the Holiness Code.

I. 1. *Occurrences.*

a. *bath* By Itself. *bath* is a common Semitic word, but it does not occur alone in Ethiopic (where it is found only in the expression *benta 'ain*, "the pupil of the eye").

The original form lying behind *bath* is *bant, bint*.[1] In Ugaritic this word appears as *bt*, pl. *bnt*,[2] in Phoenician-Punic as *bt*,[3] in Old Aramaic as (const.)

---

bath. See the bibliography under → בֵּן *bēn*, "son."

[1] *BLe*, § 618 l.
[2] *UT*, Glossary, No. 481.
[3] J. Friedrich-W. Röllig, *Phön.-Pun. Gramm.* (Rome, ²1970), § 240, with examples.

brt,[4] in Official Aramaic (never in the OT!) as *brh, br'*, const. *brt*,[5] and in Jewish Aramaic (the Targumim and the Bab. texts) as *berattā'* (but in the Galilean dialect as *bertā'*). It is also attested in Syriac (*bartā*), Mandean (*berata*), Akkadian (*bintu, bunatu, buntu;* rare and literary), Arabic (*bint*), and Old South Arabic *(bnt, bt)*.

The following synonyms should be mentioned in Akkadian: *mārtu (mer'atum, mērtu, māštu); apiltu, aplatu,* "heiress"; *bukurtu, bukratu* (only for goddesses). Egyp. *s3.t,* usually without a determinative, means one's own daughter, especially in a genealogical context (daughter of..., who...), but also denotes the mythical daughterhood of a goddess or a queen (thus *s3.t R'* as the female counterpart to the royal title); while *s3.ty* means "the two daughters," "the two children." [6]

b. *In Proper Names.* The only proper name compounded with *bath* that is certainly attested in the OT is *bath-shebha'*, "Bathsheba" (2 S. 11:3; etc.). [7] In Old Babylonian we find Bitti-ᵈDagan, Bitatum, [8] ᶠBitta-addi, [9] Bitta-kubi, [10] and Bitta-malki. [11] There are no examples from Mari. In Assyrian we find ᶠBiniti. [12] In Ugaritic we find *bthzli, btsgld, btšy,* ᶠ*bitta-rapi'*, ᶠ*bat-rapi'* and ᶠ*bitta-ṣidqi;* [13] and in Aramaic, *btzbynh* and *bt'dn.* [14]

2. *Meaning in the OT.* a. The nuances of meaning of *bath* coincide to a great extent with those of → בֵּן *bēn,* "son." Above all, *bath* means "one's own daughter" (Gen. 11:29; 19:8; Ex. 2:5; etc.). Our word "children," which includes both sexes, is usually expressed by *banim ubhanoth,* "sons and daughters" (Gen. 5:4; etc.), [15] and these two words are used in parallelism in poetic texts of the OT (Isa. 49:22; 60:4). In the expression *ke'immah bittah,* "Like mother, like daughter" (Ezk. 16:44) *bath* means "one's own daughter."

On the other hand, *bath 'abhi,* "daughter of my father," or *bath 'immi,* "daughter of my mother," means "half-sister" (i.e., two people have only the same father or the same mother, cf. Gen. 20:12; Lev. 18:9,11; 20:17; Dt. 27:22; Ezk. 22:11). *benoth banav,* "his sons' daughters" (Gen. 46:7), means granddaughters (cf. Lev. 18:10: *bath binkha,* "your son's daughter," and *bath bittkha,* "your daughter's daughter"), but *bath* alone can also have this meaning (2 K. 8:26:

---

[4] *IEJ,* 8 (1958), 228-230.
[5] *DISO,* 42.
[6] *WbÄS,* III, 411f.
[7] See I.2.e.; on *bath shua',* cf. *KBL³.*
[8] T. Bauer, *Die Ostkanaanäer* (Leipzig, 1926), 16.
[9] D. J. Wiseman, *The Alalakh Tablets* (London, 1953), Plate V 7:2,5,6,15,22,30,34-36; Plate XXXVII 367:4.
[10] *Ibid.,* No. 278:6.
[11] *Ibid.,* No. 131.
[12] K. L. Tallqvist, *Assyrian Personal Names* (Helsingfors, 1918), 275; uncertain, possibly Arabic.
[13] F. Gröndahl, *PNU,* 55, 119; see *UF,* 1 (1969), 212, where it is shown that *bt-* does not always mean "daughter."
[14] *IPN,* 14; there are no examples from Elephantine.
[15] See below, II.

Athaliah, the "daughter" of Omri). *benoth 'acheykha,* "the daughters of your brothers" (Jgs. 14:3), are hardly female cousins;[16] instead, they are the daughters of the tribal brothers. In Gen. 24:48, *bath 'achi,* "daughter of my brother," means "niece." In Gen. 37:35 and Jgs. 12:9, the *banoth* are the daughters-in-law. Similarly, in Ruth 1:13-15; 2:2,22; 3:1,16,18, the mother-in-law calls her daughters-in-law "daughter." *bath dodho,* "daughter of his uncle" (Est. 2:7), is a female cousin.

b. *bath* can also mean "(young) woman" in a very general sense. Thus the *benoth 'anshe ha'ir,* "daughters of the men of the city" (Gen. 24:13), are the young girls of the city. In Gen. 34:8, in contrast to her brothers (not the citizens of the city!),[17] Dinah is called *bittekhem,* "your daughter." *benoth 'ammekha,* "the daughters of your people" (Ezk. 13:17), and *benoth 'iri,* "the daughters of my city" (Lam. 3:51), do not denote a certain stage of life, but simply the feminine part of the nation or of the city. The *benoth tsiyyon,* "daughters of Zion" (Isa. 3:16f.; 4:4; Cant. 3:10), are the women of Jerusalem, while the *benoth ha'adham,* "daughters of men" (Gen. 6:2,4), are the women of the entire human race.

Other passages in which *bath* means girl, young woman, or woman (in general) are Gen. 30:13 (the daughters of the nation); Isa. 32:9 (par. to *nashim,* "women"); Prov. 31:29; Cant. 2:2; 6:9; Dnl. 11:17 (par. to *bath hannashim,* "the daughter of women"). In Ruth 2:8; 3:10 (Boaz to Ruth); and Ps. 45:11 (Eng. v. 10), *bath* is used in a familiar address.

c. This explains the use of *bath* as a personification of Jerusalem in the prophetic and poetic literature, which can be seen especially in the expression *bath tsiyyon,* "daughter of Zion": Isa. 1:8; 52:2 (par. to *yerushalayim,* "Jerusalem"); 62:11; Jer. 4:31; 6:2,23; Mic. 1:13; 4:10,13; Zeph. 3:14 (par. to *bath yerushalayim,* "daughter of Jerusalem"); Zec. 2:14(10); 9:9 (par. to *bath yerushalayim*); Ps. 9:15(14); Lam. 1:6; 2:1 (par. to *tiph'ereth yisra'el,* "the splendor of Israel"), 4; 4:22. This expression is given particular emphasis and clarity in the form *bethulath bath tsiyyon,* "the virgin daughter of Zion" (2 K. 19:21 par.; Lam. 2:13). The phrases *har bath tsiyyon,* "the mount of the daughter of Zion" (Isa. 10:32 [according to the emended text], par. to *gibh'ath yerushalayim,* "the hill of Jerusalem"; 16:1), and *'ophel bath tsiyyon,* "hill of the daughter of Zion" (Mic. 4:8), mean Zion. *ziqne bhath tsiyyon,* "the elders of the daughter of Zion" (Lam. 2:10), denotes the elders, *chomath bath tsiyyon,* "the wall of the daughter of Zion" (Lam. 2:8,18), the city wall of Jerusalem, and *shebhiyyah bath tsiyyon,* "captive daughter of Zion" (Isa. 52:2), the captured city. The expression *bath 'ammi,* "the daughter of my people" (Isa. 22:4; Jer. 4:11; etc.), meaning the national community, should also be mentioned here.

But other cities and nations can also be personified under the same figure: *bath tsor,* "daughter of Tyre," the city of Tyre (Ps. 45:13 [12]); (*bethulath,* from → בתולה *bethûlāh*) *bath babhel* and *bath kasdim,* "(virgin) daughter of

---

[16] Contra *KBL*[3], 158.
[17] *Ibid.*

Babylon, of the Chaldeans," the city of Babylon (Ps. 137:8; Isa. 47:1); *bath tarshish*, the city of Tarshish (Isa. 23:10); (*bethulath*) *bath tsidhon*, the city of Sidon (23:12); *bath 'edhom*, the land of Edom (Lam. 4:21f.); (*bethulath*) *bath mitsrayim*, the land of Egypt (Jer. 46:11,24); cf. also *yoshebheth bath mitsrayim*, "inhabitant of the daughter of Egypt" (46:19), and *yoshebheth bath dibhon*, "inhabitant of the daughter of Dibon" (48:18), the inhabitants of Egypt/Dibon. *bath yehudhah* (Lam. 2:2,5) means the region of Judah.

d. Like → בֵּן *bēn*, "son," [18] *bath* denotes membership in a city, a land, or a tribe: *benoth cheth*, "daughters of Heth," Hittite women (Gen. 27:46); *benoth menashsheh*, the women of Manasseh (Josh. 17:6); *benoth yisra'el*, the women of Israel (Jgs. 11:40; 2 S. 1:24); *benoth shilo*, the women of Shiloh (Jgs. 21:21); *benoth mo'abh*, the women of Moab (Nu. 25:1; on the other hand, this same expression in Isa. 16:2 means the cities of Moab); [19] *benoth kena'an*, the women of Canaan (Gen. 28:1,6,8; 36:2); and *bath levi*, a Levite woman (Ex. 2:1). The women or girls of Jerusalem are addressed as *benoth yerushalayim*, "daughters of Jerusalem" (Cant. 1:5; 2:7; 3:5,10; 5:8,16; 8:4), and *benoth tsiyyon*, "daughters of Zion" (3:11).

e. *bath* can also be used to connote a moral (or physical) characteristic. Thus a *bath beliyya'al*, "daughter of Belial," is a worthless or base woman (1 S. 1:16). *bath nadhibh*, "noble daughter" (Cant. 7:2[1]), is to be interpreted as a commendatory address: "high-born," "titled lady," and in its context it pertains to the outward appearance rather than to the intention. *bath gedhudh*, "daughter of a troop" (Mic. 4:14[5:1]), probably means [20] a warlike city. The meaning of the expression *habbath hashshobhebhah* (RSV, "faithless daughter," used of Israel in Jer. 31:22 and of Ammon in 49:4) is more difficult to determine. Recent exegetes see here an allusion not to apostasy, but to returning home. [21]

Here we should mention the feminine name Bathsheba: daughter of seven = daughter of abundance = "the abundant one" or "Fortune's favorite." [22] It is doubtful that Gomer, *bath dibhlayim* (RSV, "the daughter of Diblaim," Hos. 1:3), belongs here, and that this expression means "the girl of two fig-cakes," i.e., the cheap girl, or that it denotes a female devotee of Ishtar (fig-cakes were used in her cult, Jer. 7:18). *Dibhlayim* is probably a proper name. [23]

bath is also frequently used in expressions denoting age: *bath tish'im shanah*, lit. "a daughter of ninety years," referring to Sarah at the age of ninety (Gen. 17:17); *bath shenathah*, lit. "a daughter of a year," referring to a year-old (ewe) lamb (Lev. 14:10; Nu. 6:14; 15:27).

---

[18] Cf. → בֵּן *bēn*, III.4.

[19] See f.

[20] If the text is correct; cf. *BHS* and *KBL*[3], 170.

[21] W. Rudolph, *HAT*, 12 ([3]1968); daughter to whom homecoming beckons; A. Weiser, *ATD*, XX/XXI ([5]1966): daughter who should return home.

[22] Cf. recently J. J. Stamm, *SVT*, 16 (1967), 324.

[23] According to Rudolph, *KAT*, XIII/1, 50f., we should read *Debal-Yam* here.

f. Finally, there are numerous examples of the use of *bath* in a figurative sense. Thus the (fortified) daughter cities of a great city can be called *banoth*, "daughters":[24] Nu. 21:25,32; 32:42; Josh. 15:45,47; 17:16; Jgs. 1:27; 11:26; Neh. 11:25-31; 1 Ch. 2:23; 7:28f.; 8:12; 18:1; 2 Ch. 13:19; 28:18. *benoth mo'abh*, "the daughters of Moab," in Isa. 16:2 are the cities of Moab, "the daughters of Rabbah" in Jer. 49:2f., the cities of the Ammonites, and *benoth yehudhah*, "the daughters of Judah," in Ps. 48:12(11) and 97:8, the rural towns of Judah.

In Gen. 49:22, the (vine-)branches or shoots are called *banoth*, "daughters." *benoth hashshir*, "daughters of song," is a poetic expression for "musical notes" or "songs" (Eccl. 12:4). *'ishon bath 'ayin*, "the pupil of the daughter of the eye," is a complicated phrase; in Ps. 17:8 it means "eyeball"; but in Lam. 2:18 (where it is par. to *dim'ah*, "tears") it may mean tears that flow therefrom.

The name of the gate *bath rabbim*, "daughter of many" (Cant. 7:5[4]), is hard to interpret. Possibly there could be hidden in this expression the name of a city unknown to us, or perhaps it is a very general term meaning "a great, populous city."[25] Jackals and ostriches are called *bath hayya'anah*, "daughter of wailing" (Lev. 11:16; Dt. 14:15), and *benoth ya'anah*, "daughters of wailing" (Mic. 1:8; Job 30:29; Isa. 13:21; 34:13; 43:20; Jer. 50:39). In Mic. 1:8, these are a symbol of a wailing howl, but in other passages a common figure for destitution and destruction. *bath putsai*, "daughter of my dispersion" (Zeph. 3:10; = "my dispersed ones"), is probably a corrupt reading.

II. Position and Evaluation of a Daughter.

1. *In Comparison with a Son.* The extent to which a daughter was considered to be inferior to a son in the OT is already indicated by the fact that *ben* occurs about ten times as often as *bath*.[26] Although *banim*, lit. "sons," alone can be used for children of both sexes,[27] ordinarily *banim ubhanoth*, "sons and daughters," is used to express this, and always in this order (about 110 times!). According to ancient belief, the blessing of complete godliness must result in a greater number of sons than of daughters (Job 1:2; 42:13; cf. Ps. 127:3f.; 128:3); and although the woman is called "the mother of all living" (Gen. 3:20), the continuation of a daughter's life is less important than that of a son's (Ex. 1:16). However, sons and daughters alike are the embodiment of an abundant blessing (Ps. 144:12). In them are extended, sometimes happily and sometimes tragically, the life of parents (Dt. 28:41; Jer. 16:2; 29:6).

2. *Parental Authority to Dispose of a Daughter.* The father has the authority to dispose of his daughter. In her parents' home, the daughter is a profitable

---

[24] Cf. L. Delekat, *VT*, 14 (1964), 9-11.

[25] So W. Rudolph, *KAT*, XVII/2 (1966).

[26] According to *KBL*[3], *ben*, "son," occurs about 4850 times, and *bath*, "daughter," about 585.

[27] Cf. → בֵּן *bēn*, III.1.

laborer (Gen. 24:15; 29:9; Ex. 20:10 par.), a financial benefit that can be sold and for whom a bridal price (*mohar*) must be paid (Gen. 29:15-30; 34:12; Ex. 22:15f.[16f.], Hos. 3:2). Daughters are "given" and "taken" (Gen. 34:9,16,21; Ex. 2:21; 6:25; 34:16; Dt. 7:3; Josh. 15:16f.; Jgs. 1:12f.; 21:1,7,18; 1 S. 18:17, 19; 2 K. 14:9; etc.). Nevertheless, it would be wrong to compare the bride price with a price in the modern economic sense, esp. since the father restored it (at least in part) to his daughter as a dowry, as Gen. 31:15 shows. According to CH § 164, the dowry is even higher than the selling price of a woman. [28] If the king wishes to favor someone in a special way, he gives him his daughter in marriage (1 S. 17:25; 18:17ff.). But according to ancient law, the father can also sell his daughter as a slave (Ex. 21:7).

On the other hand, it is a "great task" to give a daughter in marriage to a good man (Sir. 7:25). To accomplish this a father must strictly guard and keep his daughter (7:24; 42:9-12). The Deuteronomic law prescribes the punishment of death by stoning for a daughter who plays the harlot in her father's house (Dt. 22:21). To be sure, Lot's behavior toward his two daughters "who had not yet known a man" (Gen. 19:8; cf. Jgs. 19:24) shows how close guarding one's daughters and surrendering them could be at times.

3. *Individual Rights of a Daughter.* However, along with the strict authority of the father, the daughter retained her own personal sphere. The words of the beautiful, proud Rebekah (Gen. 24:24) reflect a spirit of self-assurance. The father-daughter relationship is not without affection. The love between father and daughter is impressively described, e.g., in the Jephthah narrative (Jgs. 11:34-40), or in the parable of the poor man who felt toward his only little ewe lamb as he did toward a daughter (2 S. 12:3).

In contrast to the earlier law (Ex. 23:17; 34:23), the Deuteronomic law allows the daughter also to participate in the cult (Dt. 12:12,18; 16:11,14). The father is anxious lest his married daughter be ousted from her position by other wives (Gen. 31:50). If a man left no sons behind, but only daughters, they alone would have a right to his inheritance (Nu. 27:1-11; Josh. 17:3f.; cf. Job 42:15), provided, of course, that they marry only within the same tribe (Nu. 36:1-12).

4. *Danger.* A daughter is subjected to sexual taboos more than a son. Therefore, her immoral behavior also leads to more catastrophic consequences. Even the birth of a daughter brings about a twofold uncleanness in comparison with that of a son, because it is clearly believed "that the female sex was more easily accessible to and more strongly exposed to demonic influences than the male." [29] A daughter rising up against her mother is regarded as a sign of great moral ruin (Mic. 7:6). Foreign cults penetrate into Israel through the daughters of foreign nations (Nu. 25:1f.,6; Dt. 7:3; Jgs. 3:6; 1 K. 11:1ff.; 16:31-33; Mal. 2:11), and according to Gen. 6:1-4 the *benoth ha'adham,* "daughters of men," even

---

[28] On this whole matter, cf. W. Plautz, "Die Form der Eheschliessung im AT," *ZAW,* 76 (1964), 298-318.

[29] K. Elliger, *HAT,* 4 (1966), 158.

seduce the *bene ha'elohim,* "sons of God,"[30] by their beauty. In Ezk. 16:44ff. (secondary), the cities of Samaria, Jerusalem, and Sodom (personified as daughters) with their daughters are described as the sum total of debauchery.

5. *Laws in the Holiness Code.* In the law in Lev. 18, the daughter-in-law (v. 15), the father's wife's daughter, i.e., half-sister (v. 11; cf. 20:17; Dt. 27:22; Ezk. 22:11),[31] and the granddaughter (that is, the daughter of one's son or [secondary] of one's daughter, v. 10) are explicitly named among the relatives with whom sexual intercourse is forbidden. It must be assumed that originally a person's own daughter was also named.[32] It is considered particularly reprehensible for one to encourage his daughter to practice cult prostitution (Lev. 19:29). The daughter of a priest shares in the priestly holiness in a special way (21:9; 22:12f.).

H. Haag

---

[30] Cf. → בֵּן *bēn,* IV.2.c.
[31] On Lev. 18:9, cf. Elliger, *HAT,* 4 (1966), 231f., 240.
[32] Cf. K. Elliger, *ZAW,* 67 (1955), 2, 7.

בְּתוּלָה *bᵉthûlāh;* בְּתוּלִים *bᵉthûlîm*

Contents: I. In the Ancient Near East: 1. Egypt; 2. Mesopotamia; 3. Ugarit. II. Etymology. III. Meaning: 1. General Synopsis; 2. Job 31:1; 3. In the Law. IV. Summation; Observations on Isa. 7:14.

I. In the Ancient Near East.

1. *Egypt.* The Egyptian words for "girl, virgin," are *ꜥdd.t,*[1] *rnn.t,*[2] and especially *ḥwn.t.*[3] This last word is already attested in the Pyramid Texts, including the expression, "the girl in the eye," i.e., the pupil. It means "girl, virgin," in a general sense, but can also denote the young marriageable woman in particular. The Pyramid Texts speak of "the great virgin" (*ḥwn.t wr.t*) three

---

bᵉthûlāh. O. J. Baab, "Virgin," *IDB,* IV (1962), 787f.; G. Delling, "παρθένος," *TDNT,* V, 826-837; J. J. Finkelstein, "Sex Offenses in Sumerian Laws," *JAOS,* 86 (1966), 355-372; E. S. Hartom-J. J. Rabinowitz, *"betûlāh ...," EMiqr,* II (1954), 381-84; B. Landsberger, "Jungfräulichkeit: ein Beitrag zum Thema 'Beilager und Eheschliessung,'" *Symbolae iuridicae ... M. David ... edid. J. A. Ankum ...,* II (Leiden, 1968), 41-105; E. Neufeld, *Ancient Hebrew Marriage Laws* (London, 1944), 95, 100f.; A. Strobel, "Jungfrau," *BHHW,* II (1964), 914f.; G. J. Wenham, "Betulah, 'A Girl of Marriageable Age,'" *VT,* 22 (1972), 326-348; and the bibliography under → עלמה *'almāh.*

[1] *WbÄS,* I, 242.
[2] *WbÄS,* II, 435.
[3] *WbÄS,* III, 53.

times (682c, 728a, 2002a, cf. 809c); she is anonymous, appears as the protectress of the king, and is explicitly called his mother once (809c). It is interesting that Isis is addressed as *ḥwn.t* in a sarcophagus oracle that deals with her mysterious pregnancy. [4] In a text in the Abydos Temple of Seti I, Isis herself declares: "I am the great virgin." [5] In the Legend of the Birth of Hatshepsut, Queen Ahmose is characteristically presented to Amon as a virgin (*ḥwn.t*)[6] and "the most beautiful of all women." In this context it is to be observed that her husband is called a "young child," which apparently means that the young king was not able to consummate the marriage; thus the queen, although married, is a virgin. [7] Therefore, the sole fatherhood of Amon cannot be doubted. In the Legend of the Youth of Hatshepsut that follows, Hatshepsut herself is described as "a beautiful young girl" (*ḥwn.t*). [8]

In the Late Period in particular, goddesses are frequently called "(beautiful) virgins," especially Hathor, Isis, and Nephthys. As a virgin, Hathor also has virgins that wait on her. [9] It is well known that the wives of Amon in Thebes lived in celibacy as consecrated to this god alone. [10] A Ptolemaic papyrus gives an account of cultically motivated virginity. It is expressly said of the two women who played the roles of Isis and Nephthys as mourners that they should be women of a pure body, whose wombs had not been opened. [11] Summarizing, it can be stated that *ḥwn.t* is not used to denote biological virginity, but rather youthful vigor and potential motherhood. However, there are important points of contact in the Egyptian texts and representative art with the Hellenistic idea of *Isis parthénos* and the virginity of the mother-goddess.

2. *Mesopotamia*. The Akk. *batultu* [12] means primarily a young marriageable woman. [13] Only now and then do the Akkadian texts emphasize that it denotes a *virgo intacta*. [14] Otherwise, "young (unmarried) girl" always seems to be the translation necessitated by the context. [15] *batultu* does not occur as a divine epithet.

3. *Ugarit*. The Ugar. *btlt* is an epithet of the goddess ʿAnat. However, it is not entirely clear what this means. Obviously ʿAnat is not a virgin in the modern sense of the word, since she has sexual intercourse repeatedly. [16] Either this

---

4 De Buck, *CT*, II, 217d.

5 Calverley, *Abydos*, I, Plate 9.

6 *Urk.*, IV, 218, 17.

7 H. Brunner, *Die Geburt des Gottkönigs* (1964), 27ff.

8 *Urk.*, IV, 246, 6f.

9 P. Derchain, *REg*, 21 (1969), 19ff.

10 *RÄR*, 578ff.

11 Bremner-Rhind Papyrus, I, 2f.

12 *AHw*, 115; *CAD*, II, 173f.

13 Cf. *CAD*, II, 174: "primarily an age group."

14 *KAV*, 1, VIII 6, 21 (Landsberger, 58).

15 See Landsberger, 57f.

16 Cf. A. van Selms, *Marriage and Family Life in Ugaritic Literature* (London, 1954), 69, 109.

epithet emphasizes her unchangeable youth and beauty, [17] or it means that in spite of everything she has borne no children. [18] Hillers emphasizes that the virgin ʿAnat is the mourner par excellence. [19]

Bergman-Ringgren

II. Etymology. The Ugar. *btlt*, [20] Aram. *btwlh, btwlt'*, Akk. *batūlu* (masc.), *batultu* (fem.), and Arab. *batūl* (*batīl*) (fem.) are cognate with Heb. *bethulah* (also Middle Heb.). Usually the words that are translated "virgin" (with the exception of Akk. *batūlu*) are connected with Arab. *btl*, "to cut off, separate." Of course, there is nothing in the phonetic history that stands in the way of this etymology, but it encounters other difficulties: 1. It assumes that men are the indirect object of the separation (of the girl), but for the ancient Near Eastern civilization the idea of separation could apply much better to a married woman. Since the medieval Arabic lexicographers believed that *batūl* meant "virgin," it is understandable that they would adopt the etymology being questioned here, [21] but their opinion is not final in this matter. The word means "palm shoot or palm scion; one consecrated to God; virgin"; this last meaning may go back to Aramaic or Hebrew influence. 2. The Akk. *batūlu*, "younger man," and Mandean *ptwl'*, "young bachelor," cannot be derived from the assumed original meaning of *batūlu* in a roundabout way through *batūltu*. 3. The feminine does not mean "virgin" in any language exclusively (Aram.), mainly (Heb.), or generally (Akk. [and Ugar.?]). [22]

Further, when one considers that, e.g., neither Gk. *parthénos* nor Lat. *virgo* originally or exclusively meant "virgo intacta," and thus that in early linguistic stages the concept of virginity, with all the meaning that belongs to it in early linguistic associations, can frequently be expressed only negatively (e.g., Akk. *ša zikaram la īdūma*, CH § 130, [23] much like Heb. *'asher lo' yadheʿu mishkabh zakhar*, Nu. 31:18, "who never has [have] had intercourse" [RSV, "who have not known man by lying with him"]), it is best to conjecture that there was an original common Semitic word *batūl(t)*, and that it meant a young girl at the age of puberty and the age just after puberty. Then very gradually this word assumed the meaning "virgo intacta" in Hebrew and Aramaic, a development that ended in Middle Hebrew, to which the German "Jungfrau" offers an instructive parallel. It is not surprising that this process of narrowing the meaning and of making it more precise is discernible in legal language. [24]

---

[17] De Moor, *UF*, 1 (1969), 224.

[18] *UF*, 1, 182; cf. p. 224, where it is shown that the idea that ʿAnat had given birth to a calf is false.

[19] D. R. Hillers, *AB*, VIIA, 21; cf. → בעל *baʿal*, II.2.

[20] See I.3.

[21] See Lane, *s.v.*

[22] For the Heb. see below; for the Ugar. see above, I.3; for the Akk. see above, I.2; and for the Arab. see below.

[23] Cf. I.2.

[24] See below, III.3.

III. Meaning.

1. *General Synopsis.* Out of the 51 times that *bethulah* occurs in the OT, 3 times it clearly means "virgin" (Lev. 21:13f.; Dt. 22:19; Ezk. 44:22), and once it certainly does not ("Lament like a *bethulah* girded with sackcloth, for the bridegroom [*ba'al*] of her youth," Joel 1:8; this interpretation can be avoided only by the singular assumption that *ba'al* means not only "husband," but also "fiancé"). In 12 passages, almost all of which are poetic, it is connected (both in the sing. and in the pl.) with *bachur(im),* and the two expressions together mean the same thing as "young people"; here virginity plays no discernible role. In the expressions *bethulath yisra'el,* "the virgin Israel" (Jer. 18:13 + 3 times), *bethulath bath 'ammi,* "the virgin daughter of my people," *bethulath bath yehudhah,* "virgin daughter of Judah," *bethulath bath tsiyyon,* "virgin daughter of Zion," *bethulath bath babhel,* "virgin daughter of Babylon," *bethulath bath mitsrayim,* "virgin daughter of Egypt," and *bethulath bath tsidhon,* "virgin daughter of Sidon," all of which are personifications of a nation, a city, or a land, *bethulah* is probably not intended to refer to virginity; these expressions are expansions or playful modifications of the frequent two-word expressions → בת *bath yehudhah,* "daughter of Judah," *bath babhel,* "daughter of Babylon," *bath 'ammi,* "daughter of my people," etc. It is a mistake to look for a deep religious idea in *bethulath bath tsiyyon,* "virgin daughter of Zion," etc., as is clear from frequent counterparts like *bethulath bath babhel,* "virgin daughter of Babylon," etc. With regard to the other passages where *bethulah* occurs, it cannot be determined whether the various authors wanted their readers to take it to mean virginity or not. (The phrase that is added to *bethulah* a few times, "who never has had intercourse" [Gen. 24:16; Jgs. 21:12; similarly Lev. 21:3 [25]], can be restrictive ["a *bethulah,* in fact, one who..."] or descriptive ["a *bethulah,* i.e., one who..."], and thus contributes nothing to an understanding of the meaning of the word.)

2. *Job 31:1.* *bethulah* in Job 31:1 ("I have made a covenant with my eyes not to look upon the/a *bethulah*") probably means the maid 'Anat, for the following reasons: 1. It may be foolish to look upon an (unmarried) maiden (this is the meaning of the quotation of this passage in Sir. 9:5, an item in a catalog of women), but it is not sinful (Job 31:3). 2. If v. 1 referred to a human being, v. 9 ("If my heart has been enticed to a [married] woman ['*ishshah*], and I have lain in wait at my neighbor's door..."; cf. v. 11) would be superfluous, i.e., literally meaningless. 3. "God above" (v. 2) is mentioned only one other time in Job's oath of purification, viz., in vv. (26-)28, the only other passage in Job 31 where other deities threaten his absolute sovereignty. 4. An 'Anat syncretism appears in the religion of the Jews at Elephantine in the fifth century B.C., about the time that the book of Job was written, and it may have been regarded as a danger in Palestine; in this case, v. 1 would represent a reaction to this danger. 5. Finally, there may be another reference to 'Anat in the book of Job (although

[25] Cf. F. Zimmermann, *JBL,* 73 (1954), 98(ff.), n. 4.

admittedly a very weak one). Since 'Anat is called *ymmt l3mm* in the Ugaritic material, [26] it is possible that there is an oblique reference to her in the name of Job's oldest daughter Jemimah (Job 42:14). [27]

3. *In the Law.* As has already been mentioned, the three passages in which *bethulah* clearly means "virgin" are found in the law. Two of these have to do with the marriage partners of the priests. One says that a priest may marry only a virgin or a widow of a priest (Ezk. 44:22), and the other that the high priest may marry only a virgin of his own tribe (Lev. 21:13f.); here *bethulah* stands in opposition to widow, divorcee (one who had been disgraced[?]) and a prostitute. The third passage has to do with the husband's assertion that his wife was not a virgin when she married him (Dt. 22:13-21). Under normal circumstances, the parents of the girl will seek to disprove this assertion by producing before the court the sheet of the wedding night, with traces of blood as an indication of the first sexual relationship between the man and his wife; this assumes that the parents kept the sheet in their possession. (In Jewish Palestine of the second or third centuries A.D., the sheet was brought as in triumph before the newlyweds sometime during the course of the marriage festival, which lasted for several days [b*Kethubboth* 16b].) [28] This sign is called *bethulim,* "(tokens of) virginity (continuing until marriage)" (vv. 14-20). According to Landsberger's attractive explanation, [29] this more delicate concept is a derived meaning; originally *bethulim* probably meant "youth"; cf. nouns with the same form denoting age: *zequnim,* "old age," *ne'urim,* "youth," and *'alumim,* "youth." (Also, the Talmud uses the expressions *mph šl btwlym,* "sheet of virginity," b*Kethubboth* 16b, and *'wtw swdr,* "that little cloth," b*Kethubboth* 10a. In Lev. 21:13, *bethulim* means "condition of virginity".) The husband's assertion can lead to a case of criminal jurisdiction: if he cannot prove his complaint, he is whipped, pays a fine, and is forever forbidden to put away his wife, which was probably the secret intent of the accusation in the first place; but if he can, his wife is put to death. (It hardly need be added that, for anatomical or psychological reasons which could be attributed to either partner, even if blood is absent the accused woman could still be innocent.) The extraordinary harshness of the punishment on a guilty wife is based on the idea that the young woman "has committed a crime (→ נבלה *nᵉbhālāh,* "folly") in (i.e., against) Israel by playing the harlot in her father's house" (v. 21). [30] Naturally, this law cannot be a key to that found in Ex. 22:15f.(16f.), because the latter does not have to do with the seduction of a "betrothed" *bethulah.* The text of Ex. 22:15f.(16f.) does not make it clear whether the girl is a virgin or not, or whether her seducer is guilty of his first offense in this area or whether he has been guilty of it many times. From a cautious

---

[26] *CTA,* 3 [V AB], III, 9; elsewhere *ybmt.*

[27] See *UT,* 408; and G. Fohrer, *KAT,* XVI, 544.

[28] For similar Arabian customs, see S. R. Driver, *A Critical and Exegetical Comm. on Deuteronomy* (1895), 255 n.

[29] Landsberger, 57f.

[30] Cf. M. Noth, *Das System der zwölf Stämme Israels* (1930), 104-06.

philological point of view, *kemohar habbethuloth* should be translated, "according to the amount of the bride price for a young maiden," with Landsberger. [31]

IV. Summation; Observations on Isa. 7:14.

However one may interpret *bethulah* in individual cases, this word does not have a theological meaning in a real sense. In the evolution of thought from Lev. 21:7aβ to Ezk. 44:22 to Lev. 21:13-14aα,b, we find that it is incompatible with the dignity of the priestly office for priests to marry rejected (*gerushah*, "divorced") women (Lev. 21:7a), or stated coarsely, women who have already been used (including → אלמנה *'almānāh,* "a widow") (21:13f.); in the central text, women who have been used in particular by laymen (Ezk. 44:22). The passage in Ezekiel (which allows a priest to marry the widow of a priest, but not the widow of a layman) makes it clear that the viewpoint here is not anatomical, but sociological. But the real concern of Dt. 22:13-21 is not virginity, but unchastity; the element of virginity has only a procedural function, because the loss of virginity is regarded as a proof of unchastity.

Here we may deal briefly with Isa. 7:14 because of its importance in the history of interpretation: "Behold, a (the) young woman (→ עלמה *'almāh*) is pregnant (will become pregnant); she will bear a son and call him Immanuel" (or in the pl.: "young women are pregnant," etc.). *'almah* does not mean "virgin," although, of course, an *'almah* can be a "virgin." The translation "virgin" goes back to *parthénos* in the LXX. According to Kilian, [32] *parthénos* in the LXX could have been influenced by an Egyptian myth in which a pharaoh was born to a virgin. [33] The ancient sources give no evidence of a Judaized miracle story of the Alexandrian community *ca.* 200 B.C. The LXX says simply: "The virgin will become pregnant (future) and bear a son." The pregnancy lies in the future (cf. Jgs. 13:3,5); nothing indicates that the woman is also a virgin after the conception. [34]

Neither the word nor the concept of "virgin" and "virginity" is of any importance in the religious thought of the OT and in the earliest history of the interpretation of this idea.

Tsevat

---

[31] Landsberger, 62.

[32] R. Kilian, "Die Geburt des Immanuel aus der Jungfrau. Jes. 7,14," in K. S. Frank, *et al., Zum Thema Jungfraugeburt* (Stuttgart, 1970), 9-35.

[33] Cf. *ZRGG,* 12 (1960), 99.

[34] See J. A. Bewer, *JBL,* 45 (1926), 5-8; → את *'ēth,* III.

גָּאָה gā'āh; גָּאָה gē'āh; גָּאָה gē'eh; גַּאֲוָה ga'ᵃvāh;
גָּאוֹן gā'ôn; גֵּאוּת gē'ûth; גֵּוָה gēvāh

Contents: I. Etymology. II. The Use of this Root in the OT: 1. Occurrences; 2. *gevah*. III. Literal Meaning. IV. Figurative Meaning: 1. Positive; 2. Negative.

I. Etymology. 1. The root *g'h* is widespread outside of Hebrew, especially in Aramaic. In Syriac it appears in the pael and aphel, and especially in the ethpael, "to exalt oneself, be arrogant," and in a number of derivatives. This root also occurs in Mandean, where we find a peal and pael only in the active participle, the ethpael, "to be shining, outstanding," and substantival forms. In Jewish Aramaic we find the peal, "to be high," and the ethpeal, "to be exalted, boast." The same root also appears frequently in Middle Hebrew with this meaning. In Nabatean, *g'h* may be contained in the divine name *al-Gā'*, which is to be inferred from the proper names *'bd'lg'* and *'mt'lg'*.[1] Thus, we must assume that it means "the glorious one, the high one, the exalted one." To be sure, the frequently attested form *'bd'lgy'* may indicate either a deity that was worshipped in the valley (cf. Dusares as a mountain-god) or a deity that was worshipped locally, who wears the name of the place.[2] *g'h* also occurs in Ṣafaitic in the proper name *g'wn*.[3] In Akkadian we find *ga'ûm*, "to be presumptuous," once as a Canaanite word, and an adj. *ga'ûm* "presumptuous."[4]

2. The Ugar. *g'n*, which appears once in *CTA*, 17 [II D], VI, 44, is usually identified with Heb. *ga'on* in the sense of "pride." In a discussion between ʿAnat and Aqhat, the way of sin (*ntb pšʿ*) stands in parallelism with the way of pride (*ntb g'n*). Thus Ugar. *g'n* is understood only in the negative sense of "arrogance, pride, presumption."[5]

3. The root *g'h* seems also to have been known in Punic, in Plautus *Poenulus* 1027, the cry of Hanno (which is not translated by Milphio): *gune bel bal samen ierasan. gune bel* is understood universally as a cry: "magnificence of Bel!"[6] or

---

gā'āh. G. Bertram, "'Hochmut' und verwandte Begriffe im griechischen und hebräischen AT," *WO*, 3 (1964/66), 32-43; *idem*, "ὕβρις," *TDNT*, VIII, 295-307; *idem*, "ὑπερήφανος, ὑπερηφανία," *TDNT*, VIII, 525-29; P. Humbert, "Démesure et chute dans l'AT," *maqqél shaqédh. Hommage à W. Vischer* (1960), 63-82; P. L. Schoonheim, "Der alttestamentliche Boden der Vokabel ὑπερήφανος Lukas I 51," *NovT*, 8 (1966), 235-246; H. Steiner, *Die Gē'îm in den Psalmen* (diss., Lausanne, 1925).

[1] Cf. *WbMyth*, I/1, 438.
[2] Cf. Cantineau, *Le Nabatéen*, II, 76; otherwise *LidzEph*, III, 268, and E. Littmann, *Nabataean Inscriptions*, XIV, 62f., 89.
[3] *CIS*, V, 5118; Oxtoby, No. 82.
[4] Von Soden, *UF*, 4 (1972), 160.
[5] Cf. S. Loffreda, *BeO*, 8 (1966), 103-116.
[6] *DISO*, 46 ("grandeurs de Bel!").

"exaltations of Bel!" [7] This would make *gune* the plural construct of *gʾn,* which agrees exactly with the Heb. *gaʾon.*

4. The Arab. *ğāh,* "majesty, rank, honor, glory," does not belong here because it is a Persian loanword. Many Arabic lexicographers think that *ğāh* comes from *wğh.* The Tigré *ğah,* "honor, favor, excellence," is also from this root, and thus cannot be connected with *gʾh.*

5. On the other hand, Egyp. *qʾy,* "to be high," [8] corresponds in form and meaning to the Semitic root *gʾh.* It also seems to occur in Cushite; cf. Bilin and Agau *gui,* "to stand up, be exalted." [9] Possibly a biradical root *gʾ* with polar meanings, "to be or become high, deep," lies behind these forms; [10] if so, Heb. *gaiʾ,* "valley," originally could have been connected with the root *gʾh.*

II. The Use of this Root in the OT.

1. *Occurrences. gʾh* occurs 7 times altogether in the OT in 5 different passages (in Ex. 15:1,21 in the expanded form with the inf. abs. *gaʾoh gaʾah*), meaning "to be or become high, exalted"; it also appears in Sir. 10:9 in the figurative sense, "to be proud." *geʾeh* occurs as an adjectival form 8 times. Also the masc. sing. *geʾ,* which appears once in Isa. 16:6, where some think it is a secondary singular form of *geʾim,* is certainly a textual error for *geʾeh,* as 1QIsᵃ and the parallel passage in Jer. 48:29 show. Rost's proposal that we read *geʾe,* "the proud ones of," the plural construct of *geʾeh,* instead of *geʾ shemanim,* "valley of oils," in Isa. 28:1,4, [11] has also received unexpected support from 1QIsᵃ. Also it is best to read *geʾe,* "the proud ones (of the oppressors, or the proudest oppressors)," in Ps. 123:4, following the *qere,* rather than the *kethibh,* which has a hypertrophic adjectival form, *gaʾayon,* which is found only here. The substantival forms from the root *gʾh* are *geʾah, gaʾavah, gaʾon,* and *geʾuth. geʾah* occurs only once, viz., in Prov. 8:13, where it means "pride." *gaʾavah* appears 19 times (from which we should subtract Job 41:7 [Eng. v. 15] and Prov. 14:3, where one should read *gevoh* instead of *gaʾavah*), plus 6 times in Sirach (7:17; 10:6,7; 13:20; 16:8), in which the meaning can pass from "prosperity" to "majesty" to "pride, arrogance." *gaʾon,* which is found 49 times (plus Sir. 10:12; 48:18), and *geʾuth,* which occurs 8, have the same nuances of meaning. The root *gʾh* is probably also contained in the proper name *geʾuʾel,* "Geuel," in Nu. 13:15. [12] Wächter's attempt to interpret the OT verbs *sagaʾ,* "to grow," hiphil "to make great," and *sagah,* "to become great," hiphil "to make great," as originally shaphel forms of *gʾh,* [13] is worthy of consideration.

---

[7] L. H. Gray, *AJSL,* 39 (1923), 82; and M. Sznycer, *Les passages puniques en transcription latine dans le "Poenulus" de Plaute. Études et Commentaires,* 65 (1967), 144.

[8] *WbÄS,* V, 1ff.

[9] S. L. Reinisch, *Wörterbuch der Bilin-Sprache,* 132.

[10] Cf. A. Schwarzenbach, *Die geographische Terminologie im Hebr. des ATs* (1954), 33.

[11] L. Rost, *ZAW,* 53 (1935), 292.

[12] See below, IV.1.

[13] L. Wächter, *ZAW,* 83 (1971), 387f.

However, Heb. *goy,* "nation," is probably not to be connected with the root *g'h,* [14] because the loss of the aleph as the middle radical could hardly be explained if this were the case. [15] It is striking that almost all the examples of forms and constructions from the root *g'h* in the OT are found in metrically formed texts or in elevated prose. Thus this root belongs to the vocabulary of poetry, and not to everyday language.

2. *gevah.* The word *gevah* causes difficulties. It means about the same thing as *ga'avah,* as is clear from the contexts in which it occurs and from the way it is translated in some of the ancient versions, and yet the form of *gevah* shows that it cannot be cognate with the root *g'h.* The examples of this word in the OT (Jer. 13:17; Job 20:25; 22:29; 33:17) are not equally certain.

Scholars generally agree that Job 20:25 should be left out of this discussion, because this word is to be pointed *gevoh,* "his back," as the LXX suggests. But the text of Jer. 13:17 also does not seem to be entirely certain. Doniach's hypothesis that *gevah* meant "something within" = "deep inward grief, violent sorrow," [16] is not very convincing, but Volz had suggested earlier, with good reasons, that *glh,* "captivity," should be read in this text. [17] *gevah* in Job 20:25 has been understood as an interjection, "upward," ever since Ewald, Dillmann, Delitzsch, etc., and then, of course, it is derived from the root *g'h* in a literal sense. Beer and *KBL*[2] suggest that *gevah* be emended to *ge'eh* in this passage, while Fohrer reads *rumath gevah,* "pride of arrogance." [18] In Job 33:17, the LXX and Syriac translate as if *gevoh,* "his back," stood in the Hebrew text. This could be taken as an indication that the present pointing of *gvh* in the MT is a contrived attempt to improve difficult texts, as Job 20:25 seems clearly to show.

However, the problem is not made simpler by the occurrence of a form *ghevah* in Biblical Aramaic (Dnl. 4:34[37]) meaning "pride," and in 1QS 4:9, which is also to be translated "pride." In a liturgy of the three fiery tongues in 1Q29, which has been preserved only fragmentarily, there appears a *śr gvh* in fragment 13, line 3, but without sufficient context to allow an interpretation of this expression.

Barth explained the word *gevah* as a contraction of *ge'evah,* [19] but the OT has only a *ga'avah,* not a *ge'evah.* Recently, *KBL*[3] explained *gevah* as connected with the Mandean *giuta,* which comes from **gi'wat.* The form *gevah* and the well-attested form *ga'avah* are still difficult.

III. Literal Meaning. The verb *ga'ah* appears in the literal sense, "to be or

---

[14] As H. Bauer, *ZDMG,* 69 (1915), 566, tries to do by explaining *goy,* on the basis of *g'h,* as "the ones breaking open" = "the people."

[15] Cf. Th. Nöldeke, *ZA,* 30 (1915/16), 167f.

[16] N. S. Doniach, *AJSL,* 50 (1934), 177f.

[17] P. Volz, *Studien zum Text des Jeremia* (1920), 117.

[18] G. Fohrer, *KAT,* XVI, 352.

[19] J. Barth, *Nominalbildung,* § 62b.

become high," in Job 8:11, in connection with the growth of plants, especially papyrus, and in Ezk. 47:5, which states that the water of the temple river was more than 4000 ells deep, too much to pass through. The substantives *ga'avah* (RSV, "tumult," Ps. 46:4 [3]) and *ge'uth* (RSV, "raging," Ps. 89:10 [9]) are also found in connection with water. In these passages, of course, the raging of the sea is no longer to be understood simply in a literal sense, but the meaning has already come to be "strong protest, arrogance." Mythological terminology probably lies behind both these passages. *ga'on* in Job 38:11 is also understood in a similar sense as the rising of the waves. In the description of the theophany in Job 37:4, thunder is depicted as a majestic (*ga'on*) voice, and here also the emphasis is probably not so much on the literal meaning. On the other hand, in Isa. 9:17 (18) *ge'uth* has the literal meaning of "high-towering, ascending"; *ge'uth 'ashan* is a column of smoke. In a secondary gloss in Job 10:16, the verb *g'h* is used of lifting the head high (irrespective of the way in which one solves the difficulty of its relationship to the following *kashshachal*), and thus represents a development in the meaning of this root toward "being proud."

The construct expression *ge'on hayyarden*, in Jer. 12:5; 49:19 = 50:44, and Zec. 11:3, certainly does not mean the swelling of the Jordan, as G. R. Driver supposes with the aid of the Arabic, [20] but the region around the banks in the southern part of the Jordan Valley (RSV, "the jungle of the Jordan"), overgrown with abundant vegetation, which today is called ez-Zōr. [21] The "splendor" of the Jordan [22] is the thicket in which wild animals live (e.g., lions, Zec. 11:3; Jer. 49:19), and thus seems dangerous to a traveller (Jer. 12:5).

IV. Figurative Meaning.

1. *Positive.* In the figurative sense, forms of the root *g'h* appear in connection with statements about the majesty of God. In Miriam's song of victory, Yahweh is praised as highly exalted (RSV, as having triumphed gloriously, *ga'oh ga'ah*, Ex. 15:1,21), because he threw horse and rider into the sea. The same passage speaks of "the greatness of thy (Yahweh's) majesty" (*berobh ge'onekha*, Ex. 15:7). Ps. 93:1 (Yahweh is robed in *ge'uth*, RSV, "majesty") and Yahweh's summons to Job to clothe himself with God's royal robes in Job 40:10 (using *ga'on*, RSV, "majesty") [23] indicate that the attributes *ge'uth* and *ga'on* as descriptions of the glorious and majestic appearance of Yahweh play an important role in the concept of Yahweh's kingship. God's *ga'avah* (RSV, "majesty") shines forth over Israel (Ps. 68:35 [34]). The glory of Yahweh's majesty (*ga'on*) disseminates fear (Isa. 2:19, also 10,21). In the originally separate hymn in Dt. 33:2-5,26-29, which is now the framework around the tribal oracles of the Blessing of Moses, God's *ga'avah* (RSV, "majesty") on the clouds is regarded as incomparable in Dt. 33:26. Whereas the wicked does not see the

---

20 G. R. Driver, *Festschrift T. H. Robinson* (1950), 59.
21 Cf. N. Glueck, *AASOR,* 25/28 (1951), 238.
22 W. Rudolph, *HAT,* 12, 84.
23 Cf. G. Fohrer, *KAT,* XVI, 519f.

majesty (ge'uth) of Yahweh (Isa. 26:10), the exilic community shouts for joy over Yahweh's majesty (ga'on) (Isa. 24:14); cf. also Mic. 5:3(4), which speaks of the majesty (ga'on) of the name of the God of Israel. Isa. 12:5, which says that Yahweh does gloriously (ge'uth), and Dt. 33:29, where Yahweh is called Israel's pride (RSV, "triumph"; ge'uth), must also be mentioned in this connection.

The proper name ge'u'el must also be mentioned here as a hymnic predicate. The name of the spy from the tribe of Gad, ge'u'el ben makhi, "Geuel the son of Machi" (Nu. 13:15), is not a caritive form of yg'l'l,[24] nor does it come from g'wl'l by dissimilation.[25] However, the LXX Goudiēl is probably influenced by the form of the name in v. 10, and the Syr. gw'yl, the Samaritan Pentateuch gw'l, and Vulg. Guel are to be understood as phonetic transcriptions of the name ge'u'el, and thus do not point to other forms of this name. The proper names containing the root g'h in Nabatean and Ṣafaitic in particular[26] indicate that the name ge'u'el is not an isolated form at all, even if the grammatical structure is not entirely clear. In the OT, the name yehoram, "Jehoram," probably has approximately the same meaning as ge'u'el.

The interpretation of Yahweh swearing by the ga'on (RSV, "pride") of Jacob (Am. 8:7) is debated. Wolff is inclined to agree with Wellhausen that this text should be understood ironically: "Yahweh's oath is irrevocable, just as Israel's impudent arrogance is apparently irredeemable."[27] But it seems to me that Rudolph's interpretation is headed more in the right direction when he points out that Yahweh also swears by himself in Am. 4:2 and 6:8, and that ga'on as an attribute of the majesty of Yahweh is by no means unique.[28] In the first line of Am. 8:7, ga'on is probably a self-designation of Yahweh, even if the ironic idea might reflect the presumptuousness and arrogance of the people.

Nominal forms of the root g'h are also used in a positive sense of the majesty (pride, but not with a negative connotation of arrogance) of man. To be sure, this use of the root did not originate until late; at any rate, none of the examples treated here are old. The oldest example seems to be Jer. 13:9, where Jeremiah compares the waistcloth that he had buried with Israel's spoiled pride (ga'on), if ga'on is to be interpreted in the good sense. According to Isa. 4:2, the fruit of the land shall be the pride (ga'on) and glory of the survivors of Israel. Similarly, in Ps. 47:5(4) and Nah. 2:3(2),[29] the land is called the pride of Jacob or Israel, and in Isa. 60:15 we find the promise that Jerusalem will become majestic for ever (ligh'on 'olam), a cause for joy for all. This linguistic usage survives in the post-Talmudic period when ga'on is used as an honorific title of the Babylonian schoolmaster.[30]

---

[24] So F. Praetorius, ZDMG, 57 (1903), 780.
[25] So E. König, Wörterbuch, s.v.; similarly M. Noth, IPN, No. 321.
[26] Cf. above, I.1.
[27] H. W. Wolff, BK, XIV/2, 377.
[28] W. Rudolph, KAT, XIII/2, 264.
[29] But cf. BHS.
[30] Cf. "Geonim," EJ, VII (1931), 271-283.

When Babylon is called the proud splendor (RSV, "splendor and pride," *tiph'ereth ga'on*) of the Chaldeans (Isa. 13:19), this probably already reflects the idea of presumptuous pride. The same is true in Isa. 28:1,3, where the prophet pronounces woes upon the proud crown (*'atereth ge'uth*) of the drunken men of Samaria, and in Zec. 10:11, which announces the fall of the pride (*ga'on*) of Assyria (cf. also Isa. 14:11).

2. *Negative.* The Wisdom Literature has repeated warnings against pride. Therefore, personified Wisdom can say, "Pride and arrogance (*ge'ah vegha'on*) and the way of evil and perverted speech I hate" (Prov. 8:13). Yahweh tears down the house of the *ge'im*, "proud" (Prov. 15:25), casts down the throne of the *ge'im* (Sir. 10:14), and cuts off pride (*gevah*) (Job 33:17). Pride (*ga'on*) goes before destruction, and a haughty spirit before a fall. It is better to be of a lowly spirit with the poor than to divide the spoil with the proud (*ge'im*) (Prov. 16:18f.). To depart from God is the beginning of pride (*ga'on*) (Sir. 10:12).

It is not likely that we should read *ge'im*, "proud ones," instead of *goyim*, "nations," in several passages in the Psalms, as H. Steiner assumes, [31] and that *ge'im* refers to a specific group, namely, the Sadducees. Pride and arrogance are characteristics of the wicked. Thus they are depicted in the laments in the Psalter. They pursue the poor in arrogance (Ps. 10:2; read *beghe'uth*); they speak arrogantly (Ps. 17:10; cf. 31:19[18]); pride (*ga'avah*) is their necklace (Ps. 73:6), and in Ps. 140:6(5), the worshipper complains because arrogant men (*ge'im*) have hidden a trap for him. The contempt of the proud (Ps. 123:4, *kethibh;* the *qere* has "the contempt of the pride of oppressors") is hard to bear. Men cry out to God because of the pride of evil men (*mippene ge'on ra'im,* Job 35:12), that he might render to the proud their deserts (Ps. 94:2; cf. 31:24 [23]; Dnl. 4:34[37]). They shall be trapped in their pride (Ps. 59:13[12]); indeed, the heart of the proud is like a bird caught in a basket (Sir. 11:30). Thus the worshipper can pray that the foot of arrogance (*reghel ga'avah*) might not come upon him (Ps. 36:12[11]), and Ben Sira advises his hearers not to go in the way of arrogance (*ga'avah*), for arrogance is hateful before the Lord and before men (Sir. 10:6f.). A man's pride will bring him low (Prov. 29:23). Dust and ashes have no reason to be proud (*yg'h,* Sir. 10:9).

In some striking passages in the prophetic literature, Israel's self-confident attitude is condemned as the essence of pride (*ga'on*). Thus Amos announces that Yahweh abhors the pride of Jacob (Am. 6:8). That which other passages describe in detail as "despotism, unrighteousness, luxury, and military self-conceit," [32] is summed up here in the word *ga'on.* Hosea says that the presumptuous pride of Israel testifies as a witness against Israel (Hos. 5:5; and as a gloss in 7:10a). Isaiah also knows that on the day of Yahweh all that is proud (*ge'eh*) and lofty will be humbled (Isa. 2:12; cf. 13:11). Moreover, according to Zeph. 3:11 the proudly exultant ones will be removed. Pride and arrogance of heart

---

[31] Cf. also H. Herkenne, *HSAT,* V, 2, who follows Steiner's suggestion with regard to Ps. 9:6,16,18,20,21(5,15,17,19,20); 10:16; 59:6,9(5,8).

[32] H. W. Wolff, *BK,* XIV/2, 327.

prevent the inhabitants of Samaria from recognizing their true situation (Isa. 9:8[9]). Jeremiah weeps because of the pride (*gevah*) of the stubborn ones of his people (Jer. 13:17). In the threat of punishment in Lev. 26:14-38, v. 19 declares that Yahweh will break the proud power (*geʾon ʿuzzekhem*) of Israel, as he will make the sky over Palestine like iron. This same combination of *gaʾon* and *ʿoz,* "power, strength," occurs five times in Ezekiel (7:24;[33] 24:21; 30:6,18; 33:28), although in different connections. In 7:24 and 33:28 the end of Israel's proud might is announced, while in 30:6,18 Egypt's might is considered to be consecrated for destruction. Finally, Ezk. 24:21 even refers to the Jerusalem temple as *geʾon ʿuzzekhem,* "the pride of your power."

Not only do the prophets denounce the pride and arrogance of Israel, but in a similar way they also condemn the presumptuousness of foreign nations. Isa. 16:6 = Jer. 48:29 (where we find four words from the root *gʾh* in one verse) censures the haughty pride and arrogant boasting of Moab. When Moab's pride (*gaʾavah*) is trampled down, it will be like a swimmer in a dung pit (Isa. 25:11). Ezekiel also condemns the pride of Egypt in Ezk. 32:12. Isa. 23:9 announces (against Tyre) that Yahweh will defile the pride of all glory and dishonor all the honored of the earth. In this passage it is clear once again that only because of presumption does *gaʾon* turn into ruinous arrogance.

Thus, in Hebrew the root *gʾh* has a wide range of meaning. From the idea of the majesty of God it develops into the justified pride of a man, or the glory of an object, and then into arrogant pride or hubris.

D. Kellermann

---

[33] Cf. *BHS.*

גָּאַל *gāʾal;* גֹּאֵל *gōʾēl;* גְּאֻלָּה *geʾullāh*

Contents: I. 1. Etymology, Occurrences; 2. Meaning. II. Secular Use. III. Figurative, Religious Meaning: 1. Legal Nuances; 2. With *min;* 3. In Connection with the Exodus; 4. In Deutero-Isaiah; 5. *goʾel* Outside Deutero-Isaiah.

I. 1. *Etymology, Occurrences.* The root *gʾl* seems to be almost exclusively Hebrew. The only cognate appears in the Amorite proper name *Gāʾilālum.*[1]

---

gāʾal. Chr. Barth, *Die Errettung vom Tode in den individuellen Klage- und Dankliedern des ATs* (Zollikon, 1947); A. Jepsen, "Die Begriffe des 'Erlösens' im AT," *Solange es "Heute" heisst. Festschrift für R. Hermann* (1957), 153-163; A. R. Johnson, "The Primary Meaning of √גאל," *SVT,* 1 (1953) 67-77; H.-J. Kraus, "Erlösung," *RGG³,* II, 586-88; Pedersen, *ILC,* I-II, 263ff., 395ff.; O. Procksch, "λύω," *TDNT,* IV, 328-335; H. H. Rowley, "The Marriage of Ruth," *Servant of the Lord* (Oxford, ²1965), 169ff.; K. Rudolph, *KAT,* XVII, 60-65; J. J. Stamm, *Erlösen und Vergeben im AT* (1940); R. de Vaux, *AncIsr,* 21f.

[1] Huffmon, *APNM,* 179.

The examples of this root in Jewish Aramaic are based on biblical usage.[2] Therefore, the original meaning of *g'l* cannot be determined etymologically. Johnson's attempt to demonstrate that the original meaning was "to cover" or "to protect," by using examples which actually should be understood as by-forms of *g'l*, is hardly convincing. *KBL* takes as its point of departure the meaning "to lay claim to someone or to something," while Procksch begins with the meaning "to redeem," and Stamm with the meaning "to repurchase." It seems better to begin with actual linguistic usage than to postulate an original meaning.

In the OT we find the verb in the qal and niphal, the qal active participle as a substantive meaning "redeemer," and the abstract subst. *ge'ullah*.[3] There is also a root *g'l* II, which is a by-form of → גֹּעֵל *gāʿal*.

2. *Meaning.* The verb is used in two realms: on the one hand, in connection with legal and social life, and on the other, with regard to God's redeeming acts. Scholars usually start with the secular use to shed light on the religious meaning. But Jepsen emphasizes that the distinction between "secular" and "religious" was hardly intelligible to ancient man, and that one would do well to begin with an original meaning common to both realms, possibly "to restore, repair."

Later Hebrew linguistic usage inclines toward the idea of "setting free, liberating," which is found on the coins of the first Jewish revolt (*lg'lt sywn*).[4] But even in the OT, for the most part this verb is one of the "verbs of delivering (rescuing)."[5] The main word that stands in parallelism with and is almost synonymous to *ga'al* is → פָּדָה *pādhāh*, "to ransom" (Hos. 13:14; Isa. 35:10; Jer. 31:11; Ps. 69:19 [Eng. v. 18]), but *hoshiaʿ* (→ יָשַׁע *yāshaʿ*), "to save, deliver" (Isa. 60:16; Ps. 106:10), *hitstsil* (→ נָצַל *nātsal*), "to save, rescue" (Mic. 4:10), and → עָזַר *ʿāzar*, "to help" (Isa. 41:14), also occur in parallel. This is in agreement with the use of *min* to specify that from which a person is rescued or delivered, as from slavery in Egypt, exile, or distress in general (Gen. 48:16; Jer. 31:11; Hos. 13:14; Mic. 4:10; Ps. 72:14; 103:4; 106:10; 107:2).

II. Secular Use. For the secular realm it is best to begin with the ptcp. *go'el*. *go'el* is used of a man's nearest relative at a particular time. In Lev. 25:48f., it refers to a man's brother, uncle, cousin, or some other kinsman who is responsible for standing up for him and maintaining his rights. Behind this usage stands the strong feeling of tribal solidarity: not only the members of a clan, but also their possessions, form an organic unity,[6] and every disruption of this unity is regarded as intolerable and as something which must be restored or repaired.

The following specific cases are mentioned in the OT:

---

2 *KBL.*
3 See below.
4 E. Schürer, *Geschichte des jüdischen Volkes,* I (⁴1901), 767.
5 Barth, 124ff.
6 Pedersen, 263ff.; Johnson, 67f.

a. If someone sells a house or a piece of property to pay a debt, there is a right of redemption (ge'ullah), and the nearest relative at the time is bound to buy back that which was sold and thus restore the possession of the family (Lev. 25:25-34). [7] Jer. 32:6f. gives an example of the prophet redeeming the field of his uncle Hanamel (in this instance, the redemption took place before the field was sold). The book of Ruth contains another example: Boaz is the go'el of Naomi and Ruth (2:20); but there is a nearer kinsman who has the priority (3:12; 4:4). He is quite willing to buy the piece of property, but not to marry Ruth as well (which apparently was a part of the responsibilities accruing to the ge'ullah, 4:4-6). But Boaz accepts both responsibilities (4:9f.). In this instance, the legal ramifications are a little complicated, and cannot be explained in all details. [8]

b. If an Israelite sold himself to a foreigner as a slave, the right of redemption by the go'el was also applicable (Lev. 25:47-54). In this case, there was a breach in the whole nation that must be repaired.

c. If someone is murdered, his death shall be avenged by the go'el haddam, "avenger of blood," whose responsibility is to kill the murderer or a member of his clan (→ נקם nāqam). [9] The avenger of blood is first of all the dead man's son, and then other male relatives. By vengeance, the avenger of blood restores the equilibrium that had been disturbed and the wholeness that had been impaired (KBL: "redeems the guilt of the manslayer"?). The manslayer can take refuge from the avenger of blood in the cities of refuge (Nu. 35:12,19-27; Dt. 19:6,12; Josh. 20:2f.,5,9). A concrete example is given in the parable in 2 S. 14:11.

d. Lev. 27 contains a case analogous to a and b: in certain cases described in detail, votive offerings that had been dedicated to the deity can be bought back by the original owner, but its value shall be increased by 20% (vv. 13,15, 19,31). In other cases, a redemption is not possible. Jepsen finds here a restoration of the original ownership. But since padhah, "to redeem," can be used in analogous cases, it is possible that the idea of redemption is more important.

e. In one passage, Nu. 5:8, the go'el appears as a recipient of atonement money, and this, of course, in his role as responsible head of the family (clan). Some passages in which go'el is used in a figurative sense (Prov. 23:11; Jer. 50:34; Lam. 3:58; Ps. 119:154; Job 19:25) show that the go'el could appear as a helper in a lawsuit to see that justice was done to his protégé. He who does not leave behind a go'el (RSV, "kinsman") and a rēaʿ (→ רע) (1 K. 16:11) has no one who cares for his rights and honor.

III. Figurative, Religious Meaning.

1. *Legal Nuances.* Even if it is impossible to derive the religious meaning from the "secular," as Jepsen rightly emphasizes, still it must be acknowledged

[7] See the comms.

[8] See Rowley and the comms., esp. Rudolph, 64.

[9] Pedersen, 395ff.

that nuances of meaning from the legal and social realm play a role in the religious. Thus legal categories are reflected in the passages cited above under e: Yahweh is the *go'el* of the fatherless and widow and pleads their cause (→ ריב *rîbh,* Prov. 23:11; similarly Jer. 50:34); he took up the cause (*ribh*) of a worshipper and redeemed (saved, *g'l,* Lam. 3:58) his life (in the previous verses the danger of death is indicated by *bor,* "pit," and *mayim,* "water," 3:53,55, and 54); a worshipper beseeches him to plead his cause, redeem (*g'l*) him, and give him life (Ps. 119:154). Further, according to Ps. 72:14 the king is to redeem (liberate, *g'l*) the life of the poor from oppression. The parallel line in the previous verse states that he saves (*hoshiaʿ*) their life. Here, of course, the king acts as protector of their rights, although this is not explicitly stated. [10]

In some instances nuances of meaning derived from social life are not to be ignored. Thus Ps. 74:2, referring to the exodus, says that Yahweh "got (→ קנה *qānāh*) and redeemed (ransomed, *g'l*) his congregation and made them his heritage (→ נחלה *nachⁿlāh*)." This passage does not seem to have in mind a restoration, but an acquisition (so also Ruth 4:5b), although, of course, the patriarchal traditions could substantiate the idea of redemption. [11] Further, Isa. 52:3 says that Israel will be redeemed (ransomed) "without money," which implies that redemption was usually made *with* silver or gold. According to 43:3f., Yahweh gives lands and nations for the life of his people; but the occurrence of the verb *g'l* is in v. 1. [12]

2. *With min.* The passages that use *min,* "from," to specify that from which or out of which a particular thing or person is redeemed are especially instructive. In Gen. 48:16 (E, perhaps the oldest passage using the root *g'l*), Jacob (in hymnic style) praises God or his angel (→ מלאך *mal'ākh*) because he had redeemed him from all evil (*raʿ*). In v. 15, "to feed, pasture" (*rʿh*), has reference to the protection and responsibility of a shepherd. Ps. 72:14, which has already been cited above, also uses *g'l* with *min,* and speaks of redemption from violence and oppression. Jer. 31:11 mentions setting Jacob free from the hand of the enemy: Yahweh will ransom (*pdh*) and redeem (*g'l*) Jacob from the hand of those who are too strong for him, and bring him back into his land. The same idea appears in Mic. 4:10: Israel will be rescued (*nṣl*) and redeemed (*g'l*) from her enemies in Babylon (the genuineness of this verse is doubtful). [13] Ps. 107:2 speaks of deliverance from different kinds of distress: dangers in travel, imprisonment, and illness. Ps. 69:19 (18) refers to deliverance from distress in general (*tsar li,* "I am in distress," v. 18[17]) and from enemies. The object of the redemption is *nephesh,* "soul" (here *g'l* stands in parallelism to *pdh*): this is a prayer for help in distress, which is described as a deadly peril (vv. 15f. [14f.]). Here we are reminded of the passages that speak of a deliverance from death or Sheol: Ps. 103:4, where *g'l* is connected with forgiveness of sins (*pdh*

---

10 On Job 19:25, see below.
11 Stamm, 37.
12 See below, 4.
13 See the comms.

is also used in this sense once), [14] and Hos. 13:14, where again *g'l* stands in parallelism with *pdh,* and the prophet speaks of deliverance from death and Sheol (whether this verse is interpreted as a positive statement or as a question expecting a negative answer does not affect the meaning of the verb). The meaning of Isa. 63:9 is obscure, but still it is clear that it has to do with deliverance from distress (*g'l* is used in parallelism with *hoshiaʿ,* "to save"), and that *g'l* seems to be connected with pity (*chamal*) and love (*'ahabh*).

3. *In Connection with the Exodus.* Passages that use *g'l* in connection with the exodus from Egypt emphasize in particular distress by the enemy (*pdh* is used more frequently than *g'l* in speaking of the exodus, esp. in Dt. and the Deuteronomistic literature). [15] In Ex. 6:6 (P), Yahweh promises to bring his people out (*hotsi'*) from under the burdens of the Egyptians, to deliver (*hitstsil*) them from their bondage, and to "redeem" (*g'l*) them with an outstretched arm. The association with the "secular" release from the duty of slavery is evident. The only other thing that needs to be asked is whether the author also has in mind the restoration of an earlier relationship between Yahweh and Israel, since he mentions the patriarchs with whom Yahweh had already made a covenant (vv. 3f.,8). [16] The other texts using *g'l* that refer to the exodus do not trace Yahweh's choice back earlier than the liberation from Egypt: Ex. 15:13 ("thy Yahweh's election back earlier than the liberation from Egypt: Ex. 15:13 ("thy people"); 106:10 (where *g'l* appears in parallelism with *hoshiaʿ,* "to save"). Thus the people are redeemed from foreign slavery and made God's own possession.

4. *In Deutero-Isaiah.* In light of this the use of *g'l* in Deutero-Isaiah is intelligible. This prophet understands the release from Babylonian captivity as a new exodus, and thus he uses the root *g'l* to describe it. In addition, he uses *g'l* to convey the idea of restoring a broken covenant relationship. In Isa. 51:10 the word *ge'ulim,* "the redeemed," clearly refers to those who had been delivered from Egypt, and in 48:20 the redemption is described as a going forth from Babylon and a being led through deserts (v. 21), thus a new exodus. In 44:22 the redemption is connected with forgiveness of sins (as in Ps. 103). In 44:23 the act of redemption is designated as a glorification of Yahweh that summons all nature to rejoice. In 52:9 this rejoicing is depicted as rejoicing before the king, welcoming the returning Yahweh and his redeemed people. Finally, 43:1 speaks once again of the restored relationship between Yahweh and Israel: "I have redeemed you, I have called you by name, you are mine." In this connection, it is worthy of note that (just as in Lam. 3:58f.) the redemption is the subject of an oracle of salvation introduced by *'al tira',* "Fear not."

The ptcp. *go'el,* "redeemer," appears as an epithet of God nine times in Deutero-Isaiah. In seven of these cases it is used as an expansion of the messenger

---

[14] Jepsen, 157.
[15] Stamm, 18ff.
[16] Stamm, 38.

formula *koh 'amar yhvh,* "Thus says Yahweh," and twice it appears in connection with *'al tira',* "Fear not" (41:14; 54:5). Once this epithet is connected with *moshia',* "savior" (49:26). Otherwise its connection with the context is rather loose: Yahweh, the "Redeemer," helps his people (41:14; 49:7f.), defeats Babylon (43:14; 47:4), is king and everlasting God (44:6), teaches and leads (48:17). Isa. 60:16 is dependent on 49:26. An overall view of the use of *go'el* in Deutero-Isaiah shows that it is used as a stereotyped divine epithet, which can even be used without any direct connection with a specific redemption mentioned in the context.

5. *go'el Outside Deutero-Isaiah. go'el* also appears as a divine epithet in Ps. 19:15(14) and 78:35, in both instances in connection with *tsur,* "rock." God is the reliable protector who never wavers. Isa. 63:16, where Yahweh is called father (→ אב *'ābh*) and *go'el,* is worth noting. Here, also, the idea of an intimate kinship is probably present.

Finally, the meaning of Job 19:25: "I know that my *go'el* lives," is disputed. It is clear from the context that what Job anticipates here is the help of his *go'el* in a crucial lawsuit to conclusively establish his innocence. But who is his *go'el?* Since the lawsuit here stands in the context of a dispute with God, it seems unlikely that God himself would appear as vindicator and legal attorney against himself, unless a very loose train of thought is to be assumed. On the other hand, Job 16:19f. refers to a witness (*'edh*) and spokesman (*melits*) in heaven (cf. 9:33; 33:23), who seems to be someone different from God. The point in Job 19:25 is that just as there is a vindicator in an earthly lawsuit, so in Job's dispute with God there must also be one who intercedes for him, but it does not make clear who this vindicator might be. Accordingly, what we have here is an inexact statement: Job wishes to express the conviction that he must be acquitted in the end, and he clothes this thought in the figurative language of the lawsuit: someone must vindicate him to prove his innocence.

Other interpretations of Job 19:25 have been proposed. Usually the *go'el* is identified with God himself, but without following a very logical train of thought. The possibility that this passage might refer to the personal tutelary god of Job (following a Sumerian prototype) is improbable because this idea does not appear elsewhere in Israel. Moreover, the exegesis of this verse also depends on how the following statements (which have been severely mutilated in the text) are interpreted. [17]

Ringgren

---

[17] See the comms.

גָּבַהּ gābhah; גֹּבַהּ gōbhah; גָּבֹהַּ gābhōah; (גָּבֵהַּ gābhēah?);
גַּבְהוּת gabhhûth

Contents: I. Etymology, Occurrences, and Meaning in the Ancient Near East. II. Use in the OT: 1. Number and Distribution of Occurrences; 2. General Meaning; 3. Synonymous and Antithetic Ideas. III. Literal Meaning: 1. The Verb; 2. With *min, 'al,* and *be;* 3. Noun and Adjective; 4. Occurrences in Certain Names for Canaanite Cult Places. IV. Figurative Meaning and Theological Implications: 1. In Connection with Anthropological Concepts (*lebh, 'enayim, ruach, 'aph*); 2. In Other Connections.

I. **Etymology, Occurrences, and Meaning in the Ancient Near East.** The assumption of an etymological connection between the Heb. root *gbh* and Akk. *gab'u,* "height," [1] is highly problematic. *CAD* and *AHw* correctly assume that *gab'u* is to be derived from the West Semitic root *gb'* (attested in Ugar. and in Heb. *gibh'ah, gebha',* "hill, height"). The improbability of a change from the consonant *he* to *ayin* forbids an appeal to the root *gb'* for an etymological and semantic explanation of the root *gbh.* The coexistence of *gbh* and *gb'* in Ugaritic [2] and Hebrew favors the autonomy of these two roots. Similar considerations oppose the assumption of an etymological relationship between *gbh* and *gbb* (cf. Heb. *gabh,* "back, eyebrow, mound, rim, boss of a shield," Arab. *ǧubbat,* "bone structure around the eye socket"), [3] for a change from the double beth to a *bh* in the final syllable is not common. The etymological relationship between the Heb. root *gbh* and Arab. *ǧabaha* (cf. *ǧabhat,* "forehead, front, battlefront," *'aǧbahu,* "with high forehead"; [4] cf. Old South Arab. *gbht,* "forehead"), which *KBL*[3] and *GesB* assume, should not be considered unlikely simply on the basis of the way these words are spoken and written. To be sure, the original meaning of the Arab. root *ǧabaha,* "to meet, confront," speaks against this, for while there may be a semantic relationship between this Arabic root and the Heb. root *gbh* in its figurative meaning ("to be proud"), this is not the case in its literal meaning ("to be high, height"). Therefore, it is not advisable to begin the investigation of *gbh* with the Arab. root *ǧabaha.* The same arguments oppose any attempt to connect *gbh* with *gbḥ,* "having a bald forehead" (cf. Akk. *gubbuḫu,* "bald-headed"), because the primary meaning of *gbḥ* is "to be naked," while the primary meaning of *gbh* is "to be high," and this is true both in Hebrew and in other Semitic languages. Thus in both instances a similarity of meaning can be established only very artificially. The use of the root *gbh* in Jewish Aramaic, the Damascus Document, and the Qumran texts [5] is dependent on the OT usage.

---

gābhah. W. Baumgartner, "Beiträge zum hebr. Lexikon," *BZAW,* 77 (1958), 30f.; G. Bertram, "ὕψος, ὑψόω," *TDNT,* VIII, 602ff.; A. W. Schwarzenbach, *Die geographische Terminologie im Hebräischen des ATs* (1954), 6-11.

[1] So *KBL*[2] and *GesB,* but not *KBL*[3].
[2] *UT,* Glossary, 552.
[3] *KBL*[3] and *GesB.*
[4] H. Wehr, *Arab. Wörterbuch* ([3]1958).
[5] *KBL*[3]; K. G. Kuhn, *Konkordanz . . .* (1960).

The expression *qlh gbh,* "high (i.e., loud) voice" of the king, in Aramaic (Ahikar, 107), and the Aramaic ideogram for "high" in Pehlevi, [6] are probably not related to Heb. *gbh.* Thus far, only one certain example of *gbh* has been found in the Ugaritic texts: [7] *y'db yrḫ gbh* (with El as subj.), "he makes *yrḫ* (the moon-god or the moon) high" (or "exalted"; RS 24.258, 4f.).

The dearth of extrabiblical examples of the root *gbh* at best allows the conjecture that this root is native to the West Semitic languages. That it means "to be high, raise up," in these languages can also be considered certain. The same meaning in Hebrew is confirmed by the only extrabiblical example. In the Siloam Inscription, line 6, we read: "and the height (*gbh*) of the rock was 115 meters (100 ells) above the heads of the miners." [8]

II. Use in the OT.

1. *Number and Distribution of Occurrences.* The root *gbh* is found approximately 90 times in the OT. It appears only 3 times in the Pentateuch, and here exclusively in its latest strata (Dt. 3:5; 28:52 [Deuteronomistic texts]; Gen. 7:19 [P]). It occurs 12 times in the Historical Books (only in Samuel, Kings, and Chronicles), 8 times in the Psalms, 16 times in the Wisdom Literature (Job, Proverbs, and Ecclesiastes), about 50 times in the Prophets, and twice in Esther. When we consider that in the Psalms and Prophets *gbh* also frequently occurs in wisdom sayings and proverbial expressions, it follows from the statistical survey that this root is found most often in the vocabulary of wisdom sayings and is firmly established there. *gbh* is found in a broad range of time periods in OT history, and thus its absence in the earlier strata of the Pentateuch would seem to be accidental. It appears in ancient narratives (1 S. 9:2), the preexilic prophets (Am. 2:9; Zeph. 1:16; Isa. 2:11,15,17; Jer. 2:20; etc.), exilic writings (Ezk. 16:50; 17:22; Gen. 7:19 [P]; etc.), and late postexilic texts (Est. 5:14; 7:9; Dnl. 8:3). The verb occurs only in the qal (23 times) and hiphil (11 times), the noun *gobhah* is found 18 times, and the noun *gabhhuth* twice, while the adj. *gabhoah* appears 36 times. The const. *gebhah* occurs 4 times, but there is no absolute corresponding to it in the OT; thus it is questionable whether *gebhah* is another construct form of the adj. *gabhoah,* [9] or whether one should postulate another adjectival form, *gabheah.* [10]

2. *General Meaning.* The meaning "height, high," which the few extrabiblical examples clearly reveal, also clearly lies behind the use of the nouns and adjectives of the root *gbh* in the OT. Correspondingly, the use of the verb also emanates from the original meaning "to be high, make high."

3. *Synonymous and Antithetic Ideas.* In parallel statements with *gbh,* there are synonymous or related ideas that are derived from the following roots: *rum,*

6 On both of these, see *DISO.*
7 *UT,* Glossary, 548a.
8 *KAI,* 189.6.
9 So Baumgartner.
10 So *GesB* and *KBL²*; *KBL³* leaves this question undecided.

"to be high, reach high" (Ezk. 17:22f.; 31:10; Ps. 113:4f.; 131:1; Job 39:27; etc.); *qum,* "to stand up, raise up" (Isa. 10:33; *qomah:* 1 S. 16:7; Ezk. 31:3; etc.); *nasa',* "to lift, lift high" (Isa. 2:11-17—this passage has other synonymous and antithetic ideas to *gbh;* 30:25; 52:13; etc.); *ga'ah,* "to be high, become high, be arrogant" (Zeph. 3:11; Jer. 48:29; Prov. 16:18; etc.); *gadhal,* "to grow, become great, be great" (Ps. 131:1; Ezk. 31:2b,3a); *gabhar,* "to be superior" (Ps. 103:11, but the text here is questionable), and *saghabh,* "to be exalted" (Isa. 2:17b; cf. 5:16). As antithetic ideas to words from the root *gbh,* we encounter cognates of the following roots: *shaphel,* "to be low, sink down" (Isa. 2:11; 5:15f.; Ezk. 17:24; 21:31 [Eng. v. 26]; Ps. 113:5f.; etc.); *shachach,* "to be humbled" (Isa. 2:11,17; 5:15f.); *'amoq,* "to be deep" (Isa. 7:11); *kana'* (niphal), "to humble oneself" (2 Ch. 32:26); *'anah,* "to be humbled, to be miserable" (*'anavah,* "humility," Prov. 18:12).

III. Literal Meaning.

1. *The Verb.* The verb is often used to describe the greatness, height, or high position of persons, objects, places, and natural phenomena. In a special sense, it can mean "to be tall, grow tall, tower high," as in Ezk. 17:24; 19:11; 31:10,14 (of a vine or a tree). It can also denote the high location of a place: Jer. 49:16 (with *qen,* "nest," as obj.) = Ob. 4 (without *qen*); Ps. 113:5 (Yahweh's dwelling); and Isa. 7:11 (the upper world in contrast to Sheol); and the high flight of a bird: Job 5:7, where *gbh* intensifies the inf. *'uph,* "to fly"; and 39:27 (without *'uph*). In Ezk. 21:31(26), the verb appears in the hiphil in a proverb: "Exalt that which is low, and abase that which is high" (cf. 17:24). As a technical building term connected with *banah,* "to build," *gbh* denotes the height of walls (2 Ch. 33:14), or of doors (Prov. 17:19).

2. *With min, 'al, and be.* When it is used with *min* or *'al, gbh* denotes differences in height by means of comparison (1 S. 9:2; 10:23–*min;* Ezk. 31:5–*'al*). Proverbially these expressions are used to bring out the great distance of heaven from earth, or the qualitative distinction between God and man or between the plans of God and the plans of man: Isa. 55:9; Job 35:5 (*min*); Ps. 103:11 (*'al*); similarly 113:5f. In this proverbial contrast, the verb *gbh* stands at the very edge of the figurative meaning. Sometimes when *gbh* is followed by *be, be* serves to connect this verb more closely with its object, e.g., in Ezk. 31:10,14 (*qomah,* "growth"); cf. the same construction without *be* in Ezk. 19:11.

3. *Noun and Adjective.* The noun *gobhah* is used to denote the height of men (Am. 2:9; 1 S. 17:4) and trees (Am. 2:9; Isa. 10:33; Ezk. 19:11; 31:10,14). It is used repeatedly in statements about the measurements of the temple, its rooms and pieces of furniture (Ezk. 40:42; 41:8,22; 43:13, conjec.; 2 Ch. 3:4), and about the wheels of the divine throne-chariot (Ezk. 1:18). The adj. *gabhoah* is found in connection with the following: mountain (Gen. 7:19; Ezk. 17:22f.– in parallelism with the hapax legomenon *talul,* "towering, lofty," and *marom,* "towering," v. 23; 40:2; Isa. 30:25–together with *gibh'ah nissa'ah,* "towering

hill"; 40:9; 57:7–in connection with *nissa'*, "towering, lofty"; Ps. 104:18), fortified walls (Dt. 3:5; 28:52), city gate (Jer. 51:58), watchtower (Isa. 2:15), battlement (Zeph. 1:16), tree (Ezk. 17:24; 31:3 with *qomah*, "growth"), gallows (Est.
5:14; 7:9), ram's horns (Dnl. 8:3), and a man's stature (1 S. 16:7–*qomah*). The
comparative is made by using *min* with *gbh* (1 S. 9:2). The height of heaven,
an expression used to refer to the greatness of God (Job 11:8; 22:12), stands on
the periphery of the figurative use of this root.

4. *Occurrences in Certain Names for Canaanite Cult Places*. The adj. *gabhoah*
is found in two stereotyped phrases for Canaanite cult places. Sometimes it
appears with *gibh'ah*, "height, hill" (Jer. 2:20; 17:2; 1 K. 14:23; 2 K. 17:10),
and sometimes with → הַר *har*, "mountain, hill" (Jer. 3:6). The OT also uses an
expression with the adj. *ram/ramah* instead of *gabhoah* (Dt. 12:2; Ezk. 6:13;
20:28), and another without any adjective at all (Hos. 4:13; Ezk. 18:6; etc.;
2 K. 16:4) to refer to these cult places. This last form seems to be the earliest.
It probably comes from the northern kingdom, while the other two come from
Judah (Jeremiah, the Deuteronomist, and Ezekiel). The diverse terminology
of the common people in Judah and the priests of the Jerusalem temple may
be reflected in the use of the different adjectives.

IV. Figurative Meaning and Theological Implications.

1. *In Connection with Anthropological Concepts* (*lebh, 'enayim, ruach,
'aph*). The organs of the body, which are used in Hebrew to denote human
emotions and inclinations, occur so often either as objects of the verb *gbh*, or
in genitive constructions with noun forms of the root *gbh*, that it is necessary
to classify the words built from this root among the solid elements of the psychological terminology of the Israelites. The verb *gbh* is used with *lebh*, "heart,"
as its object in Ezk. 28:2,5,17; Ps. 131:1; Prov. 18:12; 2 Ch. 26:16; 32:25. Noun
forms of *gbh* stand in genitive constructions with *lebh*, "heart" (Prov. 16:5; 2 Ch.
32:26), *'enayim*, "eyes" (Isa. 2:11; 5:15; Ps. 101:5), *ruach*, "breath, spirit" (Prov.
16:18; Eccl. 7:8), and *'aph*, "nose" (Ps. 10:4). We encounter the following expressions that stand in synonymous parallelism with these statements using *gbh*:
rechabh lebhabh, "arrogant heart" (Ps. 101:5), *rum libbo*, "his heart was presumptuous" = "he was ambitious" (Jer. 48:29; Ezk. 31:10), and *'enayim ramoth*,
"haughty, proud eyes" (Prov. 6:17; cf. Isa. 2:11; 5:15). The following expressions stand in contrast with one another: *gobhah ruach*, "haughty, presumptuous
spirit," with *shephal ruach*, "lowly, humble spirit" (Prov. 16:18f.), and *gebhah
ruach*, "proud spirit," with *'erekh ruach*, "long breath, patience" (Eccl. 7:8).
There is only one passage in which *gbh* takes *lebh*, "heart," as its object in a
positive sense: "His (i.e., Jehoshaphat's) heart was courageous in the ways of
Yahweh" (2 Ch. 17:6). Apart from this one exception, in the expressions that
have been mentioned *gbh* is used to characterize the aspirations and relationships of men with God and with their fellow men in a religiously and ethically
negative sense (Prov. 16:5 in particular is severe when it says that everyone that
is proud of heart is a *to'abhath yhvh*, "an abomination to Yahweh"), and thus
should be translated "haughty, proud, presumptuous," etc.

2. *In Other Connections.* In this figurative meaning, expressions using the root *gbh* are frequently used elsewhere to describe human actions and behavior which are regarded as religiously and ethically evil. In this negative sense, they appear in particular in the prophets, wisdom sayings, cult poetry, and in rare instances in the Chronicler's work. Thus the verb is used of the proud boaster in contrast to the "humble and lowly people" (Zeph. 3:11f.), the luxuriously clothed women of Jerusalem (Isa. 3:16), and the people of Judah who will not hear Yahweh and give him the glory (*kabhodh*) (Jer. 13:15f.). Ezk. 16:50 sums up the entire list of sins committed by Sodom/Jerusalem by *gbh* and the synonymous expression, "they did abominable things before me (Yahweh)" (cf. v. 49). *gbh* is used of the king of Tyre because he claims that he possesses the qualities and characteristics of a God-King (Ezk. 28:2,5,17), of King Hezekiah because he was not grateful for being miraculously healed (2 Ch. 32:25), and of King Uzziah because he took it upon himself to perform a cultic function (2 Ch. 26:16). [11] Like the verb, the nouns and adjective from the root *gbh* are used in the religious and ethical sense to describe an evildoer (*rasha'*, Ps. 10:4), the ungodly behavior of man in general (Isa. 2:11,12, conjec., 17–in antithesis to the statement, "Yahweh alone will be exalted," *nisgabh*), man's impudent (*'athaq*) talk (1 S. 2:3), etc. [12]

In the sphere of religion and ethics, noun forms of the root *gbh* are found in a neutral sense three times at the most. In Job 41:26(34), "everything that is high" has reference to one's position in the social order. The real meaning of "high" in the expression "they are afraid of what is high" in Eccl. 12:5 remains obscure. It probably has reference to something that a person desires in his younger years, thus possibly "respect, high social position." If the textual conjecture in Ps. 90:10 is correct, the noun *gobhah* here must have the unique meaning of "maximum." The use of the root *gbh* in the negative condemnatory statements against all human striving after high position, against all pride, stands in contrast to the use of the same root in positive statements concerning the glory of God: Isa. 5:15f.–Yahweh is "exalted" in justice, in which he humbles (*shachach, shaphel*) the "proud" (*'ene ghebhohim*, "the eyes of the haughty," v. 15). The hymn in Ps. 113:5 praises Yahweh as incomparable, because he "exalted" his dwelling in the heavens (vv. 4,6). At the same time, his chosen servant (Isa. 52:13, where *gabhah* appears in parallelism with *rum*, "to exalt," and *nasa'*, "to be lifted up") and the righteous in general (Job 36:7) are "exalted." Of course, man cannot clothe himself with "glory." When God summons Job to do this, he is speaking ironically in order to make it clear to him that he is powerless (Job 40:10, where *gbh* stands in parallelism with *ga'on*, "majesty"). In a deliberately mysterious statement, the author of Eccl. 5:7(8) describes the hierarchy of those who hinder justice even when the person being oppressed is not able to see this, and he carries this hierarchy to the limit by the threefold repetition of the adj. *gabhoah*, which is used substantivally (in this passage it is necessary to restore a member that has fallen out).

Hentschke

---

[11] For additional texts with similar content, see IV.1.
[12] See IV.1.

גְּבוּל *gᵉbhûl;* **גָּבַל** *gābhal;* **גְּבוּלָה** *gᵉbhûlāh*

Contents: I. In the Ancient Near East: 1. Egypt; 2. In Mesopotamia and Among the Hittites; 3. In West Semitic Dialects. II. In the OT: 1. Etymology, Cognate Words; 2. Meaning and Use; 3. Theological Significance.

I. In the Ancient Near East.

1. *Egypt.* The Egyp. *tȝš,* "boundary," [1] in the later period also means "territory." It appears in connection with words for "boundary stone," and with modifiers like "northern, southern boundary." It denotes the boundary of a field, a province, a land, or a person (a king, the enemy). The following are familiar expressions in Egyptian literature: "the boundary reaches," "is secured"; "settle, maintain, guard, extend, pass over, the boundaries."

Another Egyptian word for "boundary" is *dr(w),* [2] which means "(extreme) end," "goal," and sometimes "territory, region." It is used, e.g., of the end of heaven and earth, and frequently appears with a figurative meaning: the limits of eternity, the limits of knowledge; it also occurs in expressions meaning "unlimited." The divine and royal epithet *nb r dr,* Lord even to the utmost limit or boundary, i.e., "Lord of all," is worthy of note.

Boundary stones between fields are mentioned in Egyptian literature, but as yet none has been discovered. [3] The boundary stones of orphans and widows are not to be removed (Amenemope, 6). Restoring provincial borders [4] is an organizational activity, which is to be compared with that of the creator-god. [5] Sixteen boundary stelae of the city territory are preserved from Amarna; they contain a proclamation in which the king vows not to abandon the territory, thus not to pass over its borders. [6]

A stela of Sesostris III in Nubia deals with the borders of the land. On this stela we read: "I established my border, in the process of which I went farther than my father.... Whichever of my sons maintains this border that has established

---

gᵉbhûl. M. Dahood, "Biblical Geography," *Greg,* 43 (1962), 73f.; A. Erman–H. Ranke, *Ägypten und ägyptisches Leben im Altertum* (1923); A. H. Grayson–E. von Schuler, "Grenze," *RLA,* III, 638-643; L. Koehler, "Der Berg als Grenze," *ZDPV,* 62 (1939), 124f.; F. R. Kraus, "Provinzen des neusumerischen Reiches von Ur," *ZA,* 51 (1955), 45-75; A. Saarisalo, *The Boundary between Issachar and Naphtali* (Helsinki, 1927); M. Saebø, "Israels Land og grenser i det Gamle Testamente," *For Israel og Evangeliet. Festschrift M. Solheim* (Oslo, 1971), 23-41 (German trans. in preparation for *ZDPV*); F. X. Steinmetzer, *Die babylonischen kudurru (Grenzsteine) als Urkundenform. Studien zur Geschichte und Kultur des Altertums,* 11/4-5 (1922); E. F. Weidner, *Politische Dokumente aus Kleinasien. Die Staatsverträge in akk. Sprache aus dem Archiv von Boghazköi. BoSt,* 1/8-9 (1923).

[1] *WbÄS,* V, 234ff.
[2] *WbÄS,* V, 585ff.
[3] Erman-Ranke, 420.
[4] Erman-Ranke, 104.
[5] Erman-Ranke, 101f.
[6] *RÄR,* 776.

my majesty is my son; he is like the son (Horus) who protected his father and maintained the borders of the one who begot him." [7] The king also set up a statue of himself on this border in order to strengthen the will of the people to resist enemy encroachment.

2. *In Mesopotamia and Among the Hittites.* There are several words for "border" in Sumerian: *bulug, kisurra,* and *zag.* Akkadian has *itû, kisurrû, kudurru, misru, pātu, pulukku,* and *tahūmu.* Most of these words mean either "border" or "territory," and sometimes it is hard to determine the exact nuance. In Middle Babylonian, *kudurru* also means "boundary-stone," [8] and *pulukku* "boundary post." [9]

The delineation of national borders was usually followed by a list of cities that lay within those borders and that were frequently also provided with garrisons for their defense. One document, which possibly came originally from the temple of Enlil at Nippur, [10] describes the provincial borders of the Neo-Sumerian kingdom with the help of landmarks like cities, villages, sanctuaries, mountains, and watercourses ("canals"). [11]

One inscription of Entemena (middle of the 3rd millennium B.C.) [12] and the so-called Synchronistic History [13] contain records of border disputes. Boundary stones, on which boundary settlements were engraved, may have existed. [14] From the classical period on, we encounter the so-called *kudurru*-stones, which guaranteed the protection of property by their divine symbols and texts; sometimes the piece of property was drawn on the stone. [15] The text of a *kudurru* ends not uncommonly with a curse on anyone who removes the boundary stone. [16]

In Hittite, the word *arha*- means both "border" and "territory." Among the Hittites, the borders of the kingdom also stood under divine protection. It was the king's responsibility to preserve and to expand the borders. Border guards under the command of a *ZAG-aš BĒLU,* "Lord of the border," were responsible for maintaining the boundary. The suzerain established the borders of the administrative areas and vassal states. [17] The course of the boundary was determined by topographical phenomena. [18] There were sacral-legal regulations for the temple areas, which belonged to the deity and whose borders were not to be touched (cf. Ex. 19:12,23). Property rights were strictly guaranteed. The borders were specified exactly in texts dealing with gifts of land and of fields. Formulas

---

[7] Erman-Ranke, 594.
[8] See below.
[9] *AHw,* 499, 879.
[10] Kraus, 68.
[11] *Ibid.,* 52.
[12] E. Sollberger, *Or,* N.S. 28 (1959), 326-350.
[13] CT 34, 38-43; Grayson, 640.
[14] Grayson, 639f.
[15] *Ibid.,* 639.
[16] E.g., Steinmetzer, 8ff.; cf. also U. Seidl, "Die babylonischen Kudurru-Reliefs," *Baghdader Mitteilungen,* 4 (1968), 1-220.
[17] Weidner.
[18] Von Schuler, 642.

of prohibition call to mind similar formulas in the OT: "Do not exceed the borders that I set for you, but maintain them"[19] (cf. Dt. 19:14).

3. *In West Semitic Dialects.* The Ugar. *gbl* occurs twice;[20] it is usually translated "mountain, rock," with reference to Arab. *ǧabal*.[21] In Phoenician and Punic, *gbl* is found with the meanings "border" and "territory," e.g., in *KAI*, 14.20, *gbl 'rṣ*, "the border of the land" (cf. Dt. 19:3).

II. In the OT.

1. *Etymology, Cognate Words.* In Hebrew the root *gbl* occurs as a verb in the qal with the meanings, "to establish a border" (Dt. 19:14), "to bound, border" (Josh. 18:20), and "to border on" (Zec. 9:2), and in the hiphil referring to the "boundary" of a cultic area (Ex. 19:12,23). The noun forms from this root in the OT are *gebhul* and *gebhulah,* both of which mean "border" and "territory," and frequently it is difficult to determine which meaning is intended in a given text.[22] The fem. *gebhulah* is used in the singular in only one passage (Isa. 28:25: the farmer puts spelt "on the border [of his field]"); elsewhere it always occurs in the plural: "territories" (Nu. 32:33; 34:2,12; Josh. 18:20; 19:49), but also with the meaning "border" with the verbs *yatsabh,* "to fix" (Dt. 32:8; Ps. 74:17), *sur* in the hiphil, "to remove" (Isa. 10:13), and *sugh,* "to remove" (Job 24:2).[23] Special meanings of *gebhul* appear in Ezk. 40:12 and 43:13,17. In the first passage, it means a low wall or border that shields the watch chamber in the eastern gate of the city of Jerusalem from the passage through the gate, and in the last two it is the elevated border around the altar.

The root *gbl* also occurs in the city name Gebal, Akk. *Gubla,* Byblos (Ezk. 27:9),[24] as well as in the gentilic *gibhli,* "the Gebalites" (Josh. 13:5; 1 K. 5:32 [Eng. v. 18]).[25] In Ps. 83:8(7) *Gebal* means the region of Edom (Arab. *Ǧibāl,* cf. also *'rṣ gbl* in 1QGenAp 21:11 or *hry gbl* in 21:29 [here = *beharram se'ir,* "in their Mt. Seir"]).[26]

The abstract *gabhluth* is found in Ex. 28:22 and 39:15 in the expression *sharshoth gabhluth,* RSV "twisted chains"; and in Ex. 28:14 we find *mighbaloth,* RSV "twisted." These words belong to the root *gbl* II, which is connected with Syr. *gᵉbal,* "to beat, hammer," Aram. *gbl,* "to knead," and Arab. *ǧiblat,* "well-spun cloth." Driver thinks this root means that the pieces are twisted together and then welded. Thus he translates *sharshoth gabhluth* "chains of welding" or "welded chains."[27] *mighbaloth* would seem to have a similar meaning.

---

[19] *KBo,* IV, 10, verso 15.
[20] *CTA,* 16 [II K], VI, 59; 3 [V AB], VI, 7.
[21] Koehler, Dahood.
[22] Cf. Eissfeldt, *KlSchr,* III (1966), 662f.
[23] Cf. Koehler, 124f.
[24] Cf. S. H. Horn, *ZAW,* 78 (1966), 75; M. Noth, *ZDPV,* 60 (1937), 283f.
[25] W. Eilers, *ZDMG,* 94 (1940), 204, n. 3.
[26] See Fitzmyer, *The Genesis Apocryphon* (Rome, ²1971), 149, 165.
[27] Driver, 254f.

2. *Meaning and Use.* It is quite natural to find *gebhul* in sections of the OT having to do with defining boundaries: Josh. 66 times, Ezk. 39 (esp. in chaps. 40–48), and Nu. 25. In other texts, this word occurs rather rarely, though a little more frequently in the historical books.

The translation "border" is natural when *gebhul* is used as the subj. of *hayah,* "to be," with the prepositions *le,* "to," *'el,* "unto," *'adh,* "up to," and *min,* "from": Gen. 10:19; Nu. 34:3ff.; Dt. 11:24; Josh. 1:4; 13:16,30; 16:5; 17:7,9; 18:12; 19:10,33; Ezk. 47:15,17; 48:28. *Gebhul* also frequently appears with verbs of motion, which define the border from point to point, so to speak: *halakh,* "to go," Josh. 16:8; 17:7; *yatsa',* "to go out, extend," Nu. 34:9; Josh. 15:3,11; 16:6; 18:11,15,17; 19:47; *yaradh,* "to go down," Nu. 34:11f.; Josh. 16:3; 17:9; 18:13,16; *sabhabh* in the niphal, "to turn about, circle," Josh. 15:10; 16:6; 18:14; 19:14; *'abhar,* "to pass on," Josh. 15:4; 18:16,19; *'alah,* "to go up," Josh. 15:6ff.; 18:12; 19:11; *pagha' be,* "to touch," Josh. 19:22,26; *shubh,* "to turn," Josh. 19:12,29,34; and *ta'ar,* "to bend," Josh. 15:9,11; 18:14,17. Some verbs like *yaradh,* "to go down," and *'alah,* "to go up," may have been chosen for topographical reasons. *pagha' be,* "to touch," is used only when the border "touches" Tabor and Carmel. Sometimes the boundaries follow natural topographical phenomena like rivers, lakes, seas, mountains, and valleys; quite frequently cities and villages form boundary points, i.e., the territory between the cities forms the boundary, not the city itself (Ezk. 47:15,17; 48:1). [28] The Levitical cities (Nu. 35:1-8; Josh. 21) seem to have been border towns that were used in defense of the borders. [29]

gebhul can be defined more precisely in different ways:

(a) According to directions (always "boundary"): *gebhul neghebh,* "southern boundary" (Nu. 34:3; Josh. 15:2,4); *gebhul yam,* "western boundary" (Nu. 34:6; Josh. 15:4,12); *gebhul tsaphon,* "northern boundary" (Nu. 34:7,9; Josh. 15:5); and *gebhul qedhemah,* "eastern boundary" (Nu. 34:10; Josh. 15:5; Ezk. 45:7).

(b) By a topographical statement ("boundary"): *gebhul 'arnon,* "the boundary formed by the Arnon" (Nu. 22:36); and *gebhul layyam,* "the bound for the sea" (Jer. 5:22).

(c) By the genitive of the name of a land, a people, or a tribe, sometimes in the sense of "boundary": *gebhul mitsrayim,* "the border of Egypt" (1 K. 5:1 [4:21]); *gebhul 'erets 'edhom,* "the border of the land of Edom" (Nu. 20:23; Josh. 15:1,21); *gebhul mo'abh,* "the boundary of Moab" (Nu. 21:13,15; 33:44; Jgs. 11:18); *gebhul bene 'ammon,* "the boundary of the children of Ammon" (Nu. 21:24; Dt. 3:16; Josh. 13:10); *gebhul hakkena'ani,* "the boundary of the Canaanites" (Gen. 10:19); and sometimes in the sense of "territory": *gebhul mitsrayim,* "the territory of Egypt" (Gen. 47:21; Ex. 10:14,19; 2 Ch. 9:26); *gebhul mo'abh,* "the territory of Moab" (Dt. 2:18; Jgs. 11:18; Isa. 15:8); *gebhul ha'emori,* "the territory of the Amorites" (Nu. 21:13; Josh. 13:4; Jgs. 1:36;

---

[28] Cf. Saarisalo, 131f.
[29] See Aharoni, *The Land of the Bible* ([2]1968), 272f.

11:22). The expression *bekhol gebhul yisra'el* always means "in the whole territory of Israel" (Jgs. 19:29; 1 S. 11:3,7; 27:1; 2 S. 21:5; 1 K. 1:3; 2 K. 10:32; 1 Ch. 21:12); similarly *bighebhul yisra'el* means "in the territory of Israel" (1 S. 7:13; Ezk. 11:10f.; Mal. 1:5). All these passages have reference to the united kingdom; 2 K. 14:25 is the only passage in which *gebhul yisra'el* stands for "the border of (North) Israel." The expression *gebhul yisra'el,* "the territory of Israel," occurs more often than *'erets yisra'el,* "the land of Israel."

gebhul is found with Israelite tribal names with the two meanings "border" and "territory": *gebhul bene 'ephrayim,* "the territory of the children of Ephraim" (Josh. 16:5); *gebhul menashsheh,* "the territory of Manasseh" (Josh. 17:7); *gebhul binyamin,* "the territory of Benjamin" (1 S. 10:2); *gebhul dan,* "the territory of Dan" (Ezk. 48:2); etc.; as well as with suffixes denoting the tribes, e.g., Josh. 13:30; 17:10; 18:5; 19:11.

(d) *gebhul* can also be defined by a genitive that designates the "territory" as the possession of persons or groups, or characterizes it in some other way: *gebhul 'artsekha,* "the border of your land" (Dt. 19:3; Ezk. 47:15, border); *gebhul nachalah* + suf., "the boundary of (their, etc.) inheritance" (Josh. 16:5; 19:10; Jgs. 2:9); *gebhul goralam,* "the territory allotted to them" (Josh. 18:11); and *gebhul 'ir miqlato,* "the boundary of his free city" (Nu. 35:26f.). In Ps. 78:54, *gebhul qodhsho,* "the region of his holiness," i.e., "his holy region," must refer to the land of Canaan; the parallel line says, "the mountain (*har*) which his right hand had won," and therefore, Dahood (with the LXX) interprets *gebhul* as "mountain" [30] (so also 1 S. 13:18; however, Ezk. 43:12 argues against this). *gebhul rish'ah,* "the territory of evil" (Mal. 1:4), is a derogatory name for Edom.

(e) In connection with the names of cities, *gebhul* always seems to mean "territory of": Ekron (Josh. 13:3), Lo-debar (13:26), Jazer (13:25), Beth-horon (16:3), Beth-shemesh (1 S. 6:12), Damascus (Ezk. 47:16f.; 48:1), Hamath (47:15,17), Hauran (47:16); it also has a similar meaning in plural forms with suffixes that refer to cities: 1 S. 5:6; 7:14; 2 K. 15:16; 18:8; Jgs. 1:18; Isa. 54:12; Ps. 147:14.

(f) *gebhul,* "territory," is used with the name of a prince: Sihon (Josh. 12:5; cf. Nu. 21:22f.), Og (Josh. 12:4); cf. the suffix form referring to Pharaoh (Ex. 7:27[8:2]; 10:4), and the king of Edom (Nu. 20:16; 22:36).

(g) *gebhul* occurs as a genitive with *qatseh,* "end," to mean the extreme boundary of a region (Gen. 47:21; Nu. 20:16; 22:36).

(h) *ughebhul,* which occurs 7 times in the OT, is a noteworthy expression. In Nu. 34:6; Josh. 15:12,47, *hayyam haggadhol ughebhul* can hardly mean "the great sea and its coastal territory" (this would be *ughebhulo*), nor can *hayyarden ughebhul* in Dt. 3:17; Josh. 13:23,27, mean "the Jordan and its territory." The translation "and the great sea also (*ve*) as a boundary," or "the Jordan as a boundary," [31] would be more conceivable. A seal inscription from *ca.* 1400 B.C.

---

[30] Dahood, 74.
[31] Cf. Holzinger, *KHC,* VI, 53; M. Ottosson, *Gilead* (Lund, 1969), 116.

with the words *qṣ wgbl,* which Goetze cautiously translates "border and territory," [32] gives little additional help.

3. *Theological Significance.* As everywhere else in the ancient Near East,
people in Israel had great respect for boundaries, both of nations and tribes and
of private property. Agreements over boundaries stood under the protection of
God, [33] and a curse awaited anyone who violated the agreement. The god of the
land guaranteed the borders of the territory where his worshippers lived. The
frequent use of the expression *gebhul yisra' el,* "the territory of Israel," points to
a conscious, most likely religious understanding of the boundary of the national
territory whose Lord and God is Yahweh. When the Philistines sent away the
ark, they watched to see whether it went up on "the way to its own territory"
(*derekh gebhulo*), in order to determine whether Yahweh had caused the misfortune among them (1 S. 6:9)–thus the territory of the ark of Yahweh is identical
with the territory of Yahweh.

But Yahweh's power also extends beyond the territory of Israel (Mal. 1:5). As
Creator, he has directed everything. He set a bound to the waters of chaos (Ps.
104:9), he placed the sand as the bound of the sea (Jer. 5:22); he determined the
bounds of the whole earth (Ps. 74:17) and fixed the bounds of all peoples (Dt.
32:8). By his power, he can also remove the boundaries between the nations and
extend the borders of Israel (Dt. 32:8). In the apportioning of territories to the
tribes, Yahweh determines the boundaries through Moses (Nu. 34) or through
casting lots (Josh. 14–19). Josh. 22:25 says that Yahweh himself determined the
borders.

With regard to private property, respect for boundary stones is emphasized in
the law. "You shall not remove your neighbor's landmark (Heb. *gebhul*)" (Dt.
19:14; cf. the curse in 27:17)–the context refers to the land as a gift of Yahweh.
Similarly we find in Proverbs: "Remove not the ancient landmark which your
fathers have set" (Prov. 22:28). Prov. 23:10 expresses the same respect for ancient inherited boundaries. Here the prohibition is connected with a warning
against breaking into the fields of the fatherless, and allusion is made to Yahweh
as the legal helper of the fatherless. [34] Yahweh himself protects the boundaries
of the widow (15:25). Job says that evildoers remove boundary stones unpunished,
and divest the fatherless, widows, and poor of their property (Job 24:2ff.). Hosea
complains because the princes of Judah remove boundaries (Hos. 5:10). Elijah's
reaction to Ahab's seizure of Naboth's vineyard (1 K. 21) indicates how serious
this crime was thought to be.

Ottosson

גִּבְעָה *gibh'āh* → הר *har*

---

[32] *BASOR,* 129 (1953), 8ff.
[33] Ottosson, *Gilead,* 36-52.
[34] Cf. Amenemope above under I.1.

גְּבַר gābhar; גְּבוּרָה gᵉbhûrāh; גְּבִיר gᵉbhîr;
גִּבּוֹר gibbôr; גֶּבֶר gebher

Contents: I. 1. In the Ancient Near East, Original Meaning; 2. Occurrences in the OT. II. The Verb: 1. Qal; 2. Piel; 3. Hithpael; 4. Hiphil. III. *gebhurah:* 1. Singular: a. As a Physical Concept and in the Military Profession; b. God's Power and Ethical Strength; c. God's Power and God's Name; d. Spiritualization of the Concept in Connection with Man; 2. Plural: The Creative and Saving Acts of God. IV. *gebhir, gebhirah.* V. *gibbor:* 1. General Usage; 2. The "Heroes" of David and David As "Hero"; 3. The Angels As "Heroes" and God As "Hero"; 4. The Expression "Godly Hero" in Isa. 9:5(6); 5. Change of Meaning. VI. *gebher:* 1. Man and Male; 2. The Spiritualization of the Concept: a. In the Formula *ne'um haggebher;* b. The New Concept in the Psalms; c. In the Book of Job; d. In the Qumran Literature.

I. 1. *In the Ancient Near East, Original Meaning.* The root *gbr* can be detected in most of the Semitic languages, if not always in some verb form, at least in derivatives. In Ugaritic, words for this root have not yet been found in texts that have been discovered so far, but it may appear in the proper name *Gbrn.* [1] The Akk. *gapāru, gapru,* [2] is found only rarely, in poetic language. In all occurrences, except in Ethiopic, where the word means "to do, make," the emphasis lies on power and strength, and frequently also on excellence and superiority, as well as on greater strength than in other cases, even if a comparative term is not always expressly mentioned. Thus, e.g., a *gebher,* and even more a *gibbor* (intensive form), has specific noteworthy characteristics that someone else has to a lesser degree or not at all. Thus, finally, we also find that certain word formations from this root are applied to God extensively.

2. *Occurrences in the OT.* In the Hebrew Bible, the verb *gabhar* occurs 24 times, *gebher* 65 times, *gibbor* 159 times, *gebhurah* and *gebhuroth* 64 times, and *gebhir* and *gebhirah* together only 17 times. Of course, there is also a large number of words, both verbs and nouns, that are synonymous with the root *gbr,* e.g., words from the roots → חָזַק *chāzaq,* → כּוֹחַ *kôach,* and → עָזַז *'āzaz;* and we also find a great number of synonymous expressions in other Semitic languages. [3]

---

gābhar. G. W. Ahlström, "Aspects of Syncretism in Israelite Religion," *Horae Soederblomianae,* 5 (1963), 61-85; P. Biard, "La puissance de Dieu," *Travaux de l'Inst. Cath. de Paris,* 7 (1960), 1-104; H. Donner, "Art und Herkunft des Amtes der Königinmutter im AT," *Festschrift für J. Friedrich* (1959), 105-145; H. Fredriksson, *Jahwe als Krieger* (Lund, 1945); W. Grundmann, "δύναμις: The Idea of Power in the OT," *TDNT,* II, 290-99; H. Kosmala, *Hebräer–Essener–Christen* (Leiden, 1959), 208-239; *idem,* "The Term Geber in the OT and in the Scrolls," *SVT,* 17 (1969), 159-169; B. Mazar, "The Military Élite of King David," *VT,* 13 (1963), 310-320; G. Molin, "Die Stellung der *gᵉbira* im Staate Juda," *ThZ,* 10 (1954), 161-175.

[1] *UT,* Glossary, No. 554.
[2] *AHw,* 281.
[3] For details, see below.

II. The Verb.

1. *Qal.* The verb not only has the simple positive meaning "to be strong," but frequently, in fact originally, a comparative sense as well. This explains why it can be connected with the comparative particle *min,* "from," when comparisons are explicitly stated (e.g., in 2 S. 1:23; similarly Ps. 65:4 [Eng v. 3]). *min* can be replaced by *'al* (Gen. 49:26; 2 S. 11:23; Sir. 36:27) or *be* (1 Ch. 5:2). Then the verb has the meaning "to be stronger than, exceed, be superior to, have the upper hand" (*'al* over the enemy, *be* among one's brethren). However, in Ps. 103:11 and 117:2, the prep. *'al* has a literal (local) meaning: "His grace governs us effectively." We find examples without any particle in Ex. 17:11; Jer. 9:2(3); Lam. 1:16; Sir. 39:21,34 (everything has its time, when it is able to come out of its apparent uselessness into the foreground and assume great significance). [4] The only passage where the verb means that man's moral strength is not very powerful in and of itself is found in the prayer of Hannah (1 S. 2:9): "not by (his own) might shall a man prevail" (cf. also the alternation in meaning in *gebhurah* and *gebher*).

2. *Piel.* In the piel, once the root *gbr* means: "to use more power (*chayalim*)" (Eccl. 10:10), and twice it has a causative meaning: "I will make them strong, and they will receive courage" (Zec. 10:6f.); "I will make them strong in Yahweh, and they will walk in his name" (10:12).

3. *Hithpael.* The hithpael of *gbr* sometimes means "to make oneself greater than another, to boast, to be proud": Job 15:25 with *'El-shaddai;* 36:9. Both of these passages in Job have to do with boasting against God. It should be noted in this connection that it is the *gebher* Job who behaves arrogantly toward God— a stylistic fine point of the author of the book. [5] The hithpael also means "to prove oneself to be strong" (Isa. 42:13, with *'al* in the battle against the enemy). In later Hebrew, it is used of a spring that becomes ever stronger (*Aboth* ii.8).

4. *Hiphil.* In Ps. 12:5 (4) we find the expression *lilshonenu naghbir,* "by our tongue (by verbosity) we have made ourselves strong." In Dnl. 9:27, the hiphil of *gbr* is used in the expression, "to make a firm agreement with the multitude of the people." The hiphil also occurs in the text of Sir. 39:34; however, this form is corrected in the margin and seems to approximate the qal in 39:21. [6]

Sometimes the verb must be translated more freely, especially when it is used figuratively. This happens frequently, but one must keep in mind in translating that the element of strength or superiority is always present. Thus *gbr* can mean "to be prominent," "to play a (the primary) role," "to be important," "to have significance," "to be of use or to be distinguished," "to exceed," "to win the victory," etc., especially in later usage (e.g., Sir. 36:27; 39:21,34).

---

[4] See also under II.4. Hiphil.
[5] See below, VI.2.c.
[6] See Smend, *Weisheit des Jesus Sirach,* Heb. section, p. 38.

III. gebhurah.

1. *Singular.* a. *As a Physical Concept and in the Military Profession.* In harmony with the original meaning of the verb *gbr,* generally speaking the cognate noun *gebhurah* means "strength," "power," etc. First, it is used of the physical strength of animals and man, e.g., of the horse (Ps. 147:10a), whose strength is in his hind legs, as the strength of man is in his thighs (*shoq,* v. 10b), and of Leviathan or the dragon (Job 41:4[12]; pl. instead of sing.). Naturally, physical strength is a gift of God (Job 39:19f.). *gebhurah* is also to be understood in the sense of powerful men in Eccl. 10:17 (cf. Jgs. 8:21) in contrast to a child king and his weak princes (v. 16), who begin the day with eating and drinking instead of doing their jobs. The first meal of the day is not supposed to be for drinking and carousing (*shethi*). Here, *gebhurah* is contrasted with drinking and drunkenness (cf. also Jer. 23:9: a *gebher* who has been overcome with wine and thus is no longer a genuine *gebher*), although sometimes the drinking of wine is recommended (but for other reasons) by the author of Qoheleth (briefly in Eccl. 10:19, as also earlier in 8:15). The Song of Deborah compares the manifestation of the love of God with the brilliance of sunrise (Jgs. 5:31). In a special way *gebhurah* is personified in a king (2 K. 18:20). In case of a war, it is not mere words, but planning and military power that decide the outcome (18:20; Isa. 36:5). Generally, *gebhurah* is also used formally of the acts of the king (1 K. 16:27; 22:46[45]; 2 K. 10:34; 13:8,12; 14:15,28). In this connection, the military power is the army (Isa. 3:25). Then *gebhurah* is synonymous with the powerful or cunning execution of a battle, with triumphal power or victory in war (Isa. 28:6; cf. Eccl. 9:11); *qol 'anoth gebhurah* is the cry of victory, the cry of joy over a victory, in distinction from *qol milchamah,* "battle cry," or *qol 'anoth chalushah,* "cry of woe" because of a defeat, or *qol 'annoth* as a common festive or joyous sound of singing, rejoicing, and dancing (Ex. 32:18f.).

b. *God's Power and Ethical Strength.* The king is the personification of power, and since God himself is a lord over all kings, including the suzerain (Aram. *melekh malkhayya',* "king of kings," Dnl. 2:37,47; Ezr. 7:12), which in turn led to the Rabbinic divine title *melekh malkhe hammelakhim,* "king of the kings of kings," his royal power (Ps. 145:11), the highest sovereign power, also extends over all generations and times (145:11-13). It is manifested in his eternal sovereignty (66:7), in his works and mighty deeds (*ma'asim, gebhuroth,* 106:2; 145:4; 150:2), and in justice (*mishpat,* 89:14f.[13f.]; cf. Isa. 42:1-4), righteousness and goodness (*tsedhaqah, tubh, chesedh,* Ps. 145:7,17; etc.; cf. Ex. 20:6). Therefore, his *gebhurah* is proclaimed and sung (Ps. 21:14[13]; 71:18; 145:4). God's wonderful power is reflected in what he has done (Isa. 33:13), and is manifested to man in the works of creation, e.g., in the mountains (Ps. 65:7[6]); elsewhere the physical strength of living creatures is his gift (Job 39:19ff.). From the activity of man, who executes his deeds in war and peace with the hand and the arm (usually the right), the mighty acts of God are also attributed to the hand (→ יד *yādh*) or arm (→ זרוע *z^erôa'*) (Ps. 89:14[13]). The figure "with a mighty hand and an outstretched arm" is old, and is used quite often, especially of the acts of God for Israel, either individually or collectively, or with interchangeable adjectives (e.g., Ex. 3:19; 6:1; Dt. 4:34; 5:15; 6:21; 7:8; 9:26; 11:2; 26:8; 34:12; Jer. 21:5; 32:21; etc.). The expression *ta'oz yadhekha, tarum yeminekha,* "strong is thy hand, high thy right hand," in Ps. 89:14(13), where we also find the expression *zeroa' 'im gebhurah,* "a mighty arm," should be mentioned here. In connection with the figure of the "strong hand," it should be observed that it is not the root *gbr* that is used for "strong," but the synonymous root → חזק *chāzaq,* and that as an adjective. The noun *chozeq* is also used in this connection (however, *bechozeq yadh,* "by strength of hand," appears only in Ex. 13:3,14,16). In other cases, however, *hzq* has not displaced the root *gbr,* especially the noun, when referring to God, and in the final analysis *gebhurah* has been preserved as a principal designation for the power of God, while the root *hzq* is limited to specific mighty acts. Other expressions that are frequently used in place of these words are *koach* and *'oz* with their various cognates.

The word *gebhurah* assumed a rather comprehensive spiritual meaning quite early, although it cannot easily be said when this took place. As has already been noted, God's *gebhurah* is frequently mentioned in connection with justice and righteousness, grace and faithfulness (e.g., Mic. 3:8; Ps. 89:14f.[13f.]). In addition, it is connected with God's spirit, wisdom and understanding, counsel and knowledge (Isa. 11:2; Job 12:13; Prov. 8:14; Sir. 42:21), where all these characteristics are activated and executed in his *gebhurah,* for without them they would all be merely theoretical.

For a fully comprehensive presentation of the statements concerning the might (power, strength, dominion) of God in the OT, naturally it would be necessary to examine not only *gebhurah,* but also all synonymous roots and their derivatives, as well as other ways of describing his might. [7]

c. *God's Power and God's Name.* The divine name Yahweh is great first of all in *gebhurah,* "might" (Jer. 10:6; cf., e.g., in addition → גדלה *gedhullāh,* "greatness," in connection with *gebhurah,* "power," in 1 Ch. 29:11, or *godhel,* "greatness," in connection with *yadhekha hachazaqah,* "thy mighty hand," and the comprehensive *gebhurah,* "mighty acts," at the end in Dt. 3:24; cf. 11:2). In other passages also, the name of Yahweh is sometimes closely connected with his *gebhurah,* with which he created heaven and earth, and which at the same time is connected with his righteousness and uprightness, etc. (cf. Ps. 89:12-15 [11-14]). By his name God saves, and by his might he vindicates (Ps. 54:3[1]); God's name and his *gebhurah* stand in synonymous parallelism here. God himself says: "I will make them know my hand and my *gebhurah* (might), and they shall know that my name is Yahweh" (Jer. 16:21). God shows his might in his saving acts; these also are done in his name (Ps. 20:7f.[6f.]). God's name is identified with his *gebhurah,* "might."

It should be no surprise, therefore, that in the Rabbinic age, when the name Yahweh was no longer uttered, the word *gebhurah* was used along with other

---

[7] Cf. the incomplete and not very clear statements of Grundmann concerning the concepts of might in the OT and in Late Judaism in *TDNT,* II, 290-99; and also Biard.

words as a substitute for the proper name of God. In this way, the name and the person of God, who has all great attributes, who is lord and sovereign over all men and by whom everything is created, and whose sovereignty has always been and will always be exercised, are best expressed. The best-known example of the use of *gebhurah* (= *dýnamis*) as a designation for God is found in the NT. Jesus uses the expression in his trial before Caiaphas (Mt. 26:64 par.), and it can hardly be any accident that Jesus is thinking of the highest power at whose right hand he will sit, since it also gives him his authority (*exousía*, Mt. 28:18). Undoubtedly, none of the other substitute names (and there are many) was able to make the fact of Jesus' authority as clear as this. Thus Jesus' "blasphemy" did not consist in uttering the name of God, but in identifying God with his own power. The Rabbinic literature contains numerous examples of the use of *gebhurah* as a term for God. (Grundmann cites only two Aramaic passages from the Targumim: [8] the assertion concerning the first must signify Targum Jerushalmi on Dt. 33:27; the other passage is insufficient, because the Targum on Jer. 16:14f. would also have to be cited to explain Lk. 22:69.) The following selections from Rabbinic quotations should suffice: *mippi haggebhurah, Siphre Num.* 15:31 (§ 112); *Shabb.* 88b; *Erub.* 54b; *Yeb.* 105b; *Meg.* 31b; *Hor.* 8a; *ARN* 37; *liphne haggebhurah, Shabb.* 87a; *lighebhurah, Sotah* 37a; *ARN* 35; *bighebhurah, Taan.* 2a (with particular emphasis on the power of God). Still another passage must be mentioned here. Since God was able to create the world by his *gebhurah* (the creation is also one of his *gebhuroth*), and since his *gebhurah* is synonymous with his name Yahweh, the Rabbis later reached the conclusion that God created it by or with his name (*Men.* 29b, the Rabbinic explanation of Isa. 26:4). Of course, the expression used in 2 Pet. 1:3 *theía dýnamis,* the divine power working in man (elsewhere in the NT, frequently *dýnamis theoú,* "the power of God" = *gebhurath yhvh* in the OT), occurs in Plato (*Leg.* iii.11, 691e), and then is also used again in the same sense in the Letter of Aristeas (§§ 157, 236, 252). However, *theoú dynasteía,* "power of God," which appears in the Letter of Aristeas (§§ 132, 141, 194) and the LXX, is not found in the NT. In the LXX, *dýnamis* often translates the words *chayil* and *tsabha',* but only rarely *gebhurah,* which is usually rendered by *dynasteía.* This is of interest in the history of religion. Apparently, the identification of *gebhurah* with *dýnamis* belongs to a later period. Philo simply calls God *dýnamis* (*Det. Pot. ins.* 83; further *Vita Mosis* i.111; *Mut. Nom. 29*), but in each case this word is accompanied by an adjective that defines it more precisely, as *theía, hē anōtátō kaí megístē,* or *hē poiētikḗ,* because otherwise a Greek reader would not have understood what was meant by *dýnamis.*

d. *Spiritualization of the Concept in Connection with Man.* Man too, who was created in the image of God, has his *gebhurah,* "might," from God, and, as we have seen, first of all in his physical strength. But as the concept of God's *gebhurah* ultimately also includes spiritual qualities which he possesses to the highest degree, man, as God's creature, shares in his power (cf. Ps. 8:6-10[5-9]).

---

[8] Grundmann, 298.

In the period of Wisdom Literature, naturally wisdom is regarded as a kind of principal concept which sums up other qualities. The book of Proverbs contains a comprehensive synopsis of everything that wisdom embraces (Prov. 8:12-21). It enumerates not only material gains, but also spiritual characteristics that are embodied in the concept of *gebhurah,* among which is wisdom (→ חכמה *chokhmāh*) as an emanation of God himself. It was already present in everything at the beginning and thus participated in creation (cf. Gen. 1:2 with Prov. 8:27f.). Accordingly, all power has its root in wisdom. God brought it into the world before the visible creation of everything and of man, and therefore it is located in the heart of man. Wisdom is better and more valuable than mere physical strength (Eccl. 9:16a), for wisdom is strength absolutely. However, man must remember that wisdom, when it is communicated to man, comes from God (Sir. 1:1). This emphasizes man's dependence on God. On the basis of this knowledge, what is man's crucial responsibility? In order to participate in the gift of wisdom (v. 10b), the fear of God is the indispensable primary condition and requirement of man. The fear of God is the beginning of wisdom (v. 12); it is wisdom's root (v. 16) and crown (v. 18). It leads to the love of God, which is glorious wisdom itself (v. 8b).

gebhurah appears in Job 12:13 in the midst of an enumeration of spiritual qualities like wisdom, counsel, and understanding. In another list (Isa. 11:2), we find the Spirit of God, the spirit of wisdom and understanding, the spirit of counsel and strength (*gebhurah*), the spirit of knowledge and—the fear of God, in which God delights (v. 3). His special joy is not in physical strength, but in those who fear him and hope in his grace (Ps. 147:10f.). Man's strength (his *gebhurah*) lies in quietness, in trusting in God, and not in relying on material possessions (Isa. 30:15f.). The fear of God, which involves obedience to his commandments, encompasses a group of spiritual characteristics that show man the right way (cf. Jer. 9:22f.[23f.]). Thus, *gebhurah* has been removed from the physical sphere and has become spiritualized. The word *gebher* also passed through a similar transition. [9] In connection with this theological change, the word *gebhurtha',* "might," appears in the Aramaic part of Daniel (Dnl. 2:20,23) immediately after *chokhmetha',* "wisdom": God possesses it and gives it to Daniel.

2. *Plural: The Creative and Saving Acts of God.* The pl. *gebhuroth* has retained its original meaning, "mighty acts, acts of victory and salvation." This word occurs in the Bible 11 times (Dt. 3:24; Isa. 63:15; Ps. 20:7[6]; 71:16; 90:10; 106:2; 145:4,12; 150:2; Job 26:14; 41:4[12]; cf. also Sir. 38:6; 42:17; 43:29). All these passages speak of the great acts of God except Ps. 90:10, where *gebhuroth* is used in a secular sense and means very old age. A second exception (Job 41:4[12]) has been mentioned under III.1.a. (cf. Sir. 43:25, of a whale?). The mighty acts of God are first his works of creation, but also his acts toward man, both his acts in the past, especially the exodus from Egypt, and other acts of salvation and deliverance that are expected in the future. The *gebhuroth* that God did in the past are proclaimed and praised, as is to be expected from the

---

[9] See below, VI.2.

particularly numerous passages in the Psalms. And if at a certain time God does not seem to be doing anything for his people, he is reminded of his earlier *gebhuroth* (Isa. 63:15ff.). Sometimes the great deeds of God, in passages where the word *gebhuroth* does not appear, are characterized as wonderful deeds (*niphla'oth*, → פלא *pālā'*; → מפתים *mōph*ᵉ*thîm*) (e.g., Ex. 3:20; Jgs. 6:13; Ps. 9:2-4 [1-3]; 71:16-18; 105:4-6; especially the work of creation, but not this alone, Ps. 136:4ff.).

IV. gebhir, gebhirah. *gebhir* appears only twice in the OT, in Isaac's blessing of Jacob (Gen. 27:29,37). Translators usually render this word "lord (ruler)." The context shows what it really means. Esau, the firstborn, has lost his birthright to Jacob, who now receives the blessing of the firstborn from his father. For this reason, Jacob has become the head of the family after Isaac, and according to the prevailing family law his brother owes him respect and obedience, which includes various services (note the explanatory words *yishtachavu*, "bow down," and *ya'abhdhu*, "serve"). But Esau will free himself later from this yoke under which he is obligated to obey his brother.

gebhirah[10] is a term applied to a woman in contrast to a girl, and indicates that she has some official position. *gebhirah* is used by Hagar to speak of Sarai (Gen. 16:4,8,9), and by the young Israelite maiden to speak of Naaman's wife (2 K. 5:3; other general examples are found in Isa. 24:2; Ps. 123:2; Prov. 30:23). *gebhirah* is also used as a title of the (Egyptian) queen,[11] i.e., the wife of the king (1 K. 11:19), or the mother of the king (1 K. 15:13 = 2 Ch. 15:16; 2 K. 10:13; Jer. 13:18; 29:2).[12] In addition, it is used figuratively of the city of Babylon, which was called the mistress of kingdoms (Isa. 47:5,7, *gebhereth*).

V. gibbor.

1. *General Usage. gibbor*, with the doubling of the middle radical, is an intensive form,[13] and thus means a particularly strong or mighty person who carries out, can carry out, or has carried out great deeds, and surpasses others in doing so. Therefore, the usual translation is "hero," especially in military activities. But it can also be used in a broader sense to refer to any special degree of physical might, power, authority, and splendor ("glory"), e.g., to the lion, which is the mightiest representative of the animal kingdom (Prov. 30:30), or to the sun, which runs its course like a *gibbor*, "strong man" (Ps. 19:6[5]; cf. Jgs. 5:31). The generation of giants, the children of the "sons of the gods," who produced them with the beautiful daughters of men, were *gibborim*, "mighty men," and "men of renown," who performed powerful deeds (Gen. 6:4). Anyone who is exceptionally important or powerful in some field is a *gibbor*, e.g., Nimrod, "a mighty hunter before the Lord" (Gen. 10:9), but who was also a

---

[10] Cf. Molin, 161f.; Donner, Ahlström, 61-85.
[11] De Vaux, *AncIsr*, 117.
[12] Cf. Ahlström.
[13] *BLe*, § 479j.

gibbor on the earth in other respects (v. 8). Even one who is a great drinker and distinguishes himself in this way is called in one passage a *gibbor* in drinking, an *'ish chayil,* "valiant man," in mixing strong drink (Isa. 5:22), but this, of course, is ironical and appears in a Woe Oracle. A *gibbor* can also be a violent man and evildoer (Ps. 52:3-5[1-3]; 120:2-4), but in the view of the Psalms, this does not apply to the true *gibbor.* Sometimes *gibbor* is used to denote the most eminent and leading man in an official vocation. So, e.g., the chief gatekeepers of the Jerusalem temple are called *gibbore hashshe'arim* (1 Ch. 9:26); at the same time, they were also men of acknowledged great ability (26:6).

Several times, *gibbor* appears in the construct followed by *chayil.* Sometimes it is difficult to find the correct meaning of *gibbor chayil,* because the word → חיל *chayil,* can have different meanings. It can mean strength (general, of a warrior, of military forces), ability (in war and in some vocation), or wealth (possessions), but the meaning must be determined by the context. Thus a *gibbor chayil* can be a wealthy man (1 S. 9:1; 2 K. 15:20), a rich landowner (Ruth 2:1), or an able man in any respect, especially with regard to work (Jeroboam I, 1 K. 11:28). In the list of families that settled in Jerusalem under Nehemiah, many are called *gibbore chayil.* Some translators understand this to mean "able men," and others, "able-bodied men" (Neh. 11:14; in this connection, 11:6 has *'anshe,* "men," instead of *gibbore;* 11:8 has the incomprehensible expression *gabbai sallai,* which probably should be read *gibbore chayil*); perhaps this expression should be understood in both senses.

By far the most frequent use of the word *gibbor* occurs in connection with military activities, especially as a designation for a warrior, either a man who is eligible for military service or is able to bear arms, or one who has actually fought in combat, who has already distinguished himself by performing heroic deeds. In this sense, *gibbor* may appear alone (1 S. 2:4; Jer. 46:12; 51:30; Hos. 10:13; Am. 2:14; Zeph. 1:14; Eccl. 9:11; etc.), or it may be expanded with similar expressions, as *'ish gibbor* (1 S. 14:52), *gibbor(e) (ha)chayil* or *chayalim* (Josh. 1:14; 8:3; 10:7; Jgs. 6:12; 11:1; 1 Ch. 7:5; 2 Ch. 13:3; 14:7[8]), *gibbor milchamah* with *'ish bachur* (2 Ch. 13:3), or other synonymous additions like *gibbor maskil* (Jer. 50:9); *'am ('ish) (ham)milchamah* (Josh. 8:3; 10:7; Ezk. 39:20); *'anshe chayil lammilchamah* (Jer. 48:14); etc. The Aram. *gibbara'* is found only once in the Bible (Dnl. 3:20). But the whole expression used in the passage, *gibbare chayil di bhechayeleh,* hardly means anything more than "powerful men in his army." Of all the derivatives from the root *gbr, gibbor* occurs most frequently in the OT. Most passages that use this word refer to military activity. This shows clearly how much wars stood in the center of ancient Israelite life.

2. *The "Heroes" of David and David As "Hero."* The "heroes of David" constitute a special group of *gibborim,* and they are mentioned frequently in the OT. [14] At the same time, a portion of this group also formed the bodyguard (*mishma'ath*) of the king (2 S. 23:23). This must have been composed of particularly strong and powerful men who were taken from the Cretans and Philistines

---

[14] Cf. de Vaux, *AncIsr,* 220; Mazar, 301f.

(also called "Cherethites and Pelethites") (2 S. 8:18; cf. 15:18; 23:23), who were probably taller and stronger in stature than the Israelites. As the king's body-guard, they were quartered in the *beth haggibborim,* "house of the heroes," but this is not mentioned as being in the city of David until Neh. 3:16. In battle, they were the most outstanding warriors (cf. 2 S. 10:7). But there are other "heroes" outside this bodyguard, and when *gibbor* is applied to them it is almost equivalent to a title or rank. First of all, we may call attention to "The Three" (2 S. 23:8-12), who were part of "The Thirty." Then the heroic acts of two others are recorded: one was the head of "The Thirty," and the other the head of the body-guard (23:18-23). Finally, "The Thirty" are listed by name (23:24-39; but the list has 31 names, not 30, and altogether the total ought to be 37 [v. 39], but there are only 36 in all [divergent statements occur in 1 Ch. 11:10-47; 27:6]). All are called "heroes" (1 Ch. 11:26). The Song of Solomon is able to record that king Solomon had a bodyguard of "60 heroes of the heroes of Israel" (Cant. 3:7). The "heroes of David" are also mentioned in the conflict over his successor to the throne as followers of Solomon (1 K. 1:8,10; 1 Ch. 29:24).

It is quite possible that David himself was regarded as a "hero," at least the people considered him one (cf. 1 S. 17:4ff.; 18:6f.,14-16). In one account, the young David is already called *gibbor chayil,* "a man of valor," and a man of war (1 S. 16:18). At the end of 2 Samuel, there appears as an addition David's song of thanksgiving and victory to Yahweh because he saved David from the hand of all his enemies. In this song we read: " . . . With the perfect (upright) *gibbor* he shows himself upright" (2 S. 22:26). In this song, David speaks wholly of himself.

But this song of David is taken up in the Psalter (Ps. 18), and there the word *gibbor* is replaced by the word *gebher.* This does not seem to be a scribal error. Although this song is also provided with the name of its author, David, in the Psalm collection, in essence the Psalm collection does not intend to relate history, but to build up the individual and the community. The average man in the com-munity is probably hardly a *gibbor,* but he can always be a *gebher,* although the word *gibbor* was also used in a spiritual sense; but the word *gebher* with its spiritual sense assumed this role entirely in the Psalms. [15] Here it should also be mentioned that David was called simply *gebher* in the heading to his "Last Words" (2 S. 23:1), but in an ancient traditional formula (*ne'um haggebher*). [16]

3. *The Angels As "Heroes" and God As "Hero."* The angels of God are called *gibbore koach,* "heroes of power," because they do God's word and carry out his commandment (Ps. 103:20 par., *mal'akhav;* cf. 1QH 8:11; 10:33f.). Thus God's judgment will also be carried out by these heroes (Joel 4:11[3:11]), and afterward the heathen will be summoned to lead all their great warriors into the battle in the Valley of Jehoshaphat. Here the word *gibbor* still clearly has a realistic, military meaning, as is also the case when it is applied to the com-mander-in-chief, *yhvh tsebha'oth,* "Yahweh of hosts" (Jer. 32:18). God himself

---

[15] See below.

[16] See VI.2.a.

fights with his hosts on Israel's behalf against her enemies, and avenges their sins which they have committed against Israel. He also has at his disposal individual angels for special tasks. He possesses an incomparable power, and he has the greatest military might. He is the *gibbor* par excellence. Not only does he go out to battle as a *gibbor,* stir up his fury, utter the battle cry, and show himself mighty (*yithgabbar*) against his foes (Isa. 42:13), but he is also a war hero in fact, as, e.g., the psalmist summons the gatekeepers to the victorious return of the honorable king (Ps. 24:7-10): "... Yahweh *'izzuz veghibbor,* strong and mighty, Yahweh a *gibbor milchamah,* a war hero." Therefore, in times of apostasy Israel is summoned to return to *'el gibbor* (Isa. 10:21). The phrase *'el gibbor* appears several times in the Bible. Viewed grammatically, the epithet *gibbor* here is used adjectivally, and sometimes other adjectives were also connected with it: *ha'el haggadhol haggibbor vehannora',* "the great, the mighty, and the terrible God," who is God of gods and Lord of lords (Dt. 10:17). This same formula with the three attributes of God also appears in the great prayer of repentance after the reading of the law under Ezra (Neh. 9:32). Sometimes the last adjective is omitted (Jer. 32:18, where the synonymous expression *yhvh tsebha'oth,* "Yahweh of hosts," is found instead), sometimes the middle word *gibbor* (Dt. 7:21; Neh. 1:5; Dnl. 9:4), and sometimes the last two words (Ps. 77:14[13]; 95:3), but the statement always refers to the great power of God and his wonderful and saving acts, for Yahweh is a *gibbor* who brings salvation (RSV, "gives victory") to his people (Zeph. 3:17).

4. *The Expression "Godly Hero" in Isa. 9:5(6).* But *'el gibbor* is used in still another context, as one of the special characteristics of the coming ruler from the house of David (Isa. 9:5[6]). Christian theology has understood this as a prediction of its Messiah, and not least because of the expression *'el gibbor,* which it considers to be unsuitable in referring to a human king. Like the other attributes mentioned in this verse, it indicates an extraordinary quality connected with the new kingdom to be created by God, a kingdom that had never existed before (v. 6[7]). In fact, it is hardly correct to translate this expression "godly hero" or "hero of God"; instead, it is a special title which will be given to the incomparable coming king (cf. Ps. 2:6-8; 89:20ff.[19ff.]; 110). [17] The qualities that are represented by these expressions are God's prerogatives and belong to his *gebhurah,* which is identified with the name of God. The coming king has wonderful counsel (with all knowledge and understanding); he will practice justice and righteousness in an everlasting kingdom of peace. It is God himself who wills this, and thus the coming king will rule in and with God's name (Isa. 9:6[7]; cf. 10:20f.).

5. *Change of Meaning.* A renunciation of everything that is called *gibbor* in the physical or any other visible sense is found in the prophet Jeremiah. If one is a *gibbor,* "mighty man," he is not to glory in his *gebhurah,* "might," or his

---

[17] On the whole problem, see Henri Frankfort, *Kingship and the Gods* (Chicago, 1948); additional literature may be found in H. Wildberger, *BK,* X, 362f., 382f.

riches or his own wisdom, but in that he understands and knows God, who alone practices steadfast love, justice, and righteousness in the earth. In these things God delights (Jer. 9:22f.[23f.]). Therefore, the person who fears God, respects his commandments and gladly complies with them will be rewarded with prosperity; God's blessings, which ultimately do not consist of wealth, rest on him. The blessing of God even extends to his descendants, who are a generation of honest and upright men that really deserve the name *gibbor* (Ps. 112). Behind this lies a strong transformation of the old idea of *gibbor* into the spiritual, just as was the case with *gebhurah* and (as will be seen) *gebher*. The emphasis no longer lies on the physical and material. However, there is only very little reference to a more spiritual interpretation of the word *gibbor,* and the mighty acts of the *gibbor* also continue to be emphasized.

VI. gebher.

1. *Man and Male.* A *gebher* is less than a *gibbor,* which is indicated first of all formally in that *gebher* is a simple, and not an intensive, form. However, *gebher* does not mean simply a man like → אדם *'ādhām* or → אנוש *'enôsh*, neither of which indicates a particular sex, nor does it mean man in general, for which the OT uses the Heb. → איש *'ish*. The word *'ish* is also known in Aramaic, but it does not occur in Biblical Aramaic. In its place we find Aram. *gebhar*, which is widely used and means simply "man," like Heb. *'ish* (Ezr. 4:21; 5:4,10; 6:8). Of course, the word *gebher* also contains the element of strength, especially in a general sense. A *gebher* without power is a self-contradiction, and is as good as dead (Ps. 88:5f.[4f.]). Similarly, a drunken *gebher* is a miserable creature (Jer. 23:9). This word is used only once of a newborn (male) child (Job 3:3), but this is a child with a special future. [18] Apart from this one exception, the *gebharim* are always grown men; children are not numbered with them (Ex. 12:37), and neither are women, of course. They are mentioned separately (Jer. 43:6; 44:20). But a *gebher* is compared with a woman if he is a helpless man, he acts like a woman, his hands are on his loins like a woman in labor, and he becomes pale (Jer. 30:6). When David assembles the Levites, the men who are 30 years of age and older are called *gebharim*. They are probably also the more important men in the Levitical families (1 Ch. 23:3; cf. 24:4 and 26:12). The younger Levites over 20 years of age who are on duty are not yet called *gebharim* in the same chapter (23:24,27). In the military service the younger soldiers, probably 20 years of age and older, are called *bachurim*, "young men" (Jer. 49:26; 50:30; etc.). However, it is important that a man, even if he is young, have a wife and children. If he has no children, he is designated as childless. Childlessness is regarded as an evil omen: a man cannot be a *gebher* (and he will not be successful in life, Jer. 22:30) without becoming a husband and having children. This ability is an essential part of the concept *gebher* from the beginning, and is never lost later. Thus the meaning of *gebher* is very close to that of → זכר *zākhār,* "male." Jeremiah prophesies that God will create something new on the earth: "a woman (*neqebhah*) courts

---

[18] See below, VI.2.c.

(attaches herself to) a *gebher"* (31:22). Of course, this passage has a figurative sense, but it obviously refers to the story of the creation of man (Gen. 1:27f.), according to which God created man as *zakhar,* "male," and *neqebhah,* "female." The word *neqebhah* refers directly to the sexual task of the woman, even if God's command to reproduce did not follow immediately. However, Jeremiah uses the word *gebher* for the male, and not *zakhar,* but sometimes he uses these two words in parallelism and synonymously (Jer. 30:6!). A passage in the Song of Deborah is somewhat stronger (Jgs. 5:30: "a womb (RSV maiden) or two for every *gebher* [man]"). *KBL* justifies the coarseness of this statement by pointing out that it represents the language of soldiers. But this did not prevent Deborah from singing the song, including this expression, which is put in the mouths of the mother of Sisera and her wise ladies of nobility (5:1,28f.).

The word *gebher* seems to have had this secondary sexual meaning, "male," from the earliest time and to have always retained it, because in Rabbinic Hebrew it is the normal word for a (powerful) penis. Also, it is no longer used as the word for "man," but serves only as the word for "cock." In this later Hebrew, then, "man" is always simply *'ish,* including a strong or courageous man, in a sense similar to our "man" in English. The same subordinate sexual meaning of the word is also found in the Aram. intensive form *gibbara'.*

2. *The Spiritualization of the Concept.* a. *In the formula ne'um haggebher.* In the OT, frequently the word *gebher* is used without implying physical strength or virility, in reference to a man who stands in a special relationship to God. The oldest example is Balaam, who is introduced simply as *gebher,* and who begins his speech with *ne'um haggebher,* "saying (or oracle) of the *gebher"* (Nu. 24:3f.,15f.). But in these cases, his dictum is not his own, but Balaam observes explicitly concerning himself that he has an open (inner) eye or a closed (outer) eye, [19] and that he hears and sees the words of God because he has the knowledge of the Most High. The Hebrew prophets do not use this formula, but are satisfied with a simple *ne'um yhvh,* "a saying (or an oracle) of Yahweh." However, the old formula appears once in connection with David, whose last words are introduced with *ne'um davidh,* "the oracle of David," and *ne'um haggebher,* "the oracle of the man" (2 S. 23:1ff.). Here also, David begins with the remark that the Spirit of Yahweh spoke in him and that his (God's) word is upon his tongue (= comes out of David's mouth). At this time, David is an old man, and Balaam too is no longer young; both proclaim God's wisdom, just as elsewhere in the OT the formula *ne'um yhvh,* "an oracle of Yahweh," expressly introduces God's oracle. The third and last example is found in Proverbs (30:1), where the *gebher* is probably an old wise man whose name is Agur. He tells how he had labored and become totally exhausted. He has to state that he is a stupid man (or a beast) and not a man, for he has not learned wisdom or knowledge from himself, he does not have divine wisdom, and to prove the impossibility of gaining

---

[19] See the Lexicons.

such wisdom he raises some questions that no man can answer. But he refers to God's words, which endure and to which one need add nothing of one's own. The true nature of a *gebher* consists in his attaining wisdom by simply trusting in God (vv. 5f.).

b. *The New Concept in the Psalms.* The word *gebher* receives a far-reaching new meaning: a man is called *gebher* when he stands in an intimate relationship with God, trusts and fears God, and does what God requires of him. The formula *ne'um haggebher,* "an oracle of the man," in the old sense of the divine utterance of a wise man dies out in the Bible. Agur is still called *gebher* in the traditional sense, but his "knowledge" is a new kind of knowledge (cf. also Eccl. 8:1,16f.). Out of his new experience, the psalmist sings "a new song": "Blessed is the *gebher* who makes Yahweh his trust," who delights in doing the will of God, in which alone is righteousness, steadfast love, and truth (Ps. 40:5,9-12[4,8-11]). In order to understand the concept intended here, it is necessary to see the *gebher* passages in their context. We also find the same thought expressed in Jer. 17:7: this *gebher* is blessed, but the *gebher* who trusts in man and turns away from Yahweh is cursed (v. 5). He is not the genuine *gebher* who turns his heart away from Yahweh, he produces nothing good (vv. 5f.). Likewise, the righteous laugh at this kind of *gebher,* who trusts in his riches and the strength of his malice instead of in God (Ps. 52:8-10[6-8]). Happy is the *gebher* who trusts in Yahweh and fears him (34:9f.[8f.]). But also blessed is he whom the Lord chastens and teaches out of his law (94:12). Then in postexilic Judaism, the "power of the Torah" came to be more and more central. [20] Of course, sometimes God allows the *gebher* to fall into the hands of oppressors and into misfortune (88:5[4]; 89:49-52[48-51]); but he cries out to God day and night (88:2 [1]), and knows that he will help him. God also treats a blameless *gebher* in a blameless manner (18:26[25]). Ps. 37 describes the deeds of the wicked and of the righteous; the wicked are destroyed once and for all, but the steps of the *gebher* are established by the Lord; God does not allow him to fall completely, but he sustains his hand (37:23f.). In some cases, the Psalms also use the general word *'ish* instead of *gebher* (e.g., Ps. 1:1), but in no way does this impair the fact that the word *gebher* had now assumed the clearly outlined meaning of a man who fears God and trusts in him. All the passages in the Psalms easily fit this definition, and provide a perfect picture of the righteous man before God. Two other passages deserve brief consideration. They appear in Pss. 127 and 128, which belong together. The former speaks of the blessing of children. Sons are a heritage of God; they are like arrows in the quiver of a warrior (*gibbor*). The reference here especially is to sons who have demonstrated their youthful strength, probably to the *gebher,* whose quiver, therefore, is full of them. *gibbor* must be understood figuratively, and once again *gebher* has reference to the virility of his youth (127:4f.). However, the next psalm affirms that this and other gifts are blessings from God for the *gebher* who fears God and walks in his way (128:1,4). Many psalms are full of ideas and subjects that describe the man who is righteous

---

[20] See *TDNT,* II, 297f.

and well-pleasing to God, but they do not always use the word *gebher*.

The book of Proverbs has a number of passages that use *gebher,* but these do not present a unified picture, because the proverbs go back to different sources. In most of the passages, the word is used in a literal sense, and the statements are based on experience and observation (6:34; 28:3,21; 29:5; 30:19). The other three passages are to be understood spiritually (20:24 = Ps. 37:23; 24:5; 30:1, *ne'um haggebher,* "an oracle of the man").

c. *In the Book of Job.* The book of Job is particularly instructive concerning the changed meaning of *gebher*. It deals with the problem of a right relationship with God, and finally answers the question of how a *gebher* proves himself to be such before God. *gebher* occurs 15 times in all in Job (3:3,23; 4:17; 10:5; 14:10,14; 16:21; 22:2; 33:17,29; 34:7,9,34; 38:3; 40:7). Along with *gebher,* the words *'adham, 'ish,* and *'enosh* (all meaning "man") appear in Job. In fact, they are found much more frequently than *gebher,* and actually the word *gebher* stands in contrast to these three words. Not only does the book of Job tell the story of Job's purification, but at the same time it also makes it clear what a *gebher* is, or what he is not. Job regards himself as a righteous *gebher,* which can clearly be ascertained from his birth on (3:3); he is a man who, according to his own testimony, has always lived a perfect life before God from the very beginning, and yet God has mistreated him. Why, then, should the *gebher* see the light of the world when his entire existence is made so impossible, when he must live without God's recognition and has no prospect in the future? Job's friends do not call him *gebher,* and when they use this word in speaking to Job, it is only to carry the idea *ad absurdum.* When they mention his birth, they speak of an *'adham* or *'enosh* or one born of a woman (5:7; 15:7,14), and they also use these words elsewhere in their speeches. They make fun of him because he calls himself a priori a *gebher* (15:7-10), and as such boasts of his wisdom, because wisdom, insight and *gebhurah,* "might," are with God alone (12:13). Job, indeed, agrees that he is merely one born of a woman, and also that as a *gebher* he participates in the final destiny of every man (14:1,10,12,14), and yet his situation is different from that of other men (9:2): God must maintain his right (16:21). This is the last time Job uses the term *gebher* in speaking of himself. Sometimes his friends use the word *gebher* in their speeches, but only to defend themselves against Job's criticism. Elihu asks: "What *gebher* is like Job, who drinks up scoffing like water?" (34:7), "for he has said, 'It profits a *gebher* nothing that he should take delight in God'" (34:9). "Men of understanding will say to me, and the (genuine) wise man will hear me" (34:34). "Job speaks without knowledge, his words are without insight" (34:35). Job is not what one would expect in a *gebher,* and Elihu concludes with this solution: the right attitude is the fear of God; God does not regard anyone who is wise in his own conceit (37:24). Job is summoned once again, this time by God, with the same (but now somewhat ironical) address: "Who is this that darkens counsel by words without knowledge? Gird up your loins like a *gebher,* I will question you, and you shall declare to me" (38:2f.; this address is repeated in 40:7). God questions Job, and Job becomes silent, confesses that he knows nothing, and repents (40:3-5; 42:2-

6). Job is not a *gebher* as he insists, at any rate, not one who excels by his own wisdom or who can dispute with God. Elihu's final word proves to be valid, and is silently supported by God. In the final analysis, true wisdom for man is humility before God and the fear of God (including the fulfillment of his commandments). The conclusion of the book of Job agrees with that of the Psalms on this point. Agur himself is called a *gebher,* but he also knows that in spite of every effort he has not learned wisdom so that he might arrive at holy knowledge (Prov. 30:1ff.; cf. Eccl. 8:16f.). God's word is real truth and all find refuge behind his shield.

The LXX in Job translates *gebher* almost always basically correctly by Gk. *anḗr,* except in 3:3; 14:14; and 33:17. In the last two passages, the LXX saw an *ánthrōpos* only in a general sense, in spite of the fact that the Hebrew original relates the situation expressly to Job as a *gebher.* In 3:3, the author calls a newborn child a *gebher,* which is very unusual. By using this word, he intended to say that the child was already determined from his birth to be a particular man, in any case as far as Job's opinion of himself is concerned. But now that Job sees the senselessness of his present existence, he wishes he had never been born, since it was with his birth that his miserable existence began. But the Greek translators understood the birth of the child here simply as the birth of a male child in the sense that the three friends thought and spoke, and thus chose the word *ársen* (= *zakhar,* "male," as in Gen. 1:27) to translate *gebher.* But the intention of the Hebrew author to express significantly an important fact concerning Job's regard for his own life is lost in this rendering.

d. *In the Qumran Literature.* Finally, the word *gebher* in the new sense became a technical term in the theology of the Qumran literature. Even though we cannot go into detail as to the place of this word in Qumran theology, still, with regard to the interpretation of the whole idea, we must point out that the Qumran literature has taken up the meanings of *gebher* commonly found in the Psalms, and the explanations of what a *gebher* is and what he is not as given in the book of Job, and has assimilated them in its own way. Like the book of Job, the Qumran writings use *'ish,* "man" (*bene 'ish,* "sons of man"), and *'adham,* "man" (*ben 'adham,* "son of man"), to denote the common man, and *'enosh,* "man," *basar,* "flesh," or *yeludh 'ishshah,* "born of woman," in particular when referring to man with emphasis on his weakness, wretchedness, or transitoriness, while they consistently use *gebher* to designate the man chosen from the *bene 'ish,* "sons of men." The Qumran *gebher* is also finally purified, like Job (1QS 4:20; 1QH 5:16; 6:8; cf. Elihu's first speech, esp. Job 33:16-28), but the perfect *gebher* will not appear until the end of the days when God creates new things (1QS 4:23-25). Everyone who is accepted in the community is naturally expected to pursue the *gebher* with good (10:18), for he is indeed his companion. Since the word *gebher* has taken on a more stereotyped and clearer meaning, the widely misunderstood passage in the so-called Thanksgiving Psalm (1QH 3:7ff.) can also be explained. Many exegetes of this text, including Dupont-Sommer, M. Black, and K. Schubert, think it refers to the birth of the Messiah, since it has borrowed various expressions from Isa. 9:5(6) and 11:2. But it does not use the expression *gibbor,* much less the complete title *'El gibbor* (the word *gibbor* appears quite frequently in the Scrolls, esp. in 1QM and 1QH, where it usually refers to a warrior, a violent man, or even an angel), but only the simple word *gebher.* Here, the author of the Hodayoth describes symbolically the sufferings under which a *gebher* is born (cf. also the expressions in the NT for rebirth or for putting on the new man). The author begins the description in the first person, and immediately after this he thanks God for saving him from the Pit (*shachath she'ol*) (on this, see the reception of the sinner and the hymn of thanksgiving of the redeemed in Job 33:23-28; cf. 33:28 with 1QH 3:19). Here the Hodayoth poet gives information about his own experience, and it is quite possible that he himself is "the Teacher of Righteousness," since Ps. 37:23f. is applied to the same teacher in the Qumran pesher. It almost goes without saying that the *gebhurath 'El,* "power of God," and the wisdom of God are mentioned and glorified frequently in the Scrolls. [21]

Kosmala

---

[21] Cf. Kosmala, *Hebräer . . .* , "The Term Geber. . . . "

| גַּד *gadh;* גָּד *gādh* |

Contents: I. 1. Etymology, Use in the Ancient Near East; 2. Meaning. II. Secular Usage: 1. As an Appellative; 2. As the Name of Persons and of a Tribe. III. Religious Usage: 1. As a Divine Name; 2. As an Epithet in Place Names; 3. Theological Relevance.

I. 1. *Etymology, Use in the Ancient Near East.* The noun *gadh* is a West Semitic word, which is probably to be derived from the root *gdd*="to cut off" (Old South Arab. "to distribute," "to decide"), [1] but it may also be a substantive not derived from a verb. In addition to Hebrew, it appears (partly as an element in compound names) also in the Mari texts, [2] in Ugaritic, [3] and in Phoenician, Punic, Aramaic, Nabatean, Palmyrenian, Syriac, Mandean, Old South Arabic, Arabic, and Ethiopic texts and inscriptions. [4]

---

gadh. W. W. Graf Baudissin, *Kyrios als Gottesname im Judentum und seine Stelle in der Religionsgeschichte,* III (1929); O. Eissfeldt, "Götternamen und Gottesvorstellungen bei den Semiten," *ZDMG,* 83 (1929), 21-36=*KlSchr,* I, 194-205; *idem,* "'Gut Glück!' in semitischer Namengebung," *JBL,* 82 (1963), 195-200=*KlSchr,* IV, 73-78; Haussig, *WbMyth,* I (1965); M. Noth, "Mari und Israel," *Geschichte und AT. Albrecht Alt zum 70. Geburtstag* (1953), 127-152; G. Wallis, "Glücksgötter," *BHHW,* I, 580.

[1] Cf. W. W. Müller, *ZAW,* 75 (1963), 307.
[2] *ARM,* I, 3.9ff.
[3] *WUS,* 65.
[4] *IPN,* 126; *KBL³,* 169.

2. *Meaning.* All the examples indicate that "fortune" is to be assumed as the original meaning. The LXX and Vulg., which translate the appellative by *týchē* and *felix* respectively (cf. Gen. 30:11), confirm this. But beyond this *gadh* also serves as a proper name for a Semitic deity or as an epithet of local deities. [5]

II. Secular Usage.

1. *As an Appellative.* In the OT a secular use of the word *gadh* is clearly attested once in Gen. 30:11 (*kethibh*). As Baudissin[6] and Eissfeldt[7] have demonstrated, against Noth,[8] *gadh* here is used as an appellative meaning "Good luck!" Furthermore, against Gunkel,[9] there is no reason to doubt that the popular etymological interpretation of the narrator correctly renders what was originally intended. Thus it can be assumed that very early (perhaps even in the common Semitic period) "fortune" was spoken of as a power or a fate, without thus identifying it with "God."

2. *As the Name of Persons and of a Tribe.* This use and interpretation of the word is confirmed by its use as a component in proper names. Thus the names *gaddi'el,* "Gaddiel" (Nu. 13:10), and *gdyv* (in the Samaritan Ostraca)[10] should probably be translated "(my) fortune is God (Yahweh)," while the *i* in *gaddi* (Nu. 13:11) and *gadhi* (2 K. 15:14,17) excludes an interpretation of *gadh* as a divine name.[11] In light of this, it is also possible to understand the proper name *gadh,* "Gad" (1 S. 22:5), and the tribal name *gadh,* "Gad" (Gen. 49:19), as representatives of the appellative meaning, and to explain them as hypocoristical terms that assume supplementation by a divine name (="the god So-and-so gives good fortune"). Thus, seen from a historical point of view, the tribal name *gadh,* "Gad," probably contains the name of a tribal leader (analogous to Simeon and Manasseh).[12]

III. Religious Usage.

1. *As a Divine Name.* A deity with the name Gad is attested for the first time in the postexilic period by the OT (Isa. 65:11), Nabatean, Palmyrenian, Safaitic, and other later proper names (e.g., *'zgd* in the Elephantine Papyri).[13] It follows from the parallelism with a deity called Meni in Isa. 65:11, who is identified as a god of destiny by examples from the ancient Near East,[14] that the deity Gad is to be understood as a god of fortune. Thus it appears that a deity

---

[5] See below, III.
[6] Baudissin, 171.
[7] Eissfeldt, *KlSchr,* IV, 77f.
[8] *IPN,* 126f.
[9] *GHK,* I/1⁶, 334.
[10] *KAI,* 184, 185.
[11] Baudissin, 171, n. 2.
[12] Contra Mowinckel, *BZAW,* 77, 149. On the tribe of Gad, cf. esp. M. Noth, *ZDPV,* 75 (1959), 14-73; and H.-J. Zobel, *BZAW,* 95 (1965), 97-101.
[13] Cf. *PW,* VII, 433-35; *DBS,* 6, 1096f.; 7, 1000; for compound Aram. names with *gaddā* in Babylonian of the 5th century B.C., see K. Tallqvist, *Assyrian Personal Names* (1918), 277a.
[14] Cf. Fohrer, *Das Buch Jesaja,* III (1964), 264f.

Gad evolved relatively late in the first millennium B.C., "when the ancient faith in the gods understood as persons began to give way to powers of fate conceived abstractly." [15] Therefore, the intention to investigate and influence fortune as human fate was connected with the worship of this deity.

2. *As an Epithet in Place Names.* In distinction from this use of *gadh* for a specific deity, the word *gadh* in the place name *ba'al gadh,* "Baal-gad" (Josh. 11:17; 12:7; 13:5), is to be interpreted simply as an epithet of the divine name Baal, which is the way a local Syro-Palestinian deity was designated more precisely. [16] Here, and in the place name *mighdal gadh,* "Migdal-gad" (Josh. 15:37), *gadh* is used in the appellative sense in a manner analogous to *ba'al pe'or,* "Baalpeor," *ba'al chatsor,* "Baal-hazor," or *ba'al tsephon,* "Baal-zephon."

3. *Theological Relevance.* Apart from the word *gadh,* the concept of "fortune" is obviously found everywhere in the OT, where prosperity and success are understood as consequences of Yahweh's intervention. In the postexilic period (when the word *chayyim,* "life," comes more and more to mean "fortune"), the substance of fortune is considered to be more than mere physical existence and its possessions, and to include especially the inner satisfaction of heart through a life governed by communion with God.

Schunck

---

[15] Baudissin, 171.
[16] Fohrer, *Jesaja,* III, 264.

גְּדִי *ge dhî;* גְּדִיָּה *ge dhiyyāh*

Contents: I. Etymology, Extrabiblical Occurrences. II. Use in the OT: 1. Occurrences; 2. Classification; 3. As a Gift; 4. In Connection with a Meal and Sacrifice; 5. The Prohibition Against Boiling a Kid in its Mother's Milk; 6. The LXX.

I. Etymology, Extrabiblical Occurrences. The Heb. *gedhi* is usually explained as a qatl noun form from *gady*[1] or *gadayu,*[2] a root with a weak third radical; fem. *gedhiyyah.* The etymology is obscure. A possible connection with *gadh,* "fortune," *gdd,* "to cut off, separate," *gez, gizzah,* "shearing," *gzh,* "to cut off," *gzz,* "to shear," etc., is equally uncertain.

---

gedhî. G. Dalman, *AuS,* VI (1939), 99f., 190, 197f., 200; D. Daube, "A Note on a Jewish Dietary Law," *JTS,* 37 (1936), 289-291; *idem, Studies in Biblical Law* (Cambridge, 1947), 83f.; Driver, *CML,* 22f., 120-25; H. Kosmala, "The So-Called Ritual Decalogue," *ASTI,* 1 (1962), 31-61, esp. pp. 50-56; M. Radin, "The Kid and its Mother's Milk," *AJSL,* 40 (1923/24), 209-218; J. Wijngaards, *Deuteronomium. BOT,* II/III (Roermond, 1971), 146ff.

[1] *BLe,* § 457p'.
[2] V. Christian, *Untersuchungen zur Laut- und Formenlehre des Hebräischen* (1953), 130.

For the Ugar. *gdy* the meaning "kid" is undisputed, [3] although the only certainty is that it refers to an animal in a series of animals that are sacrificed to Resheph. [4] It must be a small animal that is not very valuable, since only "five pitchers of oil and five baskets of dates (?)" are to be paid for 20 *gdm*. [5] In light of the few occurrences of this word, a distinction between *gd*, "musk-deer (?)," [6] and *gdy* is questionable. [7] In *CTA*, 3 [V AB], II, 2, the goddess ʿAnat is perfumed with the aroma of a kid (*gdy*), which probably refers to an unknown sacrificial rite, but this was used only rarely in Babylon because of the bad odor of the kid. [8] The occurrences in *CTA*, 17 [II D], VI, 21, and *CTA*, 20, I, 4, are textually very uncertain. Also the rubric of the sevenfold boiling of a kid ([*g*]*d*) in milk (*bḥlb*) in SS (*CTA*, 23, 14) is not entirely certain. [9] An Old Aram. *gadeh* is mentioned in the Sefire Inscription II A,2; [10] cf. also the Aram. Targum *gadyāʾ* and Syr. *gadyā*. As a loanword in Neo-Babylonian, *gadū* [11] denotes primarily a one-year-old animal (Old/Middle Bab. *lalū*, *urīṣu*), and sometimes a two-year-old kid (Late Bab. *gizzu*), and appears in particular in records of sales, trading, and debts. [12]

In addition to the Mandean *gadyaʾ* [13] and *Qam Gadya* for the month Tabit, [14] and the Pehlevic *gdy*, [15] we encounter *gdʾ* in the sacrificial tariff of Marseilles [16] with the same meaning as *ʾmr*, "lamb," and *ṣrb ʾyl*, "young ram"; cf. also Plautus *Poenulus* v.1017, *palu mer gade tha*, which is to be translated, "a splendid lamb, a kid art thou." [17]

Proper names with *gdy* are found beginning with Ugar. *bn gdy* [18] and *Ga-ad-ya*, [19] and appear in Aramaic, Neo-Babylonian, Palmyrenian, Phoenician-Punic, and Mandean. It is not clear whether this term always represents the theophorous element → גד *gadh* in these proper names, [20] as Noth thinks. [21] A Latin seal [22] illustrates the inscription *GADIA* by an engraved kid; cf. also the epithets

3 *UT*, 560; *WUS*, 631.

4 *PRU*, II, 154.

5 *UT*, 1097, 3.

6 *WUS*, 629.

7 Cf. *PRU*, II, 184.

8 Cf. B. Landsberger, *AfO*, 10 (1935/36), 158.

9 See below, II.5.

10 *KAI*, 223 A.

11 Cf. *CAD*, V, 9; *AHw*, 273.

12 E.g., *UET*, IV, 111, 1; J. N. Strassmeier, *Inschriften von Nabonidus*, 375.12; 619.11; 884.4, 10; etc.

13 *MdD*, 73b.

14 Cf. E. S. Drower, *The Mandaeans of Iraq and Iran* (Leiden, 1962), 74, 84.

15 *DISO*, 47f.; E. Ebeling, *MAOG*, 14/1 (1941), VII, 3.

16 *CIS*, 165; *KAI*, 69.9; similarly *CIS*, 3915.

17 Contra L. H. Gray, *AJSL*, 39 (1922/23), 82; M. Sznycer, *Les passages puniques en transcription latine dans le "Poenulus" de Plaute. Études et Commentaires*, 65 (Paris, 1967), 137f., 143.

18 *PRU*, V, 42.

19 *PRU*, III, 133.

20 Cf. *WbMyth*, I/1, 438f.

21 *IPN*, 126f.

22 *LidzEph*, I, 142.

Asdroúbas ho ériphos, Hasdrubal Haedus (Livius xxx.42,44), *Diónysos ho eríphios.* and *Diónysos ho aigobólos.* [23]

II. Use in the OT.

1. *Occurrences. gedhi* occurs 17 times in the OT, or perhaps 18 if we include Isa. 5:17 (conjec.), of which it is found 9 times in the construct, *gedhi 'izzim* (Gen. 38:17,20; Jgs. 6:19; 13:15; 15:1; 1 S. 16:20), and *gedhaye 'izzim* (Gen. 27:9,16). In these constructions, *gedhi* means the offspring of goats, a kid, while in the absolute it originally meant the offspring of sheep or goats, thus a lamb or a kid, like *seh;* cf. also other terms for offspring of animals, as *teli, taleh,* "lamb," *ya'arah,* "(bleating) kid," *kebhes,* "young ram," etc.

Some scholars have conjectured that *garim* in Isa. 5:17 should be emended to *gedhayim* following the LXX *árnes.* [24] But it is likely that *garim,* which is in parallelism with *kebhasim,* "lambs," should be derived from Akk. *gūrū, gurratu,* "ewe," [25] Arab. *ğarw,* and Syr. *guryā;* [26] contra Wildberger, who deletes *garim* (which was misread from *gedhayim*) as a secondary explanation of the no longer understandable *mechim,* "fat sheep." [27]

2. *Classification. gedhi* is a member of the sheep and goat family (*tso'n,* "sheep," Gen. 27:9; 38:17; cf. Cant. 1:8); in Isa. 11:6, *gedhi* is found in parallelism with *kebhes,* "lamb." In this same passage, it is also contrasted with the leopard (*namer*) and other wild beasts to convey the idea of cosmic peace. When Samson tears a lion asunder (*shissa'*) as easily as one tears a (cooked) kid in pieces and sets it out for a meal, this demonstrates his heroic power effected by the *ruach,* "Spirit" (Jgs. 14:6).

3. *As a Gift.* Tamar demands of Judah a kid as a gift for the supposed harlot (*zonah*) or cult prostitute (*qedheshah*) (Gen. 38:17,20,23 J; Eissfeldt L), for which he has to leave behind a signet and a staff as a pledge (*'erabhon*). Samson brings a kid to his wife as a gift of reconciliation, but her father does not allow her to go into her chamber (Jgs. 15:1). The interpretation of 1 S. 16:20 (where Jesse sends his son David to Saul with "five" [read *chamishshah* with Wellhausen instead of *chamor,* "ass"] loaves of bread, a skin of wine, and a kid) is disputed. Most scholars think that Jesse sent (an ass), bread, wine, and a kid as a gift to the king, but Stoebe believes these items are the provisions a man takes with him when he enters into the holy war or military service. [28] According to Tob. 2:12-14, Tobit's wife Anna receives a kid as a reward for her weaving.

4. *In Connection with a Meal and Sacrifice.* According to Gen. 27:9,16 (E, Eissfeldt J), Rebekah prepares savory food (*mat'ammim*) from two good kids

---

[23] Cf. *PW,* V/1, 1026, 1028.
[24] Cf. B. Duhm, *GHK* (⁴1922), 59.
[25] *AHw,* 299.
[26] G. R. Driver, *JTS,* 38 (1937), 38f.; cf. O. Kaiser, *ATD,* XVII (²1963), 50.
[27] H. Wildberger, *BK,* X/3 (1968), 178.
[28] H. J. Stoebe, *VT,* 7 (1957), 369.

of the flock so that Isaac will think they are Esau's game (*tsayidh*) and give his paternal blessing to the crafty Jacob. The three pilgrims going up to God at Bethel are carrying three kids, three loaves of bread, and a skin of wine as an offering or for the sacrificial meal (1 S. 10:3). A *gedhi* appears as a present (*minchah*) and a whole burnt-offering ('*olah*) in Jgs. 6:19. Gideon prepares for the messenger of Yahweh a present (*minchah,* 6:18), viz., a boiled kid and unleavened bread, to show hospitality to his guest. But as the meat and unleavened cakes lie upon the rock, fire from the rock consumes the meat and the bread (6:19-21); thus the meal intended for the guest is transformed into an '*olah* (a whole burnt-offering). [29] A similar incident takes place in connection with the hospitality that was intended for the man of God in Jgs. 13:15-19. Manoah prepares a kid and bread for the guest, but he declines and suggests the possibility of making ready ('*asah*) a whole burnt-offering ('*olah*) and offering (piel of '*alah*) it to Yahweh (13:16). Then Manoah offers an '*olah* to Yahweh upon the rock (13:19), to which an editor later added the *minchah* (cereal offering), according to Rendtorff. [30]

5. *The Prohibition Against Boiling a Kid in its Mother's Milk.* The prohibition, "You shall not boil a kid in its mother's milk," has been preserved in three passages in the OT: Ex. 23:19; 34:26; and Dt. 14:21.

a. In Ex. 23 and 34, this prohibition appears in the larger context of regulations concerning the three pilgrimage festivals of the cultic calendar (Unleavened Bread, Harvest, and Ingathering, Ex. 23:14-17), or of the making of the covenant at Sinai (Ex. 34), and in a series of special regulations concerning animal sacrifice (and firstfruits): the blood of the *zebhach* (sacrifice) shall not be offered with unleavened bread (23:18a, *lo' thizbach,* "you shall not offer"; 34:25a, *lo' thishchat,* "you shall not offer"), the fat of the festival (sacrifice) shall not remain until the morning (23:18b, *chaggi,* "my feast or festival" [=*zebhach,* "sacrifice"?]; 34:25, *zebhach chagh happasach,* "the sacrifice of the feast of the passover"), and finally a kid shall not be boiled in his mother's milk (23:19b = 34:26b). Although 23:18a,b,19b par. have to do with animal sacrifice, the absence of any connection with Yahweh in 23:19b = 34:26b speaks against an original connection with him. The relationship between Ex. 23:14ff. and 34:10ff. is hardly clear enough to help us decide which of these two passages is earlier. The concurrent parallelism in order and disparity in detail favor, instead, two different arrangements of a common original work. [31]

On the other hand, the prohibition in Dt. 14:21 stands in the context of cultic regulations concerning food: after a general prohibition against eating *to'ebhah,* "any abominable thing" (14:3), a list of clean and unclean animals that may or may not be eaten (14:3-20), and a prohibition against eating a carcass (*nebhelah,*

---

[29] Cf. R. Rendtorff, *WMANT,* 24 (1967), 94, 194.

[30] *Ibid.,* 45, 174.

[31] Jepsen, Beyerlin, Kosmala, etc.; cf. the synopsis in P. Laaf, *Die Pascha-Feier Israels. BBB,* 36 (1970), 45ff.

14:21a), we find the prohibition that literally agrees with Ex. 23:19 and 34:26; in Dt. 14:22 we have a new regulation concerning tithing. In the redaction, the prohibition in 14:21b was likely interpreted as an appendix to the cultic food regulations, which was probably suggested by the *toʿebhah* or *nebhelah* regulation in 14:3,21a.

It is impossible to prove an original connection between the individual regulations concerning animal sacrifices in Ex. 23:18f. and 34:25f. and the Passover; possible relationships appear in a later stage of the Passover tradition.

b. The prohibition against boiling a kid in his mother's milk has been connected with a fertility rite since Spencer.[32] Spencer relates the theory of an anonymous Karaite that after harvest a kid was boiled in his mother's milk, and then this milk was sprinkled over fields and fruits in order to bring about greater fertility in them. In spite of the absence of other examples,[33] this interpretation became more widespread than the view that this was a dietary regulation. But at the same time, attention was called to the custom of Jordanian Bedouins of giving a guest a kid boiled in its mother's milk as a delicacy, which is still practiced in modern times.

New light has been shed on the OT prohibition in Ex. 23:19 par. by the Ugaritic text, The Birth of Dawn and Dusk (SS), found in *CTA*, 23. This text presents a sacrificial ritual with recitations of an El epic concerning the begetting of the two sons of the gods, Shaḥar, "dawn," and Shalim, "dusk." In connection with the repotentialization of El described in the corpus, the sevenfold boiling of a kid stands in parallelism with the sevenfold pouring out of fresh water in the rubric in lines 14f.: 14. *ʾl. ʾšt. šbʿd. ǵzrm. ṭb[ḫ. g]d. bḥlb. ʾnnḥ. bḥmʾt.* 15. *wʾl. ʾgn. šbʿdm. dǵ[ṣt. yṣq]t.:* "The 'young men' shall boil a kid in milk over the fire seven times, a lamb (?)[34] in butter, and (fresh water shall be poured out) over the kettle seven times."[35] Kosmala has tried to connect Driver's reconstruction of the sevenfold pouring out of fresh water with the theory of the Karaite, explaining this rite as an attempt to maintain or increase the quantity of the fluid (milk) used to sprinkle the field and make it fruitful.[36] He admits, however, that the Ugaritic text says nothing about this. While it is unanimously agreed that the sevenfold rite was a fertility rite, scholars differ concerning its life setting and its relationship to the OT prohibition.

Gaster[37] thinks it refers to a festival or fertility of the firstfruits that was celebrated in the Gemini constellation,[38] and Gray believes it is connected with a festival of nomads and peasants associated with the harvest before the autumn

---

[32] J. Spencer, *De legibus Hebraeorum ritualibus et earum rationibus, libri tres* (Cambridge, 1685), 270f., 298-308.

[33] Cf. the synopsis in J. Frazer, *Folk-Lore in the OT*, III (London, 1919), 111-164; and Kosmala, 50-55.

[34] So Virolleaud, Cassuto, etc.; otherwise Aistleitner, Driver: "mint."

[35] Ginsberg, Driver.

[36] Kosmala, 55.

[37] T. H. Gaster, *Thespis* (New York, 1950), 225f.

[38] *Ibid.*, 409.

change of pasture. [39] Gese thinks that the rite with the frequent citation of the *hieros logos* in the presence of the king and queen was supposed to promote the blessing of children in the house. [40]

c. While G. R. Driver connects the rite prohibited in the OT with the Feast of Weeks in June, Kosmala dates the Ugaritic rite in "early spring," and calls to mind the Israelite Passover at the same time of year. However, the prohibition handed down in connection with the cult calendar in Ex. 23:19 and 34:26 would seem to exclude any confusion of the Passover with the Canaanite fertility cult. A one-year-old male lamb was used for the Passover (Ex. 12:5), and it was not to be boiled in milk or in water (12:9). Thus it may be that, after Israel's settlement in Canaan, an attempt was made to exclude any syncretistic confusion of the Passover with a similar fertility cult by an explicit prohibition; then when it no longer had any real significance, it was attached to the food regulations in Dt. 14:21, surrounded by a *to'ebhah* and *nebhelah* regulation.

6. *The LXX*. The LXX translates *gedhi* 13 times by *ériphos,* "kid," which is used elsewhere in the OT only to translate *'ez* and *sa'ir,* four times each. But in the prohibition against boiling a kid in its mother's milk, the LXX uses *arnós,* "lamb," which elsewhere is used to translate *meri'* five times and *kebhes* four. However, in harmony with the usual LXX linguistic usage, either *ériphos* or *eríphios* appears in Aquila and Codices M and A.

Botterweck

---

[39] J. Gray, *The Legacy of Canaan. SVT,* 5 (²1965), 93ff.
[40] H. Gese, "Die Religionen Altsyriens," *RdM,* 10/2 (1970), 82.

> גָּדַל gādhal; גָּדוֹל gādhôl; גְּדֻלָּה gᵉdhullāh;
>
> גֹּדֶל gōdhel; → מִגְדָּל mighdāl

Contents: I. The Word "Great" in the Languages of the Ancient Near East: 1. Egyptian;
2. Akkadian; 3. The West Semitic Languages. II. Occurrences and Meanings in Hebrew:
1. General; 2. *gadhol:* a. In Connection with Events; b. As a Determinative in the Attributive Position; c. Old and Wealthy; d. As a Predicate Noun; e. Small–Great; 3. Substantives:
a. *godhel;* b. *gedhullah;* c. *rebhu;* d. *gedholoth;* 4. The Verb *gdl:* a. Qal; b. Piel and
Pual; c. Hiphil and Hithpael. III. 1. The Greatness of God and His Works: a. The Zion
Tradition; b. In History; c. The Deuteronomistic Theology; d. The Day of Yahweh; 2. The
Greatness Given by God: a. The Promise to the Patriarchs; b. The Davidic Tradition;
c. Leaders in Israel.

I. The Word "Great" in the Languages of the Ancient Near East.

1. *Egyptian.* Egyptian has two words for "great," *wr*[1] and *ꜥꜣ.*[2] The relationship of these two words, which often stand in parallelism to each other, is not
clear. Both of them appear in all kinds of polar formulas together with *nḏs,*
"small," etc., and they also cover a wide range of meaning. They can indicate
either spatial and numerical greatness or temporal greatness. Thus, they are both
connected with "sea" and "Nile," referring in the case of the latter to the high
water level. Buildings, etc., can be *wr* and *ꜥꜣ.* With regard to temporal usage
(where these words frequently should be translated "older"), *wr,* when it refers
to gods, appears in certain stereotyped expressions, e.g., Haroëris, "Horus the
elder," "the great mourner" (Isis in contrast to Nephthys as "the little mourner").
But in these passages *wr* can also be understood in the sense of "exalted, distinguished, eminent," a meaning that also applies to *ꜥꜣ.* *wr* is found in various
priestly titles ("the great one of the seers," "the great one of the five," etc.).
Wr.t, "the great one," often appears as a title for goddesses, but later (with the
article *tꜣ*) it denotes the goddess Toeris in the form of the female hippopotamus.
ꜥꜣ.t also occurs as a title of goddesses. The Egyptian prototype of the Greek title
of Hermes, *trismégistos,* is *ꜥꜣ ꜥꜣ wr.*[3]

For a discussion of the terms *nṯr ꜥꜣ* (used of Re, Osiris, Pharaoh, etc.) and
wr (used in reference to several gods), which Junker views as an indication of a
kind of primitive monotheism in ancient Egypt, the reader should consult the
excellent remarks of Zandee.[4] He cites several examples of the parallel use of
wr and *ꜥꜣ* in divine titles. Thus Amun is "the great one (*wr*) in Heliopolis, the
great one (*ꜥꜣ*) in Thebes" (Berlin Papyrus 3055, XIV, 1). Even in the Pyramid
Texts, *wr* and *ꜥꜣ* are connected with the gods (1689c, 1690a, 2200b). A clear
distinction is made between *wr* and *ꜥꜣ* when modifying *pr,* "house," and *rn,*

---

gādhal. W. Grundmann, "μέγας," *TDNT,* IV, 529-544; E. Jenni, *"gādōl," THAT,* I, 402-409; *idem, Das hebräische Piʿel* (Zürich, 1968), 29-33, 49.

[1] *WbÄS,* I, 326ff.

[2] *Ibid.,* 161ff.

[3] See P. Boylan, *Thoth* (Oxford, 1922), 182.

[4] J. Zandee, *De Hymnen aan Amon van Papyrus Leiden I 350* (Leiden, 1947), 120ff.

"name." In the Old Kingdom, *pr ꜥ3*, "great house," is already a stereotyped expression for the royal palace, and is used (at least from the time of the New Kingdom) as a designation of the king, "Pharaoh" (→ פרעה *parʿōh*). [5] On the other hand, *pr wr*, "great house," is a name of the royal sanctuary in Upper Egypt. *rn wr* is used for the great royal title or for any of its parts, while *rn ꜥ3* stands for the primary name of a private citizen.

2. *Akkadian.* The Akk. *rabû* (which stands in antithesis to *ṣeḥru, qallu*) corresponds to Sum. *gal*, and sometimes denotes spatial greatness, sometimes rank and age. [6] When it has the former meaning, it can be used of animals, plants, parts of the body, buildings, parts of buildings, ships, weapons, vessels, a land, a mountain, a river (also of high water), sacrifices, rites, and feasts. Figuratively, it is used of sin, punishment, wrath, wisdom, powers, reputation, honor, defeat, battle, blessing, and help. When it is applied to men, frequently it should be translated "older" or "adult," e.g., *aplu* or *māru rabû*, "older son," *rabû u ṣeḥru*, "great and small," "old and young," but it is also used often in speaking of a person in high position, especially a king (*šarru rabû*, "great king," "suzerain"). [7] It appears frequently as a divine epithet, [8] e.g., *ilu rabû*, "great God," [9] *bēlu rabû*, "great lord," [10] *qarrādu rabû*, "great hero," [11] and *šadû rabû*, "great mountain" (esp. of Enlil). [12]

3. *The West Semitic Languages.* In the West Semitic languages, *gdl* is found only in Ugaritic (and here only in lists, etc., not in narrative texts: great vessel, large cattle, etc.). [13] In the Aramaic dialects and in Phoenician, the word for "great" is *rbb/rby*. [14] This root, which also denotes numerical greatness, is used of animals, buildings, parts of buildings, lords, gods, kings, men of rank, etc. The verb form means "to grow," "increase," "be numerous," and "be grown up." [15]

Bergman-Ringgren

II. Occurrences and Meanings in Hebrew.

1. *General.* Many scholars derive *gdl*, "great," from *gdl*, "to weave, twist together." [16] However, the literal use of *gdl*, "great," does not indicate any con-

---

[5] *WbÄS*, I, 516.

[6] *AHw*, 936f.

[7] Seux, 298ff.

[8] Tallqvist, *Akkadische Götterepitheta. StOr*, 7 (1938), 169f. and *passim*.

[9] *Ibid.*, 11.

[10] *Ibid.*, 51-53.

[11] *Ibid.*, 163f.

[12] *Ibid.*, 221.

[13] See *WUS*, 64; *UT*, Glossary, No. 562.

[14] *DISO*, 270f.

[15] On Biblical Aramaic, see below.

[16] Cf., e.g., *GesB;* Levy, *WTM;* J. L. Palache, *Semantic Notes on the Hebrew Lexicon* (Leiden, 1959), 18.

nection with the supposed original meaning "to weave, twist together," and thus it would seem that these represent two originally different roots. [17] The root *gdl,* "great," is not found in Akkadian. It does occur in Ugaritic, but Ugaritic uses *rb* more frequently than *gdl* to convey the idea of "great." [18] In addition, *gdl* appears once in Moabite (*mgdlt*), [19] in the Aramaic papyri from Elephantine (but only in proper names), once in a place name in Old South Arabic (*gdlm*), [20] and frequently in the El-Amarna correspondence (→ מגדל *mighdāl*). *gdl* seems to have penetrated into Jewish Aramaic from Hebrew. In any case, the root *gdl,* "great," is West Semitic, probably Canaanite. In contrast to the roots *rby/rbb* in other Semitic languages, *gdl* never means greatness of number, but always greatness of dimension and size. When it is used in connection with a collective concept (e.g., *goy,* "nation"), [21] *gdl* does not primarily convey the idea of a large number, but the greatness and extent of the entire unit envisioned. On the other hand, *rby/rbb* can denote in Hebrew not only a large number, but also greatness. In Biblical Aramaic, *rby/rbb* is used for Heb. *gdl,* "great."

On the basis of its general and formal ambiguous meaning, *gdl,* like English "great," can be connected with very different concepts. The scale of possible nuances of meaning extends all the way from literal-dimensional size (e.g., a great stone) to a figurative-abstract concept of greatness (e.g., great joy). [22] In trying to determine the meaning of *gdl* in a specific context, we must not only keep in mind the wide variety of nuances that this word may have, but also its function in the syntactical structure of the sentence or the adjoining unit of speech.

In the MT, we encounter the root *gdl* in proper names (*Giddel, Giddalti, Gedhalyahu, Yighdalyahu*), place names (→ מגדל *mighdāl*), verbal forms, and various substantival forms.

2. *gadhol.* a. *In Connection with Events.* The adj. *gadhol* occurs a little over 520 times in the OT, and in about 320 of these it is used as an attribute of an indeterminate or a determinate noun.

α. About 90 times, thus relatively often, it is used to strengthen the (indeterminate) internal object (where the verb and obj. are cognate = an etymological figure; [23] where the verb and obj. are related in meaning, but come from different roots; and in some passages that have a general verb of action, e.g., *'asah,* "to do," instead of a verb that has a specific meaning).

The miseries and defeats inflicted by men or God (*makkah,* "slaughter," Josh. 10:10,20; Jgs. 11:33; 15:8; 2 Ch. 28:5; 1 S. 6:19; 19:8; etc.; cf. *makkah rabbah,* "great plague," Nu. 11:33; 2 Ch. 13:17; cf. also Dt. 25:3, where *makkah rabbah*

---

[17] Cf. *KBL*[3].

[18] *WUS,* No. 632; *UT,* Glossary, No. 562.

[19] Cf. *DISO,* 142.

[20] ContiRossini, 121.

[21] See below, II.2.a.

[22] Cf. the attempt at a systematic grouping of the use of the adj. *gadhol* on the basis of the meanings of the various related words in *KBL*[3].

[23] Cf. *GK,* § 117q.

probably does not have reference to the number of stripes, but to a bodily punishment which is so great that it degrades the one being punished; *maggephah,* "plague," 2 Ch. 21:14); the ruin in which a nation or a city is overthrown (*shabhar,* "to smite," Jer. 14:17; cf. Jer. 4:6); the terror and fright that take hold of men (*charadhah,* "trembling," Gen. 27:33; *mehumah,* "confusion," Dt. 7:23); the retaliation that is practiced (*neqamoth,* Ezk. 25:17); the anger that God or man manifests toward someone (*qetseph,* "anger," Zec. 1:15; etc.); the discontent, the displeasure that overcomes someone (*ra'ah,* "displeasure," Jonah 4:1; Neh. 2:10; etc.); the fear that one has (*yir'ah,* Jonah 1:10,16); the jealousy with which God is jealous (*qin'ah,* Zec. 1:14; 8:2); the hate that a person has (*sin'ah,* 2 S. 13:15); the evil and injuriousness which one causes (*ra'ah,* "evil," 2 S. 13:16; Jer. 26:19; Neh. 13:27; etc.); the abominations (*to'ebhoth,* Ezk. 8:6,13,25) and the blasphemies (*ne'atsoth,* Neh. 9:18,26) that are committed; the wrong and sin that one commits (*chata'ah,* 2 K. 17:21); the feast that someone arranges (*kerah,* 2 K. 6:23; cf. the Aram. *'abhadh lechem rabh,* "he made a great feast," Dnl. 5:1; *mishteh,* "banquet," Est. 2:18; etc.); the joy in which someone may rejoice (*simchah,* Jonah 4:6; 1 Ch. 29:9; Neh. 12:43; etc.); the sacrifice that someone offers (*zebhach,* Jgs. 16:23; Neh. 12:43; etc.); the work and toil that one undertakes (*'abhodhah,* Ezk. 29:18); the work that God or a man does (*ma'aseh,* Jgs. 2:7; etc.; *mela'khah,* Neh. 6:3); the help and salvation that a man or God brings about (*yeshu'ah,* "victory," 1 S. 14:45; *teshu'ah,* "victory," 1 S. 19:5; 2 S. 23:10,12; 1 Ch. 11:14; etc.); the riches with which one is made rich (*'osher,* 1 S. 17:25; Dnl. 11:2); the spoil which one carries off (*shalal,* Ezk. 38:13); the funeral fire that is burned in honor of a deceased king (*serephah,* 2 Ch. 16:14): all these can be called *gadhol,* "great." Frequently, *gadhol* appears in attributive relationship to an internal object in connection with audible phenomena. The cry and the lament (*tse'aqah,* "cry," Gen. 27:34; Est. 4:1; etc.; *qol,* "voice," 2 S. 19:5 [Eng. v. 4]; etc.); plaintive weeping (*bekhi,* Jgs. 21:2; 2 S. 13:36; Isa. 38:3; etc.); the funeral lament (*mispedh,* Gen. 50:10); the acclamatory cry and the rejoicing of a crowd (*teru'ah,* 1 S. 4:5f.; Josh. 6:5,20; Ezr. 3:11,13; etc.); and the cry of acknowledgment (*qol,* "voice," Ezr. 10:12) are said to be great (it is not clear why this should not also be interpreted as an adverbial acc.). [24] In turn, sometimes *gadhol* is strengthened by the addition of *me'odh,* "very, exceedingly" (e.g., Gen. 27:34).

It is true that in all these passages *gadhol* modifies a noun, but it is a noun that strengthens a verb, so that *gadhol* also has an adverbial function. Thus, in these passages it is an event, an occurrence, or an act that is experienced as great or said to be great.

β. In the more than 40 passages where *gadhol* is used attributively in a prepositional phrase with *be* (once with *le,* Jer. 11:16), it has an adverbial function, as it does when it is connected with the internal object. Some of the words that are associated with *gadhol* as an internal object can also be interpreted in a prepositional sense without any perceptible difference in meaning for the expression

[24] So *GK,* § 117s.

as a whole (*qol,* "voice," Gen. 39:14; 1 S. 7:10; 28:12; etc.; *qetseph,* "wrath," Jer. 21:5; 32:37; etc.; *simchah,* "gladness," 1 Ch. 29:22; etc.; *teru'ah,* "shout, voice," 2 Ch. 15:14; etc.). In prepositional phrases with *be,* frequently *gadhol* is used of the divine activity. [25]

γ. In approximately 30 passages, *gadhol* is used to modify a subject of *hayah* when it means "to become, occur, take place, be taken," or of other verbs that can denote the beginning of an event or activity (e.g., *bo',* "to come"; *naphal,* "to fall").

Thus the OT speaks of a great slaughter and a great destruction (*maggephah,* "slaughter," 1 S. 4:17; *shebher,* "destruction," Jer. 48:3; 50:22; etc.), a great storm (*sa'ar,* "tempest," Jonah 1:4; *ruach,* "wind," 1 K. 19:11; Job 1:19), great wrath (*qetseph,* 2 K. 3:27), a great commotion (*ra'ash,* Jer. 10:22), a great rain (*geshem,* 1 K. 18:45), a great famine (*ra'abh,* 2 K. 6:25), and a great oath (*shebhu'ah,* Jgs. 21:5).

δ. In almost 30 passages, *gadhol* is used to modify a substantive that has a different syntactical function from that found in the instances mentioned above, but still has to do with an event or activity.

A sight that a man encounters (*mar'eh,* Ex. 3:3; Dnl. 10:8), the mourning that comes upon someone (*'ebhel,* Est. 4:3), deliberations that are made (*chiqre lebh,* Jgs. 5:15, conjec., cf. v. 16), a slaughter that God carries out (*tebhach,* Isa. 34:6), a distress in which Israel finds herself (*tsarah,* Neh. 9:37), and many other events mentioned above that are described substantivally, can be characterized as extraordinary by adding *gadhol.*

The possibilities mentioned thus far compose almost two-thirds of all the passages in which *gadhol* is used attributively. In all these passages, *gadhol* denotes not a static existence or an object standing by itself, but an event, an action, an occurrence. When *gadhol* is used to describe an event, it means that that event goes beyond the ordinary and usual. Here, then, *gadhol* indicates that an event is not in the stream of the usual course of history, but breaks into it, interrupts it, or goes beyond it. *gadhol* has this meaning especially when it is used in connection with those events that are due to God's activity. [26]

b. *As a Determinative in the Attributive Position.* gadhol occurs as a determinative in the attributive position first according to the general rule of the determinative, whenever the OT speaks of something in the context of great things that have already been mentioned or that have been defined elsewhere. In this case, frequently the determination is emphasized by a demonstrative pronoun or a relative clause, or is expressed by a suffix or genitive (in all, about 80 times). However, several determinative substantives with *gadhol* in the attributive do not denote a great thing defined in the immediate context, but simply a great thing that is unique, or at least original, in its greatness. Thus *gadhol* can be part of a title or a name or a stereotyped expression.

---

[25] See below, II.1.c.
[26] See below, II.1.c, d.

α. *gadhol* appears in the title "great king" (*hammelekh haggadhol,* 2 K. 18:19, 28; etc.; cf. Jth. 2:5). *melekh rabh* can also stand for *hammelekh haggadhol,* at any rate in the North Israelite dialect (Hos. 5:13, conjec.; 10:6, conjec.; with *yodh compaginis*).[27] Although the article is missing, the whole expression seems to be analogous to a proper name and thus must be understood as a determinative (so also Ps. 47:3 [2]?, cf. also the Sefire Inscription,[28] *mlk rb* = great king?).[29] *gadhol* is also found in the titles "high priest" (*hakkohen haggadhol,* Hag. 1:1, 14; etc.) and "great prince" (*hassar haggadhol,* Dnl. 12:1, referring to Michael).

β. When *gadhol* means simply something great that is localized geographically, the expression in which it appears approaches the idea of a place name: the great oak (2 S. 18:9), the great cultic high place (1 K. 3:4), and perhaps also the great tower (Neh. 3:27). This is the appropriate place to mention the two place names in which *rabh* occurs: *tsidhon rabbah,* "the great Sidon," the metropolis of Sidon (Josh. 11:8; 19:28), and *chamath rabbah,* "the great Hamath," the metropolis of Hamath (Am. 6:2). Here *rabbah* should certainly be interpreted as a determinative, although it appears without the article. *gadhol* is used quite often as an element in a geographical designation in "the Great Sea" (Nu. 34:6f.; Josh. 1:4; 9:1; Ezk. 47:15,19,20; etc.) and "the Great River" (Gen. 15:18; Dt. 1:7; 11:24– add here with *BHK, haggadhol;* Dnl. 10:4). Once the Great Sea (also, frequently *hayyam* without *gadhol*) is called *hayyam ha'acharon,* "the western (lit., behind) sea" (Dt. 11:24)–geographically this has reference to the Mediterranean Sea. Likewise, the Great River (frequently *hannahar* appears without *gadhol*) geographically refers to the Euphrates (*hu' chiddaqel,* "that is, the Tigris," in Dnl. 10:4 seems to be a gloss).[30] These two terms denote the ideal (western and eastern or northeastern) boundaries of the promised land.

γ. However, the character of the sea as a threatening chaotic and precipitous power, and of the Euphrates as a boundary of the environment given to Israel by God, beyond which, e.g., the fathers served foreign gods (Josh. 24:2,14), or from which the religious corruption of the people descended (Jer. 13:1-11;[31] cf. Isa. 8:6-8), and the literal formulation (a certain absoluteness which is obtained by a determinative and *gadhol* used attributively), make possible a stereotyped use of these two expressions. The actual geographical places (the Mediterranean Sea and the Euphrates River) are superseded cryptographically by "places" that are no longer local, but qualitative, which play a role especially in apocalypticism: the Great River becomes the place where apocalyptic visions are given (Dnl. 10:4), the place where the judgment over the earth is to originate (Rev. 9:14), and the boundary of the land that will be covered by the oppressor at the time of the judgment (Rev. 16:12); and the Great Sea becomes the abyss out of which

---

27 Cf. H. W. Wolff, *BK,* XIV/1 (²1965), 134, 222, etc.

28 *KAI,* 222 B.7.

29 Otherwise *KAI,* III², 253.

30 Cf. O. Plöger, *KAT,* XVIII, 145.

31 Cf. W. Rudolph, *HAT,* 12³, 90-95.

the four great beasts that oppose God have their origin and nature (*yamma'*
rabba', Dnl. 7:2f.; cf. Rev. 13:1f.). The expression *tehom rabbah*, "the great
Primeval Sea" (Gen. 7:11; Isa. 51:10; Am. 7:4; Ps. 36:7[6]; 78:15), is related
to this. In spite of the missing article, it would also seem to be determinative
(cf. the determinative sense in the passages cited above using *rabh* without the
article). [32] In any case, the mythological character of the great Primeval Sea,
which powerfully affects the world of men, bringing either destruction (Gen.
7:11; Isa. 51:10) or fertility and blessing (Am. 7:4; Ps. 36:7[6]; 78:15), is clear.

δ. The expression, "the great city" (*ha'ir haggedholah*, i.e., Nineveh, Jonah
1:2; 3:2; 4:11; Gen. 10:12, a gloss that originally had reference to Nineveh?), [33]
must certainly be understood in an ideal, typical sense rather than historically
and geographically. Here "the great city" is used as a representative figure to
denote the heathen world power (the situation is different in Jer. 22:8, where
devastated Jerusalem is called "this great city," with a demonstrative pron.).
This expression is also used of an apocalyptic cipher, and then means the
world power hostile to God (cf. *babhel rabbetha'*, "great Babylon," Dnl. 4:27
[30]; Jth. 1:1; Rev. 11:8; 16:19; 17:18; 18:10,16,18f.; cf. also Rev. 17:5; 14:8).
A certain kind of typology will also have to be assumed for the phrase, "the
great (and terrible) wilderness" (*hammidhbar haggadhol*, Dt. 8:15, cf. *hammidhbar haggadhol vehannora' hahu'*, "that great and terrible wilderness," 1:19;
hammidhbar haggadhol hazzeh, "this great wilderness," 2:7). These passages do
not have in mind the great wilderness any more than the actual historical region
of the earlier wandering, but rather its quality as a place of trial and encounter
with God (cf. also Rev. 12:6,14; 17:3).

In Ezk. 29:3, *hattannin* (conjec. from *tannim*) [34] *haggadhol*, "the great dragon,"
is usually understood as a figurative expression that compares the Pharaoh with
a Nile crocodile. [35] However, in the oracles concerning foreign nations in the
book of Ezekiel, especially in Ezk. 28 (concerning Tyre) and Ezk. 29–32 (concerning Egypt), there are so many cosmic-mythological elements that *hattannin*
haggadhol must also be interpreted as a mythological cipher, and possibly should
be translated "the great dragon," or something similar, and thus it can hardly
be a simple comparison with an animal. The fact that the *hattannin haggadhol*
lies not only in the midst of the streams (*bethokh ye'orav*, Ezk. 29:3), but also in
the seas (*bayyammim*, Ezk. 32:2), also points to the mythological character of
this expression. Thus, in mythological language, *hattannin haggadhol* means the
historical, actual world power in its ungodly nature (cf. similar ideas and expressions in Isa. 27:1; Job 3:8 LXX; Rev. 12:3,9; cf. also Rev. 12:4,7,13-17; 13:2,4,
11; 16:13; 20:2).

Thus, in these determinative expressions *gadhol* (like *rabh* without the article)
is used to characterize either the actual historical and actual geographical unique-

---

[32] *GK*, § 126y.

[33] Cf. H. Gunkel, *Genesis* ([3]1910), 88, etc.

[34] However, cf. W. Zimmerli, *BK*, XIII/2, 703, who interprets *tannim* as a secondary
form of *tannin*.

[35] *Ibid.*, 707f.

ness in specific titles or place names, or the suprahistorical, fundamental nature of a historically actual reality in mythological or apocalyptic ciphers.

c. *Old and Wealthy.* The formal indefiniteness of *gadhol* is made explicit by the content of the word it modifies, by its syntactical position in the construction of a sentence or an expression, and by specifically defining the word itself. *gadhol* can mean old, older, oldest (always in contrast to *qatan* in the sense of young, younger, youngest) without adding anything to it, and in this sense it can be used either as a substantive or as an attributive adjective (e.g., to *ben,* "son"; *bath,* "daughter"; *'ach,* "brother"), but always as a determinative (e.g., Gen. 27:1,15, 42; 44:12; 1 S. 17:13f.; etc.; in all about 15 times). In one passage, *rabh* without the article has the same meaning, but here it is probably determinative (Gen. 25:23, in contrast to *tsaʿir,* "younger").

gadhol can also mean the distinguished and the mighty, the rich and the esteemed, without anything being added to it (in all about 15 times). Men who are closely associated with the king are the great ones of the king (Jonah 3:7; 2 K. 10:11). *rabh* also can be used in this sense (Est. 1:8; Jer. 39:13; 41:1; cf. also the different titles of the dignitaries of the royal court with *rabh* as one element). Likewise, the Aram. *rabhrebhan* denotes the dignitaries of the king (Dnl. 4:33[36]; 5:1,3,9f.,23; 6:18[17]). Anyone who has rank and a name in the city or in the nation is among the great (2 K. 10:6; Jer. 5:5; 52:13; Nah. 3:10; Mic. 7:3; etc.). Someone who is rich or important and respected is an *'ish gadhol,* "a great man" (2 K. 5:1), or an *'ishshah ghedholah,* "a wealthy woman" (4:8). The mighty kings and leaders of the nations, into whose ranks God elevated David, are the great ones of the earth (*haggedholim 'asher ba'arets,* 2 S. 7:9 = 1 Ch. 17:8).

d. *As a Predicate Noun.* *gadhol* is used about 80 times as a predicate in a nominal clause or a clause with *hayah,* "to be," functioning as a copula. In about 12 of these instances, it appears in the predicate position modifying a noun. Things or attributes belonging to man are the subject in a third of all the passages. *gadhol* is found referring to man in the predicate position about a dozen times. It is worthy of note that in none of these passages is *gadhol* the goal or core statement of the unit.

The OT states, e.g., that the stone that covers the well is great (Gen. 29:2); it is still high day (29:7); Amnon's hatred of Tamar is greater than his earlier love for her (2 S. 13:15); Gibeon is a great city, greater than Ai (Josh. 10:2); the cities of the land are fortified and great (RSV "large," Nu. 13:28). These and other similar statements describe a situation which is certainly important for the narrative, but not central to it. Cain's prayer that his punishment be alleviated (Gen. 4:13) implies that he knows how great his wickedness is; the judgment meted out demonstrates that the wickedness of Israel and Judah (Ezk. 9:9) or the sin of the sons of Eli (1 S. 2:17) is great; in these passages, attention is focused not on the greatness of the sin, but on its consequences. Job is a great and rich man, greater than all the people of the east (Job 1:3); this, along with other statements about him, serves to introduce the person who stands in the center of what follows, but is not the theme of the book. Nabal (1 S. 25:2), Barzillai (2 S. 19:33[32]), and Naaman (2 K. 5:1) are introduced with a similar comment, but their greatness is not mentioned again in the following narrative. Moses was great and respected in the eyes of the Egyptians and the pharaoh (Ex. 11:3), and this makes it clear why the Egyptians gave their ornaments to the Israelites, [36] etc. Thus, when *gadhol* is predicated of a man or of an object pertaining to man, greatness is never the real theme of the context.

The situation is quite different, however, when *gadhol* is used in connection with God, his name, etc. Here, as a rule *gadhol* forms the nucleus of the statement which then is simply expanded by an explanation, or the intended high point toward which the whole is striving and which furnishes the key to everything else. [37]

e. *Small–Great*. The phrase *miqqatan veʿadh gadhol*, "from the least to the greatest," with its variations is found a little over 30 times in the OT, and, like similar pairs of antithetical ideas, denotes a totality. [38] Usually both of these words appear in indeterminate form (without an article or a suffix). In about half the passages where these occur together, they are connected with each other by *min–veʿadh*. In approximately three-fourths of the passages, "small" appears before "great." Therefore, the expression *miqqatan veʿadh gadhol* is to be regarded as the usual form of this expression. In this usual form, the expression always serves to denote a totality of persons, never of things. The order, "small–great," can express a certain acclivity, a movement from small to great (cf. the prepositions *min–veʿadh*): the event described does not stop with the small, but also attains the great. Originally a conclusion *a minori ad maius* may have been implied, so that the expression could be translated, "if indeed the small, then especially the great."

If the expression is dependent on a negative verb form, the combination with *min–veʿadh*, which positively embraces the intended whole, must be avoided (in 1 S. 30:19, we find the *constructio ad sensum:* "nothing was missing" has a positive meaning and therefore tolerates *min–veʿadh;* in Jer. 50:3 and 51:62, we find a similar merismus with *min–veʿadh* in a negative clause, but the intended totality is regarded positively as a logical subject). In its place, we find *ʾo*, which must be translated "(neither-) nor" (Nu. 22:18; 1 S. 22:15), or in simple syndeses by *ve* (1 S. 20:2; 25:36; 1 K. 22:31; the asyndeton in 2 Ch. 18:30 should probably be traced back to textual corruption). [39] The determinative with the article and the construct plural, or both, are used, not when the writer has in mind something small and great in a general and different sense, as the outermost members of a continuous totality that is not further divided, but two precise

---

[36] Cf. M. Noth, *ATD*, V, 73.

[37] See below, III.1.a, b, d.

[38] Cf. P. Boccaccio, "I termini contrari come espressione della totalità in ebraico," *Bibl*, 33 (1952), 173-190; A. M. Honeyman, "Merismus in Biblical Hebrew," *JBL*, 71 (1952), 11-18; and H. A. Brongers, "Merismus, Synekdoche und Hendiadys in der bibel-hebräischen Sprache," *OTS*, 14 (1965), 100-114.

[39] Cf. *BHK* and W. Rudolph, *HAT*, 21, 255.

groups standing over against one another, of which the whole is composed: the distinguished and the insignificant among the people (Ps. 115:13; Jer. 16:6); the leaders and the troops in the army (2 Ch. 18:30; in the par. text 1 K. 22:31 without the article); or large and small animals (Ps. 104:25). Apparently two groups of people in higher and lower positions appear in all passages that have a *ke–ke* construction; here, "small" and "great" are always made determinative by the article (Dt. 1:17; 1 Ch. 25:8; 26:13; 2 Ch. 31:15). This construction using *ke–ke* and the simple syndesis with *ve* (Jer. 16:6; Job 3:19) emphasize the indistinguishable identity of the group of which the intended totality is composed: the small, inexperienced, younger, less-esteemed, and the great, experienced, older, highly esteemed. The mutual participation of the two antithetical groups is emphasized in two passages where they are combined by *'im,* "with" (Ps. 104:25; 115:13).

The determinative with a suffix should be interpreted like the determinative with the article (Jer. 6:13–the secondary repetition of the text in Jer. 8:10 connects the extraordinary form of this phrase with the suffix to its usual form; Jer. 31:34; Jonah 3:5; cf. Jth. 13:13). Moreover, the suffix may suggest a certain distance from the intended totality: the speaker from those of whom he is speaking (Jer. 6:13; also 31:34?); Jonah from the penitent Ninevites (Jonah 3:5); and the faithful Judith from her disheartened countrymen (Jth. 13:13).

In seven passages, "great" appears before "small," thus deviating from the usual form. This word order can hardly be interpreted to mean that a certain writer or speaker intended to place special emphasis on the first member, the "great." This interpretation of the word order is excluded in 2 Ch. 31:15, where the construction with *ke–ke* indicates that the two groups are considered to be equal. Also the combination of the two terms by *ve* in Jer. 16:6 seems to stress the equality of the two groups in the common fate of death, so that no special emphasis on the great can be assumed. Likewise, the combination of these two words by *'o* in 1 S. 20:2 excludes any particular emphasis on the first member, the great things. The four other passages using the word order "great-small" use the *min–ve'adh* construction. These two prepositions indicate a movement. a decline, toward the second member of the formula, thus placing special emphasis on "small," while the great obviously participate in the event being described. Thus, in Est. 1:5 the nobles clearly do not stand in the foreground, because it is easy to understand why they would be invited to the king's banquet; rather, the point of the passage is that the king's kindness was not limited to the great, but also extended to the small. In Est. 1:20, it is decreed that the husbands shall be the heads of the house even to the smallest and least. Similarly, in Jonah 3:5 the word "small" is placed in the last position to show that all Ninevites put on sackcloth even to the last man (cf. Jonah 3:7f.: the people [which is obvious] and even the beasts [which is unusual and must be emphasized] must repent). Also, the final position of "small" in 2 Ch. 34:30 (which is different from the original text in 2 K. 23:2) emphasizes that all Israel to the last man, even the least, which could be entirely disregarded, must listen to the reading of the book of the covenant.

In Am. 6:11, we find "great" and "little" in the singular and the determinative, and they appear in attributive position with "house." This is probably not a variation from the meristic phrase;[40] instead, the prophet is thinking of two different houses, possibly the winter house and the summer house of the king (cf. Am. 3:15). Gen. 44:12 does not have anything to do with the expression for totality, "small-great," either. That Joseph begins by searching the sack of the eldest and ends with the youngest, the father's favorite son, is not meant to emphasize that he searched the sacks of all the men, but to dramatize the transaction and to make the discovery of the cup in the sack of the youngest the high point in the story.

3. *Substantives.* Not only is the adj. *gadhol* derived from the root *gdl,* but so also are the two substantives *godhel* and *gedhullah.* In the MT, *godhel* occurs 13 times and possibly in Ex. 15:16 (conjec.), and *gedhullah/gedhulah* appears 12 times plus once in Sir. 3:18. In addition, the feminine plural of *gadhol* is used as a substantive 11 times.

a. *godhel. godhel* has no plural. It means "greatness" as an attribute, a rather abstract and formal quality approaching a reality. It can be used positively or negatively. Isa. 9:8(9) speaks of the arrogance of heart (*godhel lebhabh,* par. to → גאוה *ga'ᵃvāh,* "pride"), from which the inhabitants of Samaria deliver their presumptuous and self-confident speeches. The same expression occurs in Isa. 10:12 (in parallelism with *rum 'enav,* "haughty pride"), where it describes the behavior of the king of Assyria, whose mission as an instrument to punish Israel he arrogantly interprets as absolute dominion brought about by his own power. In Ezk. 31:2,7,18, *godhel* (which is connected with *kabhodh,* "glory," in v. 18, and *yophi,* "beauty," in vv. 3,7f.) is used of the greatness and glory of the pharaoh (represented as the cosmic tree), which led to his arrogance and fall. Thus, when *godhel* is applied to a man, it always has reference to his presumptuousness and ungodly pride. In all the other examples, *godhel* denotes the power and exalted greatness of God, which is manifested in his historical acts (Nu. 14:19; Dt. 3:24; 5:24; 9:26; 11:2) and praised in the hymn (Dt. 32:3; Ps. 79:11; 150:2).[41]

b. *gedhullah.* The idea that the more general and more abstract *godhel* conveys only occasionally (Ezk. 31:2,7,18) is the fundamental concept suggested by *gedhullah:* it means the dominant sovereignty, the splendor around the majesty of God or a man who holds a special position. Therefore, in contrast to *godhel, gedhullah* always has a positive emphasis. In Est. 1:4, it denotes the glorious might of Ahasuerus (*yeqar tiph'ereth gedhullatho,* "the splendor and pomp of his majesty," par. to *'osher kebhodh melkhutho,* "the riches of his royal glory"); in Est. 6:3 and 10:2, the rank and dignity that the king bestowed on Mordecai; in Ps. 71:21, the respect and secure position that the (royal?) worshipper hopes to attain once again from God; in Sir. 3:18, earthly greatness, sovereignty according to the world's standard *(gedhulloth 'olam),* in view of which man must

---

[40] Contra H. W. Wolff, *BK,* XIV/2, 328; etc.
[41] See below, II.3.c.

humble himself in order to find God's mercy. In 1 Ch. 29:11, *gedhullah* appears in a list with → גבורה *gᵉbhûrāh*, "power," → תפארת *tiph'ereth*, "magnificence," → נצח *nētsach*, "splendor," → הוד *hôd*, "majesty," *mamlakhah*, "kingdom," and *mithnasse'*, "eminence," and denotes the universal rule of God.

Also, in the disturbed text in 2 S. 7:21 = 1 Ch. 17:19, *haggedhulah* does not have reference to the mighty act(s) that God did for David's sake, but conveys the idea that God gave David and his house a ruling position by election; thus, here (as in Est. 6:3) *'asah* with *gedhullah* means "to give, allot." In 1 Ch. 17:21, the Massoretes probably pointed *gdlwt* as the plural of *gedhullah* (so *gedhulloth*) in order to make it agree with the secondary *nora'oth*, "terrible things," in 2 S. 7:23. The Chronicler was probably also influenced by the feminine plural of the adj. *gadhol* found alongside *nora'oth* in Dt. 10:21; etc. (the situation is similar in 1 Ch. 17:19c). In Ps. 145:3, *gedhullah* is used of the royal splendor and glory of God. This word occurs another time in the same psalm (v. 6); here the MT and the Vulgate read the plural, while the *qere* and the other ancient versions have the singular. However, the plural destroys the chiasmus of the only two verses in this acrostic psalm connected by *ve*.

Thus, the three occurrences of the pl. *gedhullah* in the OT may be omitted, so that *gedhullah/gedhulah* always denotes splendor and sovereign majesty (of God, or of one or several men).

c. *rebhu.* The Aram. *rebhu* has the special meaning of *gedhullah* rather than the more general meaning of *godhel* in the five passages in which it appears in the MT. In Dnl. 4:19(22), like *godhel* in Ezk. 31:2,7,18, *rebhu* denotes the universal greatness and authority of the king represented as a cosmic tree. In Dnl. 4:33(36), it is used with *hadhar*, "majesty," and *ziv*, "splendor," directly and without figure to denote the sovereignty that God has restored to Nebuchadnezzar. It means the same thing in Dnl. 5:18f., where it appears in a list with *malkhu*, "kingship," *yeqar*, "glory," and *hadhar*, "majesty." According to Dnl. 7:27, this universal preeminence (here *rebhu* is found with *malkhu*, "kingdom," and *sholtan*, "dominion") will be given to the saints of the Most High (cf. 2 S. 7:23).

d. *gedholoth.* In Ps. 12:4(3), the substantival feminine plural of *gadhol*, *gedholoth*, denotes the great things the enemies of the worshipper utter boastfully and tyrannically. In Dnl. 7:8, the Aramaic equivalent means the slanderous speech of the mouth, with which the little horn is equipped *memallil rabhrebhan*, "speaking great things"; cf. *millayya' rabhrebhatha'*, "great words," Dnl. 7:11; Rev. 13:5). In Ps. 131:1, *gedholoth* is used of the great and exalted things that the worshipper denies himself when he puts his trust in God, and in Jer. 45:5, the distinguished fate, the great things, that Baruch is not to claim or expect for himself. Once *gedholoth* is applied to the great deeds of Elisha, the miracles that he did (2 K. 8:4), and in the rest of the passages where it occurs in the OT (Jer. 33:3; Ps. 71:19; 106:21; Job 5:9; 9:10; 37:5; and perhaps also 1 Ch. 17:19,21, conjec.), to the great acts of God in nature and history which transcend human design and understanding.

4. *The Verb gdl.* The verb *gadhal/*gadhel* [42] is found 121 times in the MT altogether. It occurs 54 times in the qal and in Gen. 26:13 (conjec. *gadhol*); in addition, the adj. *gadhel* [43] appears three times (apart from Gen. 26:13), and is to be identified as a qal participle. The piel is found 25 times, and in 1 K. 11:20 (conjec. *vatteghaddelehu*), 1 Ch. 17:10 (conjec. *va'aghaddelekha*), [44] and Sir. 49:11. The pual appears once, and the hiphil 34 times. In a few passages, Heb. *rabhah* means the same thing as *gdl* in the qal (Ezk. 19:2; Lam. 2:22; Job 33:12) and in the piel (Ezk. 16:7–twice). The Aramaic equivalent of *gdl* (*rabhah*) appears four times in the peal and once in the pael.

a. *Qal.* Usually verbal clauses with the so-called stative verb *gdl* in the qal are translated and interpreted no differently than nominal clauses with *gadhol* as the predicate nominative. However, "in Hebrew there is a difference between nominal clauses with the adjectival predicate... and verbal clauses with the finite verb." [45] While the nominal form of a statement with *gadhol* is used to express an opinion or evaluation in which the speaker describes the condition of the subject, the subject of "verbal clauses" (with *gdl* in the qal) "exhibits itself as great," [46] and thus such clauses have the reality and effectiveness of the subject in view, the way it presents itself to common experience. Thus *gdl* in the qal does not mean "the condition of being great," but "exhibiting oneself as great."

gdl in the qal conveys the general idea of "exhibiting oneself as great" only rarely: it is used of an outcry (Gen. 19:13), mourning (Zec. 12:11), suffering (Job 2:13), guilt or sin (Lam. 4:6; Ezr. 9:6), and of the Egyptians with large penises (Ezk. 16:26). In the majority of passages, *gdl* in the qal has a more specialized meaning. It is used of the growth of children 20 times (Gen. 21:8,20; 25:27; 38:11,14; Ex. 2:10f.; Jgs. 11:2; 13:24; Ruth 1:13; 1 S. 2:21; 3:19; 1 K. 12:8,10 = 2 Ch. 10:8,10; 2 K. 4:18; Ezk. 16:7; Job 31:18), and of an animal once (2 S. 12:3). The Heb. *rbh* in the qal has the same meaning in Ezk. 16:7 (twice). The Aram. *rbh* in the peal is used of the growth of a tree, which becomes the cosmic tree (with the overtone of arrogance and presumptuousness), in Dnl. 4:8, 17 (11,20 [twice]), and of the growth of hair and nails in Dnl. 4:30(33). In all other passages, *gdl* in the qal has to do with man's becoming important or gaining influence, wealth, and power (18 times), or with God's (his name, his power, his works) showing himself to be mighty (9 times). When *gdl* in the qal is used to describe man's becoming or being mighty, it is rarely neutral (Eccl. 2:9: the royal preacher; Gen. 41:40: Pharaoh in his royal power). Sometimes it refers to a great power that arbitrarily, unlawfully, and presumptuously demands recognition, and is successful in obtaining superiority over others (Jer. 5:27: the wicked among the people; Zec. 12:7: the house of David; Dnl. 8:9f.: the little horn); in this sense, it is very close to the inner transitive use of *gdl* in the

---

[42] Joüon, *Grammaire de l'Hébreu biblique* (²1947), § 41f.
[43] *BLe,* § 43p.
[44] Cf. the LXX and most comms.; otherwise W. Rudolph, *HAT,* 21, 130.
[45] Jenni, 26; cf. also D. Michel, *VT,* 6 (1956), 55, on *malakh/melekh.*
[46] Jenni, 32.

hiphil.[47] On the other hand, sometimes it is used to convey the idea that an individual obtains and practices greatness and respect by God's blessing or because God is with him (Gen. 24:35: Abraham; 26:13: Isaac; 48:19: Ephraim and Manasseh by the blessing of Jacob; 2 S. 5:10 = 1 Ch. 11:9: David; 1 K. 10:23 = 2 Ch. 9:22: Solomon by the wisdom given to him by God; Mic. 5:3[4]: the messianic ruler).[48] None of these passages uses greatness in the sense of a static condition, but of exercising greatness, of a dynamic efficacy and power.

b. *Piel and Pual.* Generally speaking, *gdl* in the piel means to put someone or something in the condition described by the adj. *gadhol.*[49] The particular nuances of meaning into which *gdl* in the piel falls correspond rather closely to those of *gdl* in the qal. Sometimes it refers to the activity that causes a plant or children to grow, i.e., which makes plants, etc., sprout up and children grow into adults. Thus the Nazirite lets the hair of his head grow long (Nu. 6:5); the rain or the water lets a tree grow strong (Isa. 44:14; Ezk. 31:4); and God or Jonah makes a bush grow up (Jonah 4:10). Sons, in the fulness of their youth, are like full-grown plants (Ps. 144:12: pual ptcp.; a similar comparison without *gdl* is found in Ps. 128:3 and Sir. 50:12). When *gdl* in the piel denotes the rearing of children, not only does it have reference to keeping them alive in spite of the great infant mortality rate, but also to "making something out of" the children, "letting them become something," as the two examples of parallelism between *gdl* in the piel and *rum* in the piel make clear (*rum* in the piel without *gdl* in the context of rearing children: Hos. 11:7, conjec.; Prov. 4:8). Sometimes *gdl* in the piel implies that the rearing of children was the function of wisdom and of court training (2 K. 10:6; Dnl. 1:5; in addition also 1 K. 11:8, conjec.), which agrees with other verbs that denote educational instruction. The words used in parallelism with *gdl* in the piel (*chil*, "twist, writhe," Isa. 23:4; and *yaladh*, "bear, give birth to," Isa. 49:21; 51:18; cf. Jonah 4:10, where *gdl* in the piel stands in parallelism with *'amal*, "to labor," and Nu. 11:11f., without *gdl* in the piel) show that *gdl* in the piel can also refer to the trouble and pain that the birth and rearing of children brings with it. In this trouble, frequently it is also possible to see the loving affection of the teacher. In one passage, Yahweh is the subject of *gdl* in the piel when it means "to rear" (Isa. 1:2), and in another he is the subject of the estimative *gdl* in the piel when it means "to give attention to, consider, regard as something great" (Job 7:17).[50] In two passages, Heb. *rbh* in the piel also means "to bring up, to rear" (Ezk. 19:2: a lioness rearing her whelps; Lam. 2:22: Zion rearing her children).

Eleven times, *gdl* in the piel means "to give rank and dignity to a person or to confirm him therein, mark him out, or assign him a special task." Three times this is said of a human king (Est. 3:1; 5:11; 10:2; the Aram. *rbh* in the pael means the same thing in Dnl. 2:48). In the other passages, it is God who makes

---

[47] See below, c.
[48] See below, III.2.b, c.
[49] Cf. Jenni, 275.
[50] Contra H. Wildberger, *BK,* X, 12, who is surely incorrect.

a man great in the sense that he puts him in a particular position.[51] In two passages, *gdl* in the piel is used to convey the idea that men acknowledge and joyfully confess the greatness of God that they have experienced in his acts (Ps. 34:4 [3]; 69:31[30]; the declarative piel).[52]

c. *Hiphil and Hithpael.* While *gdl* in the piel denotes bringing about the condition described by the adj. *gadhol,* generally speaking *gdl* in the hiphil means to bring about the process suggested by the finite verb in the qal: to prove oneself to be great actually and effectively.[53] The subject of *gdl* in the hiphil is always God or a man, thus always a person who is capable of carrying out his own activity (the ram in Dnl. 8:4, the he-goat in 8:8, and the horn in 8:11 are figurative terms for persons or personified powers; 1 S. 20:41 is corrupt). 1 Ch. 22:5, where the temple is the subject of *gdl* in the hiphil, is an exception. And yet, even here the temple is regarded as something working actively, which proves its world-wide significance and greatness by its own effectiveness.

α. A person never appears as an object of *gdl* in the hiphil (i.e., as a subj. that is caused to be made great) (this speaks against the conjec. *vehighdilekha,* "and he will cause thee to be great," suggested by *KBL,* etc., for 2 S. 7:11), and only in a few passages do we encounter an independent object detached from anything else used as the object of *gdl* in the hiphil (woodpile, Ezk. 24:9; shekel, Am. 8:5; perhaps here also can be mentioned the joy, Isa. 9:2[3], and the instruction, Isa. 42:21, that God can make great, and the wisdom, Eccl. 1:16, that the Preacher can make great). All other objects of *gdl* in the hiphil in the OT denote something that can almost be regarded as a part of the subject, or at least as something that is thought of as arising directly from it and continuing to belong to it or that constitutes an integral element of the efficacy of the subject expressed by *gdl* in the hiphil. Among these "objects," we find, with men as subject: *peh,* "mouth" (Ob. 12); and with God as subject: *shem,* "name" (Ps. 138:2); *chesedh,* "steadfast love, kindness" (Gen. 19:19); *yeshu'oth,* "deliverances, triumphs" (Ps. 18:51[50] = 2 S. 22:51); and *tushiyyah,* "wisdom" (Isa. 28:29). In addition, *gdl* in the hiphil is used adverbially with the inf. *la'asoth,* "to do," as an object (Joel 2:20f.; Ps. 126:2f.; 1 S. 12:24, *la'asoth* should be assumed elliptically).[54] When it is used with these "objects," *gdl* in the hiphil has less of a transitive character and more of a medial one. In reality, it means to prove oneself to be great in speaking, in manifesting oneself (*shem,* "name"), in demonstrated kindness and help, in deeds and works.

β. In approximately half of all the examples of *gdl* in the hiphil in the OT, there is no object. Here the verb has an intrinsically transitive meaning, i.e., the subject of the action and the subject of the process being brought about, viz.,

---

[51] See below, III.2.b, c.
[52] Cf. Jenni, 40-43.
[53] Cf. *ibid.,* 33-36.
[54] Cf. *GK,* § 114m and n.

bringing the greatness into operation and effectiveness, are the same. [55] With one exception (1 Ch. 22:5: the temple), the subject of the intrinsically transitive *gdl* in the hiphil is a man, and its meaning is always negative. The intrinsically transitive hiphil of *gdl* always means "to set oneself forth as great illegally, presumptuously, and arrogantly, to boast, to triumph over ('*al*) others" (15 times, 5 times without explicitly mentioning the one concerning whom the boasting was done).

In this negative sense of boasting, *gdl* in the hiphil appears above all in Individual Laments (Ps. 35:26; 38:17[16]; 41:10[9]: here '*aqebh*, "heel," should be deleted; 55:13[12]; Lam. 1:9; Job 19:5 in the accusing question of the adversary) as an element in the description of the enemy and his behavior. In these passages, the boasting of the enemy always appears in words that deride and belittle the one complaining in the distress which has already come upon him. In the context we find such words as *lachats*, "to oppress," *charaph*, "to reproach," *kalem*, "to humiliate," *samach*, "to rejoice (arrogantly)," *tsachaq*, "to laugh at," '*amar*, "to say," *millin*, "words," and direct quotations from slanderous statements. The boasting is not directed against God, but always against the lamenting worshipper. But the mention of boasting, like the description of the distress, serves in general as a motivation for God to answer the worshipper's prayer and help him. This is possible because the derision against the miserable worshipper is also a derision against God, the guarantor and ground of law and true life-giving order. [56]

We also encounter *gdl* in the hiphil in prophetic oracles of judgment against the nations located east of Israel (Moab, Jer. 48:26,42; Mt. Seir, Ezk. 35:13; Moab and the Ammonites, Zeph. 2:8), and here again always in connection with the mockery and scorn against Israel (in the context we find such words as *sachaq*, "to laugh," *charaph*, "to reproach," *cherpah*, "reproach," *gedhuphah*, "taunt," *ne'atsah*, "contempt, blasphemy," *debharim*, "words," and quotations from slanderous statements). Sometimes the boasting of this enemy is mentioned in order to substantiate the announced judgment, and then it becomes a reproach. The style of the reproach as an oracle of Yahweh, and the fundamental solidarity of God with the despised Israel which is assumed in these oracles of judgment, make it possible for God to refer to the abuse brought upon Israel directly as a boasting "against me" (Jer. 48:26,42; Ezk. 35:13). That the boasting of man always takes place literally by means of bragging scorn and slander indicates that, from the point of view of the history of genres, it has its original setting in the lament (triumphant scorn and slander fit in here as characterizing the enemy of the worshipper), [57] and only later came to be used in prophetic oracles of judgment against certain foreign nations. In the lament, the worshipper sought to move God to intervene in his behalf and help him, and thus the reason for this intervention was already assumed to be certain.

---

[55] Cf. Jenni, 46-48.

[56] Cf. H. Gunkel, *Einl. in die Psalmen. GHK,* suppl. vol. (1933), 199f.

[57] Cf. C. Westermann, "Struktur und Geschichte der Klage im AT," *ZAW,* 66 (1954), 62f.; Gunkel, *Einl. in die Psalmen,* 194f., 197, 199.

The apocalyptic description of the great adversary of God and his people is the third genre in which we encounter the intrinsically transitive *gdl* in the hiphil in the sense of boasting and arrogant conduct. In Dnl. 8:4,8, it is used of the growing power of empires that refuse to tolerate any kind of rule beside their own; in Dnl. 8:11,25, of the limitless and arrogant claim to absolute rule by the world power, whose acts of violence are hostile to God and inhumane: she no longer has any regard for someone else's law, whether it be a man's ("without warning he shall destroy many") or God's ("he shall rise up against the Prince of princes"). The connection of this sort of apocalyptic arrogance of the world power with slanderous speaking, which is no longer mentioned in Dnl. 8 (as it is in Joel 2:20, if God is not the subj. of *gdl* in the hiphil here as he is in Joel 2:21), is explicitly made in Dnl. 11:36f. (using *gdl* in the hithpael), which is essentially parallel to Dnl. 8. That the king exalts himself above every god and everything else is also clear from the fact that he "speaks astonishing things" against the God of gods (cf. also Rev. 13:5).

γ. Thus *gdl* in the hithpael in Dnl. 11:36f. has a meaning similar to that of the intrinsically transitive *gdl* in the hiphil. Also, in Isa. 10:15 *hithgaddel* is used of the claim to absolute rule by the world power, which no longer relies upon God in its boasting. Once *gdl* in the hithpael appears with God as its subject (Ezk. 38:23, in connection with *qdš* in the hiphil, "to show one's holiness," and *yd'* in the niphal, "to make oneself known"), and has reference to God's self-mani-festation, in which he proclaims his greatness and incomparability before the forum of the nations so that they might know him. [58]

III. 1. *The Greatness of God and His Works.* From a traditio-historical point of view, the statements concerning the greatness of God in the OT come from two completely different spheres. Accordingly, two different types of lin-guistic expressions can be ascertained, which view and discuss the greatness of God, sometimes from a special point of view, and sometimes within a special continuity of thought. One sphere in which the greatness of God is proclaimed is the Zion tradition, as it appears in particular in the Songs of Zion and in the Hymns of Yahweh As King in the Psalter. The other is Yahweh's historical power experienced and expressed in Israel's faith, which is attested in different literary complexes of the OT and has found its most concentrated expression in the Deuteronomistic theology as far as the use of this theme under the catch-word "greatness of God" is concerned. In the course of OT tradition, both spheres and both modes of expressing the concept of the greatness of God are mixed and mutually stimulate one another.

a. *The Zion Tradition.* The hymn, Ps. 48, begins abruptly with the proclama-tion: "Great is Yahweh," without the typical Israelite hymnic introduction. This purely nominal sentence is not an address to Yahweh, but a statement about

---

[58] On the distinction between the intrinsically transitive *gdl* in the hiphil and *gdl* in the hithpael, which is difficult to reproduce in translation, cf. Jenni, 49.

Yahweh in the 3rd person, and thus is not really a prayer to God, but a proclamation to man. The predicate nominative *gadhol* stands in the first position before the subject Yahweh, and thus is in emphatic position in the sentence. This sort of nominal sentence with *gadhol* in the predicate position does not describe a total experience like a verbal sentence with the finite verb *gdl*, but represents an opinion of the speaker as to the reality of the saying (a synthetic statement).[59]

In certain other psalms, this expression appears in another place within the structure of the hymn (Ps. 96:4; 145:3; 147:5 = 1 Ch. 16:25; and in a variant expression with "the Holy One of Israel" as subj., Isa. 12:6). In two other passages, the predicate is expanded to *'el gadhol,* "a great God" (Ps. 86:10; 95:3), and once to *melekh gadhol,* "a great king" (47:3[2]). In Ps. 135:5 and Ex. 18:11, this expression occurs after *yadha'ti* "I know, I am certain," as a kind of confession formula of an individual (*yadha'ti* is used as an introduction to a confessional statement in Ps. 119:75,152, and frequently in 1QH). Yahweh is addressed in Ps. 86:10 and Jer. 10:6. Once the subject stands in the first position before *gadhol* (Ps. 99:2). This word order with its polemical emphasis (Yahweh, and not some other god, is great; cf. also *hu' yhvh,* "this is Yahweh," 48:15[14]), the formula in the 2nd person, and the rhetorical question, "Who is great if not Yahweh?" (77:14[13]), may represent later modifications of the original form of the expression.

The syntactical connection with the context in Ps. 48 and most of the other passages where this expression occurs is relatively loose. The comparative stability of this expression, its loose mooring in the context, and its varying positions in the structure of different hymns, make it likely that the phrase, "Yahweh is great!" existed independently before it became a part of a complete hymn. In these hymns, an individual could be the speaker (Ps. 135:5; Ex. 18:11; Isa. 12:6; Ps. 145:3; 77:14[13]; 86:10: in which case this expression would be a hymnic insertion into an Individual Lament). However, as an independent proclamation, this sentence could have been uttered just as well by the worshipping congregation collectively (cf. the pl. suf. in Ps. 48:1, as well as 96:4). Apparently this expression has its permanent position in the cultic celebration on Zion (in the city of our God, Ps. 48:1; in Zion, 99:2; in your midst, Isa. 12:6; in the temple of our God, Ps. 135:2). Thus the statement, "Great is Yahweh!" seems to contain an acclamatory formula which the worshipping community on Zion used to confess the greatness of its God[60] (the existence of cultic acclamations in the Canaanite region seems to be assured by Ps. 29:9; Isa. 6:3; Ps. 99:3,5,9; etc.).

The contents that define this nominal title of Yahweh also clearly point to the Zion tradition in its pre-Yahwistic form. The greatness of God proclaimed on Zion includes in particular a universal kingship over the whole earth and over all gods. As the city of God, the mountain of the north, the center of the earth through which the earth's axis goes, and the joy of the whole earth, Zion is the

---

[59] Jenni, 26-33.

[60] On the form of the cultic acclamation, cf. Th. Klauser, "Akklamation," *RAC,* I, 216-233, with additional literature.

residence of the great king (*qiryath melekh rabh*, "the city of the great king," Ps. 48:3[2]; or of the great king over gods and men?). [61] Here Yahweh, as the *'elyon*, the Most High, is terrible, and a great king over all the earth (*melekh gadhol 'al kol ha'arets*, Ps. 47:3,8[2,7]). Here he sits on his holy throne and reigns over the nations (*malakh... 'al goyim*, Ps. 47:9[8]). The shields, i.e., kings of the earth belong to him (Ps. 47:10[9]; cf. 84:10[9]; 89:19[18]). That Yahweh is great on Zion means that he is exalted over all the peoples (*ram... 'al kol ha'ammim*, Ps. 99:2), and that, as king of the nations (*melekh haggoyim*, Jer. 10:6f.) and lord of all the earth (*'adhon kol ha'arets*, Ps. 97:5), he rules over all.

In several passages it is clear that God's kingship on Zion over the earth and over the nations includes the concept of his superiority over other gods. As the great God, Yahweh is not only king over all the world, but also and especially king above all gods (*melekh... 'al kol 'elohim*, Ps. 95:3). Not only is he terrible to the kings of the earth (Ps. 76:13[12]), but also and especially feared above all gods (Ps. 96:4). As the most high over all the earth (*'elyon 'al kol ha'arets*), he is exalted far above all gods (*'al kol 'elohim* with *'alah* in the niphal, Ps. 97:9). To be sure, in almost all the passages in which Yahweh's greatness is interpreted as sovereign rule over the gods, which originally were members of a pantheon that assembled around the supreme God, these gods have been made gods of the heathen, which are no longer gods; the unique position of superiority of the highest and greatest god came to be applied to the uniqueness of this God alone. That Yahweh is great and terrible above all gods is so true that these gods are nothing before him (→ אֱלִילִים *'elilim*, Ps. 96:5; cf. Jer. 10:6ff.; both of these passages seem to have been influenced by Deutero-Isaiah's polemic against idols). The gods that bow down before Yahweh bring shame upon those who worship their images (Ps. 97:7), so that Yahweh alone is the God who works wonders, i.e., who can really help (77:15[14]), and there is no god like him (86:8).

The greatness of Yahweh confessed and praised on Zion also contains the idea that he is the creator of the world. As the great God and the great King over all gods, he holds the depths of the earth and the heights of the mountains in his hand, he made the sea and formed the dry land, and he is the creator of man (Ps. 95:4-6). While the gods of the peoples, who are not able to do anything, are nothing in contrast to his greatness, he made the heavens (96:5). Yahweh, who is greater than all gods, does whatever he pleases in heaven and on earth, in the seas and all deeps: he makes the clouds rise, makes lightnings and rain, and brings forth the wind from the storehouses (135:6f.). His greatness carries within it that wisdom which cannot be compared with the wisdom of anyone else (Jer. 10:7f.), and which is beyond measure (Ps. 147:5). It is mentioned in his work in creation: he covers the heavens with clouds, prepares rain for the earth, makes grass grow upon the hills, gives food to the beasts and the young ravens which cry, gives snow, hoarfrost, and hail, makes water freeze and melt again, and gives his wind and rain (147:8f.,16-18).

As a universal power, the greatness of God with its creative energy also in-

---

[61] See above, I.2.b.

cludes the office of universal judge, who establishes and guarantees law and order, and prevents chaos from overcoming mankind. Yahweh, whose abode is in Salem and whose dwelling place is in Zion, whose name is great in Israel (Ps. 76:2f.[1f.]), utters judgment from the heavens, so that the earth fears and is still when God arises to establish judgment to help the poor of the earth (76:9f.[8f.]). Yahweh, whose greatness is praised on Zion, loves justice and has established equity (99:4). His law is full of righteousness, and Mt. Zion rejoices because of his judgments (48:11f.[10f.]). The motif of the assault of the nations may also belong in this context. In the towers of the residence of the great king, the God who sits enthroned on Zion shows himself a sure defense, who can expel and drive back the chaotic multitude of the nations and kings that had assembled against Zion (48:4-8[3-7]; cf. 76:4-8[3-7]).

The extent to which genuine Israelite traditions of the holy war had been introduced into his material is questionable. However, the motif of the battle against the nations is so intimately connected with the whole complex of the Zion tradition that it can be assumed without direct extra-Israelite evidence that it is a pre-Yahwistic component of the Zion theology. Consequently, the kingship of the supreme God, his creative work, and his power and judicial sovereignty which overcome chaos and establish his righteousness, thus proclaiming "Great is Yahweh!" are concepts inherited from the Canaanite, and in particular the Jerusalemite, traditions. [62]

It can probably be assumed that the form of the acclamation in which Yahweh's greatness is proclaimed comes from the pre-Yahwistic cult in Jerusalem, just like the concepts which interpret and define the meaning of the greatness of the God worshipped on Zion.

Now it is true that in a sense all these concepts of the greatness of God have their locus, viz., Mt. Zion, which is identified with the mythical Zaphon; yet they do not have their time, but express what is always valid. Thus they do not go before the greatness of God (possibly as its foundation); instead, they grow out of it, and utter in hymnic praise only more precisely and in more detail what the nominal title "great" expresses in general and without elaboration. Thus it is not valid to describe the relationship between this general concept of "greatness" and its individual aspects so as to make it mean that since God is great, he is therefore king, creator, and judge. Rather, the idea is: inasmuch as he is great, he is king over gods and nations; inasmuch as he is great, he is creator of everything and judge of the world; and conversely, inasmuch as he is king, creator, and judge, he is great. Thus the acclamation, "Great is God!" ascribes to the God worshipped on Zion the highest place in the universe of gods and nations, which he always and fundamentally occupies as great king, creator of the world, and universal judge. Originally the concept of the greatness of God had the character of permanence, or being always valid, but this has been ignored in the OT. "Great" became a title of Yahweh, who allows no other gods beside him, and therefore on the whole no longer has any place in a world of gods and men,

---

62 Cf. H. Ringgren, *Israelite Religion* (trans. 1966), 21, 79-84, 158, 271; W. H. Schmidt, *Alttestamentlicher Glaube und seine Umwelt* (1968), 116-171, with additional literature.

not even as the most High, but stands over against everything. "Great" became
the title of the God of Israel, who is not the God of the world mountain understood in a mythical setting, but the God of a people and its history.

b. *In History*. The history of the people of Israel with its God, and the experience which the individual in this people has with Yahweh, is the other realm
in which the OT speaks of the greatness of God in a second way that is quite
different from the Zion tradition.

The oldest hymn of Israel that has been handed down to us, the Song of
Miriam, speaks of the greatness of Yahweh: "Sing to Yahweh! He is highly exalted, the horse and his rider he has thrown into the sea" (Ex. 15:21; instead of
gdl, this passage uses the synonymous → גאה *gāʾāh*). Here Yahweh's exaltedness
and greatness is expressed in a simple verbal sentence, the verbal character of
which is even further intensified by the addition of the infinitive absolute (*gaʾoh
gaʾah*). Now, in contrast to the neutral nominal clause, the finite verb describes
an event, an occurrence, and thus does not delineate the attributes of Yahweh,
but gives an account of a living manifestation of his exaltedness in a concrete
event. [63] Both halves of the song are closely connected with each other syntactically by the word order in the second half of this short song (horse and rider in
the first position before the verb). From the experience of the literal deliverance
at the Red Sea, which actually took place in history, Israel comes to recognize
that it is Yahweh who has proven and is proving himself to be exalted and great.

All passages in which *gdl* appears in the qal with Yahweh as subject have the
character of event rather than mere description, and speak not out of general
principles but out of a concrete happening.

According to Ps. 35:27, an Individual Lament, the deliverance of the one being
persecuted should motivate those associated with him to acknowledge and confess: "Yahweh has shown himself to be great (*yighdal*), he who has resolved
to deliver his servant." [64] Likewise, according to Ps. 40:17(16), the deliverance
of the worshipper will cause those who seek Yahweh and love his salvation to
say: "Yahweh has shown himself to be great" (*yighdal*). According to Yahweh's
promise, people in Israel will see the punishment on boastful Edom with their
own eyes. Then, out of this experience will come the acknowledgment: "Yahweh
has shown himself to be great (*yighdal*) beyond the border of Israel" (Mal. 1:5).
Ps. 92:6(5) states that Yahweh's works have been made known (*gdl* in the qal)
as real and effective.

Because Yahweh chose David and his house, and because he gave him
superiority and kingship (*gedhullah*), [65] David knows and states in a prayer: "in

---

[63] Jenni, 27f., etc.

[64] On the impf. at the beginning of a sentence with reference to a past event, cf. D. Michel,
Tempora und Satzstellung in den Psalmen (1960), 132-37.

[65] See above, I.3.b.

this way thou hast shown thyself to be great" (*'al ken gadhalta,* 2 S. 7:22). In the future, when Yahweh confirms for ever his promise and does what he has said, his name will thus be shown to be great for ever (*gdl* in the qal, 2 S. 7:26).

Two proper names should also be mentioned here: *gedhalyahu,* "Gedaliah," "Yahweh has shown himself to be great" (2 K. 25:22ff. and Jer. 39:13ff.; 38:1; Zeph. 1:1; Ezr. 10:18; 1 Ch. 25:3,9). This kind of name, consisting of a perfect form of the verb plus a noun, is a special Israelite phenomenon appearing frequently in the monarchical period, [66] which places major emphasis on the statement in the predicate; [67] cf. also *yighdalyahu,* "May Yahweh show himself to be great." [68]

Thus this verbal form of speaking of Yahweh's greatness, which comes from Israel's believing historical experience, does not attribute to Yahweh a place in the structure of the universe of gods and men, but speaks of his incomparable activeness and efficaciousness in history.

Now of course, these two groups of statements concerning the greatness of God do not stand separate from each other in the OT, but the genuine Israelite experience of Yahweh in history is suffused into the original mythical method of speaking of the greatness of God, but without displacing it, and thus transforms it into its own understanding.

Before Ps. 104 praises the order of creation in a way similar to extra-Israelite hymns, the worshipper addresses Yahweh in this way: "O Yahweh, my God, thou art very great" (*gdl* in the qal, Ps. 104:1). The hymnic description of the eternal good in creation functions as a narrative to extol the events of creation as great deeds of Yahweh which bear witness to his living greatness. Similarly, in its description of the various aspects of creation, Ps. 147 lists the revelation of Yahweh's will to Israel, which sets the knowledge of Israel apart from all other nations (147:19f.). Like this deed, his work in nature is a demonstration of his power. But above all, the Songs of Zion and the Hymns of Yahweh As King are permeated with elements of Israel's confession of her historical faith. On the Israelite Zion, people now know of the greatness and power of Yahweh no longer simply because they cultically recite the repelling of the attack of the nations against Zion, but because in giving the land he actually subdued peoples and nations before Israel, and thus chose a heritage for Israel (Ps. 47:4f.[3f.]). Ps. 48, which presents the pre-Yahwistic Zion traditions relatively unmixed, emphasizes above all that everything that the greatness of the God enthroned on Zion means applies to Yahweh, the God of Israel: the God of whose greatness the psalm speaks is Yahweh, who leads Israel (*hu' yhvh,* "this is Yahweh," 48:15 [14]). Similarly, Ps. 99:2 emphasizes that now it is Yahweh, the God of Israel, who is great in Zion (inversion), and after quoting the old Zion traditions, this psalm speaks of Moses, Aaron, and Samuel, and of the answer that Yahweh gave to the interrogation by his priests so that Israel could keep his testimonies (99:6f.). Ps. 76, which (like Ps. 48) hardly exhibits genuine Israelite tradition, still knows

---

[66] *IPN,* 21, and n. 2.
[67] *IPN,* 20.
[68] *IPN,* 206.

that the greatness of God is not confessed and extolled on Zion alone, but in Judah and Israel as well, and applies the statements about the greatness of God to this people (76:2[1]): the God on Zion is the God of Jacob (v. 7[6]); the homage which is paid here is paid to Yahweh (v. 12[11]). In the language of the myth, Ps. 77:14-21(13-20) speaks directly of the exodus of Israel. The trembling of the water, which the myth narrates, literally took place in history when Yahweh led his people by Moses and Aaron.

The internal predominance of mythical thought and speech concerning the greatness of God is quite clear in Ps. 135:5ff. and Ex. 18:11. In Ps. 135:5ff., the acclamation "Great is Yahweh" becomes the Israelite's confession of faith (cf. the introductory yadha'ti, "I know"); the Israelite knows that it is Yahweh who exercises universal rule, because he knows of the deliverance from Egypt and the fulfilment of the land promise. Similarly, the Midianite Jethro confesses that Yahweh is great, greater than all gods, because Moses tells him of Yahweh's deeds to the Egyptians, and of Israel's deliverance from their power (Ex. 18:11). The message that Solomon sends to Hiram in 2 Ch. 2:4(5) seems also to contain this new Israelite confessional statement: the house that Solomon is to build must be great, because our God is great, greater than all gods.

Thus, the verbally expressed effect of the greatness of Yahweh, the greatness of his historical act, is attributed in the nominal style to the God of Zion, so that this act enters into the nominal sentence, "Great is Yahweh," and justifies it in its form while modifying its content. Because of Yahweh's historical acts, Israel can confess not only that these acts are great, but also that Yahweh himself is great. Now, the acclamation taken over from the pre-Yahwistic Zion cult no longer ascribes a position at the head of a universe of gods and men to the God who lives on Zaphon, but, because of the historical acts of Yahweh that had been experienced, exalts his unique and comprehensive power in history and nature.

c. *The Deuteronomistic Theology.* Ex. 14:31 (usually assigned to the Yahwist) already says that Yahweh's work with which the history of Israel as Yahweh's people began was a great work: Israel saw the great work (*hayyadh haggedholah*) which Yahweh did against the Egyptians, so that the people feared Yahweh and believed in Yahweh and in his servant Moses. But the Deuteronomistic theology notes quite frequently that the exodus from Egypt, the revelation at Horeb, and the entrance of Israel into the promised land of inheritance happened in a great way, surpassing everything of the ordinary. The formula that states that Yahweh led Israel out of Egypt with a strong hand and outstretched arm (*yadh chazaqah–zeroa' netuyah*) is often expanded by expressions using the attributive *gadhol*. Yahweh led Israel out with a strong hand and outstretched arm, and with his great power (Ex. 32:11; Dt. 4:37; 9:29; 2 K. 17:36; Neh. 1:10); with great terrors (Dt. 4:34; 26:8; Jer. 32:21); with great trials and wonders (Dt. 7:19; 29:2[3]; Josh. 24:17); with the greatness of his arm (*godhel zeroa'*, Ex. 15:16, conjec.); or simply with his greatness (*godhel*, Dt. 9:26). The initial and fundamental revelation of God on the mountain took place in great fire (4:36; 5:25); the voice of the revelation was a great (loud) voice (5:22). In these events, Yahweh caused Israel to experience his greatness, so that now it can be praised by Israel while his deeds are recited (32:3ff.; cf. Ps. 150:2). The Priestly Code adopts the Deuteronomistic terminology in modified form: Yahweh delivered Israel out of Egypt with outstretched arm and great acts of judgment (*shephatim gedholim,* Ex. 6:6; 7:4).

Then, similarly, the merciful and punitive work of Yahweh in other periods of history is characterized as a great event which Yahweh works in a great way. He punishes with great anger (*'aph,* Dt. 29:23,27[24,28]) or great wrath (*chemah,* 2 K. 22:13 = 2 Ch. 34:21), or he shows great steadfast love (*chesedh,* 1 K. 3:6; Ps. 57:11[10] = 108:5[4]; 86:13; 145:8). He delivers with the greatness of his arm (*godhel zeroa',* Ps. 79:11), and works a great work (*dabhar gadhol*) in the days of Samuel as he had done in the days of Moses (1 S. 12:16). Yahweh's work in creation is also described in the language of the Deuteronomistic exodus tradition. Just as he led Israel out of Egypt with strong hand and outstretched arm, he made heaven and earth with great power (*koach gadhol*) and outstretched arm (Jer. 27:5; 32:17).

However, the Deuteronomistic exodus theology does not yield an affirmation that can be compared with the acclamation of the Songs of Zion, "Yahweh is great." No comparable nominal predicate appears in the realm of the historical experience of the greatness of Yahweh. Perhaps the reason for this is to be sought in that here the greatness of Yahweh is experienced in the concrete events of history, and therefore a nominal sentence as a synthetic affirmation in which the speaker, in general, offers the predicate as his opinion concerning the reality of which he is speaking, is out of place.

Instead the greatness of Yahweh's historical act appears here as an attributive *gadhol.* The OT speaks of the God of Israel's history as the great and terrible God (Dt. 7:21; Neh. 1:5; Dnl. 9:4), the great God (Neh. 8:6), the great and mighty and terrible God (9:32), the great and terrible Lord (4:8[14]), the great and mighty God (Jer. 32:18), God of gods, Lord of lords, the great, the mighty, and the terrible God (Dt. 10:17). In these attributive designations of Yahweh, especially those found in postexilic prayers, Yahweh's terrible and great deeds are, as it were, components of his name, by which a person can address him, and thus his name also is great (*shem gadhol,* Josh. 7:9; 1 S. 12:22; Jer. 44:26; cf. Jer. 10:6: Deuteronomistic?). According to 1 K. 8:42 = 2 Ch. 6:32, foreigners also know of Yahweh's great name, mighty hand, and outstretched arm. According to Mal. 1:11, the name of Yahweh will be great among the nations from the rising to the setting of the sun, i.e., it will be acknowledged and revered in its greatness.

d. *The Day of Yahweh.* It follows from the historical experience of the greatness of Yahweh in his deeds that the day of Yahweh is also great. Whatever is to be said about the day (→ יוֹם *yôm*) of Yahweh, its origin and significance, it is certain that Yahweh's punitive and angry rule over men comes with it. The day of Yahweh is great because it is a day of wrath, distress, and anguish ordained by Yahweh (Zeph. 1:14ff.), a day of distress without comparison. Like the deeds of Yahweh in connection with the exodus of Israel from Egypt, and like Yahweh's name, his day is also great and terrible (*gadhol venora'*, Joel 2:11; 3:4 [2:31]; Mal. 3:23[4:5]).

2. *The Greatness Given by God.* a. *The Promise to the Patriarchs.* According to the Yahwistic promise to Abraham, God wants to make Abraham a great nation (*'asah legoy gadhol*, Gen. 12:2; *hayah legoy gadhol*, 18:18). According to the Priestly Code, the same promise is made to Ishmael (*nathan legoy gadhol*, 17:20), and according to the Elohist, to both Ishmael (*sim legoy gadhol*, 21:18) and Israel (*sim legoy gadhol*, 46:3). Israel will attain this goal "there," i.e., in Egypt. God also makes the same promise to Moses (*'asah legoy gadhol*, Ex. 32:10; Nu. 14:12; both passages are Deuteronomistic additions). Without mentioning any of the patriarchs, Dt. 4:6f. speaks of Israel as a great nation (*goy gadhol*). The Deuteronomistic insertion into the ancient confession formula, which was spoken in connection with the bringing of the firstfruits (Dt. 26:5), [69] takes up the formulation of Gen. 46:3 and says that Israel became a great nation "there," i.e., in Egypt.

The expression, "to make a man a great nation," may be understood without more precise differentiation as a promise of multiplication, which promises numerous descendants, and appears alongside the promise of the possession of the land as a second promise to the patriarchs. [70] In these passages, then, *gadhol* would mean "numerous, many," and the whole expression would not differ from that which states that one's descendants will be many (*zera'*, "seed," is never used with the root *gdl*, but frequently with *rbh*, Gen. 12:7; 13:6; 15:5; cf. also *'am rabh*, RSV, "many people," 50:20; and *'am* with *rbh*, "the people multiplied," Ex. 1:20). However, a stronger differentiation between the promises to the patriarchs, like that already suggested by Westermann, [71] is also presented here.

We could think most easily of a great number of descendants in Gen. 17:20; 21:18 (Ishmael); and 46:3; Dt. 26:5 (Israel). However, the present, which is put in the past in relationship to the anticipated future, will not be seen so much from the viewpoint of the small number as from that of meaninglessness and powerlessness, of danger and destitution, so that the future envisioned for the *goy gadhol*, "great nation," has in mind the rank, significance, and importance of the future nation, and not merely the large number of its members. Apparently, *gadhol* in Dt. 4:6f. does not mean the large number, the multitude of the people, but its unique majesty and significance, whereby it is distinguished from other nations by virtue of its peculiar relationship to its God.

But above all, it is impossible to try to find a promise of multiplication, a promise of numerous descendants, in the Yahwistic promise to Abraham in Gen. 12:1-4a. Rather, Abraham, as the one who is blessed in the universality of the nations of the world, is to become a blessing to all who acknowledge

---

[69] Cf. L. Rost, "Das kleine geschichtliche Credo," *Das kleine Credo und andere Studien zum AT* (1965), 15, 18.

[70] Cf., e.g., M. Noth, *A History of Pentateuchal Traditions* (trans. 1971), 55f.; G. von Rad, *OT Theol,* I, 169f.

[71] C. Westermann, "Arten der Erzählung in der Genesis," *Forschung am AT* (1964), 18ff.

that he is blessed. God makes Abraham's name great (*gdl* in the piel) in order to serve this purpose (Gen. 12:2). Accordingly, that God will make Abraham a great nation means that a unique place will be given to him or to the people of Israel, which is personified by him, among all the families of the earth. It is very likely that the Yahwist did not encounter this promise in the traditions that were handed down to him, but introduced them into the traditional material of the Abraham narratives (possibly in connection with the promise of numerous descendants and their superiority over their enemies, cf. Gen. 22:17; etc.) because of the experience of the empire of David and Solomon, and of the role that Israel played in his days among the nations of the world, and because he understood the distinguished position of Israel in the sense of a divine commission to mediate God's blessings to the nations. [72] Thus *goy gadhol,* "a great nation," does not primarily refer to a large population, but to the significance and importance of a nation, in Dt. 4 and Gen. 12 the universally recognized and universally significant greatness and unique position of Israel in comparison with other nations.

b. *The Davidic Tradition.* What God does for David and Israel in 2 S. 7 = 1 Ch. 17 agrees very closely with the Yahwistic promise to Abraham to make him a great nation. [73] As was promised to Abraham (Gen. 12:2), God gives David a great name like the name of the great ones of the earth (2 S. 7:9; cf. 1 Ch. 17:8), i.e., he gives him a place in the circle of the great ones of the earth. Similarly, God gives the people of Israel a name (2 S. 7:23 = 1 Ch. 17:21, conjec. *lo*), i.e., he distinguishes them from the other nations. He makes David great (*gdl* in the piel: 1 Ch. 17:10), [74] and gives to David and to the people sovereign majesty and power (*gedhullah,* 2 S. 7:21,23; 1 Ch. 17:19). [75] In both Gen. 12:2 and 2 S. 7, *gdl* denotes the distinguished position that God has given David or his people among the nations of the world.

The promised ruler of Israel, who comes from the family of David, will receive and rule over a universal kingdom by the power of Yahweh and by the grandeur of the name of Yahweh his God, so that he shall be great to the ends of the earth (*gdl* in the qal, Mic. 5:3[4]). In connection with the judgment on the ungodly world power, a universal and everlasting kingdom will be given to the people of the saints of the Most High (using *rebhu* and other designations for royal sovereign power, Dnl. 7:27).

c. *Leaders in Israel.* While *gdl* or *rbh* in 2 S. 7, Mic. 5, and Dnl. 7 have in mind the sovereign superiority of Israel or of her king in comparison with non-Israelite nations, in other passages it denotes the position of leadership that God gives to an individual among the people of Israel.

---

[72] Cf. H. W. Wolff, "Das Kerygma des Jahwisten," *EvTh,* 24 (1964), 82-88.

[73] Cf. Wolff, *ibid.,* 83; on the connections between the Davidic theology and individual themes of the Yahwist, esp. in Gen. 2 and 3, cf. E. Haag, *Der Mensch am Anfang* (1970), 101-151.

[74] Reading conjecturally with the LXX and most commentaries *va'aghaddelekha;* otherwise W. Rudolph, *HAT,* 21, 130.

[75] See above, I.3.b.

By the crossing of the Jordan, God makes Joshua great in the eyes of all Israel, i.e., he confirms Joshua in the succession of Moses as leader of the people (*gdl* in the piel, Josh. 3:7; 4:14). When it is applied to Samuel, *gdl* in the qal means (beyond natural growth in the presence of Yahweh, 1 S. 2:21) especially the importance Samuel gained in the eyes of all Israel because God made his words come to pass and thus established him as a leader in Israel (3:19). Similarly, David gains power and respect and receives the kingship over Israel because Yahweh was with him (*vayyelekh davidh halokh vegadhol*, "and David became greater and greater," 2 S. 5:10 = 1 Ch. 11:9; cf. 2 S. 5:12; according to Fohrer [76] and others, 2 S. 5:10,12 is the original conclusion of the account of David's rise; be this as it may, these verses give the central theme and purpose of this account). The word of blessing spoken concerning Solomon is that God might make his throne greater than the throne of his father (*gdl* in the piel, 1 K. 1:37,47). God makes Solomon great in the eyes of all Israel (*gdl* in the piel), and gives him such royal majesty (*hodh malkhuth*) as had not been on any king before him (1 Ch. 29:25; cf. *gdl* in the piel with reference to Solomon in 2 Ch. 1:1).

Quite generally, the OT says of the king in Israel that his glory (*kabhodh*) is great (*gadhol*) through God's help, and thus that it is God who has bestowed splendor and majesty (*hodh vehadhar;* cf. → הדר *hādhār*) upon him (Ps. 21:6[5]). According to Dnl. 4:33(36), even Nebuchadnezzar receives his royal power (*rebhu*) from Yahweh's hand. In the form of a confessional, didactic general sentence, 1 Ch. 29:12 says that, as universal Lord, God's eternal and fundamental business is to make a man great (*gdl* in the piel), i.e., to set him up as leader or ruler, and to establish him in his position as ruler.

Mosis

---

[76] G. Fohrer, *IntrodOT* (trans. 1968), 220.

גָּדַף *gādhaph;* גִּדּוּף *giddûph;* גִּדּוּפָה *giddûphāh*

Contents: I. 1. Etymology; 2. Meaning. II. Secular Usage. III. Religious Usage: 1. Blasphemy; 2. Averting Blasphemy.

I. 1. *Etymology.* The etymological explanation of the root *gdp* depends on whether it is regarded as an Aramaic loanword, [1] and beyond this whether this loanword is identical with Arab. *ğaḏafa* I, II, "to throw, cast, cut off." If so, the

---

gādhaph. H. W. Beyer, *TDNT*, I, 621-25; S. H. Blank, "The Curse, Blasphemy, the Spell and the Oath," *HUCA*, 23 (1950/51), 73-95; M. S. Enslin, *BHHW*, II (1964), 1051; A. Lemonnyer, *DBS*, 1, 981-89; J. Scharbert, *BL* (²1968), 1016f.; M. Wagner, *Die lexikalischen und grammatikalischen Aramaismen im alttestamentlichen Hebräisch. BZAW*, 96 (1966), 51a-c.

[1] As it is by Th. Nöldeke, S. Fraenkel, and M. Wagner (q.v.).

correct corresponding phonetic form of the Hebrew would be gzp[2] (cf. Old South Arab. gḏf). In the Aramaic idiom, the root gdp (with its derivatives) has an original and a figurative meaning: (a) the original meaning was "to fly" (to beat wings?), gdpʾ, "wing," Syr. "to row" (to beat oars?), Mandean gadafa, "to throw" (stones, accusations); (b) the figurative meaning was "to revile, blaspheme."

2. *Meaning.* In biblical and postbiblical Hebrew, the latter meaning is predominant (cf. Egyp. gꜣy, ḥwrw, wꜣꜣ, śḥwr, šnt), which is the case especially because the root gdp is used mainly in later OT literature; only 2 K. 19:6,22 speak against this. By way of contrast, the original meaning of violent injury (assault and battery) appears only rarely.[3] With its various renderings of this root, the LXX has emphasized the figurative sense of insult (slander): *blasphēmeín*, "to revile, blaspheme" (2 K. 19:6,22); *katalaleín*, "to speak against, slander" (Ps. 44:17 [Eng. v. 16] = codices B and S, *paralaleín*, "to chatter beside"); *oneidízein*, "to reproach, revile" (Isa. 37:6,23); *oneidismós*, "reproach, reviling" (Isa. 43:28; 51:7); *paroxýnein*, "to provoke to wrath, irritate" (Nu. 15:30); *parorgízein*, "to make (someone) angry" (Ezk. 20:27); and *megalaucheín hyperēphanía*, "to make proud boasts" (Sir. 48:18). *kondylismós*, "ill treatment" (Zeph. 2:8), and *dēlaistós*, "spoil, ruin" (Ezk. 5:15), reflect the original sense.

II. Secular Usage. gdp belongs to a family of words meaning "to slander"; cf. → קלל *qālal*, "to revile, curse," "behave in a disrespectful manner"; → נקב *nāqabh*, "to brand, stigmatize, curse." In secular usage, the sense is illuminated by the repeated use of the parallel → חרף *chāraph*, "to provoke, reproach," "revile," and its derivatives: an insult (RSV, "disgrace") against someone else (*kelimmah*, Ps. 44:16f.[15f.]). A person is treated with reviling or shame (*bosheth*, 44:16f.[15f.]; → בוש *bôsh*) in order to lower him in the eyes of a third party and lessen his reputation. In the Lament of the Individual in Ps. 44:16f.(15f.), it is the author's enemies (→ אויב *ôyēbh*; *mithnaqqem*, "avenger") that bring him disgrace, and he regards it as shame. In Zeph. 2:8, a people (Israel) also experiences a similar disgrace from its opponents (Moab and Ammon). The poetic author of Isa. 51:7 wants to comfort the righteous concerning the wrong inflicted on them by men; but elsewhere in the OT, disgrace of the unrighteous is regarded as just reward (Ezk. 5:15, the rebellious house of Israel; Isa. 43:28, the ungodly princes who are threatened with the ban).

III. Religious Usage.

1. *Blasphemy.* Of special importance is the disgrace man inflicts on God, e.g., Israel's enemies (2 K. 19:6,22 = Isa. 37:6,23) who insolently lift up their voices and their eyes against Yahweh's people. CD A 5:11f. and 1QS 4:11 (*leshon gidduphim*, "a blaspheming tongue") are to be understood in a similar sense, in the latter passage in the context of a catalog of vices. But even Israel herself is

---

[2] Gordon, *UT*, 5, 3.
[3] See below.

not immune to this kind of sin; in fact, it can originate from a conscious violation of the sacrificial Torah (Nu. 15:30), and can lead to extermination from the people of God. 1 S. 2:12-17; 3:13 (qll) tell of similar transgressions. Sacrifice offered to idols is especially sinful (Ezk. 20:27), and can result in deportation. Obviously, this sin of omission is a serious insult. The Egyptian Book of the Dead uses the root šʔt, which likewise means "to defile," for the reviling of a deity (125:38 [?],42). Akk. ṭapālu D (e.g., in Gilg. VI, 159) has a similar meaning.

In connection with the ancient Near Eastern understanding of a "word" (→ דבר dābhār), a blasphemous or reviling statement in and of itself is already a real degradation and is suffered by man as a distress, although when it comes on an ungodly person it is regarded as a punishment originating in God's righteousness, just as the abuse directed against a godly man or against the people of God can be equivalent to a blasphemy against God.

2. *Averting Blasphemy.* The man of the Old Covenant seems to have refrained from uttering a direct verbal blasphemy against God as much as possible; nonetheless he blasphemed indirectly by the sin of omission, of withholding a sacrifice (Nu. 15:30), or by offering a sacrifice to a foreign god (Ezk. 20:27). Probably what prevented a real blasphemy was the fear that the blasphemous word that was spoken would return upon the head of the blasphemer. [4] It was less necessary to have this fear when reviling a man, unless his God should take personal offense at the blasphemy and avenge it. The hope of divine retribution strengthened and comforted the righteous sufferer or the people of Israel in their affliction (Gen. 12:3; 27:29; Nu. 24:9; Zec. 2:12 [8]). In any case, when the OT openly speaks of blaspheming God, it uses a euphemism (→ ברך brk, "to bless," II. 2.i; Job 1:5, 11; 2:5,9; etc.). Accordingly, it was offensive even to mention blaspheming God.

Wallis

גָּדֵר gādhēr → חומה chômāh

---

[4] Cf. Blank, 83-85.

גּוֹג *gôgh;* מָגּוֹג *māghôgh*

Contents: I. The Gog and Magog Traditions. II. The Literary Problems in Ezk. 38–39. III. Attempts at Explaining the Names. IV. History of the Motifs in the Gog and Magog Traditions. V. Gog and Magog in Eschatological and Apocalyptic Perspective.

I. The Gog and Magog Traditions. In the table of nations in Gen. 10, the sons of Japheth are presented "in their lands, each with his own language, by their families, in their nations" (10:5). The seven sons of Japheth are: Gomer, Magog, Madai, Javan, Tubal, Meshech, and Tiras (10:2), and we encounter Togarmah among the sons of Gomer (10:3; cf. 1 Ch. 1:5f.).

In a series of prophecies in Ezk. 38–39, it is stated that "after many days," "in the latter years" (38:8), Yahweh will lead Gog of the land of Magog, chief prince of Meshech and Tubal, at the head of a great army against Israel, returned from exile. His troops include Gomer and Beth-togarmah "from the uttermost parts of the north," as well as Paras (Persia), Cush (Ethiopia), and Put (Libya?) (38:1-9). Gog devises wicked plans in arrogance, and desires only to carry off plunder from Israel. But the prophet prophesies against Gog and makes it clear to him that he will be allowed to march against Israel only in order to demonstrate Yahweh's glory (38:10-16). Gog represents the enemy announced by the earlier prophets: when he comes, an earthquake will break forth upon Israel and will destroy the land (38:17-20); but in the end this destruction will also come upon Gog (38:21-23).

Gog and his hordes will be brought against the mountains of Israel, and there they will be destroyed by Yahweh; the dead bodies will be devoured by the birds and the beasts (39:1-8).

This will continue for seven years until the weapons of the army of Gog are burned up; and after a grave has been found for Gog in the Valley of Abarim in Transjordan, burials will continue for seven months until the land is cleansed of dead bodies. Finally, Yahweh will prepare the fallen as a sacrificial meal for the birds and the beasts (39:9-20).

---

gôgh. J. G. Aalders, *Gog en Magog in Ezechiël* (Kampen, 1951); A. van den Born, "Études sur quelques toponymes bibliques," *OTS*, 10 (1954), 197-214; L. Dürr, *Die Stellung des Propheten Ezechiel in der israelitisch-jüdischen Apokalyptik. ATA*, 9/1 (1923); S. B. Frost, *OT Apocalyptic* (London, 1952), 88-92; G. Gerleman, "Hesekielsbokens Gog," *SEÅ*, 12 (1947), 148-162; H. Gressmann, *Der Ursprung der israelitisch-jüdischen Eschatologie. FRLANT,* 6 (1905); *idem, Der Messias. FRLANT,* 26 (1929), 118-134; W. Gronkowski, *Le Messianisme d'Ézéchiel* (Paris, 1930), 129-173; A. S. Kapelrud, *Joel Studies. UUÅ* (1948), 93-108; C. A. Keller, "Gog und Magog," *RGG³,* II, 1683f.; A. Lauha, *Zaphon. AnAcScFen,* B, 49, 2 (Helsinki, 1943); H.-M. Lutz, *Jahwe, Jerusalem und die Völker. WMANT,* 27 (1968); H.-P. Müller, *Ursprünge und Strukturen alttestamentlicher Eschatologie. BZAW,* 109 (1969); H. D. Preuss, *Jahweglaube und Zukunftserwartung. BWANT,* 5/7 (1968); F. Stolz, *Strukturen und Figuren im Kult von Jerusalem. BZAW,* 118 (1970); J. W. Wevers, *Ezekiel. The Century Bible* (London, 1969); W. Zimmerli, *Ezechiel. BK,* XIII (1969).

All this takes place in order that the nations may acknowledge the glory of Yahweh and understand that Israel has been punished because of her sins. But Israel herself is to know that Yahweh wants to be her God from that day forward; but after the return from exile, she must bear her humiliation and recognize that Yahweh showed himself to be the God of Israel both by the exile and by the restoration (39:21-29).

II. The Literary Problems in Ezk. 38–39. The main passage in the OT where we find the concept of Gog and Magog, Ezk. 38–39, is usually considered to be much revised. Earlier scholars usually worked with a two-source theory.[1] Gressmann's view is typical: an earlier source A consists of 38:10-16a,18-23; 39:9-20; while a later parallel source B comprises 38:3-9,16b-17; 39:1-8; both recensions are postexilic.[2] In a similar way, Dürr advances a two-source theory (A: 38:3-7,9; 39:1-8; B: 38:8,10-16,17-23; 39:9-20,21-29), but thinks that both recensions come from Ezekiel himself.[3] In more recent research, we encounter a variety of interpretations. Amidst all the diversity, one can see certain frequently recurring elements: a nucleus (whether it be from Ezekiel or not) has been revised and added to in several phases. Accordingly, Ezk. 38–39 may be regarded as an anthology of more or less related traditions. However, the attempts to separate the nucleus from the later supplements differ widely from one another. Zimmerli, e.g., thinks the oldest section is 38:1-9; 39:1-5,17-20;[4] while Lutz considers the nucleus to be only 39:1-5,17-20;[5] and von Rabenau shrinks the original component of the two chapters to 39:1-5 alone.[6]

From a traditio-historical point of view, the growth of Ezk. 38–39 must be regarded as a gradual accumulation of related motifs. Some sections probably originated with the prophet himself, while some were added later as explanatory glosses.[7] The literary structure of the final redaction is probably not as accidental as is often maintained. An alternating schema can be observed, especially in chap. 38: Gog's hordes–38:1-9; Gog's despotism–38:10-13; additional hordes–38:14-16; Yahweh punishes Israel–38:17-20; and Yahweh punishes Gog–38:21-23.[8] The literary questions cannot be treated in detail in this article. Our task will be to present a theological evaluation of the whole Gog tradition, regardless of whether certain parts of this tradition were inserted later and perhaps in an awkward way into the present literary context.

---

[1] This was still the case with Bertholet, *HAT*, 13 (1936).

[2] *Der Ursprung*, 181f.

[3] Dürr, 96-98.

[4] Zimmerli, 933-38.

[5] Lutz, 65-84.

[6] K. von Rabenau, *WZ* Halle-Wittenberg, 5/4 (1956), 677, 681; see the surveys of the research on this problem in Gronkowski, 148-161; Kuhl, *ThR,* 20 (1952), 13f.; 24 (1956/57), 28-31; Lutz, 63-65; and the comms.

[7] See esp. Fohrer, *HAT*, 13 (²1955), 212-19.

[8] See Lutz, 74-83; and von Rabenau, 676, who shows how this alternation leads to obvious contradictions.

III. Attempts at Explaining the Names. As far as the interpretation of the names Gog and Magog is concerned, the names of the nations in Gen. 10 (where Magog is mentioned) and the names of the nations that are a part of Gog's military forces in Ezk. 38 have focused the attention of scholars on the north-west, on Anatolia and the regions north of Mesopotamia. The picture is uniform if we disregard the soldiers from Persia, Ethiopia, and Libya in Ezk. 38:5, who certainly come from 27:10: [9] with a considerable degree of certainty, Meshech can be located in Phrygia, Tubal in Cilicia, Gomer in the Armenian mountains, and Togarmah in the territory east of Cilicia, (38:2,6). [10] Most of the other nations mentioned in Gen. 10:2-5 (as far as they are known) are also found in this part of the world (the Ionians, the inhabitants of Tarshish, the Kittim, the Medes, etc.). [11]

Even when the geographical location of Gog is determined, very different interpretations have been offered for the names Gog and Magog. An old inter-pretation, which is found as early as Josephus, that Gog represents the Scythians, is still advocated by Wellhausen. [12] The usual interpretation in more recent times goes back to Delitzsch, etc.: Gog is the Lydian king Gyges (Akk. *Gûgu*), who dates *ca.* 670 B.C., and consequently the land of Magog is Lydia. [13] Other schol-ars keep to the same time period, but think that Gog has reference to the dynasty of *Gagi* in the territory north of Assyria, which is mentioned in a text of Ashur-banipal. [14] Still others think it refers to a territory called *Gaga* mentioned in an Amarna letter (I, 38), which, according to the context (Ḫanigalbat and Ugarit are also mentioned), was located north of Syria, perhaps around Carchemish. [15] Among the scholars who regard Ezk. 38–39 as totally postexilic, Messel, e.g., attempts to interpret Gog as an officer in the army of the younger Cyrus (*ca.* 400 B.C.), [16] and Winckler assumes that the old name Gog (derived from *Gaga* in the Amarna letter) was used as a pseudonym for Alexander the Great. [17] In most of the attempts to explain Gog historically, the term Magog is interpreted either as an artificial form ("land of Gog"), [18] or as a "Hebraizing" of an Akk. *mātGog* (= *mātGaga* in an Amarna letter). [19] On the other hand, some scholars

---

[9] Zimmerli, 948f.; cf. 643f.; otherwise Kapelrud, 103.

[10] See Zimmerli, 652f., 788f., and 947-49.

[11] See Gunkel, *GHK*, I/1[5], 152f.; and Hölscher, *Drei Erdkarten* (1949), 45-56.

[12] J. Wellhausen, *Isr. Gesch.* (³1897), 149; cf. W. Brandenstein, *Festschrift A. Debrunner* (Bern, 1954), 64f.

[13] See J. Herrmann, *KAT*, XI, 245; Zimmerli, 942; for further information concerning Gyges cf. J. L. Myres, *PEQ*, 64 (1932), 213-19; and G. R. Berry, *JBL*, 41 (1922), 224-232, who regards Gog=Gyges as a pseudonym for Antiochus V Eupator.

[14] Dürr, 98f.; cf. Herrmann, *KAT*, XI, 244–moreover, Gagi is a proper name, and of Persian origin.

[15] H. Winckler, *Altorient. Forschungen*, II/1 (1898), 167f.; Gressmann, *Der Ursprung*, 182f.; Albright, *JBL*, 43 (1924), 380-84; cf. Dürr, 98, who equates the name Gaga in the Amarna letters with the Gagi that occurs later in the Ashurbanipal texts.

[16] N. Messel, *Ezechielfragen* (Oslo, 1945), 125f.

[17] Winckler, *et al.*; a synopsis of the different interpretations appears in H. H. Rowley, *Relevance of Apocalyptic* (new ed. London, 1963), 35-37; Zimmerli, 940-42; Herrmann, *KAT*, XI, 244f.; Fohrer, *HAT*, 13, 212f.; Wevers, 284; Keller, 1684.

[18] Kraetzschmar, *GHK*, III/3 (1900), 255; Zimmerli, 941; Keller, 1684; *KBL*[1]; etc.

think the name of the land came first, and that the name Gog was derived from it. [20]

In contrast to these various historical explanations of the terms Gog and Magog, there are certain attempts to understand these names as mythical forms: van Hoonacker thinks they are derived from Sum. *gug*, "darkness," and thus Magog = the land of darkness and Gog = the personification of darkness. [21] Others have suggested a connection between these terms and the Akkadian god Gaga, which appears in Enuma Elish. [22] More vaguely, some scholars speak of Gog as "leader and representative of the powers hostile to God," [23] or maintain that the historical names are only "masks and disguises" for "a mythical power that has nothing to do with actual history." [24] Later, Gressmann does grant the Gyges thesis as far as the origin of the name is concerned, [25] but he thinks that mythical ideas of the giant of primitive times (Og = Gog?) and of gigantic locusts lie behind this figure. [26]

Finally, some scholars try to solve the problem to some extent by text-critical considerations. According to Gerleman, Gog was inserted into Ezk. 38–39 from a pre-Massoretic version of Nu. 24:7, which read Gog instead of Agag (cf. the LXX and the Samaritan Pentateuch); the origin and meaning of this name are uncertain. [27] On the other hand, van den Born regards the expression "the land of Magog" as a marginal note that was incorporated into the text, and holds that originally the territories of Gog were understood simply as *'rṣ hmgdn,* "the territory of the Macedonian," i.e., of Alexander the Great. [28]

IV. History of the Motifs in the Gog and Magog Traditions. The attempts to interpret these names point in two directions: either historical realities or mythological ideas lie behind the Gog-Magog concept. As so often, the truth lies somewhere in between. Various motifs are used in the description of the great final battle in Ezk. 38–39: on the one hand, as in the case of Daniel, the passage has incorporated a "historical" person, Gog, whose name was known, but whose historical significance is hidden in the dim past. It has connected this person with other historical entities, lands, and kingdoms, which are far away and strange, and whose names sound mysterious. [29] On the other hand, the passage has combined these historical elements with motifs that are partly of cultic-mythological origin, [30] and are amply attested in other OT texts. The composite literary char-

---

[19] Dürr, 98f.; Herrmann, *KAT,* XI, 245; etc.
[20] König, *Mess. Weissagungen* ([2,3]1925), 261; Aalders, 31; Wevers, 284.
[21] Van Hoonacker, *ZA,* 28 (1914), 336.
[22] See Herrmann, *KAT,* XI, 244.
[23] Lauha, 71.
[24] Staerk, *ZAW,* 51 (1933), 20f.
[25] Gressmann, *Messias,* 124f.
[26] *Ibid.,* 127f.
[27] Gerleman, 157-162.
[28] Van den Born, 199f.
[29] Lauha, 25.
[30] Cf. Kapelrud, 104.

acter of these two chapters makes it easy to see how so many motifs could be brought together.

The principal motifs in Ezk. 38–39 are these:

a. "The Day of Yahweh": Although this expression itself is not used in Ezk. 38–39, the idea of a day in which Yahweh will manifest his wrath, sit in judgment, and carry out punishment through destruction clearly appears there. This idea has its origin in the ancient Israelite cult (→ יוֹם *yôm*).[31] The idea of the day of Yahweh can be regarded as a primary concept in Ezk. 38–39. Other motifs are to be considered in the framework of this concept, several of which appear in Ezk. 38–39.

b. War with Chaos and War with the Nations: The entire war situation in Ezk. 38–39 recalls, in many features, the OT descriptions of Yahweh's war against the powers of chaos, and the descriptions of Yahweh's war against the enemy peoples derived from it (war with chaos: Nah. 1:4; Hab. 3:8; Isa. 50:2f.; and many passages in the Psalms;[32] war with the nations: Isa. 14:24-27; 17:12-14; Ps. 2; 110; 68:13-19 [Eng. vv. 12-18]; etc.).[33] These battle scenes are connected with descriptions of a theophany in Ezk. 38:18-23 and in other OT passages. The war is associated with a cosmic nature catastrophe (see Zec. 14:3f.; Joel 4:15f.[3:15f.]; Isa. 24:19-23).[34] The duality which can be observed in the OT texts concerning the "war against the nations" (in the Psalms the nations themselves attack on their own initiative, while in the prophets they are often summoned by Yahweh)[35] also appears in Ezk. 38–39: in 38:1-9,14-16+17, Gog is summoned by Yahweh and is Yahweh's instrument, but in 38:10-13 he acts arbitrarily (probably influenced by Isa. 10:15ff.).[36]

c. The Foe from the North: The expression *yarkethe tsaphon* (Ezk. 38:6,15; 39:2) and the whole geographic orientation of the attack show that the idea of "the foe from the north" or "the evil from the north," known from other passages in the OT, is here in the writer's field of vision (cf. Jer. 1:13-15; 4:6ff.; 6:1ff.,22; Joel 2:20; etc.; cf. → צָפוֹן *tsāphôn* with additional literature). Ezk. 38–39 has probably borrowed this idea especially from Jeremiah.[37] In the OT tradition, this idea has undergone a historico-geographic twist, but it is certainly mythological-legendary in its origin: the evil powers of chaos that are hostile to God reside in the north, whence they are set loose.[38]

---

31 Cf. Mowinckel, *Psalmenstudien,* II (1922), 244-263; Lutz, 130-146; somewhat different in Preuss, 170-79; and Müller, 72-85.

32 See the list in Stolz, 61-63; and cf. Mowinckel, *Psalmenstudien,* II, 45-50 and 255f.

33 See the list in Stolz, 86-88.

34 Cf. Müller, 96; Lutz, 123f.; and Jeremias, *Theophanie. WMANT,* 10 (1965), 97-100.

35 Stolz, 90.

36 See Eichrodt, *ATD,* XXII, 368.

37 Zimmerli, 938f.

38 Lauha, 53-78; but cf. pp. 84-89; Kapelrud, 101-104; Ringgren, *Israelite Religion* (trans. 1966), 277f.; cf. also Zimmerli, 938f.; Lutz, 125-130; and Stolz, 90-92, who cautiously oppose a mythological interpretation.

d. Attack of the Nations upon Jerusalem: Many scholars assume that Ezk. 38–39 is based on a combination of this tradition with the one mentioned above under c. [39] The concept of a repulsed enemy attack on Jerusalem possibly has its origin in pre-Davidic Jerusalem, [40] but appears in its purest form in Pss. 46, 48, and 76. The prophetic descriptions of the enemy attack on Jerusalem (Isa. 17; 29; Joel 2; 4[3]; Zec. 12; 14) [41] probably are based on the tradition in the Jerusalem cult attested in these psalms. [42] The close connection between Ezk. 38–39 and these traditions is especially clear in 38:12, which states that the hostile attack is directed against "the navel of the earth." It is most likely that this refers to Jerusalem, [43] although this would be contrary to other passages, which speak of the "mountains of Israel" as the place of battle. [44] Furthermore, in the descriptions of frustrated enemy attacks on Jerusalem found elsewhere in the OT, there are a number of specific features which reappear in Ezk. 38–39.

e. The Sacrificial Meal: The idea that the slain will be prepared as a sacrificial meal (Ezk. 39:17-20; cf. vv. 4f.) is also found elsewhere in the OT (Jer. 46:10; Zeph. 1:7f.; Isa. 34:5-8; cf. Lam. 2:21f.). [45]

Other motifs can be mentioned: the motif of peace in the description of the burning of the weapons (Ezk. 39:9f.; cf. Isa. 9:5[6]; Ps. 46:10[9]; etc.); [46] the motif of the graves and the valley (Ezk. 39:11), which is probably etiological in nature. [47]

Thus Ezk. 38–39 has the character of a mosaic of well-known OT motifs; this fact is expressed in 38:17 and 39:8, where (probably in later additions) the Gog event is represented as a fulfilment of the predictions of earlier prophets.

V. Gog and Magog in Eschatological and Apocalyptic Perspective. It is usually maintained that Ezk. 38–39 stands at the transition from eschatology to apocalyptic. [48] This somewhat vague position is connected with the uncertainty concerning the differentiation between the nucleus that probably goes back to Ezekiel himself and later additions. [49] Frequently it is argued that the Ezekiel nucleus is of the traditional prophetic eschatological type, while the additions represent an apocalyptic tendency. [50] All this is probably a question of definition. If "apocalyptic" is interpreted as esoteric doctrine concerning the ordering of the cosmos, time, and the end of the world, then Ezk. 38–39 is not apocalyptic. Basically Ezk. 38–39 belongs to the series of OT prophecies based

---

[39] Zimmerli, 938-940; Ringgren, *loc. cit.;* Keller, 1684; Herrmann, *KAT,* XI, 252; etc.

[40] Von Rad, *OT Theol,* II (trans. 1965), 156.

[41] See Kraus, *BK,* XV, 344; Lutz, *passim;* Müller, 96-101.

[42] Kraus, *BK,* XV, 341.

[43] Stolz, 166; Fohrer, *HAT,* 13, 214.

[44] Zimmerli, 955-57.

[45] See S. Grill, *BZ,* N.F. 2 (1958), 278-283; and the comms.

[46] See Eichrodt, *ATD,* XXII, 371.

[47] Zimmerli, 965f.

[48] Gerleman, 151; Ringgren, *Israelite Religion,* 332; Frost, 90; Zimmerli, 945; Müller, 99-101; etc.

[49] Cf. II.

[50] See esp. Fohrer, *HAT,* 13, 216; Ringgren, *loc. cit.*

on the schema: punishment of Israel–chastisement of the heathen–restoration of Israel. The many motif associations indicate that Ezk. 38–39 stands in this tradition. The new element, which sets Ezk. 38–39 apart from other prophets, and which probably prepares the way for later apocalyptic speculations concerning the eons, is the idea of "the double *eschaton*," [51] i.e., "the prophet here points to something beyond what is to come next, i.e., to a second stage of the divine activity beyond that which is expected first (the gathering of the dispersed)." [52] Here the eschatological expressions *miyyamim rabbim* (38:8) and *be'acharith hayyamim* (38:16), together with the rare *be'acharith hashshanim* (38:8), which are found elsewhere in the OT, receive a more pregnant content (→ אחרית *'ach°rîth*). [53] If this idea originated with Ezekiel himself (and this is quite possible), [54] then he has given the Gog idea and the motifs connected therewith a special position in prophetic eschatology. Thus it was natural (esp. in the additions) to give everything a cosmic character and one "bordering on the bizarre."

A typical theme of Ezekiel unites the different traditions in Ezk. 38–39: the attack and suppression of Gog occurs only that Israel and the nations may acknowledge Yahweh's holiness (Ezk. 38:16,23; 39:7,[13],21-29). Thus, the Gog pericope has been set in a larger Ezekielian context (cf. 20:41; 28:25; 36:23; 37:28), [55] and an attempt has been made to achieve an internal relationship among the eschatological ideas of the book.

The "remote expectation" that characterizes Ezk. 38–39 has enabled the later Rabbinic and Christian interpretation to transfer the Gog event into an ever more remote future. [56]

Otzen

---

[51] Frost, 91.
[52] Zimmerli, 945.
[53] Cf. Müller, 100f.
[54] See Zimmerli, 945f.
[55] *Idem*, 957f.
[56] See St.-B., III, 831-840; *TDNT*, I, 789-791; Keller, 1684; and esp. for the medieval expectation, N. Cohn, *The Pursuit of the Millennium* (London, 1970).

גּוֹי gôy

Contents: I. 1. Etymology; 2. Meaning. II. 1. Use in the OT; 2. Israel As a Goy; 3. Special Religious Development.

I. 1. *Etymology*. There is widespread agreement that the Heb. word *goy* is derived from the West Semitic *gāwum/gāyum*, which is found in the Mari dialect of Akkadian. [1] According to von Soden, *gāyum* means "people"; whereas *CAD*, V, 59 gives the more precise meaning "group, (work-)gang." In the edition of the Mari documents, the editors have sometimes translated the word as "tribe" [2] and sometimes as "territory," [3] but this latter translation is disputed by Noth and Malamat. The context of the documents is not sufficiently defined to indicate whether the group of people concerned are identified by their political, territorial, or racial affiliations. Noth argues that it is a technical term for half-nomadic peoples, which had no exact counterpart in the language of settled urban communities. Malamat contends that in the Mari dialect, *gāwum/gāyum* basically refers to an ethnic-gentilic unit, to which has been added a geographic element under the royal administration. In *ARM*, VI, 28.7-9, he regards it as having a more specifically military connotation.

2. *Meaning*. From this West Semitic derivation, the primary meaning of the Heb. *goy* as "people" is fully assured, but it remains unclear to what extent the principle of identification is based on political, territorial, or gentilic consideration, and whether some element of social status is implied. [4] This is evident in the usage of the OT, where, although → עַם *'am* is used much more frequently to denote a gentilic unit, *goy* denotes a people considered either politically or racially. Speiser contends that, whereas *'am* denotes consanguinity and a com-

gôy. A. Bertholet, *Die Stellung der Israeliten und der Juden zu den Fremden* (1896); M. Birot, "Textes économiques de Mari, III," *RA*, 49 (1955), 15ff.; G. Buccellati, *Cities and Nations of Ancient Syria. StSem*, 26 (1967); A. Causse, *Du groupe ethnique à la communauté religieuse* (1937); D. O. Edzard, "Mari und Aramäer?" *ZA*, 56 (1964), 142-49; H.-M. Lutz, *Jahwe, Jerusalem und die Völker. WMANT*, 27 (1968); A. Malamat, "Mari and the Bible: Some Patterns of Tribal Organization and Institutions," *JAOS, 82 (1962)*, 143-150; idem, "Aspects of Tribal Societies in Mari and Israel," *Les Congrès et Colloques de l'Université de Liège*, 42 (1967), 129-138; M. Noth, *Die Ursprünge des alten Israel im Lichte neuer Quellen. AFNW*, 94 (1961); G. von Rad, *Das Gottesvolk im Deuteronomium. BWANT*, 3/11 (1929); L. Rost, "Die Bezeichnungen für Land und Volk im AT," *Festschrift O. Procksch* (1934), 125-148=*Das kleine Credo und andere Studien zum AT* (1965), 76-101; E. A. Speiser, "'People' and 'Nation' of Israel," *JBL, 79* (1960), 157-163=*Oriental and Biblical Studies* (1967), 160-170.

[1] *ARM*, IV, 1.13,15; VI, 28.8; Birot, I, 35; II, 5,45; III, 32,42,70; IV, 22; V, 20,31,53; cf. also the proper name Baḫluga(y)i(m), Huffmon, *APNM*, 123, 174, 180.

[2] *ARM*, IV, 1.13.

[3] *ARM*, IV, 1.15; VI, 28; cf. *RA*, 47 (1953), 127.

[4] Cf. *CAD*.

mon racial parentage, *goy* continually stresses territorial affiliation and the use of a common language. This is undoubtedly a recognizable tendency in the Hebrew use of the words, but it is not observed with complete consistency. In certain references where *'am* and *goy* occur together (e.g., Ex. 33:13; Dt. 4:6), no basic distinction between the two is intended, and the two nouns are used synonymously. Nevertheless, it remains true that Hebrew evidences a tendency for *goy* to describe a people in terms of its political and territorial affiliation, and so to approximate much more closely to our modern term "nation." *'am,* conversely, always retains a strong emphasis on the element of consanguinity as the basis of union into a people.

It is possible that in Ezk. 36:13ff. (the *kethibh* and the versions read *goyekh;* the *qere* reads *goyayikh*), *goy* designates the units of population within a land, so that the reference is to "tribes." More probably, however, we should here follow the *kethibh* and the versions in reading the singular, in which case no difficulty arises in regard to accepting the usual meaning "people, nation." In spite of the attempt by Malamat to find in the OT a more specifically military use of *goy* in Josh. 5:6; 2 K. 6:18; and metaphorically in Joel 1:6, the military connection is supplied by the context in all these cases, and it is altogether doubtful whether the term in itself was thought to have such a military meaning.

There are in the OT two geographical references where the pl. *goyim* occurs as part of the name of a region. These are *charosheth haggoyim,* "Harosheth-hagoiim," in Jgs. 4:2,13,16; and *gelil haggoyim,* "Galilee of the nations," in Isa. 8:23 (Eng. 9:1). In both cases, it is likely that the name originated in the mixed population of the regions concerned (cf. also the reference in Gen. 14:1 as *melekh goyim,* "king of Goyim"), rather than in the political division of the territory into separate units. Unfortunately, no clear evidence exists for pronouncing a clear decision on the issue. If this supposition is correct, it supports the view that *goy* contains a prominent gentilic aspect, and does not always refer to a territorial state.

II. 1. *Use in the OT.* In the OT, we find that *goy* is seldom used with pronominal suffixes (only 7 times out of more than 550 occurrences), and that the occasions when it is so used are grouped into two sections (Gen. 10:5,20, 31,32; Ezk. 36:13,14,15). In the first of these sections (Gen. 10), the pronominal suffixes refer back to the larger racial units from which the nations derive, and in the latter case to the land upon which the *goy* lives. [5] *goy* is never used with suffixes referring back to a deity, whereas such a usage is very common in the case of *'am,* where *'ammi, 'ammekha,* etc., frequently occur with reference to Yahweh (Ex. 3:7; 32:11; etc.). Nor is *goy* ever used in construct with the name of a deity, so that while Israel can be called *'am yhvh,* "the people of Yahweh" (2 S. 1:12; Ezk. 36:20), the corresponding use of *goy* is not found. We may compare also the phrase *'am kemosh,* "people of Chemosh," which is used of Moab (Nu. 21:29). This restriction in the use of the term *goy* in relation to a deity

---

[5] For the *qere* and the *kethibh,* see above.

can hardly be accidental, and no doubt reflects the stronger political coloring of *goy* in comparison with *'am.*

goy frequently occurs in parallel with other words besides *'am,* of which the most significant are *mamlakhah,* "kingdom" (Isa. 60:12; Jer. 1:10; 18:7,9; Zeph. 3:8; Ps. 46:7[6]; 2 Ch. 32:15); → משׁפחה *mishpāchāh,* "family" (Gen. 10:5,20,31, 32; Jer. 10:25; Ezk. 20:32); and → לאם *le'ōm,* "people" (Isa. 34:1; Ps. 44:15[14]; 105:44; 149:7). These indicate the general field of semantic reference, without implying complete synonymity with any one of these related terms.

Since the OT does not contain any ordered or consistent doctrine of nation-hood, we find that there is no precise definition of what constitutes a *goy.* Instead, we find that the three major aspects of race, government, and territory all contribute features of their own toward a comprehensive picture. The element of common racial origin, with its basis in consanguinity, plays an important part in the structure of a *goy,* even though it is more strongly expressed in the OT by the terms *'am* and *mishpachah.* Israel traced its origins as a *goy* back to Abraham as its patriarchal ancestor (Gen. 12:2; 17:6; 18:18; cf. the possibility of Moses' descendants becoming a nation, Nu. 14:12; Dt. 9:14). Similarly, Ishmael was to become a father of a *goy* (Gen. 17:20). This usage clearly indicates the gentilic aspect which attached to the term.

The aspect of government is also important, as is indicated by the frequent use of *goy* in parallelism with *mamlakhah,* "kingdom." In such cases, we are to think of each *goy* as constituting a separate kingdom, each ruled by its own separate *melekh* ("king"), even though the measure of independence enjoyed by such kingdoms naturally varied from case to case. It was clearly considered normal in ancient Israel for each *goy* to be ruled by its own particular *melekh,* who stood at its head (Isa. 14:6,18; 41:2; Jer. 25:14). Thus, it became a basic reason for Israel's request to God for its own king that it should be "like the *goyim* round about" (1 S. 8:5,20). Nevertheless, although it was normal that, for a people to be constituted as a *goy,* it should have a *melekh* at its head, there is nothing to indicate that this was the only form of government that could lead to such recognition. Israel certainly regarded itself as having formed a *goy* before it possessed a monarchy.[6] However, some form of independent government was clearly necessary if a people were to exist as a *goy,* and in the ancient world this was normally a monarchy. Such a government enabled the *goy* to express its own individual identity, to administer and defend its territory, and to look after its own interests in relation to other *goyim.*

The third main aspect of a *goy* that we find in the OT is that it possessed a territory of its own (Isa. 36:18-20; Ps. 105:44; 2 Ch. 32:13). Rost concluded that *goy* denotes "the whole population of the land," but this probably places too much weight upon the single aspect of possession of a territory, to the exclusion of the aspects of race and government which we have already noted. Nevertheless, possession of a territory of its own was clearly very important to a *goy.* In Ezk. 35:10, Israel's division into two *goyim* is related to its being separated into two lands (*'aratsoth*), and Ezk. 36:13-15 addresses the land as having its

---

6 See below.

own *goy*[7] which dwelt upon it. The description of the peoples deported by the Assyrians from their own lands and brought to Israel as *goyim* (2 K. 17:29,33) clearly reflects the situation of these peoples before their deportation, and not the situation into which they had come. It is probably not without importance, however, that here the Deuteronomistic history refers to these peoples in respect to their racial origin, and not in accordance with their present territorial or governmental affiliation. While the OT does not indicate any precise definition of how a community of people could be regarded as constituting a *goy,* the three aspects of race, government, and territory are all important. At any given point, one of these features could be regarded as of primary importance, but it is misleading to attempt a definition on the basis of such a single aspect. Normally all three aspects were combined in the formation of a *goy,* which thus formed the counterpart of what in the modern world would be regarded as a nation.

We also find in the OT other ways in which a *goy* expressed its individual identity, and which thereby enabled it to be recognized as such. Chief among these ways was the use of a common language (cf. esp. Gen. 10:5,20,31). We find also that the worship of a national god was important for each separate *goy* (cf. Dt. 12:30; 29:17[18]; 2 S. 7:23; 2 K. 17:29; 18:33; 19:12; Isa. 36:18; 37:12; Jer. 2:11; 2 Ch. 32:15,17). In many of these latter references, it may be assumed that a reference to the national god of each *goy* is intended, although this was not always the religious situation that pertained. Dt. 32:8 reflects the ancient tradition that the *goyim* were divided out among the sons of God by Elyon, who allocated to each its proper national boundaries. Thus, each nation was to possess its own land and its own national god. This well-ordered situation, however, did not conform to the political realities of the ancient world; and while it was assumed that each *goy* had its own god, there is no attempt to define a *goy* in relation to this. The same is true of language, so that although it is accepted that each country has its own language (Gen. 10:5ff.), there is no attempt to make this a determining factor in the constitution of a *goy.* The possession of an army was obviously also important to the life of a *goy* (cf. Josh. 5:6; 10:13; 2 K. 6:18), but there is no exclusively military use of the term to be found in the OT. Rather, the possession of an army appears as a natural function of government.

2. *Israel As a Goy.* From this general meaning of *goy* in the OT, indicating an individual national entity, we can recognize more fully its significance when applied to Israel. Abraham is promised that his descendants will become a *goy* (Gen. 12:2; cf. 17:5; 18:18), and their existence as a nation is closely tied to the promise of the possession of the land which is made to Abraham at the same time (12:7; cf. 17:8; 18:18). While the extended family of Abraham's descendants naturally constitutes an ʿ*am,* it requires a territorial acquisition and a political structure before they can truly form a *goy* among the other *goyim* of the world. Yet, the OT never precisely defines what requirements are essential for Israel's existence as a *goy,* as it does not in the case of other nations either. Dt. 26:5 loosely dates the origin of Israel's existence as a *goy* from the period of the op-

---

[7] For the sing., see above.

pression in Egypt, and the E source traces it to the formal ratification of the covenant at Sinai (Ex. 19:6). The former passage emphasizes the numerical size of the people required to form a *goy*, while the latter reference points to Israel's unique religious constitution in its covenant relationship to Yahweh as formative of its existence as a *goy*. The unique formulation of Ex. 19:6 (E), describing Israel as a *goy qadhosh*, "holy nation," and a *mamlekheth kohanim*, "kingdom of priests," affirms the religious structure of Israel as a state.

Clements

Ex. 19:6 is usually attributed to E;[8] but Noth assigns it to D, Cazelles to P dependent on D, Fohrer to the Jerusalem Priestly circle of the late monarchical period, and Wildberger to a special tradition.

The relationship of *goy qadhosh*, "holy nation," to *mamlekheth kohanim*, "kingdom of priests," is explained variously: the advocates of an objective parallelism in content interpret Israel as a community whose citizens are worshippers of Yahweh,[9] or are all priests,[10] or as priests drawing near to or approaching Yahweh,[11] or standing closer to him than the other nations,[12] or acting as a priest or mediator among the heathen nations.[13] Still others interpret *goy qadhosh* and *mamlekheth kohanim* as being more complementary of one another:[14] Israel is a holy nation that is supposed to draw near to God in the sanctuary, "because her national life is dependent upon priests..., while the other nations have kings."[15] Fohrer[16] rejects the concept of a Priestly rule over the holy nation: "As the *goy* (the constituted and governed nation) is holy, separated..., so the present ruler is priestly, i.e., holy in an advanced way...."[17] Ex. 19:5 does not speak of a general priesthood of the people of God. This understanding appears first in the NT in 1 Pet. 2:9 (cf. Rev. 1:6; 5:10; 20:6).[18]

Botterweck

Since Israel did not attain full territorial control of Canaan and independent political status until the reign of David, it is from this period that its historical existence as a *goy* is to be dated. The fact that the term is used to describe Israel before this time, therefore, is almost certainly anachronistic, and there is no clear evidence to support the view that the word was ever used by the early tribal federation of Israel to describe itself. Nevertheless, for the meaning of the term,

---

[8] G. Beer, O. Eissfeldt, J. Muilenburg, W. Beyerlin, etc.
[9] K. Galling, R. B. Y. Scott.
[10] H. L. Strack.
[11] B. Baentsch, G. Beer.
[12] P. Heinisch, J. B. Bauer.
[13] H. Holzinger, H. Schneider, A. Clamer, M. Noth, G. Auzou.
[14] W. Caspari, W. Beyerlin, W. L. Moran, H. Cazelles, etc.
[15] H. Cazelles, *DBS*, 7 (1966), 834.
[16] G. Fohrer, *ThZ*, 19 (1963), 359-362.
[17] *Ibid.*, 362.
[18] On Ex. 19:6, cf. the literature in J. H. Elliot, "The Elect and the Holy," *NTS*, 12 (1966), 50-59; and A. Deissler, *et al.*, "Der priesterliche Dienst, I," *QuaestDisp*, 46 (1970), 67-72.

it is important to bear in mind that Israel freely regarded itself as having constituted a *goy* before its acquisition of the land of Canaan and its introduction of a monarchy.

As a *goy* with a special religious character, Israel was fully conscious that it was distinct from other *goyim,* and that is possessed unique moral, political, and religious obligations (Nu. 23:9). The request that it should share the same political constitution as other nations in the form of kingship (1 S. 8:5,20) is shown as a denial of Israel's true nature. Yet, although Israel can describe itself as the *'am yhvh,* "people of Yahweh" (2 S. 1:12; Ezk. 36:20), and Yahweh frequently addresses Israel as his *'am,* there is no parallel usage with *goy.* Part of the reason for this, no doubt, is to be found in the political division of Israel into two kingdoms after Solomon's death. The actual meaning of the term *goy* would lead us to expect that each of the separate kingdoms of Israel and Judah would regard itself as forming a *goy.* Yet, it is not until Ezk. 37:22 that we find an explicit admission of this, recognizing that the once united kingdom of Israel has been divided into two *goyim* and two *mamlakhoth,* "kingdoms." With this admission, there occurs a firm promise that such a division is to end. The memory of the once united kingdom, and the belief that the act of division was a catastrophic sin (1 K. 16:2,19,26,31; etc.), as it is clearly represented in the Deuteronomistic history, undoubtedly led to a considerable reserve on the part of the historian from speaking of two *goyim* of Israel and Judah. This is well shown further in Jer. 33:24, where it is argued that Yahweh had chosen two families (*mishpachoth*), who, however, formed only one nation (*goy*).

In the postexilic Priestly Code, we find a marked restraint in the description of Israel as a *goy,* which undoubtedly reflects the fact of the beginning of the diaspora and the political situation of the Persian Age in which Israel lacked several of the normal characteristics of a *goy.* Thus, in the P account of the divine promise to Abraham, the assurance is given that the patriarch's descendants will become, not one nation, but a host of nations (Gen. 17:4; cf. 35:11; Nu. 14:12).[19] Similarly, in P, Israel's structure given to it by the event on Sinai is described as that of a "cultic community" (→ קהל *qāhāl*) and an assembly (→ עדה *'ēdhāh*). Nevertheless, it is fully clear from Ezk. 37:22 that after the exile there were circles in Israel that retained the hope of Israel's recovering full national existence as a *goy.*

3. *Special Religious Development.* In a usage in which Israel could describe itself as a *goy,* there was clearly no possibility of the term taking on a completely hostile religious meaning, although a development in this direction does begin to emerge. Alongside the lessening tendency for Israel to regard itself as forming a *goy,* we find a usage in which the term acquires an increasingly adverse religious sense. While only the first steps of this tendency are traceable in the OT, they are undoubtedly evident.

From a comparatively early period, we find a tradition expressed in Israel's cult that certain *goyim,* left historically and politically undefined, constitute a

---

[19] See above, II.2.

political threat to Israel and to its anointed king (Ps. 2:1,8; 46:7[6]). This tradition of a conflict between Yahweh and the nations was preserved in the Jerusalem cult tradition. [20] It may have originated as an Israelite adaptation of the Mesopotamian chaos-conflict motif, [21] and was related to the hope that the nations were destined to become a part of Yahweh's inheritance (Ps. 2:8; 82:8; cf. Isa. 2:2-4; Mic. 4:1-4). In the terms in which it is set out, this motif of Yahweh's conflict with the nations had a strong political accentuation, promising a great enlargement of Israel as a *goy* and removing all that threatened it. Nevertheless, it undoubtedly provided a background for a prophetic interpretation of Israel's situation, and in Isaiah is given a much more directly religious application.

Alongside this cultic motif, with its political implications, we find a more directly religious awareness, expressed in the Deuteronomic movement, that the non-Israelite *goyim* threatened Israel's existence. Here there is a strong insistence that Israel was to make no religious or political treaty with the nations who previously had possessed its land (Dt. 7:1ff.), and was not to seek to be like such nations (18:9). Although Israel was to have its own place among the *goyim* (7:7; 9:14), there is an implied hostility toward these other nations on the grounds that their religion is not pleasing to Yahweh and represents a temptation to Israel. This adverse estimate of the *goyim* is even more strongly expressed by the Deuteronomistic work, which explains the downfall of the northern kingdom of Israel as a consequence of its imitation of the ways of the *goyim* (2 K. 17:8, 11,15,33; cf. 21:2). A similar adverse estimate of the nations is found in Ezk. 20:32 (cf. 2 Ch. 28:3). Non-Israelite nations had proved themselves to be a major political threat to Israel, bringing about the downfall of the northern kingdom in 721 B.C., and Judah in 587 B.C., and this found its explanation in the belief that they had undermined Israel's unique religious constitution by the temptation of apostasy. Yet, even with this increasing tendency for the non-Israelite *goyim* to be identified as "heathen nations," at no point in the OT is the semantic development reached in which *goy* in itself means "heathen nation." Israel fully retained the recognition that it had itself once constituted a *goy,* and it preserved the hope and expectation that it would again do so. Existence as a *goy* was a goal to be desired, and the term did not itself imply any adverse religious connotation. In line with this, there is no support in the OT for the usage which emerged in Talmudic Hebrew where the sing. *goy* could denote an individual member of a non-Israelite nation. Rather, such a person is simply described in the OT as an *'ish,* "man." Nevertheless, the tendency to regard the non-Israelite nations adversely on account of their religion, combined with Israel's own political misfortunes, lent a distinctive coloring to the term *goyim.* When this is viewed in conjunction with the preference found in the OT for Israel to describe itself as an *'am,* "people," and a *mishpachah,* "family," rather than a *goy,* in view of the political overtones of the latter term, it is not difficult to see how the ground was prepared for the later Talmudic usage in which *goy* and *goyim* took on a specific and adverse religious meaning.

---

[20] Mowinckel, Johnson, Kraus, Lutz.
[21] See Mowinckel, Johnson, Kraus.

In spite of the OT assertions that Israel became a *goy* at Sinai (Ex. 19:6), or at the exodus (Dt. 26:5), which linked the term directly to Israel's belief in its divine election, Israel did not identify its election with its retaining its status as a *goy*. As an *'am*, "people," and a *mishpachah*, "family," Israel could remain the people of Yahweh, and it was only in consequence of this that it hoped to recover once again the status of a *goy*.

Clements

גְּוִיָּה *geviyyāh;* גּוּפָה *gûphāh;* גַּו *gav;* גֵּו *gēv;* גַּף *gaph*

Contents: I. Etymology. II. 1. Analysis of Occurrences in the Bible; 2. Living Body, Person: a. Man; b. Heavenly Beings; 3. Dead Body: a. Corpse, Burial–Cremation; b. Cadaver; 4. *gev, gav, gaph* (II). III. In the Qumran Literature. IV. In the LXX.

I. Etymology. *geviyyah* is probably a feminine form of the nominal root *gw(w)*, which originated in the Hebrew-Syriac sphere (Jewish Aram., Targum, Samaritan *gvyt'*; Syr. *gwāyā;* Mandean *giuta,* "bowels," [1] "abdominal cavity of Leviathan as the place of the damned" [rG 394,4; etc.], Nabatean *gvyth,* [2] "the interior of a tomb"). This root appears in the Semitic languages with various forms and meanings. The etymology is obscure.

The root *gw(w)* is not found in Akkadian, and therefore a connection with Sum. *gú,* "throat, neck, head, edge, front, bent," [3] Old Bab. *kappu/gappu,* [4] "wing, arm, hand, lungs, eyebrows, etc.," and Late- or Neo-Bab. *gabbu,* [5] which, according to *CAD,* [6] is a semifluid mass of the "brains" (?) of human and animal bodies, but can also mean "sacrificial flesh," is very questionable. A connection with Akk. *gawum,* "tribe" (→ גוי *gôy*), [7] is not obvious. In South Semitic we en-

---

geviyyāh. F. Baumgärtel–E. Schweizer, "σῶμα," *TDNT,* VII, 1044ff.; K. Bornhäuser, *Die Gebeine der Toten. BFChTh,* 26/3 (1921); E. Dhorme, *L'emploi métaphorique des noms de parties du corps en hébreu et en akkadien* (Paris, 1923=1963), 7; L. Dürr, *Ps 110 im Lichte der neueren altorientalischen Forschung* (1929); A. Merx, "'Der Honig im Cadaver des Löwen'," *Protestantische Kirchenzeitung,* 17 (1887), 389-392; M. Philonenko, "Sur l'expression 'corps de chair' dans le commentaire d'Habacuc," *Sem,* 5 (1955), 39f.; J. de Savignac, "Essai d'interprétation du psaume CX à l'aide de la littérature égyptienne," *OTS,* 9 (1951), 107-135; esp. pp. 131f.; cf. additional literature under → אדם *'ādhām;* → איש *'îsh;* → בשר *bāśār;* → נבלה *nebhēlāh;* → פגר *pegher.*

[1] *MdD,* 89a.
[2] *RES,* 2126, 3.
[3] Deimel, *SL,* III/1, 46; Delitzsch, *SG,* 102; S. Landersdorfer, *Sumerisches Sprachgut im AT* (1916), 65f.
[4] *CAD,* VIII, 185ff.
[5] *AHw,* 272.
[6] *CAD,* V, 5; cf. H. Holma, *Die Namen der Körperteile im Assyrisch-Babylonischen* (Helsinki, 1911), 152.
[7] So Fronzaroli, *AANLR,* 19 (1964), 251, n. 21.

counter this root in Arab. *ğawf*, "cavity, interior, middle, belly," [8] *ğifat*, "corpse," *ğāfa*, "to be hollow," Šhauri *egehe* and Soq. *gehe*, "breast," [9] Tigr. *gof*, "interior, heart, soul, body," [10] with which one should compare *guphah*, "body," in 1 Ch. 10:12, for *geviyyah*, "body," in 1 S. 31:12; the Aram. Hatra Inscription; [11] and Jewish Aram. *gūpā'*. [12]

By far the most frequent West Semitic examples of this root appear in the forms *gav* and *gev*, [13] and *gvy* I, [14] as a substantive meaning "interior, middle" (Job 20:25), first in the Old Aramaic Inscription of Zakar of Hamath, [15] "corporate body" (Phoen.-Pun.), [16] and then in Elephantine, Jewish Aramaic, Palmyrenian, Nabatean, Phoenician, Punic, and Christian Palestinian, used with the prefixes *be* and *le* as an adverbial indication of place, "in the midst of, in the interior, within" (cf. GenAp. 2:10). It also means "referring to this" (9 times in the *tyb-libbi* formula; [17] 23 times in the witness formula *shdi bgw*), and "inclusive," [18] and Mandean has *bgaua*, "inner part, therein," and *gauaia*, "inner, interior, esoteric." [19] The original meaning "corpse, body," is still visible in *gw* III, [20] which apparently appears in the Kraeling Papyrus XII, 24 in the sense of "handmaid, female slave." Benveniste connects this with Iranian **gav(a)*, "servant, slave," and Elamite *kam-ba(-ti-ya)*. [21] On the transition in meaning from "body" to "slave," one should compare Gk. *sŏma* = "slave." [22] For the etymological connection between *gw, gav,* and *geviyyah,* see Cross-Lambdin. [23]

There is no clear connection between this root and Egyp. *gꜣb* (from the 19th Dynasty), "arm" > *gbꜣ*, [24] or *gbgb.t* (from the New Kingdom on, used for the "reclining position of slain enemies, heaps of dead bodies"). [25]

II. 1. *Analysis of Occurrences in the Bible.* In the OT, *geviyyah* occurs 13 times, *guphah* twice, *gev* 7 times (+4 times conjec.), *gav* 4 times, and *gaph* II twice. The extrabiblical semantics are confirmed.

---

[8] Lane, 478; H. Wehr, *Arab. Wörterbuch* (³1958), 134.

[9] Leslau, *Contributions,* 14; *Lexique soqotri* (Paris, 1938), 103.

[10] Littmann-Höfner, *Wörterbuch der Tigrē-Sprache* (1962), 594.

[11] *KAI,* 256.7.

[12] *DISO,* 52; cf. G. R. Driver, *Congress Volume, SVT,* 1 (1953), 30; on the dissemination of the root in the Cushite and Chad dialects, cf. J. H. Greenberg, *The Languages of Africa* (The Hague, 1963), 53.

[13] *KBL³,* 174; *DISO,* 48; M. Wagner, *BZAW,* 96 (1966), 51d.

[14] *DISO,* 49.

[15] *KAI,* 202 B.3.

[16] *RES,* 1215; cf. Job 30:5; otherwise M. Dahood, *Bibl,* 38 (1957), 318f.

[17] Cf. Y. Muffs, *Studies in the Aramaic Legal Papyri from Elephantine* (Leiden, 1969), *passim.*

[18] G. R. Driver, *Aramaic Documents of the Fifth Century* B.C. (1954), 10, 2; Cowley, *AP;* Kraeling, *BMAP, s.v.* גו *gv.*

[19] *MdD,* 74.

[20] *DISO,* 48.

[21] E. Benveniste, *JA,* 242 (1954), 308f.

[22] J. J. Rabinowitz, *Bibl,* 39 (1958), 77f.

[23] Cross-Lambdin, *BASOR,* 160 (1960), 24, n. 21.

[24] *WbÄS,* I, 154.

[25] *Ibid.,* 165.

2. *Living Body, Person.* a. *Man.* geviyyah (like → בָּשָׂר bāśār or → שְׁאֵר she'ēr, both "flesh") means man as a whole, but does not include all that is implied by the whole and natural state. geviyyah characterizes man in his existential weakness, oppression, or trouble; perhaps the feminine form also indicates this. [26] The OT sees man in the aspect of geviyyah when, in time of real distress, e.g., during the years of Egyptian famine, after he loses his money (keseph) and livestock (miqneh habbehemah), he must finally also give his geviyyah, i.e., himself, his person, in this miserable existence of slavery in which he is near destruction, and after selling his land ('adhamah), lose the status of a free, fully enfranchised citizen (Gen. 47:18, J); cf. lammah namuth le'enekha, "Why should we die before your eyes," in 47:19a. In Neh. 9:37, Ezra mentions in his prayer that God has set foreign kings over Israel ('alenu, "over us"), who have power over (mashal) their bodies (geviyyothenu, "our bodies") and their cattle, so that they are in great distress (tsarah). The generic personal suffix in 'alenu, i.e., "us," includes the bodies, i.e., the people, and their cattle. In this context, oppression, despotism, and distress characterize the situation more precisely, so that this aspect is implied by geviyyah: it is the suffering person, the oppressed Israelite. Sirach later alters this aspect in that it is the geviyyah itself that makes the lascivious man a slave of women (Sir. 47:19).

b. *Heavenly Beings.* In Ezk. 1:11, the heavenly beings, who have the form of men, cover their bodies (geviyyothehenah) with their wings. [27] According to Isa. 6, the seraphim cover their "faces" and their "feet" (pudenda). In Ezk. 1:11, it is possible that geviyyah has the additional meaning of "person" or "form." The "man" with the appearance of a man in Dnl. 10 had a geviyyah (Dnl. does not use basar or she'er, "flesh," here), which appears through the garment, and is "like Tarshish(-stone)." tarshish, Aquila chrysólithos, has been interpreted as beryl, [28] topaz, [29] or yellow jasper; [30] in any case, it certainly characterizes "the luminous nature of this heavenly being." [31]

3. *Dead Body.* a. *Corpse, Burial–Cremation.* Like → פֶּגֶר pegher, Akk. pagru, which can mean a living body or a dead body, geviyyah also means a dead body, a corpse, or a carcass. Ps. 110:6 says that the victorious king will "fill the valleys with corpses." [32] This figure appears in the prophetic announcement of judgment as a drastic motif (Ezk. 31:12; 32:5; 35:8; cf. Isa. 5:25; 34:3; Jer. 9:21 [Eng. v. 22]; Ezk. 6:13). Nah. 3:3 uses geviyyah, pegher, and chalal, "slain," in parallelism in its apocalyptic description of the fall of Nineveh. The battlefield is

---

[26] Cf. Dhorme, 7.

[27] Cf. Zimmerli, BK, XIII, 5; BLe, § 253a'; GK, § 911.

[28] A. Jeffery.

[29] M. Delcor.

[30] N. W. Porteous.

[31] A. Bentzen, HAT, 19.

[32] So Aquila, Symmachus, Jerome, Briggs, Kraus, Dahood, etc.; on the figure of the valleys filled with dead bodies, cf. B. Meissner, BuA, I, figs. 54, 167, 168; Dürr, 22; J. de Savignac, 131f.; cf. also Homer Iliad xvi.71f.

so covered with corpses that people stumble over them. In the context of battle and discussion of war *geviyyah* denotes exclusively (*pegher* mainly) dead corpses; otherwise → נבלה *nᵉbhēlāh,* "carcass" (corpse of people and animals, figuratively of idols) is used. In 1 S. 31:10,12, *geviyyah* (and the pl. *geviyyoth*) means the corpses of those who fell in the battle against the Philistines, in particular Saul and his three sons; 1 Ch. 10:12 has *guphah* (pl. *guphoth*). There are numerous ancient Near Eastern parallels to the practice of cutting off the heads of slain enemies. [33] The people of Jabesh took the slain from the battlefield in order to bury them.

The text and meaning of 1 S. 31:12 are disputed: the MT speaks of burning (→ שׂרף *śāraph*) the *geviyyoth,* and of burying the *'atsmoth,* "bones" (→ עצם *'etsem*). Later, *geviyyah* can also mean "bones" (Sir. 49:15). Many scholars [34] defend the originality of *saraph,* "to burn," and believe that the corpses were reduced to ashes or that the entrails were burned, in order to make possible a reverent burial or a preservation of the *'atsmoth,* "bones." The interpretation of *saraph* as "anoint," "embalm," [35] is hardly correct. Others [36] suggest → ספד *sāphadh,* "to perform a dirge," as the original reading. Then the transformation of the dirge into an act of burning would represent a later disgraceful punishment of Saul for his crime. The absence of some reference to burning in 1 Chronicles may represent a conscious suppression of this despised and foreign custom.

The burial of the dead had great significance among the Israelites. Not to be buried was regarded as the distressful punishment of Yahweh (Dt. 28:26; 2 K. 9:10; Isa. 14:19; Jer. 7:33; 14:16; 16:4,6; 19:7; 22:19; 25:33; 34:20; Ezk. 29:5; etc.), and meant restlessness in the Underworld. The desire to be buried with one's fathers is very strong (Gen. 47:30; 2 S. 19:38[37]; 21:14). The slain enemy was also buried (Josh. 8:29; 10:26f.; 2 K. 9:34; Ezk. 39:11-16). In addition to family and royal graves, there were "graves of the common people" (2 K. 23:6; → קבר *qebher*). In the ancient Near East, the cremation of corpses was customary only among the Hittites. In the OT, only criminals were cremated as additional punishment (Gen. 38:24; Lev. 20:14; 21:9; Josh. 7:25); Dt. 21:23 represents an exception. The burning of the bones of the king of Edom is criticized as a sin of Moab (Am. 2:1). [37]

b. *Cadaver.* According to Jgs. 14:5ff., Samson tears a lion asunder (*ye-shasse'ehu,* 14:6); when he sought the *mappeleth,* "carcass," of the lion again after several days, he found a swarm of bees and honey in the *geviyyah,* "body," of the lion (14:8). Elsewhere, *mappeleth* is used only of the "fall of Tyre" (Ezk. 26:15,18; 27:27), the "fallen branches" of the cedars of Egypt (31:13,16), and the "fall" of the crocodile, Egypt (32:10). According to Prov. 29:16, the righteous look upon the "fall" and overthrow of the wicked. In Jgs. 14:8, *mappeleth* means

---

[33] Cf. Ackroyd, *in loc.*
[34] S. Goldman, A. van den Born, H. W. Hertzberg, R. de Vaux, *et al.*
[35] P. R. Ackroyd.
[36] Klostermann, W. Rudolph, *BHK³,* etc.
[37] Cf. *BRL,* 237-241; A.-G. Barrois, *Manuel d'archéologie biblique,* II (1953), 274-323; de Vaux, *AncIsr,* 56ff.

the "slain" lion, while *geviyyah* collectively means the cadaver or the pieces of the cadaver which apparently have already decayed.[38]

4. *gev, gav, gaph (II)*. We find *gev* with the meaning "back." The rod is for the back of those who lack sense, and of fools (Prov. 10:13; 19:29; 26:3; cf. 14:3 conjec.). The Servant of God does not try to keep smiters from beating him on the "back," nor does he hide his cheeks (*lechi*) and his face (*panim*) from them (Isa. 50:6). In 51:23, Deutero-Isaiah announces that now the time for Israel's disgraceful humiliation, in which she made her "back" like the ground and like the street for others to pass over, is past.

This connection of *gev* with the rod and humiliation would put the statue of Dagon, and thus the god Dagon himself (1 S. 5), in a pejorative light if *gevo*, "his torso," were read in v. 4, as has been proposed.[39] However, there is scarcely any justification for this conjecture.

gev and *gav* have the same meaning in the expression *hishlikh 'achare gav (gev)*, "to cast behind the back." God casts sins (*chet'*) behind his back (Isa. 38:17), i.e., he forgives them. Conversely, man casts God behind his back when he makes images (1 K. 14:9), forgets God (Ezk. 23:35), and turns his back on his Torah, "law" (Neh. 9:26).

gaph II occurs only in the law concerning slaves in the Book of the Covenant (Ex. 21:3f.), and is used to state that the *'ebhedh*, "slave," shall be released "alone" (only with his body = *beghappo*), without any possessions, at the end of his period of service.

III. In the Qumran Literature. In the Qumran literature, *lebh*, "heart," *basar*, "flesh," and *geviyyah*, "body," stand in parallelism with each other, an expansion to genuine synonymity which calls to mind Sir. 37:22f.; 41:11. Thus, the oppressed poet laments: "My strength has gone out of my body" (*miggeviy-yathi*); he says that his *lebh*, "heart," runs out like water, and his *basar*, "flesh," is dissolved like wax (1QH 8:32f.). *geviyyah* also appears in connection with celestial beings: the bodies (*geviyoth*) of the sons of the heavenly beings (*'ire hashshamayim*) were tall like the mountains (CD A 2:18f.; cf. Gen. 6:1ff.). The combination *geviyyath basar*, "body of flesh" (1QpHab 9:2; 4QpNah 2:6), is new.[40] Its equivalent in Greek, *sŏma tĕs sarkós*, is attested in Sir. 23:17 (body of a lascivious man) and 1 En. 102:5 (neutral: body); cf. Col. 1:22; 2:11. It is doubtful that this expression is merely a "rhetorical plerophory" for "body";[41] Allegro's interpretation, "fleshly natures,"[42] seems to point in the right direction.

gv occurs only in 11QPs[a] 22:7 (a Song of Zion) with the meaning "middle, breast," as the inner part of man.[43]

---

38 On this figure, cf. Herodotus v.114 (the skull of Onesilos); and the literature under
→ אֲרִי *'arî*, "lion."

39 *KBL*[3].

40 Cf. R. Weiss, *RevQ*, 4 (1963), 436.

41 K. Elliger, *BHTh*, 15 (1953), 202.

42 J. M. Allegro, *JSS*, 7 (1962), 306.

43 Cf. M. Delcor, *RevQ*, 6 (1967), 72f., 80.

IV. In the LXX. In the LXX, the terms *geviyyah* (9 times), *guphah*, *gav*, and *gev* are translated by *sōma*, "body." [44] In Jgs. 14:8 and Ps. 110:6, the LXX translates *geviyyah* by *ptōma*, "dead body, corpse," which sometimes is used to render *mappeleth* and *pegher*, and in Jgs. 14:9 by *héxis*, "exercise, practice" (so LXX[B], while LXX[A] has *stóma*, "mouth," which would mean that the honey was found in the mouth of the lion, perhaps with a view to the statement, "out of the eater came something to eat," in v. 14).

gaph II is rendered by *mónos*, "alone," in the LXX, while *gev* apparently gave these translators difficulties, for they translate it by *nōtos*, "back," in Isa. 50:6; *tá metáphrena*, "the back parts," in Isa. 51:23; and *ōmos*, "shoulder," in Prov. 19:29; and in the other passages where *gev* occurs they either mistranslate or omit it.

Fabry

---

[44] Cf. E. Schweizer, *TDNT*, VII, 1043f.

┌─────────────┐
│ גָּוַע *gāva'* │
└─────────────┘

gava', "to die, expire," really occurs only in Hebrew. A haphel form (*hg'*) occurs in the Aramaic Zakhir Inscription, meaning "to remove (a monument)." [1] The Arab. *ğā'a*, "to be empty, hungry," is even further away (however, cf. Eng. "starve," which is cognate to Ger. "sterben," "to die"). The verb *gava'* is found in Hebrew almost exclusively in later literature (P, Job, Lam., Deutero-Zec.; Josh. 22:20 is probably Deuteronomistic). In addition, we find an adjective or participle from *gv'*, "dead," in Sir. 8:7; 48:5; and a noun *gvy'h*, "death," in Sir. 38:16.

In the Pentateuch, *gava'* is found only in P. In three passages it is used in connection with *muth*, "to die" (*vayyighva' vayyamoth*, "and he breathed his last and died," Gen. 25:8,17; 35:29; cf. also 49:33). Two passages refer to the "death of all flesh" in the flood (Gen. 6:17; 7:21). Nu. 17:27f. (Eng. vv. 12f.) states that anyone who comes near the holy tabernacle of Yahweh must die; both → אבד *'ābhadh*, "to perish" (v. 27[12]), and *muth*, "to die" (v. 28[13]) are used in parallelism with *gava'* here. In Nu. 20:29, it is simply synonymous with *muth*, "to die": Aaron had died. The same applies to Lam. 1:19: "my priests and elders have died (of hunger)." Nu. 20:3 speaks of death as a punishment for sin, and the same is true of Josh. 22:20: Achan died because of his *'avon*, "iniquity." Ps. 104:29 states that man's life is dependent on God: "when thou takest away their breath (*ruach*), they pass away (die)." In Zec. 13:8, *gava'* is used in connection with *karath*, "to cut off": two-thirds of the population will be destroyed

---

[1] *KAI*, 202 B.16,19; cf. *DISO*, 49.

and "perish"; only a third will survive. Ps. 88:16(15) is a little different: "I have been afflicted (ʿani) and close to death (goveaʿ) from my youth up" (the LXX and Syr. ygʿ, "faint, weary," is probably an alleviating reading).

The other eight examples of the use of gavaʿ in the OT occur in the book of Job. Here, of course, we are dealing with elevated language, but this does not exclude the use of muth, "to die" (10 times in the poetic sections, and 3 times in the Prologue). In 3:11 and 14:10, these words even stand in parallelism: "Why did I not die (muth) at birth, come forth from the womb and expire (gavaʿ)" (similarly 10:18, where, however, only gavaʿ appears), or: "Man dies and is laid low; man breathes his last, and where is he?" All flesh dies and returns to dust, says Elihu in 34:15; and in 36:12 he states that disobedient men must die (v. 14 uses muth in the same sense). In the other passages (13:19; 27:5, 29:18), gavaʿ is synonymous with muth.

The passages in Sirach contribute nothing new to this general picture. Sir. 8:7 admonishes the wise not to rejoice over a dead man (gvʿ), for "we will all be gathered up" (ʾsp); 48:5 speaks of the resurrection of a dead person (gvʿ) from death (mmwt; par. mšʾwl, "from Sheol"); and 38:16 refers to mourning over the death (gvyʿh) of a dead person (mt).

Thus, gavaʿ expresses the usual OT attitude toward death (→ מות mûth) without connecting this word with some particular idea.

Ringgren

גּוּר gûr; גֵּר gēr; גֵּרוּת gērûth; מְגוּרִים mᵉghûrîm

Contents: I. Etymology. II. Occurrences in the OT. III. The Legal Position of the ger: 1. Reasons for Becoming a Sojourner; 2. The Position of the ger in the Monarchical Period; 3. In Deuteronomy; 4. In P; 5. In Prophetic Texts; 6. In Other Texts; 7. toshabh. IV. Specific Theological Considerations.

I. **Etymology.** Hebrew lexicography reckons with several roots gwr. In connection with an investigation of the root gwr I, "to tarry as a sojourner," the important question is whether gwr II = subordinate form of grh, "to attack,

---

gûr. E. Bammel, "Gerim Gerurim," ASTI, 7 (1968/69), 127-131; A. Bertholet, Die Stellung der Israeliten und der Juden zu den Fremden (1896); E. Fascher–J. Gaudemet, "Fremder," RAC, VIII (1972), 306-347; K. Galling, "Das Gemeindegesetz in Deuteronomium 23," Festschrift A. Bertholet (1950), 176-191; W. Grundmann, "παρεπίδημος," TDNT, II, 64f.; H. Hommel, "Metoikoi," PW, XV, 1413-1458; T. M. Horner, "Changing Concepts of the 'Stranger' in the OT," ATR, 42 (1960), 49-53; F. Horst, "Fremde, II. Im AT," RGG³, II, 1125f.; K. G. Kuhn, "προσήλυτος," TDNT, VI, 727-744; J. A. O. Larsen, "Περίοικοι," PW, XIX, 816-833; T. J. Meek, "The Translation of Gêr in the Hexateuch and Its Bearing on the Documentary Hypothesis," JBL, 49 (1930), 172-180; L. M. Muntingh, "Die Begrip 'Gêr' in die OT," NedGTT, 3 (1962), 534-558; E. Neufeld, "The Prohibitions against Loans at Interest

(continued on p. 440)

strive," and *gwr* III = subordinate form of *ygr,* "to be afraid," are independent homonymous roots, or whether possibly an original connection can be established between these roots, so that the various meanings represent special meanings of the same root. If in antiquity, "to be foreign" and "to be hostile" can be simply two different observations about the same person, one must admit the possibility that Akk. *gerû,* "to be hostile" (occurring esp. as the ptcp. *gārû,* "enemy, opponent"), [1] can be regarded as the etymon of Heb. *gwr.*

1. In Ugaritic, *gr ḥmyt ẓgrt* [2] probably means one who dwells on the walls of Ugarit. Similarly, *gr btᶾl* [3] can mean one who dwells in the temple, possibly as a fugitive. On the other hand, the verb form *wgr.nn* in *CTA,* 14 [I K], III, 110 (par. to IV, 212), cannot be interpreted with certainty. The proposed translations range all the way from "surround" [4] to "tarry," [5] "take possession of," [6] to "attack, strive." [7] The verb form *tgrgr* hardly belongs here. [8]

2. Scholars often refer to the Mesha Inscription [9] for a Moabite passage using *ger.* This account tells how Mesha captured the city of Nebo and killed everything: *7000 gbrn wgrn wgbrt wgrt wrḥmt.* Therefore, it seems little likely that *grn* and *grt* here mean male and female clients, alongside men and women, [10] for there could hardly have been a whole group of independent female clients. Presumably *grn* is to be connected with Heb. *gur,* and translated "boys" when referring to human beings, while *grt* is to be translated "girls."

3. *CIS,* I, 86 = *KAI,* 37 contains an example of *gr* in the sense of "client" in Phoenician. In the list of expenditures of a temple administration in Kition from the fourth or third centuries B.C., *grm* are mentioned along with *klbm* in A.16 and B.10. It cannot be determined satisfactorily from the context what

---

in Ancient Hebrew Laws," *HUCA,* 26 (1955), 355-412, esp. pp. 391-94; K. L. Schmidt, "Israels Stellung zu den Fremdlingen und Beisassen und Israels Wissen um seine Fremdling- und Beisassenschaft," *Jud,* 1 (1945), 269-296; K. L. and M. A. Schmidt–R. Meyer, "πάροικος," *TDNT,* V, 841-853; G. Stählin, "ξένος," *TDNT,* V, 1-36; J. de Vries, "Fremde, I. Religionsgeschichtlich," *RGG*³, II, 1124f.; H. Wildberger, "Israel und sein Land," *EvTh,* 16 (1956), 404-422, esp. pp. 417-420; *L'Étranger. Recueils de la Société Jean Bodin,* 9/10 (1958), esp. J. Gilissen, "Le statut des étrangers à la lumière de l'histoire comparative," 5-57; A. Dorsinfang-Smets, "Les étrangers dans la société primitive," 59-73; J. Pirenne, "Le statut de l'étranger dans l'ancienne Egypte," 93-103; G. Cardascia, "Le statut de l'étranger dans la Mésopotamie ancienne," 105-117; A. Abel, "L'étranger dans l'Islam classique," 331-351.

1 *AHw,* 286.
2 *CTA,* 32, 27f.
3 *CTA,* 19 [I D], III, 153.
4 Aistleitner.
5 Jirku.
6 Gordon.
7 Driver.
8 *CTA,* 23, 66 [SS II, 32].
9 *KAI,* 181.14ff.
10 So *KAI* and S. Segert, *ArOr,* 29 (1961), 240.

meaning of *gr* is to be assumed here. Lidzbarski[11] and more recently van den Branden[12] suggest the possibility of interpreting *gr* in the sense of the Heb. *gur* (as in the Mesha Inscription), here as a *catulus* = a young prostitute. As a justification for this interpretation, it may be pointed out that in the inscription in *CIS*, I, 52, which also comes from Kition, a *klbʾ* is mentioned as son of a *gr*. Compound proper names using *gr*, like *grʾ*, *grʾhl*, *grʾšmn*, *grbʿl*, *grhkl*, *grmlk*, *grmlqrt* and *grtmlq(r)t*, *grmskr*, *grskn*, *grʿštrt*, *grṣd*, and *grṣpn* indicate that, although the word *gr* certainly means "protégé, client," in Phoenician and Punic, it is used primarily of a deity.

4. Aramaic also knows the root *gwr*. In Old Aramaic, however, there is no example of the use of *gwr*, for *ʾgr* in *ʾnh ʾgr* in Sefire II C,8 is not to be derived from *gwr* III, "to fear, be anxious," with *KAI*, 223, nor from *gwr* I, "to establish oneself as a protégé," with Dupont-Sommer,[13] but is to be translated "I hire you," with Veenhof,[14] coming from a root *ʾgr* meaning "to hire."[15] Thus, there is no evidence for a verb *gwr* in the Old Aramaic of the inscriptions, but this root seems to be well attested in the later Aramaic dialects.

In Thamudic and Safaitic, the proper names *Gwr*, *Tgr*, and *Gr* should be mentioned. For Nabatean, reference can be made to *CIS*, II, 209. A tomb inscription (assuming that the usual reading and interpretation of this difficult text are accepted) mentions the authoress, *wśwh*, her sisters, daughters, and *wgr(y)hm klh*, "and all their clients," in line 6 subdivided into male and female. The way in which the male and female clients are dependent on or related to the authoress as *wśwh* is obscure. We also encounter a subst. *gyr/gr* in the Palmyrenian inscriptions.[16] In 3972, the author of the inscription prays that he and all the sons of his house will be *gyr*-protégés of the deity. In 4035, the author prays for his own welfare, the welfare of his sons, *wgrh*, "and his client." 3973 states that the Nabatean ʿUbaida built two altars and thereby gratefully remembered Zebīda, *gyrh wrḥmh*, "his patron and friend." Apparently, in Palmyra Zebīda was a host to the Nabatean soldier.[17] Finally, 4218 warns that anyone who might venture to open the tomb will have no *zrʿ wgr* in eternity. Here we find the wish that the posterity, patronage, and protection granted by a deity be denied to anyone who desecrates the tomb. Of course, one can also interpret *gr* here as client, and note that 3972 mentions the sons of the house along with the client. If "client" is meant, this inscription shows that it was an honor in Palmyra to have clients. It is clear that in Palmyra *gr* is found in the sense of sojourner, client, and patron. Of course, the extent to which the idea of *gr* is to be interpreted from Semitic or from Roman-Greek thought is questionable.

In Jewish Aramaic (esp. in the Jerusalem Targum), Christian Palestinian

11 *LidzNE*.
12 A. van den Branden, *BMB*, 13 (1956), 92.
13 So still *DISO*, 49.
14 K. R. Veenhof, *BiOr*, 20 (1963), 142-44.
15 Cf. also R. Degen, *Altaram. Grammatik* (1969), 19, 109, 120.
16 *CIS*, II, 3972,4; 3973,8; 4035,4; and 4218,5.
17 Cf. also Cooke, *NSI*, 305.

Aramaic, Mandean, and especially Syriac, the root *gwr* assumes the special meaning "to commit adultery." E.g., the substantives *gywr* and *mgyr'* still provide evidence for the meaning "proselyte, neighbor," in Christian Palestinian Aramaic, and so F. Schwally supposes that one has to assume that the original meaning was "to go in to a (female) neighbor." "This assumes a time when the individual was not only a *ger* to every other clan, but also to every other family" (*Idioticon* 17). However, one could also imagine that the sojourner lives as a person without any intimate connection with the prevailing moral laws, and therefore adultery would very easily be attributed to a breach in the relationship between two people. In German also, "fremdgehen" (go foreign) is a synonym of "ehebrechen" (commit adultery).

5. The Arabic offers interesting examples inasmuch as the verb *ǧāra* (a median *w* verb), "to depart from, commit a crime, transgress," means "to be a neighbor, to border on," in the third stem, and "to put under someone's protection," in the fourth stem. The subst. *ǧār* frequently means "neighbor," but apparently belongs to a group of words that have the contrary meaning, and can denote "protector, patron," along with the more frequently attested meaning "protective companion." [18]

6. The root is well attested in South Semitic. Thus, the verb *gr* is found once in Old South Arabic in *CIH*, 548,1, "to function as a protégé (in the temple)." [19] But the only possible example of a subst. *gr* (in Ry 507,10) will not stand up in court. Rather, the reading here must be *whgrhmw*, "their residents." The root *gwr* may appear in a series of proper names. In Ethiopic we find *gōr*, "neighbor," *tagāwara*, "to be a neighbor, to border on," and *gᵉyūr*, "sojourner."

II. Occurrences in the OT. Disregarding *gwr* II, "to attack, strive," and *gwr* III, "to be afraid," *gwr* I occurs in the qal 81 times (including Jgs. 5:17 and Isa. 54:15b). Of these, 22 passages are found in P and 13 in Jeremiah. A hithpolel form appears 3 times in the MT: 1 K. 17:20 says that Elijah dwelt with the widow of Zarephath as a *ger*, "sojourner" (*mithgorer*); however, it seems likely that the text of Jer. 30:23 should be emended to *mithcholel*, "whirling," following 23:19; and that we should read *yithgodhadhu*, "they cut themselves," in Hos. 7:14. [20] We may add to this conjecturally Jer. 5:7, where (conversely) *yithgoraru*, "they sojourned," would be an improvement over *yithgodhadhu*, "they trooped." [21] The subst. *ger* occurs 92 times, of which 36 examples are found in P (21 times in Lev. alone) and 22 in Deuteronomy. The independent ptcp. *gar*, e.g., in Ps. 105:12; 1 Ch. 16:19; and Job 19:15, is (as the Arab. *ǧār* shows) the Aramaic-Arabic development from **gawir*, while *ger* retains the Old Canaanite sound. [22] We also find a pl. form *meghurim*, made with a mem-prefix.

---

[18] Cf. Nöldeke, *Neue Beiträge zur semitischen Sprachwissenschaft* (1910), 73.
[19] Cf. Müller, 39.
[20] Cf. *BHS*.
[21] Cf. *BHS*.
[22] Cf. H. Bauer, *Zur Frage der Sprachmischung im Hebräischen* (1924), 26.

It belongs to the plural forms that denote an abstract idea. Thus, *meghurim* means "sojourning," [23] and occurs 11 times, 6 in connection with *'erets,* "land." Altogether, *meghurim* appears 7 times in P, once in Ezk. 20:38, and in Ps. 119:54; Job 18:19; Lam. 2:22; and Sir. 16:8. Finally, another abstract form, *geruth,* meaning "guest's feudal tenure," is found in Jer. 41:17. It is doubtful that the place names *ma'aleh ghur,* "Maale-gur" (RSV, "the ascent of Gur," 2 K. 9:27), *gur,* "Gur" (2 Ch. 26:7), and *yaghur,* "Jagur" (Josh. 15:21), have anything to do with the root *gur.* But it is possible that the proper name *gera',* "Gera," which is worn by three different persons in the OT, is an abbreviation of a name formed with *gr.*

III. The Legal Position of the ger. In the OT, the *ger* occupies an intermediate position between a native (*'ezrach*) and a foreigner (→ נכרי *nokhrî*). He lives among people who are not his blood relatives, and thus he lacks the protection and the privileges which usually come from blood relationship and place of birth. His status and privileges are dependent on the hospitality that has played an important role in the ancient Near East ever since ancient time. In the early period of Israel, the legal position of the *ger* is comparable with that of the metics of Greece, so that (due to certain historical events, e.g.) Canaanites or fugitives from the conquered northern kingdom living in Israel were called *ger.* However, under the sign of religious integration, the concept develops more and more toward the proselyte, the non-Israelite who becomes an adherent of the Yahweh faith.

1. *Reasons for Becoming a Sojourner.* The reasons why someone becomes a *ger,* separates himself from his clan and his home, and places himself under the legal protection of another man or group of men, are varied. The most frequent reason given in the OT is famine. Thus, Elimelech and his whole family move to Moab because of a famine in order to live there as protected citizens (Ruth 1:1). Elijah lodges with the widow of Zarephath because of a famine (1 K. 17:20). According to 2 K. 8:1, Elisha sends the woman of Shunem and her family to the fertile coastal region because of a threatening famine. Isaac remains as a *ger* with Abimelech of Gerar because of a famine (Gen. 26:3, J). And Israel's sojourn in Egypt is traced back to a famine that drove Joseph's brothers to Egypt (47:4, J). A similar account is given earlier concerning Abraham (12:10).

Military encounters can also force people to lead the life of a *ger.* Isa. 16:4 states that the outcasts of Moab seek refuge in Judah or Edom as protected citizens. It seems likely that a military encounter between the Canaanite inhabitants of Beeroth and the invading Benjaminites is concealed behind the statement in 2 S. 4:3 that the original inhabitants of Beeroth had fled to Gittaim in order to live there as *garim.* The Rechabites live as *garim* in Judah in order to preserve the nomadic ideal (Jer. 35:7). In addition, individual distress or bloodguilt can cause a person to seek protection and help among foreigners as a *ger.* Before the centralization of the cult, the Levite also could settle down as a *ger* wherever he

---

[23] Cf. C. Brockelmann, *VG,* II, § 29c.

found a place or a person or group where he could practice his profession (cf. Jgs. 17:7,8,9; 19:1,16; also Dt. 16:11,14).

2. *The Position of the ger in the Monarchical Period.* If, as Galling thinks, the nucleus of the law of the community in Dt. 23 comes from the end of the pre-monarchical period, it can be established that the treatment here of the question whether Edomites and Egyptians can be accepted into the Yahweh community, in contrast to Ammonites and Moabites, does not have the *gerim* in mind explicitly. In ancient time, however, the *ger* was probably regarded as without nationality, and as not fully entitled to become a part of the *qahal,* "congregation."

The alleged murderer of Saul, who gives David an account of Saul's death, characterizes himself as the son of an Amalekite *ger* (2 S. 1:13). This statement seems to suggest that it is quite possible for a *ger* to have a family and even to be admitted into the Israelite army, although presumably only as a mercenary. Jer. 41:17 indicates that in the time of David the king could entrust a foreigner with property, possibly from the royal domain. This passage states that after the murder of Gedaliah, Johanan and his people stopped at *geruth kimham,* located near Bethlehem in Judah, during their flight toward Egypt. The ancient versions did not understand this expression, which appears only in this text. [24] The usual interpretation, "shelter, caravansary or inn," [25] hardly conveys the original meaning of *geruth.* If *kimham* is the name of the Gileadite Chimham, whom David brought to his court in Jerusalem because of his father Barzillai (cf. 2 S. 19:32:ff.[31ff.]; 1 K. 2:7), then A. Alt is correct when he contends that *geruth* is the term meaning "a guest's feudal tenure." "Thus, the *geruth* of Chimham was a guest's feudal tenure from the royal domain for this favorite of the king, and the only surprising thing is that a place name, connected so entirely to a single situation, continued for centuries." [26] As a rule, of course, the protected citizen could acquire no property, and thus was left to the legal protection of the fully enfranchised citizen.

According to 1 Ch. 22:2, even under David the protected citizens (*gerim*), [27] no doubt primarily the pre-Israelite Canaanite population, were employed as stonecutters. 2 Ch. 2:16f.(17f.) tells how Solomon made his protected citizens burden-bearers and stonecutters. When the old Pentateuch sources regard Abraham (Gen. 12:10; 20:1; 21:23,34), Lot (19:9), Isaac (26:3), Jacob (32:5[4]), and Jacob with the brothers of Joseph (47:4,9), as sojourners, the picture that is described shows that a *ger* can have possessions (herds of cattle, manservants, and maidservants). Lot, who dwells as a *ger* in Sodom, even has his own house (19:9). On the other hand, Gen. 19:9 also shows that the *ger* is apparently undesirable as a judge. The Book of the Covenant contains a specific commandment that the *ger* is not to be oppressed (Ex. 22:20[21]; 23:9). The Sabbath law applies to him also (23:12; 20:10).

---

[24] Cf. P. Volz, *Studien zum Text des Jeremia* (1920), 281; and *BHS.*
[25] Cf. W. Rudolph, *HAT,* 12, *in loc.,* and A. Weiser, *ATD,* XX-XXI, *in loc.*
[26] *KlSchr,* III, 359.
[27] In spite of H. P. Smith, *JBL,* 24 (1905), 29, the text is not to be contested.

3. *In Deuteronomy*. It would seem that the *ger* plays an important role in Deuteronomy because at the time of the Josianic Reform in 622 B.C., the problem of the protected citizen required special attention. According to 2 Ch. 15:9, emigrants from the northern kingdom (from Ephraim, Manasseh, and Simeon), who had taken refuge as protected citizens in Judah, took part in the gathering of the people called by Asa. 2 Ch. 30:25 mentions North Israelite protected citizens in Judah as participants in Hezekiah's Passover festival (but cf. 2 Ch. 11:13f.). When Dt. 14:29; 16:11,14; 24:17,19,20,21; 26:13; and 27:19 mention the *ger* alongside orphans and widows, presumably they have in mind fugitives from the northern kingdom, who had settled in the southern kingdom from the fall of Samaria in 722 B.C. on. To some extent, the *ger* was reduced to the position of a day-laborer (24:14). The forgotten sheaf in the field (24:19), and the gleanings in the olive trees and in the vineyards (24:20,21), are allotted to the *ger,* the orphan, and the widow for their special protection. The tithe every three years (14:29 = 26:12) also belongs to the *ger*. The *ger* is to be treated righteously in judgment (1:16; 24:17; 27:19). He is mentioned in particular in the Sabbath command (5:14), the Feast of Weeks (16:11), and the Feast of Booths (16:14; the situation is different in P, cf. Lev. 23:42). According to Dt. 14:21, the *ger* can eat or sell a carcass without blame; but according to Lev. 17:15, he is told to submit to the rites of cleansing if he has eaten a carcass. Dt. 10:18 says that Yahweh loves the *ger,* and thus gives him food and clothing. Out of this, again it is concluded that the Israelites are to love the *ger* (10:19), because they themselves were sojourners in Egypt.

The Levite is a *ger* (Dt. 18:6, *gar* ptcp.). In the list of members of the cultic community by rank in Dt. 29:10(11), the *gerim* are mentioned as hewers of wood and drawers of water. As in 1 Ch. 22:2 and 2 Ch. 2:16(17), presumably this text has in mind the pre-Israelite Canaanite population. In the curses announcing the downfall of the disobedient in Dt. 28:15-46, vv. 43f. announce as a punishment that the *ger* shall mount higher and higher, so that in the end the *ger* will be the head and Israel the tail, i.e., the social order will be turned upside down. Finally, when Dt. 31:12 explicitly states that the *ger* is to be present for the solemn reading of the law, of course it does not mean that the *ger* was understood absolutely as a full-fledged member of the cultic community, but that he was exposed to the demands of the law.

4. *In P*. Not only in the old Pentateuch sources, but also in P, Abraham (Gen. 17:8; 23:4), Jacob (28:4), Isaac (35:27; 37:1), and Esau and Jacob (36:7) are designated as *gerim* (cf. also Ex. 6:4). This makes it clear on the one hand that in P also *ger* was still understood absolutely in the old sense of protected citizen, and on the other hand that the acquisition of the land of Canaan is made theologically relative.

In texts in the Priestly Code, the law concerning the *matstsoth,* "unleavened bread," in Ex. 12:19 is applied to the *ger* as well as the native. The *ger* (assuming he has been circumcised) can and should celebrate the supplementary Passover, as well as the native Israelite (Ex. 12:48f.). Even the ordinance concerning the Passover in Nu. 9:14 explicitly states that here, too, one and the same statute shall apply to the *ger* and the native. It is that much more surprising, then, when Ex. 12:45 excludes the *toshabh* from the Passover feast. Presumably, this text has in mind the uncircumcised foreigner. The *ger* is also included in the festival of the great Day of Atonement (Lev. 16:29). Only from the fact that the *ger* is not explicitly mentioned in the Feast of Booths (23:43) can one conclude that a *ger* is understood as a protected citizen in contrast to some other type of person in Israelite society, as is the case elsewhere in P. When Lev. 23:42 explicitly invites the native in Israel to celebrate the Feast of Booths, one may conclude that the protected citizen is excluded from this festival. The historical reason for dwelling in booths (23:43) helps us understand why the Feast of Booths was celebrated without the *ger*.[28] Thus, in contrast to Dt. 16:14, where the *ger* is invited to participate in the Feast of Booths, Lev. 23 occupies a more cautious position.

According to Lev. 17:8f., the protected citizen is also threatened with the death penalty if he offers an illegitimate sacrifice, i.e., a sacrifice to foreign gods. "Here, as elsewhere in P, it is certainly no longer the person living outside his family or tribe that is contrasted with the 'house of Israel', but the foreigner who for some reason has been driven from his home and now seeks admission into the Yahweh community."[29] Both the Israelite and the protected citizen are strongly forbidden to eat blood (17:10,12,13). The appendix in 17:15f. requires every native or protected citizen who has eaten anything that has died or been torn to undergo a special cleansing. The allowing of cleansing in such cases means that the old strict regulation that the flesh of an animal torn by a wild beast must be cast to the dogs (Ex. 22:30[31]) experienced a basic alleviation, but it also indicates that the permission to give a carcass to the protected citizen or foreigner (Dt. 14:21) is restricted in that now the *ger* also is subject to the laws of purification.[30] When the law concerning sexual intercourse with various relatives forbidden by marriage (Lev. 18:6-17) and sins of unchastity (18:18-23) is explicitly understood to apply to both native and immigrant (*gerim*) in 18:26, this would seem to be particularly relevant to whether the *ger* was allowed to participate in the cult. The *ger* is regarded largely as a proselyte. The same is true of Lev. 20:2, which states that any Israelite or protected citizen dwelling in Israel who sacrifices any of his children to Molech must be put to death. The *ger* is also included in the rites of cleansing with the ashes of the red heifer, which are made necessary by defilement caused by a person touching a dead person (Nu. 19).

Although the law concerning asylum in Dt. 19:1-13 does not mention the *ger*, Josh. 20:9 and Nu. 35:15 emphasize that the six asylum cities are also regarded as cities of refuge for the *ger*. In P the *ger* is one of the persons that is not to be oppressed (Lev. 19:33). He is mentioned in connection with the poor in Lev. 19:10 (cf. also 23:22 and 25:6). At the same time, however, one stratum in P knows of the *ger* who has gained possession and wealth, possibly by business or trade.[31] If an Israelite must sell himself as a slave to a protected citizen (*ger*)

---

28 Cf. Elliger, *HAT*, 4, 323.
29 *Ibid.*, 227.
30 *Ibid.*, 229.
31 *Ibid.*, 359.

or a sojourner (*toshabh*) or to a member of the family of a protected citizen, he may be redeemed (25:47f.).

The regulations concerning sacrifice in Lev. 1–7 do not explicitly mention the *ger*. This may be because to some extent the laws come from an early period when the *ger*, if he was an immigrant foreigner, was not allowed to participate in the cult. However, when the *ger* is mentioned in connection with the treatment of the quality of a sacrifice in Lev. 22:17-33, and when Nu. 15, in supplements to the regulations concerning sacrifice (Nu. 15:14,15 [twice],16,26,29,30) explicitly states that the *ger* has the same rights as the native, and that the expiatory power of the sin-offering is also given to the *ger* who lives in the midst of the whole community of the Israelites, again it is quite clear that in late strata of P the *ger* is the fully integrated proselyte. Therefore, in this portion of P one should regard all laws as also applicable to the *ger*, even if he is not explicitly mentioned. And this means that the *ger* has his place in the community as a proselyte by circumcision and mode of life.

5. *In Prophetic Texts*. It is surprising that the *ger* plays a very subordinate role in prophetic preaching. Amos and Hosea, Isaiah and Micah, do not deal with the problem of the protected citizen in any detail. This is even more remarkable because these prophets are not silent about the oppression of the weak, but lament antisocial behavior. Jeremiah, e.g., in his temple sermon (Jer. 7:6; 22:3), mentions the *ger* in reiterating the old appeal to treat the economically weak with respect. Orphan, widow, and *ger* are not to be oppressed or treated violently (cf. also Zec. 7:10 and Mal. 3:5). The emigration to Egypt due to anxiety over Nebuchadnezzar is defined more explicitly by the verb *gur* (Jer. 42:15,17,22; 43:2; 44:8,12,14,[28]). According to Jer. 43:5, those who returned from foreign countries to the land of Judah as protected citizens settle down, but they move to Egypt because they are afraid that a Babylonian expedition will come to Judah to punish them.

The subst. *ger* occurs five times in Ezekiel (14:7; 22:7,29; 47:22,23), and in three of these passages it is expanded by the participle of *gur* (14:7; 47:22,23). We may add to this one occurrence of *meghurim* in 20:38. In Ezk. 14:7, in a passage that recalls the casuistic laws which have already been encountered six times in the Holiness Code (Lev. 17:3,8,10,13; 20:2; 22:18), the *ger* is mentioned as having equal rights with the Israelite, and thus as a participant in the cult. Ezekiel's purpose here is to turn "the house of Israel" away from idolatry. *ger* here probably already denotes the proselyte, who was in danger of practicing idolatry when he first became a proselyte. Only in Ezk. 20:38 does the expression *'erets meghurim*, "land of sojournings," denote the land of exile (cf. *shene hithgoreram*, "the years of their exile," in CD A 4:5). In the other passages where this expression occurs, which are in P (Gen. 17:8; 28:4; 36:7; 37:1; Ex. 6:4), it "denotes the land of promise which had not yet been given to the fathers."[32] In Ezk. 22:7 the *ger* is listed with the widow and fatherless, and in 22:29 with the poor and needy, as persons who had been treated unjustly. The addition in

---

[32] Zimmerli, *BK*, XIII, 456.

Ezk. 47:22f. is of particular interest. According to this passage, the *ger* who begets children, i.e., has a family, is to be taken into consideration in the new allotment of the land. He is to receive an inheritance in the territory of the tribe in which he settles down, and thus he is to be integrated into that tribe. Here a change of meaning takes place. The *ger* is the proselyte who has joined the Yahweh community in Babylon, and is regarded as having equal rights with the Israelite. [33]

6. *In Other Texts.* In the decree of Cyrus in Ezr. 1:2-4, the Jew who dwells in a foreign society is called a *ger* in contrast to the people of the place, i.e., non-Jews. Here, therefore (Ezr. 1:4), the *ger* is not the proselyte, but the protected citizen. In many passages, e.g., Isa. 11:6; Ps. 5:5(4); or Lam. 4:15, commentaries and translations assume that *gur* has the general meaning, "to dwell, tarry." However, it is also possible to get a deeper understanding in these passages if the meaning of *ger* is kept in mind when translating *gur*. Thus the figure in Isa. 11:6 is improved: the wolf is the protected citizen of the lamb.

7. *toshabh.* It is not easy to determine the distinction between *toshabh* and *ger. toshabh,* the nominal form of *yashabh,* "to dwell," formed with the prefixed *t,* occurs 11 times in P (Gen. 23:4; Ex. 12:45; Lev. 22:10; 25:6,23,35,40,45,47 [twice]; Nu. 35:15), and elsewhere only in Ps. 39:13(12) and 1 Ch. 29:15 (the place name, "Tishbe," is to be read in 1 K. 17:1, following the LXX). Since the *toshabh,* "stranger," is usually mentioned in connection with the *ger,* "protected citizen," and apparently *ger vethoshabh* (RSV, "a stranger and a sojourner") (Gen. 23:4; Lev. 25:23,35,47 [twice]; Nu. 35:15) is to be regarded as a hendiadys, it is clear that these two terms were understood as closely connected. This also applies to Ps. 39:13(12) and 1 Ch. 29:15, where these two words are used in parallelism. Although *toshabh* is twice defined more precisely by the participle of *gur* (Lev. 25:6,45), and although the copula is missing in the MT of Lev. 25:47b, this can only mean that the distinction between *ger* and *toshabh* was not always recognized. Presumably *toshabh* denotes, "from the economic standpoint, the same man that is called a *ger* when speaking of his legal status, and thus one who, without any property of his own, is taken in by a fully enfranchised Israelite citizen." [34] In Lev. 25:6,40; Ex. 12:45; and Lev. 22:10, the *toshabh* appears in conjunction with the *sakhir,* "hired laborer." If the stranger (*toshabh*) and the day-laborer (*sakhir*) are excluded from participation in the Passover Feast in Ex. 12:45, but the *ger* (if he has been circumcised, Ex. 12:48) of Nu. 9:14 can and must participate in it, then *toshabh* is certainly understood merely as a foreigner, thus a non-Israelite and a nonproselyte.

IV. Specific Theological Considerations.

1. Yahweh is called a *ger* only one time in the OT. In a popular lament, presumably taken up and quoted by Jeremiah, Yahweh is asked, "Why shouldst

---

[33] *Ibid.,* 1218f.
[34] Elliger, *HAT,* 4, 293f.

thou be like a stranger in the land, like a wayfarer who turns aside to tarry for a night?" (Jer. 14:8). The drought that burdens the people moves them to make a pilgrimage and to ask Yahweh to show himself to be a helper God. Palestine is his dwelling place, which he gave to Israel as an 'erets meghurim, "land of sojournings," and in it he is like a foreigner, who does not care for the land.

2. The Israelites are commanded to treat the protected citizen kindly (Dt. 10:19; cf. Ex. 22:20[21]; 23:9), because they know what it is to be a ger (nephesh hagger, "the soul [heart] of a stranger"). Since the Israelites were foreigners in Egypt (Dt. 23:8[7]; 26:5; Isa. 52:4; Ps. 105:23; 1 Ch. 16:19), they have the responsibility of extending the law of loving their neighbor as themselves (Lev. 19:18) to the ger: "The protected citizen who sojourns with you shall be to you as the native among you, and you shall love him as yourself; for you were protected citizens (gerim) in the land of Egypt: I am the Lord your God" (Lev. 19:34).

3. Like the orphan and widow with whom he is mentioned in Ex. 22:20f. (21f.); Dt. 10:18; 14:29; 16:11,14; 24:17,19,20,21; 26:13; 27:19; Jer. 7:6; 22:3; Ezk. 22:7; Zec. 7:10; Mal. 3:5; Ps. 94:6; and 146:9, the ger is in special need of protection. Israel's God is his protective Lord. It is a sin to oppress and assault the ger.

4. The idea that man simply lives the life of a ger here on earth is of special significance. Thus, the psalmist knows that he is only a ger, "guest," and a toshabh, "sojourner," before Yahweh, like all his fathers (Ps. 39:13[12]; Luther: "your pilgrim and your citizen"). The same idea is expressed in Ps. 119:19: "I am a ger on earth." Here it must be asked what is meant by ba'arets. It seems likely that in this passage 'erets denotes the land of Palestine, and not the earth in general. In any case, Lev. 25:23 shows that the Israelites knew that Yahweh alone is owner of the land, and thus they can only be hereditary tenants of his possession, "who, like a protected citizen and stranger who has taken up his abode among them, has no power to dispose of the land alloted to them." [35] In a prayer before the assembly, David says that all riches come from God, "for we are strangers before thee, and sojourners, as all our fathers were" (1 Ch. 29:15). The distress of earthly existence leads to the recognition that God must support and help man like a patron, or else man will be lost.

D. Kellermann

---

[35] Ibid., 354.

גּוֹרָל gôrāl

Contents: I. Etymology. II. Secular Usage. III. Theological Usage: 1. Casting Lots "Before Yahweh"; 2. The Lot Oracle; 3. The Lot Ordeal; 4. Figurative Religious Meaning in the OT; 5. Change of Meaning in the Qumran Literature.

I. Etymology. Presumably *goral* means small stones that were used in connection with lot casting. The terms that describe the actual casting of lots suggest this meaning, because the lots were cast (*yadhah:* Ob. 11; Nah. 3:10), were made to fall, or fell to the earth (*naphal*, Ezk. 24:6; Jonah 1:7; Neh. 10:35 [Eng. v. 34]; 11:1; 1 Ch. 24:31; etc.). The phrases that speak of the lot being shaken (*tul* in the hophal, Prov. 16:33) and coming out (*yatsa'*, Nu. 33:54; Josh. 19:1,17,24,32,40; 21:4; 1 Ch. 24:7; 25:9; 26:14) indicate that previously the lots were kept in a container. But the OT does not mention a specific vessel in which they were kept. Usually the lot was made when it was needed, or was carried in the pocket of a person's garment. Here the lot was shaken and "made to come out." A comparison with the Arabic also shows that lots were probably made of small stones: *ǧarila*, "to be stony"; *ǧaral*, "stony ground"; *ǧarwal*, "gravel, small stone." [1] In light of religio-historical parallels, it is also possible that they were made of small pieces of wood; the pre-Islamic Arabs used wooden arrows without points [2] (Ezk. 21:26[21]; Hos. 4:12). Moreover, wood and stone could easily

---

gôrāl. J. Döller, *Die Wahrsagerei im AT. BZfr,* 10/11-12 (1923); W. Dommershausen, "Das 'Los' in der alttestamentlichen Theologie," *TrThZ,* 80 (1971), 195-206; F. Dreyfus, "Le thème de l'héritage dans l'AT," *RSPT,* 42 (1958), 3-49; O. Eissfeldt, "Wahrsagung im AT," *KlSchr,* IV (1968), 271-75; K. Elliger, "Ephod und Choschen," *VT,* 8 (1958), 19-35; T. Fahd, *La divination arabe. Études religieuses, sociologiques et folkloristiques sur le milieu natif de l'Islam* (Leiden, 1966), 138-149; I. Friedrich, *Ephod und Choschen im Lichte des Alten Orients. Wiener Beiträge zur Theologie,* 20 (1968); E. Grant, "Oracle in the OT," *AJSL,* 39 (1922/23), 257-281; M. Haran, "The Ephod according to the Biblical Sources," *Tarbiz,* 24 (1955), 380-391; A. Jirku, *Mantik in Altisrael* (Rostock, 1913); F. Küchler, "Das priesterliche Orakel in Israel und Juda," *BZAW,* 33 (1918), 285-301; J. Lindblom, "Lot-Casting in the OT," *VT,* 12 (1962), 164-178; A. Lods, "Le rôle des oracles dans la nomination des rois, des prêtres et des magistrats chez les Israélites, les Égyptiens et les Grecs," *Mélanges Maspéro,* I (1934), 91-100; J. Maier, "Urim und Tummim. Recht und Bund in der Spannung Königtum und Priestertum im alten Israel," *Kairos,* N.F. 11 (1969), 22-38; H. G. May, "Ephod and Ariel," *AJSL,* 56 (1939), 44-69; J. Morgenstern, "The Ark, the Ephod and the 'Tent of Meeting'," *HUCA,* 18 (1943/44), 1-17; F. Nötscher, *Zur theol. Terminologie der Qumran-Texte. BBB,* 10 (1956), 169-173; R. Press, "Das Ordal im alten Israel," *ZAW,* 51 (1933), 121-140, 227-255; K. H. Rengstorf, "The Concept of 'Goral' in the DSS," *Tarbiz,* 35/2 (1965f.), 108-121; E. Renner, *A Study of the Word gôrāl in the OT* (Heidelberg, 1958–typescript); E. Robertson, "The 'Urīm and Tummīm–What Were They?" *VT,* 14 (1964), 67-74; F. Schmidtke, "Träume, Orakel und Totengeister als Künder der Zukunft in Israel und Babylonien," *BZ,* 11 (1967), 240-46; J. Schoneveld, "Urim en Tummim," *OrNeer* (1948), 216-222; A. Schulz, "Die Ordalien in Alt-Israel," *Festschrift G. von Hertling* (Munich, 1913), 29-35; R. de Vaux, *AncIsr,* 349-353.

[1] Blachère-Chouémi, 1452, 1967; cf. *GesB,* 135; *KBL³,* 195.
[2] Cf. J. Wellhausen, *Reste arabischen Heidentums* (³1961), 132.

be made into lots and were accessible everywhere. According to 1 Ch. 26:13-16, lots (certainly made of stone) were marked to indicate the gates that were to be assigned to various groups of gatekeepers, whether on the east side, north side, etc. [3] In Late Egyptian, *grl,* "lot," appears as a juridical term. [4]

II. Secular Usage. In everyday life, people frequently used the lot, especially if they wanted to make an impartial decision. Furthermore, it was easy to use the lot, its use hardly required an interpretation, and it was relatively secure against manipulation. Lot casting was practiced in the secular realm. Primarily it had the character of chance and luck, even if sometimes it was believed that God was the one who made the decision in a particular case (Prov. 16:33).

The OT writers frequently mention the lot in connection with distributing goods, especially "booty" in the broadest sense of the word. The one making the complaint in Ps. 22:19(18) sees that the "enemies" persecuting him are already counting on his death. They have taken his garments, and divide them up as their booty by casting lots. According to Sir. 14:15, the descendants divide up the hereditary property by casting lots (cf. also Prov. 18:18). Behind Prov. 1:14 lies the custom thieves had of dividing up their booty by casting lots.

Lot casting was also a commonly used method in martial law. According to Nah. 3:10; Ob. 11; and Joel 4:2f.(3:2f.), victors in war disposed of the people and their property by casting lots. Ezk. 24:6 could refer to the carrying off of the inhabitants of Jerusalem in 587 B.C., which was done indiscriminately (possibly in contrast to those that were carried off in 597 B.C.). Finally, Job compares his heartless friends with men who treat persons like things: when helpless orphans are brought to them as a pledge, they see to it that they are sold by casting lots (Job 6:27).

Tasks and services were also determined by casting lots. This is the way the Levites arranged the service at the various gates of the temple (1 Ch. 26:13-16), and how the priests and singers arranged their service at the sanctuary (1 Ch. 24f.). The lot was used under Nehemiah to determine the sequence in which the various individual families were to provide the firewood for the altar (Neh. 10:35[34]). Also under Nehemiah it was decided that not only the leaders of the people would be allowed to live in Jerusalem, but also a tenth of the rest of the people. The latter consisted partly of volunteers and partly of those who were compelled to live in the holy city by the process of casting lots (Neh. 11:1f.).

The book of Esther states twice that Haman, the enemy of the Jews, cast lots in order to determine a favorable time for the massacre of the Jews (Est. 3:7; 9:24). In light of 3:7, it seems that this was the method used to determine the time: Haman cast two lots for each day (one negative and the other positive), until finally he received an affirmative reply on the thirteenth day, and then for each month, until he hit upon the month of Adar.

---

[3] Cf. Lindblom, 168.
[4] *GesB,* 135; not in *WbÄS.*

III. Theological Usage.

1. *Casting Lots "Before Yahweh."* The OT gives particular consideration to casting lots "before Yahweh." In other words, Israel is convinced that God holds the fate of man in his hands and reveals his will immediately and unambiguously through lot casting. [5] Therefore, the people of God in the OT regard lot casting as a sacral act. They inquire of Yahweh in both public and private affairs (e.g., Ex. 18:15; 33:7; Jgs. 1:1f.; etc.). Along with dreams and prophetic oracles (cf. 1 S. 28:6), the lot is regarded as the answer and final decision of Yahweh, against which there is no appeal. Of course, it is uncertain how many of the numerous inquiries of Yahweh were actually answered by casting lots.

The main intention of the "Priestly" authors in Josh. 18–20 is to declare that the distribution and allotment of the land was undertaken by Yahweh himself. They state that this was done at the central sanctuary in Shiloh, at the door of the tabernacle, and frequently emphasize that Joshua, the priest Eleazar, and the heads of the families cast lots "before Yahweh" (Josh. 18:6,8,10; 19:51; 21:1f.,8; on the allotment of the land, cf. Nu. 26:55f.; 33:54; 34:13; 36:2f.; Josh. 13:6; 14:1f.; 23:4; 1 Ch. 6:39,46,48,50[54,61,63,65]; Ezk. 45:1; 47:22; 48:29; Isa. 34:17). Dalman thinks there were two steps in the process of distributing the land. [6] First, it was decided what territory was to be given to each tribe (cf. Josh. 15:1). The size of the territory given to each tribe was determined by the number of families or conscripted soldiers belonging to it. Then, secondly, the territory belonging to each tribe was distributed among the individual families (cf. the stereotyped formula in Josh. 18 and 19: "The lot came out for the tribe of ... according to its families"). Possibly two containers, from which the marked lot stones were drawn, were used. One container had the stones with the names of the various territories on them, and the other, the stones with the names of the individual families.

According to Lev. 16, the high priest is to present two goats "before Yahweh" at the door of the tent of revelation (certainly in a special rite). Then, by casting lots, he is to ascertain which goat God wishes for himself, and which goat he wishes to be sent away to the wilderness demon, Azazel. The procedure used in casting lots here has been explained as follows: The priest puts two lot stones into a container with the names or symbols of Yahweh and Azazel upon them, and shakes it before the first goat. The lot stone that comes up (*'alah*) first designates this goat for its special purpose. The goat selected for Yahweh is offered as a sin-offering, while the other is loaded with human guilt and driven far off into the wilderness, and there he dies with the sin. [7]

Jgs. 19–21 tells of the crime of the people of Gibeah in Benjamin. The tribes of Israel assemble at the Mizpah sanctuary to decide what to do about Gibeah, and the lot plays a role in this decision. Because of the brevity of the statement in 20:9b, it is impossible to determine very precisely what was supposed to be determined by the casting of the lot. The next verse would seem to indicate that

---

[5] Heinisch, *TheolOT* (trans. 1957), 160.

[6] G. Dalman, *AuS*, II, 42.

[7] Cf. Elliger, *HAT*, 4, 212f.

it was used to determine which soldiers would fight and which would carry the provisions.

2. *The Lot Oracle.* In the sacral realm, the lot was also used in connection with the oracle and the ordeal. In ancient Israel, the lot oracle is a legitimate, priestly means of inquiring of Yahweh. [8] It is used not so much to look into the future as to bring one's own deeds into conformity with the instruction of God. E.g., in Nu. 27:21 Israel is instructed to carry on its campaigns according to Yahweh's regulations, which the priest seeks by means of the Urim-lot.

Urim here stands as *pars pro toto* for the exclusive priestly lot of the *Urim* and *Thummim*. At the present stage of research, it is thought that originally the Urim and Thummim were two cubic stones, one white and the other black, which represented the answers "Yes" or "No." [9] Accordingly, questions designed to receive a positive or negative answer were characteristically asked in connection with the Urim and Thummim. It is usually thought that one of these stones was made of limestone and the other of basalt. The words "Urim" and "Thummim" cannot be explained etymologically from the Hebrew vocabulary. Israel took them over from foreign people dwelling in the land of Canaan, but we do not know the language from which they were taken. The mimation indicates that they are very old. [10]

Later, we are told that Saul inquired of Yahweh because of the Philistines, but Yahweh did not answer him, "either by dreams, or by Urim, or by prophets" (1 S. 28:6). Between the period of the judges and that of the time of David, the Bible relates several instances in which men inquired of God. Although it cannot be proved, it is natural to assume that the Urim and Thummim were used as a means of receiving an oracle when the questions were asked in such a way as to expect a positive or negative answer (Jgs. 18:5f.; 20:26ff.; 1 S. 23:2; 2 S. 5:19).

1 S. 23 and 30 refer to still another means of obtaining an oracle, viz., the ephod ('*ephodh*). In both instances, David asks the priest Abiathar to bring the ephod to him that he might inquire of Yahweh. (Cf. 1 S. 14:18, LXX.)

There is still no convincing solution to the problem of the ephod. The main difficulty is that this word denotes different things in the OT. It is quite probable that the root word means "clothes" in the broadest sense of the word, thus some sort of material that goes around a person or an object (Jgs. 8:24-27; 17:5). This must have had a large pocket or receptacle of some sort in which the lot stones were kept, when ephod is used to mean an instrument for obtaining an oracle. 1 S. 21:10(9) must also have in mind a garment with a pocket that held the lots used for divination. This garment stood upright, and was large enough to hide something behind it, for the text states that "the sword of Goliath . . . is behind the ephod." Later (in P), the ephod is a part of the official garments of the high priest. Here it is more of a garment worn around the shoulders, but a fundamental part

---

8 A. Cody, *A History of OT Priesthood. AnBibl,* 35 (1969), 13f.

9 Cf. E. Lipiński, "'Urīm and Tummīm," *VT,* 20 (1970), 495f.

10 A. Jirku, *Bibl,* 34 (1953), 78ff.

of this garment is a breast pocket (*choshen*) with the Urim and Thummim. [11] The oldest texts of the OT refer to an *'ephodh badh,* "a linen ephod," which is a short garment that a priest girds about himself (1 S. 2:18; 22:18; 2 S. 6:14).

Thus, inquiring of the oracle-ephod with the lot stones is not basically different from using the Urim and Thummim. This conclusion is confirmed by the method that David uses in asking questions when he consults the ephod: Will Saul come down? Will the people hand me over? Shall I pursue them? Will they overtake me? (1 S. 23:11f.; 30:8). The questions are phrased so that they can be answered "Yes" or "No." The answers that are quoted are certainly expanded statements of the answers that actually came from the oracle, which were simply "Yes."

3. *The Lot Ordeal.* The lot oracle is dominated by the belief that God's wisdom determines the present and future actions of men. By way of contrast, the lot ordeal is related to man's past actions, and makes the omniscient God the guarantor that the truth will be found. Other nations in the ancient Near East also used the ordeal (cf. the heathen sailors in Jonah 1:7). The cultic lot ordeals of the Bible are not private matters, but always pertain to the whole people. Sometimes they are used to expose a guilty person, but sometimes to determine the one whom God had blessed. When Achan brought guilt on himself and the entire Israelite army by embezzling devoted things, God commanded Joshua to cast lots in order to determine the identity of the lawbreaker (Josh. 7:13f.). The same procedure is used in choosing Saul as king in 1 S. 10:20f. The circle of possible candidates becomes narrower and narrower until the choice is made. In both instances, the word *lakhadh,* "to take," is used to describe the person on whom the lot falls. However, the text of these two passages gives no detailed information as to what technique of lot casting was used or whether the Urim and Thummim were employed. A third instance of a cultic lot ordeal is related in 1 S. 14:41f. During a military campaign Jonathan, like Achan, transgresses a command, the violation of which placed one under a curse, and thus brings the wrath of God upon himself and the army. In order to determine who has aroused God's anger, Saul resorts to the lot ordeal. The LXX expands v. 41, and interprets the lot casting procedure as having been done with the holy lots, the Urim and Thummim. The MT reads *tamim,* "completeness, perfection," in Saul's ordeal prayer, while the LXX read *tummim,* "Thummim." The use of the lot ordeal in connection with the king and the people is theologically significant. Saul thinks that the guilty party will be designated by Yahweh, and that he must be delivered over to the predetermined punishment for his transgression. The people, indeed, acknowledge that Jonathan is guilty, but they plead that he not be punished because of the special service he had rendered. In the final analysis the voice of the people is the voice of God, because Jonathan slew the Philistines "with God." "Here the manifestation of the will of God stands over against the manifestation of the will of God." [12] This episode shows

---

[11] Cf. W. Eichrodt, *TheolOT,* I (trans. 1965), 113f.
[12] H. W. Hertzberg, *ATD,* X, 93.

clearly the great uncertainty that was prevalent in this period with regard to understanding the divine plan. While the lot always played a certain role in the daily life of the Israelites, the ceremonial lot casting before Yahweh and in the sanctuary was gradually replaced by prophetic preaching and priestly interpretation of the Torah (cf. Hos. 4:12; Sir. 33:3). [13] The lot oracle also seems to have come to an end with the exile, although the Talmud states that it ceased with Solomon (Mishnah *Soṭa* ix.12). [14] At the time of the composition of the Priestly Code, the Urim and Thummim had certainly already lost their original function, and are included among the garments of the high priest as symbols of his judicial authority (Ex. 28:30; Lev. 8:8; Dt. 33:8; Ezr. 2:63; Neh. 7:65; Sir. 45:10).

4. *Figurative Religious Meaning in the OT.* Yahweh had once allotted the land to the individual tribes and families of his people by means of casting lots. It is easy to understand then that a parcel of land apportioned by lot casting was itself called a "lot." Thus, Yahweh's great deed of giving the land is kept in memory by this technical term, and provides the basis for the spiritualization of this term. [15] "Lot" appears with the meaning "land, territory (territorial boundary)," in Josh. 15:1; 16:1; 17:1,14,17; Ps. 125:3; Mic. 2:5.

In Ps. 16:5f., the word "lot" is used figuratively of the fate of man, which God holds in his hands. The worshipper can trust in Yahweh, because God is the ground of his existence. The same idea is also expressed by the synonyms → חֵלֶק *chēleq* (possession), → חֶבֶל *chebhel* (measuring cord), and → נַחֲלָה *nachªlāh* (inheritance) all of which originally referred to casting lots for the land. In Wisd. 2:9, also, "lot" (Gk. *klḗros*) denotes the individual "lot" in life of the unrestrained hedonist.

In the prophetic doom oracle in Isa. 57:3-6, he who practices idolatry is threatened with a corresponding punishment: the fate of the accused takes place where he sinned. Here, "lot" in the sense of fate also includes a retribution which the Lord apportions to the ungodly. The retributive nature of the lot is also expressed in the woe against Assyria in Isa. 17:14. The sudden destruction of the enemy army is "the lot of those that plundered and despoiled Israel." According to Jer. 13:20-27, Yahweh's punitive retribution will come upon the wanton woman, Jerusalem. She will be reviled for her adulterous deeds. Spiritual qualities or, quite generally, the blessing of God stand in the foreground of the remunerative retribution in Ben Sira (Sir. 11:22). Punitive retribution is announced as a threatening principle (25:19). Dnl. 12:13 is an exhortation to Daniel to look forward confidently to his lot at the end, since he will certainly be raised to everlasting life. The LXX confirms the idea of eschatological retribution when it renders "lot" here by "glory" (*dóxa*). Wisd. 3:14 and 5:5 also promise the righteous a joyful reward in the hereafter.

---

[13] Eissfeldt, *KlSchr*, IV, 272.
[14] Cf. Robertson, 69f.
[15] Renner, 39-71; Dreyfus, 13ff.

In ancient Jewish literature, the "lot" is also used figuratively. E.g., the line of thought begun in Dnl. 12:13 is continued in 1 Enoch (37:4; 48:7; 58:5).

5. *Change of Meaning in the Qumran Literature.* In the Qumran texts, *goral* is used exclusively in the figurative sense. When it means "punishment" and "reward" ("retribution"), there is a distinction between a *goral qedhoshim* ("lot of the saints," 1QS 11:7), a *goral 'olam* ("everlasting destiny," 1QH 3:22), as well as a *goral 'or* ("lot of light," describing a life in light, 1QM 13:9) and a *goral 'aph* ("destiny of wrath," judgment of wrath, 1QH 3:27f.).

goral also experiences a change in meaning in the Qumran literature from what is found in the OT or in Rabbinic literature. Thus, *goral* can mean "a decision, a resolution," which is made without casting lots (1QS 5:3; 6:16,18,22; 9:7; CD 13:4). And from this meaning, it is transferred to the rank (office) granted by the decision (1QS 1:10; 2:23; 1QSa 1:9,20). Furthermore, it denotes the community (party, adherents) in which a decision is binding: *goral 'el* = the party of God (1QS 2:2; 1QM 1:5; 15:1; 17:7); *goral 'emeth* = the adherents of truth (1QM 13:12); *goral beliyya'al* = the followers of Belial (1QS 2:5; 1QM 1:5); and *goral choshekh* = the men of darkness (1QM 1:11).

1QM 1:13 (three lots; cf. 17:16) and 1:14 (the seventh lot) are obscure; perhaps they have to do with a military formation. [16]

Dommershausen

[16] Nötscher, 173.

| גָּזַל *gāzal;* גֶּזֶל *gēzel;* גָּזֵל *gāzēl;* גְּזֵלָה *gᵉzēlāh* |

Contents: I. Etymology, Meaning. II. OT Linguistic Usage. III. Specific Theological Usage.

I. Etymology, Meaning. The root *gzl* appears not only in biblical and post-biblical Hebrew, but also in other Semitic languages, including Ugaritic (in proper names),[1] Phoenician (*ngzlt,* "to be torn down"), Aramaic (e.g., Syr. *gelaz,* "to snatch away, steal"), and Arabic (*ǧazala,* "to cut off").[2] On the basis of the occurrences of this root in the various Semitic languages, it can be assumed that its original meaning was "to snatch away violently."

II. OT Linguistic Usage. In the OT, the root *gzl* is found in verb forms of the qal and niphal, and in the derivative nouns *gezel, gazel,* and *gezelah.* The OT confirms the original meaning "to snatch away violently," especially in three passages: 2 S. 23:21 (par. 1 Ch. 11:23); Mic. 3:2; and Job 24:9, which speak of

[1] See *WUS,* No. 641.
[2] Cf. *GesB, KBL.*

snatching a spear out of the hand of an enemy, tearing the skin off (the body of) a man, and snatching the fatherless child from his mother's breast, respectively. *gzl*, whose meaning to some extent approximates the ideas suggested by → גנב *gānabh*, "to steal," *chataph*, "to seize," → פשט *pāshaṭ*, "to strip off, flay," → נהג *nāhagh*, "to drive off," and → בזז *bāzaz*, "to spoil, plunder," clearly describes the forceful tearing away of an object from its owner or its place by a person or persons who are stronger than the object or its owner. Then, as is clear from its occasional connection with legal themes and from Mic. 3:2 and Job 24:9, *gzl* usually denotes an illegal action which manifests power and overcomes a person or a thing. This is also evident from the fact that the word → עשק *'āshaq*, "to oppress, extort," or *'osheq*, "oppression, extortion," is frequently used in connection with the root *gzl* (cf. Lev. 5:23 [Eng. 6:4]; 19:13; Dt. 28:29; Jer. 21:12; 22:3; Ezk. 18:18; 22:29; Mic. 2:2; and also Lev. 5:21[6:2]; Ps. 62:11 [10]; Eccl. 5:7[8]).

Thus, as an action affecting a specific object (sometimes with a more explicit statement concerning its separation from the place or person to whom it belongs: using a prepositional phrase with *min*–Gen. 31:31; Dt. 28:31; cf. also 2 S. 23:21 = par. 1 Ch. 11:23; Mic. 3:2; and Job 24:9; or the acc.–Isa. 10:2, unless *bammishpat*, "in justice," is the correct reading here), *gzl* denotes a powerful, unlawful snatching away or stealing of people (Gen. 31:31: daughters; Jgs. 21:23: wives), animals (Dt. 28:31: ass; Job 24:2: flocks; see also Mal. 1:13 [pass. ptcp.]: what has been taken [= the sacrificial animal]), and things (Gen. 21:25: well of water; Mic. 2:2: fields; Job 20:19: houses). In the last group, the emphasis lies especially on the powerful and unjust acquisition of these things.

In the figurative sense, *gzl* denotes the removal of justice (Isa. 10:2; cf. Eccl. 5:7[8]), and, without any legal emphasis, robbing one of sleep (Prov. 4:16), and the taking away or absorption of snow water (Job 24:19).

As an action directed against a specific person and injurious to him, *gzl* denotes robbing someone of something (Lev. 19:13: a neighbor; Jgs. 9:25: those who pass by; Prov. 22:22: the poor; Prov. 28:24: father and mother; Dt. 28:29: you shall be robbed), and thus the active participle is used of the robber (Ps. 35:10, of the poor), and the passive participle of the one being robbed (Jer. 21:12; 22:3, by the oppressor).

Some form of the verb with an internal object in the form of a noun from the same root (figura etymologica) is used to express a robbery in the emphatic absolute sense (to commit a robbery) (*gezelah*, Lev. 5:23[6:4]; Ezk. 18:7,12,16, conjec. 18; *gazel*, Ezk. 22:29; cf. Ps. 69:5[4]).

The derivative nouns *gezel*, *gazel*, and *gezelah* denote stealing, robbery, or the spoil (Eccl. 5:7[8]; Lev. 5:21[6:2]; Isa. 61:8; Ps. 62:11[10]; Sir. 16:13; Ezk. 33:15; Isa. 3:14).

III. **Specific Theological Usage.** As its occurrences in the social accusations of the prophets, in the context of legal maxims, lists of regulations and prohibitions, and in precept-like demands or instructions show, the theological emphasis of *gzl* is connected above all with the aspect of injustice, and refers either to the deed itself or to the wrongdoer or to one affected by the deed. In particular, the theological emphasis is to be divided into three main areas.

In the area of Wisdom thought, *gzl*, which was evidently classified and resisted here primarily as an antisocial behavior that destroyed community (cf. Prov. 28:24 and 22:22, probably influenced by Egyptian Wisdom), is regarded as an action involving Yahweh's retribution (so according to the Wisdom elements in Ps. 62:11ff.[10ff.]), or (as the view represented by Job's friends reveals) as a typical characteristic of the ungodly criminal, who is struck by the retributive righteousness of God (Job 20:19). In contrast, however, in Job's statement of his position *gzl* is used to refer to a behavior which indeed is wicked, but which incomprehensibly is not met with divine retribution, but is evidently tolerated and permitted by God (24:2,9), so that finally Qoheleth can soberly tell his audience not to be amazed when justice and right are violently taken away (Eccl. 5:7[8]). On the other hand, Jesus ben Sira again maintains that retribution by divine judgment is the inevitable consequence of *gzl* (Sir. 16:13).

According to the prophetic view, *gzl,* as it is directed against the socially weak that are under divine protection and hurls them into destruction, calls for Yahweh to act immediately in punishing those responsible for this crime by means of his historical acts (Isa. 3:14; 10:2; Mic. 2:2; Ezk. 22:29), and to save the oppressed (Jer. 21:12; 22:3; cf. also the confession of the innocent sufferer who has been falsely accused in Ps. 35:10). *gzl* is also a characteristic of the ungodly criminal, whom Yahweh calls into account and who is punished with death when he refuses to be converted as the only possible means of salvation (Ezk. 18:7,12, 16,18; 33:15). The prophets interpret criminal robbery as something that God hates (Isa. 61:8), and declare that an offering taken by violence is useless and unacceptable to Yahweh (Mal. 1:13).

In the area of priestly, cultic theology, *gzl* is used to describe the condition of the man who is struck by Yahweh's curse because of his disobedience to the divine commandments and statutes (Dt. 28:29,31). And then, in the context of the giving of the priestly sacrificial law, *gzl* is understood as sin and embezzlement against Yahweh, which can be expiated only by restitution and the sacrifice of a sin offering (Lev. 5:21,23[6:2,4]). Finally, in the Holiness Code, *gzl* in general is prohibited as an act that is out of harmony with the holiness of Israel which Yahweh desires (Lev. 19:13).

In spite of the various theological emphases associated with *gzl,* the content and form of the statements using this root in the different areas are similar, which indicates that the various areas had a mutual influence on one another.

Schüpphaus

גָּזַר *gāzar;* גֶּזֶר *gezer;* גְּזֵרָה *gᵉzērāh;* מַגְזֵרָה *maghzērāh*

Contents: I. Original Meaning: 1. Etymology; 2. Spectrum of Occurrences; 3. Identity of the Root. II. Pre-Theological Usage: 1. Formative Function; 2. Critical Role; 3. The "Separated" Region. III. The "Excluded" Man: 1. Exile; 2. Collective Separation; 3. Separation of the Individual.

I. Original Meaning.

1. *Etymology.* Examples of the root *gzr* appear in South and Northwest Semitic, but as yet not in East Semitic. The later dialects seem to reflect a semantic difference, since a Middle Heb.-Aram. *gzr,* "to decide," stands over against Arab. *ǵazara,* "to cut off, slaughter," and Ethiop. *gazara,* "to cut." However, the former is due to a change of meaning of a secondary sort.[1] In the Ugar. expression *'gzrym,*[2] Aistleitner[3] sees the "images of Yam."[4] However, Gray thinks it refers to "the Morning and Evening Star 'cutting off,' i.e., delimiting the day."[5] Apart from these different interpretations, it is certain that Ugar. *gzr* means "to cut, cut straight."[6] In spite of the similar consonants and a certain synonymity of meaning ("to be partial"),[7] Egyp. *gśꜣ* (attested from the Middle Kingdom on) can hardly be regarded as a Semitic loanword. All additional detailed information concerning the root *gzr* can be gained only from the OT.

2. *Spectrum of Occurrences.* A study of this root in the OT reveals that it is used both as a verb and as a noun. *gzr* occurs in the qal in 1 K. 3:25,26; 2 K. 6:4; Ps. 136:13; Job 22:28; and possibly also Hab. 3:17 (perhaps a qal pass.)[8] and Isa. 9:19 (Eng. v. 20) (probably not from a different root).[9] Niphal forms of this root appear in Isa. 53:8; Ezk. 37:11; Ps. 88:6(5); Lam. 3:54; 2 Ch. 26:21; and Est. 2:1. The noun forms that appear are **gezer* (Gen. 15:17; Ps. 136:13), *gezerah* (Lev. 16:22; Ezk. 41:12,14,15; 42:1,10,13 [twice]; Lam. 4:7), and *maghzerah* (2 S. 12:31).[10]

---

gāzar. L. Delekat, "Zum hebräischen Wörterbuch," *VT,* 14 (1964), 11-13; J. Gray, *The Legacy of Canaan. SVT,* 5 (²1965), 98; J. L. Palache, *Semantic Notes on the Hebrew Lexicon* (1959), 19.

[1] Cf. Palache, 19, who observes a similar root in Akk. *parāsu,* "separate > decide."
[2] *CTA,* 23 [SS], 23, 58, 61.
[3] J. Aistleitner, *Die mythologischen und kultischen Texte von Ras Schamra* (1959), 59.
[4] Cf. also *WUS,* 643.
[5] Gray, 98, n. 7.
[6] On the proper name *gzry,* cf. *PNU,* 130.
[7] *WbÄS,* V, 205.
[8] Cf. M. Dahood, *Ugaritic-Hebrew Philology* (Rome, 1965), 21.
[9] Cf. Delekat, 13, n. 3; Gray, 98, n. 7.
[10] On the place name Gezer ("isolated room"), cf. *KBL³,* 180.

3. *Identity of the Root.* According to Delekat, Lam. 3:54; Ezk. 37:11; Ps. 88:6(5); 2 Ch. 26:21; Hab. 3:17; and Isa. 53:8 have undergone a secondary revision. He supposes that a root *gzr,* meaning "to destroy, vanish," which occurs in Ps. 31:23(22) (and which he postulates in Jonah 2:5), lies behind the present MT as the original reading. [11] However, an investigation of all these examples suggests the possibility that *gzr,* which originally meant "to cut," may be interpreted in every case to mean "to cut off, destroy," and "to cut straight, decide."

II. Pre-Theological Usage.

1. *Formative Function.* The root *gzr* is used to describe the mechanical activity of "felling trees" in 2 K. 6:4 (2 S. 12:31 speaks of the *maghzerah,* "ax"). Isa. 9:19(20) seems to go a step beyond this ("to cut off something in order to eat it"?). According to Hab. 3:17, the cattle of the oppressed are "cut off, torn" (not simply "lost") from the herd. In order to seal a covenant, a smoking fire pot and a flaming torch are passed between the pieces of flesh (*gezarim,* Gen. 15:17). In an etymological figure, Ps. 136:13 speaks of "dividing" the waters of the Red Sea at the time of the exodus. Formerly, the "style," the form of Israel's elite, had been like a precious stone (Lam. 4:7). Therefore, the secular spectrum exhibits all aspects of literal "cutting."

2. *Critical Role.* Solomon's verdict of "exemplary wisdom" [12] is that the controversial child is to be "divided" (1 K. 3:25f.). This act is supposed to solve the problem. The figurative meaning of *gzr,* "to decide," is found later in Job 22:28 and Est. 2:1 as a result of this usage. In this way the root *gzr* attains a critical quality.

3. *The "Separated" Region.* The scapegoat laden with the sins of Israel is sent away into the wilderness, and thus he carries away the people's guilt into a "separated region" (*'erets gezerah,* Lev. 16:22). This expression may mean an "unfruitful land," [13] but it may also denote a region that is located quite apart from the cultic camp. The independent word *gezerah* denotes a part of the temple region in Ezekiel (41:12,14f.; 42:1,10,13), but according to Zimmerli, it is "probably a descriptive word," which can mean "a region which is not accessible to the common man, who has not been consecrated, like the Gk. *témenos.*" [14]

III. The "Excluded" Man.

1. *Banishment.* One's understanding of 2 Ch. 26:21 is connected with one's interpretation of Lev. 16:22, except that in 2 Ch. 26:21 *gzr* indicates the separation from the cultic realm more clearly: the leprous Uzziah is "excluded" (*nighzar*) from the house of Yahweh. The thought here is not very different from

---

[11] Delekat, 11-13.
[12] Von Rad.
[13] *KBL³,* 180.
[14] Zimmerli, *BK,* XIII, 1038.

a type of excommunication: thus, the niphal form is also suitable to a sacral, legal situation.

2. *Collective Separation.* In Ps. 88:6(5), before Yahweh, the worshipper deplores the fate of the dead, who are "'carried away' (*nighzaru*) by thy hand." The relationship of this statement to the corresponding expression in the preceding line, "whom thou dost remember no more," also speaks against a different derivation: *nighzar* means separation from life by death, presumably brought about by God. A sharper description of this figure and idea appears in the quotation found in Ezk. 37:11b, which is probably an element of the popular lament. In a vision of the field of the dead, the exiles are described figuratively as those who are "cut off": "all three phrases of this quotation express the hopeless drying up, perishing, and being cut off."[15] The climax and the absolute use of *nighzar*[16] emphasize the consciousness of a complete separation from land and life.

3. *Separation of the Individual.* It is only a step from this confession of the defeated people to the statement that the Servant of Yahweh will be "'cut off' out of the land of the living" (*nighzar me'erets chayyim*, Isa. 53:8a). Here also, the language as a whole argues against a correction. Like the '*ebhedh*, "Servant" (v. 10), the one who complained that water had closed over his head (Lam. 3:54) is also saved by Yahweh: the confession '*amarti nighzarti*, "I said, I am lost" (perhaps a "familiar expression"),[17] represents the final cry of despair before the element of the "certainty of hearing" is introduced (v. 55).

Görg

---

[15] *Ibid.*, 897.

[16] This correction is suggested in *KBL³*, 180, and goes back to F. Perles, *OLZ*, 12 (1909), 251f.: this leaves *nighzar navlenu*, "our thread of life is cut off"; cf. also Zimmerli, *BK*, XIII, 887.

[17] Cf. Delekat, 11.

גחל *ghl*; גֶּחָלִים *gechālîm*; גַּחֲלֵי־אֵשׁ *gachᵃlê-'ēsh*; גַּחֶלֶת *gacheleth*

Contents: I. 1. Etymology; 2. Occurrences. II. Usage in Everyday Life and in Idioms. III. Theological Significance: 1. In the Cult; 2. In Oracles of Judgment; 3. In Theophanies.

I. 1. *Etymology.* The root *ghl* is attested in only a few Semitic languages. With some degree of certainty, it can be related to Amharic *gāla*, "to be red-hot,"[1] and Yemenite *ǧaihal* > *miǧhal*, "firewood."[2] The connection with *khl*,[3] Akk. *guḫlu*,[4] is certainly incorrect.

---

[1] E. Ullendorff, *An Amharic Chrestomathy* (Oxford, 1956), 129.

[2] Ch. Rabin, *Ancient West-Arabian* (London, 1951), 26.

[3] *KBL²*, 430f.

[4] *AHw*, 288, 296; *CAD*, V, 71, 125.

The root ğḥl is also related to ğḥm (sound change from l to m) (Gen. 22:24); cf. Arab. ğaḥīm or ğaḥmat, "bright flame"; Tigr. gaḥama, "to char." [5]

2. *Occurrences.* In the OT the root ğḥl appears only in some derivatives: a. *gechalim* (the pl. of a postulated *gechchal)* occurs nine times: once each in 2 Samuel and Isaiah (44:16, conjec. from v. 19), twice each in Ezekiel and Psalms, and three times in Proverbs. The LXX translates this word by *ánthrakes* (Prov. 26:21, sing.) and *ánthrakes pyrós* (in Prov. 6:28; 25:22).

b. *gachale* is the plural construct of a postulated *gachchal,* which does not occur elsewhere. It appears in combination with → אֵשׁ *'ēsh* six times: twice each in Leviticus and Ezekiel, and once each in 2 Samuel and Psalms; and in combination with *rethamim,* "broom tree," once in Ps. 120:4. The LXX translates this expression by *ánthrakes pyrós* and by *ánthrakes erēmikoí* in Ps. 120:4.

c. *gacheleth* is the only form of this root that has been preserved in the singular. [6] It occurs twice in the OT: 2 S. 14:7; Isa. 47:14. In the first passage the LXX translates by *ánthrax,* "coal," and in the second by *ánthrakes pyrós,* "coals of fire."

KBL[3], 180, thinks that the meaning of this root in every case is "live coals (charcoal)," [7] in contrast to nonburning wood coals (*pecham*), and in this way limits its range of meaning to a specific manner of production.

II. Usage in Everyday Life and in Idioms.

1. Along with fire (→ אֵשׁ *'ēsh*), which rapidly consumes the wood, the lasting coal that results plays a great role in everyday life. It is used to melt copper (Ezk. 24:11), and is necessary for baking and roasting; everything would be consumed by an open fire: "Half of it I burned in the fire (*bemo 'esh*), I also baked bread on its coals (*gechalav*) and roasted flesh" (Isa. 44:19; cf. v. 16). In the cold winter months, it gives scanty warmth (Isa. 47:14; cf. Jer. 36:22f.), usually as the only source of heat in houses, since an open fire is too dangerous in closed areas, and outlets for smoke were not built until relatively late, and then only in isolated places. The coal normally required here comes exclusively from burned wood (Isa. 44:19; Ezk. 24:11) or preheated charcoal (Prov. 26:21; cf. Lev. 16:12; and for the late period, Mishnah *Tamid* ii.5, 9; etc.). [8] As a result, *gechalim* and *pecham* can be used synonymously, as the expression *gachale 'esh,* "coals of fire" (Lev. 16:12; 2 S. 22:13 = Ps. 18:13 [Eng. v. 12]; Ezk. 1:13; 10:2), suggests; cf. *pacham 'esh* or *pachame 'esh,* "coals of fire," in Ps. 11:6, following the con-

---

[5] Littmann-Höfner, *Wörterbuch der Tigrē-Sprache* (1962), 565b.
[6] Cf. *BLe,* § 607c.
[7] However, cf. *KBL,* 179!
[8] Cf. Dalman, *AuS,* IV, 4f.

jecture of Bickell. The embers of the coals of the broom tree are preferred, because its very hard wood guarantees especially intense and lasting heat, which also explains why arrows are sharpened with these embers (Ps. 120:4).

2. Daily association and experience with coal explain why it is used in idioms and figurative expressions. For example, a person cannot walk on hot coals without burning his feet (Prov. 6:28). As wood for fire and coals (*pecham*) for hot embers (*leghechalim*), so is a quarrelsome man for kindling strife (26:21). Good deeds that a person does for his enemy are like coals heaped on his head (25:22). The coal that gives warmth and life stands behind the metaphor in 2 S. 14:7: "thus they would quench my coal which is left (i.e., kill my son)."

III. Theological Significance.

1. *In the Cult.* Coal is required in the cult in connection with the offering of incense, which was burned each morning and each evening (Ex. 30:7f.). According to Lev. 16:12, a priest takes a censer full of hot coals from the altar of burnt-offering, sprinkles fragrant herbs upon it, and brings it within the veil. The cloud of smoke coming from this is supposed to make invisible the mercy seat (of the ark), which is especially dangerous to look at because of the divine presence or appearance, and thus protect the high priest from the appearance of Yahweh. The procedure described here does not take into consideration the special altar of incense described in Ex. 30:1-10; instead, it simply presupposes the one altar of Ex. 27:1-8. [9]

2. *In Oracles of Judgment.* In statements concerning God's judging and punitive intervention, coals play an important role along with fire (→ אש *ʾēsh*). In comparison to the consuming fire, they signify an intensification (as in Ezk. 24:11), and signal the totality of destruction and the finality of judgment.

a. The sphere of daily life is the setting for the oracles of judgment in Isa. 47:14; Ezk. 24:11; and Ps. 120:4: the deceptive tongue will be destroyed as by a warrior's sharp arrows and glowing coals of the broom tree. These two figures are to be interpreted as a hysteron proteron (reversal of natural order). Thus, the element of intensification is already visible stylistically: in the especially powerful glowing coals of the broom tree Yahweh allows the deceitful tongue to sharpen its deadly arrows well, which, although intended for others, will ultimately strike that tongue and destroy it. [10] Yahweh will destroy all filthiness like an empty pot whose bronze melts in the coals (Ezk. 24:11). In the end, there will be no fire to sit before and no coal for warming oneself (Isa. 47:14b): every living thing will die.

---

[9] K. Elliger, *HAT,* 4, 209f., 213.
[10] Cf. H. Gunkel, *Einl. in die Psalmen* (1933), 537ff.

b. Ezk. 10:2 calls to mind Lev. 16:12 combined with Gen. 19:24: [11] the man
clothed in linen is to go into the temple, fill his hands with coals (probably from
the altar of incense), and scatter them over the city in order to destroy it completely. The fire kindled in honor of Yahweh is changed into the coals of his
anger, which destroy his own city with a special destructive power. And when
the man clothed in linen leaves the temple with the coals, the glory of Yahweh
also leaves the sanctuary and thus delivers it up to destruction. [12]

c. The motifs involving coal discussed thus far are rooted in the experiences
of everyday life and based on the idea of a coal that comes from wood or charcoal. An entirely different realm of ideas stands behind the words of judgment
in Ps. 11:6; 140:11(10); Prov. 25:22; and the description of the theophany in
Ps. 18:13(12)=2 S. 22:13. [13] The coal that is about to fall on the evildoer (Ps.
140:11[10]), or which Yahweh will rain on the evildoer (11:6), is from an entirely
different source. The prototype of this idea of the destructive intervention of
Yahweh is the old narrative of the destruction of Sodom and Gomorrah (Gen.
19:24): Yahweh rains down fire and brimstone on these cities and destroys them
completely. It is likely that a volcanic eruption is the real background of this
event. Thus *gechalim* (Ps. 140:11[10]) means "glowing stones" or "glowing
lava." [14]

The text of Ps. 11:6 is corrupt. Most scholars have adopted the conjectural
reading *pacham 'esh,* "coal of fire," or (following Bickell) *pachame 'esh,* "coals
of fire." But in view of Ps. 140:11(10) and what has been said about it above, it
seems better to read *gechalim,* "coals," or *gachale 'esh,* "coals of fire," here.

A later echo of this idea of judgment is to be found in Prov. 25:22: good
deeds that a person does for his enemy are like coals which he heaps upon his
head. [15]

3. *In Theophanies.* When Yahweh himself appears for judgment, he appears
in powerful cosmic theophanies (cf. Ps. 18:8-16[7-15]=2 S. 22:8-16; Ps. 77:17-
20[16-19]; Isa. 29:6; etc.). "Coals" play a significant role in OT descriptions of
theophanies along with fire (→ אֵשׁ *'ēsh*), lightning, smoke, and consuming fire.

a. "Coals" appears twice in the very ancient storm theophany in Ps. 18:8-16
(7-15) par.: vv. 9 and 13 (8 and 12).

"Smoke went up from his nostrils, and devouring fire from his mouth; glowing
coals flamed forth from him" (v. 9[8]). The line dealing with "coals" is usually
regarded as a secondary expansion. [16] In reality, this is a cultic addition: the coals
which burn before Yahweh are nothing other than the fire kindled in his honor
in the temple, transformed into the coals of his anger, which now brings about the

---

[11] See below, c.

[12] W. Zimmerli, *BK,* XIII, 233.

[13] See below, 3.

[14] Cf. already Gunkel, *GHK,* II/2, 41.

[15] Perhaps following an Egyptian prototype; see H. Ringgren, *ATD,* XVI, 103; cf. S
Morenz, *ThLZ,* 78 (1953), 187-192; L. Ramaroson, *Bibl,* 51 (1970), 230-34.

[16] H.-J. Kraus, *BK,* XV, 138.

final judgment with special destructive power. Here also the motif of coals has
an intensifying function and is occasioned by Lev. 16:12 in combination with
Ezk. 10:2. In any case, this explanation is more natural than the suggestions that
"whatever the fiery breath of His anger reached became coals, were kindled, and
burned like coals."[17] The situation is different in v. 13(12): "Out of the brightness before him there broke through his clouds hailstones and coals of fire."
Here the "coals" are a part of the original text. This makes it very difficult to
interpret this verse, thus explaining why commentators usually pass over it in
polite silence. *gachale 'esh* is mentioned in connection with hail. The simplest
interpretation would be "hail and lightning." Then *gachale 'esh* is understood
as being synonymous with lightning, or is used to amplify the destructive power
of lightning (as in Ps. 18:9[8]; Ezk. 24:11). But it is likely that the idea of a
storm is abandoned in the use of coals here, and a volcanic element is introduced (cf. Ps. 11:6; 140:11[10]). In this case, Ps. 18:13(12) contains a combination of motifs taken from the appearance of a storm and from a volcanic eruption.
But this combination is already represented in the fundamental theophany at
Sinai (Ex. 19), to which Ps. 18:8-16(7-15) is also related theologically (cf. Ex.
19:16,19; 20:18,21 [E]; with 19:18; 20:18 [J]).

Be this as it may, in the theophanies of judgment that shake the foundations
of the earth, Yahweh's burning anger is made concrete and his irresistible power
is made manifest. The motif of coals in the OT is composed of two elements:
the glowing coals or lava stones, with which Yahweh covers whole cities, or
which he hurls down on the evildoer, reveal his wrath to a special degree, and
the continuing heat of the coals manifests the finality of his judgment, from
which no one can escape.

b. "Coals" are mentioned only once in later texts, in the vision of Ezekiel's
call (Ezk. 1:13). Here their use is wholly in keeping with the traditional elements
of the description of theophanies. It is not possible to find a special meaning for
"coals" in this passage.[18]

Fuhs

---

[17] C. A. and E. G. Briggs, *Psalms, I. ICC;* similarly F. Nötscher, *Psalmen, EB,* 43.
[18] W. Eichrodt, *ATD,* XXII, 7; G. A. Cooke, *Ezekiel. ICC,* 15; Zimmerli, *BK,* XIII, 54f.

גִּיחוֹן **gîchôn**

Contents: I. Spring in Jerusalem. II. River of Paradise. III. Streams of the City of God.

I. Spring in Jerusalem. *gichon*, "Gihon," is the name of a spring in Jerusalem, the modern 'Ain Umm ed-Dereğ, "the spring of steps," which Christians called 'Ain Sittī Maryām, "the spring of Mary." The cognate verb *giach*, "to burst forth," is used of the bursting forth of water from the "womb" in Job 38:8, and in a similar mythical way in 40:23. Therefore, it probably means "to gush forth."

The fact that Gihon is a proper name shows that a spring was of great importance to a city. But this can also be concluded from the extensive tunnel system of accesses and diversions in Ophel, which to some extent come from the pre-Israelite period.[1] These probably played a role in David's conquest of Jerusalem (cf. the corrupt text in 2 S. 5:8 with the *tsinnor* interpreted as a "water shaft").[2] Since there is an old wall tower above the Gihon spring, Kenyon thinks that the water gate of Old Jerusalem was located here, which was used in peace time but was closed in war time.[3] According to 2 K. 25:4, apparently a conduit led the outflow of the Gihon spring along the hillside to water the "king's garden." Finally, Hezekiah built the most magnificent tunnel in Jerusalem to guard against the Assyrian threat; he "closed the upper outlet of the waters of Gihon and directed them down to the west side of the city of David" (2 Ch. 32:30; cf. also vv. 3f. and 33:14). Thus, Hezekiah's tunnel brought the water of the Gihon spring from the Kidron Valley to the Tyropoeon Valley, where the modern Pool of Siloam is located (originally this pool was probably a covered water reservoir). From this point, the water flowed into another underground canal along the western slope of Ophel toward the south.[4] The Siloam Inscription, which was discovered in 1880, attests to the joy of those who built the tunnel over the success of their work.[5] The Gihon spring was the place where Solomon was anointed king–an important event in Israel's history (1 K. 1:33-40).

---

gîchôn. G. A. Barrois, "Gihon (Spring)," *IDB*, II (1962), 396; Th. A. Busink, *Der Tempel von Jerusalem*, I (Leiden, 1970), 81, 90; G. Cornfeld–G. J. Botterweck, *Die Bibel und ihre Welt*, II (1969), "Wasserversorgung"; M. Dahood, *Psalms*, III. *AB*, XVII A (1970), 119f.; G. R. Driver, "Water in the Mountains!" *PEQ*, 102 (1970), 83-91; K. Kenyon, *Jerusalem: Excavating Three Thousand Years of History* (1968), 15f., 31, 69-71; H.-J. Kraus, *Psalmen. BK*, XV (³1966); H. Lesêtre, "Gihon," *DB*, III (1903), 239-241; M. Saebø, *Sacharja 9-14. WMANT*, 34 (1969), 300-305, 116, 121ff.; H. Schmid, "Jahwe und die Kulturtraditionen von Jerusalem," *ZAW*, 67 (1955), 168-197, esp. 187f.; J. Simons, *Jerusalem in the OT* (Leiden, 1952), 157-194; F. Stolz, *Strukturen und Figuren im Kult von Jerusalem. BZAW*, 118 (1970), 217; H. Vincent, *Jérusalem de l'AT*, I (1954), 260-64; C. Westermann, *Genesis. BK*, I (1970), 293-98; W. Zimmerli, *Ezechiel. BK*, XIII (1969), 1186-1201.

[1] Cf. Simons, 162-194.
[2] Similarly Busink, 81, 90.
[3] Kenyon, 31.
[4] *Ibid.*, 69ff.
[5] *KAI²*, 189.

The OT does not give any reason why this place was chosen for Solomon's anointing. It probably goes back to an ancient custom, possibly dating from the Jebusite period. It is possible that a similar unexplained motif in Ps. 110:7 may be connected with anointing at the spring: "he will drink from the brook by the way; therefore he will lift up his head." Many scholars think this simply refers to a refreshment of the king in battle (cf. v. 6). But since Ps. 110 is a Song of Accession to the Throne (vv. 1,3), the drink could also be a part of the rite of the festival, [6] which may have a parallel in Ugaritic material. [7] Drinking and lifting up the head could be expressions meaning that God strengthens and "lifts up" the king, as we find in Ps. 89:20 (Eng. v. 19) (of David); 92:11(10) (in connection with anointing); 3:4(3); 75:8(7); etc. Thus, because of the relationship between the ideas in Ps. 110 and the prophecy of Nathan in 2 S. 7:12-16 (son, being begotten, priesthood, everlasting dominion), the spring, as a traditional place for anointing kings, was important for the succession of David to the throne and for his dynasty.

II. River of Paradise. While *gichon,* "Gihon," occurs 5 times in the MT of the OT as the name of a spring, once it denotes the second river that goes out of → עֵדֶן *'ēdhen,* "Eden." In spite of the indication that the rivers flowing out of Eden were understood geographically (Gen. 2:11f.), this does not seem to be the only way they were interpreted. *gichon* is not the name of a real river, and the same is true of *pishon,* "Pishon" (*push,* "to stamp, spring, jump"). Further, Gunkel calls attention to the fact that the Tigris is mentioned before the Euphrates, and thus the other two rivers are to be sought in the "mythical" north. [8] In any case, the context indicates that all the watercourses of the earth come from Eden. Therefore, we must consider whether perhaps the spring of Jerusalem is connected mentally with the river of Paradise that has the same name, so that Zion was looked upon as the center of the world, from which all watercourses come, symbolizing salvation from God.

III. Streams of the City of God. The Song of Zion, Ps. 46, shows that presumably, in ancient time, people spoke of "watercourses" in the city of Yahweh (vv. 5f.[4f.]): "a river whose streams make glad the city of God, the holy habitation of the Most High." We cannot be sure whether the concept of the power of fertility of the god Shalem stands behind the idea of the fertility-giving river. [9]

If Gen. 2:10ff. praises the place of the garden of God because of its abundant supply of water which is able to supply the earth with its four great rivers, and if Ps. 46 extols the city of God as the place that maintains life by God's rivers of water, then Ezk. 47 praises in particular the wonder of a fulness of blessing springing forth from small beginnings. [10]

---

[6] Mowinckel, *Psalmenstudien,* II, 101.

[7] *CTA,* 19 [I D], 152.

[8] Gunkel, *Genesis* ([7]1966), 8f.

[9] Stolz, 217.

[10] Zimmerli, 1186-1201.

It is obvious that the "water issuing from below the threshold of the temple" in Ezk. 47:1 represents an idealization of the *gichon*. This water becomes ever wider and deeper, makes the water of the Dead Sea fresh, and causes paradisiacal fertility (47:9,12). According to Joel 4:18(3:18), "a fountain (spring) shall come forth from the house of Yahweh and water the valley of acacias (Shittim)." Ps. 65:10(9) says that this blessing comes from God. Here, also, the reference to Zion and the temple is clear (vv. 2,5[1,4]). The rite of drawing water was practiced at the Feast of Tabernacles (*Sukkah* iv.9).[11] Mowinckel thinks this custom is "probably very old."[12] He traces it back to the promise in Isa. 12:3: "With joy you will draw water from the wells of salvation" (cf. Ps. 36:9f.[8f.]). In Isa. 55:1, Yahweh invites those who are thirsty to come to him, and v. 3b mentions the promise to David. But anyone who is unfaithful to Yahweh is like a person who "forsakes the fountain (spring) of living water" (Jer. 2:13; 17:13; Isa. 8:6).

Like Isa. 55:1,5, Zec. 14:8 introduces a universal element into our picture. It states that there is a spring that flows the year round in Jerusalem, and its water overflows into the western and the eastern sea. This denotes salvation for all the earth, because Yahweh will become king over all the earth (v. 9). This description differs from Ezk. 47 in that it does not mention the temple as the place where the spring is located (although it does assume this), the river flows in two directions, and the reference to the rivers of Paradise is clearer. The life-giving river flows out of Jerusalem all year round, and it will make the land, which was "like a desert," return, revive, and become fruitful. The distinction is even clearer if one differentiates between three sources, with Saebø: the original source (vv. 6,7b), a second traditional source influenced by Ezekiel (vv. 8,10aα,11), and a third traditional source (vv. 7a,9,10aβ b) which speaks primarily of Yahweh's kingship and the exaltation of Jerusalem.[13] Since Yahweh gives the nations native rights in Zion, they can say of Zion with Ps. 87:7: "All my springs are in you" (assuming that one retains the MT).[14] Passages such as this, which combine the concept of salvation in the End Time, where God rules over all nations, with the picture of the water of Zion glorified paradisiacally, permit the assumption that *gichon* in its twofold use is more than merely a geographical designation.

One who admits references to motifs on the basis of similarities of words could also appeal to the passage in Isa. 2:2-5 for the concept of the magnificent universality of salvation. Here the nations "flow" (*nahar*, 2:2–Gen. 2:10ff.) to Zion, and the torah (law, instruction) of Yahweh "goes forth" (*yatsa'*) from there (2:3–Gen. 2:10; Ezk. 47:1). Jesus ben Sira, who describes the wisdom of the law as an ever expanding stream and the bottomless sea (Sir. 24:23-33 in the LXX; cf. esp. vv. 30-32), and compares it with the four rivers of Paradise (together with the Jordan, vv. 25-27), probably saw this connection. He saw it explicitly in connection with Ezk. 47 and the *gichon*, and then attributed to it a theologically significant symbolism.

Eising

---

11 St.-B., II, 799-805.
12 Mowinckel, *Psalmenstudien*, II, 100f.
13 Saebø, 304f.
14 Cf. Kraus, *BK*, XV, 452f.

גִּיל gyl; גִּילָה gîlāh

Contents: I. In Ancient Near Eastern Languages: 1. Egyptian; 2. Akkadian; 3. West Semitic. II. 1. The Root; 2. Etymology; 3. Meaning. III. 1. Occurrences; 2. Conjectures; 3. Frequency in Various Parts of the OT; 4. Verb Forms; 5. Constructions. IV. 1. Synonyms; 2. Antonyms; 3. Ancient Versions. V. 1. "Secular" Usage; 2. Early History; 3. "Sacral" Usage.

I. In Ancient Near Eastern Languages.

1. *Egyptian.* The abundance of Egyptian words that are usually translated "joy," "to rejoice," etc. is astonishing.[1] Frequently we find a group of more or less synonymous words for joy in descriptions of the festive mood which is experienced in the main feasts at the temple. We find these words in the temple of Isis at Philae: "Heaven is in a festive mood, the earth in a happy disposition, the temples are sustained by radiant joy, the gods are in exultation, the goddesses rejoice, men are joyful when they see this, their great memorial."[2] The term translated "happy disposition" or "radiant joy" here means literally "malachite" or "colored glass," but is used figuratively as an expression for "radiant joy," which is the opposite of "carnelian," possibly "grief."[3] Some expressions for "joy" contain the word "heart" (*ib*), thus indicating that joy is anchored in the inner part of man (*ʒw.t-ib, wnf-ib, ndm-ib,* etc.).[4]

2. *Akkadian.* It is probably not accidental that Heb. *gyl* belongs to the same class of roots as Akk. *riāšum (râšu).* A part of the *ayin-yodh* verb belongs to the class of verbs denoting "bodily functions,"[5] which also includes expressions which we interpret as psychical processes. Thus *râšu*[6] means "to rejoice, exult," and differs from *ḫadû,* "to rejoice,"[7] in that it is not connected with *libbu,*

---

gyl. R. Bultmann, "ἀγαλλιάομαι," *TDNT,* I, 19-21; F. Crüsemann, *Studien zur Formgeschichte von Hymnus und Danklied in Israel. WMANT,* 32 (1969), 19-80; D. W. Harvey, in *Israel's Prophetic Heritage. Essays in Honor of J. Muilenburg* (New York, 1962), 116ff.; P. Humbert, "Laetari et exultare dans le vocabulaire religieux de l'AT," *RHPR,* 22 (1942), 185-214=*Opuscules d'un hébraisant* (Neuchâtel, 1958), 119-145; L. Kopf, "Arabische Etymologien und Parallelen zum Bibelwörterbuch," *VT,* 9 (1959), 247-287, esp. pp. 249f., 276f.; J. J. Stamm, "Zum Personennamen Abigail," *Hebräische Wortforschung. Festschrift für W. Baumgartner. SVT,* 16 (1967), 316ff.; C. Westermann, "גִּיל 'jauchzen'," *THAT,* I, 415-18.

[1] See *WbÄS,* VI, 55, *s.v.* "Freude, sich freuen," cf. *ibid.,* 84, *s.v.* "Jubel, jubeln"–references are made to approximately fifty different roots here.

[2] H. Junker, *Der grosse Pylon des Tempels der Isis* (1958), 110, 1ff.

[3] *WbÄS,* II, 56, *mfkȝ.t;* V, 391, *ṯḥn.*

[4] For the important motif of joy in connection with Isis, who appears not only as a mourner but also as a goddess of joy, see J. Bergmann, *Ich bin Isis* (Uppsala, 1968), 141ff.

[5] Von Soden, *Grundriss der akkadischen Grammatik* (1952), § 101o.

[6] *AHw,* 979f.

[7] *CAD,* VI, 25ff.

"heart," *kabittu*, "liver," etc. Thus, *râšu* (like *šululu*, from *alālu*) [8] has reference to joy which is expressed audibly, while *ḥadû* places more emphasis on the feeling, and also denotes goodwill, pleasure, etc. *ḥadû* is often connected with *râšu* and *šululu*, e.g., in EnEl II, 112, 114: "My father, rejoice (*ḥadû*) and exult (*šululu*); you will conquer Tiamat." In the *kalû* ritual, Nisaba is addressed as the one who causes the fields to rejoice (the context also speaks of *ḥegallu*, "plenty"). [9] Marduk takes a road of exultation (*šululu*), joy (*rišāti*), and homage to Babylon, the people greet his splendor with exultation (*šululu*). [10] The whole world rejoices and exults at the mention of the name of Ashurbanipal. [11] In oaths, very often we encounter wishes like this: "May Enlil rejoice over you, may Ea be joyful over you"; [12] such a wish is directed to a deity and is intended to attain his mercy.

3. *West Semitic*. In the Ugaritic texts we encounter *g(y)l*, [13] *ḥd(y)*, and *šmḥ*. The last two are found in parallelism in *CTA*, 18 [III D], I, 8f. (the context is broken) and 3 [V AB], V, 28ff.: "Do not rejoice, do not be joyful" (I will defeat you). *šmḥ* is used of joy over a victory (5, II, 20; 3, II, 26), the death of Baal (6, I, 39), the resurrection of Baal (6, III, 14), the building of Baal's temple (4, II, 28; V, 82, 97; VI, 35), and the life and immortality of Keret (16, I, 14; II, 99).

In Aramaic and Phoenician inscriptions we encounter *ḥdy*, [14] while *šmḥ* appears only rarely (Pun.). [15]

Bergman–Ringgren

II. 1. *The Root*. Outside Hebrew, the root *gyl* occurs for certain only in Ugaritic; [16] therefore, it does not seem to be found in East Semitic and South Semitic languages.

2. *Etymology*. Some scholars have attempted to determine the original meaning of *gyl* by appealing to roots in Arabic which have a similar form. Th. Nöldeke, J. Palache, [17] and P. Humbert [18] connect it with Arab. *ǧāla* (*ǧwl*), "to turn, revolve." Humbert argues that *gyl* means "to rejoice," and connects it with the ecstatic cries of cult participants or dervishes "whirling" in their dances. Kopf goes in a different direction by connecting *gyl* with Arab. *ǧalla* (*ǧll*), "to be great, high, exalted." Thus, he thinks *gyl* means "to rejoice," because this provides a credible

---

[8] *CAD*, I, 331f.

[9] Thureau-Dangin, *Rituels accadiens* (1921), 26.

[10] IV R 20, No. 1,12ff.; see *BAss*, 5, 340f.

[11] M. Streck *Assurbanipal. VAB*, VII (1916), 260, 13.

[12] Ebeling, *Die akk. Gebetsserie 'Handerhebung'* (1953), 64, line 23.

[13] See below, II.1.

[14] *DISO*, 82.

[15] *Ibid.*, 308.

[16] *CTA*, 16 [II K], I-II, 15, 99: *ngln*, // *nšmḥ*.

[17] See *KBL³*, 182.

[18] P. Humbert, 213, or 144.

etymology, and other verbs meaning "to rejoice" have an earlier meaning, "to be high" (e.g., *samach, rum*). Neither of these two derivations is convincing. [19]

3. *Meaning.* Since *gyl* is frequently parallel to and even synonymous with → שָׂמַח *śāmach*, "to rejoice," → שׂישׂ/שׂושׂ *śûś/śîś*, "to exult," → רָנַן *rānan*, "to cry aloud," → עָלֵז *ʿālaz*, "to exult," → רוּעַ *rûaʿ* in the hiphil, "to shout," → פָּצַח *pātsach*, "to break forth with joyous shout," → *hālal*, "to praise," etc., it seems most likely that it has reference to an act of expressing joy in spontaneous, enthusiastic cries. It is no longer possible to know whether the various verbs or substantives ever denoted different kinds of joyful cries. The usual translation of *gyl* by "rejoice" or "exult" conveys the meaning only approximately. There is an increasing synonymity between the verbs meaning "to rejoice" in the postexilic period. [20] According to Rudolph, the "onomatopoetic" character of the root is clear from the difficult *yaghilu*, "they (the idolatrous priests) shall exult," in Hos. 10:5. [21] He suggests that *gyl* is a *verbum anceps* (a two-edged verb), which can mean "to rejoice" or "to lament with a shrill cry." But this can hardly be established on the basis of Hos. 10:5 alone. [22]

III. 1. *Occurrences.* The verb *gyl* appears 45 times in the MT, and the cognate substantives *gil* and *gilah* together occur 10 times. The proper name *ʾabhighayil*, "Abigail," "my Father is Joy" (17 times), also seems to contain this root. [23] The Qumran literature has six examples of the verb, and two of the noun *gilah*. [24] The subst. *gil* occurs once in the Oxyrhynchus Papyri. [25]

2. *Conjectures.* The MT is uncertain in eight passages: Hos. 9:1 (read *ʾal taghel*, "thou shalt not rejoice," instead of *ʾel gil*, "unto rejoicing"); 10:5 (read *yelilu*, "they will howl," instead of *yaghilu*, "they will rejoice"?); Isa. 9:2 (Eng. v. 3) (read *haggilah*, "the rejoicing," instead of *haggoy loʾ*, "the nation, not"); Mic. 1:10 (read *ʾal taghilu*, "you shall not rejoice," instead of *ʾal taggidhu*, "you shall not tell"?); Ps. 2:11 (read *beraghelav*, "on his feet," instead of *veghilu*, "and rejoice" + *br*); [26] 43:4 (read *simchathi ʾaghilah*, "[in God] my joy let me rejoice," instead of *simchath gili*, "my exceeding joy"); Job 3:22 (read *ʾele ghal*, "over a heap," instead of *ʾele ghil*, "unto joy"); and Isa. 35:2 (read *gilah*, the abs., instead of *gilath*, the const.). If we adopt these suggested emendations, the occurrences of the root *gyl* in the OT are changed only slightly: 46 verb forms and 8 noun forms, a total of 54 occurrences.

3. *Frequency in Various Parts of the OT.* *gyl* and its derivatives are not distributed equally throughout the biblical books. They occur 25 times in the

---

[19] On the root *gl*, cf. further G. J. Botterweck, *BBB*, 3 (1952), 32-36.

[20] On the meaning of *samach* and *sus/sis*, see below, III.1.

[21] W. Rudolph, *KAT*, XIII/1 (1966), 196.

[22] Rudolph, like many others, thinks that *gilu*, "rejoice," in Ps. 2:11 is a textual error.

[23] See Stamm.

[24] See K. G. Kuhn, *Konkordanz zu den Qumrantexten* (1960), 44c; *Nachträge*, 187a.

[25] *VT*, 1 (1951), 51, line 7.

[26] See *BHK/BHS*.

prophets, 23 times in the Psalms (with 1 Ch. 16:31), 5 times in Proverbs, and once each in Canticles and Job, a total of 55 times. Consequently, this root is not found in the Pentateuch, the historical books, Ezekiel, and probably Jeremiah (48:33 is secondary). At least the following texts using this root come from the preexilic period: Hos. 9:1; 10:5 (text ?); Isa. 9:2b(3b); Hab. 1:15; 3:18; Ps. 21:2 (1); 45:16(15); 2:11(?). gyl occurs in postexilic texts in Deutero-Isaiah (41:16; 49:13), Trito-Isaiah (61:10; 65:18,19); Joel (1:16; 2:21,23); and Zechariah (9:9; 10:7); as well as in secondary passages in Isaiah (16:10; 25:9; 29:19; 35:1f.); Jeremiah (48:33); and Zephaniah (3:17). In the remaining passages in which this root appears (Ps. 9:15[14]; 13:5f.[4f.]; 14:7=53:7[6]; 16:9; 31:8 [7]; 32:11; 35:9; 43:4[?]; 48:12[11]; 51:10[8]; 65:13[12]; 89:17[16]; 96:11; 97:1,8; 118:24; 149:2; Prov. 2:14; 23:24f.; 24:17; Job 3:22[?]; Cant. 1:4) a preexilic date is very problematic.

4. *Verb Forms.* The use of the verb gyl (found only in the qal in the OT; the hiphil also appears in 1QM 12:13 and 19:5, but with an intransitive meaning)[27] indicates a remarkable limitation in its forms, which express either a present or a future action:

It is used in the present sense (denoting a habitual act or a condition) 11 times: Isa. 9:2(3); Hos. 10:5; Hab. 1:15; Ps. 16:9; 21:2(1); 48:12(11); 89:17(16); 97:8; Prov. 2:14; 23:24f.; cf. Ugar. *ngln;*[28] 1QM 17:8; 1QH 9:35.

It occurs in the future sense (conveying the idea of a promise or expectation) 10 times: Ps. 14:7=53:7(6); 35:9; Isa. 29:19; 35:1f.; 41:16; 65:19; Zeph. 3:17; Zec. 10:7; with a negative, Ps. 13:5(4); cf. 1QH 12:22.

It appears as a cohortative 6 times: 1st person sing.–Hab. 3:18; Ps. 9:15(14); 31:8(7); 1st person pl.–Ps. 118:24; Isa. 25:9; Cant. 1:4; cf. 1QM 13:13.

It is found in the imperative 8 times: fem. sing.–Isa. 49:13; Joel 2:21; Zec. 9:9; pl.–Ps. 32:11; Isa. 65:18; 66:10; Joel 2:23; Ps. 2:11 (text ?); cf. 1QM 12:13; 19:5.

It occurs in the jussive 8 times: 3rd person sing.–Ps. 13:6(5); 96:11; 97:1; 1 Ch. 16:31; Isa. 61:10; 3rd person pl.–Ps. 51:10(8); 149:2; with a negative, Prov. 24:17; Hos. 9:1 (with the emended text); Mic. 1:10 (with the emended text).

Accordingly, gyl is not used to express individual, isolated events of the past; only verbs closely connected with gyl, like *samach, rua', sus,* and *ranan,* are used in this way.

5. *Constructions.* Frequently gyl and its derivatives stand alone in the sentence, i.e., without any direct reference to the cause or object of the "rejoicing": cf. Hos. 9:1; Hab. 1:16; Joel 1:16; Zec. 9:9; Ps. 14:7=53:7(6); 43:4; 51:10(8); 65:13(12); 96:11; 97:1; Prov. 23:24f.

When there is such a reference, as a rule gyl is used with *be,* "in" (21 times), but also twice each with *'al,* "upon, at," and *lema'an,* "for the sake of, on account

---

[27] Contra *KBL*[3], 182a.
[28] See above, II.1.

of" (Ps. 48:12[11]; 97:8). *ki* clauses giving a reason ("for, because") occur in Ps. 13:5(4); 16:9f.; Isa. 49:13; 65:18; Joel 2:21,23. Independent clauses in the immediate context can express the reason for the "rejoicing" (e.g., *yhvh malakh taghel ha'arets*, "Yahweh reigns, let the earth rejoice," Ps. 97:1; cf. 96:10f.; *gili me'odh... hinneh malkekh yabho'*, "Rejoice greatly,... lo, your king comes," Zec. 9:9).

Humbert's analysis of the various constructions using *gyl*[29] is lacking in many respects, and needs to be supplemented and corrected.

Usually the subject of *gyl* is man as an individual or in specific groups or communities. In statements concerning the future (Isa. 35:1f.) and in hymnic "calls to rejoice" (Ps. 96:11; 97:1; Isa. 49:13; Joel 2:21), even certain aspects of nature may be said to rejoice (cf. Ps. 65:13 [12]). God appears as the subject of *gyl* only in Isa. 65:19 and Zeph. 3:17 (referring to Jerusalem, the people of God); cf. 1QH 9:35; 1QM 3:11.

IV. 1. *Synonyms*. From the postexilic period on, the verbs *samach*, *sus*, *ranan*, *rua'* in the hiphil, *halal* in the piel, *'alaz*, *patsach*, *shir*, "to sing," *zamar* in the piel, "to make melody (music)," *yadhah* in the hiphil, "to give thanks, praise," and their derivatives are to be regarded as "synonyms" of *gyl*. Most frequently, *gyl* stands in parallelism with *samach*, "to rejoice" (36 times; the same is true in Ugar.); in the majority of these cases *samach* occurs in the first line (25 times; this is also the case in Ugar. and 4 times in 1QM). Less frequently, *gyl* is found in parallelism with *sus*, "to rejoice, exult" (8 times), and *ranan*, "to cry aloud" (4 times; both also appear in parallelism with *gyl* in 1QM). *gyl* is used in parallelism with *rua'* in the hiphil, "to shout aloud" (Zec. 9:9); *halal* in the hithpael, "to praise" (Isa. 41:16); *'alaz*, "to exult" (Hab. 3:18); *shir*, "to sing" (Ps. 13:6[5]); *patsach*, "to break forth with joyous shout" (Isa. 49:13); and *saphar*, "to recount" (Ps. 9:15[14]).

Crüsemann argues that the verbs *samach*, *gyl*, *sus*, *rua'*, *ranan*, *'alaz*, *patsach*, and *tsahal*, "to cry shrilly," all denote manifestations of joy "without spoken and sung words." This is the feature that distinguishes them from the verbs used in the imperative hymn, such as *shir*, *halal* in the piel, *zamar*, *yadhah* in the hiphil, *zakhar* in the hiphil, "to call upon, praise," *naghadh* in the hiphil, "to declare, tell," and so forth, for which articulate language is typical.[30] It must also be asked to what extent this distinction in meaning plays a role in the passages where *gyl* appears in parallelism with these words. In comparison with *gyl*, *samach*, as a comprehensive word for "joy," covers a much wider range of meaning.

2. *Antonyms*. Prominent words, moods, sounds, and gestures of the mourner are used to express the opposite of *gyl* and its synonyms, especially → אבל *'ābhal*, "to mourn," → בכה *bākhāh*, "weep," → ספד *sāphadh*, "lament," and → צום *tsûm*, "fast." The summons to rejoice (*samach*, *gil*) over Jerusalem in Isa. 66:10 is

---

29 Humbert, 137.
30 Crüsemann, 47-58.

addressed to those who now mourn (*'abhal*) over her. In a similar way, the
mourning, dried up ground (*'adhamah*) (Joel 1:10) is summoned to rejoice (2:21).
The contrast between *gil* and *'abhal* in Hos. 10:5 does not fit the context. [31] According to Isa. 65:18f., the people of Jerusalem will hear *gilah*, "rejoicing," and
masos, "joy," instead of *ze'aqah*, "distress," and *bekhi*, "weeping"; cf. also the
contrasts in Ps. 30:6(5) (*bekhi–rinnah*, "weeping"–"joy"); Isa. 22:2,4 (*bekhi–
'allizah*, "weep"–"exultant"); Ps. 137:1,3 (*bkh–smḥ*, "wept"–"mirth"); Isa. 25:8f.
(*dim'ah–gil*, "tears"–"be glad"); and Joel 1:13-16; 2:12-17,23 (*bakhah*, "weep,"
tsum, "fast," *saphadh*, "lament," *za'aq*, "cry out," etc.–*gil*, "rejoice"). Because
of the textual corruption in Mic. 1:10, it is not certain whether a wordplay is
intended on the place names (*bakhah–gil*, "weep"–"rejoice"). [32]

3. *Ancient Versions.* Three Greek words are used to translate *gyl* in the
LXX: *agalliáomai*, "to exult, be glad," and its derivatives (27 times); *chaírō*,
"rejoice, be glad," and its derivatives (10 times); and *euphraínō*, "gladden,
cheer," and its derivatives (5 times). These same words are used to translate
samach, *sus*, *ranan*, *'alaz*, etc., and therefore the LXX does not interpret *gyl* in
a specific way. The Vulgate understands *gyl* (and sometimes *ranan*, *rum* in the
polel, "extol," etc.) as expressing the most intensive type of joy (*exultare*,
"exult"), in contrast to *samach* (*laetari*, "rejoice"), *sus* (*gaudere*, "rejoice, be
glad"), etc.

V. 1. *"Secular" Usage.* *gyl* and its cognates play an important role in certain
genres of the prophetic oracle and of the temple lyric poetry, [33] but they are by
no means limited to these types. In many passages, the "rejoicing" has nothing
to do with Yahweh or his deeds, but with a wide variety of experiences in "secular" life: bringing in the harvest (Isa. 16:10; Jer. 48:33; cf. *ranan*, *rua'* in the
hiphil, and *shir* in Ps. 65:9,14[8,13]); dividing the spoils of war (Isa. 9:2b[3b]);
the queen at her marriage (Ps. 45:16[15]); the royal bridegroom (Cant. 1:4);
the growth of one's own children (Prov. 23:24f.); the triumph of evil (Prov. 2:14)
and of world powers (Hab. 1:15); the misfortune of the godly (Ps. 13:5[4]) or of
one's enemy (Prov. 24:17); and the happiness of those in misery over being allowed to die (Job 3:22; cf. *samach* and *sis*, even if *gal* should be read instead
of *gil*). [34]

This "secular" use of *gyl* (13 times) does not seem to have been continued in
Middle Hebrew (yet cf. Sir. 30:22 in the diminished sense of "gladness" of heart),
although it shows that *gyl* and its derivatives appear in the colloquial speech of
preexilic and postexilic times.

2. *Early History.* The passages using *gyl* that are probably the oldest (Ugar.; [35]
Hos. 9:1; 10:5) seem to indicate a connection with pre-Israelitic cult practices.

---

[31] See above, III.2.
[32] See above, III.2.
[33] See above, III.3.
[34] See above, III.2.
[35] See above, II.1.

Following the example of Graham, [36] Humbert, [37] and Harvey, [38] Wolff [39] and Rudolph [40] in particular have maintained that there is an intimate connection between *gyl* (and *samach*) and the Canaanite fertility cults. According to Humbert, *gyl* is a word loaded with "heathen" overtones, which came to be used in the cultic and prophetic language of the postexilic period only after long opposition from Yahwism. The arguments in favor of this idea are unsatisfactory.

The isolated occurrence of *gyl* in Ugaritic does not favor this idea either, because the Keret Legend (text 125-128) "does not reveal any type of connection with fertility rites." [41] As far as Hos. 9:1 is concerned (*'al taghel ka'ammim,* "exult not like the peoples," according to the emended text), it should be kept in mind that this passage (in prophetic reversal of the hymnic "summons to rejoice") does not oppose the cultic expression of joy as such, but the expression of joy in connection with the Baal cult. [42] Also, no far-reaching conclusions can be made from *yaghilu 'al kebhodho,* "they shall rejoice over its (i.e., the calf of Beth-aven) glory," in Hos. 10:5, because of the uncertain text.

3. *"Sacral" Usage.* The use of *gyl* is theologically significant especially when it has reference to Yahweh, his deeds, way of behavior, or attributes. The following appear as the basis and subject of "rejoicing": Yahweh himself (Hab. 3:18; Isa. 29:19; 41:16; 61:10; Zec. 10:7; Joel 2:23; Ps. 35:9; 89:17[16]; 149:2; in conjunction with verbs in parallelism, Ps. 32:11; 43:4 emended); Yahweh's help (*yeshu'ah,* "deliverance," Ps. 9:15[14]; 13:6[5]; 21:2[1]; Isa. 25:9; and indirectly in Ps. 51:10[8]; 65:13[12]; Isa. 66:10; Joel 1:16), steadfast love (*chesedh,* Ps. 31:8[7]), and judgment (*mishpat,* 48:12[11]; 97:8); the appearance of his glory (*hadhar/kabhodh,* Isa. 35:1f.), and "the day which Yahweh has made" (Ps. 118:24). [43]

In spite of these numerous examples of the use of *gyl* in connection with the deeds of Yahweh (36 times, but only in the Psalms and the prophetic books), there is nothing to support the view that originally and essentially *gyl* meant "joy over an act of God." [44] The thesis that originally *gyl* denoted an expression of joy in the context of a Canaanite fertility cult [45] has just as little to support it. *gyl* and its cognates have a positive or a negative meaning, depending on the particular context in which they occur. The reasons for the absence of the root *gyl* in large portions of the OT traditions must be sought elsewhere.

Barth

---

36 W. C. Graham, *AJSL,* 47 (1931), 237ff.
37 P. Humbert, 207ff., or 140ff.
38 D. W. Harvey, 116ff.
39 H. W. Wolff, *BK,* XIV/1, 163, 197, 228.
40 Rudolph, *KAT,* XIII/1, 171.
41 O. Eissfeldt, "Ugarit," *RGG*³, VI, 1105.
42 Cf. Westermann, 418.
43 For reasons with *ki* or with independent clauses, see above, III.5.
44 Cf. Westermann, 417.
45 Humbert, etc.

גָּלָה gālāh; גּוֹלָה gôlāh; גָּלוּת gālûth

Contents: I. Occurrences, Meaning, Etymology: 1. Outside the OT; 2. In the OT. II. Secular Usage: 1. As a Term Meaning "To Be Away," "Go Away," "Lead Away"; 2. As a Term Meaning "To Be Open," "To Open," "Uncover": a. To Become Visible; b. To Become Audible. III. Religious Usage: 1. Parallel Ideas; 2. "To Be Open," "To Open," "Uncover," Referring to: a. The Eyes (Vision); b. The Ears (Audition); c. A Secret; d. Yahweh Himself. IV. Theological Considerations: 1. glh and the Theme, "The Revelation of God in the OT"; a. Distribution of the Term; b. Its Contribution to This Theme; 2. golah As a Designation for the Postexilic Cult Community.

I. Occurrences, Meaning, Etymology.

1. *Outside the OT.* Outside the OT, the verb glh occurs in Ugaritic and Phoenician. It is also found in Egyptian Aramaic, Jewish Aramaic, Syriac, Mandean, Arabic, Ethiopic, and Akkadian (as a foreign word). [1] Arabic has a noun derived from this root, *ğāliyat,* and Jewish Aramaic has a noun derived from it, *glwt.*

All six examples of *gly* in Ugaritic are in the perfect tense of the root. Five of these appear in the stereotyped expression, *y/tgly š₂d ʔl wy/tbʔ qrš mlk ʾb šnm,* [2] "he/she arrived at the mountain of El and came to the hall of the king, the father of years (?)." As here, so also in the last section of *CTA,* 16 [II K], VI, 4, *gly* is closely connected with *bʾ,* which is used four times in all in lines 2-3, 5, and which stands right next to *gly* in line 4: *tgly wtbʔ.* Gordon translates this verb, "to leave." [3] Thus, he thinks that *gly* is cognate to Arab. *ğalā,* "to emigrate," and that it is not synonymous with, but rather antithetical to, *bʾ,* "to come, arrive." [4] However, several Ugaritologists advocate an interpretation of

gālāh. O. Betz, *Offenbarung und Schriftforschung in der Qumransekte* (1960); W. Eichrodt, "Offenbarung, II. Im AT," *RGG³,* IV, 1599-1601; Y. M. Grintz, "Because they exiled a whole exile, to deliver to Edom," in *idem, Studies in Early Biblical Ethnology and History. Beth Mikra,* 13/1 (1969), 354-56 (Modern Heb.); H. Haag, "'Offenbaren' in der hebräischen Bibel," *ThZ,* 16 (1960), 251-58; *idem,* "Offenbarung, I. Im AT," *BL²,* 1242-48; R. Knierim, "Offenbarung im AT," *Probleme biblischer Theologie. Festschrift G. von Rad* (1971), 206-235; A. Oepke, "ἀποκαλύπτω, C. Revelation in the OT," *TDNT,* III, 571-77; E. Pax, ΕΠΙΦΑΝΕΙΑ. *MThS,* 1/10 (1955), 100-101; R. Rendtorff, "Offenbarung im AT," *ThLZ,* 85 (1960), 833-38; *idem,* "Offenbarungsvorstellungen im Alten Israel," *Offenbarung als Geschichte,* ed. W. Pannenberg (³1965)=*KuD,* Beiheft 1, 21-41; (G.) R(inaldi), "'zn (ʾōzen)," *BeO,* 9 (1967), 144; R. Schnackenburg, "Offenbarung, II. In der Schrift," *LThK²,* VII, 1106-1109; H. C. M. Vogt, *Studie zur nachexilischen Gemeinde in Esra-Nehemia* (1966), 22-43; 157f.; S. Wagner, "I. Sam. 9,15: 'Jahwe aber hatte das Ohr des Samuel geöffnet ...'," *Schalom. Festschrift A. Jepsen* (1971)=*Aufsätze und Vorträge zur Theologie und Religionswissenschaft,* 51, 65-72; W. Zimmerli, "'Offenbarung' im AT," *EvTh,* 22 (1962), 15-31.

[1] *KBL³.*
[2] *CTA,* 6 [I AB], I, 34-36; etc.
[3] *UT,* Glossary, No. 579.
[4] So T. H. Gaster, *Thespis* (1950), 288.

gly synonymous with *b'*, as, "to go after,"[5] "arrive at,"[6] "enter,"[7] "break in, penetrate,"[8] "approach, arrive at, enter,"[9] "step over (a threshold),"[10] or the like.

In Phoenician, the imperfect of the root *glh* occurs. The Aḥiram Inscription has as the object of *glh*, *'rn*,[11] and the Yeḥawmilk Inscription, *mstrv*.[12] In both cases, *glh* denotes the "uncovering" or "opening" of a sarcophagus or a hiding place.

In the other Semitic languages, the verb means "to open," "make manifest," or "emigrate," "go into exile," and the nouns are rendered by "colony of emigrants," or by "exile" or "exiles."

2. *In the OT*. The verb occurs about 180 times in Biblical Hebrew, 9 times in Biblical Aramaic, and 40 times in the Qumran literature. In Biblical Hebrew, the verb appears 44 times in the qal, 30 in the niphal, 57 in the piel, twice in the pual, 38 in the hiphil, 7 in the hophal, and twice in the hithpael. In Biblical Aramaic, it is found 7 times in the peal and twice in the haphel. The noun *golah* occurs 42 times in the Hebrew OT and twice in the Qumran literature (1QM 1:2, 3), and the noun *galuth* is found 15 times in the Hebrew OT, 4 times in the Aramaic part of the OT, and once in the Qumran material (1QpHab 11:6).

Arranged according to the frequency of occurrence, the Greek words used to translate the verb forms of *glh* are these: the qal–*apokalýptō*, "to uncover, reveal," *aichmalōtízō*, "to capture," *aichmálōtos*, "captive," *apoikízō*, "to send away, emigrate," *metoikízo*, "to deport, resettle," *aichmalōsía*, "captivity," *aichmalōteúō*, "to capture," *anakalýptō*, "to uncover, unveil," *anegnōsménos*, "read aloud, published," *apokinéō*, "to remove, put away from," *apoikía*, "colony," *eisakoúō*, "to listen to, obey," *helkýō*, "to drag or draw out," *epitássō*, "to order, command," *metoikesía*, "deportation," *prostássō*, "to order, command," *paúō*, "to stop, cease"; niphal–*apokalýptō*, "to uncover, reveal," *anakalýptō*, "to uncover, unveil," *ekkalýptō*, "to uncover, reveal," *anoígō*, "to open," *apérchomai*, "to go away, depart," *epiphaínomai*, "to appear," *phanerós*, "visible, clear," *horáō*, "to see," *aichmálōtos*, "captive," *próstagma deíknymi*, "to make know or explain a commandment"; piel–*apokalýptō*, "to uncover, reveal," *anakalýptō*, "to uncover, unveil," *apágō*, "to lead away," *katakalýptō*, "to cover, veil," *poiéō*, "to do, make"; pual–*apokalýptō*, "to uncover, reveal"; hiphil–*apoikízō*, "to send away, emigrate," *metoikízō*, "to deport, resettle," *metaírō*, "to go away," *aichmalōtízō*, "to capture"; hophal–*apoikízō*, "to send away, emigrate," *katoikízō*, "to settle, establish"; hithpael–*gymnóō*, "to strip, lay bare." This summary makes two things clear. On the one hand, *glh* has a wide variety of nuances of meaning; and on the other, these nuances revolve around

---

[5] Aistleitner, *WUS*.

[6] Jirku, *Texte*.

[7] Eissfeldt, *El im ugaritischen Pantheon* (1951), 30, and n. 4.

[8] Ginsberg, *Keret* (1946), 31; Driver, *CML*, 146b.

[9] Pope, *El in the Ugaritic Texts* (1955), 64-65.

[10] Gray, *The Krt Text* (²1964), 27.

[11] *KAI*, 1.2.

[12] *KAI*, 10.14f.

the two basic concepts, "to uncover," "reveal," and "to emigrate," "go away," "go into captivity." As Pope correctly remarks,[13] there is no serious reason to suppose two different roots *glh*. Emigration or exile can be understood as an uncovering of the land, and thus "revealing," "uncovering," could be the original meaning of *glh* (cf. Phoen.),[14] but one could also argue conversely. This would mean that *glh* should be interpreted as a verb of motion and traced back to Ugar. *gly*.

The Heb. nouns *golah* and *galuth,* which the LXX usually translates by *apoikesía,* "emigration," *metoikesía* "deportation," or *aichmalōsía,* "captivity," mean "exile" or "those who are exiled, exiles," and the same is true of the Biblical Aram. noun *galu,* "exile." They are derivatives of the root *glh* meaning "to go into exile," and are of as little help in determining the original meaning of this root as the occurrences of *glh* in the other Semitic languages.

II. Secular Usage. That the original meaning of *glh* must be sought behind the concepts "to reveal," "uncover," and "to emigrate," "go into exile," points to the prominent secular meaning of the verb, and thus explains the dominant secular use of this root in the OT.

1. *As a Term Meaning "To Be Away," "Go Away," "Lead Away."* The roots *sur,* "to pass away," in Am. 6:7 and Isa. 49:21, and *'arabh,* "to waste away, vanish," in Isa. 24:11, are used as synonyms of our verb *glh*. Hezekiah's statement, "my dwelling is plucked up (*nasa'* in the niphal) and removed from me" (Isa. 38:12), and the description of the fate of the ungodly in Job 20:28, "the possessions of his house will be carried away, dragged off in the day of God's wrath,"[15] show that *glh*, which can be connected with *min,* "from," or can be used alone, means "to be away" or "go away."

With the same content, then, *glh min* occurs in the explanation of Ichabod's name, "the glory has departed from Israel" (1 S. 4:21,22); Hos. 10:5, "it (the glory) must depart from it"; Lam. 1:3, "Judah has gone into exile because of affliction and hard servitude"; Mic. 1:16, "they shall go from you into exile"; and the expression "to go into exile away from his land" (*glh me'al 'adhmatho,* 2 K. 17:23; 25:21; Am. 7:11,17; Jer. 52:27), in connection with which the accusative of place can appear, as in 2 K. 17:23 (so also in 2 K. 24:15; Am. 1:5; with *'el,* "unto," in Ezk. 12:3). *glh,* "to go away," appears alone in Jgs. 18:30 (the land), Isa. 5:13 (my people), Jer. 1:3 (Jerusalem), Ezk. 39:23 (Israel), and Am. 5:5 (Gilgal).

In David's speech to Ittai, "you are an exile 'from' your home" (2 S. 15:19), and in Nah. 2:8 (Eng. v. 7), one should read the qal instead of the pual.[16]

The hiphil and hophal of *glh* mean exclusively, "to lead away (into captivity)" (the same is true of the haphel in Aram., Ezr. 4:10; 5:12), or "to be led away,"

---

[13] Pope, *El,* 64.
[14] Haag, *ThZ,* 251.
[15] Otherwise Fohrer, *KAT,* XVI, 325.
[16] On this and the interpretation of Prov. 27:25, see the comms.

and almost without exception refer to the exiles of Israel and Judah (otherwise only in 2 K. 16:9: Damascus; Am. 1:6: Gaza; 2 K. 17:11: the dispersion of foreign nations before Israel by Yahweh).

2. *As a Term Meaning "To Be Open," "To Open," "Uncover." glh* means "to be open," "to open," "uncover." This is also verified by verbs that appear in synonymous parallelism with *glh,* viz., *chasaph,* "to strip off" (Isa. 47:2; Jer. 49:10); *paqadh,* "to punish" (Lam. 4:22); *ra'ah,* "to see" or "be seen" (2 S. 22:16 = Ps. 18:16[15]; Isa. 40:5; 47:3; Nah. 3:5; Job 38:17; cf. Ezk. 16:37; 21:29 [24]; Hos. 2:12[10]), and similar terms, but even more clearly by verbs used in antithetic parallelism to *glh,* viz., *chabhah* in the niphal, "to hide oneself" (Jer. 49:10); *kasah,* "to cover," "to veil" (Isa. 26:21; Prov. 11:13; 26:26), and *sathar,* "to hide" (Isa. 16:3; Prov. 27:5; cf. Jer. 49:10: *mistarav,* "his hiding places"). It is also supported by Jer. 32:11,14, which mentions both the "sealed" (*chathum*) and the "open" (*galuy*) deed.

a. *To Become Visible.* The oracle of salvation in Isa. 49:9 shows that the concepts "to be open" and "to open" are used of the appearance of light or of daylight. Here the prophet says to the prisoners, "Come forth" (*tse'u*), and to those who are in darkness, "Come to light" (*higgalu*). And Job 12:22 praises Yahweh as the God "who uncovers the deeps out of darkness, and brings deep darkness to light." The most frequent object of *glh* in the piel (the pass. of which is the niphal) is *'ervah,* "shame," "nakedness." In this connection, the phrase "to uncover the shame" means either "to commit fornication" (Ex. 20:26; Lev. 18:6-19; 20:11,17-21; Ezk. 16:36,37; 22:10), which is emphasized in Ezk. 23:18 by the synonymous parallelism between *galah* (in the piel) *taznuth,* "to carry on harlotry openly," and *galah 'ervah,* "to uncover (RSV flaunt) nakedness," or "to rape" (Ezk. 23:10,29), as is clear from the parallelism between "your nakedness shall be uncovered" and "your shame shall be seen" in Isa. 47:3. The expression "to uncover one's nakedness" is found in connection with "uncovering the fountain of her blood" in Lev. 20:18, and "uncovering the skirt of his father" in Dt. 23:1(22:30); 27:20. We encounter a series of similar expressions as figures for fornication, shame, and utmost insult in the prophetic literature: Isa. 57:8, "uncover the bed," Hos. 2:12(10), "uncover lewdness (shame)," Isa. 47:2, "strip off the robe" and "uncover the legs," and Jer. 13:22 and Nah. 3:5, "lift up the skirts."

Other objects of *glh* in the piel, "to uncover," include "the feet" (Ruth 3:4,7), "the outer garment" of the crocodile (Job 41:5[13]), "the foundations" of Samaria (Mic. 1:6), "the foundation" of a wall (Ezk. 13:14), "the foundations" of the world (2 S. 22:16 = Ps. 18:16[15]), "the gates" of death (Job 38:17), and "the covering (that served as a protection for Judah)" (Isa. 22:8).

glh in the niphal + *'el* means "to show oneself to someone" (1 S. 14:8,11: Jonathan and his armorbearer to the Philistines), and + *le,* "to uncover oneself before someone" (2 S. 6:20: David before his maidens). Again, in these passages *glh* conveys the idea of becoming visible or becoming seen, as is emphasized even further in 2 S. 6:20 by *le'ene,* "before the eyes of." The hithpael also supports this in Gen. 9:21, where Ham saw the nakedness of Noah as he lay in the midst of his tent (v. 22), and in Prov. 18:2, which says that the fool "uncovers his heart," i.e., "displays his folly." [17]

b. *To Become Audible.* The phrases using *glh* that have to do with uncovering transgressions, etc., point to the element of hearing in this root. When the OT speaks of uncovering "iniquity (RSV, corruption)" (Hos. 7:1; Job 20:27; Lam. 2:14), "sins" (*chatto'th,* Lam. 4:22), "wickedness" (*ra'ah,* Prov. 26:26), "transgressions" (*pesha',* Ezk. 21:29[24]), and the "blood" of the slain (Isa. 26:21), a legal situation is always assumed (this is explicit in Prov. 26:26, which refers to the "legal assembly," *qahal*), in which the hidden crime is discussed. Jeremiah's desire to see God's vengeance on his fellow citizens from Anathoth, founded on the statement, "for to thee I have committed my cause" (→ רִיב *rîbh*), also presupposes this kind of situation, inasmuch as it is addressed to Yahweh, "who judgest righteously" (Jer. 11:20; 20:12). [18]

It is clear that the expression *glh* → סוֹד *sôdh,* "to reveal secrets" (Prov. 11:13; 20:19; 25:9), has in mind speaking, for "to reveal secrets" is to divulge them, and these passages characterize the person who does this as a slanderer in 11:13 and 20:19, and as a gossip in 20:19b.

Finally, another argument that justifies the conclusion that *glh,* "to be open," "to open," includes the twofold concept of becoming visible and becoming audible is that *'ayin,* "eye," and *'ozen,* "ear," both appear as objects of this verb. The expression, "to open the eyes," [19] which, to be sure, is found only in religious contexts, stands in contrast to several occurrences of the expression, "to open someone's ear," in the sense of "proclaiming something to someone," [20] in the secular realm: 1 S. 20:2 (Saul to Jonathan); 20:12,13 (Jonathan to David); 22:8 (twice; Saul's men to Saul); 22:17 (*qere;* the priests to Saul); Ruth 4:4 (Boaz to his kinsman who had the right of redemption). This last passage is of interest, because Boaz's inquiry to his kinsman who had the right of possession with regard to the acquisition of the property of Elimelech, which is introduced by *le'mor,* "saying," follows the expression, "I thought I would tell you of it." [21] We also encounter *glh le,* "to proclaim something to someone," "to make known," in Isa. 23:1 and Est. 3:14.

III. Religious Usage. In the preceding section, in showing the specific meanings of *glh,* we have already referred to a number of passages which, strictly speaking, use *glh* in a religious sense, because in these texts Yahweh, Elohim, or the like is subject of *glh.* The prophetic literature in particular speaks of uncovering the pudenda or something similar. [22] Jer. 33:6 should be included in these passages. We may also mention the statements that God sent Israel into

---

[17] Ringgren, *ATD,* XVI.
[18] Otherwise Rudolph, *HAT,* 12.
[19] Cf. III.2.a.
[20] Cf. Rinaldi.
[21] Cf. III.2.b.
[22] Cf. II.2.a.

exile (2 K. 17:11; Jer. 29:4,7,14; Ezk. 39:28; Am. 5:27; Lam. 4:22; 1 Ch. 5:41 [6:15]), which are very few in number when compared with the passages in which a human being appears as the subject of *glh*. All these statements belong to the secular realm directly, and thus indicate that, apart from the changed subject-object relationship, there is no functional difference between the secular and religious usage of *glh*.

1. *Parallel Ideas.* In Isa. 56:1, *bo'*, "to come," occurs in synonymous parallelism with *glh* in the niphal. This is noteworthy, because nowhere else in the OT do these words appear in such a relationship, although they may stand in juxtaposition in the Ugaritic texts. [23] In harmony with the secular linguistic usage, Dt. 29:28(29) contrasts the "secret things" with the "things that are revealed." In the religious realm, we also find examples in which *glh* is related to verbs meaning "to see," "look," "gaze upon": → ראה *rā'āh* in the qal, "to see" (Nu. 22:31; Isa. 40:5); in the niphal, "to appear" (1 S. 3:21); → נבט *nābhat* in the hiphil, "to behold" (Ps. 119:18); → חזה *chāzah*, "to see" (Nu. 24:4,16); as well as to verbs meaning "to speak" and "to hear": Job 36:10,11. It is true that there are no examples of *glh* being used in connection with *nabhat* and *chazah* in secular texts. Also, the parallelism between *glh* and → ידע *yādha'*, "to know," in Ps. 98:2 is unique.

This survey shows that the religious usage of *glh* is closely connected with the secular. But beyond this, it is now at least clearly suggested that when *glh* is used in the religious realm, it receives a new content which is made explicit by the selection of parallel terms to go with it, which give it the quality of a technical term for revelation in the OT.

2. *"To Be Open," "To Open," "Uncover."* As we have noted above, [24] *glh*, whose original meaning was "to be open," "to open," includes the elements of seeing and hearing. This helps explain why this verb was taken over into religious linguistic usage, because according to OT thought the revelation of God takes place in the form of a vision or an audition or of both together.

a. *Referring to the Eyes (Vision).* *glh* is used to describe the state of visionary emotion in the two Yahwistic Songs of Balaam (Nu. 24:4,16), where it says that the seer "sees the vision of Shaddai, falling down, but having his eyes uncovered." In spite of the fact that these two verses mention "hearing the words of El and knowing the knowledge of Elyon," and that on this basis it could be supposed that Balaam not only saw a vision but also heard a divine word, the content of these two songs is against this assumption, for they are presented as descriptions of figures that have been seen or as pictorial events, but not as reproductions of a divine word. If El, or more precisely El Shaddai, here is the author of the vision, in the J narrative it is Yahweh who "opened the eyes of Balaam that he might see the angel standing in the way" (Nu. 22:31), and who thus brought

[23] Cf. I.1.
[24] Cf. II.2.

about the following dialogue between the angel and the seer (vv. 32-35). Thus, in contrast to the pure vision in these songs, in the narrative material there is, as it were, a mixture of visionary and auditory elements.

The expression "to open the eyes" is used in a prayer in Ps. 119:18: "Open my eyes, that I may behold wondrous things out of thy Torah (law)." This text does not have in mind a visionary event. The worshipper yearns for "instruction";[25] he prays that understanding of the Torah (law), "judgment" and "knowledge," may be made known to him in the written word.[26] Nor is this passage referring to revelation, although the theme of the knowledge of God and of his acts is a part of its narrower circle. In the postexilic hymn, Ps. 98,[27] the "marvelous deeds" of v. 1 are explained in v. 2: "Yahweh has made known his help, he has revealed his righteousness in the sight of the *goyim* (nations)"; and v. 3 states that "the ends of the earth" see all this, and so they are to praise God with "all the earth" (v. 4). Consequently, revelation is an event in which Yahweh alone is subject. Its content is determined by the proclamation of God's salvation in his marvelous deeds, by the revelation of his righteousness; and its purpose is to bring foreigners to a knowledge of the divine majesty and thus to an acknowledgment of Yahweh in believing praise.

Finally, the passages in the Aramaic portion of the book of Daniel that use *glh* in the peal, "to disclose," "to reveal," should be mentioned here. Apart from the hymnic expression in 2:22: "he reveals deep and mysterious things,"[28] in all the other passages, *raz,* "mystery," appears as the object of *glh* (2:19,28-30,47). The way in which God reveals his mystery is in a vision of the night (2:19), which is given to Daniel so that he might tell Nebuchadnezzar what will happen at the end of the days. And since the king ultimately acknowledges Daniel's God when he hears Daniel's word (2:47), the determinative elements for revelation as vision also become evident here.

b. *Referring to the Ears (Audition).* A second sphere of ideas, emphasizing the auditory side of the revelatory event, is suggested by the expression, "to open someone's ear" (1 S. 9:15; 2 S. 7:27 = 1 Ch. 17:25; Job 33:16; 36:10,15). That this expression comes from the secular realm is clear from the "dominant concept" of the subject in the Samuel passages, which strongly emphasize that it is Yahweh who is acting here.[29] The object of Yahweh's action is the ear of Samuel (1 S. 9:15), David (2 S. 7:27 = 1 Ch. 17:25), and men (the Job passages). As in secular linguistic usage (Ruth 4:4), this phrase can be connected to the content of the revelation by *le'mor,* "saying" (1 and 2 S.), or by *vayyo'mer,* "and he said" (Job 36:10), but its meaning can also be clarified by parallel phrases: "they are sealed in their discipline" (RSV, "and he [God] terrifies them with warnings"; 33:16; 36:15), meaning "they turn away from injustice and are saved from the Pit" (33:17), or "to redeem him by his distress." With regard to 1 S. 9:15,

---

25 Gunkel, *Einl. in die Psalmen* (1933).
26 H. Schmidt, *HAT,* 15.
27 Fohrer, *IntrodOT* (trans. 1968), 290.
28 On the obj., cf. II.2.
29 Brockelmann, *Synt.* § 48, 123.

Wagner discusses the question (raised by the secular use of our expression with the meaning "to tell, proclaim something to someone") whether *le'mor* should be understood as "and he said," and thus opening the ear as purely a hearing event, or whether (as frequently in the OT) it functioned almost as a colon, and consequently this expression denotes not merely a hearing event, but an "apperception event, an understanding, a comprehension, the setting in motion of an important act, that which makes obedience possible." [30] Wagner correctly decides in favor of the latter meaning. [31] The Job passages (to which Wagner could also have referred) clearly point in this direction, since they also connect the opening of the ear with obedience.

As we have said, the act of Yahweh that takes place in the opening of the ear sets in motion an act of obedience on the part of man, which is connected with what he has heard from Yahweh. If the Job passages have to do with turning away from sin, the passage 1 S. 9:15f. deals with nothing less than the installation of the kingship of Saul and thus of Israelite kingship in general, and the promise of Nathan in 2 S. 7 depicts the divine legitimation of the dynastic principle in connection with David's succession to the throne. It is evident from this that Yahweh's activity of *glh 'ozen,* "opening the ear," indicates a functional relationship, "which is irreversible and has far-reaching consequences." [32]

If we review what we have learned thus far, it can rightly be stated that the expression, "Yahweh opened someone's ear," can be regarded as a technical term for revelation, because it has a breadth of meaning. It is characterized as a comprehensive event, which is initiated by Yahweh when he opens a man's ear and imparts a word to him, and is actualized by obedient execution on the part of the hearer. Revelation seizes the whole man and is intimately intertwined with history.

However, there is one detail that distinguishes the Samuel passages from each other. In 1 S. 9:15 Yahweh speaks directly to Samuel, but in 2 S. 7:27 Nathan mediates the word of Yahweh to David. David's statement that God had revealed to him, "I will build you a house" (2 S. 7:27), refers back to the identical word of Yahweh to Nathan in v. 11. Thus it may be said in general that a man who has been called can impart revelation to one of his fellows, and that the latter can regard this as a word spoken to him by Yahweh directly.

c. *A Secret.* Another expression already known to us from the secular or, more precisely, the Wisdom linguistic usage, *glh sodh,* "to reveal a secret," occurs in Am. 3:7. As a wisdom saying, this meant, "to divulge a secret wantonly." This does not fit the Amos passage. It says that Yahweh does nothing without instructing the prophets. He reveals his plan to them beforehand. Thus this word probably does not come from Amos, but is close to the Deuteronomistic theology, [33] and thus is valuable for the relationship it indicates between the word of

---

[30] Wagner, 68.
[31] So also Rinaldi: to make someone understand.
[32] Wagner, 69.
[33] Weiser, *ATD,* XXIV; Wolff, *BK,* XIV/2; otherwise Robinson, *HAT,* 14.

Yahweh and the deed of Yahweh, and for the significance this has for understanding the work of the prophets. Because of the knowledge that has been given to them, they must proclaim the divine deeds (cf. Lam. 2:14). They are the bridge over which Yahweh establishes an intimate relationship with his people.

d. *Yahweh Himself.* Finally, the niphal of *glh,* in combination with *'el,* "unto," *le,* "to," *be,* "in," or appearing alone, is used as a specific technical term for revelation. Here once again, we are dealing with expressions that come from the secular realm, which mean "to show oneself to someone," "to uncover oneself before someone," etc. [34] The idea of "showing oneself" may be intended in Gen. 35:7 (E; note *nir'eh,* "appear," in v. 1), because the reason it gives for calling the place El-bethel, "because there Elohim had revealed himself to him when he fled from his brother," refers back to Gen. 28:10-22* (E), which speaks of a vision that Jacob saw and of the vow that he carried out in 35:1ff., but not of a word of God which had been given to him. Here *glh* can mean emphatically that God came forth out of seclusion, that he became visible. But this does not cover everything in the passage. Since God's turning to Jacob is expressed by answering Jacob's prayer and being with him wherever he goes (35:3), and leads Jacob and "his household" to serve this new God (35:2,4), *glh* here means more than an apparent manifestation of God. This revelation is articulated in the promise to Jacob, which makes possible and determines the continuation of the history of God with Israel. [35]

glh in the niphal also has this comprehensive meaning in 1 S. 2:27; 3:7,21. 1 S. 2:27 is the beginning of a message of a man of God to Eli introduced by *koh 'amar yhvh,* "Thus Yahweh has said" (vv. 27-36): "I revealed myself to the house of your father when they were in Egypt.... And I chose (→ בחר *bāchar*) him out of all the tribes of Israel to be my priest." This section has traces of a Deuteronomistic revision, [36] as indicated by the style, which follows the model of the prophetic speech forms, and the threat against the house of Eli following this introductory statement, whose structure is like that of prophetic oracles. The relationship between the revelation of God and the choice to the priesthood, which has not previously been observed, certainly belongs here, since the Deuteronomist was probably the first to use *bachar,* "to choose," as a technical theological term. This passage is important to an understanding of revelation, because it traces the call to priestly office back to revelation.

Prophetic concepts appear in 1 S. 3:7,21. While Samuel is sleeping in the Shiloh temple, "the word (→ דבר *dābhār*) of Yahweh is revealed to him." Its content is a threat against the house of Eli (vv. 11-14), and thus it is a parallel to 2:27-36. According to this, revelation is a gift imparted with the divine word. It qualifies Samuel to be a "prophet of Yahweh" in all Israel (3:20), and causes Shiloh to become the favorite Israelite sanctuary (v. 21). There is an echo of the prophetic style in Dnl. 10:1.

Finally, the use of *glh* in the niphal by itself as an OT technical term for revela-

---

[34] Cf. II.2.a.

[35] Cf. Rendtorff, *KuD,* 25; Zimmerli, 16.

[36] Eissfeldt, *The OT* (trans. 1965), 270, 280, 299; Fohrer, *IntrodOT,* 224.

tion is verified by the combination of *glh* in the niphal with a preposition or a particle. This can be seen in Isa. 22:14. The reproach and threat, which certainly comes from Isaiah, "Surely this iniquity will not be forgiven you till you die," is introduced by the statement, "Yahweh Sebaoth has revealed himself in my ears." This statement has nothing to do with the expression about "opening the ears," for, like *beshilo,* "at Shiloh," in 1 S. 3:21, *be'oznai,* "in my ears," has in mind the place of Yahweh's revelation, and not the object. Here, the secular expression with the niphal used by itself, meaning "to uncover oneself," is carried over into the religious realm. By using the statement, "Yahweh has revealed, uncovered, himself in my ears," the prophet makes it clear that he understands the following announcement of punishment as something that Yahweh himself decrees. "Here, the word of threat which echoes in the ears of the prophet, intruding upon the event, is depicted as the place of revelation." [37] By the means at his disposal, the prophet must proclaim or announce what Yahweh's concrete will is.

Additional passages in Deutero- and Trito-Isaiah speak of revelation as a proclamation of Yahweh's will. Isa. 40:5 contains the concluding statement of the little unit beginning in vv. 3f., which calls upon Israel to prepare a way for Yahweh through the desert "in order that the glory (→ כבוד *kābhôdh*) of Yahweh may be revealed, and all flesh shall see it." Thus, the revelation of the glory of Yahweh involves determining the way by which the captives will return home from Babylon, for the call to prepare the way is also an announcement that the exile is at an end. Therefore, just as the way of Yahweh and the road of those returning from exile are the same, so also the return of the exiles and the revelation of the glory of Yahweh are the same. Thus, revelation is a wondrous event initiated by Yahweh, which takes place before *all* eyes (even those of the heathen), and makes it clear that Yahweh's majesty triumphs over all seclusion (cf. Isa. 52:10). Isa. 53:1 asks the question, "Who has believed what we have heard? And to whom has the arm of Yahweh been revealed?" Here, the "arm of Yahweh" is used in a figurative sense for the strength or power of God, which is expressed in his saving deeds for Israel. The content of revelation is the disclosure of what Yahweh does for Israel. As Isa. 52:15 pointedly states, this can be "seen" and "perceived," "announced" and "believed" (→ אמן *'āman*).

Isa. 56:1 also speaks of the imminent revelation of the salvation of Yahweh: "Soon my help (RSV salvation) will come, and my righteousness (RSV deliverance) be revealed." In contrast to Deutero-Isaiah, this statement is based not on hope, but on the "admonition to 'do righteousness'" in v. 1, which culminates in keeping the sabbath (v. 2). [38] Revelation and law are connected with each other even more directly in Dt. 29:28(29), a verse containing a final admonition: "The secret things belong to Yahweh our God; but the things that are revealed belong to us and to our children for ever, that we may do all the words of this Torah (law)." [39]

---

[37] Zimmerli, 16.
[38] Westermann, *ATD,* XIX.
[39] Cf. Haag, *ThZ,* 253.

IV. Theological Considerations.

1. *glh and the Theme, "The Revelation of God in the OT."* Finally, when
we attempt to summarize the contribution *glh* makes to the theme of "the revelation of God in the OT," it is helpful to present a brief survey of the distribution
of this term in the OT in the religious sense.

a. *Distribution of the Term. glh* appears five times in the Hexateuch in the
religious sense: three times in J (only in the Balaam narrative!), and once each
in E and Deuteronomy. In the historical books, there are four occurrences in
1 Samuel, one indicating Deuteronomistic influence and two prophetic. The only
passage in 2 Samuel is also closely related to prophetic ideas. In the prophetic
books, *glh* is used once in Isaiah. The only passage in Amos indicates Deuteronomistic influence. Along with two examples in Deutero-Isaiah and one in Trito-
Isaiah, *glh* occurs twice in the postexilic psalms, three times in Job, and eight
in Daniel. Thus, of these 28 occurrences, 10 are preexilic, 16 postexilic, and 2
Deuteronomistic. The results of this statistical analysis are obvious. *glh* is not a
term characteristic of a particular author or a particular time. If anything, *glh*
in the religious sense exhibits a certain nearness to preexilic prophetism, which
could explain its use in E, the books of Samuel, and the Deuteronomic-Deuteronomistic literature, as well as the easily established increase of occurrences in
the exilic and postexilic periods. Further, when we consider that the book of
Daniel belongs to Apocalyptic Literature, and that approximately 50 percent
of the examples of *glh* in the Qumran literature belong to the religious realm,
this may corroborate our conjecture that *glh* attained greater significance as a
technical term for revelation only in the later course of Israelite-Judean history.

b. *Its Contribution to This Theme.* With regard to the contribution of *glh*
to the theme of "revelation in the OT," the oft-repeated statement that the religious use of *glh* has been taken over from the secular is important because,
according to the view of the OT, the revelation of God can be described only
"in 'profane, secular language'." This is fundamental to a correct understanding
of biblical revelation. [40]

In light of this, it is significant that the oldest occurrence of *glh,* from the
viewpoint of content and literary style, appears in the description of Balaam's
reception of a vision. Since Balaam is a foreigner, and (judging from the names
El, Elyon, and Shaddai) his God originally belonged to the Canaanite pantheon,
the idea of divine revelation in a vision could be non-Israelite in origin. Of course,
nothing can be proved from a single passage. However, the fact that the J narrative suppresses the visionary element in favor of the auditory [41] points in this
direction. Thus, Yahweh shows himself, appears, in order to say something. In
Israelite thought, the entire emphasis is placed on the word of God.

1 S. 9:15 may emphasize this further. Wagner is certainly correct in saying
that this passage contains one of the oldest examples in which *glh* describes a

[40] Wagner, 66f.; contra Rendtorff, 23.
[41] Cf. Zimmerli, 16f.

revelatory act of Yahweh. [42] This confirms with regard to content the conclusion Eissfeldt reached on the basis of literary criticism, that the narrative in 1 S. 9:1–10:16 is intimately related to J in the Hexateuch. [43] The word that Yahweh causes Samuel to hear is all important, and it authorizes him to anoint Saul *naghidh*, "prince," over the people of God, in order that he might save them from the Philistines. Thus, on the one hand revelation involves the speaking of Yahweh and the hearing of Samuel, but also, on the other hand, the execution of Yahweh's commission to Samuel, in which is manifested God's saving will for Israel. Accordingly, revelation is defined not as a mere appearance, as God becoming visible, but as a manifestation of God intruding upon an event, as a word of God that shapes history, makes known the course of history, and takes place in the course of this history. [44]

Thus, *glh* became a theologically filled concept, which is able to express the main features of the Israelite understanding of revelation. And also at a later time this verbal root came to be used as a technical term for revelation in the prophetic literature and in the literature intimately related to it. Furthermore, the word intruding into history, now as a word of threat, is the place where the revelation of God occurs. However, in contrast to the Samuel passage, the word of God is no longer merely a direct introduction to the act of the person empowered thereby, but much more the announcement of the divine act itself, a proclamation of the will of God mediated by the prophet, the purpose of which is to make Israel see the consequences of her deeds, and, if possible, to bring her back to the way of obedience.

In light of this, it is possible on the one hand to define the course of history itself explicitly as the revelation of Yahweh, and from this to get an understanding of the majesty of God, but now also applying to non-Israelites, and on the other hand to attain an understanding of the law which finds in the written Torah the revealed will of God, binding for all time. Both ways are attested in the exilic and postexilic periods, and thus characterize the understanding of revelation belonging to this era.

A final alteration takes place in the apocalyptic literature. Probably in a looser, and yet still purely formal, relationship to the oldest prophetic concepts, it understands revelation to mean the disclosure of particular secrets mediated to the apocalypticist in nocturnal visions (the passages in Dnl. and the Qumran literature, as 1QH 1:21; etc.). In the Qumran community, a principal element of these revealed secrets is the interpretation of the OT disclosing the events to take place in the End Time. In this connection, the Qumran sect regards as revelation not the Torah or the other parts of the OT, but only their own understanding. [45]

2. *golah As a Designation for the Postexilic Cult Community*. A brief word must also be said concerning the theological evaluation of the term *golah* in the

---

[42] Wagner, 67.

[43] Recently in his *The OT*, 243.

[44] Cf. Wagner, 69.

[45] Cf. 1QS 1:9; 8:15; 9:13; as well as Betz, Schnackenburg, and Haag, *BL*, 1246f.

Chronicler's work. [46] The Chronicler also knows and uses the meaning "exile," "exiles," which was suggested above. [47] But in Ezr. 9–10, he also connects *golah* with "remnant," and extends it to include the whole Jerusalem cult community in order to contrast it with the Samaritans. "Those who belong to this cult community, repeatedly pardoned by God and established by God, are a part of 'those who returned home' and of 'the remnant'." [48]

Zobel

---

46 Cf. Vogt.
47 Cf. I.2.
48 Vogt, 158.